Lecture Notes in Computer Science   4767

Commenced Publication in 1973
Founding and Former Series Editors:
Gerhard Goos, Juris Hartmanis, and Jan van Leeuwen

Farhad Arbab   Marjan Sirjani (Eds.)

International Symposium on Fundamentals of Software Engineering

International Symposium, FSEN 2007
Tehran, Iran, April 17-19, 2007
Proceedings

 Springer

Volume Editors

Farhad Arbab
CWI, Leiden University
Kruislaan 413, Amsterdam, The Netherlands
E-mail: Farhad.Arbab@cwi.nl

Marjan Sirjani
University of Tehran, IPM
North Karegar Ave., Tehran, Iran
E-mail: msirjani@ut.ac.ir

Library of Congress Control Number: 2007936606

CR Subject Classification (1998): D.2, D.2.4, F.4.1, D.2.2

LNCS Sublibrary: SL 2 – Programming and Software Engineering

ISSN   0302-9743
ISBN-10   3-540-75697-3 Springer Berlin Heidelberg New York
ISBN-13   978-3-540-75697-2 Springer Berlin Heidelberg New York

Springer is a part of Springer Science+Business Media

springer.com

© Springer-Verlag Berlin Heidelberg 2007
Printed in Germany

Typesetting: Camera-ready by author, data conversion by Scientific Publishing Services, Chennai, India
Printed on acid-free paper   SPIN: 12175260   06/3180   5 4 3 2 1 0

Preface

The present volume contains the post-proceedings of the second IPM International Symposium on Fundamentals of Software Engineering (FSEN), Tehran, Iran, April 17–19, 2007. This event, FSEN 2007, was organized by the School of Computer Science at the Institute for Studies in Fundamental Sciences (IPM) in Iran, in cooperation with the ACM SIGSOFT and IFIP WG 2.2, and was additionally supported by the University of Tehran, Sharif University of Technology, and the International Scientific Meetings Office (ISMO). This symposium brought together researchers and practitioners working on different aspects of formal methods in software engineering. FSEN 2007 covered many aspects of formal methods, especially those related to advancing the application of formal methods in the software industry and promoting their integration with practical engineering techniques.

A truly international program committee of top researchers from 23 different academic institutes in 9 countries selected the technical content of this symposium. We received a total of 73 submissions, out of which the PC selected 22 as regular papers and 8 as short papers to be published in the post-proceedings, and 6 papers accepted for poster presentations at the symposium. Each submission was reviewed by at least 3 independent referees, for its quality, originality, contribution, clarity of presentation, and its relevance to the symposium topics. We had 93 registered participants at the symposium from 12 countries.

We had 4 distinguished keynote speakers at FSEN 2007: James C. Browne, University of Texas at Austin, Texas, USA, on *Unification of Verification and Validation Methods for Software*; Masahiro Fujita, University of Tokyo, Japan, on *Hardware-Software Co-design for SoC with Separated Verification Between Computation and Communication;* Davide Sangiorgi, University of Bologna, Italy, on *Bisimulation in Higher-Order Languages*; and Peter D. Mosses, Swansea University, Wales, UK, on *Fundamentals of Semantics Engineering*.

In conjunction with FSEN 2007, the Working Group 2.2 of IFIP organized 2 full-day tutorials by internationally recognized researchers on the semantics of programming languages (Peter D. Mosses), and the semantics of concurrency (Davide Sangiorgi). These well-attended and well-received tutorials strengthened the impact of FSEN 2007, and we would like to take this opportunity to express our appreciation for the contribution of IFIP WG 2.2 and the tutorial speakers.

We are grateful for the support and the assistance of the IPM staff in the organization of this symposium, especially Dr. Larijani, Dr. Sarbazi-Azad, Ms. Arfai and Mr. Shahrabi. We thank the members of the program committee for their time, effort, and contributions to making FSEN 2007 a quality symposium. Last but not least, our thanks go to our authors and workshop participants, without whose submissions and participation FSEN 2007 would not have materialized.

April 2007   Farhad Arbab
                                                               Marjan Sirjani

Organization

Program Chairs

Farhad Arbab, CWI, Netherlands; Leiden University, Netherlands; University of
Waterloo, Canada
Marjan Sirjani, University of Tehran, Iran; IPM, Iran

Program Committee

Gul Agha, University of Illinois at Urbana - Champaign, USA
Farhad Arbab, CWI, Netherlands; Leiden University, Netherlands; University of
Waterloo, Canada
Mohammad Ardeshir, Sharif University of Technology, Iran
Christel Baier, University of Bonn, Germany
Frank S. de Boer, CWI, Netherlands; Leiden University, Netherlands
Marcello Bonsangue, Leiden University, Netherlands
Mario Bravetti, University of Bologna
James C. Browne, University of Texas at Austin, USA
Michael Butler, University of Southampton, UK
Nancy Day, University of Waterloo, Canada
Masahiro Fujita, University of Tokyo, Japan
Maurizio Gabbrielli, University of Bologna, Italy
Jan Friso Groote, Technical University of Eindhoven, Netherlands
Radu Grosu, State University of New York at Stony Brook, USA
Michael Huth, Imperial College of London, UK
Joost Kok, Leiden University, Netherlands
Marta Kwiatkowska, University of Birmingham, UK
Mohammad Reza Meybodi, AmirKabir University of Technology, Iran
Seyed-Hassan Mirian-Hosseinabadi, Sharif University of Technology, Iran
Ugo Montanari, University of Pisa, Italy
Mohammad Reza Mousavi, Technical University of Eindhoven, Netherlands
Ali Movaghar, IPM, Iran; Sharif University of Technology, Iran
Andrea Omicini, University of Bologna, Italy
George Papadopoulos, University of Cyprus, Cyprus
Jan Rutten, CWI, Netherlands; Vrije University Amsterdam, Netherlands
Sandeep Shukla, Virginia Tech, USA
Marjan Sirjani, IPM, Iran; University of Tehran, Iran
Carolyn Talcott, SRI International, USA

Local Organization

Hamidreza Shahrabi, IPM, Iran (Chair)
Samira Tasharofi, IPM, Iran; University of Tehran, Iran
Hossein Hojjat, IPM, Iran; University of Tehran, Iran

Referees

Sumit Ahuja	Jan Friso Groote	Niloofar Razavi
Elisabeth Ball	Hossein Hojjat	Michel Reniers
Simonetta Balsamo	Hamed Iravanchi	Abdolbaghi Rezazadeh
Massimo Bartoletti	Mohammad Izadi	Shamim Ripon
Debayan Bhaduri	Mohammad-Mahdi	Jan Rutten
Armin Biere	Jaghouri	Werner Sandmann
Stefano Bistarelli	Kevin Kane	Laura Semini
Frank S. de Boer	Stephanie Kemper	Gaurav Singh
Benedikt Bollig	Ramtin Khosravi	Marjan Sirjani
Maria Paola Bonacina	Minyoung Kim	Colin Snook
Pascal Bouvry	Alexander Knapp	Jeremy Sproston
Pyrros Bratskas	Christian Kohler	Andres Stam
Mario Bravetti	Adam Koprowski	Martin Steffen
Adam Brown	Marcel Kyas	Mark-Oliver Stehr
James Browne	Timo Latvala	Syed Suhaib
Michael Butler	Moreno Marzolla	Meng Sun
Marco Carbone	Deepak Abraham	Sameer Sundresh
Liping Chen	Mathaikutty	Paolo Tacchella
Pericles Leng Cheng	Kirill Mechitov	Edward Turner
Tom Chothia	Seyyed Hassan Mirian	Aimilia Tzanavari
Dave Clarke	Mohammad-Reza	Yaroslav Usenko
Claudio Sacerdoti Cohen	Mousavi	Daniele Veracca
John Colley	Ali Movaghar	Fons Verbeek
David Costa	Gethin Norman	Eric Verbeek
Pieter Cuijpers	Farhad Oroumchian	Erik de Vink
Marco Danelutto	Karel Van Oudheusden	Dimitrios Vogiatzis
Nancy Day	David Parker	Marc Voorhoeve
Wan Fokkink	Nearchos Paspallis	Michael Weber
Matthias Fruth	Hiren Patel	Muck van Weerdenburg
Fatemeh Ghassemi	Bas Ploeger	Marco Wiering
Vittorio Ghini	Jaco van de Pol	Hans Zantema
Cinzia di Giusto	Jose Proenca	

Sponsoring Institutions

ACM Special Interest Group on Software Engineering (SIGSOFT)
International Federation for Information Processing (IFIP WG 2.2)

International Scientific Meetings Office (ISMO)
Iran Telecommunications Research Center (ITRC)
Hi-Tech Industries Center of Iran
Electronic Computing Machine Service Company

University of Tehran
Sharif University of Technology
Centrum voor Wiskunde en Informatica (Center for Mathematics and
    Computer Science - CWI)

Table of Contents

Finite Abstract Models for Deterministic Transition Systems: Fair Parallel Composition and Refinement-Preserving Logic

Harald Fecher and Immo Grabe

Christian-Albrechts-University at Kiel, Germany
{hf,igb}@informatik.uni-kiel.de

Abstract. Since usually no scheduler is given at the programming or modeling language level, abstract models together with a refinement notion are necessary to model concurrent systems adequately. Deterministic transition systems are an appropriate model for implementations of (concurrent) reactive programs based on synchronous communication. In this paper, we develop a suitable setting for modeling and reasoning about deterministic transition systems. In particular, we (i) develop a class of abstract models together with a refinement notion; (ii) define parallel composition guaranteeing fairness; and (iii) develop a 3-valued logic with a satisfaction relation that is preserved under refinement.

1 Introduction

The execution of concurrent reactive programs, where the scheduler is given, e.g., by the operating system, behaves (if no real random generator exists) deterministically up to the environment, i.e., the system behaves in the same way whenever the environment behaves in the same way (including points in time). Deterministic transition systems, where no two transitions leaving the same state have the same label, are an appropriate model for reactive systems based on synchronous communication, whenever the environment will provide at most one action (resp. will request at most one of the actions provided by the system) at once. For example, they are in particular an appropriate model for implementations of a UML state machine [1], where only synchronous communication between the state machine and its event pool, which can provide at most one 'event' at the same time, occurs.

Deterministic transition systems are also appropriate as model for components of closed concurrent systems, whenever every component has its own scheduler, i.e., determines which process(es) of the component performs the next action. Here, a global scheduler decides if a (and which) communication between the component and its environment takes place or if an internal computation takes place.

Models for programming languages that contain concurrency are usually nondeterministic, since the scheduler is not known at that level (i.e., will be provided by the operating system). Therefore, those models as well as models for

F. Arbab and M. Sirjani (Eds.): FSEN 2007, LNCS 4767, pp. 1–16, 2007.

modeling languages should contain nondeterminism, which will be resolved (via refinements) in later design phases and/or by the operating system until deterministic computations are reached. Properties valid on the abstract level, i.e., on the model containing nondeterminism, should be preserved under refinement to maintain the relation between the model and the system. Furthermore, a model for the abstract level should provide a compact and finite description of sets of implementations, especially to improve verification. Moreover, it should be closed under standard operators to be suitable for defining semantics of programming languages and for compositional reasoning. Note that often programmers, software engineers, and computer scientists stay on the abstract level and never reach the concrete level in their contribution to the software development process. Nevertheless, it is important to know what exactly the systems are, since the definition of, e.g., sound satisfaction at the abstract level heavily depends on this information.

Contribution. We develop a setting for modeling and reasoning about deterministic transition systems.
   In particular:

- We develop a class of abstract models together with a refinement notion, where exactly the deterministic transition systems are the concrete ones. Our model allows finite/compact modeling by (i) abstracting labels, (ii) having a predicate over labels indicating whether the removal of all transitions having a label is allowed as a refinement step or not, and (iii) having Streett acceptance conditions for restricting infinite computations.
- We define parallel composition for our model that (i) preserves refinement, (ii) preserves satisfiability (i.e., the existence of a refining implementation), and (iii) guarantees fairness, in that, roughly speaking, every component as well as internal synchronization gets an infinite number of opportunities to execute. Here, Streett acceptance conditions are naturally generated by parallel composition between deterministic transition systems.
- We develop a logic together with its satisfaction relation. The logic has as its basic operator $\langle\!\langle \alpha \rangle\!\rangle q$ indicating that α can be executed and after executing α property q is guaranteed to hold. This logic yields a 3-valued satisfaction relation on our model, but is 2-valued on concrete abstractions (implementations). We show soundness, i.e., that satisfaction is preserved under refinement. Furthermore, deciding our satisfaction relation is in NP and approximates the EXPTIME-hard language inclusion problem which asks whether all implementations that refine abstraction $\mathcal{M}$ satisfy property ϕ. The PSPACE-complete LTL model checking problem is also approximated.

Related work. Kripke structures (with Streett fairness constraints) together with trace inclusion as refinement notion are used as abstract settings for linear time, where implementations are traces. In this context, LTL [2] is an appropriate logic. Abstract models used for abstraction of linear time settings are not appropriate for our purpose, since they do not model the branching time sensitivity obtained by communications on different actions.

Transition systems with (forward or backward) simulation [3, 4] are not an appropriate setting for abstraction of deterministic transition systems, since deterministic transition systems can be refined further and, therefore, refinement preserving satisfaction relations are in general not 2-valued on them. Therefore, alternating refinement [5] also yields no appropriate setting for our purpose, since it coincides with simulation on labeled transition systems.

On the other hand, transition systems with ready simulation [6] yield an appropriate setting if deterministic transition systems are the implementations. The predicate over labels and the fairness constraint in our setting allow a more compact representation than ready simulation, which will be illustrated later. Note that ready simulation coincides with our refinement notion for the canonical embedding of transition systems into our setting. Transition systems are already extended in [7, 8] by a predicate over labels indicating divergence (infinitely many internal computations are possible). Therefore, the relation introduced there, called *prebisimulation*, does not yield a comparable refinement notion. The refinement notions of failure, failure trace, ready, and ready trace inclusion [9] are also appropriate settings if deterministic transition systems are the implementations. Their trace based approach makes it hard to define an approximated, compositional satisfaction relation that is preserved under refinement.

Standard branching time logics, which are interpreted on transition systems, are, e.g., CTL [10] and the μ-calculus [11]. But these logics are not appropriate for our setting, since these logics are not preserved under ready simulation: the property that "there is a transition labeled a such that b is possible afterwards" holds in the labeled transition system $\square \xleftarrow{b} \square \xleftarrow{a} \square \xrightarrow{a} \square$ but not in its refinement $\square \xrightarrow{a} \square$. μ-automata [12], (disjunctive) modal transition systems [13, 14] and their variants [15, 16, 17, 18] are used as abstraction model for transition systems in order to improve verification of full branching time properties, as, e.g., in [19, 20, 21]. These models are not appropriate for our purpose, since they consider transition systems rather than deterministic transition systems as implementations. Consequently, these models contain additional complex structures that are unnecessary if the implementations are guaranteed to be deterministic. For example, a state in a modal transition system can have more than one outgoing must-transitions, which makes it, e.g., hard to determine satisfiability w.r.t. deterministic transition systems.

To the best of our knowledge there is no abstract model (beside the model developed here) that can create finite abstraction of labeled (deterministic) transition systems in case infinitely many different transition labels are used.

Outline. Our model together with its refinement notion is formally introduced in Section 2, whereas in Section 3 the parallel composition is presented. Section 4 introduces the logic together with the satisfaction relation and Section 5 presents illustration how the setting can be used for modeling and for verification. Section 6 concludes the paper and discusses future work.

2   Synchronously-Communicating Transition Systems

Here, we present the model of interest, including the refinement notion. In the following, $|M|$ denotes the cardinality of a set M, $\mathbb{P}(M)$ denotes its power set, and $\overline{M} = \{\overline{m} \mid m \in M\}$ denotes the set of conames of M. Furthermore, let $\mathcal{Act}$ be the set of actions such that (i) $\mathcal{Act}$, $\{\tau\}$, and $\{\Delta\}$ are pairwise disjoint and (ii) $\forall h \in \mathcal{Act} : \overline{h} \in \mathcal{Act} \wedge \overline{\overline{h}} = h$.[1] Here, $\overline{h} \in \mathcal{Act}$ is the co-action on which $h \in \mathcal{Act}$ synchronizes, τ indicates an internal computation, and Δ indicates that a not yet specified communication is possible. Note that in reactive programs fairness depends more on the communication than on the states. Therefore, defining fairness constraints on transitions rather than on states leads to a smoother approach. Formally, our abstract model for (programming and modeling languages of) deterministic, concurrent, reactive systems based on synchronous communication is:

Definition 1 (STS). *A synchronously-communicating transition system (STS) $\mathcal{M}$ is a tuple $(S, S^{\mathrm{i}}, \Omega, T, \gamma, e, \mathbb{S})$ such that*

- *$(s \in)S$ is its set of states,*
- *$S^{\mathrm{i}} \subseteq S$ is its nonempty set of initial states,*
- *$\Omega \subseteq \mathcal{Act}$ is its set of explicitly modeled communication,*
- *$(t \in)T$ is its set of transitions,*
- *$\gamma : T \to S \times (\mathcal{Act} \cup \{\tau, \Delta\}) \times S$ is its transition relation;*
  to simplify later definitions, we assume that every initial state is a target of an τ-transition, i.e., $\forall s' \in S^{\mathrm{i}} : \exists t, s : \gamma(t) = (s, \tau, s')$, (those transitions, from a non-reachable state s, are often omitted in later illustrations)
- *$e : S \to \mathbb{P}(\mathcal{Act} \cup \{\tau\})$ is its action existence predicate,*
- *$\mathbb{S} \in \mathbb{P}(\mathbb{P}(T) \times \mathbb{P}(T))$ a finite set representing a Streett acceptance condition.*

$\mathcal{M}$ is called finite *if $|S| + |\Omega| + |T| + |\bigcup_{s \in S} e(s)|$ is finite.*

Before we give comments on the above definition, we introduce the following notations: The components of a STS $\mathcal{M}$ are denoted by S, S^{i}, Ω, T, γ, e, $\mathbb{S}$ and tagged with indices if needed. We write $\mathrm{src}_{\mathcal{M}}(t)$ for the source, $\mathrm{lab}_{\mathcal{M}}(t)$ for the label, and $\mathrm{tar}_{\mathcal{M}}(t)$ for the target of $t \in T$ (where subscript $\mathcal{M}$ is omitted if it is clear from the context), i.e., if $\gamma(t) = (s, \alpha, s')$ then $\mathrm{src}(t) = s$, $\mathrm{lab}(t) = \alpha$, and $\mathrm{tar}(t) = s'$. Furthermore, $\mathcal{O}_{\mathcal{M}}(s)$ denotes the set of labels that occur on transitions leaving s, i.e., $\mathcal{O}(s) = \{\mathrm{lab}(t) \mid t \in T \wedge \mathrm{src}(t) = s\}$.

  Transitions having labels α outside Ω can be matched by α or by the default label. The following function is used later to model this circumstance:

$$\widetilde{\gamma}(t) \stackrel{\text{def}}{=} \begin{cases} \{\overline{\mathcal{A}} \setminus \Omega\}\{(\mathrm{src}(t), h, \mathrm{tar}(t)) \mid h \in \mathcal{Act} \setminus \Omega\} & \text{if } \mathrm{lab}(t) = \Delta \\ \{\gamma(t)\} & \text{otherwise} . \end{cases}$$

Predicate e is used to obtain compact abstractions, especially for the definition of the parallel composition. Here, $h \in e(s) \cap \mathcal{Act}$ indicates that the existance of

---

[1] Note that overlined labels $(\overline{h})$ can be omitted if an undirected synchronous communication is used.

a transition labeled with h is guaranteed iff $h \in e(s)$. Similarly, the existence of a transition labeled with τ is only guaranteed iff $\tau \in e(s)$. Otherwise, a process, where no internal computation exists (can only communicate), is an allowed refinement. That predicate e really yields more compact representation than ready simulation is illustrated by the following example:

Example 2. Consider the STS $\longrightarrow\boxed{a}\overset{a}{\longrightarrow}\boxed{}\,^{a_1,\ldots,a_n}$. In order to describe the same set of deterministic transition system of this STS via ready simulation at least $1 + 2^n$ states are necessary, since the non initial state has to be modeled by using all possible subsets of $\{a_1, \ldots, a_n\}$. Furthermore, $2^n + 2^n(\sum_{i=0}^{n}(i \cdot \binom{n}{i}))$ transitions instead of the $1 + n$ of the STS are needed, since per label and state either all or none states of the $1 + 2^n$ derived states from the non-initial state have to be reached. For example, if $n = 2$ then the following transition system describes the same set of deterministic transition system via ready simulation:

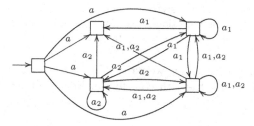

The Streett acceptance condition for model $\mathcal{M}$ is a predicate $\mathrm{Acc}_{\mathcal{M}}$ that characterizes the *allowed* infinite sequences of transitions, those $(t_n)_{n \in \mathbb{N}}$ satisfying *"for all $(E, F) \in \mathbb{S}$ set $\{n \in \mathbb{N} \mid t_n \in E\}$ is infinite or set $\{n \in \mathbb{N} \mid t_n \in F\}$ is finite"*. We chose a Streett condition since they are closed under, and naturally appear in, parallel composition, which is not the case for RabinChain or Rabin fairness conditions. Moreover, a Streett condition guarantees that checking formulas of our logics, introduced later, for such models is in NP. Two STSs are illustrated in Figure 1. We continue by introducing implementations formally:

Definition 3 (Concrete STS). *A concrete STS is a STS $\mathcal{M}$ such that*

- *there is exactly one initial element, i.e., $|S^i| = 1$,*
- *every communication is explicitly modeled, i.e., $\Omega = \mathcal{A}ct$,*
- *the default label is not used, i.e., $\forall t \in T : \mathrm{lab}(t) \neq \Delta$,*
- *a transition exists iff its existence predicate holds, i.e., $\forall s \in S : \mathcal{O}(s) = e(s)$,*
- *the underlying transition system is deterministic, i.e.,*
  $\forall t, t' \in T : (\mathrm{src}(t) = \mathrm{src}(t') \wedge \mathrm{lab}(t) = \mathrm{lab}(t')) \Rightarrow t = t'$, and
- *no acceptance condition exists, i.e., $\mathbb{S} = \emptyset$.*

The STS $\breve{\mathcal{N}}$ of Figure 1 is, e.g., a concrete STS, whereas $\widehat{\mathcal{N}}$ of that figure is not concrete. We turn to defining a refinement notion between models, using game based definition, similar as, e.g., in [22], since fairness can be nicely handled by

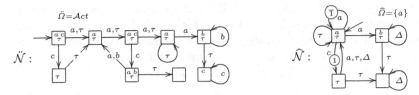

Fig. 1. Two synchronously-communicating transition systems. Here, $\mathcal{A}ct = \{a, b, c\}$. Targets of transitions having no source indicate initial states. The elements of $e(s)$ are written inside the state borders of s. Transitions labeled with tuples describe a set of transitions each having a label from that tuple. A circled number i (resp., $\bar{i}$) on transition t denotes that t is contained in the first (resp., second) component of the i-th Streett condition pair.

Table 1. Moves of refinement game at configuration $(t_1, t_2) \in T_1 \times T_2$. Refinement plays are sequences of configurations generated thus.

Transition: Player II chooses $t_1' \in T_1$ such that $\mathrm{tar}(t_1) = \mathrm{src}(t_1')$; Player I responds
    with $t_2' \in T_2$ such that $\mathrm{tar}(t_2) = \mathrm{src}(t_2')$ and $\mathrm{lab}(t_1') = \mathrm{lab}(t_2') \vee (\mathrm{lab}(t_1') \in \mathcal{A}ct \setminus \Omega_2 \wedge$
    $\mathrm{lab}(t_2') = \Delta)$; the next configuration is (t_1', t_2').
Existence predicate: Player II chooses $a \in e_2(\mathrm{tar}(t_2))$; Player I wins iff $a \in e_1(\mathrm{tar}(t_1))$.

games. For a sequence of tuples Φ we write $\Phi[i]$ for the sequence obtained from Φ through projection onto the i-th coordinate. Note that $\mathrm{Acc}_{\mathcal{M}}$ is defined on page 5.

Definition 4 (Refinement)

- *Finite refinement plays for models $\mathcal{M}_1$ and $\mathcal{M}_2$ have the rules and winning conditions as stated in Table 1. An infinite play Φ is a win for Player I iff $\mathrm{Acc}_{\mathcal{M}_1}(\Phi[1]) \Rightarrow \mathrm{Acc}_{\mathcal{M}_2}(\Phi[2])$ holds; otherwise, it is won by Player II.*
- *Model $\mathcal{M}_1$ refines $\mathcal{M}_2$ iff $\Omega_2 \subseteq \Omega_1$ and Player I has a strategy for the corresponding refinement game between $\mathcal{M}_1$ and $\mathcal{M}_2$ such that for all $t_1 \in T_1$ with $\mathrm{tar}(t_1) \in S_1^i$ there is $t_2 \in T_2$ with $\mathrm{tar}(t_2) \in S_2^i$ and Player I wins all refinement plays started at (t_1, t_2) with her strategy.*

Every label explicitly modeled at the abstract level has to be explicitly modeled at a more concrete level ($\Omega_2 \subseteq \Omega_1$). The necessity of a communication action (or computation) at the abstract level must be maintained at the concrete level (see Table 1). Furthermore, every action that is possible at the concrete level must have already been possible at the abstract level, possibly via the default label if the label does not have to be explicitly modeled at the abstract level (see Table 1). The acceptance on the concrete level has to be maintained at the abstract level in an infinite play.

Example 5. $\mathcal{N}$ of Figure 1 refines $\widehat{\mathcal{N}}$ of that figure (the 4 upper states on the left side are abstracted by the upper left state, the upper right by the upper right, the two bottom left by the bottom left, and the two bottom right by the bottom right one).

The refinement notion of simulation on transition system is embedded into our setting by mapping e always to the empty set, whereas the notion of ready simulation is embedded by mapping $e(s)$ always onto $\mathcal{O}(s)$.

Note that if an STS $\mathcal{M}$ refines a concrete STS it is not necessarily the case that $\mathcal{M}$ has to be concrete, e.g., refines .

Theorem 6. *Refinement is reflexive and transitive. Moreover, refinement yields an equivalence relation on concrete STSs.*

Note that the complexity of checking refinement is high, since [Streett $\Rightarrow$ Streett] does not reduce in general to Rabin or Streett conditions, i.e., in general no Player has a memoryless winning strategy. Nevertheless, this is not very problematic for our purpose, since in practice refinement will be guaranteed by construction: using refinement patterns for top-down developments and using abstraction techniques, like predicate abstraction [23], for bottom-up developments. To us it is more important to obtain efficient satisfaction check, which we get.

Definition 7 (Satisfiability). *Suppose $\mathcal{M}$ is an STS, then $\mathcal{M}$ is satisfiable if there is a concrete STS that refines $\mathcal{M}$.*

For example, the STSs of Figure 1 are satisfiable, whereas is not.

3 Parallel Composition

Only parallel composition, which is the most complex one, and no further operators, like hiding, is presented.[2] Parallel operators following different views, where, e.g., a CSP [24] based communication instead of a CCS [25] based handshake communication is used, can also be straightforwardly defined on STS. Below we write π_i for the projection onto the i-th coordinate of an ordered tuple.

Definition 8 (Parallel composition). *Suppose $\mathcal{M}_1$ and $\mathcal{M}_2$ are two STSs such that, without loss of generality, S_1, T_1 as well as S_2, T_2 are disjoint and $\Omega_1 = \Omega_2 = \mathcal{A}ct$. Then the parallel composition $\mathcal{M}_1 \| \mathcal{M}_2$ is the STS $(S_1 \times S_2, S_1^i \times S_2^i, \Omega_1, T, \gamma, e, \mathbb{S})$, where*

- $T \subseteq (T_1 \times S_2) \cup (S_1 \times T_2) \cup (T_1 \times T_2)$, *where only those t are taken for which $\gamma(t)$, given in Table 2, is defined,*

$$
- e(s_1, s_2) = \begin{cases} \{\tau\} & \text{if } e^-_{(s_1,s_2)} \wedge e^+_{(s_1,s_2)} \\ \{\tau\} \cap (e_1(s_1) \cup e_2(s_2)) & \text{if } \neg e^-_{(s_1,s_2)} \wedge e^+_{(s_1,s_2)} \\ \{\tau\} \cup e_1(s_1) \cup e_2(s_2) & \text{if } e^-_{(s_1,s_2)} \wedge \neg e^+_{(s_1,s_2)} \\ e_1(s_1) \cup e_2(s_2) & \text{if } \neg e^-_{(s_1,s_2)} \wedge \neg e^+_{(s_1,s_2)} \end{cases}
$$

with $e^-_{(s_1,s_2)}$ if communication is guaranteed, i.e., $e(s_1) \cap \overline{e(s_2)} \cap \mathcal{A}ct \neq \emptyset$, and $e^+_{(s_1,s_2)}$ holds if communication is possible, i.e., $\mathcal{O}(s_1) \cap \overline{\mathcal{O}(s_2)} \cap \mathcal{A}ct \neq \emptyset$,

---

[2] Note that in order to define sequential composition, the definition of STS has to be extended such that termination can be modeled.

Table 2. Transition relation of the parallel composition

$$\frac{(s_1, h, s_1') \in \tilde{\gamma}_1(t_1) \quad (s_2, \overline{h}, s_2') \in \tilde{\gamma}_2(t_2) \quad h \in \mathcal{A}ct}{\gamma(t_1, t_2) = ((s_1, s_2), \tau, (s_1', s_2'))}$$

$$\frac{\gamma_1(t_1) = (s_1, \alpha, s_1')}{\gamma(t_1, s_2) = ((s_1, s_2), \alpha, (s_1', s_2))} \qquad \frac{\gamma_2(t_2) = (s_2, \alpha, s_2')}{\gamma(s_1, t_2) = ((s_1, s_2), \alpha, (s_1, s_2'))}$$

- $\mathbb{S} = \bigcup_{i \in \{1,2\}} \{((\{t \in T \mid \pi_i(t) \in E\}, \{t \in T \mid \pi_i(t) \in F\}) \mid (E, F) \in \mathbb{S}_i\} \cup$
  $\{(\mathrm{Co}_1 \cup \mathrm{NC}_1, \mathrm{Co}^{\|}), (\mathrm{Co}_2 \cup \mathrm{NC}_2, \mathrm{Co}^{\|}), (\mathrm{Sy} \cup \mathrm{NS}, \mathrm{Co}^{\|})\}$
  where for $i \in \{1, 2\}$, $\mathrm{Co}^{\|} = \{t \in T \mid \mathrm{lab}(t) = \tau\}$ *is the set of all transitions*
  obtained by internal computtions, $\mathrm{Co}_i = \{t \in \mathrm{Co}^{\|} \mid \pi_i(t) \in T_i \wedge \mathrm{lab}(\pi_i(t)) = \tau\}$ *are those transitions obtained by internal synchronization of* $\mathcal{M}_i$, $\mathrm{Sy} = \{t \in \mathrm{Co}^{\|} \mid \pi_1(t) \in T_1 \wedge \mathrm{lab}(\pi_1(t)) \neq \tau\}$ *are those transitions obtained by synchronization of* $\mathcal{M}_1$ *and* $\mathcal{M}_2$, $\mathrm{NC}_i = \{t \in T \mid \tau \notin e(\pi_i(\mathrm{src}(t)))\}$ *are those transitions where no internal computation is guaranteed in the* i-*th component of its source, and* $\mathrm{NS} = \{t \in T \mid \neg e^{-}_{(\mathrm{src}(t))}\}$ *are those transition where no synchronization is guaranteed in its source.*

A label is explicitly modeled if it is explicitly modeled by both sides. The transitions of the parallel composition are (i) the tuple of the transitions from both sides, if they correspond to communication between the two components and (ii) the transitions of each side not corresponding to communication between the two sides combined with all states of the other side. The latter kind of transitions is described by the last two rules in Table 2, whereas the first rule of this table describes the synchronization between the two components, which yields an internal computation. A computation is guaranteed in state (s_1, s_2) if at least one side guarantees a computation or an synchronization is guaranteed. A communication action is guaranteed if it is guaranteed by at least one side and no synchronization is possible. The latter point is reasonable, since the scheduler for communication may always favor a synchronization instead of an external communication.

The Streett condition of each side is preserved and the scheduler gives (if infinite computations take place) every component as well as every synchronization an infinite number of opportunities to execute, i.e., these computations infinitely often occur or they are infinitely often disabled. These fairness constraints correspond to weak fairness. Strong fairness, where, e.g., one component executes infinitely often unless its computation is continuously disabled at the global scheduling points (i.e., points different from communication with the environment), can be obtained as follows: Replace the last three tuples in $\mathbb{S}$ by $\{(\mathrm{Co}_1, \mathrm{PC}_1), (\mathrm{Co}_2, \mathrm{PC}_2), (\mathrm{Sy}_1, \mathrm{PH})\}$, where PH ($\mathrm{PC}_i$) consists of those transitions where an synchronization is possible in (the i-th component of) its source. Note that in case of communications the scheduler (for the weak as well for the strong variant) is not completely fair: If both sides always provide h then it is possible that the environment only communicates via h with the left component. Extra constraints can be added to $\mathbb{S}$ in order to restrict the scheduler further. Also different weak fairness constraints can be defined, e.g., by taking only those position into account, where an internal computation takes place (restrict NC_i and NS to elements from $Co^{\parallel}$ and add into the first components of the Streett pairs those transitions where no internal computation is guaranteed at their sources). The kind of application determines which parallel operator is the appropriate one.

It is easily seen that $\mathcal{M}_1 \| \mathcal{M}_2$ indeed yields an STS and that $\|$ is commutative (e^- and e^+ turns out to be symmetric). An example of parallel composition is given in Figure 2. As seen in that example, the parallel composition of two

Fig. 2. Parallel composition of two STS. For notations we refer to Figure 1.

concrete STS does not yield in general a concrete STS. This is reasonable, since the distribution of the concurrent computation is not yet given. Refinement and satisfiability is preserved under parallel composition:

Theorem 9 (Refinement preservation). *Let* $\mathcal{M}_1$, $\mathcal{M}'_1$, $\mathcal{M}_2$, *and* $\mathcal{M}'_2$ *be STSs with* $\mathcal{M}_1$ *refines* $\mathcal{M}'_1$ *and* $\mathcal{M}_2$ *refines* $\mathcal{M}'_2$. *Then* $\mathcal{M}_1 \| \mathcal{M}_2$ *refines* $\mathcal{M}'_1 \| \mathcal{M}'_2$.

Theorem 10 (Satisfiability preservation). *Suppose* $\mathcal{M}_1$ *and* $\mathcal{M}_2$ *are two satisfiable STS. Then* $\mathcal{M}_1 \| \mathcal{M}_2$ *is satisfiable.*

4   EF-Logic

We define a satisfaction relation between our models and a tree automata version similar to [26]. An automaton description of the logic rather than a BNF-grammar is used, since this allows an appropriate satisfaction definition via games even if the model has fairness constraints.

Definition 11 (EF automata). *An exists-forall automaton (EF automaton) is a tuple* $\mathcal{A} = (Q, q^i, \delta, \Theta)$, *where*

- $(q \in)Q$ *is a finite, nonempty set of states,*
- $q^i \in Q$ *is its initial automaton state,*
- δ *is a transition relation, which maps an automaton state to one of the following forms, where* q, q_1, q_2 *are automaton states and* $\alpha \in Act \cup \{\tau, \tilde{\Delta}\}$:
  true $|$ false $| q | q_1 \tilde{\wedge} q_2 | q_1 \tilde{\vee} q_2 | \langle\!\langle \alpha \rangle\!\rangle q | [\alpha]q$, *and*
- $\Theta: Q \to \mathbb{N}$ *is an acceptance condition with finite image.*

$\mathcal{A}$ *is guarded if every cycle in the underlying graph of automaton* $\mathcal{A}$ *contains an element that is labeled with* $\langle\!\langle \alpha \rangle\!\rangle$ *or* $[\alpha]$ *for some* α.

Label q only moves to a next state; it is used to obtain effective transformation of fixpoint formulas in terms of a BNF-grammar representation into a EF automaton representation [26]. $\tilde{\wedge}$ ($\tilde{\vee}$) corresponds to the logical *and* (respectively, *or*). Formula $\langle\!\langle\alpha\rangle\!\rangle q$ with $\alpha \neq \tilde{\Delta}$ means that α is present and after its execution the property of q is guaranteed to hold. Its dual formula $[\alpha]q$ with $\alpha \neq \tilde{\Delta}$ indicates that either no α is possible or after the execution of α the property of q is guaranteed to hold. Furthermore, $[\tilde{\Delta}]q$ indicates that after any possible communication the property of q is guaranteed to hold. Consequently, its dual operator $\langle\!\langle\tilde{\Delta}\rangle\!\rangle q$ holds if a communication is possible such that the property of q is guaranteed to hold afterwards. In other words, $[\tilde{\Delta}]q$ ($\langle\!\langle\tilde{\Delta}\rangle\!\rangle q$) encodes some special infinite conjunctions (respectively, disjunctions).

Definition 12 (Dual automaton). *The dual EF automaton of an EF automaton $\mathcal{A}$, written $\mathcal{A}^{\mathrm{dual}}$, is $(Q, q^i, \delta^{\mathrm{dual}}, \Theta^{\mathrm{dual}})$, where $\forall q : \Theta^{\mathrm{dual}}(q) = \Theta(q) + 1$ and δ^{dual} is obtained from δ by replacing* true *by* false, $\tilde{\wedge}$ *by* $\tilde{\vee}$, $\langle\!\langle\alpha\rangle\!\rangle$ *by* $[\alpha]$, *and vice versa.*

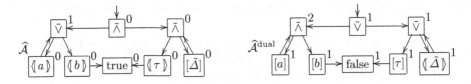

Fig. 3. An alternating tree automata and its dual one. Accepting values are depicted next to states. $\widehat{\mathcal{A}}$ says that (i) if only a happens, b has to be possible after a finite number of steps and (ii) after any communication a computation remains guaranteed. $\widehat{\mathcal{A}}^{\mathrm{dual}}$ states that (i) after any a-communication b is never enabled or (ii) there is a finite sequence of communications such that no computation is possible thereafter.

An alternating tree automaton and its dual one is depicted in Figure 3. Throughout this paper, we restrict ourselfs without loss of generality to guarded automata (formulas) [11]. Also, for any bounded sequence $\boldsymbol{n}$ of elements in $\mathbb{N}$ we write $\sup(\boldsymbol{n})$ for the largest m that occurs in $\boldsymbol{n}$ infinitely often. Let $\mathrm{map}(f, \Phi)$ be the sequence obtained from the sequence Φ by applying function f to all elements of Φ pointwise. In the following, we give a satisfaction definition generalizing the intuition of satisfaction on concrete STS to general STS such that it is preserved under refinement. Note that this satisfaction relation is also the suitable approximative satisfaction relation for ready simulation (remind that transition systems can be embedded such that our refinement restricted to this embedding coincides with ready simulation).

Definition 13 (Satisfaction)

- *Finite satisfaction plays for model $\mathcal{M}$ and EF automaton $\mathcal{A}$ have the rules and winning conditions as stated in Table 3. An infinite play Φ is a win for Player I iff $[\mathrm{Acc}_{\mathcal{D}}(\Phi[1]) \Rightarrow \sup(\mathrm{map}(\Theta, \Phi[2]))$ is even]; otherwise, it is won by Player II.*

Table 3. Moves of satisfaction game at configuration $(t, q) \in T \times Q$, specified through a case analysis on the value of $\delta(q)$. Satisfaction plays are sequences of configurations generated thus.

true: is won by Player I.   false: is won by Player II.

q': the next configuration is (t, q').

$q_1 \tilde{\wedge} q_2$: Player II picks a q' from $\{q_1, q_2\}$; the next configuration is (t, q').

$q_1 \tilde{\vee} q_2$: Player I picks a q' from $\{q_1, q_2\}$; the next configuration is (t, q').

$[\alpha]q'$ and $\alpha \neq \tilde{\Delta}$: Player II picks t' such that $\text{tar}(t) = \text{src}(t')$ and $\text{lab}(t') = \alpha \vee (\alpha \in Act \setminus \Omega \wedge \text{lab}(t') = \Delta)$; the next configuration is (t', q').

$[\tilde{\Delta}]q'$: Player II picks t' such that $\text{tar}(t) = \text{src}(t')$ and $\text{lab}(t') \in Act \cup \{\Delta\}$; the next configuration is (t', q').

$\langle\!\langle \alpha \rangle\!\rangle q'$ and $\alpha \neq \tilde{\Delta}$: Player II wins if $\alpha \notin e(\text{tar}(t))$; otherwise the play continues as in case $[\alpha]q'$.

$\langle\!\langle \tilde{\Delta} \rangle\!\rangle q'$: Player I picks $h \in Act$; the play continues as in case $\langle\!\langle h \rangle\!\rangle q'$.

- *The model $\mathcal{M}$ satisfies the automaton $\mathcal{A}$, written as $\mathcal{M} \models \mathcal{A}$, iff Player I has a strategy for the corresponding satisfaction game between $\mathcal{M}$ and $\mathcal{A}$ such that for any $t \in T$ with $\text{tar}(t) \in S^i$ Player I wins all satisfaction plays started at (t, q^i) with her strategy.*

We give some comments on the non standard steps used in Table 3: In $[\alpha]q'$ with $\alpha \neq \tilde{\Delta}$ any transition labeled with α and in case the label is not explicitly modeled also any transition labeled with the default label has to be matched, since it can be refined to one having this label. If $\alpha = \tilde{\Delta}$ then any transition labeled different from τ has to be matched. In $\langle\!\langle \alpha \rangle\!\rangle q'$ the transition has to be existent, which is guaranteed by $\alpha \in e(\text{tar}(t))$. Furthermore, all possible transitions have to be matched, which is handled via $[\alpha]q'$. The latter point is necessary, since a concrete refinement is deterministic and the corresponding concrete transition only has to be matched by one transition at the abstraction. In $\langle\!\langle \tilde{\Delta} \rangle\!\rangle q'$ a communication action has to be existent that always leads to a state satisfying q'. The acceptance condition for satisfaction plays between a model $\mathcal{M}$ and an automaton $\mathcal{A}$ is a variant of those familiar from the literature: An infinite play Φ is a win for Player I iff either the projection of Φ onto the automata $\mathcal{A}$ is accepting in $\mathcal{A}$ (i.e., $\sup(\text{map}(\Theta, \Phi[2]))$ is even), or the projection of Φ onto $\mathcal{M}$ is non-accepting in M (i.e., $\neg\text{Acc}_{\mathcal{D}}(\Phi[1])$). Note that the possible infinite choice in rule $\langle\!\langle \tilde{\Delta} \rangle\!\rangle$ can be easily reduced to a finite one whenever $\mathcal{M}$ is finite. Furthermore, negation of a formula is modeled via the dual automaton:

Theorem 14 (2-valuedness). *Suppose $\mathcal{A}$ is a guarded EF automaton and $\ddot{\mathcal{M}}$ is a concrete STS, then $\ddot{\mathcal{M}} \models \mathcal{A} \iff \neg(\ddot{\mathcal{M}} \models \mathcal{A}^{\text{dual}})$.*

The satisfaction relation on general STS is inherently 3-valued, since (i) any instance $\mathcal{M} \models \mathcal{A}$ attempts to establish whether all refinements $\mathcal{M}'$ of $\mathcal{M}$ satisfy $\mathcal{A}$ and (ii) some, but not all, refinements of $\mathcal{M}$ may satisfy $\mathcal{A}$ in q. The winning conditions for the satisfaction game are Rabin conditions as they have form [Streett $\Rightarrow$ RabinChain] which reduces to Rabin; so deciding $\mathcal{M} \models \mathcal{A}$ is in NP for finite models. We prove soundness of $\mathcal{M} \models \mathcal{A}$ as an approximation of the EXPTIME-hard relation which asks whether all concrete STS $\breve{\mathcal{M}}$ that refine $\mathcal{M}$ satisfy $\mathcal{A}$. In particular, we approximate the PSPACE-complete LTL model checking problem [27], since LTL, as well as the linear μ-calculus, can be embedded into our logic if we transform unlabeled transition systems having predicates as STS by (i) labeling all transitions with τ, (ii) encoding predicates via labeled transitions, and (iii) putting $e(s) = \mathcal{O}(s)$.[3]

Theorem 15 (Soundness). *Let $\mathcal{A}$ be a guarded EF automaton and $\mathcal{M}_1$ and $\mathcal{M}_2$ be two STSs such that $\mathcal{M}_1$ refines $\mathcal{M}_2$ and $\mathcal{M}_2 \models \mathcal{A}$. Then $\mathcal{M}_1 \models \mathcal{A}$.*

Example 16. The automaton $\widehat{\mathcal{A}}$ of Figure 3 is satisfied by the STS $\widehat{\mathcal{N}}$ of Figure 1, and thus by Theorem 15 also by $\widecheck{\mathcal{N}}$ of Figure 1. The three-valuedness of the satisfaction relation can be seen, since neither all concrete refinements of $\widehat{\mathcal{N}}$ satisfy $\langle c \rangle$true nor its dual one, $[c]$false. The approximation of our satisfaction definition is seen by the fact that $\langle c \rangle$true $\vee$ $[c]$false is not satisfied by $\widehat{\mathcal{N}}$, but by all of its concrete refinements.

Corollary 17. *A STS $\mathcal{M}$ is not satisfiable if $\mathcal{M}$ satisfies an EF automaton as well as its dual one.*

5   Application

Here, we present two small examples illustrating the advantages of our setting. One in the context of modeling the other one in the context of verification.

5.1   Modeling

Suppose a program as well as a firewall that prechecks the incoming messages for the program are executed on a single processor computer. The program can beside its internal computation always react on an incoming message from the firewall. This is done via handshake communication of the firewall action $\bar{p}$ (pass) and the program action p. After such a handshake communication the program directly replies to the environment via action $\bar{r}$ (reply). The firewall is able to receive a message from the environment via action g (get) at the initial state. Then it either drops it (and goes back to the initial state) or $\bar{p}$ is enabled. In the later case, further get actions can be received. Additionally, after $\bar{p}$ the initial state is reached or messages can still be passed on. Furthermore, at every point in time internal computation is possible. The program and firewall are modeled by the STS of Figure 4 (a), respectively (b).

As already illustrated in Figure 2, Streett fairness constraint are obtained after parallel composition of the models of the program and the firewall. This is reasonable, since we are only interested in operating systems that give the program

---

[3] To be precise, we have NP over the number of transitions, whereas LTL is PSPACE-complete over the number of states. Nevertheless, we can straightforwardly adapt our satisfaction definition w.r.t. state-based fairness. In other words, we really have an NP approximation of the PSPACE-complete LTL model checking problem.

Fig. 4. (a) A program, (b) an abstract firewall model, and (c) a less abstract firewall modeled as STS, where $\Omega = \{p, \bar{p}, g, \bar{r}\}$ in all three models

as well as the firewall infinitely often the opportunity to execute. It is straightforward to see that the current firewall specification satisfies the EF automata from Figure 5. Now the model of the firewall is made more precise by modeling one

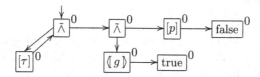

Fig. 5. An alternating tree automata. It says that (i) a message can only be passed to the program if the firewall received one and (ii) if no message is received so far, the firewall must be able to receive one.

having a message buffer of size two. This leads to the STS of Figure 4 (c). Then one can see that this is indeed a refinement of the previous firewall model. Hence, it also satisfies the EF automaton of Figure 5 by Theorem 15.

5.2   Abstraction

Consider the firewall implementation of Figure 6 (a), where (i) the message is added to the buffer, x, if the maximal buffer size, y, is not exceeded, otherwise the message is lost; (ii) the maximal buffer size can be extended by one via an internal computation if the maximal buffer size is currently reached; and (iii) a message in a buffer can be removed and passed on. It is obvious that this firewall is indeed deterministic and that it satisfies the property of the automaton from Figure 5. Nevertheless, it cannot be automatically verified, since the underlying state space is infinite. A predicate abstraction [23] technique yielding STSs, which is not yet formally defined, is illustrated in Figure 6 (b). This abstract

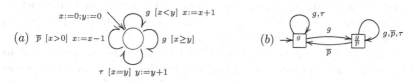

Fig. 6. (a) A firewall implementation in terms of a state machine and (b) its abstraction w.r.t. predicate $x = 0$ in terms of STSs, where $\Omega = \{p, \bar{p}, g, \bar{r}\}$

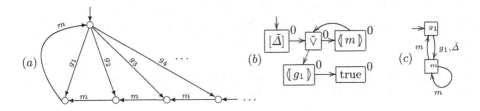

Fig. 7. A deterministic transition systems (a) for which no finite abstraction in terms of modal transition system exists that satisfies EF-automata (b), which describes that after the first action either infinitely many m-actions are possible or g_1 is possible after finitely many m-actions. On the other hand, the STS (c) satisfies EF-automata (b) and is an abstraction of (a).

STS is finite and indeed satisfies the automaton from Figure 5 as required. Note that modal transition systems [13] are not sufficient as abstract model to verify this property by using predicate $x = 0$ for abstraction, since no outgoing must transition from the abstract state $x = 0$ exists. In other words at least unnecessary complex abstractions (greater state space) have to be derived. That modal transition also fails is in some cases is illustrated in Figure 7. Disjunctive modal transition systems [14], which are sufficient, are unnecessary complex, since additional must hypertransitions are needed.

In order to handle arbitrary liveness properties the predicate abstraction can be extended with ranking functions, as it is done in [15], where arbitrary transitions systems are the implementations. By this abstraction technique, Streett acceptance condition naturally occur by construction. Note that by using this ranked predicate abstraction technique, STS are complete in the sense that if a deterministic transition satisfies an EF automaton $\mathcal{A}$, then there is a ranked predicate abstraction such that the obtained STS abstraction also satisfies $\mathcal{A}$.

6   Conclusion

Synchronously-communicating transition systems (STS), which are a suitable setting for modeling and reasoning about deterministic transition systems, were presented. In particular, we presented a refinement notion, fair parallel composition, and 3-valued satisfaction on a logic for STSs. Therefore, whenever implementations behave deterministically and synchronous communication is considered, STSs (i) are appropriate as semantical model of programming and modeling languages and (ii) yield an appropriate foundation for verification via abstraction as well as via compositional reasoning.

Future work will be an extension of STSs such that also asynchronous and shared variable communication, as well as termination is possible. Here, a combination of transition systems with termination [28, 29] and I/O-automata [30] might be a good starting point. Furthermore, an adaption where sets of actions rather than single actions are used as labels is also of interest, since this allows to model that communication on different actions can take place (via parallel components) at the same time step.

Acknowledgments. This work is in part financially supported by the DFG FE 942/1-1 project Refism and by the EU IST-33826 project CREDO.

References

[1] Object Management Group: UML Superstructure Specification, v2.0 formal/05-07-04 (2005)

[2] Manna, Z., Pnueli, A.: The Temporal Logic of Reactive and Concurrent Systems. Springer, New York (1992)

[3] Park, D.: Concurrency and automata on infinite sequences. In: Deussen, P. (ed.) Theoretical Computer Science. LNCS, vol. 104, pp. 167–183. Springer, Heidelberg (1981)

[4] Lynch, N., Vaandrager, F.: Forward and backward simulations: I. Untimed systems. Information and Computation 121, 214–233 (1995)

[5] Alur, R., Henzinger, T., Kupferman, O., Vardi, M.Y.: Alternating refinement relations. In: Sangiorgi, D., de Simone, R. (eds.) CONCUR 1998. LNCS, vol. 1466, pp. 163–178. Springer, Heidelberg (1998)

[6] Bloom, B., Istrail, S., Meyer, A.: Bisimulation can't be traced. J. ACM 42(1), 232–268 (1995)

[7] Walker, D.J.: Bisimulation and divergence. Information and Computation 85(2), 202–241 (1990)

[8] Milner, R.: A modal characterization of observable machine-behaviour. In: Astesiano, E., Böhm, C. (eds.) CAAP 1981. LNCS, vol. 112, pp. 25–34. Springer, Heidelberg (1981)

[9] Glabbeek, R.v.: The linear time–branching time spectrum I. The semantics of concrete, sequential processes [31], pp. 3–99

[10] Clarke, E.M., Emerson, E.A.: Design and synthesis of synchronization skeletons using branching-time temporal logic. In: Kozen, D. (ed.) Logics of Programs. LNCS, vol. 131, pp. 52–71. Springer, Heidelberg (1982)

[11] Kozen, D.: Results on the propositional μ-calculus. Theor. Comput. Sci. 27, 333–354 (1983)

[12] Janin, D., Walukiewicz, I.: Automata for the modal mu-calculus and related results. In: Hájek, P., Wiedermann, J. (eds.) MFCS 1995. LNCS, vol. 969, pp. 552–562. Springer, Heidelberg (1995)

[13] Larsen, K.G., Thomsen, B.: A modal process logic. In: LICS, pp. 203–210. IEEE Computer Society Press, Los Alamitos (1988)

[14] Larsen, K.G., Xinxin, L.: Equation solving using modal transition systems. In: LICS, pp. 108–117. IEEE Computer Society Press, Los Alamitos (1990)

[15] Fecher, H., Huth, M.: Ranked predicate abstraction for branching time: Complete, incremental, and precise. In: Graf, S., Zhang, W. (eds.) ATVA 2006. LNCS, vol. 4218, pp. 322–336. Springer, Heidelberg (2006)

[16] Shoham, S., Grumberg, O.: 3-valued abstraction: More precision at less cost. In: LICS, pp. 399–410. IEEE Computer Society Press, Los Alamitos (2006)

[17] Dams, D., Namjoshi, K.S.: The existence of finite abstractions for branching time model checking. In: LICS, pp. 335–344. IEEE Computer Society Press, Los Alamitos (2004)

[18] Dams, D., Namjoshi, K.S.: Automata as abstractions [32], pp. 216–232
[19] Huth, M.: Refinement is complete for implementations. Formal Asp. Comput. 17(2), 113–137 (2005)
[20] Grumberg, O., Lange, M., Leucker, M., Shoham, S.: Don't know in the μ-calculus [32], pp. 233–249
[21] de Alfaro, L., Godefroid, P., Jagadeesan, R.: Three-valued abstractions of games: Uncertainty, but with precision. In: LICS, pp. 170–179. IEEE Computer Society Press, Los Alamitos (2004)
[22] Henzinger, T.A., Majumdar, R.: Fair bisimulation. In: Schwartzbach, M.I., Graf, S. (eds.) ETAPS 2000 and TACAS 2000. LNCS, vol. 1785, pp. 299–314. Springer, Heidelberg (2000)
[23] Graf, S., Saidi, H.: Construction of abstract state graphs with PVS. In: Grumberg, O. (ed.) CAV 1997. LNCS, vol. 1254, pp. 72–83. Springer, Heidelberg (1997)
[24] Hoare, C.A.R.: Communications Sequential Processes. International Series in Computer Science. Prentice Hall (1985)
[25] Milner, R.: Communication and Concurrency. International Series in Computer Science. Prentice-Hall (1989)
[26] Wilke, Th.: Alternating tree automata, parity games, and modal μ-calculus. Bull. Soc. Math. Belg. 8(2), 359–391 (2001)
[27] Sistla, A.P., Clarke, E.M.: The complexity of propositional linear temporal logics. Journal of the ACM 32(3), 733–749 (1985)
[28] Bergstra, J.A., Fokkink, W., Ponse, A.: Process algebra with recursive operations [31], pp. 333–389
[29] Fecher, H., Majster-Cederbaum, M.: Event structures for arbitrary disruption. Fundamenta Informaticae 68(1,2), 103–130 (2005)
[30] Lynch, N., Tuttle, M.: An introduction to input/output automata. CWI-Quarterly 2(3), 219–246 (1989)
[31] Bergstra, J.A., Ponse, A., Smolka, S.A. (eds.): Handbook of Process Algebra. North-Holland, Amsterdam (2001)
[32] Cousot, R. (ed.): VMCAI 2005. LNCS, vol. 3385, pp. 17–19. Springer, Heidelberg (2005)

Slicing Abstractions[*]

Ingo Brückner[1], Klaus Dräger[2], Bernd Finkbeiner[2], and Heike Wehrheim[3]

[1] Carl von Ossietzky Universität, 26129 Oldenburg, Germany
ingo.brueckner@informatik.uni-oldenburg.de
[2] Universität des Saarlandes, Fachrichtung Informatik, 66123 Saarbrücken, Germany
{draeger,finkbeiner}@cs.uni-sb.de
[3] Universität Paderborn, Institut für Informatik, 33098 Paderborn, Germany
wehrheim@uni-paderborn.de

Abstract. Abstraction and slicing are both techniques for reducing the size of the state space to be inspected during verification. In this paper, we present a new model checking procedure for infinite-state concurrent systems that interleaves automatic abstraction refinement, which splits states according to new predicates obtained by Craig interpolation, with slicing, which removes irrelevant states and transitions from the abstraction. The effects of abstraction and slicing complement each other. As the refinement progresses, the increasing accuracy of the abstract model allows for a more precise slice; the resulting smaller representation gives room for additional predicates in the abstraction. The procedure terminates when an error path in the abstraction can be concretized, which proves that the system is erroneous, or when the slice becomes empty, which proves that the system is correct.

1 Introduction

Much of the progress in automated software verification during the past decade has been driven by the invention of *predicate abstraction* together with methods like Craig interpolation that automatically find the right predicates [1,2,3,4,5,6,7]. Predicate abstraction reduces a potentially infinite state space to the finite set of valuations of a tuple of state predicates. In the *abstraction refinement* loop, one first builds an initial abstract model from some given set of predicates. Then the abstract model is verified, which may result in a proof of correctness (no counter example), a proof of incorrectness (an abstract counter example that can be concretized), or a spurious counter example (an abstract counter example that cannot be concretized). In the latter case, additional predicates are extracted from the proof of spuriousness, and the next iteration of the loop starts with the extended set of predicates.

The advantage of predicate abstraction is its *precision*: when successful, the refinement loop automatically produces a set of predicates that eliminates all

[*] This work was partly supported by the German Research Council (DFG) as part of the Transregional Collaborative Research Center "Automatic Verification and Analysis of Complex Systems" (SFB/TR 14 AVACS, www.avacs.org).

F. Arbab and M. Sirjani (Eds.): FSEN 2007, LNCS 4767, pp. 17–32, 2007.
© Springer-Verlag Berlin Heidelberg 2007

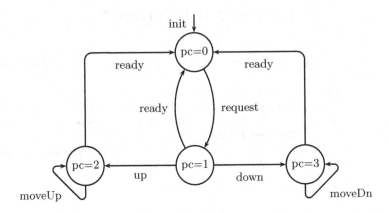

Fig. 1. Control flow graph of a simple elevator

spurious counter examples. On the other hand, the abstract systems generated by predicate abstraction tend to become prohibitively large: the size of the abstract system, and hence the complexity of the verification step of the loop, grows exponentially with the number of predicates.

In this paper, we address this problem by interleaving abstraction refinement steps with *slicing*. Slicing syntactically tracks the dependencies between variables and transitions in a system and completely removes irrelevant parts. While slicing alone cannot be used as a proof technique, it has the advantage that it never increases the size of the state space and may lead to significant reductions.

Figure 1 shows the control flow graph of a simple elevator example, which will be used in the following to illustrate our method. The elevator accepts a request for a certain floor, then moves up or down accordingly, and finally, after reaching the requested floor, is ready for a new request. The transitions of the elevator are specified in Table 1. The system variables include the program counter *pc*, the current floor *current*, the currently requested floor *req*, and a nondeterministic input variable *input* (*input* is constrained to be in the valid range *input* ≤ *Max* when the elevator is ready to receive its next request). We verify the correctness of the elevator by showing that the error condition *current* > *Max* is never satisfied.

The verification of the elevator is shown in Figures 2 and 3. (We will refer to these figures throughout the paper to illustrate the individual steps.) Our procedure maintains an explicit representation of the abstract model. Rather than requiring, as in many other approaches, a simulation preorder between system and abstraction, we call an abstraction *sound* if the system is correct iff the abstraction has no concretizable error path. The process starts with a default abstraction shown as Step 1 of Figure 2: there are four abstract nodes, corresponding to the four different evaluations of *init* (a predicate characterizing the initial states) and *error* (a predicate characterizing error states). The edges in the abstraction allow for all possible paths between *init* and *error* states that are "minimal" in the sense that they do not visit a second *init* or *error* state. The advantage of this restriction is that redundant computation segments,

Table 1. Initial condition, error condition, and transitions of a simple elevator

init	$pc=0 \wedge current \leq Max \wedge input \leq Max$
error	$current > Max$
request	$pc=0 \wedge pc'=1 \wedge current'=current \wedge req'=input$
ready	$pc \geq 1 \wedge req=current \wedge pc'=0 \wedge current'=current \wedge req'=req \wedge input' \leq Max$
up	$pc=1 \wedge req > current \wedge pc'=2 \wedge current'=current \wedge req'=req$
down	$pc=1 \wedge req < current \wedge pc'=3 \wedge current'=current \wedge req'=req$
moveUp	$pc=2 \wedge req > current \wedge pc'=2 \wedge current'=current + 1 \wedge req'=req$
moveDn	$pc=3 \wedge req < current \wedge pc'=3 \wedge current'=current - 1 \wedge req'=req$

such as any downward movement of the elevator (which needs to be followed by an upward movement before an error can possibly be reached), are quickly eliminated from the abstraction.

Predicates, obtained by Craig interpolation, are used to refine the abstraction locally, i.e., by splitting individual nodes. In parallel, slicing reduces the size of the abstraction by dropping irrelevant states and transitions from the model. (In Figures 2 and 3, components that are eliminated by slicing are shown in dashed lines.) The effects of abstraction and slicing complement each other. As the refinement progresses, the increasing accuracy of the abstract model allows for a more precise slice; the resulting reduction gives room for additional predicates in the abstraction. In the example, the procedure terminates after Step 6, when the slice becomes empty, proving that the system is correct.

2 Related Work

Abstraction. There is a rich literature on predicate abstraction and the abstraction refinement loop [1,2,3,4,5]. The key difference between our approach and classic predicate abstraction is that we use new predicates to split individual nodes, while predicate abstraction interprets every predicate in every abstract state. Our approach can be seen as a generalization of *lazy abstraction* [6,7], which incrementally refines the state space with new predicates as the control flow graph is searched in a forward manner to find an error path. New predicates in lazy abstraction only affect the subgraph reachable from the current node. Lazy abstraction thus exploits locality in branches of the control flow graph while our approach exploits locality in individual nodes of the abstraction.

Our abstraction process is similar to *deductive model checking* [8], which also refines an explicit abstraction by splitting individual nodes. While we only handle simple error conditions, deductive model checking provides rules for full linear-time temporal logic. The key difference is that deductive model checking is only partly automated and in particular relies on the user to select the nodes and predicates for splitting.

Slicing. Program slicing, introduced by Weiser [9], is a static analysis technique widely used in debugging, program comprehension, testing, and maintenance.

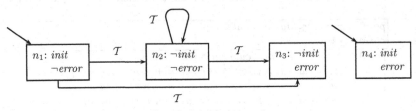

Step 1: Initial abstraction.

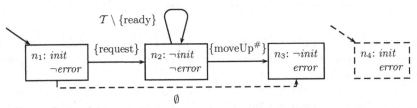

Step 2: After slicing. The transition relation moveUp on edge (n_2, n_3) simplifies to
$\text{moveUp}^{\#} = pc{=}2 \wedge req > current \wedge pc'{=}2 \wedge current'{=}current + 1$.

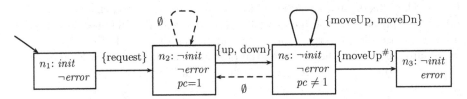

Step 3: After splitting node n_2 with predicate $pc{=}1$ and slicing.

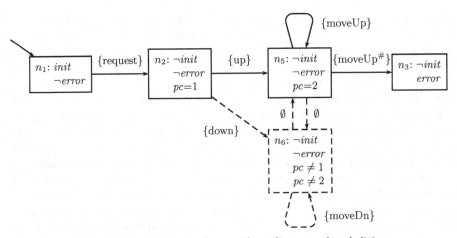

Step 4: After splitting node n_5 with predicate $pc{=}2$ and slicing.

Fig. 2. Steps 1–4 of the verification of the simple elevator. Components shown in dashed
lines are deleted in the slice.

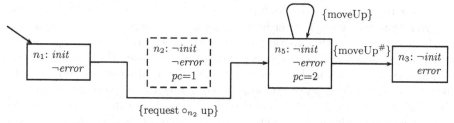

Step 5: Node n_2 is bypassed via transition relation request $\circ_{n_2}$ up.

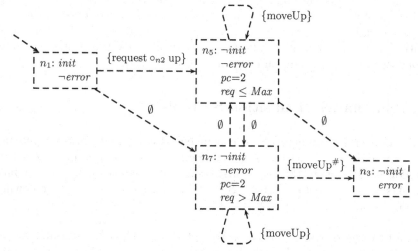

Step 6: After splitting node n_5 with predicate $req \leq Max$ and slicing.

Fig. 3. Steps 5 and 6 of the verification of the simple elevator. Components shown in dashed lines are deleted in the slice. Since the slice after Step 6 is empty, the system is correct.

Essentially, slicing extracts the parts of a program which might affect some given slicing criterion (e.g. a variable at some point). Slicing has become one of the standard reduction techniques in finite-state model checking (for instance in SAL [10], Bandera [11], Promela [12], IF [13]). More recently, slicing has been used in automated abstraction refinement as a preprocessing step on abstract error paths (thus analyzing individual paths, not the full abstraction). *Path slicing* [14] removes irrelevant parts of the abstract error path before the path is passed to the theorem prover to verify if the path can be concretized.

Usually, the slice is determined by a dependency analysis on the control flow graph of the program. A more refined technique, taking additional information about the property under interest into account, is *conditioned slicing* [15]. Here, an assumption about the initial (forward conditioning) or final states (backward conditioning) is added in the form of a predicate, and slicing then only keeps the statements which can be executed from an initial state or which lead to a final state satisfying the predicate.

Closest to our work is the backward conditioning approach of [16] (used for program comprehension, not verification). Backward conditioning proceeds by a symbolic execution of the program and the use of a theorem prover to prune the execution paths which do not lead into a desired final state. The analysis is however always carried out on the concrete program, not its abstraction, and the technique will – due to its objective of program comprehension – preserve *all* paths to the given final states. A use of conditioned slicing in verification can be found in [17], where the condition is extracted from a temporal logic formula of the form $G(p \rightarrow q)$. The predicate p is used as a condition for forward conditioning, the technique is then building a refined program dependence graph (based on the control flow graph). A conditioning method operating on an abstraction of the program is presented in [18]. On this abstraction it can be determined under which conditions one statement might affect another (while for verification we need to find out whether some condition might hold at all or not).

3   Preliminaries: Transition Systems

We use a general representation of concurrent systems as transition systems, which can be defined using an assertion language based on first-order logic. In the following we denote the set of first-order formulas over a set of variables V by $Ass(V)$. A *transition system* $S = \langle V, init, T \rangle$ consists of the following components:

- V: a finite set of system *variables*. We define for each system variable $v \in V$ a primed variable $v' \in V'$, which indicates the value of v in the next state. We call the set $Ass(V)$ of assertions over the system variables the set of *state predicates* and the set $Ass(V \cup V')$ of assertions over the system variables and the primed variables the set of *transition relations*. For a state predicate φ, let φ' denote the assertion where each variable v is replaced by v'.
- $init(V)$: the *initial condition*, a state predicate characterizing all states in which the computation of the system can start.
- T: the *transition set*. Each transition $\tau(V, V') \in T$ is a conjunction $\tau(V, V') = \bigwedge_i g_i(V) \land \bigwedge_i t_i(V, V')$ of *guards* g_i and *transition relations* t_i. In the special case where, for a given set W of variables, τ is of the form $\tau(V, V') = \bigwedge_i g_i(V) \land \bigwedge_{v \in W}(v' = e_v(V))$, i.e., each variable in W is assigned a value defined over V, we say that τ is a *guarded W-assignment*. We assume that T always contains the idling transition $\tau_{idle} = \bigwedge_{v \in V} v = v'$.

A *state* of S is a valuation of the system variables V. A *run* is an infinite alternating sequence $s_0, \tau_0, s_1, \tau_1, \ldots$ of states and transitions such that $init(s_0)$ holds and for all positions $i \geq 0$, $\tau_i(s_i, s_{i+1})$ holds.

We assume that the correctness criterion for S is given as an *error condition* $error(V)$, a predicate which characterizes all error states. We say S is *correct* if there is no run $s_0, \tau_0, s_1, \ldots$ of S that has a position $i \geq 0$ such that $error(s_i)$ holds.

4   Abstraction

Our abstractions are graphs where the nodes are labeled with sets of predicates and the edges are labeled with sets of transition relations.

Definition 1. *An* abstraction $\mathcal{A} = \langle N, E, \nu, \eta \rangle$ *of a transition system* $S = \langle V, init, \mathcal{T} \rangle$ *consists of the following components:*

- *a finite set N of nodes,*
- *a set $E \subseteq N \times N$ of edges,*
- *a labeling $\nu : N \to 2^{Ass(V)}$ of nodes with sets of predicates, and*
- *a labeling $\eta : E \to 2^{Ass(V,V')}$ of edges with sets of transition relations.*

A node $n \in N$ of the abstraction is an *initial* node if its label $\nu(n)$ contains the initial condition *init*, and an *error node* if its label $\nu(n)$ contains the error condition *error*. In the following, let $I = \{n \in N \mid init \in \nu(n)\}$ denote the set of initial nodes, and $F = \{n \in N \mid error \in \nu(n)\}$ the set of error nodes.

A *path* of an abstraction is a finite alternating sequence $n_0, \tau_0, n_1, \tau_1, \ldots, \tau_{k-1}, n_k$ of nodes and transitions such that for all $0 \leq i < k, \tau_i \in \eta(n_i, n_{i+1})$. An *error path* is a path $n_0, \tau_0, n_1, \tau_1, \ldots, \tau_{k-1}, n_k$ such that $n_0 \in I$ is an initial node and $n_k \in F$ is an error node.

An abstract path $n_0, \tau_0, n_1, \tau_1, \ldots, \tau_{k-1}, n_k$ is *concretizable* in S if there exists a finite sequence of states $s_0, s_1, \ldots, s_k$ such that for every position $0 \leq i \leq k$ and every state predicate $q \in \nu(n_i)$, $q(s_i)$ holds and for every position $0 \leq i < k$, $\tau_i(s_i, s_{i+1})$ holds. We call the alternating sequence of system states and transitions $s_0, \tau_0, s_1, \tau_1, \ldots, \tau_{k-1}, s_k$ the *concretization* of $n_0, \tau_0, n_1, \tau_1, \ldots, \tau_{k-1}, n_k$. An abstract error path that is not concretizable is called *spurious*. An abstraction $\mathcal{A}$ of a transition system S is *sound* if there exists a concretizable error path in $\mathcal{A}$ if and only if S is not correct. Our abstraction refinement procedure starts with a sound initial abstraction and then preserves soundness in each transformation.

Definition 2. *The* initial abstraction $\mathcal{A}_0 = \langle N, E, \nu, \eta \rangle$ *of a transition system* $S = \langle V, init, \mathcal{T} \rangle$ *consists of the following components:*

- $N = \{ie, \overline{i}e, i\overline{e}, \overline{i}\overline{e}\}$
- $E = \{(i\overline{e}, \overline{i}\overline{e}), (i\overline{e}, \overline{i}e), (\overline{i}\overline{e}, \overline{i}e), (\overline{i}\overline{e}, \overline{i}\overline{e})\}$
- ν : $ie \mapsto \{init, error\}, \overline{i}e \mapsto \{\neg init, error\}, i\overline{e} \mapsto \{init, \neg error\}, \overline{i}\overline{e} \mapsto \{\neg init, \neg error\}$,
- $\eta : e \mapsto \mathcal{T}$ *for all* $e \in E$.

The initial abstraction is shown as Step 1 of Figure 2. As explained in the introduction, no concretization of a path in the abstraction visits an initial or error state twice. This is consistent with our definition of soundness, which only requires the existence of *some* concretizable error path. Given an error path that visits initial or error nodes multiple times, we can always construct an error path that visits both only once, by considering the segment between the last initial node and the first error node.

Proposition 1. *The initial abstraction $\mathcal{A}_0$ of a transition system S is sound.*

Proof. By definition, the concretization of an error path of $\mathcal{A}_0$ is the prefix of a run of S that leads to a state that satisfies the error condition. Hence, the existence of a concretizable error path implies that S is not correct. Suppose, on the other hand, that S is not correct, i.e., there exists a run $s_0, \tau_0, s_1, \tau_1 \ldots$ such that $error(s_k)$ holds for some $k \in \mathbb{N}$. Let i be the greatest index between 0 and k such that $init(s_i)$ holds, and let j be the smallest index between i and k such that $error(j)$ holds. The subsequence $s_i, \tau_i, s_{i+1}, \tau_{i+1}, \ldots, s_k$ defines a concretizable abstract path $n_i, \tau_i, n_{i+1}, \tau_{i+1}, \ldots, \tau_{k-1}, n_k$ as follows: for all $l = i, \ldots, k$, $n_l = ie \Leftrightarrow init(s_l) \wedge error(s_l)$; $n_l = \overline{i}e \Leftrightarrow \neg init(s_l) \wedge error(s_l)$; $n_l = i\overline{e} \Leftrightarrow init(s_l) \wedge \neg error(s_l)$; $n_l = \overline{ie} \Leftrightarrow \neg init(s_l) \wedge \neg error(s_l)$. Since $n_i \in I$ and $n_k \in F$, $n_i, \tau_i, n_{i+1}, \tau_{i+1}, \ldots, \tau_{k-1}, n_k$ is an error path. $\square$

Soundness of the abstraction is preserved by all of the following transformations on the abstraction. Due to lack of space, we prove this only for the most complex type of simplification, namely Simplify Transition.

5   Slicing

Slicing removes irrelevant components from the abstraction. We define four different types of slicing operations: Elimination of transitions, elimination of nodes, simplification of transition relations, and the introduction of bypass transitions.

5.1   Eliminating Transitions

The abstraction may contain transitions that are irrelevant because the predicates on the source and target nodes of the edge contradict the transition relation. Such transitions are eliminated in the slice:

Inconsistent Transition. Let $\mathcal{A} = \langle N, E, \nu, \eta \rangle$ be an abstraction that contains a transition relation $\tau \in \eta(m, n)$ on some edge $(m, n) \in E$ such that the formula $\bigwedge_{q \in \nu(m)} q \wedge \tau \wedge \bigwedge_{q \in \nu(n)} q'$ is unsatisfiable. We remove τ, resulting in the abstraction $\mathcal{A}' = \langle N, E, \nu, \eta' \rangle$, where $\eta'(m, n) = \eta(m, n) \setminus \{\tau\}$ and $\eta'(e) = \eta(e)$ for $e \neq (m, n)$.

Empty Edges. The removal of transition relations may result in edges with empty labels. Such edges can be removed, transforming $\mathcal{A} = \langle N, E, \nu, \eta \rangle$ into the abstraction $\mathcal{A}' = \langle N, E', \nu, \eta|_{E'} \rangle$, where $E' = \{e \in E \mid \eta(e) \neq \emptyset\}$.

In Step 2 of the elevator example, all transition relations on the edge between nodes n_1 and n_3 are contradicted by the predicates on the nodes: there is no transition that leads directly from an initial state to an error state (the only transition enabled in the initial state is request, which does not modify *current*). As a result, all transitions are removed from the label, and the empty edge is removed from the abstraction.

5.2   Eliminating Nodes

Nodes are removed from the abstraction if they are either labeled with an in-consistent combination of predicates or do not occur on any error paths.

Inconsistent Node. Let $\mathcal{A} = \langle N, E, \nu, \eta \rangle$ be an abstraction that contains a node $n \in N$ such that $\bigwedge_{q \in \nu(n)} q$ is unsatisfiable. We remove n, resulting in the abstraction $\mathcal{A}' = \langle N', E', \nu|_{N'}, \eta|_{E'} \rangle$, where $N' = N \setminus \{n\}$ and $E' = E \cap (N' \times N')$.

Unreachable Node. Let $\mathcal{A} = \langle N, E, \nu, \eta \rangle$ be an abstraction that contains a node $n \in N$ which is unreachable from initial nodes or from which no error node can be reached. We remove n, resulting in $\mathcal{A}' = \langle N', E', \nu|_{N'}, \eta|_{E'} \rangle$, where $N' = N \setminus \{n\}$ and $E' = E \cap (N' \times N')$.

In Step 2 of the elevator example, the inconsistent node n_4 is removed (the conjunction $init \wedge error$ is unsatisfiable). Unreachable nodes are removed in Step 4 (node n_6), Step 5 (node n_2), and Step 6 (the entire abstraction).

5.3   Simplifying Transition Relations

The next slicing mechanism removes constraints from transition relations that are irrelevant for the existence of a concretizable error path. For this purpose we assign to each node $n \in N$ a set of *live* variables $L(n) \subseteq V$, containing all variables whose value may possibly affect the existence of a concretizable path from n to the error.

As usual in slicing, the set of live variables is computed by a fixpoint computation. Initially, the live variables of a node $n \in N$ are those appearing in its labeling $\nu(n)$ and in the enabling conditions of the transitions on outgoing edges: $L_0(n) = vars(\nu(n)) \cup \bigcup_{(n,m) \in E, \tau \in \eta(n,m)} vars(enabled(\tau))$.

Then, this labeling is updated according to dependencies through transition relations on edges. For a predicate q we let $vars(q)$ denote the set of its free variables. For a transition relation τ and a set of variables X we let $depend_\tau(X)$ denote the set of variables that potentially influence the value of variables in X when τ is taken: for $\tau = \bigwedge_i g_i(V) \wedge \bigwedge_i t_i(V, V')$, $depend_\tau(X) = W \cap V$, where W is the smallest set of variables such that $X' \subseteq W$, for all i, $vars(g_i) \subseteq W$, and for all i with $vars(t_i) \cap W \neq \emptyset$, $vars(t_i) \subseteq W$. The labeling is updated as follows until a fixpoint is reached: $L_{i+1}(n) = L_i(n) \cup \bigcup_{(n,m) \in E, \tau \in \eta(n,m)} depend_\tau(L_i(m))$.

Given the set of live variables for all nodes, we can simplify the transition relations by eliminating constraints over irrelevant variables. We assume that the conjunction of all such constraints is satisfiable (which can be achieved by a prior application of transformation Inconsistent Transition).

Simplify Transition. Let $\mathcal{A} = \langle N, E, \nu, \eta \rangle$ be an abstraction and let $L(n) \subseteq V$ indicate the set of live variables for each node n. The simplification $simplify(\tau, m, n)$ of a transition τ on an edge $(m, n) \in E$ is obtained by removing from τ all conjuncts ϕ with $vars(\phi) \cap (L(m) \cup L(n)') = \emptyset$. In the special case of a guarded W-assignment τ, the simplification $simplify(\tau, m, n)$ is obtained by removing from τ all conjuncts $v' = e_v(V)$ with $v \notin L(n)$. Simplifying all transitions results in the new abstraction $\mathcal{A}' = \langle N, E, \nu, \eta' \rangle$ where $\eta'(m, n) = \{simplify(\tau, m, n) \mid \tau \in \eta(m, n)\}$ for all $(m, n) \in E$.

In Step 2 of the elevator example, node n_3 is labeled with the set $\{pc, current, input\}$ and nodes n_1 and n_2 are labeled with the full set of variables. As a result, the transition relation moveUp on the edge from n_2 to n_3 is simplified to moveUp$^{\#}$ by dropping the conjunct $req'=req$.

Proposition 2. *Let $\mathcal{A} = \langle N, E, \nu, \eta \rangle$ be a sound abstraction of a transition system $\mathcal{S} = \langle V, init, T \rangle$, and let $\mathcal{A}'$ be the result of applying Simplify Transition. Then $\mathcal{A}'$ is again a sound abstraction.*

Proof. We show that $\mathcal{A}$ has a concretizable error path iff $\mathcal{A}'$ has. The implication from $\mathcal{A}$ to $\mathcal{A}'$ is straightforward since *simplify* eliminates conjuncts from transition relations and thus every concretization of an error path in $\mathcal{A}$ is a concretization of the corresponding modified error path in $\mathcal{A}'$.

For the reverse direction assume $n_0, \tau_0, n_1, \tau_1, \ldots, n_k$ to be a concretizable error path in $\mathcal{A}'$ with concretization $s_0, \ldots, s_k$. Let $\widehat{\tau_i}$ be the corresponding non-simplified version of τ_i in $\mathcal{A}$. We inductively construct a concretization $\widehat{s_0}, \ldots, \widehat{s_k}$ of $n_0, \widehat{\tau_0}, n_1, \widehat{\tau_1}, \ldots, n_k$. For a state s and a set of variables $X \subseteq V$, we write $s|_X$ to stand for the valuation s restricted to X. We use the operator $\oplus$ to conjoin valuations over disjoint sets of variables. The construction of the concretization starts with $\widehat{s_0} = s_0$. $\widehat{s_0}$ can be written as $s_0|_{L(n_0)} \oplus t_0$ for some valuation t_0 of variables in $V \setminus L(n_0)$. Then we set $\widehat{s_1}$ to $s_1|_{L(n_1)} \oplus t_1$, where t_1 is a valuation of $V \setminus L(n_1)$ such that $\phi(t_0, t_1)$ for all removed conjuncts ϕ of $\widehat{\tau_0}$. Such a t_1 exists since we assumed that the conjunction of all ϕ is satisfiable and ϕ furthermore contains no variables from $enabled(\widehat{\tau_0})$. Then $\widehat{\tau_0}(\widehat{s_0}, \widehat{s_1})$ since ϕ does not constrain variables in $L(n_1)$ (definition of *depends*) and the enabledness of $\widehat{\tau_0}$ is independent of ϕ ($vars(enabled(\widehat{\tau_0})) \subseteq L(n_0)$). This construction can similarly be continued for all states. $\square$

5.4 Bypass Transitions

The following construction allows us to bypass (and, as a consequence, often eliminate) nodes in the abstraction. For a node n with an incoming transition τ_1 and an outgoing transition τ_2, we define the bypass relation $(\tau_1 \circ_n \tau_2)(V, V') = \exists V'' . \tau_1(V, V'') \wedge \nu(n)(V'') \wedge \tau_2(V'', V')$. If $W = L(n)$ is the set of live variables of n and τ_1 is a guarded W-assignment $\tau_1(V, V') = \bigwedge_i g_i(V) \wedge \bigwedge_{v \in W}(v' = e_v(V))$, then $\tau_1 \circ_n \tau_2$ can be simplified to $(\tau_1 \circ_n \tau_2)(V, V') = \bigwedge_i g_i(V) \wedge \nu(n)[e_v/v](V) \wedge \tau_2[e_v/v](V, V')$.

Bypass Transition. Let $\mathcal{A} = \langle N, E, \nu, \eta \rangle$ be an abstraction and let $\tau \in \eta(m, n)$ be a transition on some edge $(m, n) \in E$. Transition τ can be modified to bypass node n, resulting in the new abstraction $\mathcal{A}' = \langle N, E', \nu, \eta' \rangle$, where $E' = E \cup \{(m, n') \mid (n, n') \in E\}$, $\eta'(m, n) = \eta(m, n) \setminus \{\tau\}$ and $\eta'(m, n') = \eta(m, n') \cup \{\tau \circ_n \tau_2 \mid \tau_2 \in \eta(n, n')\}$.

In Step 5 of the elevator example, node n_2 is bypassed via request $\circ_{n_2}$ up. As a result, n_2 becomes unreachable and is eliminated.

6 Abstraction Refinement

We first introduce the refinement step for a given predicate and node and then discuss how both can be obtained automatically by error path analysis.

6.1 Node Splitting

Given some new predicate q, we split an abstract node labeled φ into two new nodes, one labeled $\varphi \cup \{q\}$, the other $\varphi \cup \{\neg q\}$.

Node split. Let $\mathcal{A} = \langle N, E, \nu, \eta \rangle$ be an abstraction of a transition system $\mathcal{S} = \langle V, init, \mathcal{T} \rangle$, and let $n \in N$ be some abstract node and $q(V)$ some predicate. The *node split* of $\mathcal{A}$ with respect to n and q is the new abstraction $\mathcal{A}' = \langle N', E', \nu', \eta' \rangle$, where

- $N' = N \cup \{n'\}$ where n' is a fresh node $n' \notin N$;
- $E' = \bigcup_{e \in E} edgesplit(e)$, where

$$edgesplit(e) = \begin{cases} \{(n,n),(n,n'),(n',n),(n',n')\} & \text{if } e = (n,n), \\ \{(m,n),(m,n')\} & \text{if } e = (m,n), m \neq n, \\ \{(n,m),(n',m)\} & \text{if } e = (n,m), m \neq n, \text{ and} \\ \{e\} & \text{otherwise,} \end{cases}$$

- $\nu'(m) = \begin{cases} \nu(n) \cup \{q\} & \text{if } m = n \\ \nu(n) \cup \{\neg q\} & \text{if } m = n', \text{ and} \\ \nu(m) & \text{otherwise;} \end{cases}$

- $\eta'(e') = \eta(e)$ for all $e' \in edgesplit(e)$

The elevator example involves several node splits. For instance, in Step 3, the split of node n_2 with predicate $pc = 1$ adds the new node n_5.

6.2 Error Path Analysis

The verification process terminates as soon as the abstraction has a concretizable error path (in which case the system is incorrect) or no error paths at all (in which case the system is correct). The refinement process is therefore driven by the analysis of spurious error paths.

Our technique is based on *Craig interpolation*. For a given pair of formulas $\varphi(X)$ and $\psi(Y)$, such that $\varphi \wedge \psi$ is unsatisfiable, a Craig interpolant $\Upsilon(X \cap Y)$ is a formula over the variables common to φ and ψ such that Υ is implied by φ and $\Upsilon \wedge \psi$ is unsatisfiable. Craig interpolants can be automatically generated for a number of theories, including systems of linear inequalities over the reals combined with uninterpreted function symbols [19].

In order to obtain the new predicate, we use a variation of a standard error path *cutting* technique [20] from predicate abstraction, which splits the path into two subsequences such that the new predicate is an interpolant for the first-order formulas corresponding to the first and second parts. To ensure that the new predicate affects as many error paths as possible, we focus on minimal spurious sub-paths:

For a spurious error path $n_0, \tau_0, n_1, \tau_1, \ldots, \tau_{k-1}, n_k$, we call a sub-path $n_i, \tau_i, n_{i+1}, \tau_{i+1}, \ldots, \tau_{j-1}, n_j$ with $0 \leq i < j \leq k$ *minimal* if the sub-path is not concretizable but both $n_{i+1}, \tau_{i+1}, \ldots, \tau_{j-1}, n_j$ and $n_i, \tau_{i+1}, \ldots, n_{j-1}$ are concretizable.

We translate error paths to first-order formulas in the following way. Let, for each $i \in \mathbb{N}$, V_i be a set of fresh variables such that for each $v \in V$, V_i contains a corresponding fresh variable $v_i \in V_i$. Given a finite path $\boldsymbol{p} = n_0, \tau_0, n_1, \tau_1, \ldots, \tau_{k-1}, n_k$ in an abstraction $\mathcal{A}$ (such that $\tau_i \in \eta(n_i, n_{i+1})$ for all $0 \leq i < k$), we define two first-order formulas

$$\Gamma_1(\boldsymbol{p}) = \nu(n_0)(V_0) \wedge \tau_0(V_0, V_1) \wedge \nu(n_1)(V_1) \wedge \tau_1(V_1, V_2) \wedge \ldots \wedge \nu(n_{k-1})(V_{k-1}),$$
$$\Gamma_2(\boldsymbol{p}) = \tau_{k-1}(V_{k-1}, V_k) \wedge \nu(n_k)(V_k).$$

We analyze a given spurious error path $n_0, \tau_0, n_1, \tau_1, \ldots, \tau_{k-1}, n_k$ in two steps:

1. We find a minimal sub-path $\boldsymbol{p} = n_i, \tau_i, n_{i+1}, \tau_{i+1}, \ldots, \tau_{j-1}, n_j$. This determines the node $n = n_{j-1}$ which will be split.
2. We compute the interpolant of $\Gamma_1(\boldsymbol{p})$ and $\Gamma_2(\boldsymbol{p})$. The interpolant $\Upsilon(V_{j-1})$ defines the new predicate $q = \Upsilon(V)$ on which we split node n.

After Step 2 of the elevator example, we obtain the abstract error path $\boldsymbol{p} = n_1, \text{request}, n_2, \text{moveUp}^{\#}, n_3$. The error path is minimal, since both $n_1, \text{request}, n_2$ and $n_2, \text{moveUp}^{\#}, n_3$ are concretizable. Hence, n_2 is selected for the split. The interpolant of $\Gamma_1(\boldsymbol{p})$ and $\Gamma_2(\boldsymbol{p})$ is the predicate $pc_1 = 1$, which is implied by $\Gamma_1(\boldsymbol{p})$ (it occurs in $\text{request}(V_0, V_1)$) and contradicts $\Gamma_2(\boldsymbol{p})$ ($pc_1 = 2$ occurs in $\text{moveUp}^{\#}(V_1, V_2)$).

7   Experiments

We have implemented the new model checking procedure as a small prototype tool named SLAB (for *Slicing abstractions*). SLAB is implemented in Java (JRE 1.5) and relies on Andrey Rybalchenko's *CLP-Prover* [21] for satisfiability checking and interpolant generation. In Table 2, we give running times of SLAB for a collection of standard benchmarks. Our experiments were carried out on an Intel Pentium M 1.80 GHz system with 1 GByte of RAM. For comparison, we also give the running times of the *Abstraction Refinement Model Checker* ARMC [22] and the *Berkeley Lazy Abstraction Software Verification Tool* BLAST [23] where applicable. Our benchmarks include a finite-state system (Deque), an infinite-state discrete system (Bakery), and a real-time system (Fisher).

Table 2. Experimental results for SLAB vs. ARMC and BLAST: number of iterations of the refinement loop and running times in seconds on the benchmarks Deque (with $5, \ldots, 9$ cells), Bakery (with $2, \ldots, 5$ processes), and Fisher (with $2, 3, 4$ processes). (BLAST is not applicable to the real-time system Fisher.)

specification	SLAB iterations	SLAB time (s)	ARMC time (s)	BLAST time (s)
Deque 5	6	1.34	3.80	2.23
Deque 6	6	1.92	27.65	5.64
Deque 7	8	2.70	255.63	13.64
Deque 8	8	3.15	1277.85	36.63
Deque 9	10	4.80	timeout	90.17
Bakery 2	29	6.30	2.56	9.26
Bakery 3	47	33.53	24.97	1943.17
Bakery 4	71	128.53	988.69	timeout
Bakery 5	96	376.56	timeout	timeout
Fisher 2	42	9.26	3.37	N/A
Fisher 3	335	126.05	339.21	N/A
Fisher 4	2832	2605.85	timeout	N/A

Deque. The *Deque* benchmark is an abstract version of a cyclic buffer for a double-ended queue. We model the cells of the buffer by n flags, where *true* indicates a currently allocated cell. Initially, all but the first flag are *false*. Adding or deleting an element at either end is represented by toggling a flag under the condition that the values of the two neighboring flags are different: $(true, true, false) \leftrightarrow (true, false, false)$ and $(false, true, true) \leftrightarrow (false, false, true)$. The error condition is satisfied if there are no unallocated cells left in the buffer.

Bakery. The *Bakery* protocol [24] is a mutual exclusion algorithm that uses *tickets* to prevent simultaneous access to a critical resource. Whenever a process wants to access the shared resource, it acquires a new ticket with a value v that is higher than that of all existing tickets. Before the process accesses the critical resource, it waits until every process that is currently requesting a ticket has obtained one, and every process that currently holds a ticket with a lower value than v has finished using the resource. An error occurs if two processes access the critical resource at the same time.

Fisher. Fisher's algorithm, as described in [25], is a real-time mutual exclusion protocol. Access to a resource shared between n processes is controlled through a single integer variable *lock* and real-time constraints involving two fixed bounds $C1 < C2$. Each process uses an individual (resettable) clock c to keep track of the passing of time between transitions. Each process first checks if the lock is free, then, after waiting for no longer than bound C1, sets *lock* to its (unique) id. It then waits for at least C2, and if the value of the lock is unchanged, accesses the critical resource. When leaving, it frees up the lock. As in the previous

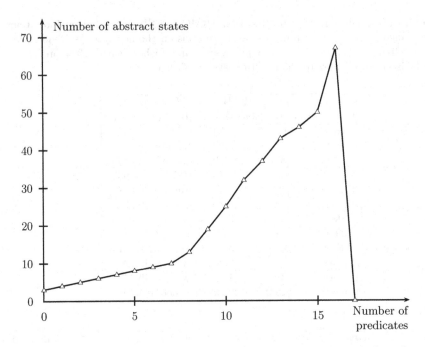

Fig. 4. Relation of the number of abstract states and the number of predicates in intermediate abstractions during the verification of the Bakery protocol with three processes

benchmark, an error occurs if two processes access the critical resource at the same time.

On our benchmarks, SLAB outperforms both ARMC and BLAST, and scales much better to larger systems. It appears that the abstract state space constructed by SLAB grows much more slowly in the number of predicates than the (fully exponential) state space considered by standard predicate abstraction: Figure 4 depicts the relation between the number of predicates and the number of abstract states in intermediate abstractions from the verification of the Bakery protocol with three processes.

8   Conclusions

We have presented a new model checking procedure for infinite-state concurrent systems that combines automatic abstraction refinement with slicing. Our experiments show that the two methods indeed complement each other well: As the refinement progresses, the increasing accuracy of the abstract model allows for a more precise slice; because the size of the resulting abstraction grows more slowly (in the number of predicates) than in standard predicate abstraction, our approach scales to larger systems.

Similar to lazy abstraction [6,7], the new approach exploits the inherent *locality* of the system. While lazy abstraction incrementally adds new predicates during a traversal of the control flow graph, ensuring that the additional predicates affect only the currently traversed sub-branch of the control flow graph, our approach refines individual nodes of the abstraction.

The state set that is partitioned according to a new predicate is thus not identified by a particular control flow location, as in lazy abstraction, but changes *dynamically* as the abstraction refinement progresses: with increasing precision of the existing abstraction, the state sets partitioned by new predicates become smaller and smaller. As a result, the abstraction process is independent of a particular control structure and can be applied to any transition system, including those with concurrent or infinite control.

References

1. Graf, S., Saidi, H.: Construction of abstract state graphs with PVS. In: Grumberg, O. (ed.) CAV 1997. LNCS, vol. 1254, pp. 72–83. Springer, Heidelberg (1997)
2. Colón, M.A., Uribe, T.E.: Generating finite-state abstractions of reactive systems using decision procedures. In: Vardi, M.Y. (ed.) CAV 1998. LNCS, vol. 1427, pp. 293–304. Springer, Heidelberg (1998)
3. Ball, T., Rajamani, S.K.: Automatically validating temporal safety properties of interfaces. In: Proc. SPIN 2001, pp. 103–122. Springer, New York (2001)
4. Clarke, E.M., Grumberg, O., Jha, S., Lu, Y., Veith, H.: Counterexample-guided abstraction refinement. In: Emerson, E.A., Sistla, A.P. (eds.) CAV 2000. LNCS, vol. 1855, pp. 154–169. Springer, Heidelberg (2000)
5. Das, S., Dill, D.L.: Counter-example based predicate discovery in predicate abstraction. In: Aagaard, M.D., O'Leary, J.W. (eds.) FMCAD 2002. LNCS, vol. 2517, Springer, Heidelberg (2002)
6. Henzinger, T., Jhala, R., Majumdar, R., Sutre, G.: Lazy abstraction. In: Proc. POPL 2002, pp. 58–70. ACM Press, New York (2002)
7. McMillan, K.L.: Lazy abstraction with interpolants. In: Ball, T., Jones, R.B. (eds.) CAV 2006. LNCS, vol. 4144, pp. 123–136. Springer, Heidelberg (2006)
8. Sipma, H.B., Uribe, T.E., Manna, Z.: Deductive model checking. Formal Methods in System Design 15(1), 49–74 (1999) (Preliminary version appeared). In: Proc. 8th Intl. Conference on Computer Aided Verification. LNCS, vol. 1102, pp. 208–219. Springer-Verlag, Heidelberg (1996)
9. Weiser, M.: Program slicing. In: Proceedings of the 5th International Conference on Software Engineering, pp. 439–449. IEEE Press, Los Alamitos (1981)
10. Ganesh, V., Saidi, N.S.H.: Slicing SAL. Technical report, SRI International (1999), http://theory.stanford.edu/
11. Dwyer, M.B., Hatcliff, J., Hoosier, M., Ranganath, V., Robby, W.T.: Evaluating the effectiveness of slicing for model reduction of concurrent object-oriented programs. In: Hermanns, H., Palsberg, J. (eds.) TACAS 2006 and ETAPS 2006. LNCS, vol. 3920, pp. 73–89. Springer, Heidelberg (2006)
12. Millett, L., Teitelbaum, T.: Issues in slicing PROMELA and its applications to model checking, protocol understanding, and simulation. Software Tools for Technology Transfer 2(4), 343–349 (2000)

13. Bozga, M., Fernandez, J.C., Ghirvu, L., Graf, S., Krimm, J.P., Mounier, L.: IF: An Intermediate Representation and Validation Environment for Timed Asynchronous Systems. In: Wing, J.M., Woodcock, J.C.P., Davies, J. (eds.) FM 1999. LNCS, vol. 1708, pp. 307–327. Springer, Heidelberg (1999)
14. Jhala, R., Majumdar, R.: Path slicing. In: Proc. PLDI 2005, pp. 38–47. ACM Press, New York (2005)
15. Canfora, G., Cimitile, A., Lucia, A.D.: Conditioned program slicing. Information and Software Technology Special Issue on Program Slicing 40, 595–607 (1998)
16. Fox, C., Danicic, S., Harman, M., Hierons, R.M.: Backward Conditioning: A New Program Specialisation Technique and Its Application to Program Comprehension. In: IWPC, pp. 89–97. IEEE Computer Society, Los Alamitos (2001)
17. Vasudevan, S., Emerson, E.A., Abraham, J.A.: Efficient Model Checking of Hardware Using Conditioned Slicing. ENTCS 128(6), 279–294 (2005)
18. Hong, H., Lee, I., Sokolsky, O.: Abstract slicing: A new approach to program slicing based on abstract interpretation and model checking. In: SCAM, pp. 25–34. IEEE Computer Society, Los Alamitos (2005)
19. McMillan, K.L.: Applications of Craig interpolants in model checking. In: Halbwachs, N., Zuck, L.D. (eds.) TACAS 2005. LNCS, vol. 3440, pp. 1–12. Springer, Heidelberg (2005)
20. Henzinger, T.A., Jhala, R., Majumdar, R., McMillan, K.L.: Abstractions from proofs. In: Proc. POPL 2004, pp. 232–244. ACM Press, New York (2004)
21. Rybalchenko, A.: CLP-prover (2006), http://mtc.epfl.ch/~rybalche/clp-prover/
22. Podelski, A., Rybalchenko, A.: ARMC: the logical choice for software model checking with abstraction refinement. In: Hanus, M. (ed.) PADL 2007. LNCS, vol. 4354, Springer, Heidelberg (2006)
23. Henzinger, T.A., Jhala, R., Majumdar, R., Sutre, G.: Software Verification with BLAST. In: Ball, T., Rajamani, S.K. (eds.) SPIN 2003. LNCS, vol. 2648, pp. 235–239. Springer, Heidelberg (2003)
24. Lamport, L.: A new solution of Dijkstra's concurrent programming problem. Communications of the ACM 17(8), 435–455 (1974)
25. Manna, Z., Pnueli, A.: Clocked transition systems. Technical Report STAN-CS-TR-96-1566, Computer Science Department, Stanford University (1996)

Nuovo DRM Paradiso:
Towards a Verified Fair DRM Scheme

M. Torabi Dashti[1], S. Krishnan Nair[2], and H.L. Jonker[3]

[1] CWI Amsterdam
dashti@cwi.nl
[2] Vrije Universiteit Amsterdam
srijith@few.vu.nl
[3] Technische Universiteit Eindhoven
hjonker@win.tue.nl

Abstract. We formally specify the recent DRM scheme of Nair et al. in the μCRL process algebraic language. The security requirements of the scheme are formalized and using them as the basis, the scheme is verified. The verification shows the presence of security weaknesses in the original protocols, which are then addressed in our proposed extension to the scheme. A finite model of the extended scheme is subsequently model checked and shown to satisfy its design requirements, including secrecy, fairness and resisting content masquerading. Our analysis was distributed over a cluster of machines, allowing us to check the whole extended scheme despite its complexity and high non-determinacy.

1 Introduction

Recent years have seen a rapid increase in the popularity of personal devices capable of rendering digital contents. Large content providers as well as independent artists are looking forward to these new opportunities for selling their copyrighted materials, necessitating the development of systems to protect digital contents from illegal access and unauthorized distribution. Technologies used to enforce policies controlling usage of digital contents are referred to as Digital Rights Management (DRM) techniques. A major challenge in DRM is enforcing the policies after contents have been distributed to consumers. This problem is currently addressed by limiting the distribution of protected contents only to the so-called *compliant* devices (e.g. iPods), that by construction are guaranteed to always enforce the DRM policies associated with the contents they render.

A unique concept of DRM-preserving content *redistribution* was proposed in [1], hereafter called NPGCT scheme, where users act also as content redistributors. This potentially allows consumers to not only buy the rights to use a content, but also to redistribute the content in a controlled manner. From a security point of view, this is technically challenging, since the resulting system forms a peer-to-peer network of independent devices, each of them a consumer, an authorized distributor, and also a potential attacker. Recent sobering experience [2] has shown that DRM techniques are inherently complicated and if

F. Arbab and M. Sirjani (Eds.): FSEN 2007, LNCS 4767, pp. 33–48, 2007.

carelessly enforced can infringe on customers', as well as vendors', rights. These serve as motivation for using formal methods to verify the NPGCT scheme to provide both content vendors and customers a certain degree of confidence in the security and fairness of the system.

Contributions. Our contribution in this paper is twofold. First, on the security side, we formally specify the NPGCT protocols and analyze them. Our analysis reveals two security flaws in the scheme. We then propose an extended scheme, dubbed *Nuovo DRM*, to address these issues. A formal specification and verification of Nuovo DRM is subsequently presented and (a finite model of) the scheme is shown to indeed achieve its design goals.

Second, we use state-of-the-art formal tools and techniques to handle the verification problem of DRM schemes. We use the μCRL process algebraic language [3] and toolset [4] to specify the protocol participants and the intruder model. Due to the complexity and sheer size of the schemes, we resorted to a distributed instantiation of the toolset [5] to generate and minimize the corresponding state spaces. In particular, since the Nuovo DRM scheme is highly non-deterministic due to the presence of several fall-back scenarios, with the inclusion of an intruder model to the system, it easily runs into the limits of single-machine state space generation. To the best of our knowledge, we are the first to formally verify a whole DRM scheme. Moreover, we adapt the standard formal model of intruder, namely the Dolev-Yao model [6], to reflect the restricted behavior of compliant devices in DRM systems.

Related work. Nuovo DRM contains an optimistic fair exchange protocol. Optimistic fair exchange protocols have been introduced in [7] and since then have attracted much attention. The closest fair exchange protocol to our scheme is perhaps the probabilistic synchronous protocol of [8], as it relies on trusted computing devices in exchange. In contrast to [8], we present a deterministic asynchronous protocol that achieves strong (as opposed to probabilistic) fairness, but, as a drawback, relies on impartial agents to secure unsupervised exchanges.

In this paper we do not address modeling semantics and derivations of rights associated with DRM-protected contents, which constitutes a whole separate body of research, e.g. see [9]. We focus on formal analysis of transactional properties of DRM schemes. Related to this, there are several papers on model checking (usually small instances of) optimistic fair exchange protocols, e.g. [10,11,12]. What makes our study unique is the size of the system that is automatically analyzed here, as well as, capturing some DRM-specific features of the system, e.g. compliant devices, in the model. Constraint solving for checking fair exchange protocols has been proposed in [13]. This can detect type-flaw attacks, but is restricted to checking safety properties. Theorem-proving approaches to checking fairness of protocols [14,15,16] can provide a complete security proof at the cost of heavy human intervention, and thus cannot be easily integrated in the protocol design phase.

Structure of the paper. We start by explaining the notations and (cryptographic) assumptions used in the paper, in Section 2. Section 3 summarizes the NPGCT scheme, which provides the basis for our refined scheme. Section 4 presents the Nuovo DRM scheme, its assumptions and its goals. Nuovo DRM is then formally analyzed in Section 5 and shown to achieve its goals. Finally, Section 6 concludes the paper with some possible future research directions.

2   Notations and Assumptions

Trusted devices assumptions. Compliant devices are tamper-proof hardware, possibly operated by malicious owners, that follow only their certified software. We assume that compliant devices are able to locally perform *atomic* actions: multiple actions can be logically linked in these devices, such that either all or none of them are executed. They also contain a limited amount of secure scratch memory and non-volatile storage. These requirements are typically met by current technologies (e.g. iPods). A legitimate content provider, (abusively) referred to as trusted third party (TTP), is assumed impartial in its behavior and eventually available to respond to requests from compliant devices.

Cryptographic assumptions. In our analysis the cryptographic operations are assumed to be ideal à la Dolev-Yao [6]: we assume access to a secure one-way collision-resistant hash function h; therefore $h(x)$ uniquely describes x. A message m encrypted with symmetric key K is denoted $\{m\}_K$, from which m can only be extracted using K. Notations $pk(X)$ and $sk(X)$ denote the public and private keys of entity X, respectively. In asymmetric encryption we have $\{\{m\}_{sk(X)}\}_{pk(X)} = \{\{m\}_{pk(X)}\}_{sk(X)} = m$. Encrypting with $sk(X)$ denotes signing and, for convenience, we let m be retrievable from $\{m\}_{sk(X)}$.

Notations. C and D denote compliant customer devices, respectively owned by $owner(C)$ and $owner(D)$. P denotes a trusted legitimate content provider. A DRM-protected content is denoted by M. The finite set of all protected contents is denoted $Cont$. It is assumed that unique descriptors (e.g. hash values) of all $M \in Cont$ are publicly known. The (finite) set of all possible rights in the protocols is denoted $Rgts$. The term $R_X(M)$ represents the rights of device X for content M.

3   The NPGCT DRM Scheme

The NPGCT scheme was proposed as a DRM-preserving digital content redistribution system where a consumer doubles up as a content reseller. In this section we briefly describe the NPGCT scheme and then present the results of its formal analysis. For a detailed specification of NPGCT see [1].

3.1   NPGCT Protocols

The scheme consists of two main protocols: the first distributes contents from provider P to client C, the second allows C to resell contents to another client D.

Provider-customer protocol (P2C). The protocol is initiated by the owner of C who wants to buy item M with rights R from provider P. From [1]:

1. $C \to P$: Request content
2. $C \leftrightarrow P$: Mutual authentication, [payment]
3. $P \to C$: $\{M\}_K, \{K\}_{pk(C)}, R, \sigma, \Lambda$
   σ=meta-data of M, $\Lambda=\{h(P, C, M, \sigma, R)\}_{sk(P)}$

Here Λ acts as a certification that C has been granted rights R and helps in proving C's right to redistribute M to other clients. It also binds the meta-data σ to the content, which prevents masquerading attacks on M.

Customer-customer protocol (C2C). This part of the protocol is initiated by the owner of D who wants to buy M with rights R' from C. From [1]:

1. $D \to C$: Request content
2. $C \leftrightarrow D$: Mutual authentication
3. $C \to D$: $\{M\}_{K'}, \{K'\}_{pk(D)}, R_C(M), R', \sigma, \Lambda, \Lambda'$
   $\Lambda' = \{h(C, D, M, \sigma, R')\}_{sk(C)}$
4. D : Verifies σ, Λ' and $R_C(M)$ using Λ
5. $D \to C$: ψ, [payment]
   $\psi = \{h(C, P, \{M\}_{K'}, \sigma, R')\}_{sk(D)}$

By ψ, D acknowledges that it has received M with rights R', while Λ and Λ' form a chain that helps to prove that D has been granted rights R'.

3.2   Formal Analysis of NPGCT

We have formally specified and model checked the NPGCT scheme. In this section, due to space constrains, we only present the results of this analysis. The assumptions and security goals of the scheme, their formalization, the protocol specification toolset and the model checking technology used here are similar to those used for Nuovo DRM, which are discussed in the following sections. Details of this analysis along with found attack traces are available online [17].

Two security flaws in the NPGCT scheme were revealed in our analysis. First, in the P2C (and similarly the C2C) protocol, a malicious customer could feed rights from a previous session to the trusted device, because the authentication phase is not extended to guarantee freshness of the content-right bundle that is subsequently delivered. This flaw allows C to accumulate rights without paying P for it. As a remedy, fresh nonces from the authentication phase can be used in Λ to ensure the freshness of the whole exchange, c.f. Section 4.

Second, in the C2C protocol, payment is not bound to the request/receive messages exchanged between two customers. Thus, once D receives M in step 3, the owner of D can avoid paying C by aborting the protocol. Since this exchange is unsupervised, the owners of compliant devices are forced to trust each other to complete transactions. While it is reasonable to extend such trust to a legitimate content provider, it should not be assumed for device owners in C2C exchanges.

4   The Nuovo DRM Scheme

This section describes an extension to the NPGCT, dubbed Nuovo DRM, which in particular addresses the security concerns identified in Section 3.2. Here we confine to informal descriptions; a formal specification is discussed in Section 5.

4.1   Nuovo DRM's Goals

We require the Nuovo DRM scheme to achieve the following goals (the same goals as those used to analyze the NPGCT scheme in Section 3.2):

G1. Effectiveness. A protocol achieves effectiveness iff when honest participants run the protocol, it terminates successfully, i.e. a desired content-right bundle is exchanged for the corresponding payment order. Effectiveness is a sanity check for the functionality of the protocol and is therefore checked in a reliable communication system with no attacker.

G2. Secrecy. Secrecy states that no outsider may learn "secret" items, which are usually encrypted for intended receivers. Nuovo DRM (similar to NPGCT) limits the distribution of protected contents by encrypting them for intended compliant devices. This scheme must thus guarantee that a DRM-protected content never appears in plain to any non-compliant device.

G3. Resisting content masquerading. Content masquerading occurs when content M is passed off as content M', for $M \neq M'$. Preventing this attack ensures that an intruder cannot feed M' to a device that has requested M.

G4. Strong fairness. Assume Alice owns m_A and Bob owns m_B. Informally, strong fairness states that if Alice and Bob run a protocol to exchange their items, finally either both or neither of them receive the other party's item [18]. Strong fairness usually requires the contents exchanged in the system to be *strongly generatable*: in Nuovo, a content provider can provide the exact missing content if the exchange goes amiss. Strong fairness also guarantees *timeliness*, which informally states that, in a finite amount of time, honest protocol participants can safely terminate their role in the protocol with no help from malicious parties. As this is a liveness property[1], resilient communication channels (assumption A2 below) are necessary for fairness to hold [7]. For an in-depth discussion of fairness in exchange we refer the interested reader to [7].

4.2   Nuovo DRM's Assumptions

Nuovo DRM is based on the following assumptions:

A1. Consumer compliant devices are assumed tamper-proof. Owners of compliant devices are however untrusted. They may collude to subvert the protocol.

---

[1] Properties of systems can be divided into two classes: *safety* properties, stating unwanted situations do not happen, and *liveness* properties, stipulating desired events eventually happen. For a formal definition of these property classes see [19].

They can, in particular, arbitrarily switch off their own devices ("crash failure model" in distributed computing terminology).

A2. We assume an asynchronous resilient communication model with no global clock, i.e. the communication media deliver each transmitted message intact in a finite but unknown amount of time. Resilience is necessary when aiming for fairness [20], and is realizable under certain reasonable assumptions [21].

A3. There exists a hierarchy of public keys, with the public key of the root embedded in each compliant device and available to content providers. Using such an infrastructure, a device can prove its identity or verify other devices' identities without having to contact the root. Participant identities (C, D and P) implicitly refer to these authentication certificates issued by the root.

A4. Protocol participants negotiate the price of content in advance. In Nuovo DRM, the price of the content being traded is bundled with the requested rights.

4.3   Nuovo DRM Protocols

As in NPGCT, our scheme consists of two main protocols: the first distributes content from provider P to client C, the second allows C to resell content to another client D.

Provider-customer protocol (P2C). The owner of C wants to buy item M with rights R from content provider P. Here C and P, but not $owner(C)$, are assumed trusted.

$$
\begin{aligned}
&1.\ owner(C) \rightarrow C : P,\ h(M),\ R \\
&2.\qquad\quad C \rightarrow P : C,\ n_C \\
&3.\qquad\quad P \rightarrow C : \{n_P,\ n_C,\ C\}_{sk(P)} \\
&4.\qquad\quad C \rightarrow P : \{n_C,\ n_P,\ h(M),\ R,\ P\}_{sk(C)} \\
&5.\qquad\quad P \rightarrow C : \{M\}_K,\ \{K\}_{pk(C)},\ \{R,\ n_C\}_{sk(P)}
\end{aligned}
$$

In the first step, the hash of the desired content, retrieved from a trusted public directory, with a right and the identity of a legitimate provider are fed to the compliant device C. Following assumption A4, $owner(C)$ and P have already reached an agreement on the price. Whether P is a legitimate provider can be checked by C and vice versa (see assumption A3). In step 2, C generates a fresh nonce n_C and sends it to P, which will continue the protocol only if C is a compliant device. Message 4 completes the mutual authentication between C and P. This also constitutes a *payment order* from C to P. After receiving this message, P checks if R is the same as previously agreed upon (assumption A4) and only if so, stores the payment order (for future/immediate encashing) and performs step 5 after generating a random fresh key K. When C receives message 5, it decrypts $\{K\}_{pk(C)}$, extracts M and checks if it matches $h(M)$ in message 1, and n_C is the same as the nonce in message 2. If these tests pass, C updates $R_C(M)$ with R, e.g. R is added to $R_C(M)$. Note that $R_C(M)$ is not necessarily R: C could already have some rights associated with M, for instance, acquired from an earlier purchase. Since we abstract away from rights semantics (see our related work), the update phase is left unspecified here.

We now define a set of *abstract* actions to highlight important steps of the protocol. These are used in the formalization process to define desired behaviors of the protocol. For the P2C protocol, C performs the abstract action $request(C, h(M), R, P)$ at step 4, indicating the start of the exchange from C's point of view. At step 5, P performs $issue(P, h(M), R, C)$, denoting the receipt of the payment order and sending the content to C. Finally C performs $update(C, h(M), R, P)$ upon accepting message 5, denoting the successful termination of the exchange from C's point of view. These abstract actions are further discussed in Section 5.

Customer-customer protocol (C2C). The owner of D wants to buy item M with rights R' from another compliant device C. This protocol can be seen as a fair exchange protocol where C and D want to exchange a content-right bundle for its associated payment so that either both or none of them receive their desired items. In deterministic protocols, however, achieving fairness is proved to be impossible without a TTP [22]. Assuming that most participants are honest and protocols go wrong infrequently, it is reasonable to use protocols which require TTP's intervention only when a conflict has to be resolved. These are usually called *optimistic* fair exchange protocols [7] and contain two sub-protocols: an optimistic sub-protocol is executed between untrusted devices, and if a participant cannot finish this protocol run, it will initiate a recovery sub-protocol with a designated TTP.[2] Our C2C protocol is an optimistic fair exchange protocol which uses the content provider P as the TTP. The optimistic exchange sub-protocol is as follows:

1. $owner(D) \rightarrow D : C, h(M), R'$
2. $\qquad D \rightarrow C : D, n_D$
3. $\qquad C \rightarrow D : \{n'_C, n_D, D\}_{sk(C)}$
4. $\qquad D \rightarrow C : \{n_D, n'_C, h(M), R', C\}_{sk(D)}$
5. $\qquad C \rightarrow D : \{M\}_{K'}, \{K'\}_{pk(D)}, \{R', n_D\}_{sk(C)}$

This protocol is similar to the P2C protocol and only the abstract actions are described here: at step 4, D takes the action $request(D, h(M), R', C)$ when sending out the message which represents its payment. At step 5, C performs $issue(C, h(M), R', D)$ and in the same atomic action updates the right associated with M (reflecting that some part of $R_C(M)$ has been used for reselling M) and stores the payment order signed by D. Note that the atomicity of these actions is necessary to guarantee that C does not store the payment order without simultaneously updating the right $R_C(M)$. Upon accepting message 5, D performs $update(D, h(M), R', C)$.

---

[2] Fair exchange is attained by ensuring either successful termination (recovery) or failure (abortion) for both parties. In Nuovo DRM, if neither party terminates successfully, nothing is exchanged and failure is already attained. Hence, no particular "abort" protocol is necessary.

In this protocol, a malicious *owner(C)* can abort before sending message 5 to D or this message can get lost due to a hardware failure. To prevent such unfair situations for D, we provide a recovery mechanism to obtain the lost content.

Recovery sub-protocol. The goal is to bring the compliant device D back to a fair state in case of a failure in delivering message 5 in the C2C protocol. D can start a recovery session with the content provider P at any time after sending message 4 in the C2C protocol. If a connection with the provider is not available, D saves the current state and simply waits till it becomes available. Once the recovery protocol has been initiated, D ignores messages from the optimistic run of C2C. The purpose of the recovery is to ensure that D receives the content and rights that *owner(D)* wanted (and ostensibly paid for).

5^r. $D : resolves(D)$
6^r. $D \rightarrow P : D, n'_D$
7^r. $P \rightarrow D : \{n'_P, n'_D, D\}_{sk(P)}$
8^r. $D \rightarrow P : \{n'_D, n'_P, \langle n_D, n'_C, h(M), R', C\rangle, R'', P\}_{sk(D)}$
9^r. $P \rightarrow D : \{M\}_{K''}, \{K''\}_{pk(D)}, \{R'', n'_D\}_{SK(P)}$

In this protocol D and P behave as if D is purchasing the M-R'' content-right bundle from P using the P2C protocol, except that, in message 8^r, D reports the failed C2C exchange it had with C. The following abstract actions are performed here: $request(D, h(M), R', P)$ is performed by D at step 8^r. At step 9^r, P performs $issue(P, h(M), R', D)$ and upon accepting message 9^r, D performs $update$ $(D, h(M), R', P)$. The way P resolves (payments of) failed exchanges deserves detailed explanation. This however falls beyond the scope of our formal analysis and, due to space constraints, is omitted here; see [17] for a detailed discussion.

One can argue that the recovery sub-protocol may also fail due to lossy communication channels. As a way to mitigate this, persistent communication channels for content providers can be built, e.g., using an FTP server as an intermediary. The provider would upload the content, and the device would download it from the server. In order to guarantee fairness, such resilient communication channels are generally unavoidable [7] (c.f. assumption A2).

As a final note, we emphasize that only tamper-proof compliant devices are considered here (assumption A1). These protocols can be trivially attacked if the devices are tampered with (e.g. a corrupted D would be able to initiate a recovery protocol even after a successful exchange). Methods for revoking circumvented devices and resisting systematic content pirating are described in [23,1].

5   Formal Analysis

In this section we describe the steps followed to formally verify that Nuovo DRM achieves its design goals. Our approach is based on finite-state model checking [24], which (usually) requires negligible human intervention and, moreover, produces concrete counterexamples, i.e. attack traces, if the design fails to satisfy a desired property. It can therefore be effectively integrated into the design phase. However, a complete security proof of the system cannot, in general, be established by model checking. For an overview on formal methods for verifying security protocols see [25]. Our formal verification can be seen as a sequence of steps: first, we specify the protocol and the intruder model in the μCRL process algebraic language and generate the corresponding model using the μCRL toolset (version 2.17.12). Second, we state the desired properties in the regular (alternation-free) μ-calculus, and, finally, check the protocol model with regard to the properties in the CADP toolset. Below, these steps are described in detail.

5.1   Formal Specification of Nuovo DRM

The complex structure of Nuovo DRM calls for an expressive specification language. We have formalized the Nuovo DRM scheme in μCRL, a language for specifying and verifying distributed systems and protocols in an algebraic style [3]. A μCRL specification describes a labeled transition system (LTS), in which states represent process terms and edges are labeled with actions. The μCRL toolset [4,5], together with CADP [26] which acts as its back-end, features visualization, simulation, symbolic reduction, (distributed) state space generation and reduction, model checking and theorem proving capabilities.

We model a security protocol as an asynchronous composition of a finite number of non-deterministic named processes. These processes model roles of honest participants in the protocol. Processes communicate by sending and receiving messages. A message is a pair $m = (q, c)$, where q is the identity of the intended receiver process (so that the network can route the message to its destination) and c is the content of the message. To send or receive a message m, a participant p performs the actions $\mathbf{send}(p, m)$ or $\mathbf{recv}(p, m)$, respectively. Apart from $\mathbf{send}$ and $\mathbf{recv}$, all other actions of processes are assumed internal, i.e. not communicating with other participants. These are symbolic actions that typically denote security claims of protocol participants (e.g. *update* in Section 4.3). Here, we only present a μCRL specification of the honest customer role in the P2C protocol. For a complete specification of Nuovo DRM see [23]. We start with a very short introduction to μCRL.

The μCRL specification language. In a μCRL specification, processes are represented by process terms, which describe the order in which the actions may happen in a process. A process term consists of action names and recursion variables combined by process algebraic operators. The operators '$\cdot$' and '$+$' are used for the sequential and alternative composition ("choice") of processes, respectively. The process $\sum_{d \in \Delta} P(d)$, where Δ is a (infinite) data domain, behaves as $P(d_1) + P(d_2) + \cdots$.

The customer process. In μCRL spec 1 we specify the customer's compliant device role in the P2C protocol of the Nuovo DRM scheme. In this specification, *Nonce* and *Key* represent the finite set of nonces and keys available in the protocol, respectively. The set Ω is C's local collection of content-right bundles, n_C denotes the nonce that is available to C in the current protocol round, and the function $nxt : Nonce \rightarrow Nonce$, given a seed, generates a fresh random nonce.

To simplify the presentation we remove the identities of senders and intended receivers from messages. Note that any discrepancy in the received content is automatically detected in this code: in the last message, if the first part does not agree with the initial $h(M)$, the message will not be accepted.

μCRL spec 1. Customer device in the P2C protocol

$$C(\Omega, n_C) = \sum_{\substack{R \in Rgts \\ M \in Cont}} \mathbf{recv}(P, h(M), R).\mathbf{send}(C, n_C).$$

$$\sum_{n \in Nonce} \mathbf{recv}(\{n,\ n_C,\ C\}_{sk(P)}).$$

$$\mathbf{send}(\{n_C,\ n,\ h(M),\ R,\ P\}_{sk(C)}).request(C, h(M), R, C).$$

$$\sum_{K \in Key} \mathbf{recv}(\{M\}_K,\ \{K\}_{pk(C)},\ \{R,\ n_C\}_{sk(P)}).update(C, h(M), R, P).$$

$$C(\Omega \cup \{\langle M, R\rangle\}, nxt(n_C))$$

Communication models. We consider two different communication models. The first is a synchronous communication model that is used to verify the effectiveness property (goal G1). In this model there is no intruder and all participants are honest. A process p can send a message m to q only if q at the same time can receive it from p. The synchronization between these is denoted **com**, which formalizes the "$p \rightarrow q : m$" notation of Sections 3 and 4. In order to verify the properties G2–G4, an asynchronous communication model is used where the intruder has complete control over the communication media. When a process p sends a message m with the intention that it should be received by q, it is in fact the intruder that receives it, and it is only from the intruder that q may receive m. The communications between participants of a protocol, via the intruder, is thus asynchronous and, moreover, a participant has no guarantees about the origins of the messages it receives.

Intruder model. We follow Dolev and Yao's approach to model the intruder [6], with some deviations that are described below. The Dolev-Yao (DY) intruder has complete control over the network: it intercepts and remembers all transmitted messages, it can encrypt, decrypt and sign messages if it knows the corresponding keys, it can compose and send new messages using its knowledge and it can remove or delay messages in favor of others being communicated. As it has complete control over communication media, we assume it plays the role of the communication media. All messages are thus channeled through the intruder. Under the perfect cryptography assumption, this intruder has been shown to be the most powerful attacker model [27]. In our formalization, this intruder is a non-deterministic process that exhausts all possible sequences of actions, resulting in an LTS which can subsequently be formally checked. Note that the intruder is not necessarily an outside party: it may be a legitimate, though malicious, player in the protocol.

The intruder model used here is different from the DY intruder in two main aspects (for a formal specification of our intruder model see [23]). These differences stem from the characteristics of the DRM scheme and its requirements:

I1. Trusted devices, that play a crucial role in these protocols, significantly limit the power of the intruder[3]. However, the intruder has the ability to deliberately turn off its (otherwise trusted) devices. This has been reflected in our model by allowing the devices controlled by the intruder to non-deterministically choose between continuing and quitting the protocol at each step, except when performing atomic actions. Therefore, in the model, all non-atomic actions a of the devices operated by the intruder are rewritten with $a + off$. Thus, the intruder cannot turn compliant devices off while these devices are performing an atomic action. We verify the protocols in the presence of this enriched intruder model to capture possible security threats posed by these behaviors.

I2. Liveness properties of protocols can in general not be proved in the DY model, since the intruder can block all communications. To achieve fairness, which inherently comprises a liveness property (see Section 4.1), optimistic fair exchange protocols often rely on a "resilient communication channels" (RCC) assumption, e.g. see [28]. RCC guarantee that all transmitted messages will *eventually* reach their destination, provided a recipient for them exists [7]. The behavior of our intruder model is limited by RCC, i.e. it cannot indefinitely block the network.[4] Since the intruder is a non-deterministic process in our model, to exclude executions that violate RCC, we impose a fairness constraint [5] on the resulting LTS. Besides, the action **com**†, used in Section 5.3, represents communications not required by RCC. A protocol has to achieve its goals even when executions containing **com**† actions are avoided. A formal treatment of these issues is beyond the scope of this paper and can be found in [29].

As a minor deviation from DY, to indicate violation of the secrecy requirement, the intruder process performs the abstract action *revealed* when it gets access to a non-encrypted version of any DRM-protected content. This action is of course not triggered when the intruder merely renders an item using its trusted device, which is a normal behavior in the system.

5.2 Regular μ-Calculus

The design goals of Nuovo DRM (G1-G4) are encoded in the regular μ-calculus [30]. This logic covers the Nuovo DRM's design goals in its entirety, both safety and liveness, and naturally incorporates data parameters that are exchanged in the protocols. The alternation-free fragment of the regular μ-calculus can be efficiently model checked [30], and all the formulas that we have verified are in this fragment. Below, a short account of this logic is presented.

---

[3] In our formalization we ignore the possibility of tampering trusted devices. Countermeasures for such cases are discussed in [23,1].

[4] For instance, a wireless channel provides RCC for mobile devices, assuming that jamming can only be locally sustained.

[5] Two different notions of fairness are used in this paper: fairness in exchange (see G4) and fairness constraint of an LTS, which informally states that each process of the system has to be given a fair chance to execute [24].

Regular μ-calculus consists of *regular formulas* and *state formulas*. Regular formulas, describing sets of traces, are built upon *action formulas* and the standard regular expression operators. We use '.', '$\vee$', '$\neg$' and '*' for concatenation, choice, complement and transitive-reflexive closure, respectively, of regular formulas. State formulas, expressing properties of states, are built upon propositional variables, standard boolean operators, the possibility modal operator $\langle \cdots \rangle$ (used in the form $\langle R \rangle \mathsf{T}$ to express the existence of an execution of the protocol for which the regular formula R holds), the necessity modal operator $[\cdots]$ (used in the form $[R]\mathsf{F}$ to express that, for all executions of the protocol, the regular formula R does not hold) and the minimal and maximal fixed point operators μ and ν. A state satisfies $\mu X. F$ iff it belongs to the minimal solution of the fixed point equation $X = F(X)$, F being a state formula and X a set of states. The symbols F and T are used in both action formulas and state formulas. In action formulas they represent *no action* and *any action* and in state formulas they denote the empty set and the entire state space, respectively. The wild-card action parameter '$-$' represents any parameter of an action.

5.3   Analysis Results

In this section we describe the results obtained from the formal analysis of the Nuovo DRM scheme. Our analysis has the following properties: the intruder is allowed to have access to unbounded resources of data (like fresh nonces), should it need them to exploit the protocol. We consider only a finite number of concurrent sessions of the protocol, i.e. each participant is provided a finite number of fresh nonces to start new exchange sessions. Although this does not, in general, constitute a proof of security for a protocol, in many practical situations it suffices. As security of cryptographic protocols is not decidable (e.g. see [31]), a trade-off has to be made between completeness of the proofs and their automation. Our analysis method is fully automatic. Following [6], we assume perfect cryptography and do not consider attacks resulting from weaknesses of the cryptographic apparatus used in protocols. Type-flaw attacks[6] are also omitted from our analysis. These can, in any case, be easily prevented [32].

Our formal analysis consists of two scenarios. The first verifies effectiveness (G1) while using the synchronous communication model of Section 5.1. The second scenario uses the asynchronous communication model of Section 5.1 to verify the remaining properties (G2-G4). Both scenarios consist of two compliant devices C and D that are controlled (but not tampered) by the intruder of Section 5.1. Below, P, as always, represents the trusted content provider. The formulas in the following results use abstract actions to improve the readability of the proved theorems. These actions are explained in Sections 4.3 and 5.1. A complete formalization of these actions can be found in [23].

Honest scenario S_0: The communication network is assumed operational and no malicious agent is present. C is ordered to buy an item from P. Then, C resells

---

[6] A type-flaw attack happens when a field in a message that was originally intended to have one type is interpreted as having another type.

the purchased item to D. This scenario was checked using the EVALUATOR 3.0 model checker from the CADP toolset, confirming that it is deadlock-free, and effective as specified below.

Result 1. *Nuovo DRM is effective for scenario S_0, meaning that it satisfies the following properties:*

1. Each purchase request is inevitably responded.

$$\forall m \in Cont, \ r \in Rgts. \ [\mathsf{T}^*.request(C, m, r, P)] \ \mu X.((\langle \mathsf{T} \rangle \mathsf{T} \ \wedge \ [\neg update(C, m, r, P)]X)$$
$$\wedge$$
$$[\mathsf{T}^*.request(D, m, r, C)] \ \mu X.((\langle \mathsf{T} \rangle \mathsf{T} \ \wedge \ [\neg update(D, m, r, C)]X)$$

2. Each received item is preceded by its payment.

$$\forall m \in Cont, \ r \in Rgts.$$
$$[(\neg issue(P, m, r, C))^*.update(C, m, r, P)]\mathsf{F} \ \wedge \ [(\neg issue(C, m, r, D))^*.update(D, m, r, C)]\mathsf{F}$$

Dishonest scenario S_1: The intruder controls the communication network and is the owner of the compliant devices C and D. The intruder can instruct the compliant devices to purchase items from the provider P, exchange items between themselves and resolve a pending transaction. Moreover, the compliant device C can non-deterministically choose between following or aborting the protocol at each step, which models the ability of the intruder to turn the device off (see I1 in Section 5.1). We model three concurrent runs of the content provider P, and three sequential runs of each of C and D. The resulting model was checked using the EVALUATOR 3.0 model checker from the CADP toolset and the following results were proven.

Result 2. *Nuovo DRM provides secrecy in scenario S_1, i.e. no protected content is revealed to the intruder (see Section 5.1).*

$$\forall m : Cont. \ [\mathsf{T}^*.revealed(m)]\mathsf{F}$$

Result 3. *Nuovo DRM resists content masquerading attacks in S_1, ensuring that a compliant device only receives the content which it has requested.*

$$\forall a \in \{C, D\}, \ m \in Cont, \ r \in Rgts. \ [(\neg request(C, m, r, D))^*.update(C, m, r, D)]\mathsf{F} \ \wedge$$
$$[(\neg request(D, m, r, C))^*.update(D, m, r, C)]\mathsf{F} \ \wedge$$
$$[(\neg request(a, m, r, P))^*.update(a, m, r, P)]\mathsf{F}.$$

Besides, the intruder cannot feed the self-fabricated content m_0 to compliant devices:

$$\forall a \in \{C, D\}, \ r \in Rgts. \ [\mathsf{T}^*.update(C, m_0, r, D)]\mathsf{F} \ \wedge$$
$$[\mathsf{T}^*.update(D, m_0, r, C)]\mathsf{F} \ \wedge$$
$$[\mathsf{T}^*.update(a, m_0, r, P)]\mathsf{F}.$$

Result 4. *Nuovo DRM provides strong fairness in S_1 for P, i.e. no compliant device receives a protected content, unless the corresponding payment has been made to P.*

$$\forall a \in \{C, D\}, \ m \in Cont, \ r \in Rgts. \ [(\neg issue(P, m, r, a))^*.update(a, m, r, P)]\mathsf{F}$$
$$\wedge$$
$$[\mathsf{T}^*.update(a, m, r, P).(\neg issue(P, m, r, a))^*.$$
$$update(a, m, r, P)]\mathsf{F}$$

Result 5. *Nuovo DRM provides strong fairness in S_1 for D, as formalized below*[7]:

1. *As a customer: if a compliant device pays (a provider or reseller device) for a content, it will eventually receive it.* [8]

   Note that there are only finitely many TTPs available in the model, so the intruder, in principle, can keep all of them busy, preventing other participants from resolving their pending transactions. This corresponds to a denial of service attack in practice, which can be mitigated by putting time limits on transactions with TTPs. As we abstract away from timing aspects here, instead, the action $last_{ttp}$ is used to indicate that all TTPs in the model are exhausted by the intruder. In other words, as long as this action has not occurred yet, there is still at least one TTP available to resort to.

$$\forall m \in Cont, \ r \in Rgts. \ [\mathsf{T}^*.request(D,m,r,P).(\neg(update(D,m,r,P)))^*]$$
$$\langle(\neg com^\dagger(-,-,-))^*.(update(D,m,r,P))\rangle\mathsf{T}$$
$$\wedge$$
$$\forall m \in Cont, \ r \in Rgts. \ [\mathsf{T}^*.request(D,m,r,C).(\neg(resolves(D) \vee update(D,m,r,C)))^*]$$
$$\langle(\neg com^\dagger(-,-,-))^*.(resolves(D) \vee update(D,m,r,C))\rangle\mathsf{T}$$
$$\wedge$$
$$[(\neg last_{ttp})^*.request(D,m,r,C).(\neg last_{ttp})^*.resolves(D).$$
$$(\neg(update(D,m,r,P) \vee last_{ttp}))^*]$$
$$\langle(\neg com^\dagger(-,-,-))^*.update(D,m,r,P)\rangle\mathsf{T}$$

2. *As a reseller: no compliant device receives a content from a reseller device, unless the corresponding payment has already been made to the reseller.*

$$\forall m \in Cont, \ r \in Rgts. \ [(\neg issue(D,m,r,C))^*.update(C,m,r,D)]\mathsf{F}$$
$$\wedge$$
$$[\mathsf{T}^*.update(C,m,r,D).(\neg issue(D,m,r,C))^*.update(C,m,r,D)]\mathsf{F}$$

Note that the strong fairness notion that is formalized and checked here subsumes the timeliness property of goal G4, simply because when D starts the resolve protocol, which it can autonomously do, it always recovers to a fair state without any help from C.

Theorem 1. *Nuovo DRM achieves its design goals in scenarios S_0 and S_1.*

Proof. G1 is achieved based on result 1. Result 2 implies G2. Result 3 guarantees achieving G3. Results 4 and 5 guarantee G4.

6   Conclusions

We have formally analyzed the NPGCT DRM scheme and found two vulnerabilities in its protocols. The scheme is subsequently extended to address these

---

[7] Strong fairness for C is not guaranteed here, as it can quit the protocol prematurely. A protocol guarantees security only for the participants that follow the protocol.

[8] The fairness constraint used in the formulas corresponds to the strong notion of fairness in [33]: $\forall \theta. \ F^\infty enabled(\theta) \Rightarrow F^\infty executed(\theta)$.

vulnerabilities. The extended scheme, namely Nuovo DRM, as many other DRM systems, is inherently complicated and, thus, error prone. This calls for expressive and powerful formal verification tools to provide a certain degree of confidence in the security and fairness of the system. We have analyzed and validated our design goals on a finite model of Nuovo DRM. There is of course no silver bullet: our formal verification is not complete as it abstracts away many details of the system. For instance, as future work, we are considering analyzing the account-ability of the provider, which is taken as non-disputable in this study, addressing possible anonymity concerns of customers and incorporating the payment phase into the formal model. We are currently working on a practical implementation of Nuovo DRM using existing technologies, see [17].

Acknowledgments. We are grateful to Bruno Crispo and Wan Fokkink, for their comments on earlier versions of this paper, and to Bert Lisser for his help with distributed state space generation.

References

1. Nair, S., Popescu, B., Gamage, C., Crispo, B., Tanenbaum, A.: Enabling DRM-preserving digital content redistribution. In: 7th IEEE Conf. E-Commerce Technology, pp. 151–158. IEEE CS, Los Alamitos (2005)
2. Halderman, J., Felten, E.: Lessons from the Sony CD DRM episode. In: The 15th USENIX Security Symposium, pp. 77–92 (2006)
3. Groote, J.F., Ponse, A.: The syntax and semantics of μCRL. In: Algebra of Communicating Processes 1994. Workshops in Computing Series, pp. 26–62. Springer, Heidelberg (1995)
4. Blom, S., Fokkink, W., Groote, J.F., van Langevelde, I., Lisser, B., van de Pol, J.: μCRL: A toolset for analysing algebraic specifications. In: Berry, G., Comon, H., Finkel, A. (eds.) CAV 2001. LNCS, vol. 2102, pp. 250–254. Springer, Heidelberg (2001)
5. Blom, S., Calame, J., Lisser, B., Orzan, S., Pang, J., van de Pol, J., Torabi Dashti, M., Wijs, A.: Distributed analysis with μCRL. In: TACAS 2007 (to appear, 2007)
6. Dolev, D., Yao, A.: On the security of public key protocols. IEEE Trans. on Information Theory IT-29(2), 198–208 (1983)
7. Asokan, N.: Fairness in electronic commerce. PhD thesis, Univ. Waterloo (1998)
8. Avoine, G., Gärtner, F., Guerraoui, R., Vukolic, M.: Gracefully degrading fair exchange with security modules. In: Dal Cin, M., Kaâniche, M., Pataricza, A. (eds.) EDCC 2005. LNCS, vol. 3463, pp. 55–71. Springer, Heidelberg (2005)
9. Pucella, R., Weissman, V.: A logic for reasoning about digital rights. In: CSFW 2002, pp. 282–294. IEEE CS, Los Alamitos (2002)
10. Gürgens, S., Rudolph, C., Vogt, H.: On the security of fair non-repudiation protocols. In: Boyd, C., Mao, W. (eds.) ISC 2003. LNCS, vol. 2851, pp. 193–207. Springer, Heidelberg (2003)
11. Kremer, S., Raskin, J.: A game-based verification of non-repudiation and fair exchange protocols. In: Larsen, K.G., Nielsen, M. (eds.) CONCUR 2001. LNCS, vol. 2154, pp. 551–565. Springer, Heidelberg (2001)
12. Shmatikov, V., Mitchell, J.: Finite-state analysis of two contract signing protocols. Theor. Comput. Sci. 283(2), 419–450 (2002)

13. Kähler, D., Küsters, R.: Constraint solving for contract-signing protocols. In: Abadi, M., de Alfaro, L. (eds.) CONCUR 2005. LNCS, vol. 3653, pp. 233–247. Springer, Heidelberg (2005)
14. Abadi, M., Blanchet, B.: Computer-assisted verification of a protocol for certified email. In: Cousot, R. (ed.) SAS 2003. LNCS, vol. 2694, pp. 316–335. Springer, Heidelberg (2003)
15. Bella, G., Paulson, L.C.: Mechanical proofs about a non-repudiation protocol. In: Boulton, R.J., Jackson, P.B. (eds.) TPHOLs 2001. LNCS, vol. 2152, pp. 91–104. Springer, Heidelberg (2001)
16. Evans, N., Schneider, S.: Verifying security protocols with PVS: widening the rank function approach. J. Logic and Algebraic Programming 64(2), 253–284 (2005)
17. Krishnan Nair, S., Torabi Dashti, M.: DRM paradiso (2007), http://www.few.vu.nl//∼srijith/paradiso/andformal.phptherein
18. Pagnia, H., Vogt, H., Gärtner, F.: Fair exchange. Comput. J. 46(1), 55–75 (2003)
19. Alpern, B., Schneider, F.: Defining liveness. Technical Report TR 85-650, Dept. of Computer Science, Cornell University, Ithaca, NY (October 1984)
20. Fischer, M., Lynch, N., Paterson, M.: Impossibility of distributed consensus with one faulty process. J. ACM 32(2), 374–382 (1985)
21. Basu, A., Charron-Bost, B., Toueg, S.: Simulating reliable links with unreliable links in the presence of process crashes. In: Babaoğlu, Ö., Marzullo, K. (eds.) WDAG 1996. LNCS, vol. 1151, pp. 105–122. Springer, Heidelberg (1996)
22. Even, S., Yacobi, Y.: Relations amoung public key signature systems. Technical Report 175, Computer Science Department, Technicon, Haifa, Israel (1980)
23. Jonker, H., Nair, S.K., Dashti, M.T.: Nuovo DRM paradiso. Technical Report SEN-R0602, CWI, Amsterdam, The Netherlands (2006), ftp.cwi.nl/CWIreports/SEN/SEN-R0602.pdf
24. Clarke, E., Grumberg, O., Peled, D.: Model Checking. MIT Press, Cambridge (2000)
25. Meadows, C.: Formal methods for cryptographic protocol analysis: Emerging issues and trends. IEEE J. Selected Areas in Communication 21(1), 44–54 (2003)
26. Fernandez, J.C., Garavel, H., Kerbrat, A., Mateescu, R., Mounier, L., Sighireanu, M.: CADP: A protocol validation and verification toolbox. In: Alur, R., Henzinger, T.A. (eds.) CAV 1996. LNCS, vol. 1102, pp. 437–440. Springer, Heidelberg (1996)
27. Cervesato, I.: Data access specification and the most powerful symbolic attacker in MSR. In: Okada, M., Pierce, B.C., Scedrov, A., Tokuda, H., Yonezawa, A. (eds.) ISSS 2002. LNCS, vol. 2609, pp. 384–416. Springer, Heidelberg (2003)
28. Kremer, S., Markowitch, O., Zhou, J.: An intensive survey of non-repudiation protocols. Computer Communications 25(17), 1606–1621 (2002)
29. Cederquist, J., Torabi Dashti, M.: An intruder model for verifying liveness in security protocols. In: FMSE 2006, pp. 23–32. ACM Press, New York (2006)
30. Mateescu, R., Sighireanu, M.: Efficient on-the-fly model-checking for regular alternation-free μ-calculus. Sci. Comput. Program. 46(3), 255–281 (2003)
31. Comon, H., Shmatikov, V.: Is it possible to decide whether a cryptographic protocol is secure or not? J. of Telecomm. and Inform. Tech. 4, 3–13 (2002)
32. Heather, J., Lowe, G., Schneider, S.: How to prevent type flaw attacks on security protocols. In: CSFW 2000, pp. 255–268. IEEE CS, Los Alamitos (2000)
33. Francez, N.: Fairness. Springer, Heidelberg (1986)

Formalizing Compatibility and Substitutability in Communication Protocols Using I/O-Constraint Automata

Mahdi Niamanesh and Rasool Jalili

Department of Computer Engineering
Sharif University of Technology
Tehran, Iran
{niamanesh@mehr,jalili}@sharif.edu

Abstract. A communication protocol consists of a sequence of messages used by peer entities to communicate. Each entity in a network is equipped by at least one protocol stack. Due to the need for on-the-fly reconfiguration of protocol stack in future communication and computation devices, formalizing substitutability and compatibility of protocol entities are important in correctness assessment of dynamic reconfiguration. In this paper, we extend Constraint Automata and propose I/O-Constraint Automata to model behavior of protocols and propose enough formalism for substitutability and compatibility relations between protocols. We introduce input-blocking property of communication protocols, and show that in the context of communication protocols simulation relation is not strong enough for notion of substitutability. We show the relation between substitutability and compatibility to reason about the correctness in substitution of a protocol with a new one.

1   Introduction

Every system in a network has at least one protocol stack to communicate with other systems. Each protocol stack is materialized through one or more components, to which we refer as protocol components. Considering the OSI model [1] of a protocol stack, the application layer is located on the top layer and its mission is to transfer the application data to its peer application layer in the other system. The underlying peer protocols in two systems exchange proper sequence of messages in order to transfer upper layer data.

Future communication and computation devices require a dynamic- reconfigurable protocol stack to operate in different situations and contexts. In dynamic-reconfigurable protocol stack, protocol entities can be changed at run-time. Many research projects such as [2,3,4] have been carried out to offer a dynamic reconfigurable protocol stack.

In this context, substitutability problem is defined as the verification of whether a protocol component can be replaced with another component transparently. For this reason, two criteria should be verified for correctness[5]; First,

F. Arbab and M. Sirjani (Eds.): FSEN 2007, LNCS 4767, pp. 49–64, 2007.

any updated protocol component must continue to provide all messages offered by its earlier counterpart, and secondly intended correctness properties should be valid for the new component.

Compatibility problem studies the verification of inter-operation of two communicating peer components. It is important to note that, correct substitution of a new component with an old one, provides compatibility of the new component and the peer of the old one[6]. We believe that substitutability and compatibility are two key properties in the development of dynamic-reconfigurable systems, because they allow one to reason about the correctness of reconfiguration.

In this paper, we briefly describe Constraint Automata introduced in [7] and properties of communication protocols related to substitutability and compatibility problems, in Section 2. In Section 3, we introduce I/O-Constraint Automata to model behavior of communication protocol. We believe that I/O-Constraint Automata with its names-set and constraints, is an appropriate formalism to model communication protocols. Section 4 proposes enough formalisms for specification of substitutability and compatibility of protocols. We propose communication automaton of two constraint automata for the notion of compatibility; Moreover, we show that simulation notion in automata is not strong enough for the substitutability of two protocols. This section presents a formalism for backward-compatibility relation between protocols. In Section 5, we discuss related work. Finally, we conclude in Section 6, expressing our current and future work.

2   Background

One widespread approach to model behavior of protocol components is using automata. We extend and use Constraint Automata introduced by Arbab et al [7] for modeling protocol components and also substitutability and compatibility notions. In this section, we briefly describe Constraint Automata and its underlying semantic, Timed Data Streams.

2.1   Timed Data Streams

Timed Data Stream (TDS) is used to represent the sequence of timestamped snapshot of data-exchanging activities being done in a port. To define it formally, suppose $Data$ is a fixed, non-empty, and finite set of exchanging data. The set of all timed data streams over $Data$ is given by:

$$TDS = \{\langle \alpha, a \rangle \in Data^\omega \times \mathbb{R}_+^\omega | \forall k \geq 0 : a(k) \leq a(k+1) and \lim_{k \to \infty} a(k) = \infty\}$$

in which $V^\omega = \{\alpha | \alpha : \{0, 1, 2, ...\} \to V\}$ (for $V = Data, \mathbb{R}_+$), are the set of all streams over $Data$ and $\mathbb{R}_+$. Data stream $\alpha \in Data^\omega$ is denoted as $\alpha = \alpha(0), \alpha(1), \ldots$. Moreover, notation α' is used as derivative for α stream and denotes $\alpha(1), \alpha(2), \alpha(3), \ldots$. Thus, a timed data stream $\langle \alpha, a \rangle$ consists of a data stream α and a time stream a consisting of increasing positive real numbers that go to infinity. The time stream a indicates for each data item $\alpha(k)$ the moment $a(k)$ at which it appears for input, output or internal use. The presented TDS specifies infinite streams, which corresponds to infinite "runs".

To each port A_i, a timed data stream is associated and for a given name-set $Names = \{A_1, ..., A_n\}$, all TDS-tuples are defined as follows:

$$TDS^{Names} = \{(\langle \alpha_1, a_1 \rangle, ..., \langle \alpha_n, a_n \rangle) : \langle \alpha_i, a_i \rangle \in TDS, i = 1, ..., n\}$$

2.2 Constraint Automata

Constraint automata use a finite set N of $Names$, which stands for a set of all ports. The transitions of constraint automata are labeled with pairs consisting of a subset N of ports $\{A_1, ..., A_n\}$ and a data constraint g, which can be viewed as a symbolic representation of sets of data-assignments. Formally, data constraints are propositional formula built from the atoms $A = d$, where data item d is assigned to port A. Data constraints are given by the following grammar:

$$g ::= true \mid A = d \mid g_1 \wedge g_2 \mid \neg g$$

Logical equivalence $\equiv$ and logical implication $\leq$ of data constraints are defined as:

$$g_1 \equiv g_2 \text{ iff for all data-assignments } \delta : \delta \models g_1 \Longleftrightarrow \delta \models g_2$$
$$g_1 \leq g_2 \text{ iff for all data-assignments } \delta : \delta \models g_1 \Longrightarrow \delta \models g_2$$

In above formulas, δ is in the form of $[A \mapsto \delta_A : A \in N]$, which is used to describe the data-assignment that assigns to every TDS-name $A \in N$ the value $\delta_A \in Data$. The symbol $\models$ stands for the obvious satisfaction relation, which results from interpreting data constraints over data-assignments.

Definition 1 (Constraint Automata). *A constraint automaton over the data domain Data is a tuple $A = (Q, Names, \rightarrow, Q_0)$ where:*

- *Q, is a set of states*
- *$Names$, is a finite set of port names*
- *$\rightarrow$, is a subset of $Q \times 2^{Names} \times DC \times Q$, called the transition relation of A*
- *$Q_0 \subset Q$, is the set of initial states.*

It is common to write $q \xrightarrow{N,g} p$ instead of (q, N, g, p), in which N is the name-set and g is the data constraints over N acting as a guard of the transition. DC is an abbreviation for $DC(N, Data)$, which denotes the set of data constraints over ports N.

Constraint automaton is considered as acceptor for TDS-tuple that takes an input-stream $\theta \in TDS^{Names}$ and generates an infinite run for θ, that is a sequence $q_0, q_1, q_2, \ldots$ of automaton-states that can be obtained via transitions whose name-sets and guards match θ.

Bisimulation and Simulation. To define bisimulation, let $A = (Q, Names, \rightarrow, Q0)$ be a constraint automaton and R an equivalence relation on states of automata, Q. R is called a bisimulation for A if for $q_1, q_2 \in Q$, all pairs $(q1, q2) \in R$, all R-equivalence classes $P \in Q \backslash R$, and every $N \subset Names$:

$$dc(q_1, N, P) \equiv dc(q_2, N, P)$$

in which, $dc(q, N, P)$ is a disjunction of all data constraints for all transitions from q into a state in P with nodes N. States q_1 and q_2 are called bisimulation equivalent (denoted $q_1 \sim q_2$) iff there exists a bisimulation R with $(q_1, q_2) \in R$. Moreover, two constraint automata A_1 and A_2 with the same set of names, are called bisimulation equivalent (denoted $A1 \sim A2$) iff for every initial state $q_{0,1}$ of A_1 there is an initial state $q_{0,2}$ of A_2 such that $q_{0,1}$ and $q_{0,2}$ are bisimulation equivalent, and vice versa. Here, A_1 and A_2 must be combined into a large automaton obtained through the disjoint union of A_1 and A_2.

To define simulation relation, let $A = (Q, Names, \rightarrow, Q_0)$ be a constraint automaton and R a binary relation on Q. R is called a simulation for A if for $q_1, q_2 \in Q$, all pairs $(q1, q2) \in R$, all R-upward closed sets $P \subset Q$, and every $N \subset Names$:

$$dc(q_1, N, P) \leq dc(q_2, N, P)$$

P is called R-upward closed iff for all states $p \in P$ and $(p, p') \in R$ we have $p' \in P$. A state q_1 is simulated by another state q_2 (and q_2 simulates q_1), denoted as $q_1 \preceq q_2$, iff there exists a simulation R with $(q_1, q_2) \in R$. A constraint automaton A_2 simulates another constraint automaton A_1 (denoted as $A_1 \preceq A_2$) iff every initial state of A_1 is simulated by an initial state of A_2.

2.3   Communication Protocol

A communication protocol defines the rules for transmission of data blocks, each known as a Protocol Data Unit (PDU), from one node in a network to another node. Protocols are normally defined in a layered manner and provide all or part of the services specified by a layer of the OSI reference model[1]. A protocol specification defines operations of the protocol and consists of three parts[8]:

- Definition of the format for protocol control information which forms the PDU header
- Definition of rules for transmitting and receiving PDUs
- Definition of services provided by the protocol layers

Internal services and mechanisms in protocols, such as error handling in a protocol entity, are provided for its upper layer; They are transparent to its peer entity and realized through input and output messages. Accordingly, we give a simple definition for protocol:

Definition 2 (Protocol). *A protocol is a set of input and output messages having predefined formats, plus some rules governing the exchange of messages.*

While given definition of protocol does not consider timing issues (e.g. timeout and resending mechanisms), it fulfills our requirements in this paper.

In practice, each protocol entity has a minimum set of functionalities corresponding to a set of input and output messages. Over time, one or more extensions corresponding to some new or updated services in protocol entity are added or replaced. These extensions may change set of input or output messages. Inter-operation of two peers requires their commitment on the main functionalities. If the new version can transparently inter-operate with the peer of the old version, it is called backward-compatible extension.

Backward Compatibility. Backward-compatible extensions are used to modify protocols without coordinating the distribution of new versions. It causes to limit the distribution and standardizing costs. In a backward-compatible extension the component is modified in such a way that it can transparently inter-operate with existing versions [9]. This generally implies no essential changes in the component. TCP slow-start [10] and ESMTP [11] are examples of such a change. In a slightly more relaxed version of backward-compatibility, no changes are made to the fixed part of the header of protocol. Instead, either some fields are added to the variable length options field at the end of the header, or existing header fields are used for multiple purposes(overloaded).

3   I/O-Constraint Automata

In this paper, we modify Constraint Automata (CA) [7] in such a way that can separately express the sequence of input, output and internal messages, and the constraints governing messages. We call the new automata, I/O-Constraint Automata (or I/O-CA in short). The main motivations for using CA and introducing an extension, to model communication protocols are:

- Unlike I/O Automata [12] and Interface Automata [13] transitions in I/O-CA are data-dependent, which is useful (w.r.t Definition 2) in modeling protocol messages;
- The TDS-language generated by CA (and so I/O-CA) can be considered to specify data streams that can flow through the communication protocol;
- Data constraints on transitions can be used to specify formats and constraints of data and control messages;
- For pragmatic reasons, it is desirable to separate input, output and internal messages in protocols.

We suppose that every protocol is implemented as a component (protocol component) and its behavior is specified with an automaton (protocol automaton), namely I/O-CA. Each message type in the protocol has an equivalent port or name in its corresponding I/O-CA. Unlike original CA, ports in I/O-CA are distinct into three disjoint sets (like Interface Automata[13]), input, output, and internal to clearly distinguish protocol input, output and internal streams. In sequel, whenever it is understood from the context, we use the term "protocol" instead of protocol automaton or protocol component.

To formalize behavior of a protocol component by means of timed data streams, we use the names $A_1^I, ..., A_n^I$ for the input ports, $A_1^O, ..., A_n^O$ for the output ports, and $A_1^H, ..., A_n^H$ for the internal ports. The input and output ports connect components to each other or to the environment of the system. Each port is dedicated to one specific type of message.

For every given name-set of ports $Names$, we show set of all input ports, output ports and internal ports with $Names^I$, $Names^O$ and $Names^H$ respectively. To each port A_i, a timed data stream is associated. That is, for a given name-set $Names$ in which, $Names^I = \{A_1^I, ..., A_n^I\}$, $Names^O = \{A_1^O, ..., A_m^O\}$, $Names^H = \{A_1^H, ..., A_k^H\}$, we define input, output and internal streams as follows:

$$TDS^{Names^I} = \{(\langle \alpha_1, a_1 \rangle, ..., \langle \alpha_n, a_n \rangle) : \langle \alpha_i, a_i \rangle \in TDS, i = 1, ..., n\}$$

$$TDS^{Names^O} = \{(\langle \beta_1, b_1 \rangle, ..., \langle \beta_m, b_m \rangle) : \langle \beta_i, b_i \rangle \in TDS, i = 1, ..., m\}$$

$$TDS^{Names^H} = \{(\langle \gamma_1, c_1 \rangle, ..., \langle \gamma_l, c_l \rangle) : \langle \gamma_i, c_i \rangle \in TDS, i = 1, ..., l\}$$

3.1   Example: Alternating Bit Protocol

Alternating Bit Protocol (ABP) is a simple form of the Sliding Window Protocol (SWP) with a window size of 1. It is a connection-less protocol for transferring messages in one direction between a pair of protocols. Many popular communication protocols such as TCP and HDLC are based on SWP. The message sequence numbers simply alternate between 0 and 1 [1]. The sender simply sends messages numbered $d(0)$, the data d attached with a bit "0", or $d(1)$, the data d attached with a bit "1"; the content of messages is not identified. These are acknowledged with ack(1) or ack(0) respectively. Figure 1 shows a corresponding I/O-CA for a ABP-sender, noted as $A(ABP) = (Q, Names, \rightarrow, Q_0)$. There is one input port that supports message types A, $Names^I = \{A\}$. Message type is a pre-defined format for a message, for example A may be one byte-message. Also, there is one output port that supports message type D, $Names^O = \{D\}$. We use annotations "in", "out" and "int" for indices of ports to distinguish their input, output or internal types. Each message type or port has a timed data stream. For example TDS for port A is a set like $TDS(A) = \{\langle '00000010', t_0 \rangle, \langle '00000100', t_1 \rangle, ...\}$.

3.2   Execution Model for Communicating I/O-CA

There are two interaction (synchronization) models for two communicating peer components[14].

  i. Input-Blocking, Output-Blocking: Whenever a component is ready to perform an input/output transition, it has to wait (is blocked) until a peer is ready. Systems based on this type of synchronization are called "blocking systems".

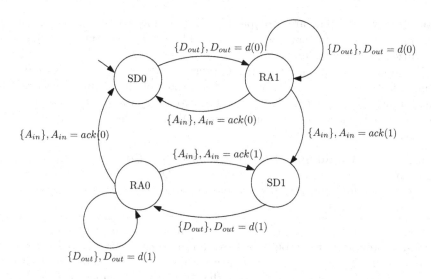

Fig. 1. Protocol Automata for Alternating Bit Protocol (ABP) sender

ii. Input-Blocking, Output-Non-Blocking: Whenever a component is ready to perform an output transition, it is free to do so. Whenever a component is ready to perform an input transition, it has to wait until the peer is ready. These systems are called "non- blocking systems".

In both models, the component is blocked when it requires an input message. We call this property "input-blocking". Moreover, in non-blocking systems, we assume that input ports can *receive* all type of messages but never *delivers* incorrect message type.

Interaction in communication protocols are usually based on non-blocking model. For safety considerations, incorrect inputs are not considered for delivery in order not to cause the protocol component to behave abnormal. For an example, in TCP protocol, when a TCP sender component sends a SYN message to its peer (TCP receiver), it waits (is blocked) for receiving a $SYN - ACK$ message. Any other message type may be received by the TCP sender, but in this state, it only accepts and delivers appropriate $SYN - ACK$ message from the peer.

To model the inter-operation of two communicating peer protocol components, we use two I/O-CA that communicate through a FIFO and error-free communication channels (with unbounded buffers). We call communication of two peers "parallel execution" which takes place in a closed system. That is, for two protocol components P_1 and P_2, inputs for *input ports* of P_1 (P_2) are provided only from the component P_2 (P_1), and outputs of *output ports* of P_1 (P_2) are given only to P_2 (P_1). For every output port such as D_{out} in one component, if there is an input port D_{in} in its peer component in which it can use (deliver) D_{out}'s messages, we call port D_{out} is "utilized" in the communication by the port D_{in}. In addition, for two ports D_{out} as an output and D_{in} as an input port, we call they are "compatible", if their message types are the same. It is important to note that, for two compatible ports, the output port may not be utilized in any communication.

We propose an automaton called *Communication Automata* to specify the communication behavior of two automata. States of the Communication Automaton are the consistent global states of two automata and transitions show the legal input/output actions for the ports. We define the Communication Automaton as follows:

Definition 3 (Communication-Automaton).   *The communication-auto-maton of two I/O-CA* $A_1 = (Q_1, Names_1, \rightarrow_1, Q_{0,1})$ *and* $A_2 = (Q_2, Names_2, \rightarrow_2, Q_{0,2})$ *is built by applying our pruning algorithm on the Cartesian product automaton* $A = A_1 \times A_2$.

The objective of the *pruning algorithm* is to remove all incorrect traces from the Cartesian product automaton to achieve an automaton with global consistent states. Intuitively, an incorrect trace is a trace that has an input port that can not utilize any preceding output port in that trace. Such an input port causes the trace to be blocked for infinite time and should be removed from the automata.

Our pruning algorithm traverses the automaton and marks all compatible input and output pairs of ports. At first, all the ports are unmarked. Specifically, the algorithm has two steps:

1. In each transition of A (Cartesian product automaton) and for each input port, look for an unmarked compatible port or marked compatible port on a self loop transition (transition with the same source and sink node) in the same or preceding transitions (path from the initial states to that transition) and mark both input and output ports; if there is no compatible port, remove the transition from the automaton.
2. Remove all the states (and their transitions) that are not reachable from any initial state.

Moreover, in production of two automata, we should have following preconditions, to avoid abusing of names:

$$Names_1^H \cap Names_2 = \phi, \qquad Names_2^H \cap Names_1 = \phi,$$
$$Names_1^O \cap Names_2^O = \phi, \qquad Names_1^I \cap Names_2^I = \phi$$

In the definition, two automata synchronize on their compatible input and output ports. Non-blocking property of I/O-CA allows automaton to send its output whenever it is ready. As a result, a pair of input and output ports should be synchronized either on the same transition or in a path of transitions that the output port precedes the input port. Figure 2 shows the communication automaton for two communicating I/O-CA. In the figure, we used the short notation "$D+$" for producing a proper data item from output port D, and "$D-$" for consuming a proper data through input port D. The notation "$D + -$" as a label for a transition indicates two compatible ports D_{in} and D_{out} sends and receives data at the same time.

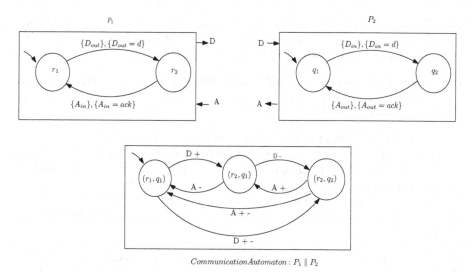

Communication Automaton : $P_1 \parallel P_2$

Fig. 2. Communication automaton for a parallel execution of two peer automata

In I/O-CA, there is no final states and we define the safety of communication based on the infinite run of two communicating I/O-CA. It is easy to check that if the communication automaton of two communicating I/O-CA has a cyclic graph, then two I/O-CA can have an infinite run. This is because in every traces of the communication automaton, before each input port there is a compatible output port that causes the trace not to be blocked. As a result, we give the following corollary for safety of a communication automaton:

Corollary 1 (Safe Communication Protocol). *Let* $A_1 = (Q_1, Names_1, \rightarrow_1, Q_{0,1})$ *and* $A_2 = (Q_2, Names_2, \rightarrow_2, Q_{0,2})$ *be two automata.* $A = A_1 \parallel A_2 = (Q, Names, \rightarrow, Q_0)$ *is safe iff* A *has a cyclic graph.*

4   Compatibility and Substitutability

In this section, we explain compatibility of two I/O-CA based on their communication automaton. We exploit simulation relation for definition of substitutability and backwards-compatibility notions in communication protocols.

4.1   Compatibility

Compatibility of two parallel executable automata implies the amount of ability of each automaton in utilizing messages of its peer. We define compatibility of two automata based on their communication-automaton. The definition exploits the non-blocking model of interaction of two communicating I/O-CA.

We define two specific types of compatibility, strong and weak. In a strong compatibility, two peer protocol components utilize all provided messages of each other. This situation occurs when all outputs of the components are carried out in a "correct" way. In a weak compatibility, there is at least one output of a peer component that is not utilized by the other peer.

Definition 4 (Compatibility of two I/O-CA). *Let* $A_1 = (Q_1, Names_1, \rightarrow_1, Q_{0,1})$ *and* $A_2 = (Q_2, Names_2, \rightarrow_2, Q_{0,2})$ *be two automata. Let* $A = A_1 \parallel A_2 = (Q, Names, \rightarrow, Q_0)$:

- A_1 *and* A_2 *have weak compatibility, noted* $A_1 \parallel_{wc} A_2$, *iff* A *is safe and has at least one output port that is not utilized in the communication automaton.*
- A_1 *and* A_2 *have strong compatibility, noted* $A_1 \parallel_{sc} A_2$, *iff* A *is safe and all output ports are utilized in the communication automaton.*
- *For* $\Gamma \subseteq (Names_1 \cap Names_2)$, A_1 *and* A_2 *have* Γ-*satisfiable compatibility, noted* $A_1 \parallel_\Gamma A_2$, *iff all ports in* Γ *are utilized during the communication automaton.*

Example 1. Figure 3 depicts I/O-CA for some example components, P_1, P_2, P_3, and P_4. Each component has its own input and output ports. We have used annotations "in" and "out" to distinguish input and output ports. The set $Data = \{d, ack, eack\}$ shows the data items that can be sent or delivered in all components. According to the figure, component P_1 simply sends a data d from port D and waits for port A to get data item ack. Component P_2 delivers data item d through port D and sends a data item ack. In component P_3, in state t_2 the component waits to receive $eack$ message and then ack message to send next data item d. In component P_4, in state s_2 component either accept ack or $eack$ message and then sends a data item d.

Considering the automata, we have following results based on the definition for compatibility:

- P_1 and P_2 are strongly compatible components: $P_1 \parallel_{sc} P_2$ or $P_1 \parallel_\Gamma P_2$ in which $\Gamma = \{D, A\}$
- despite extra input type E for P_4, we have $P_4 \parallel_{sc} P_2$ or $P_4 \parallel_\Gamma P_2$ in which $\Gamma = \{D, A\}$. Note that, based on our definition for the strong compatibility, it is not necessary for the peer of P_4 to produce messages for the input port E.

4.2   Behavioral Substitutability

In this subsection, we define behavioral substitutability of two protocol automata and formalize the backwards-compatibility notion of substitutability in protocols.

Based on simulation relation we define substitutability relation between two automata.

Definition 5 (Strong substitutability of two protocols). *Let* $A_1 = (Q_1, Names_1, \rightarrow_1, Q_{0,1})$ *and* $A_2 = (Q_2, Names_2, \rightarrow_2, Q_{0,2})$ *be two automata,* A_2 *is strongly substitutable with* A_1, *noted* $A_1 \sqsubseteq_{ss} A_2$, *iff* $Names_1 = Names_2$ *and* $A_1 \sim A_2$; *(* A_1 *and* A_2 *are bisimilar)*

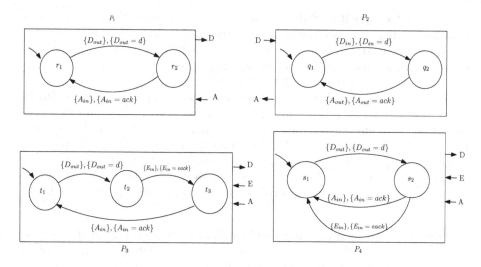

Fig. 3. Examples for protocol component automata

For ordinary labeled transition systems checking bisimilarity or checking whether one simulates another can be done in polynomial time [15]. For I/O-CA, standard algorithms for labeled transition systems (and finite automata) can be modified. However, as CA deals with logical equivalence and implication, the algorithmic treatment of the branching time relations (bisimulation and simulation) is more difficult than for ordinary labeled transition systems where only the existence of transitions with certain target states is important. As the proofs in [7] the problems of checking whether two CA are bisimilar or one automaton simulate another one, are coNP-Hard. Here, we use I/O-CA for modeling protocols, which have finite set of messages and states; therefore, the complexity of checking bisimulation and simulation relations are polynomial.

Simulation and bisimulation in behaviors of two component automata are usually used as a sufficient condition for substitutability problem (e.g. [16]). Herein, as our I/O-CA are input-blocking/output non-blocking systems, we show with an example that the simulation relation is not strong enough for substitutability problem.

Example 2. Considering Figure 3 and protocol automata for protocols P_1, P_2, P_3, and P_4 we have:

- protocol P_3 simulates protocol P_1, $P_1 \preceq P_3$, but we cannot substitute it with P_1; This is because of the extra input requirement (namely *eack*) together with input-blocking property of I/O-CA.
- protocol P_4 simulates protocol P_1, $P_1 \preceq P_4$, and we can substitute it with P_1; Extra input requirement (*eack*) does not always block the execution of the protocol, because state s_2 may proceed with alternative input (*ack*).

The given example leads us to find a condition, weaker than bisimulation, for substitutability notion.

Backward Compatible Substitution. Backward-compatibility property of a protocol component is an essential requirement to perform a transparent dynamic reconfiguration in a single node of a network [9]. Here, we want to formalize backward-compatibility based on our automata model for a protocol component to present a sufficient condition for substitutability.

To enable a new protocol to inter-operate with the peer of the old protocol component, is should provide at least all the previous output messages and should not have any extra input. The only remaining problem which may be a risk in backward-compatibility of a new protocol and the peer of the old protocol is the extra requirements of new protocol. Regarding the input blocking property of protocols, as mentioned in Section 3.2, there is no problem with the extra output messages of the new protocol and only extra input requirements should be satisfied.

Definition 6 (Backward compatible substitution of a protocol). *For automata A_1 and A_2, A_2 is a backward-compatible substitution for A_1, noted as $A_1 \sqsubseteq_{bs} A_2$ iff following conditions are hold:*

- $A_1 \preceq A_2$, *(A_2 simulates A_1)*
- *For any $q_i, q_j \in STATE(A_1) \cap STATE(A_2)$, in which $STATE(A_k)$, is the set of states for automaton A_k ($k = 1, 2$), and any transition path $q_i \leadsto^* q_j$, ($i \neq j$) in which all transitions are in $ST(A_2) \backslash ST(A_1)$ either the transition path has not any input port or there is at least one alternative transition path from q_i to q_j exists in A_1. Transition path $q_i \leadsto^* q_j$ means a sequence of transitions starts from q_i and ends in q_j.*

Example 3. Considering Figure 3 and protocol automata for protocols P_1, P_2, P_3, and P_4 we have:

- with respect to the Definition 6, $P_1 \sqsubseteq_{bs} P_4$, because the extra transition in P_4 has no input port,
- $P_1 \not\sqsubseteq_{bs} P_3$ because of the extra transition in P_3 with an input port (note that, $P_1 \preceq P_3$)

Based on the definitions for strong substitutability and backward-compatible substitutability we give the following corollaries:

Corollary 2 (Hierarchy of substitutability relations). *The substitutability relations form a hierarchy: $\sqsubseteq_{ss} \Rightarrow \sqsubseteq_{bs}$*

Corollary 3. *For all constraint automata A_1, A_2 and A_3 we have:*
$A_1 \sqsubseteq_x A_1$, and if $A_1 \sqsubseteq_x A_2$, and $A_2 \sqsubseteq_x A_3$ then $A_1 \sqsubseteq_x A_3$ (for $x = ss$ and bs)

Proof. It is clear the relation $\sqsubseteq_{ss}$ is reflexive. Transitivity property of $\sqsubseteq_{ss}$ is deduced from transitivity of bisimulation relation. For realizing transitivity property of $\sqsubseteq_{bs}$ relation, we should note that, based on the definition for backward-compatible substitution, $\sqsubseteq_{bs} \Rightarrow \preceq$.

We show the existing link between compatibility and substitutability concepts, and namely their combination, which seems necessary, when we deal with incremental design of components. Backward compatibility guarantees the transparency of changes in behavior of automaton. As a result, we can expect no effect in compatibility between two parallel executing automata. The following theorem studies the preservation of compatibility by substitutability, dealing with the two compatibility relations together with the two substitutability relations given in this paper.

Theorem 1 (Compatibility preservation by substitutability). *For automata A_1, A_2 and A_3, in which $A_i = (Q_i, Names_i, \rightarrow_i, Q_{0,i})$:*

1. $(A_1 \parallel_{sc} A_3) \quad \bigwedge \quad (A_1 \sqsubseteq_{ss} A_2) \quad \Rightarrow \quad (A_2 \parallel_{ss} A_3)$
2. $(A_1 \parallel_{\Gamma_{13}} A_3) \quad \bigwedge \quad (A_1 \sqsubseteq_{bs} A_2) \quad \Rightarrow \quad (A_2 \parallel_{\Gamma_{23}} A_3)$ *such that,* $\Gamma_{13} \subseteq \Gamma_{23}$

Proof. Part 1. It is enough to prove for each transition of A_2, there is a corresponding transition (path) in A_3 in which they can synchronize in communication automaton. Let $q_{j,2} \rightarrow q_{j+1,2}$ be a transition in A_2, we can find $q_{k,1}$ and $q_{l,1}$ in A_1 that are similar to $q_{j,2}$ and $q_{j+1,2}$. The transition (path) between $q_{k,1}$ and $q_{l,1}$ have a corresponding transition in A_3, that can be synchronized with $q_{j,2} \rightarrow q_{j+1,2}$.

Part 2. From the definition for $\sqsubseteq_{bs}$ we realize that A_2 is similar to A_1. Therefor, in their corresponding communication automaton all the ports in Γ_{13} exist and also Γ_{23} may have more ports than Γ_{13}.

5   Related Work

Most works in the field of modeling behavior of components [17] address component compatibility and adaptation in a distributed environment and are often based on process calculi [18]. Different automata models also exist to formally explain behavior of components; I/O Automata [12] (suitable for modeling distributed and concurrent systems), Interface Automata [13] (for documentation and validation of systems made of components communicating through their interfaces) and Component Interaction Automata [14] (formal verification-oriented component-based specification language with special emphasis on compositionality in components) are example of such models.

Some researches [19,16] put a specific emphasis on the substitutability and compatibility problems. In [16], the authors focus on a compositional mathematical automata model for behavioral programs to correct use of extended components in frameworks. The problem of compatibility is used to check the correctness of compositionality of components. In [20] Labeled Petri Net is used to model behavior of components. Substitutability of two components has been defined based on subtyping of provided and required observable services. For compatibility of two components, authors have used production of petri net models of components. In [5] authors aim to present an automated and compositional procedure to solve the substitutability problem in the context of evolving software systems. For checking correctness of software upgrades a technique based on simultaneous use of over and under approximations obtained via existential and universal abstractions together with a dynamic assume-guarantee reasoning algorithm has been proposed. Authors use Interface Automata in [6] and refinement or subtyping relations for substitutability and production of two automata for compatibility problem.

We use I/O-Constraint Automata (an extension to Constraint Automata [7]) to model behavior of protocol components. I/O-Constraint Automata employ set of input, output and internal port names and data constraints over the ports. Data-dependent transitions and ports are used to model data flow in the communication protocols. To solve the substitutability problem in protocols, we use bisimulation relation between two protocol automata and show that simulation relation is not strong enough for substitutability assessment in the context of protocols. We introduce input-blocking property of protocols and define backward-compatible substitution. For compatibility, like related work we use product automaton of two automata with attention to the input-blocking property.

6   Conclusion and Future Work

In this paper, we proposed I/O-Constraint Automata to model behavior of protocols. Based on this model, we defined the substitutability and compatibility relations. We demonstrated that in the context of communication protocols simulation relation is not strong enough for notion of substitutability. Based on the results of this paper, there is a strong relation between substitutability and compatibility. The relation helps to reason about the correctness in substitution of two communicating protocols. We introduced input-blocking property in communication protocols and formally defined backward-compatibility notion which is useful in designing new protocols and checking backward-compatibility between protocols.

Our work on formalizing protocol components relies on our currently and future experience with a framework for dynamic-reconfigurable architecture for protocol stack. In this framework, protocol entities are realized through one software component that includes formal specification of protocol and its implementation. Such a component model allowed us to study substitutability and compatibility of protocol components.

References

1. Tanenbaum, A.S: Computer Networks. Prentice Hall, Englewood Cliffs, NJ (1996)
2. Lee, Y., Chang, R.: Developing dynamic-reconfigurable communication protocol stacks using java. Software Practice Experience 6(35), 601–620 (2005)
3. Michiels, S., Matthijs, F., Walravens, D., Verbaeten, P.: Dips: A unifying approach for developing system software. In: Williams, A.D. (ed.) Proceedings - The Eigth Workshop on Hot Topics in Operating Systems, IEEE Computer Society, Los Alamitos (2001)

4. AN, L., Pung, H.K., Zhou, L.: Design and implementation of a dynamic protocol framework. Journal of Computer Communications (2005)
5. Sharygina, N., Chaki, S., Clarke, E., Sinha, N.: Dynamic component substitutability analysis. In: Fitzgerald, J.A., Hayes, I.J., Tarlecki, A. (eds.) FM 2005. LNCS, vol. 3582, pp. 512–528. Springer, Heidelberg (2005)
6. Clarke, E., Sharygina, N., Sinha, N.: Program compatibility approaches. In: Proceedings of the Formal Methods for Components and Objects symposium (2006)
7. Arbab, F., an J Rutten, C B., Sirjani, M.: Modeling component connectors in reo by constraint automata. In: FOCLASA 2003, ENTCS, pp. 25–41 (2004)
8. Jacobson, V., Braden, R., Zhang, L.: Tcp extensions for high-speed paths. RFC 1185 (1990)
9. O'Malley, S., Peterson, L.: Tcp extensions considered harmful. RFC 1263 (1991)
10. Allman, M., Paxson, V., Stevens, W.: Tcp congestion control. RFC 2881 99(7), 1–100 (1999)
11. Klensin, J., Freed, N., Rose, M., Stefferud, E., Crocker, D.: Smtp service extensions. RFC 1425, United Nations University, Innosoft International, Inc., Dover Beach Consulting, Inc., Network Management Associates, Inc., The Branch Office (1993)
12. Lynch, N.: An introduction to input/output automata. CWI Quarterly 2(3), 219–246 (1989)
13. de, A L., Henzinger, T.: Interface automata. In: Matsui, M. (ed.) FSE 2001. LNCS, vol. 2355, Springer, Heidelberg (2002)
14. Varekova, P., Zimmerova, B.: Component-interaction automata for specification and verification of component interactions. In: Romijn, J.M.T., Smith, G.P., van de Pol, J. (eds.) IFM 2005. LNCS, vol. 3771, pp. 71–75. Springer, Heidelberg (2005)
15. Henzinger, M., Henzinger, T., Kopke, P.: Computing simulations on finite and infinite graphs. In: Proc. FOCS 1995, pp. 453–462 (1995)
16. Moisan, S., Ressouche, A., Rigult, J.: Towards formalizing behavioral substitutability in component frameworks. In: SEFM 2004. Second International Conference on Software Engineering and Formal Methods, pp. 122–131 (2004)
17. Allen, R., Garlan, D.: A formal basis for architectural connection. ACM Trans, on Software Engineering and Methodology 6(3), 213–249 (1997)
18. Plasil, F., Visnovsky, S.: Behavior protocols for software components. IEEE Trans. on Software Engineering 28(11) (2002)
19. Liskov, B., Wing, J.: A behavioral notion of subtyping. ACM Trans. on Programming Languages and Systems 16(6), 1811–1841 (1994)
20. Hameurlain, N.: On compatibility and behavioural substitutability of component protocols. In: SEFM 2005. The 3rd IEEE International Conference on Software Engineering and Formal Methods, pp. 394–403. IEEE Computer Society, Los Alamitos (2005)
21. Arbab, F., Baier, C., de Boer, F., Rutten, J.: Models and temporal logics for timed component connectors. In: Proc. SEFM 2004, IEEE CS Press, Los Alamitos (2004)
22. Hoare, C.A.R.: Communicating sequential processes. Prentice-Hall, Englewood Cliffs (1985)
23. Satyanarayanan, M.: Pervasive computing: Vision and challenges. In: IEEE PCM, pp. 10–17. IEEE Computer Society Press, Los Alamitos (2001)
24. Stewart, R., Xie, Q., Morneault, K., Sharp, C., Schwarzbauer, H., Taylor, T., Rytina, I., Kalla, M., Zhang, L., Paxson, V.: Stream control transmission protocol. RFC 2960 (2000)

25. Niamanesh, M., Jalili, R.: Formalizing compatibility and substitutability in communication protocols using i/o-constraint automata. In: FSEN 2007. IPM International Workshop on Foundations of Software Engineering (Theory and Practice) (accepted 2007)
26. Niamanesh, M., Dehkordi, F.H., Nobakht, N.F., Jalili, R.: On validity assurance of dynamic reconfiguration in component-based program. In: FSEN 2005. Proceedings of IPM International Workshop on Foundations of Software Engineering (Theory and Practice) (7) (2005)

Is Your Security Protocol on Time ?[*]

Gizela Jakubowska[1] and Wojciech Penczek[2]

[1] Szczecin University of Technology,
Faculty of Computer Science and Information Systems
gjakubowska@wi.ps.pl
[2] Institute of Computer Science, PAS, and
Institute of Informatics, Podlasie Academy
penczek@ipipan.waw.pl

Abstract. In this paper we offer a novel methodology for verifying correctness of (timed) security protocols. The idea consists in computing the time of a correct execution of a session and finding out whether the Intruder can change it to shorter or longer by an active attack. Moreover, we generalize the correspondence property so that attacks can be also discovered when some time constraints are not satisfied. As case studies we verify generalized authentication of KERBEROS, TMN, Neumann Stubblebine Protocol, Andrew Secure Protocol, WMF, and NSPK.

1 Introduction

Security (or authentication) protocols define the rules of exchanging some messages between the parties in order to establish a secure communication channel between them, i.e., they provide the mechanism aimed at guaranteeing that the other party is who they say they are (*authentication*), that confidential information is not visible to non-authorised parties (*secrecy*), and that the information exchanged by two parties cannot be altered by an intruder (*integrity*). There are several approaches to verification of untimed security protocols, see e.g., [1,2,3,4,5]. Quite recently there have also been defined approaches to verification of time dependent protocols [6,7,8,9]. Our approach is closer to the work by Corin at al. [10], where security protocols are directly modeled in terms of networks of timed automata extended with integer variables, and verified with UppAal [11]. The authors address timeouts and retransmissions, but do not show how one can model timestamps [12] in such an approach.

There are several methods for finding attacks on security protocols. One can check whether the authentication property is satisfied, but this is not sufficient for discovering several 'authentication-independent' types of attacks. So, knowing the type of an attack one check whether it can occur or not. But, how to look for entirely unknown (types of) attacks ? Clearly, we can test the knowledge of the Intruder in order to find out whether he possesses some 'insecure' information. This requires either to use a special (epistemic) formalism for expressing

[*] The authors acknowledge partial support from the Ministry of Science and Information Society Technologies under grant number 3 T11C 011 28 and N516 038 31/3853.

F. Arbab and M. Sirjani (Eds.): FSEN 2007, LNCS 4767, pp. 65–80, 2007.

properties or to encode the knowledge of the Intruder into the states of the model, which leads to either making verification or the model itself more complicated. Moreover, no feedback for implementators follows from such a method of checking correctness. This paper[1] offers a novel method for finding attacks of any type either known or unknown. Our method consists in computing the time of a correct execution of a session and finding out whether the Intruder can change it to shorter or longer by an active attack. This method can be applied to both the timed as well as untimed protocols. To this aim and in order to make our modelling closer to real applications, the model of a protocol involves delays and timeouts on transitions by setting time constraints on actions to be executed. Timestamps are not necessary for using our method, but we take the opportunity to show how to tackle protocols with timestamps as well.

Our experimental results show that the known replay attacks on KERBEROS and Neumann Stubblebine protocol [14] are found using the classical correspondence property, whereas an attack on TMN [15] and a type flaw attack on Andrew Secure RPC Protocol (ASP) [14] requires verifying our generalised (timed) property. While playing with timing constraints, in addition to finding attacks, we can also identify time dependencies in protocols for which some known attacks can be eliminated. An example of such a protocol is Needham-Schroeder Public-Key (NSPK), where one can find an attack [16] using the correspondence property, but this attack disappears when we introduce timeouts and set them in an appropriate way. Formally, our method consists in translating a Common Language specification of a security protocol, possibly with timestamps, to one of the higher-level language IL[2] [17], and then again translating automatically the specification (obtained) in IL to a timed automaton without integer variables[3].

The rest of the paper is organized as follows. Section 2 introduces security protocols and the Dolev-Yao model of the Intruder In Section 3 timing aspects of the protocols are discussed. Our timed authentication property is defined in Section 4. The implementation in IL is described in Section 5. The experimental results and conclusions are presented in Section 6 and Section 7.

2   Modelling Security Protocols and the Intruder

In this section we introduce basic syntax for writing security protocols and discuss the Dolev-Yao model of the Intruder assumed in this paper.

We describe the protocols using a standard notation [14], called Common Syntax (CS, for short) developed for cryptographic protocols [15]. Usually, protocols involve two, three or four roles, which we denote with the capital letters A, B for the principals, and with S or S' for the servers.

---

[1] Some preliminary results [13] were presented at CS&P'06.

[2] IL is the acronym for the Intermediate Language (ver. 1.0).

[3] Thanks to that in addition to UppAal we can also use model checkers like Kronos [18] or VerICS [19] accepting timed automata (or their networks) without integer variables.

Let a protocol Q be represented by a finite sequence of instructions:

1. $X_1 \longrightarrow Y_1 : M_1$

...

n. $X_n \longrightarrow Y_n : M_n$

where $X_i, Y_i \in \{A, B, S, S'\}$ and $X_i \neq Y_i$ for $1 \leq i \leq n$, $Y_i = X_{i+1}$ for $1 \leq i < n$, and M_i is called a *message* variable[4]. The informal meaning of the instruction $A \longrightarrow B : M$ is that a principal of role A sends a message, which is a value of the variable M, to a principal of role B. Each message variable M is composed of variables ranging over identifiers representing principals ($\mathcal{PV}$), keys ($\mathcal{KV}$), nonces ($\mathcal{NV}$), and possibly timestamps ($\mathcal{TV}$), and their lifetimes ($\mathcal{LV}$).

Formally, the message variables are generated by the following grammar:

$Message ::= Component \times Component^*$
$Component ::= Cipher \mid Atom$
$Cipher ::= \{Component^*\}_K$
$Atom ::= P \mid N \mid K \mid T \mid L,$
where $P \in \mathcal{PV}$, $N \in \mathcal{NV}$, $K \in \mathcal{KV}$, $T \in \mathcal{TV}$, and $L \in \mathcal{LV}$.

For $X, Y \in \{A, B, S, S'\}$, K_{XY} is a *key* variable of X and Y, N_X is a *nonce* variable of X, T_X is a *timestamp* variable of X, and L_X is a *lifetime* variable of X. Moreover, by R we denote a *random number* variable. A message M can be encrypted with a key K, denoted by $\{M\}_K$. For example $\{T_X, N_X\}_{K_{XY}}$ is a message variable containing the timestamp variable T_X and the nonce variable N_X encrypted with the key variable K_{XY}.

The *keys* shared between an agent and a server (e.g., K_{AS}, K_{BS}) or between two agents (e.g., K_{AB}) are considered. The *nonces* represent random non-predictable numbers that are declared to be used only once by a concrete agent. The *timestamps* are unique identifiers whose values are provided by the (local) clock of its issuing entity and determine the time when a given message is generated. A value related to a timestamp is a *lifetime* defining how long since the timestamp creation it is acceptable to use each of the components of the messages the timestamp relates to. Next, we give an example of the protocol which is considered in the following sections.

Example 1. The protocol ASP [20] is the following sequence of four instructions:

1. $A \longrightarrow B : M_1 = A, \{N_A\}_{K_{AB}};$
2. $B \longrightarrow A : M_2 = \{N_A + 1, N_B\}_{K_{AB}};$
3. $A \longrightarrow B : M_3 = \{N_B + 1\}_{K_{AB}};$
4. $B \longrightarrow A : M_4 = \{K'_{AB}, N'_B\}_{K_{AB}}.$

In the first message A (Initiator) sends a nonce N_A, which B (Responder) increments and returns as the second message together with his nonce N_B. If A is satisfied with the value returned, then he returns B's nonce incremented by

---

[4] We will frequently refer to variables via their names like *message, principal, nonce, key,* and *timestamp* if this does not lead to confusion.

1. Then, B receives and checks the third message and if it is matched, then he sends a new session key to A together with a new value N_B' to be used in a subsequent communication.

A concrete *message* consists of components which are built of atomic cryptographic primitives that are elements of the following finite sets of identifiers: $\mathcal{P} = \{s, a, b, c, \iota, \ldots\}$ — *principal*, also called agents or participants, $\mathcal{SK} = \{k_{as}, k_{bs}, k_{ab}, \ldots\}$ *symmetric keys*, $\mathcal{AK} = \{k_a, k_b, k_a^{-1}, k_b^{-1}, \ldots\}$ — *asymmetric keys*, let $\mathcal{K} = \mathcal{SK} \cup \mathcal{AK}$ be the set of all the keys, $\mathcal{N} = \{n_a, n_b, n_a', n_b', \ldots\}$ — *nonces*, $\mathcal{T} = \{t_a, t_b, t_s, \ldots\}$ — *timestamps*, $\mathcal{L} = \{l, l', \ldots\}$ — *lifetimes*, $\mathcal{R} = \{r_a, r_b, \ldots\}$ — *random numbers*[5].

By a *protocol run* we mean a finite sequence of instructions resulting from a fixed number of possibly parallel sessions of the protocol. In a *session* of the protocol the variables are instantiated by concrete identifiers (names) of the principals and of the message elements. By a *component's type* we understand the sequence of the types of its atoms together with the braces. For example the type of the component $c = \{k, p, l\}k$ is $\{\mathcal{K}, \mathcal{P}, \mathcal{L}\}\mathcal{K}$ and the type of the component $c = \{\{p, l\}k\}k$ is $\{\{\mathcal{P}, \mathcal{L}\}\mathcal{K}\}\mathcal{K}$. Notice that for each protocol there is a finite set of the types of components that can be used for composing all the messages in this protocol. These types of components are denoted by $C_1, C_2, \ldots, C_n$.

2.1 Modelling the Intruder

Notice that the set $\mathcal{P}$ contains the identifier ι used for denoting the Intruder. The Dolev-Yao model of the Intruder is assumed [21]. One of the capabilities (besides exploiting intercepted messages) is that the Intruder can impersonate each agent executing the protocol, so he can play each of the roles of the protocol. Even thought the Intruder has got his own keys, nonces etc., he can also try to use all the information he is receiving in the protocol run as his own (e.g., nonces). When the Intruder impersonates an agent x $(x \in \mathcal{P} \backslash \{\iota\})$, we denote this by $\iota(x)$.

Intruder: Knowledge, Processes and Actions. Typically, the following Dolev-Yao capabilities of the Intruder are assumed [21]:

- He eavesdrops every letter passing through the *Net*, duplicates it and stores a copy in his local memory *IK*, called *database* or Intruder *knowledge*.
- He can affect intercepted letters by changing their headers (rerouting), replaying a letter, replacing an original letter with a modified or a new one, and finally send it or just delete intercepted letter.
- He can create any brand new letter built upon his knowledge.
- He can derive new facts basing only on his actual knowledge. This means he can decrypt and decompose any message only if he possesses a proper key.
- He can also exploit the malicious agent, who can initialize some sessions of the protocol. The Intruder can use his knowledge.

---

[5] We provide a variant of our implementation where the sets $\mathcal{N}$ and $\mathcal{K}$ are unified into the set $\mathcal{R}$.

An Optimized Intruder. The crucial point in an efficient modelling of the Intruder is to restrict his capabilities as much as possible, but without eliminating any of the possible attacks. One obvious restriction is that the Intruder generates messages of such a type and pattern, which can be potentially accepted by some agent. This means that the Intruder should be only sending messages, which are correct. So, intercepted messages are only modified by replacing some components with other components of the same type and pattern, which can be generated using the Intruder's knowledge and then send over to the responder. However, when the Intruder acts as an initiator[6] (for example sending the message $\mathcal{M}_1$ or $\mathcal{M}_3$ in KERBEROS), generating a completely new message can bring him to success. Our restriction on the Intruder's behaviour follows the rules of the optimized and the lazy Intruder of [21,2,13].

3   Timing Aspects

In this section we discuss all the timing aspects we consider in the implementations of security protocols.

Timeout. After sending a message M_i, a principal $p \in \mathcal{P}$ playing a role X, where $X \in \{A, B, S\}$, in a session j of a protocol is waiting for a response message[7]. The maximal period of time the sender is allowed to wait for it is called *a timeout* we denote as $t_{out,i}(j)$. Then, the next action of the principal p is executed if a response message had been received before the timeout passed. When the timeout is reached, and no response message has arrived, the principal who sends the message M_i in the session j can execute one of the following alternative actions: resending a message (called a *retransmission*) or starting the same session again (called *reset of a session*).

When verifying cryptographic protocols with timestamps, it is desirable to check their safety with respect to the timestamps and analyse their relationship with timeouts fixed in the protocol. It is well known that in some types of protocols it is not possible to set a timeout for each message. In such a case a timestamp indicating the time of creating a message is useful. Then, the receiver can decide whether the message is fresh or not, depending on the value of the timestamp and its lifetime L.

Time of Creating a Message M_i. For each principal $p \in \mathcal{P}$ we set a time of performing each mathematical operation like encryption - $\tau_{enc}(p)$, decryption - $\tau_{dec}(p)$, and generating random values - $\tau_{gen}(p)$. This way we can compute the time $\tau_{M_i}(p)$ of creating any message M_i by the principal p.

$$\tau_{M_i}(p) = (n_1 * \tau_{dec}(p)) + (n_2 * \tau_{enc}(p)) + (n_3 * \tau_{gen}(p)),$$

---

[6] He can initiate a session either from the beginning or from a middle of the protocol.

[7] Note, however, that there are messages without a corresponding response. This depends on the construction of a protocol and there are protocols without any response message (e.g., WMF protocol).

where $n_2(n_3)$ is the number of the operations of encryption (generating random values, resp.) to be performed in order to generate a message M_i, whereas n_1 is the number of the operations of decryption after receiving M_{i-1} (of the previous step of the protocol). The Intruder's time of composing a message using components he has intercepted in previous steps of the protocol is denoted by $\tau_{com,M_i}(\iota)$, but when it is assumed to be equal for all the messages it is denoted with $\tau_{com}(\iota)$.

Delay. The delay τ_d represents the time of message transmission from sender to receiver. As we have said before, all the messages are passing through the Intruder's part of the model, so how long it takes from sending to receiving a message depends on the value of a delay and the actions the Intruder performs. We assume that $\tau_d \in \langle \tau_{d,min}, \tau_{d,i} \rangle$ and the $\tau_{d,min}$ is a minimal delay of the network we have set before the run of the protocol. In order to simplify the formalism we assume that the minimal delay is the same for all the message transmissions [8]. The value of $\tau_{d,i}$ represents the maximal delay for a step i of the protocol (transferring a message M_i) and it is computed with respect to the timeouts (lifetimes) which cover the sequences of actions this step belongs to, the times of composing the messages that are sent in these sequences of actions, and $\tau_{d,min}$. The details of computing $\tau_{d,i}$ are given later in this section.

Time of a Session. This is an expected time of performing all the steps of a protocol including the time of a transmission of messages through the net. It is specified as a time interval $\langle T_{min}, T_{max} \rangle$, where $T_{min}(T_{max})$ is the minimal (maximal, resp.) time of an execution of all the actions allowing for all the possible delays. Below, we give a definition of the graph of the message flow in a protocol $\mathcal{Q}$ of n instructions and its one session $\mathcal{R}$:

1. $X_1 \longrightarrow Y_1 : M_1$ 1. $p_1 \longrightarrow q_1 : m_1$

   ...   ...

n. $X_n \longrightarrow Y_n : M_n$ n. $p_n \longrightarrow q_n : m_n$

where p_i (q_i) is the principal sending (receiving, resp.) m_i, for $1 \le i \le n$.

Let $tstamp(M_i)$ be the timestamp variable (if exists) of the message M_i, and let l_i be the value of the lifetime granted for $tstamp(M_i)$ in m_i. For example, if $M_i = \{X, L_X\}_{K_{XS}}, \{T_X, N_X\}_{K_{XY}}$, then $tstamp(M_i) = T_X$ and if $m_i = \{x, l_x\}_{k_{xs}}, \{t_x, n_x\}_{k_{xy}}$, then $l_i = l_x$.

In the graph defined below (Def. 1), the vertices represent control points of the message flow in the protocol such that the vertex $2i - 1$ corresponds to sending the message i, whereas the vertex $2i$ to receiving this message, for $i \in \{1, \ldots, n\}$. There are four types of edges in the graph denoted with E_j for $j \in \{1, 2, 3, 4\}$. Each edge $(2i - 1, 2i)$ of E_1 represents a transfer of the message i through the net. This edge is labelled with the minimal and maximal time of this transfer.

---

[8] We usually assume that $\tau_{d,min}$ is close to 0.

Each edge $(2i, 2i + 1)$ of E_2 represents a composition of the message i and it is labelled with the time of this composition. The edges of E_3 (E_4) correspond to timeouts (lifetimes, resp.). The intuition behind the edge (i, j) of E_3 or E_4 is that it covers all the edges of E_1 and E_2 between the vertices from the set $\{i, \ldots, j\}$.

Definition 1. *The four-tuple $G = (V, l_V, E, l_E)$ is a weighted labelled acyclic graph of the message flow in the session $\mathcal{R}$, where*

- $V = \{1, 2, \ldots, 2n\}$ *is the set of the vertices,*
- $l_V : V \longrightarrow \{+, -\} \times \mathcal{P}$ *is a vertex labelling function such that*
  $l_V(2i - 1) = -p_i$ *(p_i is the principal sending the message i) and*
  $l_V(2i) = +q_i$ *(q_i is the principal receiving the message i) for $1 \leq i \leq n$.*
- $E \subseteq V \times V$ *is a set of the directed labelled edges, where $E = E_1 \cup E_2 \cup E_3 \cup E_4$, $E_2 \cap (E_3 \cup E_4) = \emptyset$, $E_1 \cap E_3 = \emptyset$, and*
  - $E_1 = \{(2i - 1, 2i) \mid 1 \leq i \leq n\}$.
    E_1 *contains the edges representing the minimal and the maximal times of transferring messages through the net.*
  - $E_2 = \{(2i - 2, 2i - 1) \mid 1 < i \leq n\}$.
    E_2 *contains the edges representing the times of composing the messages.*
  - $E_3 = \{(2i - 1, 2j) \mid l_V(2j) = +p_i, 1 \leq i < j \leq n$, *where j is the smallest such a number for i}.*
    E_3 *contains the edges representing the timeouts between sending the message m_i and receiving the response message m_j by p_i.*
  - $E_4 = \{(2i - 1, 2j) \mid tstamp(M_i) = tstamp(M_j), \ 1 \leq i \leq j \leq n\}$.
    E_4 *contains the edges representing the lifetime l_i of the timestamp sent in the message m_i and then received in each message m_j.*
- $l_E : E \longrightarrow N \cup (N \times N) \cup (N \times N \times N) \cup (\{\tau_M\} \times N \times \mathcal{P})$ *is an edge labelling function s.t.*
  an edge $(2i - 1, 2i) \in E_1 \setminus E_4$ is labelled with $\langle \tau_{d,min}, \tau_{d,i} \rangle$ for $1 \leq i \leq n$, ($\tau_{d,min}$ is fixed, whereas the value of $\tau_{d,i}$ is computed if there is a lifetime or a timeout covering[9] the edge $(2i - 1, 2i)$, otherwise is equal to ∞),
  an edge $(2i - 1, 2i) \in E_1 \cap E_4$ is labelled with $\langle \tau_{d,min}, \tau_{d,i} \rangle, l_i$ for $1 \leq i \leq n$,
  an edge $(2i - 2, 2i - 1) \in E_2$ is labelled with $\tau_{M_i}(p_i)$ for $1 < i \leq n$,
  an edge $(2i - 1, 2j) \in E_3 \cap E_4$ is labelled with $min\{t_{out,i}, l_i\}$,
  an edge $(2i - 1, 2j) \in E_3 \setminus E_4$ is labelled with $t_{out,i}$, and
  an edge $(2i - 1, 2j) \in E_4 \setminus E_3$ is labelled with l_i, for $1 \leq i \leq j \leq n$,
  where $\tau_{d,i}$ is calculated as follows.
  For each $i \in \{1, \ldots, n\}$ define:
  - a set of the timeout- or lifetime-edges covering the edge $(2i - 1, 2i)$ of transferring the message m_i,

$$\mathbf{LT}_i = \{(k, l) \in E_3 \cup E_4 \mid k \leq 2i - 1 \wedge l \geq 2i\} \tag{1}$$

- the minimal time of executing all the operations covered by the timeout (lifetime) $l_E((k, l))$, where p_i is the principal composing the message M_i.

---

[9] This means that there is an edge (k, l) in $E_3 \cup E_4$ s.t. $k \leq 2i - 1$ and $2i \leq l$.

$$tca(k,l) = \sum_{i=(k+1)/2+1}^{l/2} (\tau_{M_i}(p_i) + \tau_{d,min}) + \tau_{d,min} \tag{2}$$

For each $(k,l) \in \mathbf{LT}_i$:

$$\mathbf{lt}_{(k,l)} = max\{\tau_{d,min}, l_E((k,l)) - tca(k,l) + \tau_{d,min}\} \tag{3}$$

For each $i \in \{1, \ldots, n\}$:

$$\tau_{d,i} = min\{\mathbf{lt}_{(k,l)} \mid (k,l) \in \mathbf{LT}_i\}. \tag{4}$$

Notice that we do not consider the time of composing the first and decomposing the last message. It is sufficient to measure the time between sending the first message and receiving the last one. Moreover, if a timeout or a lifetime is incorrectly set, i.e., it does not allow for sending a message, say M_i, after the time delay $\tau_{d,min}$, then we set $\tau_{d,i}$ to be equal to $\tau_{d,min}$ as well. But, later when computing the minimal and maximal possible time of executing one session (T_{min} and T_{max}), we use this information for setting both the times to 0.

Notice that $\tau_{d,i}$ (in the formula (4)) is computed as the minimum over all the times allowed by the timeout- and lifetimes-edges covering the transfer of the message m_i. This is clearly correct as $\tau_{d,i}$ can never exceed the minimal value of a timeout (lifetime)-edge covering the transfer of m_i.

In [10] the four typical message flow schemas for cryptographic protocols are presented. Their taxonomy is focused on timeout dependencies, so it does not deal with timestamps in the message flow schemas. As our goal is to apply the method to all the types of protocols without any restriction on their specifications or contents of the messages we introduce lifetime parameters that were not specified in [10]. Next, for each protocol to be verified, we build the corresponding graph according to Definition 1. Then, T_{min} and T_{max} are computed. T_{min} is taken as the weight of the minimal path in this graph, which corresponds to a sequential execution of all the actions within their minimal transmission time. However, if $l_E((k,l)) - tca(k,l) < 0$ for some $i \in \{1, \ldots, n\}$ and $(k,l) \in \mathbf{LT}_i$, then we set $T_{min} := 0$.

T_{max} is the maximal possible time of executing one session of the protocol taking into account all the timeouts and lifetimes. The idea behind computing T_{max} is as follows. For each transition $(2j-1, 2j)$ of E_1 we find its maximal possible delay, denoted by $\tau_{max,j}$, provided all the preceding transfers of the messages from m_1 to m_{j-1} have taken their maximal possible delays. The value of $\tau_{max,j}$ is computed similarly to $\tau_{d,j}$, but for all the transitions $(2i-1, 2i)$ of E_1 prior to $(2j-1, 2j)$, we take the values of $\tau_{max,i}$ instead of $\tau_{d,min}$. This requires to slightly modify the formulas $\mathbf{LT}_{(k,l)}$ into $\mathbf{LT}^j_{(k,l)}$. Then, T_{max} is defined as the sum of $\tau_{max,1}$ and all $\tau_{max,j}$ and $\tau_{M_i}(p_i)$ for $j \in \{2, \ldots, n\}$. But, if $\tau_{max,j} < \tau_{d,min}$ for some $j \in \{1, \ldots, n\}$, then we set $T_{max} := 0$. Below, we formalize the above algorithm in the following inductive definition.

We start with setting $\tau_{max,1} := \tau_{d,1}$.

Next, for $j \in \{2, \ldots, n\}$ we will use the following definitions to calculate $\tau_{max,j}$. For $(k, l) \in \mathbf{LT}_j$:

$$\mathbf{lt}^j_{(k,l)} = l_E((k,l)) \; - \sum_{i=(k+1)/2+1}^{l/2} (\tau_{M_i}(p_i) + \tau_{i-1}) \tag{5}$$

$$\text{where } \tau_i = \begin{cases} \tau_{max,i}, & for\ i \leq j, \\ \tau_{d,min}, & otherwise \end{cases}$$

Finally:

$$\tau_{max,j} = min\{\mathbf{lt}^j_{(k,l)} \mid (k,l) \in \mathbf{LT}_j\}, \tag{6}$$

$$T_{min} := \begin{cases} \tau_{d,min} + \sum_{j=2}^n (\tau_{M_j}(p_j) + \tau_{d,min}), & (\forall 1 \leq j \leq n)\ \tau_{max,j} \geq \tau_{d,min} \\ 0, & otherwise \end{cases} \tag{7}$$

$$T_{max} := \begin{cases} \tau_{max,1} + \sum_{j=2}^n (\tau_{max,j} + \tau_{M_j}(p_j)), & (\forall 1 \leq j \leq n)\ \tau_{max,j} \geq \tau_{d,min} \\ 0, & otherwise \end{cases} \tag{8}$$

Example 2. The message flow graph for ASP is shown in Fig. 1. The graph contains 8 vertices as there are 4 instructions in the protocol. There are no edges corresponding to lifetimes as timestamps are not used in the protocol. Notice that the timeout $t_{out,1}$, labelling the edge $(1,4)$, covers the three edges: $(1,2)$ - representing the sending of M_1 from a to b, $(2,3)$ - composing M_2 by b, and $(3,4)$ - the sending of M_2 from b to a. The timeout $t_{out,2}$, labelling the edge $(3,6)$, covers the three edges: $(3,4)$ - representing the sending of M_2, $(4,5)$ - composing M_3 by a, and $(5,6)$ - the sending of M_3 from a to b. Finally, the timeout $t_{out,3}$, labelling the edge $(5,8)$, covers the three edges: $(5,6)$ - representing the sending of M_3, $(6,7)$ - composing M_4 by b, and $(7,8)$ - the sending of M_4 from b to a.

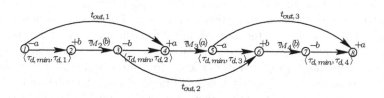

Fig. 1. The message flow graph for *ASP*

Assuming proper timeouts settings, the simplified formulas for T_{min} and T_{max} derived from (3)-(8) for the graph presented in Fig. 1 are as follows: $T_{min} = \tau_{M_2}(b) + \tau_{M_3}(a) + \tau_{M_4}(b) + 4 * \tau_{d,min}$, $T_{max} = t_{out,1} + \tau_{M_3}(a) + t_{out,3}$. If at least one of the timeouts is too short, then T_{min} and T_{max} are set to 0.

4   Authentication Property

We start with giving a definition of an attack [22] on an authentication protocol. We do not consider a *passive attack* [22] which is only based on monitoring the communication channel. Then, we formulate an extension of the authentication property for which we show that it implies an attack on a protocol.

Definition 2. *An* **active attack** *is one where the adversary attempts to delete, add, or in some other way alter the transmission on the channel.*

The actions of the Intruder leading to an active attack are called **active actions**.

Typically security protocols are verified against the (entity) authentication property [23,24], which can be formulated as the following correspondence property:

If a principal x has finished N sessions with a principal y in a protocol run, then the principal x must have started at least N sessions with the principal y.

When the above relation is symmetric we capture the *mutual entity authentication*. In this paper we suggest the *timed authentication property*, which consists of the above property and the following extension:

If a session of a protocol run between two principals x and y started at the time T_{start}, then it can be finished only within the time interval $\langle T_{start} + T_{min}, T_{start} + T_{max} \rangle$.

Notice that if a protocol ends before the specified T_{min}, then this may be a result of omitting at least one of the instructions or/and performing at least one of the instructions faster than it was expected. But, if a protocol ends after the specified T_{max}, then this may be caused by some additional actions, a modification of the timestamp, or an execution of at least one of the instructions slower than it was assumed. As the honest participants are not able to change the way they execute the protocol, the only possibility for an unexpected speed up or slow down in the execution of the protocol is due to an active action of the Intruder. So, if a session ends before the minimal time or after the maximal time specified causing that the timed authentication property does not hold, then there is an active attack in the meaning of Definition 2.

It is worth mentioning that the timed authentication property allows for detecting attacks even when the standard correspondence property is satisfied. To this aim observe that the correspondence property holds for a protocol whose session has started but has not terminated, but it fails only if a session has been terminated but it had not been started. Notice that there are attacks in which the Intruder impersonating the Responder leads to a successful end of a session, so that the correspondence property holds. By playing with the times of executing Intruder's actions we can show that there is a session which is finished before its minimal time T_{min}, which means that the timed authentication property fails.

5   Implementation

The roles A and B of the protocol Q are translated to disjoint parametrized IL processes $Proc_{X(p)}(j)$, where $p \in \mathcal{P}$ is the agent playing the role $X \in \{A, B\}$, and $j \in N$ is the number of a session. Notice that it is possible to run more than one[10] instance of each role by each agent of $\mathcal{P}$. The role S (S') is translated to the process $Proc_S$ ($Proc_{S'}$, resp.), which is not parametrized as it is possible to specify only one instance of each of them for all the possible sessions of the protocol. Each process $Proc_{X(p)}(j)$ and $Proc_S$ is specified by a set of local variables $V_p = \{N, K, L, T\}$, which are called *protocol variables*, a set of locations Q_p of the internal states of p which represents the local stage of the protocol execution, the initial location q_p^0 in which all the necessary initial values of the protocol variables are set, and a set of (timed) transitions $T_p(j)$ which correspond to the steps executed by the principal p playing his role in the session j.

The time interval specified for the transition indicates the period of time in which the transition is allowed to be fired since its enabling. The processes running in parallel are synchronized through a set of buffers B and global variables V_G. Communication between the participants is realized via two sets of buffers, called $\mathbf{B}^{IN}$ and $\mathbf{B}^{OUT}$. A sender puts the message i into the buffer of B_i^{OUT} which is denoted as $Send(B_i^{OUT}, m)$, whereas a receiver accepts the message i from the buffer of B_i^{IN} denoted as $Accept(B_i^{IN}, m)$. The Intruder transfers messages from $\mathbf{B}^{OUT}$ to $\mathbf{B}^{IN}$, so that he can easily control the flow and contents of the messages.

All the processes of Intruder are operating on a special set IK of buffers, called *Intruder's knowledge*. The buffers are used for storing all the messages passing through the net according to the types of components. But, if components corresponding to some cryptographic primitives have not been defined for a verified protocol, then the buffers for them are created additionally. Such an organization allows the Intruder for an easy access to desired data types in order to compose new correct messages. In case of ASP we have the following buffers: B_{C_1}, B_{C_2}, and B_{C_3} corresponding to the three types of components, whereas $B_{\mathcal{K}}$ (for keys) and $B_{\mathcal{N}}$ (for nonces) would be added as there are no components corresponding to the primitives of $\mathcal{K}$ and $\mathcal{N}$. The automated procedures of the Intruder's behaviour are described in [25]. The process of composing messages is based on two main procedures: *ComposeHeader* and *ComposeComponent* that use the components stored in IK in order to compose all the possible correct messages. The decomposing process consists of *DecomposeMessage* and *DecomposeComponent* procedures. The first one splits messages into components which are then analysed by the second procedure. The plain and encrypted components are stored in IK. If the Intruder happens to be in the possession of the proper key to decrypt a component, then this component is decomposed into subcomponents that are saved in IK.

The timing aspects discussed are modelled by timed transitions. To implement a timeout, for each session j we introduce the variable $Tmr_i(j)$ that indicates the state of a process $Proc_{X(p)}(j)$ ($p \in \mathcal{P}$ and $j \in N$) after the sending of message M_i[11]. Moreover, we implement the process $TmOut_i(j)$ which is responsible for managing the value of this variable. When the process $Proc_{X(p)}(j)$ sends a

---

[10] We assume that the number of sessions is bounded.

[11] Note that only one role in a session j can send a message M_i.

message and starts a timer of the timeout by setting $Tmr_i(j)$ to 1, the transition $t1$ in the process $TmOut_i(j)$ gets enabled and fired after the time reaches $t_{out,i}(j)$. This transition changes the value of $Tmr_i(j)$ back to 0. The process $Proc_{X(p)}(j)$ is able to receive an expected message as long as $Tmr_i(j)$ equals to 1. When this condition fails to hold, the process returns to the state $Init$ and generates new initial values like keys, nonces, and other random variables.

To implement a timestamp, the global variable T_i is introduced and initially set to 0. This variable represents the state of the timestamp i which may by either 'valid' or 'not valid'. The process $Timestamp_i$ is responsible for managing the value of T_i. When timestamp i is generated, T_i is set to i and the transition from $Init$ to $NotValid$ gets enabled (see Fig. 2). Then, after exactly L_i units of time the transition from $Init$ to $NotValid$ is forced, and it sets back T_i to 0. When the agent receives a message, he tests the corresponding timestamp by reading its identifier from the buffer and then checking the value of the variable T_i of the timestamp. If the value is equal to i and the message is found as *matched*, then it is accepted. Otherwise, the message is not accepted. An outdated timestamp cannot be validated anymore.

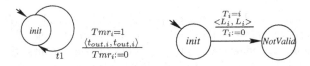

Fig. 2. The automata models of the processes $TmOut_i$ and $Timestamp_i$

A set of processes $Property_{xy}(j)$ in IL, one for each session j, is used to model the timed authentication property. The process $Property$ for one session is shown in Fig. 3. There are three possible locations (in addition to $Init$) each process $Property$ can be in: $AUTH$, ERR, and C_ERR. The state $AUTH$ is reached when the last message in a protocol is accepted within the correct time interval. The transition to the state ERR is caused when either the protocol ends too early or too late, whereas the state C_ERR is reached when the correspondence property is not satisfied. The pair of global variables $start$ and end is used to synchronize the participants' processes with the process $Property$. When the protocol starts, the variable $start$ is set to 1, the transition from Init to $AUTH$, and both the transitions from $Init$ to ERR become enabled. Each of them is fireable within the time interval specified, but it is fired only when the variable end has changed its value to 1 (during this time interval).

To implement the (basic) correspondence property, for each pair (x, y) of principals, where $x, y \in \mathcal{P} \setminus \{server\}$, we use the global variable $V_{AUTH}(x, y)$ whose value is equal to 0 at the beginning of a protocol run. Then, at the beginning of each new session for x and y the variable $V_{AUTH}(x, y)$ is incremented by 1, and at the end of each session the variable $V_{AUTH}(x, y)$ is decremented by 1. As long as the value of $V_{AUTH}(x, y)$ is non-negative the (basic) correspondence property holds.

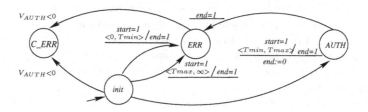

Fig. 3. The schema of the process $Property_{xy}$

6   Experimental Results

Our experiments are performed in order to show how values of time constraints influence safety of protocols as well as how they can be used to find or eliminate flaws in these protocols. We used the following two tools: VerICS [19] and Kronos [18]. Both of them have been fed with product automata generated by VerICS. For the protocols ASP, KERBEROS, NSP, and TMN the results are displayed in Fig. 4, where reachability of the states *AUTH, ERR,* and *C_ERR* depends on values of the timed parameters.

In order to find an attack we set the time for each of the Intruder's actions to belong to the time interval $\langle 0, T_{max} \rangle$. We test each protocol against the property shown in Fig. 3. When the state *ERR* (or *C_ERR*) of the property is reached, we look through the path leading to this state in the product automaton to get the time intervals for time parameters for which the attack has been discovered. This may result in finding an execution of the protocol, which is finished before the specified minimal time of a session. This way flaws are found in ASP [14] and

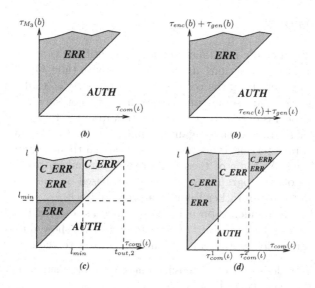

Fig. 4. The experimental results for ASP(a), TMN(b), NSP(c), and KERBEROS(d)

TMN [15] as for both the protocols the state ERR is reachable (see Fig. 4 (a),(b)). We have also checked the relationships between the lifetime of a timestamp and $\tau_{com}(\iota)$[12]. In Fig. 4 (a) the relationship between $\tau_{com}(\iota)$ and the time of finishing ASP is presented. If composing a new message by the Intruder takes less time than composing a message of type $\mathcal{M}_3$ by the principal b, then the protocol is finished before T_{min}.

For both the protocols NSP and KERBEROS if $\tau_{com}(\iota) < l$, then the correspondence property does not hold (see Fig. 4 (c),(d)). Moreover, the results for NSP show that when l does not allow for finishing the protocol (it is too short) but the time $\tau_{com}(\iota)$ is shorter than l, the protocol is finished before the time specified and the state ERR becomes reachable. The minimal value of the lifetime of a timestamp allowing to finish the protocol is denoted as l_{min}.

For KERBEROS the state ERR becomes reachable as well if additionally $\tau_{com}(\iota) < \tau_{com}^1(\iota)$ or $\tau_{com}(\iota) > \tau_{com}^2(\iota)$, where $\tau_{com}^1(\iota) = T_{min} - \tau_{M_4}(b)$ and $\tau_{com}^2(\iota) = T_{max} - \tau_{M_4}(b)$.

The protocol WMF[13] is another example for which we show that the timed property can be unsatisfied while the correspondence property still holds. This is the case when the time of a session is exceeded and is not limited even by a timestamp. So, the state ERR of the property is reached, for the following time constraint $\tau_{com}(\iota) + \tau_{d,1} + \tau_{d,2} < l_1$, where l_1 is the lifetime set for m_1.

While playing with timing constraints, in addition to finding attacks, we can also identify time dependencies for which some known attacks in protocols can be eliminated. Consider the protocol NSPK, where one can find an attack [16] using the correspondence property. This attack can be eliminated when the timeouts are set in an appropriate way. The condition is as follows: $(\tau_{d,i} - \tau_{d,min}) < \tau(M_i)(\iota)$ for $i = \{1, 3\}$. Recall that $\tau_{d,i}$ depends on the corresponding timeouts.

7   Conclusions

In this paper we offered a novel methodology for verifying correctness of (timed) security protocols whose actions are parametrized with time. Our main contribution consists in generalizing the correspondence property so that several attacks can be discovered when some time constraints are not satisfied. The verified model of a protocol is obtained via a translation from CL to the high level specification language IL, and then again to timed automata. We have introduced several time parameters into the model and discussed their meaning for the protocols considered. As some of these parameters depend on principal's abilities (e.g., the times of cryptographic operations) we based our methodology on one session of a protocol run rather than on a protocol itself.

Our timed correspondence property is specified as a timed IL process where the insecure states are constrained by time intervals. We showed how to build the message flow graph for a protocol session with respect to the timed parameters

---

[12] This is the Intruder's time of composing a message using components he has intercepted in previous steps of the protocol.

[13] 1. $A \longrightarrow S : A, \{T_A, B, K_{AB}\}_{K_{AS}}$ 2. $S \longrightarrow B : \{T_S, A, K_{AB}\}_{K_{BS}}$.

discussed in order to calculate the essential values used in the property. The definition of such a graph is applicable to most of the protocols [14,15].

The verification based on checking the reachability of the error states for the timed correspondence property leads us to find attacks that cannot be discovered using the standard correspondence property. The experimental results for the protocols ASP and TMN confirm that the timed property is not satisfied as both the protocols can be finished before the specified minimal time of a session.

Using this property it is also possible to find an insecure relationship between timed parameters, which may show weak points of the protocol. We showed a subtle relationship between lifetimes of the timestamps and timeouts in NSP and KERBEROS, while for KERBEROS these parameters can be tuned carefully to avoid an unexpected finish of the protocol.

Moreover, time constrains are used to find time dependencies for which some known attacks in protocols can be eliminated.

References

1. Armando, A., Compagna, L.: SATMC: A SAT-based model checker for security protocols. In: Alferes, J.J., Leite, J.A. (eds.) JELIA 2004. LNCS (LNAI), vol. 3229, pp. 730–733. Springer, Heidelberg (2004)
2. Basin, D.A., Mödersheim, S., Viganò, L.: OFMC: A symbolic model checker for security protocols. International Journal of Information Security 4, 181–208 (2005)
3. Boreale, M., Buscemi, M.G.: Experimenting with STA, a tool for automatic analysis of security protocols. In: SAC 2002. Proc. of the 2002 ACM Symposium on Applied Computing, pp. 281–285. ACM, New York (2002)
4. Armando, A., Basin, D., Boichut, Y., Chevalier, Y., Compagna, L., Cuellar, J., Drielsma, P.H., Heám, P., Kouchnarenko, O., Mantovani, J., Mödersheim, S., von Oheimb, D., Rusinowitch, M., Santiago, J., Turuani, M., Viganó, L., Vigneron, L.: The AVISPA tool for the automated validation of internet security protocols and applications. In: Etessami, K., Rajamani, S.K. (eds.) CAV 2005. LNCS, vol. 3576, pp. 281–285. Springer, Heidelberg (2005)
5. Kurkowski, M., Penczek, W., Zbrzezny, A.: Sat-based verification of security protocols via translation to networks of automata. In: MoChart IV. LNCS (LNAI), vol. 4428, pp. 146–165. Springer, Heidelberg (2007)
6. Delzanno, G., Ganty, P.: Automatic verification of time sensitive cryptographic protocols. In: Jensen, K., Podelski, A. (eds.) TACAS 2004. LNCS, vol. 2988, pp. 342–356. Springer, Heidelberg (2004)
7. Evans, N., Schneider, S.: Analysing time dependent security properties in CSP using PVS. In: Cuppens, F., Deswarte, Y., Gollmann, D., Waidner, M. (eds.) ESORICS 2000. LNCS, vol. 1895, pp. 222–237. Springer, Heidelberg (2000)
8. Gorrieri, R., Locatelli, E., Martinelli, F.: A simple language for real-time cryptographic protocol analysis. In: Degano, P. (ed.) ESOP 2003 and ETAPS 2003. LNCS, vol. 2618, pp. 114–128. Springer, Heidelberg (2003)
9. Lowe, G.: Casper: A compiler for the analysis of security protocols. Journal of Computer Security 6, 53–84 (1998)
10. Corin, R., Etalle, S., Hartel, P.H., Mader, A.: Timed model checking of security protocols. In: FMSE 2004. Proc. of the 2004 ACM Workshop on Formal Methods in Security Engineering, pp. 23–32. ACM Press, New York (2004)

11. Bengtsson, J., Larsen, K.G., Larsson, F., Pettersson, P., Yi, W., Weise, C.: New generation of UPPAAL. In: Proc. of the Int. Workshop on Software Tools for Technology Transfer (1998)
12. Jakubowska, G., Penczek, W., Srebrny, M.: Verifying security protocols with timestamps via translation to timed automata. In: CS&P 2005. Proc. of the International Workshop on Concurrency, Specification and Programming, pp. 100–115. Warsaw University (2005)
13. Jakubowska, G., Penczek, W.: Modelling and checking timed authentication of security protocols. In: CS&P 2006. Proc. of the Int. Workshop on Concurrency, Specification and Programming, vol. 206(2) of Informatik-Berichte, pp. 280–291. Humboldt University (2006)
14. Clark, J.A., Jacob, J.L.: A survey of authentication protocol literature. Technical Report 1.0 (1997)
15. Security protocols open repository (2003), http://www.lsv.ens-cachan.fr//spore
16. Lowe, G.: An attack on the needham-schroeder public-key authentication protocol. Information Processing Letters 56, 131–133 (1995)
17. Doroś, A., Janowska, A., Janowski, P.: From specification languages to timed automata. In: CS&P 2002. Proc. of the Int. Workshop on Concurrency, Specification and Programming, vol. 161(1) of Informatik-Berichte, pp. 117–128. Humboldt University (2002)
18. Daws, C., Olivero, A., Tripakis, S., Yovine, S.: The tool KRONOS. In: Alur, R., Sontag, E.D., Henzinger, T.A. (eds.) Hybrid Systems III. LNCS, vol. 1066, pp. 208–219. Springer, Heidelberg (1996)
19. Dembiński, P., Janowska, A., Janowski, P., Penczek, W., Półrola, A., Szreter, M., Woźna, B., Zbrzezny, A.: VerICS: A tool for verifying timed automata and Estelle specifications. In: Garavel, H., Hatcliff, J. (eds.) ETAPS 2003 and TACAS 2003. LNCS, vol. 2619, pp. 278–283. Springer, Heidelberg (2003)
20. Burrows, M., Abadi, M., Needham, R.: A logic of authentication. ACM Trans. Comput. Syst. 8, 18–36 (1990)
21. Armando, A., Compagna, L.: An optimized intruder model for SAT-based model-checking of security protocols. ENTCS 125, 91–108 (2005)
22. Menezes, A.J., van Oorschot, P.C., Vanstone, S.A.: Handbook of Applied Cryptography. CRC Press, Boca Raton, USA (2001)
23. Panti, M., Spalazzi, L., Tacconi, S.: Using the NuSMV model checker to verify the kerberos protocol. In: Simulation Series. Society for Computer Simulation, vol. 34, pp. 230–236 (2002)
24. Woo, T.Y.C., Lam, S.S.: A semantic model for authentication protocols. In: SP 1993. Proc. of the 1993 IEEE Symposium on Security and Privacy, pp. 178–194. IEEE Computer Society, Los Alamitos (1993)
25. Jakubowska, G., Penczek, W.: Verifying timed properties of security protocols. Technical Report 991, ICS PAS, Ordona 21, 01-237 Warsaw (2006)

Adapting the UPPAAL Model of a Distributed Lift System

Wan Fokkink[1,2], Allard Kakebeen, and Jun Pang[3]

[1] Vrije Universiteit, Section Theoretical Computer Science, Amsterdam,
The Netherlands
[2] CWI, Embedded Systems Group, Amsterdam, The Netherlands
[3] Universität Oldenburg, Safety-Critical Embedded Systems, Oldenburg, Germany
wanf@cs.vu.nl, allard_kakebeen@hotmail.com,
jun.pang@informatik.uni-oldenburg.de

Abstract. Groote, Pang and Wouters (2001) analyzed an existing distributed lift system using the process algebraic toolset μCRL. Pang, Karstens and Fokkink (2003) analyzed a redesign of this system using the timed automata based toolset UPPAAL. We adapt and extend this UPPAAL model. Firstly, we refine the synchronization mechanism between lifts, to explain a new problem that was reported by the developers of the lift system, and to propose a solution for it. Secondly, we allow a lift to enter a halt state, after which the entire system should make an emergency stop, for instance because a lift meets a maximum height threshold. Using the UPPAAL model checker we verified that the adapted lift system satisfies the system requirements.

1 Introduction

Verifying the correctness of the protocols that regulate the behavior of distributed systems is usually a formidable task, as even simple behaviors become wildly complicated when they are carried out in parallel. Formal verification is a suitable approach to check whether a specification of such a protocol meets its requirements. In a formal model of a real-life system, details irrelevant to the requirements under scrutiny can be abstracted away. With the formal model at hand, one is able to reason about the system in a systematic and automatic way, using e.g. a model checker or theorem prover. This formal reasoning can detect errors and suggest ways in which the system can be improved or optimized.

To achieve more confidence regarding the verified system, detected flaws in the formal model can be repaired, the model can be refined by adding more details, and extensions of the functionality can be included in the model. In this paper, we report on some modeling and verification experiences gained by adapting the UPPAAL model from [1,2] of a distributed lift system.

This lift system is used in real life for lifting lorries, railway carriages, buses etc. A system consists of a number of lifts: each wheel is supported by one lift, and each lift has its own micro-controller. This system is being designed and implemented by a small Dutch company (for commercial reasons we are not at

F. Arbab and M. Sirjani (Eds.): FSEN 2007, LNCS 4767, pp. 81–97, 2007.
© Springer-Verlag Berlin Heidelberg 2007

liberty to reveal the company name). A special protocol has been developed to let the lifts, which are connected in a ring network, operate synchronously. It consists of an initialization phase, in which all lifts get a unique identity, and a normal operation phase. When in the latter phase say an UP button on a lift is pushed, this lift leads the synchronous upward movement of all lifts until its UP button is released again. Special situations, such as when UP buttons at different lifts are pushed at the same time, have to be taken into account.

In order to explain and repair some detected bugs in the lift system, it was initially specified in the process algebraic language μCRL, and analyzed by means of model checking using the μCRL toolset [3]. This work was reported in [4,5]. In a redesign of the lift system, to include the recommendations from [5], the developers experienced a new problem. Since this problem involved exact timing information, and details of the system that had been abstracted away in the μCRL model, a more detailed model was specified in UPPAAL [6]. Using the graphic simulation tool in UPPAAL, the reason for the problem in the redesign was explained, and a solution was proposed. Moreover, it was shown using model checking that the UPPAAL model with this new solution satisfied all requirements. The solution was incorporated in the latest release of the lift system in early 2004. This work was reported in [1].

At the end of 2004, the developers of the lift system involved us in two matters regarding the coming release. Firstly, the developers reported that a new bug could sometimes occur when an UP button was pressed and almost immediately released again. We refine the synchronization mechanism between lifts in the UPPAAL model from [1], to capture this new problem and propose a solution for it. Secondly, the developers wanted a more polished solution for the situation where the system has to make an emergency stop because, for instance, one of the lifts meets a maximum height threshold. This feature of the system had been abstracted away in the μCRL and the original UPPAAL model. In our new UPPAAL model, we allow a lift to enter a special "halt" state, which is spread to the other lifts, upon which they all halt. The main challenge is how to move from this halt state to a standby state, as this requires that the main authority shifts back from the lift that initiated to halt state to the lift that controlled the movement.

During the adaptation of the UPPAAL model, we made several initial design errors, which were detected in the model checking phase. In this paper we explain our ultimate solutions for the synchronization mechanism and the halt state, and report on some of the initial design errors. Moreover, during the model checking exercise we detected a flaw in the UPPAAL model from [1] (which does not occur in the real implementation of the lift system). This flaw in the model had gone unnoticed due to a too restrictive test automaton in that paper. We explain how this flaw in the model can be repaired. We have shown using the UPPAAL model checker that our solutions are correct, at least for ring networks of size three, and with respect to the scenarios in our test automata.

A first aim of the current paper is to add yet another experience report on the use of formal methods in industry. Our collaboration with the company that builds the lift system has continued over the last five years. This experience is quite unique, in the sense that formal methods and tools (μCRL and UPPAAL) have been applied to the original lift system and its redesigns in three subsequent case studies. Over the years, the team of developers remained the same, but the team from the formal methods side has changed at each case study. In Section 6 we will draw some conclusions on the use of formal methods in long term industrial development, on the basis of these case studies.

A second aim is to communicate our experiences with adapting an UPPAAL model. Also it is explained how we used the UPPAAL model checker, with the help of test automata and decoration variables [7,8].

The developers acknowledge the usefulness of formal verification for their redesign. The new synchronization mechanism was included in the latest release of the lift system. Our specification of the special halt state will become part of the next release. The developers are now more confident in the correct functioning of the redesigned lift system. They stress that applying formal methods in the early design phases would save them testing effort and cost.

The paper is structured as follows. In Section 2, we provide an informal high-level description of the lift system, together with an explanation of our UPPAAL model of this system. Section 3 presents the system requirements that we want to verify. In Section 4 we present the refined synchronization mechanism between lifts, and explain in detail how we model checked the resulting UPPAAL model. In Section 5 we present the extension with a special halt state for emergency situations, and again describe the model checking exercise. Section 6 contains the conclusions. And finally Appendix A contains the most important automata of the UPPAAL model of the lift system.

2 UPPAAL Model of the Lift System

2.1 High-Level System Description

The lift system consists of an arbitrary number of lifts. Each lift supports one wheel of a vehicle. Different lift systems may have a different number of lifts, but this has no influence on the analysis, since this network should operate in the same way regardless how many lifts are connected.

Every lift has its own buttons. Three buttons are taken into account in the model: SETREF, UP and DOWN. Pressing a SETREF button on a lift is the only way a run of the system can start. If an UP or DOWN button on a certain lift is pressed, all lifts in the system are meant to move up or down at the same time. If the UP button at a lift has been pressed, the DOWN button at this same lift cannot be pressed before the UP button is released.

Movement of the lift system is controlled by means of a micro-controller. Each lift has its own micro-controller, called station here. Stations can adopt four different states: STARTUP, STANDBY, UP and DOWN. The state of a station can change in two ways: when a button on the lift is pressed, or by receiving a message from the network.

In the lift system, the data field of the messages transferred over the bus contains two pieces of information: the position of the sender station and the type of the message. There are two types of messages: state messages and sync messages. State messages broadcast the state of the sending station to the other stations, while sync messages initiate physical movement. In response to a sync message, the receiving station transfers its state to the motor of the lift, which causes movement. If the station is in the state UP, the lift will move up a fixed distance; if it is in DOWN, the lift will move down.

All stations are connected to a CAN (Controller Area Network) bus [9]. The CAN bus is a multi-master serial bus with error detection capabilities. The bus transmits messages to the stations. Whenever a station wants to send a message, it is said to claim the bus. Stations can receive messages at any moment, but when a station wants to send a message it has to wait until it is its turn to claim the bus. In the CAN bus, all stations can claim the bus at each cycle and several stations can claim the bus simultaneously. A non-destructive arbitration mechanism is used to determine which station may send its message. The resulting usage of the bus is ordered, meaning that the stations take fixed turns to send their messages. To achieve this orderly usage of the bus, before the lift system can start to operate, a start-up phase is performed in which each station finds out its position in the network and the total number of lifts in the network. This start-up phase is part of our UPPAAL model, but we abstract away from it here, as it is identical to the specification of the start-up phase in the original UPPAAL model. See [1] for a detailed description of the start-up phase.

When the start-up phase has finished, each station has been assigned a unique position and is in the state STANDBY, and the SETREF button is disabled. Then the normal operation phase starts, which is described in some detail in the remainder of this section. During normal operation, stations claim the bus in the same order cycle after cycle. A station knows whether it is its turn to claim the bus by checking the position of the sender station in the last received message. The state of a station changes from STANDBY to UP or DOWN when its UP or DOWN button is pressed, respectively. A station where this happens is called an active station. The active station sends an up or down message, according to the button that was pressed at the station. Each passive station changes its state according to the messages it receives, and when it is its turn to claim the bus it broadcasts its state. These state messages are received by all other stations, and the ordered sending of messages makes sure that the active station counts no more than one message from each station. When the active station counts enough up (or down) messages, it concludes that all lifts are ready to move. Then the active station broadcasts a sync message, after which in each cycle (as long as the active station continues to broadcast sync messages) all lifts move one unit of distance. In contrast to passive stations, the state of the active station can only change when the pressed button is released again. In that case its state changes to STANDBY and the station becomes passive again.

2.2   UPPAAL Model

UPPAAL [6] is a toolset for verifying timed systems, which are modeled as networks of timed automata [10], extended with global shared variables. Clock variables can be associated to a transition or a node. In a transition, clock variables can be reset or used in a guard. There are a graphical editor for system specification, a simulator and a model checker. During the design phase, the simulator is used to validate the dynamic behavior of each design sketch, in particular for fault detection, and later on for debugging the generated diagnostic traces. The verifier mainly checks for invariants and reachability properties. It does so by exploring the state space of a system using on-the-fly techniques. Symbolic techniques are used to reduce the verification of modal logic formulas to solving simple reachability constraints.

The UPPAAL (version 3.4.11) model of the lift system consists of four automata: *Bus*, *Timer*, *Station* and *Interface*. The automaton *Bus* models the CAN bus, and the automaton *Timer* models time delays. For each lift in the system we create two automata: *Station* and *Interface*, where *Station* models the microcontroller, while *Interface* captures the pressing and releasing of buttons on the lift. These last two automata can be found at the end of this paper, in Appendix A. The complete UPPAAL model is available at . http://seshome.informatik. . uni-oldenburg.de/ jun/lift/. Here we only provide sufficient explanations to present our adaptations of the original UPPAAL model and the analysis of this adapted model. A more detailed explanation and motivation can be found in [11].

Fast and main loop. Each station performs two different loops. In the so-called *fast loop*, a station can get a message from the bus, and when it is a station's turn to claim the bus, it sends a message to the bus intended for the other stations. Furthermore, the active station can count state messages and initiate movement of the whole system, by means of a sync message. In a *main loop*, a station synchronizes with its interface, to obtain information about which button on the lift (if any) has been pressed or released. Such a main loop takes place after a fixed number of cycles from the fast loop.

The two loops were implemented separately because communication with the bus is relatively fast. The separation leads to faster communication between the lifts, which is essential for the safe functioning of the system, as else the response time of the system would become too slow.

The precise time delays of the two loops in the actual lift system are taken into account in the UPPAAL model, and will be discussed below.

Flags. In [1], two flags CHANGE and ACTIVE were introduced in the automaton *Station*, as an improvement over two flags in the implementation of the lift system. The developers of the lift system acknowledged that this improvement solved a detected bug in the system, and included the new flags in its redesign.

When ACTIVE is set, the corresponding station is active; otherwise, the station is passive. CHANGE of a station is set when at this station a button is pressed or released; this update is communicated to the station through the main loop. The CHANGE flag is used to remember that the ACTIVE flag at this station must change from passive to active, or vice versa. CHANGE is reset together with a setting or resetting of ACTIVE (or if in the meantime a button is released or pressed again). This first change happens as soon as the station gets its turn to claim the bus, and the incoming message carries the state STANDBY.

Bus. We omit a precise description of the internals of the automaton *Bus*, and view it as a black box that regulates the distribution of messages in the fast loop. In the UPPAAL model, there are two channels for communication between the bus and the stations, and global shared variables are used for data transfer over these channels. When a station wants to send a message to the bus, it has to instantiate values for some global variables, for instance the sender's identity and state. When communication takes place, the values of those variables are saved to local variables of the bus. In a similar fashion, messages are sent from the bus to the stations.

Timer. Transitions normally do not take time in UPPAAL, but they do in the lift system. Each main loop consumes 1 millisecond. After each main loop, the station waits 0.5 millisecond to get messages from the bus. During the fast loop, the receiving and sending messages take 1 millisecond. Before sending a sync message, stations delay 1.5 millisecond. And before sending a state message, stations delay 2 milliseconds. The automaton *Timer* expresses this time consumption by means of transitions; this idea is borrowed from [12].

3   Requirements

The desired behavior of the lift system is captured in five requirements it has to fulfill, taken from [1]. These requirements were formulated together with the developers of the system.

1. *Deadlock freeness:* The system never ends up in a state where it cannot perform any action.
2. *Liveness I:* If all buttons are released, the system will eventually get to a state in which all lifts are standby.
3. *Liveness II:* If exactly one UP (or DOWN) button is pressed and not released, then all lifts will eventually move up (or down).
4. *Safety I:* If one of the lifts moves, then all other lifts move simultaneously (that is, within one cycle of the fast loop) in the same direction.
5. *Safety II:* If the lifts move, then an appropriate button was pressed.

The model checker of UPPAAL allows to check formulas over a rather weak temporal logic. In particular, *Liveness II* and *Safety I* cannot be expressed in this logic. In [7,8] an approach was developed for model checking such properties via reachability testing. The idea is to transform the property into a so-called *test automaton*, which is placed in parallel to the UPPAAL model of the system.

Such a test automaton is typically built from a specific scenario (e.g., a fixed sequence of button presses and releases), and contains a 'bad' state which can only be reached if the corresponding property is violated.

The test automaton may need some extra information that is not being maintained in the UPPAAL model of the system (such as how often a certain loop has been taken). This information can be added to the model, without influencing its functional behavior, in the form of so-called *decoration variables*.

In our verifications of two versions of the UPPAAL model of the lift system, which will be described in Sections 4 and 5, we made extensive use of test automata and decoration variables. We performed model checking with respect to networks of two or three lifts.

In the test automata, station 1 will play the role of active station. That is, the UP button at station 1 is the first button to be pressed, making station 1 active. We note that this is not a real limitation, in the sense that the network is fully symmetric (i.e., all stations exhibit the same behavior).

4   Sync Flag

The developers of the lift system informed us that a deadlock had occurred. After some testing at their premises, empirical evidence showed that it may occur if an UP (or DOWN) button is released shortly after it was pressed. Since this deadlock was not detected using the UPPAAL model from [1], it appeared that a crucial aspect of the system was missing in that model. The developers were of the opinion that the bug was most likely in the synchronization mechanism between the stations.

Discussions with the developers brought to light the fact that synchronization of the stations is implemented in a somewhat different fashion than as was specified in the UPPAAL model. In the real system there is an extra SYNC flag at each station, which is missing in the UPPAAL model.

When the active station counts enough up (or down) messages, in the UPPAAL model, this station initiates movement straight away by sending a sync message to the other stations. But in the real system, at each station there is an extra SYNC flag, which is set if the state of the station is UP (or DOWN) and there is no obstruction to send output to the motor. Each station reports in the messages it sends whether its SYNC flag is set, and the active station only sends a sync message when the SYNC flag is set at each station. When output is sent to the motor, the SYNC flag at that station is reset. The SYNC flag guarantees that output ports of the stations to their motors are in sync. Otherwise it might be the case that one station moves while another does not, for instance because the latter reached its highest position.

At first sight, it makes sense to abstract away from the SYNC flag in the UPPAAL model, as it does not take into account obstructions to the output ports. However, the SYNC flag can have an influence on the functional behavior, even in the absence of such obstructions. We therefore adapted the UPPAAL model from [1] to include the SYNC flag, and analyzed by means of the UPPAAL model checker whether the adapted model satisfies the requirements from Section 3.

Deadlock freeness can be expressed in the modal logic of UPPAAL:

`A[] not deadlock`

where `deadlock` is a predefined predicate in UPPAAL that holds for all deadlock states. We checked this property with respect to a number of scenarios (i.e., test automata). Initially this property was violated. Analysis of the error trace showed that, in line with reports from the developers, the deadlock may occur if an UP (or DOWN) button is released shortly after it has been pressed. Namely, as said before, the SYNC flag is reset when output is sent to the motor. But if the UP button is released shortly after it has been pressed, it may be the case that a SYNC flag at some station is set, but never reset, because no output is sent to the motor. The simple solution for this problem is to reset SYNC flags also when a button is released. We included this solution in our UPPAAL model, upon which no further deadlocks were detected.

Parallel button presses do not have an effect. That is, suppose that a button at some station is pressed. If (before the release of this button) a button at another lift is pressed and released, then this does not affect the states of the stations. We formulated this in a test automaton, in which initially the UP button at station 1 is pressed, expressed by the flag `press1!`. This button press makes station 1 active; the guard `Active[1]==1` makes sure that this happens before the UP button at station 2 is pressed (`press2!`), as else station 2 might get active instead of station 1. Finally the button at station 2 is released (`release2!`). The `bad` state can be reached if as a result the state of one of the stations is not in sync with the button state of the active station 1. The test automaton uses a decoration variables `countcycle`, which in the model is increased by one at every fast loop, together with a parameter `NCYCLE` (which we instantiated with 6 for two lifts, and with 13 for three lifts). The guard `countcycle<=NCYCLE` on the last transition guarantees that the scenario covers only a bounded number of fast loops, as otherwise the property could not be model checked. Without the guard `countcycle==1` on the second transition the `bad` state could be reached, as it requires one cycle of the fast loop before all stations have attained the same state as `buttonstate[1]`.

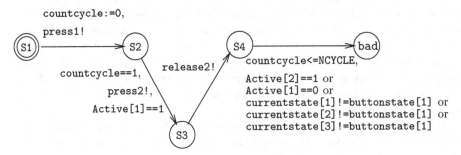

A model checking exercise with respect to our model in parallel to the test automaton above (for three lifts) showed that the `bad` state in the test automaton cannot be reached. In view of this positive model checking result, in the test automata to follow regarding the liveness and safety requirements, we do not take into account parallel button presses.

Liveness I was checked for a number of scenarios. Below a test automaton is presented in which first the UP button at station 1 is pressed (making it active), next the UP button at station 2 is pressed, then the button at station 1 is released (making station 2 active), and finally the button at station 2 is released. As before, `countcycle` and `NCYCLE` are used to make the scenario bounded. The `bad` state can be reached if after `NCYCLE` fast loops the stations are not all standby. (Again we instantiated `NCYCLE` with 6 for two lifts, and with 13 for three lifts).

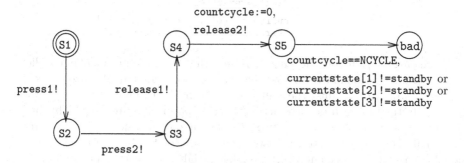

A model checking exercise with respect to our model in parallel to the test automaton above (for three lifts) showed that the `bad` state in the test automaton cannot be reached.

Liveness II was verified using a test automaton in which the UP button at station 1 is pressed and not released; *Liveness II* requires that eventually all lifts will start moving. As before, `countcycle` and `NCYCLE` are used to make the scenario bounded. In the model, the decoration variable `visitmovement` is increased by one every time a lift starts moving. Furthermore, N denotes the number of lifts in the system. If the UP button at station 1 is pressed and not released, and at the deadline (`countcycle==NCYCLE`) not all lifts have started moving (`visitmovement<N`), then the `bad` state is reached.

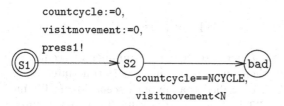

A model checking exercise with respect to our model in parallel to the test automaton above showed that the `bad` state in the test automaton cannot be reached.

The test automaton that was used in [1] for checking *Safety I* captures a quite restricted collection of scenarios. We constructed the following more elaborate test automaton. It has a similar structure as the previous test automaton. Suppose that the UP button at station 1 is pressed. The `bad` state can only be reached if ultimately (`countcycle==NCYCLE`) all lifts move (`visitmovement==N`) while not all stations are in the same state (`currentstate[1]!=currentstate[2]` or `currentstate[1]!=currentstate[3]`).

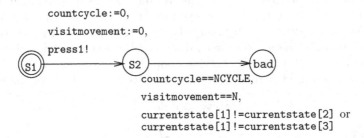

To our surprise, a model checking exercise with respect to our model in parallel to the test automaton above showed that *Safety I* was violated. We also checked this test automaton against the UPPAAL model from [1], and there too it was violated. In the model, lifts could actually move in opposite directions! This bug did not occur in a network with two lifts, but it did in a network with three lifts. Analysis of the error trace showed the reason for the bug: in the UPPAAL model (unlike the implementation), a global variable in the CAN bus maintains the message state; each station can read this variable. With three lifts, it is possible that a station receives a state message without processing it yet. Then another station may send a message to the bus, overwriting the message state variable before the first station reads it. The solution for this problem is simply to conform to the implementation, by introducing a message state variable at each station. We included this solution in our UPPAAL model, upon which *Safety I* was satisfied.

Finally, we verified *Safety II* in the same fashion as in [1]. The idea is to put a 'false' guard on all transitions in the *Interface* automaton that represent a button being pressed, and to add a flag `move` to the node capturing movement in the *Station* automaton, which is set if this node is visited. Now *Safety II* can be verified using the following modal formula:

$$A[] \text{ move } == 0.$$

We also verified *Safety II* with respect to a number of scenarios in which a button is pressed and then released within a short time interval, expressed by the parameter `SHORT`. We verified that in such scenarios no lift moves. In the test automaton below, `SHORT` was given the value 3 (in case of three lifts).

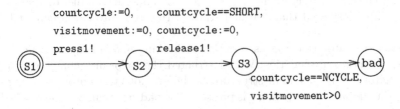

5 HALT State

In the implementation of the lift system, the situation is taken into account where the system has to make an emergency stop, for instance because one of the lifts meets a minimum or maximum height threshold. This feature of the system was abstracted away in the UPPAAL model in [1]. The developers of the lift system asked us to propose a more polished solution for emergency stops, because in their implementation emergency stops were dealt with in a rather ad hoc fashion.

We extended the *Station* automaton, by allowing it to enter a special HALT state, which is spread to the other lifts, upon which they all halt. Adapting the model can be split into three tasks: (1) achieve HALT in the detecting station, (2) communicate this HALT state to the other stations, and (3) leave the HALT state to continue normal operation from the STANDBY state.

Detecting HALT. In the *Station* automaton, we added a transition which allows a station (nondeterministically) to detect a halt notification, after which it changes its state to HALT. Initially, we allowed this transition to be taken only when the lift is in movement. However, according to the developers, in real life detection may also happen when a button was pressed but no movement has taken place yet. Therefore the latter was added as an extra possibility.

Spreading HALT. The HALT state is spread to the other stations via the fast loop. When a station in state HALT gets its turn to claim the bus, it sends out a halt message, which makes the other stations take on the HALT state too.

Leaving HALT. The hardest part is leaving the HALT state once the button that initiated the last movement has been released. The active station, at which this button was pressed, then needs to return to the STANDBY state to resume normal operation. It must therefore ignore further incoming halt messages from the other stations. So if a station is in HALT state, and its ACTIVE and CHANGE flags are both set (meaning that it is the active station and the button has been released), it adopts the STANDBY state, and spreads this state to the other stations via the fast loop.

We analyzed by means of the UPPAAL model checker whether the adapted model, including the HALT state, satisfies the requirements from Section 3. Two requirements need the proviso that HALT is not detected.

1. *Liveness II*: If exactly one UP (or DOWN) button is pressed and not released, *and* HALT *is not detected*, then all lifts will eventually move up (or down).
2. *Safety I*: If one of the lifts moves, *and* HALT *is not detected*, then all other lifts simultaneously move in the same direction.

Furthermore, together with the developers of the system we formulated one extra liveness requirement and one extra safety requirement.

1. *Liveness III*: After HALT is detected, it is always possible for the system to get to a state where all stations are STANDBY.
2. *Safety III*: If HALT is detected, then within a certain amount of time a state is reached where no lift moves.

Deadlock freeness, *Liveness I* and *Safety II* could be verified as in the previous section. For the other requirements, a global decoration variable `halted` was introduced, to signal the detection of HALT. In the test automata for *Liveness II* and *Safety I*, we added a guard to ensure that the `bad` node can only be reached if `halted` is not set. With these adapted test automata, *Liveness II* and *Safety I* could be verified without problem.

Liveness III was checked against a test automaton that is similar to the test automaton that we used for *Liveness I* in the previous section. The main difference is that a guard `halted==1` was added, to express that HALT has been detected. A model checking exercise with respect to our model in parallel to the resulting test automaton showed that the `bad` state cannot be reached.

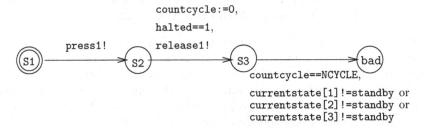

For *Safety III*, initially we required that after a detection of HALT, all lifts would stop moving within one cycle of the fast loop. However, this turned out to be too strict as it is not satisfied by the real-life system. Namely, if the lifts are moving, and the station detecting HALT has just sent a state message to the bus, it may be that two cycles of the fast loop are needed before all lifts have halted. *Safety III* with "four cycles of the fast loop" substituted for "a certain amount of time" does hold (in case of three lifts). That is, all stations except the one that detects HALT move at most twice after this detection; so in general there can be at most $2N-2$ movements from the moment HALT is detected. In the model, the value of the decoration variable `visitmovement` (which is increased by one at every movement of a lift) is set to zero as soon as `halted` is set. The `bad` state is reached if `visitmovement>=2N-1` and `halted==1`. We successfully checked the following test automaton against our model.

Time and memory consumption. Uppaal recommends to use "memtime" (see `http://freshmeat.net/projects/memtime/`) for measuring time and memory consumption. It is also remarked: "Please note that the result on memory is obtained by polling (with variable periods), which means that programs terminating very quickly may give different results for different executions."

The experiments were performed with Uppaal 3.4.11 on a PC with a AMD Athlon(TM) 64 Processor 3200+ of 2GHz, and with 1GB memory. Time and memory consumption were extracted using the Uppaal command line: "veri-fyta" with options "depth first search", "conservative space optimization", and "cheap inclusion checker". The time and memory consumption for checking each separate requirement, for a network of three lifts with NCYCLE = 13, is presented in Table 1.

Table 1. Time and memory consumption

	time (seconds)	memory (KB)
Deadlock freeness	10.7	64,588
Liveness I	35.2	399,256
Liveness II	6.2	76,980
Liveness III	19.0	234,936
Safety I	6.1	85,052
Safety II	12.7	157,672
Safety III	10.4	141,612

6 Concluding Remarks

In this paper, we have reported on an industrial case study in which formal techniques were applied for the analysis of a distributed system for lifting trucks. Our work can be considered as one more piece of evidence that formal verification techniques are sufficiently mature to be applied in the design of industrial systems. In particular embedded controllers appear to be well-suited for formal modeling and verification with model checking, as they tend to combine a high degree of complexity with a manageable state space.

A formal model is always an abstraction of the real system. The good thing is that this enables to study the core of a system, without superfluous details that may needlessly obscure the picture and increase the state space. A drawback however is that one may abstract away too much. In our case study, we saw two examples of this, regarding the UPPAAL model from [1]. Firstly, abstracting away from the SYNC flag meant that a bug in the implementation was missed. Secondly, using one global shared variable instead of different local shared variables at all stations induced a serious flaw in the model.

The latter flaw brings us to the use of test automata, as this flaw was initially missed due to a too restrictive test automaton. UPPAAL's modal logic is not very expressive. It is well-known that test automata can come to the rescue, to express different scenarios of a property that is outside the scope of the modal logic. However, this comes at a price. First of all, it means that only a subset of scenarios is verified, so that concrete test automata tend to be less general than the high-level requirements. Furthermore, building a good test automaton can be quite laborious. Last but not least, a test automaton can itself be too restrictive or even flawed. Still, test automata do allow to adequately capture critical/typical user interactions with the system. On one hand, more general test automata can describe more interactions, but on the other hand, checking them requires much more running time and memory usage, and can make the verification impossible, as we experienced. It is up to the user to try and find a good balance in this trade-off.

A disappointment for us was that, even with respect to relatively simple test automata, UPPAAL was only able to verify a network of up to three lifts. For a network of four lifts, it simply ran out of memory. A solution to this problem may be to use symbolic, compositional or on-the-fly methods, or symmetry reduction. Especially the latter approach could be fruitful here, in view of the symmetric nature of the ring topology of the lift system; as future research we intend to use the symmetry reduction method for UPPAAL from [13].

A strong point of formal models is that it is relatively easy to extend or adapt them, and then verify the adapted model. We experienced that it is very useful to have the ability to try different solutions to a problem (in this case the extra HALT state), and verify with model checking whether a solution is satisfactory. This was far easier than it would have been for the developers of the system to implement these different solutions and perform a substantial testing effort.

One has to keep in mind that an adaptation of the model can give rise to an adaptation of requirements, or to new requirements. Here we had to adapt *Liveness II* and *Safety I*, and introduced new requirements *Liveness III* and *Safety III*, for the extended model that includes a HALT state.

For us, the excellent graphical interface of UPPAAL has been invaluable, as it enabled the developers of the lift system to fully understand and comment on our formal models. We would like to emphasize the importance of establishing a good relationship between a formal methods group and a team of engineers. This relationship should be built on mutual trust and technical insight. Too often, a formal verification effort within industry is limited to a single case study. In general it would be much more fruitful to perform a series of case studies with the same group of engineers, and ideally with subsequent releases of the same system. This way the engineers get better acquainted with the formal methods approach, and the formal methods people get a better technical insight. Even more important, this way the results of a formal analysis can have a direct impact on the design of a system, and the strengths of formal models come to light. Namely, while developers may struggle to adapt the implementation and have to spend considerable testing effort, adaptation of the formal model and the subsequent model checking exercise tend to take relatively little effort.

Acknowledgments. We thank the developers of the lift system for their collaboration and fruitful discussions. Henk Barendregt and Frits Vaandrager provided useful feedback.

References

1. Pang, J., Karstens, B., Fokkink, W.J.: Analyzing the Redesign of a Distributed Lift System in UPPAAL. In: Dong, J.S., Woodcock, J. (eds.) ICFEM 2003. LNCS, vol. 2885, pp. 504–522. Springer, Heidelberg (2003)
2. Karstens, B.: Formal Verification of the Redesign of a Distributed Lift System using UPPAAL. MSc thesis, Utrecht University (June 2003), Available at www.phil.uu.nl/preprints/scripties/list.html

3. Blom, S.C.C., Fokkink, W.J., Groote, J.F., van Langevelde, I.A., Lisser, B., van de Pol, J.C.: μCRL: A Toolset for Analysing Algebraic Specifications. In: Berry, G., Comon, H., Finkel, A. (eds.) CAV 2001. LNCS, vol. 2102, pp. 250–254. Springer, Heidelberg (2001)
4. Groote, J.F., Pang, J., Wouters, A.G.: A Balancing Act: Analyzing a Distributed Lift System. In: Proc. FMICS 2001, pp. 1–12 (2001)
5. Groote, J.F., Pang, J., Wouters, A.G.: Analysis of a Distributed System for Lifting Trucks. Journal of Logic and Algebraic Programming 55(1-2), 21–56 (2003)
6. Larsen, K.G., Pettersson, P., Wang, Y.: UPPAAL in a Nutshell. Software Tools for Technology Transfer 1(1–2), 134–152 (1997)
7. Aceto, L., Burgueno, A., Larsen, K.G.: Model Checking via Reachability Testing for Timed Automata. In: Steffen, B. (ed.) ETAPS 1998 and TACAS 1998. LNCS, vol. 1384, pp. 263–280. Springer, Heidelberg (1998)
8. Aceto, L., Bouyer, P., Burgueno, A., Larsen, K.G.: The Power of Reachability Testing for Timed Automata. Theoretical Computer Science 300(1-3), 411–475 (2003)
9. Gmbh, R.B.: Postfach 30 02 40, D-70442 Stuttgart, Germany. CAN Specification. Version 2.0 (1991)
10. Alur, R., Dill, D.L.: A Theory of Timed Automata. Theoretical Computer Science 126(2), 183–235 (1994)
11. Kakebeen, A.: Extension and Formal Verification of a Distributed Lift System in UPPAAL. MSc thesis, Radbout Universiteit Nijmegen (August 2005), Available at www.cs.vu.nl/~wanf/kakebeen.doc
12. Havelund, K., Larsen, K.G., Skou, A.: Formal Verification of a Power Controller using the Real-time Model Checker UPPAAL. In: Katoen, J.-P. (ed.) AMAST-ARTS 1999, ARTS 1999, and AMAST-WS 1999. LNCS, vol. 1601, pp. 277–298. Springer, Heidelberg (1999)
13. Hendriks, M., Behrmann, G., Larsen, K.G., Niebert, P., Vaandrager, F.W.: Adding Symmetry Reduction to UPPAAL. In: Larsen, K.G., Niebert, P. (eds.) FORMATS 2003. LNCS, vol. 2791, pp. 46–59. Springer, Heidelberg (2004)

A UPPAAL Automata of the Lift Model

We present the two most important automata of our UPPAAL model. Start-up phase and the automata *Bus* and *Timer* are left out.

The automaton *Interface*, which is depicted in Figure 1, captures the buttons on a lift.

The automaton *Station* is depicted in two separate parts, which are joined together at the initial node normaloperation. At this node, two loops of a station can be performed: the main loop and the fast loop.

The main loop, which is depicted in Figure 2, is a short loop in which the automaton *Station* synchronizes with its *Interface*. Executing the main loop is the only way the station can get information about which button on the lift (if any) is pressed or released. This main loop takes place after a fixed number of fast loops, which is modeled as a constant CYCLES in the UPPAAL model. A counter cyclecounter is used to record the number of fast loops that have happened after the last main loop. When cyclecounter==CYCLES, the main loop takes place and cyclecounter is reset to 0. If the station detects a difference between

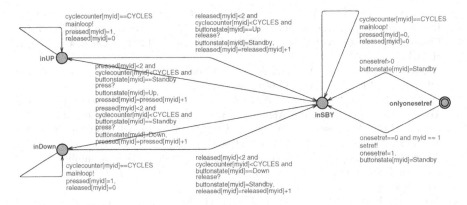

Fig. 1. The automaton *Interface*

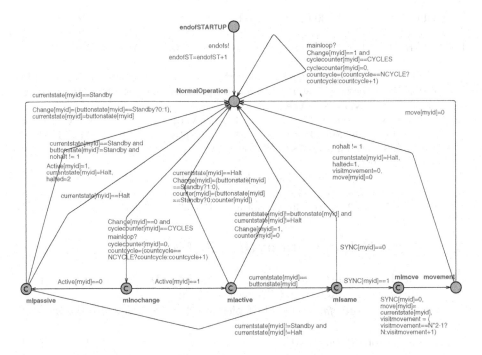

Fig. 2. Part of the automaton *Station*: Main loop

its current state (modeled by the variable `currentstate`) and the state of the *Interface* (modeled by variable `buttonstate`), the station may change its state and adopt the one from the *Interface*.

In the fast loop, which is depicted in Figure 3, a station can do several things. First a station can get messages from the bus. Second, a station can send a message to the other stations, if it gets the turn to use the bus. Third, the active

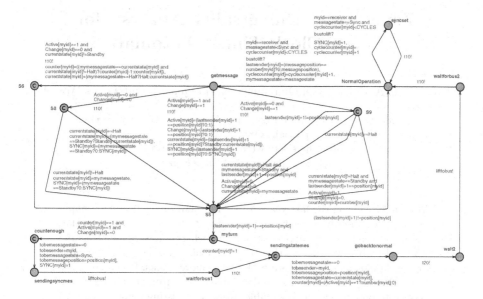

Fig. 3. Part of the automaton *Station*: Fast loop

station can count state messages and initiate a movement of the whole system. In that case the active station will enter the node **activemovement**, while the other stations get a sync message and enter the node **passivemovement**.

Zone-Based Universality Analysis for Single-Clock Timed Automata

Parosh Aziz Abdulla[1], Joël Ouaknine[2], Karin Quaas[1], and James Worrell[2]

[1] Department of Computer Systems, Uppsala University, Sweden
{parosh,karin}@it.uu.se
[2] Oxford University Computing Laboratory, UK
{joel,jbw}@comlab.ox.ac.uk

Abstract. During the last years, timed automata have become a popular model for describing the behaviour of real-time systems. In particular, there has been much research on problems such as language inclusion and universality. It is well-known that the universality problem is undecidable for the class of timed automata with two or more clocks. Recently, it was shown that the problem becomes decidable if the automata are restricted to operate on a single clock variable. However, existing algorithms use a region-based constraint system and suffer from constraint explosion even for small examples. In this paper, we present a zone-based algorithm for solving the universality problem for single-clock timed automata. We apply the theory of better quasi-orderings, a refinement of the theory of well quasi-orderings, to prove termination of the algorithm. We have implemented a prototype based on our method, and checked universality for a number of timed automata. Comparisons with a region-based prototype confirm that zones are a more succinct representation, and hence allow a much more efficient implementation of the universality algorithm.

1 Introduction

Timed automata have emerged as one of the most popular models for specification and analysis of real-time systems. An execution of such an automaton can be viewed as a *timed word* consisting of a sequence of events and their associated timestamps. Furthermore, different properties of the automaton can be expressed as languages of timed words. Since their introduction by Alur and Dill [1], timed automata have been used as the foundation for several verification algorithms and tools (see [2] for a survey). One of the most fundamental results about timed automata is the undecidability of the universality problem: Given a timed automaton $\mathcal{A}$, is the language of $\mathcal{A}$ universal? (i.e., is every timed word accepted by $\mathcal{A}$?). This problem is undecidable when the automaton $\mathcal{A}$ is allowed to have two or more clocks. In this context it is natural to seek subclasses of timed automata, with reduced expressive power, for which universality (or the more general problem of language inclusion) is decidable [3,4,2,5,6,7].

In particular, the paper [8] shows that both the universality and language inclusion problems are decidable for the class of timed automata which are restricted to operate on a single clock. The paper uses a variant of *regions* as a

F. Arbab and M. Sirjani (Eds.): FSEN 2007, LNCS 4767, pp. 98–112, 2007.

symbolic representation for sets of states in the universality algorithm; and uses the theory of *well quasi-orderings*, for proving termination of the algorithm. Despite the positive result in [8], deriving an algorithm which has a reasonable efficiency is still a difficult challenge. In fact, it is shown in [9] that the universality problem has a non-primitive recursive complexity for single-clock timed automata. In addition, it is well-known that the region representation is in general very inefficient and tends to explode even on very small examples.

In this paper, we propose a new formalism based on *zones* as a symbolic representation of sets of states in the universality algorithm. Our motivation is twofold. On one hand, several existing verification algorithms for classes of systems with well quasi-ordered state spaces perform well in practice when combined with efficient symbolic representations (despite non-primitive recursive complexities). Examples include lossy channel systems [10] and timed Petri nets [11]. On the other hand, zones often provide a much more compact representation of states than regions. Therefore, zones are used for instance in the design of existing tools for verification of real-time systems, such as KRONOS [12] and UPPAAL [13].

We solve the universality problem, by adapting the standard subset construction method. In particular we compute *configurations*: each configuration is the set of states which the automaton reaches through the execution of one timed word. We use zones as symbolic representations of (infinite) sets of configurations. One important aspect of the universality problem is that there is no bound on the number of clock variables in the zones which arise in the analysis. This makes the algorithm much more difficult to design compared to other zone-based algorithms such as the ones used in the above mentioned tools. A main challenge then is to show that the algorithm is still guaranteed to terminate. To achieve this, we show that zones are *well quasi-ordered*. More precisely, we show that, for each infinite sequence of zones $Z_0, Z_1, Z_2, \ldots$, there are i and j with $i < j$ such that the non-universality of Z_j is "entailed" by the non-universality of Z_i. To show the well quasi-ordering of zones, we follow the methodology of [14], and show that zones in fact satisfy a stronger property than well quasi-ordering, namely that they are *better quasi-ordered*.

We have implemented a prototype based on our method and have checked a number of timed automata for universality. Comparisons with a region-based prototype confirm that zones are a more succinct representation, and hence universality analysis is much more efficient when it operates on zones rather than regions.

Outline. In the next section, we give some preliminaries of timed automata. In Section 3 we consider the universality problem for configurations. In Section 4, we introduce zones, and in Section 5, we describe the zone-based universality algorithm. In Section 6, we show that the algorithm is guaranteed to terminate. We devote Section 7 and Section 8 to describe how to implement the different steps of the algorithm; more precisely, we show how to compute successors of zones in the algorithm, and how to check the entailment relation on zones. In Section 9, we report some experimental results. Finally, we give some conclusions and directions for future work in Section 10.

2 Timed Automata

In this section, we recall the basic definitions for timed automata, and concentrate on the class where the automata operate on a single clock.

We use $\mathbb{N}$ and $\mathbb{R}_+$ to denote the sets of natural numbers and non-negative reals respectively. For $\nu \in \mathbb{R}_+$, let $\lfloor \nu \rfloor$ and $fract\,(\nu)$ be the integral resp. fractional part of ν.

Timed Words. Let Σ be a finite alphabet. A *timed event* is a pair (t, a), where $t \in \mathbb{R}_+$ is called the *timestamp* of the *event* $a \in \Sigma$. A *timed word* is a finite sequence $t = (t_0, a_0)(t_1, a_1)(t_2, a_2) \ldots (t_n, a_n)$ of timed events whose sequence of timestamps $t_0 t_1 t_2 \ldots t_n$ is non-decreasing. We write $T\Sigma^*$ for the set of finite timed words over the alphabet Σ.

Timed Automata. We consider timed automata which operate on a single clock (in the sequel referred to as clock c). We define the set Φ of clock constraints to be conjunctions of formulas of the form $c \sim k$, $k \sim c$, where $k \in \mathbb{N}$ and $\sim \in \{<, \leq, >, \geq\}$. A *timed automaton* is a tuple $\mathcal{A} = (\Sigma, S, s_{init}, F, E)$, where

- Σ is a finite alphabet of events,
- S is a finite set of control states,
- $s_{init} \in S$ is the initial control state,
- $F \subseteq S$ is a set of accepting control states,
- $E \subseteq S \times S \times \Phi \times \Sigma \times \{tt, ff\}$ is a finite set of edges. An edge (s, s', ϕ, a, R) allows an a-labelled transition from s to s', provided that the precondition ϕ on clock c is met. Afterwards, c is either reset to 0 (if $R = tt$), or its value remains unchanged (if $R = ff$).

We let $cmax$ be the maximum natural number which appears on the edges of the automaton. A *global state* q of $\mathcal{A}$ is a pair (s, ν), where $s \in S$ is a control state and $\nu \in \mathbb{R}_+$ represents the value of clock c. We use $state\,(q)$ and $val\,(q)$ to denote s and ν. We say that q is *accepting* if $state\,(q) \in F$. The *initial global state* q_{init} is of the form $(s_{init}, 0)$.

Transition System. We define a transition relation on global states. For a global state q, we let $q + \delta$ be the global state q' such that $state\,(q') = state\,(q)$ and $val\,(q') = val\,(q) + \delta$. A *timed transition* is of the form $q \xrightarrow{\delta}_T q'$, where $q' = q + \delta$. A *discrete transition* is of the form $(s, \nu) \xrightarrow{a}_D (s', \nu')$ such that there is an edge (s, s', ϕ, a, R) in E and the following conditions are satisfied: (i) ν satisfies ϕ; (ii) $\nu' = 0$ if $R = tt$; and (iii) $\nu' = \nu$ if $R = ff$. We write $q \xrightarrow{\delta, a} q'$ to denote that $q \xrightarrow{\delta}_T q + \delta \xrightarrow{a}_D q'$. For a global state q, a *run* (of $\mathcal{A}$) from q is a finite sequence of transitions

$$q_0 \xrightarrow{\delta_0, a_0} q_1 \xrightarrow{\delta_1, a_1} q_2 \xrightarrow{\delta_2, a_2} \cdots \xrightarrow{\delta_{n-1}, a_{n-1}} q_n \tag{1}$$

where $q_0 = q$. The run is *accepting* if q_n is accepting. We use $L(q)$ to denote the set of timed words of the form $(t_0, a_0)(t_1, a_1) \ldots (t_{n-1}, a_{n-1})$ such that there is an accepting run from q of the above form and $t_j = \sum_{i=0}^{j} \delta_i$ for each $j : 0 \leq j < n$.

We say that q is *universal* if $L(q) = T\Sigma^*$. In the *universality problem*, we are given an automaton, and are asked whether the initial global state is universal or not.

3 Configurations

To solve the universality problem for global states, we study a more general problem, namely the universality problem for (sets of) *configurations*.

Configurations. A *configuration* γ is a finite set of global states. A configuration is said to be *accepting* if some $q \in \gamma$ is accepting. We lift the transition relation from global states to configurations. We use $\gamma \xrightarrow{\delta}_T \gamma'$ to denote that $\gamma' = \{q' | \exists q \in \gamma.\ q \xrightarrow{\delta}_T q'\}$. The definitions of the relations $\xrightarrow{a}_D$ and $\xrightarrow{\delta, a}$ are extended to configurations in a similar manner. For a configuration γ, a *run* (of $\mathcal{A}$) from γ is a finite sequence of transitions

$$\gamma_0 \xrightarrow{\delta_0, a_0} \gamma_1 \xrightarrow{\delta_1, a_1} \gamma_2 \xrightarrow{\delta_2, a_2} \cdots \xrightarrow{\delta_{n-1}, a_{n-1}} \gamma_n \qquad (2)$$

where $\gamma_0 = \gamma$. The run is *accepting* if γ_n is accepting. We define $L(\gamma)$ in a similar manner to the case of global states. We say that γ is *universal* if $L(\gamma) = T\Sigma^*$. Notice that $L(\gamma) = \bigcup_{q \in \gamma} L(q)$.

Sets of Configurations. A set Γ of configurations is said to be *accepting* if all its members are accepting. We use $\Gamma \xrightarrow{\delta}_T \Gamma'$ to denote that $\Gamma' = \{\gamma' | \exists \gamma \in \Gamma.\ \gamma \xrightarrow{\delta}_T \gamma'\}$. The definitions of the other transition relations are extended analogously. Also the notions of a run, an accepting run, $L(\Gamma)$, and universality, are extended in a similar manner to the case of sets of configurations.

We write $\Gamma \Longrightarrow \Gamma'$ to denote that $\Gamma \xrightarrow{\delta}_T \Gamma'' \xrightarrow{a}_D \Gamma'$ for some δ, a, and Γ''. We define $(\Gamma \Longrightarrow)$ to be the set $\{\Gamma' | \Gamma \Longrightarrow \Gamma'\}$.

Region Equivalence. For configurations γ and γ', and a bijection $h : \gamma \mapsto \gamma'$, we write $\gamma \equiv_h \gamma'$ to denote that the following conditions are satisfied for each $q, q_1, q_2 \in \gamma$:

- *state* $(q) = state\ (h(q))$.
- *val* $(q) \le cmax$ iff *val* $(h(q)) \le cmax$.
- if *val* $(q) \le cmax$ then $\lfloor val\ (q) \rfloor = \lfloor val\ (h(q)) \rfloor$.
- if *val* $(q) \le cmax$ then *fract* $(val\ (q)) = 0$ iff *fract* $(val\ (h(q))) = 0$.
- if *val* $(q_1) \le cmax$ and *val* $(q_2) \le cmax$ then *fract* $(val\ (q_1)) \le fract\ (val\ (q_2))$ iff *fract* $(val\ (h(q_1))) \le fract\ (val\ (h(q_2)))$.

We write $\gamma \equiv \gamma'$ to denote that $\gamma \equiv_h \gamma'$ for some h. The relation $\equiv$ is an equivalence, and is a modification of the standard region equivalence on global states. The latter relates (multi-clock) global states, while we here relate sets of global states each with a single clock. The following lemma is an adaptation from the classical theory of timed automata [1].

Lemma 1. *For configurations γ_1, γ_2, and γ_3, if $\gamma_1 \xrightarrow{\delta, a} \gamma_2$ and $\gamma_1 \equiv \gamma_3$, then there is a γ_4 such that $\gamma_3 \xrightarrow{\delta, a} \gamma_4$ and $\gamma_2 \equiv \gamma_4$.*

Entailment. We define an *entailment* relation $\sqsubseteq$ on (sets of) configurations. For configurations γ and γ', we write $\gamma \sqsubseteq \gamma'$ to denote that there is a $\gamma'' \subseteq \gamma'$ such that $\gamma'' \equiv \gamma$. For sets of configurations Γ and Γ', we use $\Gamma \sqsubseteq \Gamma'$ to denote that for each $\gamma' \in \Gamma'$, there is a $\gamma \in \Gamma$ such that $\gamma \sqsubseteq \gamma'$. We write $\Gamma \equiv \Gamma'$ to denote that both $\Gamma \sqsubseteq \Gamma'$ and $\Gamma' \sqsubseteq \Gamma$. The following lemma follows from Lemma 1.

Lemma 2. *Let Γ_1, Γ_2, Γ_3 be sets of configurations. If $\Gamma_1 \Longrightarrow \Gamma_2$ and $\Gamma_3 \sqsubseteq \Gamma_1$, then there is a set of configurations Γ_4 such that $\Gamma_3 \Longrightarrow \Gamma_4$ and $\Gamma_4 \sqsubseteq \Gamma_2$.*

For a set Γ of configurations, we define the *distance* $dist(\Gamma)$ of Γ to be the smallest n such there is a sequence $\Gamma_0 \Longrightarrow \Gamma_1 \Longrightarrow \Gamma_2 \Longrightarrow \cdots \Longrightarrow \Gamma_n$, where $\Gamma_0 = \Gamma$, and Γ_n is not accepting. In other words, $dist(\Gamma)$ gives the shortest distance through $\Longrightarrow$ from Γ to a non-accepting set of configurations. If Γ is universal then we define $dist(\Gamma) = \infty$. Notice that $dist(\Gamma) = 0$ iff Γ is not accepting. The following two lemmas relate (non-)universality of a set Γ of configurations to the (non-)universality of its successors.

Lemma 3. *For a set Γ of configurations, if $0 < dist(\Gamma) < \infty$ then there is a $\Gamma' \in (\Gamma \Longrightarrow)$ such that $dist(\Gamma') < dist(\Gamma)$.*

Lemma 4. *For a set Γ of configurations, Γ is universal iff Γ is accepting and each $\Gamma' \in (\Gamma \Longrightarrow)$ is universal.*

Notice that if $\Gamma \sqsubseteq \Gamma'$ and Γ' is not accepting then Γ is not accepting. This, together with Lemma 2, implies the following lemma. The lemma shows the relation between the entailment relation and the distance function.

Lemma 5. *For sets Γ and Γ' of configurations, if $\Gamma \sqsubseteq \Gamma'$ then $dist(\Gamma) \leq dist(\Gamma')$.*

4   Zones

We will use zones as a symbolic representation of (infinite) sets of configurations in our universality algorithm. We assume a timed automaton $\mathcal{A} = (\Sigma, S, s_{init}, F, E)$. For each $s \in S$, we will use a set X^s of variables ranging over $\mathbb{R}_+$. We use X to denote the set $\bigcup_{s \in S} X^s$. For $x \in X^s$, we use *type* (x) to denote the control state s.

Zones. A *zone condition* φ is one of the forms $x \sim k$, $k \sim x$, or $y - x \sim k$, where $\sim \in \{\leq, <\}$, $x, y \in X$, and k is an integer. A *zone* Z is a finite conjunction of zone conditions. Sometimes, we consider a zone Z to be a set and write, for instance, $(x \sim k) \in Z$ to indicate that $x \sim k$ is one of the conjuncts in Z. We use *Var* (Z) to denote the set of variables which occur in Z.

Consider a zone Z, a configuration γ, and a mapping $h : Var(Z) \mapsto \gamma$. We write $\gamma \models_h Z$ to denote that, for each $x, y \in Var(Z)$, the following conditions are satisfied:

- $type(x) = state(h(x))$.
- if $(x \sim k) \in Z$ then $val(h(x)) \sim k$.
- if $(k \sim x) \in Z$ then $k \sim val(h(x))$.
- if $(y - x \sim k) \in Z$ then $val(h(y)) - val(h(x)) \sim k$.

We write $\gamma \models Z$ to denote that $\gamma \models_h Z$ for some h. We use $[\![Z]\!]$ to denote the set $\{\gamma \mid \gamma \models Z\}$. Intuitively, each variable in $Var(Z)$ represents one global state. The configurations in $[\![Z]\!]$ contain global states whose control states are defined by the types of the corresponding variables, and whose clock values are related according to the zone conditions.

We say that Z is *universal* if $[\![Z]\!]$ is universal. Similarly, we say that Z is *accepting* if $[\![Z]\!]$ is accepting. Let Y be a set of variables. By $Z[Y]$, we mean the zone we get from Z by removing all conjuncts which contain a variable in Y. For a set $\mathcal{Z}$ of zones, we use $\mathcal{Z}[Y]$ to denote the set $\{Z[Y] \mid Z \in \mathcal{Z}\}$.

For zones Z and Z', abusing notation, we use $Z \equiv Z'$ resp. $Z \sqsubseteq Z'$ to denote that $[\![Z]\!] \equiv [\![Z']\!]$ resp. $[\![Z]\!] \sqsubseteq [\![Z']\!]$, and use $dist(Z)$ to denote $dist([\![Z]\!])$. We use $Post(Z)$ to denote a finite set $\mathcal{Z}$ of zones such that $\bigcup_{Z' \in \mathcal{Z}}[\![Z']\!] = ([\![Z]\!] \Longrightarrow)$. In Section 7, we show that such a set exists and is computable. A zone Z is said to be *consistent* if $[\![Z]\!] \neq \emptyset$.

Lemma 6. *For a zone Z, we can check whether Z is consistent or not.*

Notice that an inconsistent zone is trivially universal.

Normal Form. A zone Z is said to be in *stable* if the following four conditions are satisfied:

- If $(y - x \leq k_1) \in Z$ and $(z - y \leq k_2) \in Z$ then $(z - x \leq k_3) \in Z$ for some $k_3 \leq k_1 + k_2$.
- If $(x \leq k_1) \in Z$ and $(y - x \leq k_2) \in Z$ then $(y \leq k_3) \in Z$ for some $k_3 \leq k_1 + k_2$.
- If $(y - x \leq k_1) \in Z$ and $(k_2 \leq y) \in Z$ then $(k_3 \leq x) \in Z$ for some $k_3 \geq k_2 - k_1$.
- If $(y - x \leq k_1) \in Z$ then $(k_2 \leq x) \in Z$ for some $k_2 \geq -k_1$.
- Similar conditions hold in the case of strict inequalities.

A zone Z is said to be in *normal form* if all the constants appearing in the definition of Z are less than or equal to $cmax$. It is straightforward [15] to show the following

Lemma 7. *For each zone Z, we can construct:*

- *a stable zone Z_S such that (i) $Var(Z_S) = Var(Z)$; and (ii) $\gamma \models_h Z_S$ iff $\gamma \models_h Z$ for each γ and h*
- *A zone Z_N in normal form such that $Z_N \equiv Z$.*

Notice that the first part of the lemma implies that $[\![Z_S]\!] = [\![Z]\!]$. We use $Stabilize(Z)$ and $Norm(Z)$ to denote Z_S and Z_N respectively. For a set $\mathcal{Z}$ of zones, we define $Stabilize(\mathcal{Z}) = \{Stabilize(Z) \mid Z \in \mathcal{Z}$ and Z is consistent$\}$.

5   Algorithm

The zone-based universality algorithm is defined as follows:

Algorithm 1. Zone-Based Universality Checking
Input: A zone Z_{init}.
Output: Is Z_{init} universal?

        ToExplore := $\{Z_{init}\}$
        Explored := $\emptyset$
        while ToExplore $\neq \emptyset$
           remove some Z from ToExplore
           if Z is not accepting **then**
               return (false)
           else if $\exists Z' \in$ Explored. $Z' \sqsubseteq Z$ **then**
               discard Z
           else
               ToExplore := ToExplore $\bigcup \{Norm(Z')|\ Z' \in Post(Z)\}$
               Explored := $\{Z\} \bigcup \{Z'|\ Z' \in$ Explored $\wedge (Z \not\sqsubseteq Z')\}$
        return (true)
        end

The algorithm inputs a zone Z_{init}, and should check whether Z_{init} is universal or not. The algorithm maintains two sets of zones: a set ToExplore, initialized to $\{Z_{init}\}$, of zones which have not yet been analyzed; and a set Explored, initialized to the empty set, of zones which contains information about the set of zones which already have been analyzed. The algorithm preserves the following two invariants:

- some zone in (ToExplore $\bigcup$ Explored) is non-universal iff Z_{init} is non-universal; and
- If Z_{init} is non-universal, then $\exists Z \in$ ToExplore. $\forall Z' \in$ Explored. $dist(Z) < dist(Z')$.

Due to the invariants, the following two conditions can be checked during each step of the algorithm:

- if ToExplore becomes empty then the algorithm terminates with a positive answer; and
- if a non-accepting zone is detected then the algorithm terminates with a negative answer.

If neither of the two conditions is satisfied, the algorithm proceeds by picking and removing a zone Z from ToExplore. Two possibilities arise depending on the value of Z:

- If there exists a zone $Z' \in$ Explored with $Z' \sqsubseteq Z$, then we discard Z. The first invariant is preserved by Lemma 5. If Z_{init} is non-universal, then the second invariant and Lemma 5 imply that there is still some $Z'' \in$ ToExplore

such that $dist(Z'') < dist(Z') \leq dist(Z)$. This means that the second invariant will also be preserved by this step.
- Otherwise, we generate the zones in $Post(Z)$, normalize each one of them (Lemma 7), and then put it in ToExplore. The first invariant will be preserved by Lemma 4, while the second invariant will be preserved by Lemma 7, Lemma 5, and Lemma 3.

Partial correctness of the algorithm follows immediately from the invariant. It remains to show that:

- The algorithm terminates (done in Section 6).
- We can compute $Post$ and can check the entailment relation $\sqsubseteq$ on zones (done in Section 7 and Section 8).

Remark. Observe that the correctness of the algorithm is preserved in case we replace $\sqsubseteq$ in the algorithm by any ordering $\sqsubseteq'$ such that $\sqsubseteq' \subseteq \sqsubseteq$ (i.e., $Z \sqsubseteq' Z'$ implies $Z \sqsubseteq Z'$).

6 Termination

Using the methodology of [16] it can be shown that the universality algorithm of Section 5 is guaranteed to terminate in case $\sqsubseteq$ is a *well quasi-ordering (WQO)*. Following the framework of [14], we show that $\sqsubseteq$ in fact satisfies a stronger property than WQO; namely that it is a *better quasi-ordering (BQO)*.

6.1 WQOs and BQOs

A *quasi-ordering*, or a *QO* for short, is a pair $(A, \preceq)$ where $\preceq$ is a reflexive and transitive (binary) relation on a set A. A QO $(A, \preceq)$ is a *well quasi-ordering*, or a *WQO* for short, if for each infinite sequence $a_1, a_2, a_3, \ldots$ of elements of A, there are $i < j$ such that $a_i \preceq a_j$. For a set $B \subseteq A$, we define $\min(B)$ to be a subset of B which satisfies the following two properties:

- for each $a \in B$ there is a $b \in \min(B)$ with $b \preceq a$.
- the elements of $\min(B)$ are not related by $\preceq$, i.e., there are no $a, b \in \min(B)$ with $a \preceq b$.

If there are several sets satisfying the above two conditions, then we assume that $\min(B)$ gives an arbitrary (but fixed) such a set. Notice that if $\preceq$ is a WQO then $\min(B)$ is finite.

Given a QO $(A, \preceq)$, we define a QO $(A^*, \preceq^*)$ on the set A^* such that $x_1 \, x_2 \, \cdots \, x_m \preceq^* y_1 \, y_2 \, \cdots \, y_n$ if and only if there is a strictly monotone injection h from $\{1, \ldots, m\}$ to $\{1, \ldots, n\}$ such that $x_i \preceq y_{h(i)}$ for each $i : 1 \leq i \leq m$. We define the relation $\preceq^{\mathcal{P}}$ on the set $\mathcal{P}(A)$ of finite subsets of A, so that $A_1 \preceq^{\mathcal{P}} A_2$ if and only if $\forall b \in A_2 : \exists a \in A_1 : a \preceq b$.

Lemma 8. *For sets $A_1, A_2 \subseteq A$, we have $A_1 \preceq^{\mathcal{P}} A_2$ iff $\min(A_1) \preceq^{\mathcal{P}} \min(A_2)$.*

In the following lemma we state some properties of BQOs[1] [14,17].

Lemma 9. *1. Each BQO is WQO.*
2. If A is finite then $(A, =)$ is BQO.
3. If $(A, \preceq)$ is BQO then $(A^*, \preceq^*)$ is BQO.
4. If $(A, \preceq)$ is BQO then $\left(\mathcal{P}(A), \preceq^P\right)$ is BQO.
5. If $(A, \preceq_1)$ is BQO and $\preceq_1 \subseteq \preceq_2$ then $(A, \preceq_2)$ is BQO.

(Sets of) Configurations are BQO. Fix an automaton $\mathcal{A} = (\Sigma, S, s_{init}, F, E)$
For a global state q, we define the *signature* $sign(q)$ to be a pair $(s, k) \in S \times \{0, 1, 2, \ldots, 2 \cdot cmax + 1\}$, where $s = state(q)$ and k is defined as follows:

- $k = 2 \cdot \lfloor val(q) \rfloor$ if $val(q) \leq cmax$ and $fract(val(q)) = 0$.
- $k = 2 \cdot \lfloor val(q) \rfloor + 1$ if $val(q) < cmax$ and $fract(val(q)) > 0$.
- $k = 2 \cdot cmax + 1$ if $val(q) > cmax$.

For a configuration γ, we define $sign(\gamma)$ to be a word over $S \times \{0, 1, \ldots, 2 \cdot cmax + 1\}$ of the form $r_0 r_1 \cdots r_n$ such that the following properties are satisfied:

- $\{sign(q) \mid q \in \gamma\} = r_0 \cup r_1 \cup \cdots \cup r_n$.
- If $q \in r_i$ and $q' \in r_j$ then $fract(q) \leq fract(q')$ iff $i \leq j$.

The signature can be viewed as an encoding of the region to which the configuration belongs. The ordering among the sets inside the word reflects the relative ordering of the fractional parts. The control states, the integral parts of the clock values, and whether the fractional part is equal to zero, are all stored inside the signature of each global state. Observe that a signature is not an exact encoding of region, as the former keeps track of the fractional parts of clocks greater than $cmax$, while a region equates all such clock values. We define an ordering on configurations induced by signatures as follows. Consider configurations γ and γ' such that $sign(\gamma) = r_0 r_1 \cdots r_m$ and $sign(\gamma') = r'_0 r'_1 \cdots r'_n$. We use $\gamma \preceq \gamma'$ to denote that there is a strictly monotonic[2] injection $h : \{0, \ldots, m\} \mapsto \{0, \ldots, n\}$ such that $r_i \subseteq r'_{h(i)}$ for each $i : 0 \leq i \leq m$. The above mentioned relation between regions and signatures is captured in the following lemma (a formal proof can be given in a similar manner to see [18] or [8]).

Lemma 10. *For configurations γ and γ' if $\gamma \preceq \gamma'$ then $\gamma \sqsubseteq \gamma'$*

We observe that the signature of each configuration is a finite word over finite sets over a finite alphabet (namely finite sets over $S \times \{0, 1, 2, \ldots, 2 \cdot cmax + 1\}$). Consequently, Lemma 9 (Property 2 and Property 3) gives the following:

Lemma 11. $\preceq$ *is a BQO on the set of configurations.*

From Lemma 10, Lemma 11, and Lemma 9 (Property 5) we get the following:

---

[1] The technical definition of BQOs is quite complicated and can be found in e.g. [14]. The actual definition is not needed for understanding the rest of the paper, and is therefore omitted here.
[2] Strict monotonicity means that $i < j$ implies $h(i) < h(j)$.

Corollary 1. $\sqsubseteq$ *is a BQO on the set of configurations.*

From the definition of $\sqsubseteq$ on zones, Corollary 1, Lemma 8, and Lemma 9 (Property 4) we get the following

Lemma 12. $\sqsubseteq$ *is a BQO on zones.*

Lemma 12 and Lemma 9 (Property 1) give the following:

Corollary 2. $\sqsubseteq$ *is a WQO on zones.*

7   Computing Successors

In this section, we show how to compute $Post(Z)$ for some zone Z. We compute $Post(Z)$ as $Post_D(Post_T(Z))$, where $Post_T$ and $Post_D$ characterize timed resp. discrete successors of Z.

Timed Successors. For a zone Z, we let $Post_T(Z)$ denote the zone Z' such that $[\![Z]\!] \xrightarrow{\delta}_T [\![Z']\!]$. In other words, Z' characterizes the set of configurations which are timed successors of configurations in $[\![Z]\!]$. To compute Z', we first compute the zone Z'' where Z'' is stable and where $[\![Z'']\!] = [\![Z]\!]$ (Lemma 7). We can derive $Post_T(Z)$ from Z'' by deleting all clock conditions of the forms $x \leq k$ and $x < k$ in Z''. This gives the following:

Lemma 13. *For a zone Z, we can compute $Post_T(Z)$.*

Discrete Successors. Fix a timed automaton $\mathcal{A} = (\Sigma, S, s_{init}, F, E)$ and a zone Z. Informally, the idea of computing $Post_D(Z)$ is as follows. We recall that each variable in $x \in Var(Z)$ represents one global state q in a configuration $\gamma \in [\![Z]\!]$. The global state q (represented by x) produces a (possibly empty) set of successors. More precisely, each edge $e = (s, s', \phi, a, R)$ which "matches" x may produce a successor global state q'. Here, x and e are considered to be matching if $type(x)$ is identical to the source control state s in e. Notice that a successor is generated only if $val(q)$ satisfies ϕ. In this manner, a configuration γ produces a set of successors, reflecting the different successors of the individual global states in γ. We formalize the above reasoning in a number of steps.

First, we define the set of matching variables and edges. For a variable $x \in Var(Z)$ and a label $a \in \Sigma$, we let $E(x, a)$ be the set of edges whose source control state is $type(x)$ and whose label is a. For an $a \in \Sigma$, we define the set $Z \odot a = \{(e, x) \mid x \in Var(Z) \wedge e \in E(x, a)\}$. For each pair $(e, x) \in (Z \odot a)$, we use a fresh variable $y_{(e,x)}$ (i.e., $y_{(e,x)}$ is not a member of $Var(Z)$). We define $type(y_{(e,x)})$ to be the target control state of e. Intuitively, for $e = (s, s', \phi, a, R)$, the set $Z \odot a$ contains all pairs (e, x) which are matching, i.e., $type(x) = s$. Each such a pair can potentially generate a new global state, represented by a new variable $y_{(e,x)}$ in $Post_D(Z)$. Since the control state of the new global state will be s', the type of $y_{(e,x)}$ is also defined to be s'.

For $(e, x) \in Z \odot a$ with $e = (s, s', \phi, a, R)$, we define $Z \otimes (e, x)$ to be one of the following sets:

- if $R = f\!f$ then $Z \otimes (e, x) = \{(y_{(e,x)} = x) \wedge \phi(x)\ ,\ \neg\phi(x)\}$.
- if $R = tt$ then $Z \otimes (e, x) = \{(y_{(e,x)} = 0) \wedge \phi(x)\ ,\ \neg\phi(x)\}$.

Intuitively, for each pair (e, x), there are two possibilities: either (i) the guard ϕ is satisfied, in which case we generate a new global state represented by the new variable $y_{(e,x)}$ in $Post(Z)$; or (ii) ϕ is not satisfied in which case no new variable is added to $Post(Z)$. If a new global state is added then, depending on the value of R, there are two possibilities: either (i) its clock value is equal to the clock value of the original global state; or (ii) its clock value is equal to 0. In the first case we add the condition $y_{(e,x)} = x$, while in the second case we add the condition $y_{(e,x)} = 0$.

For $a \in \Sigma$, we define $Z \otimes a$ to be the set of zones of the form

$$\left(\bigwedge_{(e,x) \in (Z \odot a)} \phi_{(e,x)} \right) \wedge Z$$

where $\phi_{(e,x)} \in (Z \otimes (e, x))$ for each $(e, x) \in (Z \odot a)$. Finally, we define:

$$Z \oplus a = \ (Stabilize\ (Z \otimes a))\,[Var\,(Z)]$$

Each member of $Z \otimes a$ is a zone which represents the conjunction of the original zone Z with one of the zones in $Post_D(Z)$. To obtain the new zone, we abstract from the variables of Z. The purpose of stabilization is to avoid losing information when removing the elements of $Var\,(Z)$. The following lemma shows correctness of the above construction.

Lemma 14. $Post_D(Z) = \displaystyle\bigcup_{a \in \Sigma} Z \oplus a.$

8   Checking Entailment

In this section, we describe how to implement the entailment relation $\sqsubseteq$ on zones. In fact, there are two methods of computing $Z_1 \sqsubseteq Z_2$. The first method is to generate the regions in Z_1 and Z_2, and compare them for entailment. This method is still less sensitive to constraint explosion than regions-based methods (methods which only use regions), since only a subset of the regions (namely the ones in Z_1 and Z_2) need to be stored at a time. Another method (which we have used in our experimentation) is to construct a logical formula (in a decidable theory) which gives a characterization of the entailment relation. More precisely, the formula corresponds to an ordering $\sqsubseteq'$ on zones which implies $\sqsubseteq$. As indicated in Section 5, the correctness of the universality algorithm will be preserved using the new ordering $\sqsubseteq'$. However, the algorithm will not be guaranteed to terminate unless $\sqsubseteq'$ itself is a WQO. This is due to the fact that zones may avoid being discarded although they are entailed (according to $\sqsubseteq$) by other zones. The use of $\sqsubseteq'$ may still be motivated if they run efficiently on more examples in practice.

Here, we use formulas in a decidable logic which we call *Difference Bound Logic (DBL)*. The atomic formulas are either of the form $x \leq k$ or of the form $y - x \sim k$, where x and y are variables interpreted over $\mathbb{R}_+$ and $k \in \mathbb{N}$. Furthermore the set of formulas is closed under the propositional connectives. It is easy to see that validity of DBL-formulas is NP-complete.

Given a zone Z with $Var(Z) = \{x_1, \ldots, x_m\}$, it is sometimes convenient to view Z as a predicate $Z(x_1, \ldots, x_m)$ on the set $\mathbb{N}^m$. Observe that $\gamma \models_h Z$ iff $Z(h(x_1), \ldots, h(x_n))$ holds. For zones Z_1 and Z_2, a renaming from Z_1 to Z_2 is a mapping $\mathcal{R} : Var(Z_1) \mapsto Var(Z_2)$ such that $type(x) = type(\mathcal{R}(x))$. We use $Ren(Z_1)(Z_2)$ to denote the set of renamings from Z_1 to Z_2.

Lemma 15. *For zones Z_1 and Z_2 with $Var(Z_1) = \{x_1, \ldots, x_m\}$ and $Var(Z_2) = \{y_1, \ldots, y_n\}$, if*

$$\forall y_1, \ldots, y_n. \left(\begin{array}{c} Z_2(y_1, \ldots, y_n) \implies \\ \bigvee_{\mathcal{R} \in Ren(Z_1)(Z_2)} Z_1(\mathcal{R}(x_1), \ldots, \mathcal{R}(x_m)) \end{array} \right)$$

then $Z_1 \sqsubseteq Z_2$.

Notice that the above is a DBL-formula.

Remark. Lemma 15 defines an ordering $\sqsubseteq'$ which implies $\sqsubseteq$. More precisely, in $\sqsubseteq'$ we take into consideration clock differences even for clocks whose values are greater than $cmax$. In fact, we can modify $\sqsubseteq'$ so that it coincides with $\sqsubseteq$. This can be achieved by modifying the disjunction through adding formulas which equate clock values greater than $cmax$. This can be expressed as a DBL-formula in a straightforward manner. In this manner, the termination of the algorithm will still be guaranteed when using $\sqsubseteq'$.

9 Experimentation

We have implemented two prototypes to check universality for single-clock timed automata. One of the implementations is based on zones, whereas the other one uses a more compact representation of zones, called Difference Decision Diagrams (DDD), and is based on a package developed at the Technical University of Denmark [19]. We have used these prototypes to check several timed automata for universality. As a reference tool, we used the region-based implementation developed at the Oxford University Computing Laboratory.

In Table 1 we present the results of the tests. For each timed automaton, we give the number of control states, edges, $cmax$, whether universality holds or not, and the execution time for each of the three methods. We use "not term." to indicate that the program did not terminate after more than 24 hours, or that the program stopped without solving the problem due to an out-of-memory exception. All tests were conducted on a Sun workstation with 4.0 GB memory and a 1.0 GHz UltraSPARC-IIIi processor. For both the zone- and region-based implementations we used Java version 1.5.0_05. The DDD-based implementation is compiled with gcc version 2.7.2.3.

Table 1. Experimental results

$|S|$	$|E|$	$cmax$	univ?	Region	Zone	DDD
3	4	1	no	21 ms	13 ms	10 ms
3	4	25	no	364 ms	13 ms	0 ms
3	4	50	no	636 ms	14 ms	10 ms
3	4	10000	no	4 hr 49 min 38 sec 601 ms	13 ms	10 ms
10	22	2	yes	639 ms	61 ms	70 ms
10	22	6	yes	550 ms	41 ms	50 ms
10	22	25	yes	1 sec 526 ms	40 ms	70 ms
10	29	135	yes	20 s 981 ms	4 sec 418 ms	not term.
10	29	235	yes	1 min 9 sec 20 ms	3 sec 558 ms	not term.
10	29	335	yes	2 min 24 sec 21 ms	3 sec 746 ms	not term.
10	38	335	yes	1 min 43 sec 175 ms	20 sec 184 ms	not term.
10	44	35	no	3 sec 181 ms	4 min 28 sec 762 ms	1 sec 10 ms
10	44	170	no	27 sec 227 ms	2 min 57 sec 715 ms	670 ms
10	44	560	no	1 min 25 sec 289 ms	6 sec 758 ms	870 ms
10	44	1635	no	41 min 20 sec 623 ms	3 sec 523 ms	320 ms
10	44	2635	no	2 hr 44 sec 135 ms	10 sec 300 ms	1 sec 600 ms
10	44	3635	no	2 hr 1 min 26 sec 921 ms	14 sec 174 ms	1 sec 580 ms
10	44	5635	no	5 hr 21 min 9 sec 24 ms	13 sec 457 ms	1 sec 680 ms
10	44	11635	no	not term.	15 sec 207 ms	1 sec 540 ms
10	30	9335	yes	not term.	3 sec 599 ms	not term.
20	53	4335	yes	not term.	7 sec 061 ms	not term.
25	63	3000	yes	not term.	40 sec 324 ms	not term.
20	53	4335	no	not term.	13 sec 132 ms	12 sec 410 ms
10	30	9880	no	not term.	11 sec 52 ms	300 ms
25	65	10000	no	not term.	1 sec 225 ms	480 ms
25	65	10000	no	not term.	10 min 27 sec 614 ms	2 sec 670 ms

In 16 out of 26 tests the execution time of the DDD-based program is smaller than that of the other programs. However, the zone-based prototype is almost as efficient as the DDD-based prototype, as the differences between the execution times are very small, i.e., within a time span of no more than seconds in most of the cases. This is in contrast to the significant differences between the run times of region- and zone-based implementations, varying between milliseconds and hours. As expected, the region-based implementation performs badly for high values of $cmax$. Notice that the run times of both the DDD- and the zone-based prototypes remain relatively stable under changes of the value of $cmax$.

10   Conclusions and Future Work

We have presented a zone-based algorithm for solving the universality problem for timed automata with a single clock. We prove termination of the algorithm using the theory of better quasi-orderings, a refinement of the theory of well quasi-orderings. One interesting direction for future work is to extend the algorithm so that we solve the more general problem of language inclusion. Another challenge is to extend the algorithm to deal with the case of general (multi-clock) timed automata. In fact, we can modify the notion of zones by adding extra information to keep track of clocks which belong to the same state inside a configuration. In such a case, computing successors and checking entailment can be carried out in a similar manner to the methods of this paper. However, the entailment relation will not be a well quasi-ordering, and therefore the universality algorithm will no more be guaranteed to terminate. This is expected since the problem is undecidable for multi-clock timed automata. Despite this, using zones may make the algorithm terminate sufficiently often so that it becomes practically interesting even for the general case.

References

1. Alur, R., Dill, D.: A theory of timed automata. Theoretical Computer Science 126, 183–235 (1994)
2. Alur, R., Madhusudan, P.: Decision problems for timed automata: A survey. In: Bernardo, M., Corradini, F. (eds.) Formal Methods for the Design of Real-Time Systems. LNCS, vol. 3185, Springer, Heidelberg (2004)
3. Alur, R., Fix, L., Henzinger, T.: Event-clock automata: A determinizable class of timed automata. Theoretical Computer Science 211, 253–273 (1999)
4. Alur, R., Torre, S.L., Madhusudan, P.: Perturbed timed automata. In: Morari, M., Thiele, L. (eds.) HSCC 2005. LNCS, vol. 3414, Springer, Heidelberg (2005)
5. Alur, R., Feder, T., Henzinger, T.: The benefits of relaxing punctually. Journal of the ACM 43, 116–146 (1996)
6. Henzinger, T., Manna, Z., Pnueli, A.: What good are digital clocks? In: Kuich, W. (ed.) ICALP 1992. LNCS, vol. 623, Springer, Heidelberg (1992)
7. Ouaknine, J., Worrell, J.: Universality and language inclusion for open and closed timed automata. In: Maler, O., Pnueli, A. (eds.) HSCC 2003. LNCS, vol. 2623, Springer, Heidelberg (2003)
8. Ouaknine, J., Worrell, J.: On the language inclusion problem for timed automata: Closing a decidability gap. In: Proc. LICS 2004, 20th IEEE Int. Symp. on Logic in Computer Science, IEEE Computer Society Press, Los Alamitos (2004)
9. Abdulla, P.A., Deneux, J., Ouaknine, J., Worrell, J.: Decidability and complexity results for timed automata via channel machines. In: Caires, L., Italiano, G.F., Monteiro, L., Palamidessi, C., Yung, M. (eds.) ICALP 2005. LNCS, vol. 3580, Springer, Heidelberg (2005)
10. Abdulla, P.A., Jonsson, B.: Verifying programs with unreliable channels. Information and Computation 127(2), 91–101 (1996)
11. Abdulla, P.A., Nylén, A.: Timed Petri nets and BQOs. In: Colom, J.-M., Koutny, M. (eds.) ICATPN 2001. LNCS, vol. 2075, pp. 53–70. Springer, Heidelberg (2001)
12. Yovine, S.: Kronos: A verification tool for real-time systems. Journal of Software Tools for Technology Transfer 1(1-2) (1997)
13. Larsen, K., Pettersson, P., Yi, W.: UPPAAL in a nutshell. Software Tools for Technology Transfer 1(1-2) (1997)
14. Abdulla, P.A., Nylén, A.: Better is better than well: On efficient verification of infinite-state systems. In: Proc. LICS 2000, 16th IEEE Int. Symp. on Logic in Computer Science, pp. 132–140. IEEE Computer Society Press, Los Alamitos (2000)
15. Bengtsson, J., Larsson, F.: Uppaal a tool for automatic verification of real-time systems. Technical Report 96/97, DoCS, Uppsala University (1996)
16. Abdulla, P.A., Čerāns, K., Jonsson, B., Tsay, Y.K.: Algorithmic analysis of programs with well quasi-ordered domains. Information and Computation 160, 109–127 (2000)

17. Marcone, A.: Foundations of bqo theory. Transactions of the American Mathematical Society 345(2) (1994)
18. Abdulla, P.A., Jonsson, B.: Verifying networks of timed processes. In: Steffen, B. (ed.) ETAPS 1998 and TACAS 1998. LNCS, vol. 1384, pp. 298–312. Springer, Heidelberg (1998)
19. Møller, J., Lichtenberg, J.: Difference decision diagrams. Master's thesis, Department of Information Technology, Technical University of Denmark, Building 344, DK-2800 Lyngby, Denmark (1998)

Compositional Semantics of System-Level Designs Written in SystemC

Niloofar Razavi[1,2] and Marjan Sirjani[1,2]

[1] Department of Electrical and Computer Engineering
University of Tehran, Karegar Ave., Tehran, Iran
[2] School of Computer Science, Institute for Studies in Theoretical Physics and
Mathematics (IPM)
Niavaran Square, Tehran, Iran
n.razavi@ece.ut.ac.ir, msirjani@ut.ac.ir

Abstract. In this paper, we propose a component-based approach to
verify system-level designs. The coordination language Reo is selected as
an Architecture Description Language (ADL) to model system designs
written in SystemC. In our approach we map a SystemC design to a Reo
circuit, and then construct the corresponding constraint automata which
show the behavior of the system and can be used for analysis purposes.
The elegance of our approach is in using Reo and constraint automata as
a pair to capture the structure and the behavior of the system together.
We checked the correctness of our approach by comparing the SystemC
simulation kernel behavior with the behavior of the glue code we proposed.

Keywords: hardware design, formal verification, Reo, constraint automata, SystemC.

1 Introduction

Variants of general-purpose programming languages, like SystemC [1] are increasingly used to specify system-level designs that have both hardware and software parts. Using these languages, the decision concerning hardware/software
partitioning may be deferred to later stages. SystemC also enables the design
team to design systems at a high level of abstraction. This higher level of abstraction gives the designers a fundamental understanding early in the design
process of the interactions of the entire system and enables better and earlier
verification [1].

Most engineering designs can be viewed as systems, i.e., as collections of several components whose combined operation provides useful services. Components
can be heterogeneous in nature and their interaction may be regulated by some
simple or complex means. So, the application of component-based modeling in
design and verification of hardware systems seems to be practical [2,3,4].

Here we use a unified method based on components for system-level design,
considering hardware and software, and different levels of abstraction. Using

F. Arbab and M. Sirjani (Eds.): FSEN 2007, LNCS 4767, pp. 113–128, 2007.

a verifiable component-based language, we provide formal verification support. Existing approaches and tools for verifying hardware/software co-designs mainly apply non-formal approaches or handle only low-level specifications. But formal verification is getting more and more attention as a technique to verify/validate the hardware/software co-designs sufficiently [5,6,7].

The specification languages typically fall into two classes with diverse pros and cons [8]. The first set of specification languages is called Architecture Description Languages (ADLs). The second set consists of general formal models usually based on the automata theory. The essential drawback of the ADLs is that their specification power is limited by the underlying model which is often not general enough to preserve all the interaction properties which might arise through the component composition. Additionally, the verification within an ADL framework usually supports a verification of only a small fixed set of properties often unique for the language [8]. The automata-based models (as opposite to ADLs) are highly formal and general, and usually supported by automated verification tools (model-checkers in particular). However, these models are designed for modeling of component interaction only and therefore are unable to describe the interconnection structure of hierarchical component architecture which also influences the behavior [8].

In this work, Reo [9] and constraint automata [10] are used for modeling system designs written in SystemC. The supporting tools and techniques can be used for formal verification. We use Reo as an ADL language to model the systems and then construct the corresponding constraint automata which show the behavior of the systems and can be used for analysis purposes. The power and elegance of our approach is in using Reo and constraint automata as a pair to capture the structure and the behavior of the systems together. The behavior of the system components can be modeled directly by constraint automata without coping with the details of their internal structure. The coordination and communication between components are captured by Reo circuits. The capability of Reo in modeling synchrony and asynchrony together, makes the language suitable for designing hardware systems.

In this paper we show how a SystemC code can be mapped to Reo circuits. The process is as follows:

- Get system designs written in SystemC
- Model the behavior of the SC_METHOD and SC_THREAD processes in the design by constraint automata
- Use Reo channels to connect SC_METHOD and SC_THREAD processes in the design together and visualize the architecture of the system
- Obtain the behavior of the system compositionally by joining the constraint automata of the processes and the constraint automata of the Reo circuits used in the model

We show how the processes in a SystemC code are mapped to constraint automata and how the communication between processes is modeled by Reo circuits and then mapped into constraint automata. By this approach, given a

SystemC code, we have a visual representation of the design architecture and its behavior.

This work is based on the work proposed in [11] but is significantly extended according to the further results gained by working on SystemC designs and SystemC simulation kernel semantics. In [11], the system is first partitioned into combinational and sequential hardware and software components and then Reo is used for connecting the components. Here, we do not need to partition the system and the connecting Reo circuit is designed based on the types of the processes in SystemC designs.

We can alternatively start the design process from the architecture of the system captured as a Reo circuit (instead of a SystemC code) and then proceed to obtain the constraint automata of the whole system to be able to analyze the behavior of the system.

Outline of the paper. In the next section we have an overview of the related work. Then, a brief background of SystemC, Reo and constraint automata is presented in Section 3. Section 4 explains our approach where Reo circuits are made from SystemC designs. The mapping of SystemC processes to constraint automata is also presented in this section. Section 5 is a short conclusion and a view of our future work.

2   Related Work

Related projects mainly concern defining SystemC semantics and verifying SystemC designs. For instance, Salem presented the formal semantics of a synchronous subset of SystemC using denotational semantics [12]. The subset includes modules, processes, threads, *wait* statement, ports and signals. The author proposes a formal model for SystemC *delta* time and gives a semantic definition for the languages two-phase scheduler. The work in [12], however, provides the description of the above parts only using general syntactic rules. It does not provide any specific definitions for basic SystemC components and processes [5].

In [7], an approach is given in order to translate SystemC models into a Petri-net based representation. The Petri-net model is then used for model checking of properties expressed in a timed temporal logic. The authors focused on the translation of some SystemC mechanisms like method calls, scheduler, signals and wait statements into the proposed representation. The approach is particularly suitable for models at a high level of abstraction, such as transaction-level. The Petri-net models become very complicated even for small SystemC designs and can not visualize the behavior of the designs clearly.

Kroening and Sharygina [6] translate SystemC models into Labeled Kripke Structures (LKS). Their approach does not take either timing or signal aspects into account. Their work is more focused on an abstraction-refinement approach based on automatic hardware/software partitioning.

The work of Vikram [13], derives the Finite State Machine (FSM) model of the SystemC designs. In that approach, the design in SystemC is first translated to C. Then, the FSM is generated from the C code. This approach is problematic in the sense that translating SystemC to C is not always feasible. The technique can not be applied to SystemC considering the object oriented nature of the library and that not all of the SystemC is synthesizable [14].

In [5], a methodology is presented to verify SystemC designs based on a definition for SystemC semantics using Abstract State Machines (ASMs) [15]. In this methodology the SystemC design is abstracted into hypergraphs to keep a simplified view of the design including only processes status, activation conditions and order of execution. The latter is then modeled with ASMs and compiled with the AsmL tool in order to generate a finite state machine that can be used for formal verification by external tools linked to ASM, such as model checkers or theorem provers.

In our previous work [11], we used Reo [9] for specification of system level designs. Constraint automata can be constructed from Reo circuits and can be formally verified. In that work, only the coordination and communication between different components of a system are modeled in Reo, and nothing is said about modeling the components themselves. Here, we focus on the modeling of behavior of the SystemC processes as components and also elaborate on the mapping between coordination and communication extracted from SystemC codes and Reo circuits. We start from SystemC designs, visualize the architecture of the systems using Reo and analyze them by constraint automata. Our method is easy to use and can be used in different levels of abstraction. It also supports compositional and formal verification of SystemC designs based on the tools developed for analyzing constraint automata.

3   Background

3.1   SystemC

SystemC was originally developed for specification of low-level designs. The main motivation of SystemC is that a circuit model can be compiled using a regular C++ compiler, and then simulated efficiently. The SystemC language includes all constructs allowed in C++, although a very small subset is actually synthesizable.

Modularization in SystemC is implemented by means of C++ classes: the SystemC construct, SC_MODULE, is simply a pre-processor macro for a class definition. The behavior of a module is specified by defining one or more processes which are executed concurrently. A process is either an SC_METHOD, an SC_THREAD, or an SC_CTHREAD.

A process has a list of events that activate the process. This list of events is called the sensitivity list of the process. SC_METHOD processes never suspend internally. They can never invoke *wait* and must avoid using calls to blocking methods. Whenever an event occurs on any of the signals to which an SC_METHOD process is sensitive, the SC_METHOD process will run atomically and return.

SC_THREAD processes are started once and only once by the simulator. Once a thread starts to execute, it is in complete control of the simulation until it chooses to return control to the simulator. SystemC offers two ways to pass control back to the simulator. One way is to simply exit and the other way is the *wait* statement. When an SC_THREAD process exits, it is terminated for the rest of the simulation. The *wait* suspends the SC_THREAD processes until it is again activated by an event. Therefore, SC_THREAD processes typically contain an infinite loop containing at least one *wait*.

SC_CTHREAD is a variation on the SC_THREAD and has the requirement of being sensitive to a clock. For every SC_CTHREAD process, a corresponding SC_Thread process with the same behavior can be substituted. So, in our approach, we only consider the Method and Thread processes.

Events may be generated explicitly by a process (notifying an SC_EVENT), or implicitly by changing signal values.

The simulation kernel of SystemC has a two-dimensional timing. One dimension is the actual physical time and the other is *delta* time. *Delta* time is used to model the concurrent execution of the hardware systems. So, if processes that are running concurrently, change the values of some signals, the values of the signals shall be updated simultaneously after a *delta* time delay which is a zero-real-time interval.

3.2   Reo

Reo is a model for building component connectors in a compositional manner [9]. Reo *connectors* are constructed in the same spirit as logic and electronics circuits: take basic elements and connect them. Basic connectors in Reo are *channels*. Each channel has exactly two ends, which can be a *sink* end or a *source* end. A *sink* end is where data flows out of a channel, and a *source* end is where data flows into a channel.

Channels are connected to make a circuit. Connecting (or *joining*) channels is putting channel ends together in a *node*. So, a *node* is a set of coincident channel ends. The semantics of a node is as follows. A component can write data items to a source node that it is connected to. The write operation succeeds only if all (source) channel ends coincident on the node accept the data item, in which case the data item is transparently written to every source end coincident on the node. A source node, thus, acts as a *replicator*. A component can obtain data items, by an input operation, from a sink node that it is connected to. A take operation succeeds only if at least one of the (sink) channel ends coincident on the node offers a suitable data item; if more than one coincident channel end offers suitable data items, one is selected nondeterministically. A sink node, thus, acts as a nondeterministic *merger*.

The simplest channels used in these connectors are synchronous (Sync) channels, represented as simple solid arrows (Figure 1.a). A Sync channel has a source and a sink end, and no buffer. It accepts a data item through its source end iff it can simultaneously dispense it through its sink. A lossy synchronous (LossySync) channel is similar to a Sync channel, except that it always accepts all data items through its source end. If it is possible for it to simultaneously dispense the data item through its sink (e.g., there is a take operation pending on its sink) the channel transfers the data item; otherwise the data item is lost. LossySync channels are depicted as dashed arrows (Figure 1.b). FIFO1 is an asynchronous channel with the bounded capacity of 1 (Figure 1.c). The small box in the middle of the arrow represents its buffer.

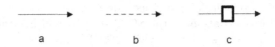

Fig. 1. A Set of Basic Reo Channels

3.3   Constraint Automata

Constraint automata [10] is proposed as compositional semantics for Reo, based on timed data streams [16]. Each element of a timed data stream is a pair of time and a data item, where the time indicates when the data item is being input or output. A transition ma be fired when a data item is observed at a port of the component and according to the observed data, the automaton may change its state. A constraint automaton (over the data domain Data) is a tuple $A = (Q, Names, \longrightarrow, Q_0)$ where Q is a finite set of states, $Names$ is a finite set of names, $\longrightarrow$ is a finite subset of $Q \times 2^{Names} \times DC \times Q$, called the transition relation of A, and $Q_0 \subseteq Q$ is the set of initial states. In the transition relation, DC represents the data constraints.

Each channel in Reo, and the merger nodes are mapped to a constraint automaton. Some examples of this mapping are depicted in Figure 2. Constraint automata have some operations (i.e. join and hide), that allow joining of the constraint automata [10].

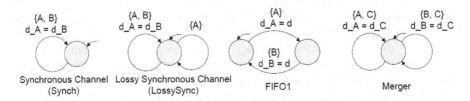

Fig. 2. Constraint automata for some basic Reo channels, and merger node

To simplify constraint automata where data plays a significant role in computation, a parameterized notation of constraint automata is proposed in [10]. The transitions of a parameterized constraint automaton may have an action set which consists of some expressions. An expression is built from constants $d \in Data$, the symbols d_B for $B \in Names$, variables and operators for the chosen data domain (e.g., boolean operator $\vee$, $\wedge$, etc. for $Data = (0,1)$ and arithmetic operators $+$, $-$, etc. for $Data = N$). The expressions in the action set of each transition are executed when the transition is fired.

4   Mapping SystemC Designs to Reo Circuits

In our approach, we get the description of a system in SystemC. Then we distinguish the constituent components of the system and their communication relation. The processes in a SystemC design, either SC_METHOD or SC_THREAD, build up the components of the system. Each process is modeled as a constraint automaton using the control graph of the process. The communication and coordination is modeled by Reo circuits. The behavior of the whole system is compositionally obtained by joining the constraint automata of the processes and the constraint automata of the Reo circuits. We first studied the SystemC simulation kernel carefully and mapped it to constraint automata. The simulation kernel of SystemC is responsible for executing a concurrent model in a sequential system. We consider the results in this mapping and instead of coping with all the details of simulation kernel we put the Reo circuits as the glue code between the components. Using Sync channels in Reo circuits allows the components of the model to be executed concurrently and helps us to abstract *delta* time in SystemC simulation. Although these two approaches is consistent, the second one is simpler and gives us better visualization of the architecture of the systems.

4.1   Determining the Constituent Components

We get the description of a system in SystemC from which the components of the system are determined. Each process of a SystemC design (SC_METHOD or SC_THREAD) is considered as a component of the system.

Each SC_METHOD is mapped to a component which has an input port for each signal in the sensitivity list of the process and an output port for each signal to which it writes into. Components related to SC_THREAD processes have an input port for each signal which they call *wait* statement on it, and an output for each signal that they writes to it.

4.2   Constraint Automata of the Components

After determining the components of the system, a constraint automaton is derived for each component. These constraint automata are captured through the paths and sub-paths in the control graph of the related processes. In the following, first we show how the paths and sub-paths are defined in the control graph of the processes. Then we explain how the constraint automata of the SC_METHOD processes and the constraint automata of SC_THREAD processes are derived respectively.

Two variables are considered for each signal; *data* and *Value*. The *data* variable is temporary and read only. It can be used only on the transitions which has the corresponding signal in their name set. It contains the current value of the signal and is shown as *data_signalName*. On the other hand, the *Value* variable contains the current value of the signal and even can be used in a transition that does not have the signal in its name set. The name of this variable is equal to the name of the related signal. Whenever a new value is written to a signal, the corresponding *Value* variable gets the new value.

Paths and Sub-paths in Processes. SystemC is a C++ class library. There-fore any C++ construct can be used in describing the behavior of a process. By considering the statements in the body of a process, a control graph is obtained. There are different paths in the control graph, starting from the first statement and going through the consequent statements. The paths are formed by selec-tion statements. We consider these paths to construct the constraint automaton of each process and call them *processpaths*. A condition and an action set is considered for each process path. The condition set is obtained by integrating all the selection conditions in the process path. The action set consists of all the statements except selection statements in the path. Figure 3 is a small ALU

```
SC_MODULE(Alu_Module) {
    sc_in⟨bool⟩ reset;
    sc_in⟨int⟩ op;
    sc_in⟨int⟩ in_data;
    sc_out⟨int⟩ out_data;
    sc_int I;
    SC_CTOR(Alu_Module) {
        SC_METHOD(alu_Method);
        Sensitive⟨⟨reset⟨⟨op;
    }

path 1: condition = {reset=1}
    action = {I:=0, out_data:=0 }
path 2: condition = {reset⟨⟩1, op=1}
    action = {I:=1, out_data:=in_data+1}
path 3: condition = {reset⟨⟩1, op=2}
    action = {I:=2, out_data:=in_data+2}
path 4: condition = {reset⟨⟩1, op⟨⟩1, op⟨⟩2}
    action = {I:=0}
```

```
void Alu_Module : alu_Method() {
    if (reset.read() == 1) {
        I =0;
        out_data.write(0);
    }
    else {
        switch(op) {
        case 1 :
            I = 1;
            out_data.write(in_data + I );
            break;
        case 2 :
            I = 2;
            out_data.write(in_data + I );
            break;
        case default :
            I=0;
        }
    }
}
```

Fig. 3. A Simple ALU Design in SystemC

design. The ALU has three input and one output ports. The *alu_Method* which is an SC_METHOD process, describes the behavior of the ALU and is sensitive to *reset* and *op* signals. If the value of the *reset* signal is equal to one, the ALU puts a zero value on its output. Otherwise, the value of the *op* signal determines the kind of operation that the ALU has to do. If the *op* signal has the value one(two), *in_data* data is added to one(two) and put on the *out_data* signal. In the case that the value of *op* signal is not equal to one or two, nothing is done by the ALU, causing the *out_data* to retain its value. The paths of the example are shown in Figure 4. These paths are also demonstrated as condition-action pairs in Figure 3.

The paths of an SC_METHOD process do not contain any blocking statement, but the paths of an SC_THREAD may contain several blocking statements. If a path consists of n blocking statements, it can be broken to n sub-paths in such a way that each sub-path contains exactly one blocking statement from which the sub-path starts. Figure 5 shows a special counter design. The counter has two inputs and one output. The *counter_Thread* is an SC_THREAD process and demonstrates the counter behavior. The counter is a sequential component and counts the number of the clock cycles in which the *input* becomes zero. The paths

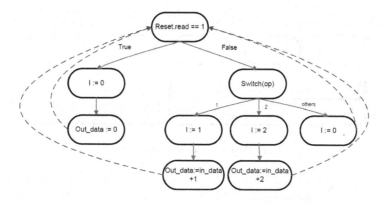

Fig. 4. Paths of the alu_Method

```
SC_Module(Counter_Module) {          void Counter_Module : counter_Thread() {
    sc_in⟨bool⟩ clk;                     for( ; ; ) {
    sc_in⟨int⟩ input;                        wait(input);
    sc_out⟨int⟩ output;                      if (input == 0) {
                                                 count++;
    sc_int count=0;                              wait();
                                                 output.write(count);
                                             }
    SC_CTOR(Counter_Module) {            }
        SC_THREAD(counter_Thread);   }
        Sensitive⟨⟨clk.neg();
    }
}
```

path 1: condition={input ⟨⟩ 0}   action={}
path 2: condition={input = 0}   action={count += 1, output := count}
sub-path1 of path 2 : waits on input condition={input = 0} action={count += 1}
sub-path2 of path 2 : waits on clk   condition={} action={output := count}

Fig. 5. A Special Counter Design in SystemC

of the *counter_Thread* process are shown in Figure 6. The paths/sub-paths are also demonstrated in Figure 5.

Constraint Automata of SC_METHOD Processes. The Name set of the constraint automaton of an SC_METHOD process is the set of signals that the process writes to plus the signals in the sensitivity list of the process. Figure 7 shows the algorithm to construct the constraint automata of SC_METHOD processes. The constraint automaton of an SC_METHOD process has only one state which is initial state. The transitions are added to the constraint automaton of the process using the paths of the control graph. The occurrence of events on each combination of the signals in the sensitivity list of the process, can activate the process independently. Therefore, for each path, at most $2^N - 1$ transitions will be added; where N is the number of the signals in the sensitivity list of the process. The name set of the transitions are different combinations of the signals

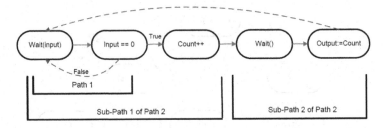

Fig. 6. Paths of the counter_Thread

```
BEGIN
   Create Initial State: S0
   FOR each path in the control graph
      FOR each combination of the signals in the sensitivity list
         Add a transition :          S0 → S0
         Name ₃ = {signals in the combination, signals which are written in the path }
         Condition ₃ = condition set of the path
         Action ₃ = action set of the path
      EndFor
   EndFor
END
```

Fig. 7. Algorithm to Construct Constraint Automata of SC_METHOD Processes

in the sensitivity list plus the signals which are written in the related path. The data constraint and the action sets of the transitions are equal to the condition set and the action set of the path, respectively.

For loops (and nested loops), we have one transition initializing the indexes of the loop, and a transition to check their values. Also a transition is considered for the last iteration of the loop which returns to a state from which the loop starts. The constraint automaton of the *alu_Method* is shown in Figure 8.

Constraint Automata of SC_THREAD Processes. The Name set of the constraint automaton of an SC_THREAD process is the set of signals that the process writes to or waits on. Figure 9 shows the algorithm to construct the constraint automata of SC_THREAD processes. For each sub-path, there exists a transition. The name set of each transition is the set of signals on which the wait statement is called. The data constraint and action sets of the these transition are equal to the condition and action sets of the corresponding sub-path, respectively. The transitions of the first sub-paths start from the initial state. For each subsequent sub-path, a state is added from which the transition of the sub-path starts. The final transition of the path must be ended at the initial state.

Here, loops are treated like the loops in SC_METHOD processes with a little bit difference, considering blocking statements in them. The constraint automaton of the *counter_Thread* is shown in Figure 10.

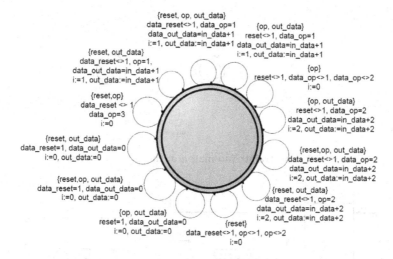

Fig. 8. Constraint Automaton of the alu_Method

```
BEGIN
  Create Initial State: S0
  State : current_state
  FOR each path in the control graph
    current_state = S0
    FOR each sub-path of the path
      IF there exists any sub-path after it
        Create a new State : S
        Add a transition :                        current_state → S
        Name ₃ = {signals on which the process is waiting, signals which are written in the sub-path }
        Condition ₃ = condition set of the sub-path
        Action ₃ = action set of the sub-path
        current_state = S
      Else
        Add a transition :                        current_state → S0
        Name ₃ = {signals on which the process is waiting, signals which are written in the sub-path }
        Condition ₃ = condition set of the sub-path
        Action ₃ = action set of the sub-path
        current_state = S0
      EndIF
    EndFor
  EndFor
END
```

Fig. 9. Algorithm to Construct Constraint Automata of SC_THREAD Processes

4.3   Modeling the Communication Between Components Using Reo

In the previous section, we used constraint automata for modeling the behavior of the components of SystemC designs. Here, we show how Reo can be used as an ADL to show the components (as black boxes) and the communication between them. Reo circuits are used as glue codes to connect the components all together and make the whole system. The behavior of the whole system is obtained by joining the constraint automata of the components and the constraint automata of the Reo circuits used in the model.

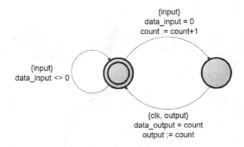

Fig. 10. Constraint Automaton of the counter_Thread

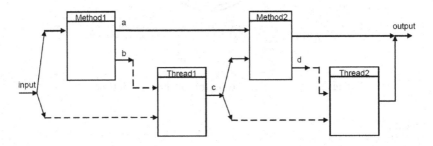

Fig. 11. An Example of Components Connection Using Reo

Sync channels, LossySync channels, mergers and replicators are used to connect the components of a SystemC together. The inputs and outputs of the components related to SC_METHOD processes, must be provided through Sync channels. An event on each input of a SC_METHOD process would cause the process to run atomically and provide its outputs immediately. So, using Sync channels at the input and output ports of the components related to SC_METHOD processes is appropriate.

The inputs and outputs of the components related to SC_THREAD processes are provided through LossySync and Sync channels, respectively. The component

```
SC_Module(Module1) {
    sc_in⟨int⟩ a;
    sc_out⟨int⟩ o;

    void Method1{
        o = a * 10;
    }

    SC_CTOR(Module1) {
        SC_METHOD(Method1);
        Sensitive(⟨a;}
}
```

```
SC_Module(Module2) {
    sc_in⟨int⟩ m,n;
    sc_out⟨int⟩ x;

    void Method1{
        x = m + n;
    }

    SC_CTOR(Module2) {
        SC_METHOD(Method2);
        Sensitive(⟨m,n;}
}
```

```
SC_Module(Module3) {
    sc_in⟨int⟩ b, d;
    sc_out⟨int⟩ c;

    void Thread1{
        for( ; ; ) {
            wait(d); c = 0;
            wait(b); c = 1;
        }
    }

    SC_CTOR(Module3) {
        SC_THREAD(Thread1);}
}
```

Fig. 12. Some Modules Written in SystemC

of a SC_THREAD process has an input for each of the signals on which it waits. If the process is waiting on a signal and an event occurs on that signal, the LossySync channel at the related input port, will act as a Sync channel and the process will continue running. In the case that the process is waiting on a signal and an event occurs on another signal which is also the input of the process, the event is lost in the LossySync channel and nothing is done by the process. This behavior of the LossySync comes from the maximal progress concept in constraint automata.

Since the outputs of the SC_THREAD processes are provided immediately through the execution of the process, Sync channels are appropriate to be used at the output ports of the components related to these processes.

A signal may provide input for more than one component. According to its behavior, a replicator can handle this situation. A merger is used in the situation where there are more than one driver for a signal. Figure 11 shows a schema of components interconnection using Reo circuits.

```
int sc_main(int argc, char* argv[]){     int sc_main(int argc, char* argv[]){     int sc_main(int argc, char* argv[]){
  sc_signal(int) a,b,c,tmp;                sc_signal(int) a,n,x;                    sc_signal(int) a,b,n,c,x;
  Module1 mod1("Module1");                 Module1 mod1("Module1");                 Module1 mod1("Module1");
  Module3 mod3("Module3");                 Module2 mod2("Module2");                 Module2 mod2("Module2");
  mod1.a(a);                               mod1.a(a);                               Module3 mod3("Module3");
  mod1.o(tmp);                             mod1.o(tmp);                             mod1.a(a);
  mod3.b(b);                               mod2.m(tmp);                             mod1.o(tmp);
  mod3.d(tmp);                             mod2.n(n);                               mod2.m(tmp);
  mod3.c(c);                               mod2.x(x);                               mod2.n(n);
...}                                     ...}                                       mod2.x(x);
                                                                                    mod3.b(b);
                                                                                    mod3.d(tmp);
                                                                                    mod3.c(c);
                                                                                  ...}
```

Fig. 13. Some Designs Made of Modules in Figure 12

Some Examples. Figure 12 contains the description of three modules in SystemC. *Module1* has one input, *a*, and one output, *o*. The behavior of this module is shown by an SC_METHOD process which is sensitive to *a*. *Module2* has two inputs, *m* and *n*, and one output, *x*. The behavior of this module is also shown by an SC_METHOD process. The SC_METHOD process is sensitive to all of the inputs of the module. *Module3* has two inputs, *b* and *d*, and one output, *c*. The behavior of this module is shown by an SC_THREAD process which waits on *d* and *o*, repeatedly.

Figure 13 shows three small SystemC designs made of the modules described in Figure 12. In the first design the instances of *Module1* and *Module2* are connected to each other. The second design contains one instance of *Module1* and one instance of *Module2*. The last design has an instance of all the modules of Figure 12. Figure 14 shows the Reo circuits used in connecting the components of the designs in Figure 13.

As can be seen, the inputs and outputs of the SC_METHOD processes are provided through Sync channels and the inputs and outputs of the SC_THREAD processes are provided through LossySync and Sync channels, respectively.

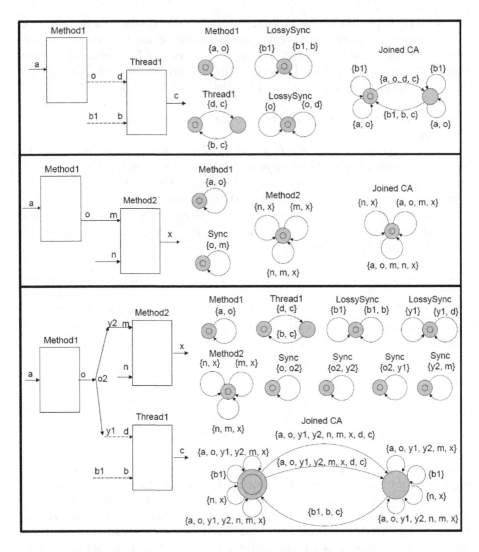

Fig. 14. Some Examples of Components Interconnection Using Reo

Figure 14 contains the constraint automata of the processes and the constraint automata of Reo circuits used in each design. For each design, a constraint automaton is derived by joining the constraint automata of the constituent processes and Reo circuits, which shows the behavior of the designs.

5   Conclusion and Future Work

We introduced a compositional and component-based approach for modeling and verifying system-level designs. This approach allows to describe the architecture of a SystemC design in high levels of abstraction, using Reo as an ADL language. The architecture is then mapped to automata which can be formally verified. So, we can benefit from ADL languages and automata-based languages at the same time. We mapped the system designs written in SystemC to Reo circuits and then compositionally construct their behavior using constraint automata. Then we can use the common formal techniques for formal verification of constraint automata.

This work concentrates on mapping of SystemC to Reo and constraint automata. The mapping is independent of the size of the system designs. There may be problems in analyzing large constraint automata resulted from a big SystemC design. Considering the ongoing research and work on model checking constraint automata, we will soon have better tools for analyzing larger constraint automata.

For proposing our approach, we worked on mapping the SystemC simulation kernel to constraint automata. The constraint automaton of the simulation kernel can be a substituent for the Reo circuit which serves as the glue code between components. We checked and saw the equivalency of the constraint automata of the whole system resulted from applying each method (putting the proposed Reo circuit or the constraint automata of the simulation kernel). The proof of this equivalency shall be provided in our future work. As an alternative, the design process can start from a Reo circuit instead of the hardware description languages like SystemC. We plan to study the possible methods for deriving SystemC codes from Reo circuits.

Acknowledgement

The research of the authors is supported by a grant from IPM (No.CS1384-3-04). We also wish to thank Iran Telecommunication Research Center for grant on this project. The work of the last author is also supported by CWI (within the project "Synthesis and Analysis of Connector Components (SYANCO)" DN 62-613).

References

1. Black, D.C., Donovan, J.: SystemC: From the Ground Up. Kluwer Academic Publishers, Boston, MA (2004)
2. Shukla, S.K., Doucet, F., Gupta, R.: Structured component composition framework for embedded system design. In: International Conference on High Performance Computing, pp. 663–678 (2002)
3. Doucet, F., Shukla, S., Otsuka, M., Gupta, R.: Balboa: A component-based design environment for system models. In: IEEE Transactions on Computer-Aided Design of Integrated Circuits and Systems, pp. 1597–1612. IEEE Computer Society Press, Los Alamitos (2003)
4. Arato, P., Mann, Z., Orban, A.: Component-based hardware-software co-design. In: Proceedings 17th International Conference on Architecture of Computing Systems (2004)

5. Gawanmeh, A., Habibi, A., Tahar, A.: Enabling systemc verification using abstract state machines. In: Proceedings of Forum on Specification and Design Languages, pp. 19–22 (2004)
6. Kroening, D., Sharygina, N.: Formal verification of SystemC by automatic hardware/software partitioning. In: Proceedings of Formal Methods and Models for Codesign, pp. 101–110. IEEE, Los Alamitos (2005)
7. Cortes, L.A., Eles, P., Peng, Z.: Verification of embedded systems using a petri net based representation. In: Proceedings 13th International Symposium on System Synthesis, pp. 149–155 (2000)
8. Brim, L., Cerna, I., Varekova, P., Zimmerova, B.: Component interaction automata as a verification-oriented component-based system specification. In: Proceedings of Specification and Verification of Component-Based Systems, pp. 31–38 (2005)
9. Arbab, F.: Reo: A channel-based coordination model for component composition. Mathematical Structures in Computer Science 14, 329–366 (2004)
10. Baier, C., Sirjani, M., Arbab, F., Rutten, J.J.: Modeling component connectors in reo by constraint automata. Science of Computer Programming 61, 75–113 (2006)
11. Razavi, N., Sirjani, M.: Using reo for formal specification and verification of system designs. In: Proceedings of MEMOCODE 2006, pp. 113–122. IEEE, Los Alamitos (2006)
12. Salem, A.: Formal semantics of synchronous systemc. In: Proceedings of Design, Automation and Test in Europe, pp. 10376–10381 (2003)
13. Saun, V.S.: Fsm derivation from systemc. Technical report, CSE Department of Indian Instititute of Technology, Delhi (2004)
14. Habibi, A., Moinudeen, H., Tahar, S.: Generating finite state machines from systemc. In: Proceedings of Design, Automation and Test in Europe, pp. 76–81 (2006)
15. Borger, E.: Abstract state machines: A method for high-level system design and analysis. Springer, Heidelberg (2003)
16. Arbab, F., Rutten, J.: A coinductive calculus of component connectors. In: Wirsing, M., Pattinson, D., Hennicker, R. (eds.) Recent Trends in Algebraic Development Techniques. LNCS, vol. 2755, pp. 34–55. Springer, Heidelberg (2003)

Reusing Requirements:
The Need for Extended Variability Models

Ramin Tavakoli Kolagari and Mark-Oliver Reiser

Technische Universität Berlin, Fakultät IV, Lehrstuhl Softwaretechnik,
Franklinstraße 28/29, 10587 Berlin, Germany
{tavakoli, moreiser}@cs.tu-berlin.de

Abstract. The paper describes a product-line-oriented approach to reusing requirements for systems with highly complex variability. Software product lines are a powerful means to manage comprehensively of all artifacts produced during system development for reuse. Hence, classical product line approaches provide mechanisms to handle requirements for reuse. But especially in the context of automotive systems, we face the challenge of creating reusable requirements specifications that each contain variability; reuse for requirements specifications of this kind means handling variability of variability models. This paper describes techniques for generating requirements specifications with variability from a so-called *requirements library*. The research results described originate from a process improvement initiative at DaimlerChrysler. The presented approaches are therefore pragmatic and aimed at current industrial practice but are formally based on a category-theoretical notation. Driven by practical issues, the paper comes up with extended means for variability modeling and a new notion of variability, broadening the scope of what can be managed by product lines.

Keywords: automotive systems, complex variability, requirements engineering, software product lines, variability modeling.

1 Introduction

The complexity of automobile electronics is due to both the distribution of a variety of interacting functions over a number of different components and a concomitantly large number of interfaces and the high degree of variation resulting from inevitable product differentiation.

This results in multiple fields of action. On the one hand, high quality demands must be placed on specifications owing to the level of complexity. On the other hand, efficiency when creating specifications in the face of short development cycles is becoming increasingly important.

In most cases, it is not possible to adopt the specifications of earlier models, mainly owing to the technology's constant further development and because the distribution of functions among components frequently differs from model to model for reasons of overall optimization, which can lead to very different system architectures right

F. Arbab and M. Sirjani (Eds.): FSEN 2007, LNCS 4767, pp. 129–143, 2007.

across the model range. What is required, instead, is a method that allows existing specification modules to be adapted and reconfigured. Up to now, the field of textual specifications reuse has provided only limited methodical support for wide-spread industrial use, particularly in the context of developing automobile electronics.

A successful technique for supporting the reuse of all kinds of development artifacts are software product lines. Carmakers have, in fact, experienced substantial benefits from product line approaches applied to the fabrication and mechanical engineering of vehicles. Engines and floor panels, Antilock Braking Systems and lamps are all being shared across a widening range of cars — indeed, across different marques and company boundaries.

Compared with the success of reusing mechanical and electrical components the reuse of software has proved harder to achieve. Luxury cars contain an increasing amount of software, which accounts for a rapidly growing percentage of the total cost of design and production. This is particularly true of the car's control software, which is organized in electronic control units (ECUs). These communicate on an internal network or bus such as a CAN bus (itself now a standardized commodity item).

Each ECU is, as far as the carmaker is concerned, specified and procured as a unique component for each type of car. Top-of-the-range models are distinguished from the rest — both cheaper models from the same carmaker and rival models of other marques — by the innovativeness and desirability of their ECUs' features.

This situation is problematic because there is no methodical support for reusing artifacts (in particular requirements) beyond different ECUs, which would allow economies of scale – especially in the context of automotive model ranges: we use the term model range in order to describe a set of cars that have a high degree of commonalities, e.g. all currently produced A-classes are a model range. The cars of a model range can differ from one another, but also model ranges differ from one another, e.g. all A-classes differ from all C-classes.

The classical definition of a software product line is based on such product families that are similar to model ranges and requires explicit activities to manage the commonalities and differences between the products (see Section 2 for details).

Each product of an automotive model range is a vehicle, and each vehicle contains ECUs. These ECUs realize the overall variability of the model range, which means that each ECU is a product family. Classical product line and variability modeling approaches provide mechanisms for handling these kinds of product families. But, as outlined above, from the point of view of a carmaker the problem is not describing the variability of one model range but reusing development artifacts across specific model ranges; reuse here means using development artifacts in different product families. These product families can also differ in their underlying variability approach, so carmakers need a technique to express variability and commonality of product families – a technique not provided by classical product line approaches.

In this paper, we present a *requirements library* to manage variability and commonality of product families at the requirements level. The problem of highly complex variability is not described in the research literature, except for a previous publication of ours on multi-level feature trees [1]. The results presented in this paper originate from a process improvement initiative at DaimlerChrysler [2]. Since it is intended to implement the results in the practical work of the business units, the presented solutions are pragmatic and geared to industrial practice. The basic idea of the paper – arranging requirements for the ECUs of different model ranges in one requirements library – is based on developers' experience. This paper provides a systematic framework for the experience-based "method" and describes it comprehensively. This is important to make the idea available for broad industrial use and to enhance classical product line techniques.

Although highly complex variability in this sense is today a problem mainly in the automotive domain and other domains producing highly differentiated embedded systems for mass customization (like the mobile phone industry), the problem will become more relevant in other software domains in the near future: software will be increasingly developed in software product lines in order to benefit from intensive reuse and fast development cycles. In a situation where the developed products themselves are product lines, techniques are needed to handle commonalities and variability between product lines.

The remainder of the paper introduces a comprehensive technique for managing requirements for systems with highly complex variability. Section 2 provides a survey of literature is provided, discussing other variability techniques. Section 3 describes the current status of requirements reuse as an experience-based requirements library method. Section 4 describes requirements reuse within the systematic use of the requirements library and gives a definition of the notion of model-range-spanning variability, i.e. extended variability. Detailed requirements variability modeling is introduced in Section 5 where it is also illustrated by small examples from the automotive domain that already clarify the problem although the examples themselves are quite simple. Section 6 discusses related approaches and Section 7 concludes with a discussion of the presented approach and points out future research needs.

2 Survey of Literature on Software Product Lines and Variability Modeling

The method described below deals with adjustments to specifications and to the process of creating specifications in order to simplify the reuse of model-range-spanning requirements. As a practical example, this paper will examine the wipe/wash function in a passenger car. Almost all passenger cars support this function in one form or another; however the model-specific implementation of this function is frequently different because even if the function and operation is uniform, the technical implementation still varies from model to model. This problem is discussed in general under the keyword "Software Reuse". There are a range of proposed solutions, from a component-oriented approach (e.g. [3]) to abstraction and traceability (e.g. [4]) to a compact, systematic approach in which all artifacts arising during the development of the system are associated with one another (e.g. [5], [6], and [7]).

The appeal of a "software product line approach" is that only the core elements of the product are available as core assets and, as such, form the heart of the reuse: these core elements are adopted and enhanced to incorporate detailed system-specific information, some of which is already identified by variation points, without anticipating design decisions. A software product line can therefore be defined as "a set of software-intensive systems sharing a common, managed set of features that satisfy the specific needs of a particular market segment or mission and that are developed from a common set of core assets in a prescribed way" [7].

The starting point for the reuse of detailed requirements specifications is often a feature list for the organization and an overview of the characteristics of all electrical and electronic systems, on the basis of which decisions relation to the model-range-independent development of electrical or electronic functions are made. This technique of working with features is frequently suggested as a way of supporting a product line approach (e.g. [8]), although the rigorous application of features is also subject to criticism because the structured approach based on working with features [9] is clearly reaching its limits, much like structured analysis [10]. Furthermore, the features concept is currently used in various domains, sometimes even within organizations, with different connotations. Currently, there are attempts to unify feature models (e.g. [11]) and equip them with comprehensive expressiveness (e.g. [12]). The present paper tries to show how these current efforts to enhance expressiveness and use of feature models can support requirements reuse in complex variability situations. It shows the interplay of flexibility and abstraction – e.g. as provided by multi-level feature trees – and explicit variability modeling within the artifact of requirements, a necessity in order to manage highly complex variability for the reuse of requirements specifications.

3   Current Status in Practice: The Intuitional Use of a "Requirements Library"

To implement a useful reuse mechanism for electrical and electronic passenger car systems, it was important for us to include current research and experience in this area of the industry as well as to examine current procedures used to create specifications to ensure that our proposal addresses these issues. In addition to an intensive study of the relevant literature, we therefore studied six specifications for complex interior ECUs from various models in order to provide answers to questions relating to the reuse of requirements, the systematic changing and evolution of requirements as well as the types of variability and options for displaying variability. To reinforce our findings from the specifications' review we conducted several interviews with requirements engineers developing the requirements specifications.

The primary activities involved in the development of ECUs on the manufacturing side are the creation of the specifications, the assignment of a supplier to implement the ECUs and the inspection, testing and integration of the ECU into the vehicle concept. In this case, a team typically supervises an ECU for the various model ranges in which changing requirements within the environment must be acted upon and implemented. In addition to the further development of systems for new models, there is naturally always a need to develop innovative features, which takes up a disproportionate amount of time.

The strict team orientation leads to intensive cooperation among developers and an implicit bundling of knowledge about the application domains. Functional changes as well as solutions to technical problems are discussed on an ad-hoc basis and incorporated into the specifications. This cooperation results in the development over time of a common understanding of functions, which acts as a strong force in molding identity. Even if this is sometimes manifested in a team-specific specification culture, there are considerable benefits to be reaped from this working method because it is based on efficient communication.

Along with competencies in requirements engineering, ECU engineers have acquired high levels of competence in the areas of inspection and integration with regard to the electrical and electronic design of ECUs. As a result, the specifications have acquired a very technical orientation and are specified to a level that makes them less suitable for reuse, with the consequence that they have a short life cycle based on the rapid pace of technological development. Nevertheless, we observed a high degree of similarity in the specifications used as test items in our study, although they were certainly subject to system-specific variations: similarity measures of approx. 15% to 90% were found at text module level. The variations between the specifications with high similarity measures were attributable to technical variations, variations relating to parameterization or new functions. Marginal reuse quotients were more likely to be recorded in cases where the specifications were written by different teams.

The reasons for changing or evolving features or function descriptions were frequently based on decisions that concerned this model range and that addressed the ECU under examination as well as the interface with other control units. Established model-range-independent functions such as the wipe/wash function were only occasionally changed in terms of their functionality. We identify this as an important starting point for supporting reuse.

Based on our own demand to propose a reuse approach closely related to current practical requirements specification processes, we decided to examine the specifications in the same way as the developers themselves had previously dealt with variability, and we discovered that the specifications described the systems with all the possible special equipment, options and alternatives for this model range (the outer shell covering all functions for this model). The current vehicle configuration is stored in the ECUs using local parameters; or it is passed to the individual functions at runtime using messages issued by a selected ECU or may not be issued at all. In the case of reduced equipment, we identified two typical patterns used in the specification of behavior in the event of missing hardware or software: the function specifications described either different function branches that depended on the vehicle configuration or an emergency operation procedure for hardware or software detected as missing – e.g. owing to the absence of specific signals. In the latter case, only the diagnostic module is informed of the configuration, thus suppressing the generation of entries in the fault memory; the actual function specification can remain unchanged.

Since development teams are organized with respect to the ECUs they develop, each team is confronted with differences of the ECUs for different model ranges. Thus the developers were in fact aware of the need to also describe different variability behavior of the ECUs for different model ranges. This becomes obvious because of a very specific dependency referred to in different requirements specifications: the "*independency*". This kind of dependency is only needed if there is a comparison between different variability models – i.e. product families – in place, as shown explicitly in the next section. The case of repeated occurrence of this dependency in different requirements specifications makes it obvious that the developers have a kind of abstract requirements library in their minds and explicitly describe differences between variability approaches of model ranges (see Fig. 1); the "independency" is needed to show that in this model range the dependency behavior between two variable items differs from another model range (which may be in the mind of the reader of the specification).

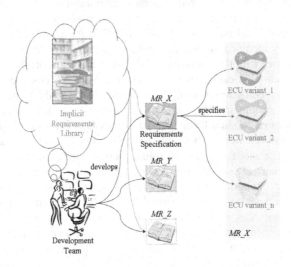

Fig. 1. The development team uses the requirements library implicitly to describe requirements specifications for ECUs of different model ranges (*MR_X*, *MR_Y*, and *MR_Z*). Each requirements specification for a model range describes a set of different ECU variants in order to realize the variability of a model range.

Hence, the main results were:

- development of one ECU for different model ranges within one development team
- intuitional reuse of requirements and functions for technically different ECUs
- development teams facilitate the description of variability of model ranges by using certain patterns (e.g. description of outer shell covering all functions of the ECU instead of describing the possible variants of the model range products)

In the next section, a systematic methodical basis for the requirements library is elaborated.

4 Requirements Reuse in a Requirements Library

The challenge for us was to find a successful product line approach to be applied in industries where mostly only requirements play an important role, because the other software development artifacts like software architecture or code are developed by suppliers, as is the case in the automotive industry.

"A system that is used will be changed" states Lehman in [13] – and system changes are actually what chiefly drive the need for systematic reuse. Reuse means handling changes; systematic reuse essentially means handling expected changes.

Thus one has to ask how changes occur, which changes are right and desirable, and which changes are occasional, uncoordinated or historically conditioned, and hence possibly dispensable.

Thus, if a product is changed in the course of time, these questions should be asked at all development levels producing artifacts because it may be possible that at each level there arises the wish to realize individual solutions or approaches or the need for abbreviations or simplifications as a result of short development schedules. These temporary changes should not become methodical, e.g. by putting them as a specific and reusable variant in a reuse platform; this means that techniques must be provided to prevent developers from making short-term solutions part of a reuse framework.

If reuse means that future changes are supported beneficially, reuse essentially comprises two aspects with respect to our discussion:

- Constructively, it means that we must first identify those changes that are relevant and that must be communicated to every stakeholder, e.g. by putting these changes in a platform.
- Application of this idea means that only those changes will have an impact on future product development that are reasonable for the product line, e.g. by providing innovative features or by making system features independent of the specific system architecture. This means that individual or short-term solutions are marginalized and play a less relevant role in daily development work.

Especially the constructive aspect of this interpretation of reuse is crucial for textual requirements. Language is a social asset that is used by humans to present themselves, to enunciate personal ideas. Language is then, an important form of expression for every individual and a main way to show individuality. This social aspect of language vehemently contradicts the objective of reuse to minimize individual (and thus short-term) differences. The existence of such a conflict of goals is also supported by the findings of the previous section, where we described the analysis of requirements specifications and found a wide range of similarity quotients: a small portion of functionally different requirements and a large portion of differently expressed requirements, describing mostly the same thing.

Reusing requirements involves special demands with respect to the handling of requirements. In practice it is not normally possible to make a clear distinction between problem and solution space. That is why requirements – unlike the demands of requirements engineering textbooks –not only describe problems but already give solutions. This is in fact acceptable if requirements engineers record their own expertise in doing so. In the case of reuse, a strictly solution-oriented description of requirements may result in short-lived requirements because technology develops rapidly and each reference to a concrete technology might cause rejection of the requirement in the next development step. This means that requirements must be described independently of specific technical solutions or architectures because the level of functional and non-functional requirements is less affected by changes than technological issues. Thus requirements can describe functional solutions and still be reused if the function itself is well established and the requirement does not refer to a technical solution or assumes a specific system architecture.

Another aspect peculiar to requirements – especially requirements for automotive systems – must be observed for successful reuse: cars are developed in model ranges, and model ranges comprise a set of vehicles differing from one another by optional equipment, design and country variants. This kind of variability we call model-range-specific variability.

Model-range-specific variability signifies variable items of requirements specifications for a model range. Forms of model-range-specific variability are:

- *variability through optional equipment*
- *variability through special vehicles (police cars, taxis ...)*
- *variability through country-specific equipment*
- *variability through specific design (cabriolet, estate ...)*

This specific variability has not only a bearing on the whole vehicle but also on each ECU of the vehicle because the ECUs react with different functional ranges on the variability. Specific variability can be expressed by classical variability and feature models (e.g. [8], and [9]).

The present paper is about adapting specifications of ECUs to facilitate the reuse of model-range-spanning variability.

Model-range-spanning variability signifies variabilities between model ranges. These variabilities can affect functional ranges as well as model-range-specific variability.

This definition of model-range-spanning variability is the basis for the requirements library. The requirements library provides a pool of architecture-independent specification modules, which, supported by tools, can be combined to form model-range-specific system specifications or components thereof.

The requirements library consists mainly of abstract and technical requirements abstracting from concrete design decisions. Requirements use parameters and signals in order to be adapted smoothly for different model ranges. Requirements reuse within the requirements library is driven by selecting features, which in turn preselect abstract requirements in the database. Decisions met by requirements engineers further refine and complete the preselection.

During the transition from the features to the requirements descriptions, a switch also takes place from a customer-oriented view to a system development view. The requirements are sufficiently decomposed into technical requirements to make them suitable for distribution across system architectures. We draw a distinction between the abstract and technical levels of the requirements descriptions, which are both described independently of the system architecture, i.e. they contain neither requirements to ECU assignments nor signal addressing.

The abstract level of the requirements library only describes the targeted functionality and the required parameters and signals. Most of the decisions relating to the selection of possible alternatives and options should be made in this not overly detailed view of the vehicle systems. Only at the technical level are details added (e.g. behavior in the event of errors, value ranges and coding of signals and parameters, binding times ...).

5 Requirements Variability Modeling

Variability modeling for requirements reuse differs from current variability modeling approaches: the variability model is not used to configure, say design elements for a product family; instead, it directly influences the selection of requirements. And in the case of automotive requirements specifications one is confronted with the need to manage model-range-spanning variability. Furthermore, requirements specifications offer an abstract view of the described system, similar to feature models. These are the reasons why we decided to describe requirements variability directly within the artifact of requirements.

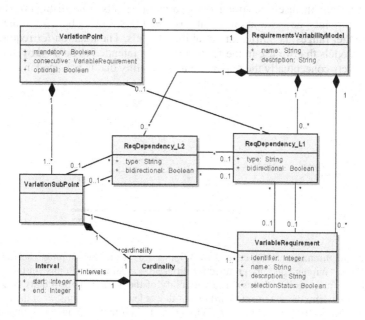

Fig. 2. The basic elements of the requirements variability model are variable requirements. Requirements can be grouped by variation-sub-points, expressing the variability of the requirements by cardinalities (cf. [12]). Variation-sub-points are grouped by variation points. Two kinds of dependencies can be expressed in the requirements variability model: level-1 dependencies, e.g. between variable requirements or variable requirements and variation points; or level-2 dependencies, e.g. between variation-sub-points, between level-1 dependencies or between variation-sub-points and level-1 dependencies.

Requirements variability must cope with both, model-range-spanning and model-range-specific variability because requirements are used between different model range specifications and each requirements specification must also describe the specific variability. We can state that

- each requirements specification is a requirements library, and
- each requirements library comprising only model-range-specific variability is a product (i.e. model range) specification.

Provided a stable requirements library exists, the main task of a requirements engineer shifts from *developing requirements specifications* to *deriving requirements specifications* (including the derivation of a variability definition for the model range). Deriving product specifications from a requirements library effectively means a stepwise decrease of model-range-spanning variability. The requirements variability model described below is formalized (syntactically as well as semantically) in a category-theoretical notation in [2] that can be used for a language-independent implementation. The tool described in the last part of this section is also based on this formalization.

The basic elements of the requirements variability model are (variable) requirements, see Fig. 2. This means that the variability model is directly implemented within the requirements database. Variable requirements are arranged in variation-sub-points, which are themselves arranged in variation points. The distinction between variation-sub-points and variation points is needed to describe requirements for different model ranges, i.e. different variability models. The notation for requirements variability models that we use in the following is not intended to be used by end-users. It rather depicts conceptually the requirements variability that is managed in tools.

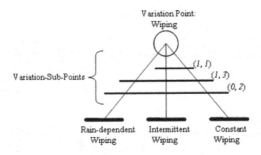

Fig. 3. The requirements "Rain-dependent Wiping" to "Constant Wiping" belong to the Variation Point "Wiping" and are grouped by different Variation-Sub-Points (in this example we have three Variation-Sub-Points). The variability of the Variation-Sub-Points is described by cardinalities, where the statement (n, m) means that at least n and at most m of the respective requirements can be chosen. "Intermittent Wiping" and "Constant Wiping" are grouped by the first Variation-Sub-Point, whereas the other two Variation-Sub-Points comprise all three requirements.

Fig. 3 gives an example of a variation point and three variation-sub-points. If the requirements library includes a model as depicted in Fig. 3, this means that there are model ranges in whose vehicles either "Intermittent Wiping" or "Constant Wiping" is available; "Intermittent Wiping" and "Constant Wiping" are excluding alternatives in this case (Variation-Sub-Point $(1, 1)$). There are also model ranges whose vehicles include at least one and at most three of all three wiping modes (Variation-Sub-Point $(1, 3)$), and there are also model ranges whose vehicles include zero to at most two of all three wiping modes (Variation-Sub-Point $(0, 2)$).

The variation point "Wiping" can be instantiated with respect to a specific variability modeling (i.e. one can chose one of the variation-sub-points) or with respect to a specific selection of requirements that is a correct instantiation of either of the variation-sub-points. Fig. 4 shows two possible instantiations of the variation point "Wiping".

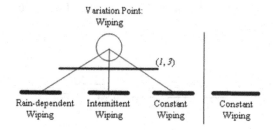

Fig. 4. Two possible instantiations of the Variation Point "Wiping" of Fig. 3 are shown. In the left part of the figure, the variation point is instantiated and includes only one variation-sub-point, i.e. one variability model. In the right part of the figure, the variation point is instantiated by instantiating correctly one of the variation-sub-points. This ensures that the variation point is fully bound and no variability is left.

In order to keep the search space in the instantiation process small, we distinguish between three kinds of variation points:

- A variation point can be *mandatory*, i.e. one of its variation-sub-points or a correct instance of one of the variation-sub-points must be instantiated for each specification derived from the requirements library.
- A variation point can be *optional*, meaning that the whole variation point with its variation-sub-points and all the requirements can be left out when instantiating a specification from the requirements library.
- A variation point can be *consecutive*, meaning that the whole variation point must be selected only if the respective requirement (the requirement having an includes-dependency to the variation point) is chosen.

Fig. 5 illustrates this point.

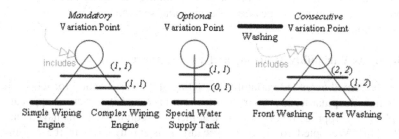

Fig. 5. A *Mandatory* Variation Point is depicted by an includes-dependency without a source element. Here it can either be instantiated to a variation point offering a "Simple Wiping Engine" or a "Complex Wiping Engine" as alternatives or to a rudimentary variation point offering mandatory a "Complex Wiping Engine". Furthermore the variation point can be instantiated to a correct instantiation of either of its variation-sub-points (e.g. "Simple Wiping Engine"). An *Optional* Variation Point is given if no dependency is linked to the variation point. It can be left out completely or is instantiated to either of its variation sub points or to the requirement itself (being a correct instance of at least one variation sub point). A *Consecutive* Variation Point is given if a requirement includes this variation point.

Fig. 5 introduces includes-dependencies of level-1. Fig. 6 illustrates the use of level-2 dependencies.

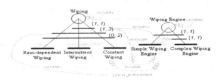

Fig. 6. The figure depicts the variation points "Wiping" and "Wiping Engine", both mandatory variation points, depicted by the includes-dependency. But there are also dependencies between these variation points. A level-1 dependency is the includes-dependency from "Constant Wiping" to "Simple Wiping Engine". This dependency is excluded by a level-2 dependency from the variation-sub-point (*1, 3*) of the "Wiping" variation point. The reason is another level-2 dependency from the variation-sub-point (*1, 3*) of "Wiping" to the lower (*1, 1*) variation-sub-point of "Wiping Engine", always including the "Complex Wiping Engine". Since the level-1 includes-dependency is excluded in this case, there exists another level-2 dependency from the variation-sub-point (*1, 3*) of the "Wiping" variation point to the alternative dependency – in this case the is-independent-dependency – a specific dependency of extended variability models.

In Fig. 6, a specific level-1 dependency is depicted: the is_independent-dependency. This kind of dependency is motivated by practical considerations (cf. Section 3) and needed for a systematic description of the variability model. It is only applicable as a level-1 dependency, whereas all the other possible level-1 dependencies (like includes, excludes and influences) can also be used as level-2 dependencies.

The complete details of extended variability models could not presented in this paper for reasons of length; for more details (including the use of category theory to describe a comprehensive framework of syntax and semantics of variability models), readers are referred to [2].

Requirements Variability Modeling and Tool Support

We have presented extended variability modeling and its application for requirements libraries in conceptual terms. To try out the approach and its practical applicability, we applied the approach [14] to the commercial requirements management tool DOORS [15]. We opted for DOORS because it is wildly used in the automotive industry. Also it is easily extendable because it provides a script language *DOORS eXtension Language* (*dxl*) making a huge number of tool-internal functions available. The study, which also includes a set of rules concerning the use of the model, contains a compact program allowing the use of extended variability models in DOORS. By using DOORS-specific links for the realization of level-1 dependencies, the concept can be elegantly visualized for the user.

The applicability of the approach in a tool as shown in the study is an important step towards practical implementation of the approach: process improvement initiatives often start with the introduction of a new tool directly supporting the accomplishment of several process steps. The need for a systematic reuse process for requirements specifications is obvious, with systems facing increasingly complicated, high quality demands of customers and short development cycles. The applicability of the reuse approach presented in this paper and the possibility of implementing the approach easily in a tool describe a practical approach to successfully meeting current challenges in requirements reuse of embedded systems with highly complex variability.

6   Related Work

In [16], Bühne et al. describe the problem that classical feature models fail to meet the demands for specifying automotive model ranges because there are multiple criteria applying to whole model ranges. Consequently, they propose enhancing feature models to describe feature models for model ranges, design, country, and special vehicle variants. This, in fact, is an approach to solving the problem of differing variability for different model ranges. With respect to the method described in this paper, the following differences were identified:

- The resulting feature model is invariably oriented to the past because the developed feature model only describes complete model ranges, as opposed to describing basic structures of more than one model range in one variability model, as proposed in this paper. Hence, this kind of feature model is not suitable for specifying future model ranges or country variants.
- The proposed feature model comprises a fixed set of criteria, each constituting one perspective on how the systems might be variable. But this set of criteria could change, in which case maintenance of the model is very challenging because many dependencies are encapsulated in the different layers of the model and are therefore not visible.
- Such a feature model does not directly support the reuse of requirements or specifications because no requirements are described. Feature models cannot replace requirements specifications – at most they supplement requirements. Since feature models provide an abstract view of the system and the system-specific variability (cf. Section 4) and can be adapted flexibly, they are of special interest to management and software architecture developers, allowing them to gain a first impression of the system. But in the case of carmakers, software architecture plays a secondary role because it is largely developed by suppliers.
- Last but not least, the underlying idea of these feature diagrams is difficult to align with current thinking of requirements engineers in automotive industrial practice: partitioning perspectives on feature models into model range, design or country variant is not really suitable for engineers because the current industrial process (cf. Section 3) assumes a model-range-oriented approach in which design and country variants are nothing more than optional equipment. This industrial approach is, in fact, reasonable because design or country variability does not differ conceptually from optional-equipment variability.

In summary, the approach presented in this paper is more focused on the specific needs of the automotive domain and also comprises treatment of requirements, not only feature models.

Therefore, we suggest using different criteria, flexibly introduced, to preconfigure feature trees from multi-level feature trees with respect to specific characteristics of the set of products under examination [17] (cf. also Section 3).

7 Conclusion

In supporting the creation of model-range-specific electrical and electronic systems, the requirements library pursues a practice- and reuse-oriented approach. It is geared to both software product lines and component-oriented approaches.

The European research project ATESST (http://www.atesst.org) further develops the architecture description language for automotive systems EAST-ADL (http://www.east-eea.net/) addressing among other things, highly complex variability. The techniques presented in this paper will be included in the EAST-ADL2, developed in ATESST.

Future work will focus primarily on integration of the presented requirements library and other variability modeling approaches in order to equip the requirements-artifact-oriented requirements library with more abstract – and therefore more flexible – techniques. The already mentioned multi-level feature trees [1] in particular can be used to provide a more abstract view of the system. In fact, since multi-level feature trees also include techniques for handling highly complex variability, they provide a comprehensive view of the variability of the requirements library.

Future work will, however address the link not only to a more abstract view of the requirements library but also to more concrete artifacts than requirements. Rapidly changing system architectures for different model ranges are a special challenge for the automotive industry. The requirements library can be seen as a new step in a progression of standardization efforts by automotive developers to abstract from concrete ECUs. The introduction of OSEK (http://www.osek-vdx.org/) allowed abstraction from one specific ECU. The current efforts of Autosar (http://www.autosar.org) aim at abstraction from a single combination of ECUs. The requirements library can now be used to abstract from a set of different combinations of ECUs. Further research is needed to implement a connection to the design layer, mapping the requirements to different system architectures based on architecture validation.

References

1. Reiser, M.-O., Weber, M.: Managing Highly Complex Product Families With Multi-Level Feature Trees. In: RE 2006. Proceedings of 14th IEEE International Requirements Engineering Conference, Minneapolis, pp. 146–155. IEEE Computer Society, Los Alamitos (2006)
2. Tavakoli Kolagari, R.: Requirements Engineering für Software-Produktlinien eingebetteter, technischer Systeme. PhD Thesis in Experimental Software Engineering, Vol. 18, Fraunhofer IRB Verlag (2006)

3. Atkinson, C., Bayer, J., Muthig, D.: Component-Based Product Line Development: The KobrA Approach. In: Donohoe, P. (ed.) Software Product Lines: Experiences and Research Directions, pp. 289–309. Kluwer Academic Publishers, Norwell (2000)
4. von Knethen, A., Paech, B., Kiedaisch, F., Houdek, F.: Systematic Requirements Recycling through Abstraction and Traceability. In: Proceedings of the IEEE Joint International Requirements Engineering Conference, Essen, pp. 273–281. IEEE Computer Society Press, Los Alamitos (2002)
5. Bayer, J., Flege, O., Knauber, P., Laqua, R., Muthig, D., Schmid, K., Widen, T., DeBaud, J.-M.: PuLSE: A Methodology to Develop Software Product Lines. In: Proceedings of the Fifth Symposium on Software Reusability: Bridging the Gap between Research and Practice, Los Angeles, pp. 122–131 (1999)
6. Bosch, J.: Design and Use of Software Architectures: Adopting and evolving a product-line approach. Addison-Wesley, ACM Press Books, Harlow (2000)
7. Clements, P., Northrop, L.: Software Product Lines: Practices and Patterns. The SEI Series in Software Engineering. Addison-Wesley, Boston (2002)
8. Hein, A., Schlick, M., Vinga-Martins, R.: Applying Feature Models in Industrial Settings. In: Donohoe, P. (ed.) Software Product Lines: Experiences and Research Directions, pp. 47–70. Kluwer Academic Publishers, Norwell (2000)
9. Kang, K.C., Cohen, S.G., Hess, J.A., Novak, W.E., Petersen, A.S.: Feature-Oriented Domain Analysis (FODA) Feasibility Study. Technical Report CMU/SEI-90-TR-21, Software Engineering Institute of the Carnegie Mellon University, Pittsburgh (1990)
10. DeMarco, T.: Structured Analysis and System Specification. Prentice Hall, Englewood Cliffs (1978)
11. Schobbens, P.-Y., Heymans, P., Trigaux, J.-C., Bontemps, Y.: Feature Diagrams: A Survey and A Formal Semantics. In: RE 2006. Proceedings of 14th IEEE International Requirements Engineering Conference, Minneapolis, pp. 139–148. IEEE Computer Society, Los Alamitos (2006)
12. Czarnecki, K., Kim, P.: Cardinality-Based Feature Modeling and Constraints: A Progress Report. In: Proceedings of the International Workshop on Software Factories At OOPSLA, San Diego (2005)
13. Lehman, M.M.: On Understanding Laws, Evolution, and Conservation in the Large-Program Life Cycle. Journal of Systems and Software 1(3), 213–231 (1980)
14. Heß, S.A.: Erweitertes Variationspunkte-Abhángigkeiten-Modell für den Erstellungs- und Wiederverwendungsprozess von Spezifikationen mit hoher Restvariabilität. Master Thesis, University of Ulm (2005)
15. Telelogic DOORS website: http://www.telelogic.com/products/doorsers/index.cfm
16. Bühne, S., Lauenroth, K., Pohl, K., Weber, M.: Modeling Features for Multi-Criteria Product-Lines in Automotive Industry. In: (ICSE 2004 Workshop, SEAS) Proceedings of the Workshop on Software Engineering for Automotive Systems, Edinburgh (2004)
17. Reiser, M.-O., Weber, M.: Using Product Sets to Define Complex Product Decisions. In: Obbink, H., Pohl, K. (eds.) SPLC 2005. LNCS, vol. 3714, pp. 21–32. Springer, Heidelberg (2005)

Test Selection Criteria for Quantifier-Free First-Order Specifications*

Marc Aiguier[1], Agnès Arnould[2], Pascale Le Gall[1], and Delphine Longuet[1]

[1] IBISC CNRS FRE 2873 - University of Évry Val d'Essonne
523 place des terrasses de l'Agora, F-91000 Évry
{marc.aiguier,pascale.legall,delphine.longuet}@ibisc.univ-evry.fr
[2] SIC - University of Poitiers
SP2MI, F-86962 Futuroscope Cedex
arnould@sic.univ-poitiers.fr

Abstract. This paper deals with test case selection from axiomatic specifications whose axioms are quantifier-free first-order formulae. Test cases are modeled as ground formulae and any specification has an exhaustive test data set whose successful submission means correctness, provided that the software under verification can be modeled as a first-order structure over the same signature. As it has already been done for positive conditional equational specifications, we derive test cases from selection criteria based on axiom coverage. Our selection criteria allows us to select test cases by iteratively unfolding an initial target test purpose, given as a formula. The initial reference test set is iteratively split into successive subsets. Each subset of test cases is defined by constraints which are increasingly introduced by the unfolding procedure to ensure an appropriate matching between the current test purpose under unfolding and specification axioms. Our unfolding procedure is sound (no test is added) and complete (no test is lost) with respect to the starting test purpose. It is exemplified on a simple example.

Keywords: Specification-based testing, quantifier-free first-order specifications, selection criteria, test purpose, axiom coverage, unfolding, proof tree normalization.

Introduction

Specification-based testing is a particular case of black-box testing which consists in performing the system under test with some input data in order to state whether its behaviour is conformant to a rigorous specification (*i.e.* given as a formal text provided with a clear semantic). Formal specifications make possible the automation of both test case generation from selection criteria and evaluation

---

* This work is performed within a French national project STACS (*Spécification et Test, Abstraits et Compositionnels, de Systèmes*) in collaboration with the French Atomic Energy Commission (CEA). This project is devoted to automatically generate test data sets for Input Output Symbolic Transition Systems.

F. Arbab and M. Sirjani (Eds.): FSEN 2007, LNCS 4767, pp. 144–159, 2007.

of test executions as successful or not. Selection criteria for specification-based testing generally allow to cover specification requirements (*e.g.* axioms, transitions or states). The computation of the success/failure verdict of test execution tools follows from the comparison between the outputs given by the system under test and the expected ones defined by the formal specification. Besides the possibility of computing verdicts for a test case execution, using formal specifications allows one to properly define the conformance relation, which states what it means for a system to conform to its specification. Such a conformance relation depends on both test hypotheses on the system, which allow to consider it as a formal model, and observability restrictions on the system. These observability restrictions are used to select test cases which can be interpreted as successful or not when performed by the system under test. For instance, in the framework of testing from algebraic specifications, "observable" test cases are any ground equations provided with an equality predicate within the programming language used to implement the system under test. When such conditions (test hypotheses on systems and observability restrictions) are precisely stated, it becomes possible to formally define the testing activity [1,2]. In particular, correctness can be defined up to these conditions by characterizing an exhaustive test set, whose success is equivalent to system correctness. Moreover, a testing process can be qualified as sound if selected test cases cannot discard correct systems, and as complete if any non-correct system can be detected by at least one test case. In fact, these notions of soundness and completeness may be slightly adapted depending on whether they are applied to an exhaustive test set, to a selection criterion, or to a subset of tests targeted by a test purpose [3].

Testing from algebraic specifications has already been extensively studied [1, 2, 4, 5, 6, 7, 8, 9, 10, 11, 12, 13]. Correctness issues have been investigated in presence of non-observable types whose equality can only be observed through observable contexts, *i.e.* by applying some composition of functions yielding an observable result. Selection issues have also been investigated. They consist in either directly covering axioms by instantiating variables with some chosen data or unfolding axioms in order to make a case analysis of function definition. In this last case, test cases for a functionality under test are extracted from the specification by building input data which match the different cases defined by the specification. For example, when functions are recursively specified, the analysis can be refined as many times as the tester chooses to do it. The main drawback of such a selection strategy is that the specification under consideration has to be under a restrictive form, namely positive conditional formulae [4,5,6].

In this paper, we propose a family of selection criteria based on axiom unfolding for a larger class of axiomatic specifications: quantifier-free first-order formulae. The enlargement is twofold. First, we do not reduce atomic formulae to equations and consider any kind of predicates. Secondly, formulae are not restricted to Horn clauses (called conditional positive formulae when dealing with equational logic). Our primary goal was to consider the whole classical first-order language. However, we immediately eliminate the existential quantifier. Indeed, testing a formula of the form $\exists X, \varphi(X)$ would amount to exhibit a witness value

a such that $\varphi(X)$ is interpreted as true by the system when substituting X by a. Of course, there is no general way to exhibit such a pertinent value, but notice that astonishly, exhibiting such a value would amount to simply prove the system with respect to the initial property. Thus, existential properties are not testable. Some works on specification-based testing [7,8] have already considered a similar class of formulae. They propose a mixed approach combining black-box and white-box testing to deal with the problem of non-observable data types. From the selection point of view, they do not propose any particular strategy, but only the substitution of axiom variables for some arbitrarily chosen data. On the contrary, following the specification-based testing framework proposed in [1], we characterize an exhaustive test set for such specifications. Moreover, by extending the unfolding-based selection criteria family defined for conditional positive equational specifications, we define a sound and complete unfolding procedure devoted to the coverage of quantifier-free first-order axioms.

The paper is organized as follows. In Section 1, we recall standard notations about quantifier-free first-order specifications. Section 2 gives relevant definitions of [1] concerning our framework of testing. In Section 3, an exhaustive test set for quantifier-free first-order specifications is characterized. Section 4 proposes an unfolding procedure allowing us to define a family of selection criteria for the considered class of specifications. Finally, in Section 4.3, the selection criteria based on the unfolding procedure is proved to be both sound and complete.

1   Preliminaries

1.1   Quantifier-Free First-Order Specifications

A *(first-order) signature* $\Sigma = (S, F, P, V)$ consists of a set S of sorts, a set F of operation names each one equipped with an arity in $S^* \times S$, a set P of predicate names each one equipped with an arity in S^+ and an S-indexed set of variables V. In the sequel, an operation name f of arity $(s_1 \ldots s_n, s)$ will be denoted by $f : s_1 \times \ldots \times s_n \to s$, and a predicate name p of arity $(s_1 \ldots s_n)$ will be denoted by $p : s_1 \times \ldots \times s_n$. Given a signature $\Sigma = (S, F, P, V)$, $T_\Sigma(V)$ and T_Σ are both S-sets of *terms with variables in V* and *ground terms*, respectively, freely generated from variables and operations in Σ and preserving arity of operations. A *substitution* is any mapping $\sigma : V \to T_\Sigma(V)$ that preserves sorts. Substitutions are naturally extended to terms with variables. Σ-*atomic formulae* are formulae of the form $p(t_1, \ldots, t_n)$ with $p : s_1 \times \ldots \times s_n$ and $t_i \in T_\Sigma(V)_{s_i}$ for each i, $1 \leq i \leq n$. A Σ-*formula* is a quantifier-free first-order formula built from atomic formulae and Boolean connectives $\neg$, $\wedge$, $\vee$ and $\Rightarrow$. As usual, free variables of quantifier-free formulae are implicitly universally quantified. A Σ-formula is said *ground* if it does not contain variables. Let us denote $For(\Sigma)$ the set of all Σ-formulae. A *specification* $Sp = (\Sigma, Ax)$ consists of a signature Σ and a set Ax of quantifier-free formulae built over Σ. Formulae in Ax are often called *axioms*.

A Σ-*model* $\mathcal{M}$ is an S-indexed set M equipped for each $f : s_1 \times \ldots \times s_n \to s \in F$ with a mapping $f^{\mathcal{M}} : M_{s_1} \times \ldots \times M_{s_n} \to M_s$ and for each predicate $p : s_1 \times \ldots \times s_n$ with an n-ary relation $p^{\mathcal{M}} \subseteq M_{s_1} \times \ldots \times M_{s_n}$. $Mod(\Sigma)$ is the category objects of which are all Σ-models. Given a Σ-model $\mathcal{M}$, a Σ-interpretation in M is any mapping $\nu : V \to M$. Interpretations are naturally extended to terms with variables. A Σ-model $\mathcal{M}$ *satisfies* for an interpretation ν a Σ-atomic formula $p(t_1, \ldots, t_n)$ if and only if $(\nu(t_1), \ldots, \nu(t_n)) \in p^{\mathcal{M}}$. The *satisfaction* of a Σ-formula φ for an interpretation ν by $\mathcal{M}$, denoted $\mathcal{M} \models_{\nu} \varphi$, is inductively defined on the structure of φ from the satisfaction for ν of atomic formulae of φ and using classic semantic interpretations of Boolean connectives. $\mathcal{M}$ validates a formula φ, denoted $\mathcal{M} \models \varphi$, if and only if for every interpretation $\nu : V \to M$, $\mathcal{M} \models_{\nu} \varphi$. Given $\Psi \subseteq For(\Sigma)$ and two Σ-models $\mathcal{M}$ and $\mathcal{M}'$, $\mathcal{M}$ is Ψ*-equivalent to* $\mathcal{M}'$, denoted $\mathcal{M} \equiv_{\Psi} \mathcal{M}'$, if and only if we have: $\forall \varphi \in \Psi$, $\mathcal{M} \models \varphi \iff \mathcal{M}' \models \varphi$. Given a specification $Sp = (\Sigma, Ax)$, a Σ-model $\mathcal{M}$ is an *Sp-model* if for every $\varphi \in Ax$, $\mathcal{M} \models \varphi$. $Mod(Sp)$ is the full subcategory of $Mod(\Sigma)$, objects of which are all Sp-models. A Σ-formula φ is a *semantic consequence* of a specification $Sp = (\Sigma, Ax)$, denoted $Sp \models \varphi$, if and only if for every Sp-model $\mathcal{M}$, we have $\mathcal{M} \models \varphi$. $Sp^{\bullet}$ is the set of all semantic consequences.

Given a set of quantifier-free formulae $\Psi \subseteq For(\Sigma)$, let us denote $\mathcal{H}_{T_{\Sigma}}$ the Σ-model, classically called the Herbrand model of Ψ,

- defined by the Σ-algebra, whose carrier is T_{Σ} and whose operation meaning is defined for every operation $f : s_1 \times \ldots \times s_n \to s \in F$ by the mapping $f^{\mathcal{H}_{T_{\Sigma}}} : (t_1, \ldots, t_n) \mapsto f(t_1, \ldots, t_n)$, and
- determined by the set of ground atomic formulae $p(t_1, \ldots, t_n)$ such that $\Psi \models p(t_1, \ldots, t_n)$.

It is easy to show that $\Psi \models \varphi \Leftrightarrow \mathcal{H}_{T_{\Sigma}} \models \varphi$ for every ground formula φ, and then $\mathcal{H}_{T_{\Sigma}} \in Mod((\Sigma, \Psi))$.

A calculus for quantifier-free first-order specifications is defined by the following inference rules, where $\Gamma \mathrel{\vdash\mkern-9mu\sim} \Delta$ is a sequent such that Γ and Δ are two sets of quantifier-free first-order formulae:

$$\frac{}{\Gamma, \varphi \mathrel{\vdash\mkern-9mu\sim} \Delta, \varphi} \text{Ax}$$

$$\frac{\Gamma \mathrel{\vdash\mkern-9mu\sim} \Delta, \varphi}{\Gamma, \neg\varphi \mathrel{\vdash\mkern-9mu\sim} \Delta} \text{Left-}\neg \qquad \frac{\Gamma, \varphi \mathrel{\vdash\mkern-9mu\sim} \Delta}{\Gamma \mathrel{\vdash\mkern-9mu\sim} \Delta, \neg\varphi} \text{Right-}\neg$$

$$\frac{\Gamma, \varphi, \psi \mathrel{\vdash\mkern-9mu\sim} \Delta}{\Gamma, \varphi \wedge \psi \mathrel{\vdash\mkern-9mu\sim} \Delta} \text{Left-}\wedge \qquad \frac{\Gamma \mathrel{\vdash\mkern-9mu\sim} \Delta, \varphi \quad \Gamma \mathrel{\vdash\mkern-9mu\sim} \Delta, \psi}{\Gamma \mathrel{\vdash\mkern-9mu\sim} \Delta, \varphi \wedge \psi} \text{Right-}\wedge$$

$$\frac{\Gamma, \varphi \mathrel{\vdash\mkern-9mu\sim} \Delta \quad \Gamma, \psi \mathrel{\vdash\mkern-9mu\sim} \Delta}{\Gamma, \varphi \vee \psi \mathrel{\vdash\mkern-9mu\sim} \Delta} \text{Left-}\vee \qquad \frac{\Gamma \mathrel{\vdash\mkern-9mu\sim} \Delta, \varphi, \psi}{\Gamma \mathrel{\vdash\mkern-9mu\sim} \Delta, \varphi \vee \psi} \text{Right-}\vee$$

$$\frac{\Gamma \mathrel{\vdash\mkern-9mu\sim} \Delta, \varphi \quad \Gamma, \psi \mathrel{\vdash\mkern-9mu\sim} \Delta}{\Gamma, \varphi \Rightarrow \psi \mathrel{\vdash\mkern-9mu\sim} \Delta} \text{Left-}\Rightarrow \qquad \frac{\Gamma, \varphi \mathrel{\vdash\mkern-9mu\sim} \Delta, \psi}{\Gamma \mathrel{\vdash\mkern-9mu\sim} \Delta, \varphi \Rightarrow \psi} \text{Right-}\Rightarrow$$

$$\frac{\Gamma \mathrel{\vdash\mkern-9mu\sim} \Delta}{\sigma(\Gamma) \mathrel{\vdash\mkern-9mu\sim} \sigma(\Delta)} \text{Subs} \qquad \frac{\Gamma \mathrel{\vdash\mkern-9mu\sim} \Delta, \varphi \quad \Gamma', \varphi \mathrel{\vdash\mkern-9mu\sim} \Delta'}{\Gamma, \Gamma' \mathrel{\vdash\mkern-9mu\sim} \Delta, \Delta'} \text{Cut}$$

Observe that the inference rules associated to Boolean connectives obviously define an automatic process that allows to transform any sequent $\mathrel{\vdash\mkern-9mu\sim} \varphi$, where φ is a quantifier-free formula, into a set of sequents $\Gamma \mathrel{\vdash\mkern-9mu\sim} \Delta$ where every formula in Γ and Δ is atomic. Let us call such sequents *normalized sequents*.

Moreover, we can show that every proof tree can be transformed into a proof tree of same conclusion and such that both Cut and Subs rules never occur under rule instances associated to Boolean connectives. This transformation is obtained from basic transformations, for example:

$$\cfrac{\cfrac{\Gamma \vdash \Delta,\psi,\varphi}{\Gamma,\neg\varphi \vdash \Delta,\psi}\text{ Left-}\neg \quad \Gamma',\psi \vdash \Delta'}{\Gamma,\Gamma',\neg\varphi \vdash \Delta,\Delta'}\text{ Cut} \quad \rightsquigarrow \quad \cfrac{\cfrac{\Gamma \vdash \Delta,\psi,\varphi \quad \Gamma',\psi \vdash \Delta'}{\Gamma,\Gamma' \vdash \Delta,\Delta',\varphi}\text{ Cut}}{\Gamma,\Gamma',\neg\varphi \vdash \Delta,\Delta'}\text{ Left-}\neg$$

The other basic transformations are defined in the same way. Therefore, using proof terms for proofs, with a recursive path ordering $>^{rpo}$ to order proofs induced by the well-founded relation (precedence) $>$ on rule instances

$$\text{Cut, Subs} > \text{Left-@, Right-@, where @} \in \{\neg, \wedge, \vee, \Rightarrow\}$$

we show that the transitive closure of $\rightsquigarrow$ is contained in the relation $>^{rpo}$, and thus that $\rightsquigarrow$ is terminating.

This last result states that every sequent is equivalent to a normalized sequent, which allows to only deal with normalized sequents. Therefore, in the following, we will suppose that specification axioms are normalized sequents.

1.2   Running Example

By way of illustration, we give a specification of sorted lists of positive rationals.

We first give a specification of naturals, built from constructors 0 and successor s. Addition add and multiplication $mult$ on naturals are specified as usual, as well as the predicate "less than" ltn. The constructor operation $\_/\_$ then builds rationals from couples of naturals. Two rationals x/y and u/v are equal (eqr predicate) if $mult(x,v)$ and $mult(u,y)$ are equal. Since we consider only positive rationals, x/y is less than u/v (ltr predicate) if $mult(x,v)$ is less than $mult(u,y)$.

Lists of rationals are then built from constructors $[]$ and $\_::\_$ as usual. The insertion $insert$ of a rational in a sorted list needs to consider four cases: the list is empty; the first element of the list is equal to the rational to insert, and then the element is not repeated; the first element of the list is greater than the rational to insert, and then it is inserted at the head; the first element of the list is less than the rational to insert, then the insertion is tried in the rest of the list. The membership predicate $isin$ is specified saying that there is no element in the empty list, and that searching for an element in a non-empty list comes to find it at the head of the list or to search it in the rest of the list.

The behaviour of operations add, $mult$ and $insert$ is classically specified by equations. When dealing with first-order logic, this requires to introduce three equality predicates $=_{Nat}: Nat \times Nat$, $=_{Rat}: Rat \times Rat$ and $=_{List}: List \times List$, each one equipped with the following axioms:

$$x =_@ x$$
$$x =_@ y \Rightarrow y =_@ x$$
$$x =_@ y \wedge y =_@ z \Rightarrow x =_@ z$$
$$x_1 =_{@_1} y_1 \wedge \ldots \wedge x_n =_{@_n} y_n \Rightarrow f(x_1,\ldots,x_n) =_@ f(y_1,\ldots,y_n)$$
$$x_1 =_{@_1} y_1 \wedge \ldots \wedge x_n =_{@_n} y_n \wedge p(x_1,\ldots,x_n) \Rightarrow p(y_1,\ldots,y_n)$$

where $@, @_i \in \{Nat, Rat, List\}$, $f : @_1 \times \ldots \times @_n \rightarrow @$ and $p : @_1 \times \ldots \times @_n$. In order not to make heavy specifications, another approach is to transform any operation $f : s_1 \times \ldots \times s_n \rightarrow s$ into a predicate $f : s_1 \times \ldots \times s_n \times s$ and then to make the equality implicit. This is the approach we will follow in the specification below. Another consequence of such an approach is to make the use of our algorithm of selection criteria, based on axiom unfolding, easier because less axioms are considered.

spec RATLIST =
    sorts *Nat, Rat, List*
    ops $0 : Nat$;
           $s : Nat \rightarrow Nat$;
           $\_/\_ : Nat \times Nat \rightarrow Rat$;
           $[\,] : List$;
           $\_::\_ : Rat \times List \rightarrow List$;
    preds *add* $: Nat \times Nat \times Nat$;
             mult $: Nat \times Nat \times Nat$;
             ltn $: Nat \times Nat$;
             eqr $: Rat \times Rat$;
             ltr $: Rat \times Rat$;
             insert $: Rat \times List \times List$;
             isin $: Rat \times List$
    vars x, y, z, u, v, n, m: *Nat*; e: *Rat*; l, l': *List*
    • $add(x, 0, x)$
    • $add(x, s(y), s(z)) \Leftrightarrow add(x, y, z)$
    • $mult(x, 0, 0)$
    • $add(x, u, z) \wedge mult(x, y, u) \Rightarrow mult(x, s(y), z)$
    • $ltn(0, s(x))$
    • $\neg\, ltn(x, 0)$
    • $ltn(s(x), s(y)) \Leftrightarrow ltn(x, y)$
    • $mult(x, s(v), n) \wedge mult(u, s(y), n) \Rightarrow eqr(x/s(y), u/s(v))$
    • $ltn(m, n) \wedge mult(x, s(v), m) \wedge mult(u, s(y), n) \Rightarrow ltr(x/s(y), u/s(v))$
    • $insert(x/s(y), [\,], x/s(y) :: [\,])$
    • $eqr(x/s(y), e) \Rightarrow insert(x/s(y), e :: l, e :: l)$
    • $ltr(x/s(y), e) \Rightarrow insert(x/s(y), e :: l, x/s(y) :: (e :: l))$
    • $ltr(e, x/s(y)) \wedge insert(x/s(y), l, l') \Rightarrow insert(x/s(y), e :: l, e :: l')$
    • $\neg\, isin(x/s(y), [\,])$
    • $isin(x/s(y), e :: l) \Leftrightarrow eqr(x/s(y), e) \vee isin(x/s(y), l)$
end

Axioms are then transformed into normalized sequents, as explained above. For example, the normalization of the right-to-left implication of the axiom $isin(x/s(y), e :: l) \Leftrightarrow eqr(x/s(y), e) \vee isin(x/s(y), l)$ leads to two normalized sequents as follows:

$$\cfrac{\cfrac{eqr(x/s(y),e) \;\vdash\; isin(x/s(y),e::l) \quad isin(x/s(y),l) \;\vdash\; isin(x/s(y),e::l)}{eqr(x/s(y),e) \vee isin(x/s(y),l) \;\vdash\; isin(x/s(y),e::l)} \;\text{Left-}\vee}{\vdash\; eqr(x/s(y),e) \vee isin(x/s(y),l) \Rightarrow isin(x/s(y),e::l)} \;\text{Right-}\Rightarrow$$

1. $\vdash\!\!\!\sim add(x, 0, x)$
2. $add(x, s(y), s(z)) \vdash\!\!\!\sim add(x, y, z)$
3. $add(x, y, z) \vdash\!\!\!\sim add(x, s(y), s(z))$
4. $\vdash\!\!\!\sim mult(x, 0, 0)$
5. $add(x, u, z), mult(x, y, u) \vdash\!\!\!\sim mult(x, s(y), z)$
6. $\vdash\!\!\!\sim ltn(0, s(x))$
7. $ltn(x, 0) \vdash\!\!\!\sim$
8. $ltn(s(x), s(y)) \vdash\!\!\!\sim ltn(x, y)$
9. $ltn(x, y) \vdash\!\!\!\sim ltn(s(x), s(y))$
10. $mult(x, s(v), n), mult(u, s(y), n) \vdash\!\!\!\sim eqr(x/s(y), u/s(v))$
11. $ltn(m, n), mult(x, s(v), m), mult(u, s(y), n) \vdash\!\!\!\sim ltr(x/s(y), u/s(v))$
12. $\vdash\!\!\!\sim insert(x/s(y), [\,], x/s(y) :: [\,])$
13. $eqr(x/s(y), e) \vdash\!\!\!\sim insert(x/s(y), e :: l, e :: l)$
14. $ltr(x/s(y), e) \vdash\!\!\!\sim insert(x/s(y), e :: l, x/s(y) :: e :: l)$
15. $ltr(e, x/s(y)), insert(x/s(y), l, l') \vdash\!\!\!\sim insert(x/s(y), e :: l, e :: l')$
16. $isin(x/s(y), [\,]) \vdash\!\!\!\sim$
17. $isin(x/s(y), e :: l) \vdash\!\!\!\sim eqr(x/s(y), e), isin(x/s(y), l)$
18. $eqr(x/s(y), e) \vdash\!\!\!\sim isin(x/s(y), e :: l)$
19. $isin(x/s(y), l) \vdash\!\!\!\sim isin(x/s(y), e :: l)$

2   A General Framework of Testing from Formal Specifications

The work presented in Section 4 comes within the general framework of testing from formal specifications defined in [1]. Here, we succinctly introduce this framework, then we instantiate it to the formalism we have just defined in Section 1.

The interpretation of test cases submission as a success or failure is related to the notion of program correctness. Following previous works [1, 4, 9, 10, 11], test cases are formulae and programs are Σ-models. Therefore, test cases interpretation is defined by formula satisfaction. When a test case is submitted to a program, it has to yield a verdict (success or failure). Hence, test cases have to be directly interpreted as "true" or "false" by a "computation" of the program. These "executable" formulae are called *observable*.

Let $Sp = (\Sigma, Ax)$ be a specification and $Obs \subseteq For(\Sigma)$ any set of observable formulae. Let P be a program which is denoted by a Σ-model of $Mod(\Sigma)$. Then *test cases* are observable formulae, which are *successful* for P if and only if P validates them (i.e. performs them and interprets them as "true"). A *test set* T is then a set of test cases. T is said to be *successful* for P if and only if $\forall \varphi \in T, P \models \varphi$.

Following an observational approach [14], to be qualified as correct with respect to a specification Sp, a program is required to be observationally equivalent to a model of $Mod(Sp)$, up to the observable formulae of Obs.

Definition 1 (Correctness). *P is correct for Sp via Obs, denoted by Correct$_{Obs}$(P, Sp), if and only if there exists a model $\mathcal{M}$ in Mod(Sp) such that $\mathcal{M} \equiv_{Obs} P$.*

Definition 2 (Exhaustiveness). *Let* $\mathcal{K} \subseteq Mod(\Sigma)$. *A test set* T *is* exhaustive *for* $\mathcal{K}$ *with respect to* Sp *and* Obs *if and only if*

$$\forall P \in \mathcal{K}, P \models T \Longleftrightarrow Correct_{Obs}(P, Sp)$$

The existence of an exhaustive test set means that Sp is testable via Obs since correctness can be asymptotically approached by submitting a (possibly infinite) test set. Hence, an exhaustive test set is appropriate to start the process of selecting a finite test set with a reasonable size. However, depending on the nature of Sp, Obs and $\mathcal{K}$, an exhaustive test set does not necessarily exist. For instance, in [12], we have shown that for positive conditional algebraic specifications, when Obs is restricted to ground equations, $Sp^{\bullet} \cap Obs$ is only exhaustive for algebras satisfying a strong condition, called initiality, which, roughly speaking, means that the program under test behaves like the initial algebra of $Mod(Sp)$ for all ground instances of equations occurring in premises of axioms of Sp. The problem is that showing such a property on a program may be as difficult as proving its correctness, and then restricts its testability.

In Section 3, we will show that in the presence of a specification Sp with quantifier-free axioms, and when the set of observable formulae Obs is the set of all ground first-order formulae, the exhaustiveness of $Sp^{\bullet} \cap Obs$ holds without conditions on programs, that is $\mathcal{K} = Mod(\Sigma)$.

Test sets can be compared with respect to their ability to reject (or to accept, from a dual point of view) programs. Two test sets are then said to be equivalent if and only they accept exactly the same programs.

The challenge of testing then consists in managing (infinite) test sets. In practice, experts apply some selection criteria on a reference test set in order to extract a test set of sufficiently reasonable size to be submitted to the program. The underlying idea is that all test sets satisfying a considered selection criterion reveal the same class of incorrect programs, intuitively those corresponding to the fault model captured by the criterion. For example, the criterion called "uniformity hypothesis" over a test set T postulates that any chosen value is equivalent to another one in T.

A classic way to select test data with a selection criterion C consists in splitting a given starting test set T into a family of test subsets $\{T_i\}_{i \in I_{C(T)}}$ such that $T = \cup_{i \in I_{C(T)}} T_i$ holds. A test set satisfying such a selection criterion simply contains at least one test case for each non-empty subset T_i. Intuitively, all test cases in T_i are supposed equivalent to reveal incorrect programs with respect to the fault model captured by T_i. Hence, the selection criterion C is a coverage criterion according to the way C is splitting the initial test set T into the family $\{T_i\}_{i \in I_{C(T)}}$. This is the method that we will use in this paper to select test data, known under the term of *partition testing*.

For instance, the selection criterion we will define in the sequel of this paper consists in splitting a test set into subsets according to specification axioms. If we come back to the RATLIST specification, the *insert* predicate is specified inductively by four axioms. Testing a formula consists in finding input data, that is, ground substitutions to apply to the formula in order to submit it to the program, bringing into play at least once each of these four axioms. Therefore, the set of test cases associated to $insert(r, L, L')$, where r, L and L' are variables, can be split into four subsets:

1. The set of tests associated to the substitution $L \mapsto [\,]$, coming from the axiom $insert(x/s(y), [\,], x/s(y) :: [\,])$.
2. The set associated to the case where the rational to insert is equal to the first element of the list, that is, associated to the substitution $r \mapsto x/s(y)$, $L \mapsto e :: l$ with $eqr(x/s(y), e)$, coming from the axiom $eqr(x/s(y), e) \Rightarrow insert(x/s(y), e :: l, e :: l)$.
3. The set associated to the case where it is less than the first element, that is, the substitution $r \mapsto x/s(y)$, $L \mapsto e :: l$ with $ltr(x/s(y), e)$, coming from axiom $ltr(x/s(y), e) \Rightarrow insert(x/s(y), e :: l, x/s(y) :: e :: l)$.
4. The set associated to the case where it is greater than it, that is, the substitution $r \mapsto x/s(y)$, $L \mapsto e :: l$ with $ltr(x/s(y), e)$, coming from the axiom $ltr(e, x/s(y)) \wedge insert(x/s(y), l, l') \Rightarrow insert(x/s(y), e :: l, e :: l')$.

The process can be pursued on each above subset.

Definition 3 (Selection criterion). *A selection criterion C is a mapping*[1] $\mathcal{P}(Sp^{\bullet} \cap Obs) \rightarrow \mathcal{P}(\mathcal{P}(Sp^{\bullet} \cap Obs))$. *For a test set T, we denote $|C(T)| = \cup_{i \in I_{C(T)}} T_i$ where $C(T) = \{T_i\}_{i \in I_{C(T)}}$.*
T' satisfies C applied to T, denoted by $T' \sqsubset C(T)$, if and only if:

$$\forall i \in I_{C(T)}, T_i \neq \emptyset \Rightarrow T' \cap T_i \neq \emptyset$$

A selection criterion consists of a mapping that splits test sets into families of test sets. The selection criterion is satisfied as soon as the considered test set contains at least one test case within each (non-empty) set of the resulting family. To be pertinent, a selection criterion should ensure some properties between the starting test set and the resulting family of test sets:

Definition 4 (Properties). *Let C be a selection criterion and T be a test set.*

– *C is said sound for T if and only if $|C(T)| \subseteq T$;*
– *C is said complete for T if and only if $|C(T)| = T$.*

The properties of soundness and completeness are essential for an adequate selection criterion: soundness ensures that test cases will be selected within the starting test set (i.e. no test is added) while completeness ensures that we capture all test cases up to the notion of equivalent test cases (i.e. no test is lost).

3   An Exhaustive Test Set

Here, we show that for every quantifier-free first-order specification $Sp = (\Sigma, Ax)$, $Sp^{\bullet} \cap Obs$ is an exhaustive test set for $Mod(\Sigma)$, when Obs is the set of all ground formulae built over Σ.

---

[1] For a given set X, $\mathcal{P}(X)$ denotes the set of all subsets of X.

Theorem 1. *Let $Sp = (\Sigma, Ax)$ be a specification. Then $Sp^{\bullet} \cap Obs$ is exhaustive for $Mod(\Sigma)$.*

Proof. Let P be a program, *i.e.* $P \in Mod(\Sigma)$, such that $P \models Sp^{\bullet} \cap Obs$. Let us show that $Correct_{Obs}(P, Sp)$.

Note $Th(P) = \{\varphi \in Obs \mid P \models \varphi\}$. Let $\mathcal{H}_{T_{\Sigma}} \in Mod(\Sigma)$ be the Herbrand model of $Th(P)$. By definition, we have that $P \equiv_{Obs} \mathcal{H}_{T_{\Sigma}}$. Let us then show that $\mathcal{H}_{T_{\Sigma}} \in Mod(Sp)$. Let φ be an axiom of Sp. Let $\nu : V \to \mathcal{H}_{T_{\Sigma}}$ be an interpretation. By definition, $\nu(\varphi)$ is a ground formula. By hypothesis, $P \models \nu(\varphi)$ and then $\mathcal{H}_{T_{\Sigma}} \models \nu(\varphi)$. We conclude that $\mathcal{H}_{T_{\Sigma}} \models_{\nu} \varphi$.

Suppose that there exists $\mathcal{M} \in Mod(Sp)$ such that $\mathcal{M} \equiv_{Obs} P$. Let $\varphi \in Sp^{\bullet} \cap Obs$. By hypothesis, $\mathcal{M} \models \varphi$, then $P \models \varphi$ as well. $\square$

4   Selection Criteria Based on Axiom Unfolding

In this section, we study the problem of test case selection for quantifier-free specifications, by adapting a selection criteria based on unfolding of positive conditional formulae in the algebraic specification setting [6].

4.1   Test Sets for Quantifier-Free Formulae

The selection method that we are going to define takes inspiration from classic methods that split the initial test set of any formula considered as a test purpose. Succinctly, for a quantifier-free first-order formula φ, our method consists in

1. splitting the initial test set for φ into many test subsets, called *constrained test sets for φ*, and
2. choosing any input in each non-empty subset.

First, let us define what test set and constrained test set for a quantifier-free formula are.

Definition 5 (Test set). *Let φ be a quantifier-free formula, called test purpose. The* test set for φ, *denoted by T_{φ}, is the set defined as follows:*

$$T_{\varphi} = \{\rho(\varphi) \mid \rho : V \to T_{\Sigma}, \rho(\varphi) \in Sp^{\bullet} \cap Obs\}$$

Note that φ may be any formula, not necessarily in $Sp^{\bullet}$.

Example 1. Here are some test purposes for the signature of specification RATLIST, with examples of associated test cases.

$add(x, 0, x)$. Since $add(x, 0, x)$ is an axiom, all ground instances of this formula are test cases: $add(0, 0, 0)$, $add(6, 0, 6)$, *etc.*

$eqr(u, v)$. This predicate is under-specified, the case where a rational is of the form $x/0$ is not taken into account, so there cannot be tests on this case. Test cases may be: $eqr(1/2, 1/2)$, $eqr(3/6, 4/8)$, *etc.*

$add(m, n, r) \Rightarrow mult(m, 2, r)$. Only cases where $add(m, n, r)$ is not satisfied or
where $m = n$ are semantic consequences of the specification. The interesting test cases are those where $m = n$ such as $add(2, 2, 4) \Rightarrow mult(2, 2, 4)$,
$add(5, 5, 10) \Rightarrow mult(5, 2, 10)$, etc.
$insert(r, l, [\,])$. The formula is never satisfied for any ground instance of r and l,
so there is no possible test case.

Definition 6 (Constrained test set). *Let φ be a quantifier-free formula, C
be a set of quantifier-free formulae called Σ-constraints, and $\sigma : V \to T_\Sigma(V)$ be
a substitution. A test set for φ with respect to C and σ, denoted by $T_{(C,\sigma),\varphi}$, is
the set of ground formulae defined by:*

$$T_{(C,\sigma),\varphi} = \{\rho(\sigma(\varphi)) \mid \rho : V \to T_\Sigma, \rho(\sigma(\varphi)) \in Sp^\bullet \cap Obs, \forall \psi \in C, \rho(\psi) \in Sp^\bullet \cap Obs\}$$

The couple $\langle (C, \sigma), \varphi \rangle$ is called a constrained test purpose.

Note that the test purpose φ of Definition 5 can be seen as the constrained test
purpose $\langle (\{\varphi\}, id), \varphi \rangle$.

Example 2. Let us denote a substitution $\sigma : V \to T_\Sigma(V)$ mapping a set $X = \{x_1, \ldots, x_n\}$ to a set $Y = \{y_1, \ldots, y_n\}$, such that $\sigma(x_i) = y_i$ for all i, $1 \leq i \leq n$,
by $[x_1 \mapsto y_1, \ldots, x_n \mapsto y_n]$.
   Examples of constrained test purposes may be the following:

$$\langle (\emptyset, [x \mapsto s(u)]), add(x, 0, x) \rangle$$

$$\langle (\{ltn(3, x)\}, id), add(x, 0, x) \rangle$$

$$\langle (\{ltn(x, z)\}, [u \mapsto x/s(y), v \mapsto z/s(y)]), ltr(u, v) \rangle$$

$$\langle (\{ltn(m, n), mult(x, s(z), m), mult(w, s(y), n)\}, [u \mapsto x/s(y), v \mapsto w/s(z)]), \\ ltr(u, v) \rangle$$

As another example, to come back to the example of splitting the test set
associated to $insert(r, L, L')$ into four subsets, we can express each of four test
subsets in terms of constrained test purposes as follows:

$$\langle (\emptyset, \sigma_1), insert(r, L, L') \rangle$$
$$\langle (\{eqr(x_0/s(y_0), e_0)\}, \sigma_2), insert(r, L, L') \rangle$$
$$\langle (\{ltr(x_0/s(y_0), e_0)\}, \sigma_3), insert(r, L, L') \rangle$$
$$\langle (\{ltr(e_0, x_0/s(y_0)), insert(x_0/s(y_0), l_0, l'_0)\}, \sigma_4), insert(r, L, L') \rangle$$

where

	r	L	L'
σ_1	$x_0/s(y_0)$	$[\,]$	$x_0/s(y_0) :: [\,]$
σ_2	$x_0/s(y_0)$	$e_0 :: l_0$	$e_0 :: l_0$
σ_3	$x_0/s(y_0)$	$e_0 :: l_0$	$x_0/s(y_0) :: (e_0 :: l_0)$
σ_4	$x_0/s(y_0)$	$e_0 :: l_0$	$e_0 :: l'_0$

Only this kind of constrained test sets, built from a case analysis of the specification axioms, will be of interest. The aim of the unfolding procedure we will
introduce in the next section is to build such test sets.

4.2   Unfolding Procedure

In practice, the initial test purpose is unconstrained. The aim is to replace it with a set of constrained test purposes. This is what the unfolding procedure does, matching the initial formula with the specification axioms, when it is possible.

Therefore, the unfolding procedure inputs are:

- a quantifier-free specification $Sp = (\Sigma, Ax)$ where axioms of Ax have been transformed into normalized sequents;
- a quantifier-free formula φ seen as the initial constrained test purpose $\langle(\emptyset, id), \varphi\rangle$;
- a family Ψ of couples $(\mathcal{C}, \sigma)$ where $\mathcal{C}$ is a set of Σ-constraints in the form of normalized sequents, and σ is a substitution $V \to T_\Sigma(V)$.

The first set Ψ_0 only contains the couple composed of the set of normalized sequents obtained from the quantifier-free formula φ under test and the identity substitution.

The unfolding procedure is expressed by the following two rules:[2]

$$\textbf{Reduce}\frac{\Psi \cup \{(\mathcal{C} \cup \{\Gamma \vdash \Delta\}, \sigma')\}}{\Psi \cup \{(\sigma(\mathcal{C}), \sigma \circ \sigma')\}} \quad \exists \gamma \in \Gamma, \exists \delta \in \Delta \text{ s.t. } \sigma(\gamma) = \sigma(\delta), \sigma \text{ mgu}$$

$$\textbf{Unfold}\frac{\Psi \cup \{(\mathcal{C} \cup \{\psi\}, \sigma')\}}{\Psi \cup \bigcup_{(c,\sigma) \in Tr(\psi)} \{(\sigma(\mathcal{C}) \cup c, \sigma \circ \sigma')\}}$$

where $Tr(\psi)$ for $\psi = \gamma_1, \ldots, \gamma_m \vdash \delta_1, \ldots, \delta_n$ is the set defined by:

$$\left\{ \left(\begin{array}{c} \{(\sigma(\gamma_{p+1}), \ldots, \sigma(\gamma_m), \sigma(\zeta_i) \vdash \sigma(\delta_{q+1}), \ldots, \sigma(\delta_n)\}_{1 \leq i \leq k} \\ \cup \{(\sigma(\gamma_{p+1}), \ldots, \sigma(\gamma_m) \vdash \sigma(\xi_i), \sigma(\delta_{q+1}), \ldots, \sigma(\delta_n)\}_{1 \leq i \leq l} \end{array}, \sigma \right) \middle| \begin{array}{l} \psi_1, \ldots, \psi_p, \xi_1, \ldots, \xi_l \vdash \zeta_1, \ldots, \zeta_k, \varphi_1, \ldots, \varphi_q \in Ax, \\ 1 \leq p \leq m, \forall 1 \leq i \leq p, \sigma(\psi_i) = \sigma(\gamma_i), \\ 1 \leq q \leq n, \forall 1 \leq i \leq q, \sigma(\varphi_i) = \sigma(\delta_i), \\ \sigma \text{ unifier}, k, l \in \mathbb{N} \end{array} \right\}$$

The **Red** rule eliminates tautologies from constraints sets. Intuitively, the **Unfold** rule consists in replacing the formula ψ with a set c of constraints, which are what remains of the axiom after unification. Then testing $\sigma(\psi)$ comes to test the formulae of c. The particular case where no formula has to be cut is taken into account, since k and l may be equal to zero. $Tr(\psi)$ is then a couple $(\emptyset, \sigma)$, and it is the last step of unfolding for this formula.

Each unification with an axiom leads to a couple (c, σ), so the initial formula ψ is replaced with as much sets of formulae as there are axioms to which it can be unified. The definition of $Tr(\psi)$ being based on unification, this set is computable if the specification Sp has a finite set of axioms. Therefore, given an

---

[2] The most general unifier (or mgu) of two terms γ and δ is the most general substitution σ such that $\sigma(\gamma) = \sigma(\delta)$.

atomic formula ψ, we have the selection criterion C_ψ that maps any $T_{(C,\sigma'),\varphi}$ to $(T_{(\sigma(C\setminus\{\psi\})\cup c,\sigma\sigma'),\varphi})_{(c,\sigma)\in Tr(\psi)}$ if $\psi \in C$, and to $T_{C,\varphi}$ otherwise.

We write $\langle \Psi, \varphi \rangle \vdash_U \langle \Psi', \varphi \rangle$ to mean that Ψ' can be derived from Ψ by applying **Reduce** or **Unfold**. An unfolding procedure is then a program, inputs of which are a quantifier-free first-order specification Sp and a quantifier-free formula φ, and uses the above inference rules to generate the sequence

$$\langle \Psi_0, \varphi \rangle \vdash_U \langle \Psi_1, \varphi \rangle \vdash_U \langle \Psi_2, \varphi \rangle \ldots$$

Example 3. We want to test the formula $isin(r, L) \Rightarrow insert(r, L, L')$.

$$\Psi_0 = \{ (\{isin(r, L) \mathrel{|\!\sim} insert(r, L, L')\}, id) \}$$

$$\begin{aligned}
\Psi_1 = \{ &(\emptyset, \sigma_1), \ (16) \\
&(\{eqr(x_0/s(y_0), e_0) \mathrel{|\!\sim} insert(x_0/s(y_0), e_0 :: l_0, l_0'), \\
&\phantom{(\{}isin(x_0/s(y_0), l_0) \mathrel{|\!\sim} insert(x_0/s(y_0), e_0 :: l_0, l_0')\}, \sigma_2), \ (17) \\
&(\{isin(x_0/s(y_0), e_0 :: l_0) \mathrel{|\!\sim} insert(x_0/s(y_0), l_0, l_0')\}, \sigma_3), \ (19) \\
&(\emptyset, \sigma_4), \ (12) \\
&(\{isin(x_0/s(y_0), e_0 :: l_0) \mathrel{|\!\sim} eqr(x_0/s(y_0), e_0)\}, \sigma_5), \ (13) \\
&(\{isin(x_0/s(y_0), e_0 :: l_0) \mathrel{|\!\sim} ltr(x_0/s(y_0), e_0)\}, \sigma_6), \ (14) \\
&\{isin(x_0/s(y_0), e_0 :: l_0) \mathrel{|\!\sim} ltr(e_0, x_0/s(y_0)), \\
&\phantom{\{}isin(x_0/s(y_0), e_0 :: l_0) \mathrel{|\!\sim} insert(x_0/s(y_0), l_0, l_0')\}, \sigma_7) \ (15) \}
\end{aligned}$$

where

	r	L	L'	x	y	e	l	l'
σ_1	$x_0/s(y_0)$	$[]$		x_0	y_0			
σ_2	$x_0/s(y_0)$	$e_0 :: l_0$	l_0'	x_0	y_0	e_0	l_0	
σ_3	$x_0/s(y_0)$	l_0	l_0'	x_0	y_0		l_0	
σ_4	$x_0/s(y_0)$	$[]$	$x_0/s(y_0) :: []$	x_0	y_0			
σ_5	$x_0/s(y_0)$	$e_0 :: l_0$	$e_0 :: l_0$	x_0	y_0	e_0	l_0	
σ_6	$x_0/s(y_0)$	$e_0 :: l_0$	$x_0/s(y_0) :: e_0 :: l_0$	x_0	y_0	e_0	l_0	
σ_7	$x_0/s(y_0)$	$e_0 :: l_0$	$e_0 :: l_0'$	x_0	y_0	e_0	l_0	l_0'

Each couple of Ψ_1 is labelled by the number of the axiom used for the unfolding of the initial formula.

The first couple $(\emptyset, \sigma_1)$ comes from the unification of the initial formula with the axiom $isin(x/s(y), []) \mathrel{|\!\sim}$. Since $isin(r, L) \mathrel{|\!\sim} insert(r, L, L')$ with $r = x/s(y)$ and $L = []$ is a direct consequence of this axiom, no constraint is generated but the substitution.

If L is not the empty list, the initial formula $isin(r, L) \mathrel{|\!\sim} insert(r, L, L')$ is true if and only if $L = L'$. Its unfolding when L is not empty will then lead to two kinds of constraints: those where $L = L'$ that will become test cases since they are consequences of the specification, and those where $L \neq L'$ that will not lead to test cases. For example, the fifth couple $(\{isin(x_0/s(y_0), e_0 :: l_0) \mathrel{|\!\sim} eqr(x_0/s(y_0), e_0)\}, \sigma_5)$ is a potential test case since $isin(x_0/s(y_0), e_0 :: l_0)$ and $eqr(x_0/s(y_0), e_0)$ are true simultaneously for any ground substitution. On the contrary, the sixth couple, whose constraint formula is $isin(x_0/s(y_0), e_0 ::$

l_0) $\hspace{-0.3em}\sim\hspace{-0.8em}\mid\hspace{0.3em}$ $ltr(x_0/s(y_0), e_0)$, will never lead to a test case. Indeed, when $x_0/s(y_0)$ is in the list $e_0 :: l_0$, then it cannot be less than e_0, for any ground substitution.

The unfolding procedure cannot distinguish between these two kinds of constraints, however, before being submitted to the program, a ground substitution ρ is applied to constrained test purposes. Since by definition, $\rho(\psi)$ has to be a consequence of the specification, constraints where $L \neq L'$ will not be submitted as test cases to the program.

A second unfolding of, for example, the formula $isin(x_0/s(y_0), e_0$ :: $l_0)$ $\mid\hspace{-0.8em}\sim$ $eqr(x_0/s(y_0), e_0)$ would lead to the following set:

$$\{\ (\{eqr(x_0/s(y_0), e_0)\ \mid\hspace{-0.8em}\sim\ eqr(x_0/s(y_0), e_0)$$
$$isin(x_0/s(y_0), l_0)\ \mid\hspace{-0.8em}\sim\ eqr(x_0/s(y_0), e_0)\}, \sigma'_1),\ (17)$$
$$(\{isin(x_0/s(y_0), e_1 :: e_0 :: l_0)\ \mid\hspace{-0.8em}\sim\ eqr(x_0/s(y_0), e_0)\}, \sigma'_2),\ (19)$$
$$(\{isin(x_0/s(y_0), u_0/s(v_0) :: l_0)\ \mid\hspace{-0.8em}\sim\ mult(x_0, s(v_0), n_0),$$
$$isin(x_0/s(y_0), u_0/s(v_0) :: l_0)\ \mid\hspace{-0.8em}\sim\ mult(u_0, s(y_0), n_0)\}, \sigma'_3),\ (10)$$
$$(\{isin(x_0/s(y_0), l_0)\ \mid\hspace{-0.8em}\sim\ \}, \sigma'_4)\ (17)\ \}$$

The tautology $eqr(x_0/s(y_0), e_0)$ $\mid\hspace{-0.8em}\sim$ $eqr(x_0/s(y_0), e_0)$ would be naturally deleted with the **Reduce** rule.

Here, our unfolding procedure has been defined in order to cover behaviours of one test purpose, represented by the formula φ. When we are interested in covering more widely the exhaustive set $Sp^\bullet \cap Obs$, a strategy consists in ordering quantifier-free first-order formula with respect to their length, as follows:

$$\Phi_0 = \{\ \mid\hspace{-0.8em}\sim\ p(x_1, \ldots, x_n)\ \mid\ p : s_1 \times \ldots \times s_n \in P, \forall i, 1 \leq i \leq n, x_i \in V_{s_i}\}$$

$$\Phi_{n+1} = \{p(x_1, \ldots, x_n), \Gamma \mid\hspace{-0.8em}\sim \Delta,\quad \Gamma \mid\hspace{-0.8em}\sim \Delta, p(x_1, \ldots, x_n)\ \mid$$
$$\Gamma \mid\hspace{-0.8em}\sim \Delta \in \Phi_n, p : s_1 \times \ldots \times s_n \in P, \forall i, 1 \leq i \leq n, x_i \in V_{s_i}\}$$

Then, to manage the size (often infinite) of $Sp^\bullet \cap Obs$, we start by choosing $k \in \mathbb{N}$, and then we apply for every i, $1 \leq i \leq k$, the above unfolding procedure to each $p(x_1, \ldots, x_n), \Gamma \mid\hspace{-0.8em}\sim \Delta$ and $\Gamma \mid\hspace{-0.8em}\sim \Delta, p(x_1, \ldots, x_n)$ belonging to Φ_i. Of course, this requires that signatures are finite so that each set Φ_i is finite too.

4.3   Soundness and Completeness

Here, we prove the two properties that make the unfolding procedure relevant for selection of appropriate test cases, i.e. that the selection criterion defined by the procedure is sound and complete for the initial test set we defined.

Test sets for quantifier-free formulae are naturally extended to sets of couples Ψ as follows:

$$T_{\Psi, \varphi} = \bigcup_{(\mathcal{C}, \sigma) \in \Psi} T_{(\mathcal{C}, \sigma), \varphi}$$

Theorem 2. *If* $\langle \Psi, \varphi \rangle \vdash_U \langle \Psi', \varphi \rangle$, *then* $T_{\Psi, \varphi} = T_{\Psi', \varphi}$.

The proof may be found in [15].

5   Conclusion

In this paper, we have extended a selection criterion, based on unfolding of positive conditional axioms in the algebraic specification setting, to quantifier-free first-order specifications. Our unfolding procedure consists in dividing an initial test set into subsets and then selecting test cases within each subset. We have then proved that this unfolding is complete. Moreover, we have shown that given a quantifier-free first-order specification Sp, $Sp^\bullet \cap Obs$ is an exhaustive set whatever the system under test is.

Research on this unfolding procedure is mainly continued on two aspects. First, we are specializing our unfolding procedure by handling equality (when it occurs) in a efficient way. Indeed equality often occurs in software specifications. When dealing with first-order logic, the axiomatization of equality leads to uniformly tackle this predicate as the others, without taking advantage of the efficient, natural and concise kind of reasoning which is attached to, namely, replacement of equal by equal. We are then adapting our unfolding procedure by defining it from sequent calculus $LK_=$ or $G_=$ [16]. Finally, our goal is to propose a framework of functional testing with selection criteria including primitive structuration, following [8, 13].

References

1. Le Gall, P., Arnould, A.: Formal specification and test: correctness and oracle. In: Haveraaen, M., Dahl, O.-J., Owe, O. (eds.) Recent Trends in Data Type Specification. LNCS, vol. 1130, pp. 342–358. Springer, Heidelberg (1996)
2. Gaudel, M.: Testing can be formal, too. In: Mosses, P.D., Schwartzbach, M.I., Nielsen, M. (eds.) CAAP 1995, FASE 1995, and TAPSOFT 1995. LNCS, vol. 915, pp. 82–96. Springer, Heidelberg (1995)
3. Tretmans, J.: Test generation with inputs, outputs and repetitive quiescence. Software—Concepts and Tools 17(3), 103–120 (1996)
4. Bernot, G., Gaudel, M.C., Marre, B.: Software testing based on formal specifications: a theory and a tool. Software Engineering Journal 6(6), 387–405 (1991)
5. Marre, B.: Loft: a tool for assisting selection of test data sets from algebraic specifications. In: Mosses, P.D., Schwartzbach, M.I., Nielsen, M. (eds.) CAAP 1995, FASE 1995, and TAPSOFT 1995. LNCS, vol. 915, pp. 799–800. Springer, Heidelberg (1995)
6. Aiguier, M., Arnould, A., Boin, C., Le Gall, P., Marre, B.: Testing from algebraic specifications: Test data set selection by unfolding axioms. In: Grieskamp, W., Weise, C. (eds.) FATES 2005. LNCS, vol. 3997, pp. 203–217. Springer, Heidelberg (2006)
7. Machado, P.: On oracles for interpreting test results against algebraic specifications. In: Haeberer, A.M. (ed.) AMAST 1998. LNCS, vol. 1548, Springer, Heidelberg (1998)
8. Machado, P.: Testing from structured algebraic specifications. In: Rus, T. (ed.) AMAST 2000. LNCS, vol. 1816, pp. 529–544. Springer, Heidelberg (2000)
9. Arnould, A., Le Gall, P.: Test de conformité: une approche algébrique. Technique et Science Informatiques, Test de logiciel 21, 1219–1242 (2002)

10. Arnould, A., Le Gall, P., Marre, B.: Dynamic testing from bounded data type specifications. In: Hlawiczka, A., Simoncini, L., Silva, J.G.S. (eds.) Dependable Computing - EDCC-2. LNCS, vol. 1150, pp. 285–302. Springer, Heidelberg (1996)
11. Bernot, G.: Testing against formal specifications: a theoretical view. In: Abramsky, S. (ed.) TAPSOFT 1991, CCPSD 1991, and ADC-Talks 1991. LNCS, vol. 494, pp. 99–119. Springer, Heidelberg (1991)
12. Aiguier, M., Arnould, A., Le Gall, P.: Exhaustive test sets for algebraic specification correctness. Technical report, IBISC - Université d'Évry Val d'Essonne (2006)
13. Machado, P., Sannella, D.: Unit testing for CASL architectural specifications. In: Diks, K., Rytter, W. (eds.) MFCS 2002. LNCS, vol. 2420, pp. 506–518. Springer, Heidelberg (2002)
14. Hennicker, R., Wirsing, M., Bidoit, M.: Proof systems for structured specifications with observability operators. Theoretical Computer Science 173(2), 393–443 (1997)
15. Aiguier, M., Arnould, A., Le Gall, P., Longuet, D.: Test selection criteria for quantifier-free first-order specifications. Technical Report, -01, IBISC - Université d'Évry Val d'Essonne (2007), Available at http://www.ibisc.fr/ dlonguet/ Publications/RR-AALL07.pdf
16. Gallier, J.H.: Logic for Computer Science: Foundations of Automatic Theorem Proving. Harper & Row, New York (1986)

Formal Testing of Systems Presenting Soft and Hard Deadlines*

Mercedes G. Merayo, Manuel Nez, and Ismael Rodrguez

Dept. Sistemas Informáticos y Computación
Universidad Complutense de Madrid, E-28040 Madrid, Spain
mgmerayo@fdi.ucm.es,mn@sip.ucm.es,isrodrig@sip.ucm.es

Abstract. We present a formal framework to specify and test systems presenting both soft and hard deadlines. While hard deadlines must be always met on time, soft deadlines can be sometimes met in a different time, usually higher, from the specified one. It is this characteristic (to formally define *sometimes*) what produces several reasonable alternatives to define appropriate *implementation relations*, that is, relations to decide wether an implementation is correct with respect to a specification. In addition to introduce these relations, we define a testing framework to test implementations.

1 Introduction

Formal methods refer to techniques based on mathematics for the specification, development, and verification of systems. The use of formal methods is especially relevant in reliable systems where, due to safety and security reasons, it is important to ensure that errors are not included during the development process. Formal methods are particularly effective when used early in the development process, at the requirements and specification levels, but can be used for a complete formal development of a system. In this regard, and considering specification formalism, we may mention the (original) notions of process algebras, Petri nets, and Moore/Mealy machines. Once the roots were well consolidated other considerations were taken into account. The next step was to deal with quantitative information such as the *time* underlying the performance of systems or the *probabilities* resolving the non-deterministic choices that a system may undertake. These characteristics gave raise to new models where time and/or probabilities were included (for example, [1,2,3,4,5,6,7,8] among many others).

The formal representation of systems allows to rigorously analyze their properties. In particular, it allows to establish the *correctness* of the system with

---

* This research was partially supported by the Spanish MEC projects MASTER/TERMAS TIC2003-07848-C02-01 and WEST/FAST TIN2006-15578-C02-01, the Junta de Castilla-La Mancha project PAC06-0008, the Comunidad de Madrid project to fund research groups CAM-910606, and the Marie Curie project MRTN-CT-2003-505121/TAROT.

F. Arbab and M. Sirjani (Eds.): FSEN 2007, LNCS 4767, pp. 160–174, 2007.

respect to a specification or the fulfillment of a specific set of required conditions, to check the semantic *equivalence* of two systems, to analyze the *preference* of a system to another with respect to a given criterion, to predict the possibility of *incorrect behaviors*, to establish the *performance* level of a system, etc. In this line, formal testing techniques allow to test the correctness of a system with respect to a specification. Formal testing originally targeted the functional behavior of systems, such as determining whether the tested system can, on the one hand, perform certain actions and, on the other hand, does not perform some unexpected ones. The application of formal testing techniques to check the correctness of a system requires to identify the *critical* aspects of the system, that is, those aspects that will make the difference between correct and incorrect behaviors. While the relevant aspects of some systems only concern *what* they do, in some other systems it is equally relevant *how* they do what they do. Thus, formal testing techniques are recently also dealing with *non-functional* properties such as the probability of an event to happen or the time that it takes to perform a certain action (for example, [9,10,11,12,13,14,15,16]).

One of the problems when specifying timed systems is that it is not always easy to precisely establish the time bounds associated with the tasks that the system performs. Thus, it is sometimes useful to allow some degree of *indecision* in such specifications. In this line, *stochastic models* (for example, [17,18,19,20,21,22,23]) allow to specify constraints such as *with probability p the task must finish before t time units have passed*. So, the specifier does not need to provide the precise point of time associated with a task, but a probabilistic estimation of the time value(s). However, there are situations where the specifier either does not have such probabilistic information or does not want to provide such information because it might unnecessarily complicate the model. In this case, it seems that the most appropriate way to specify time constraints is to use *time intervals*, that is, the specifier provides a set of possible time values, instead of just one, but without quantifying the probability that each value of the interval has. Moreover, it may happen that while testing the correctness of a system the tester allows some *imprecision* in the temporal behavior of the system. For example, if the specifier cannot precisely define the temporal constraints of a system, the tester can also have problems to determine what is the exact notion of passing a test *on time*. Moreover, it can be admissible that the execution of a task sometimes lasts more than expected: If most of the times the task is performed on time, a couple of delays can be tolerated. This is the idea of a *soft* deadline, in contrast with *hard* deadlines that have to be always met on time. Finally, another reason for the tester to allow imprecisions, it may happen that the artifacts measuring time while testing a system are not as precise as desirable. In this case, an apparent wrong behavior due to bad timing can be in fact correct since it may happen that the *watches* are not working properly.

In this paper we propose a formal framework to specify and test systems where time considerations can fall in some of the cases commented in the previous paragraph. Time will be introduced in specifications by extending classical finite state machines with time intervals associated to the performance of actions.

Intuitively, transitions in finite state machines indicate that if the machine is in a state s and receives and input i then it will produce and output o and it will change its state to s'. An appropriate notation for such a transition could be $s \xrightarrow{i/o} s'$. If we consider our timed extension of finite state machines, a transition such as $s \xrightarrow{i/o} [t_1,t_2]s'$ means that if the machine is in state s and receives the input i, it will perform the output o and reach the state s', and it will take a time greater than or equal to t_1 but smaller than or equal to t_2.

Testing, as well as the definition of implementation relations, will depend on measuring time values and accepting the performance of the system if the time behavior is correct *up to* an admissible error. The possible definition of *admissible* will give raise to several alternative implementation relations and several notions of passing a test. However, there is still a last issue that must be taken into account when dealing with systems where time requirements are given by means of intervals. Since we assume a black-box testing framework, we cannot check that the intervals governing the behavior of the implementation are correctly related with the ones corresponding to the implementation. In fact, the execution of a test will return the time that it took to be performed, not the associated time interval. As a consequence, since we assume that time intervals are non-negative real numbers, we would need an infinite number of observations from a transition of the implementation (with an unknown time interval) to assure that its time interval is correct with the respect to the one of the specification (which it is accessible).

Even though there are several papers devoted to formal testing of timed systems [10,9,11,12,15,16], we are aware of only one work where the topic of *non-strict* deadlines is considered in a testing framework. In [24], a probabilistic formalism is used to approximate the idea of soft deadline. However, their approach is not very related to ours since, on the one hand, they are based on [25,26], and, on the other hand, they use a probabilistic approach, based on [27], to deal with soft deadlines. Testing relations to compare processes are based on the responses of the processes to *all* the tests, while we apply tests, derived from specifications, to implementations to determine whether the implementation is *somehow* correct with respect to the specification. As we mentioned before, stochastic models allow to partially simulate soft deadlines. In this line, there are two proposals to test stochastic systems [28,29]. Since they are also inspired by [25,26], these contributions are not related to the one presented in this paper.

The rest of the paper is organized as follows. In Section 2 we introduce our notion of timed finite state machine and give some auxiliary notation. In Section 3 we give our timed conformance relations. In Section 4 we show how tests are defined and applied to implementations. Finally, in Section 5 we give our conclusions and some lines for future work.

2   Extending Finite State Machines with Time Intervals

In this section we introduce our notion of timed finite state machine, that we call IFSM, and some concepts that will be used along the paper. The main difference with respect to usual FSMs consists in the addition of *time* to indicate the lapse between offering an input and receiving an output. First we introduce notation related to time intervals, sets, and multisets.

Definition 1. We say that $d = [a_1, a_2]$ is a *time interval* if $a_1 \in \mathbb{R}_+$, $a_2 \in \mathbb{R}_+ \cup \{\infty\}$, and $a_1 \leq a_2$. From now on we assume that for all $r \in \mathbb{R}_+$ we have $r < \infty$, $r + \infty = \infty$, and $\frac{r}{\infty} = 0$. We consider that $\mathcal{I}_{\mathbb{R}_+}$ denotes the set of time intervals. We write $\pi_i(d)$, for $i \in \{1, 2\}$, to denote the value a_i.

Given two time intervals $d_1 = [a_{11}, a_{12}]$ and $d_2 = [a_{21}, a_{22}]$, $d_1 + d_2$ denotes the time interval $[a_{11} + a_{21}, a_{12} + a_{22}]$. Addition of time intervals can be generalized to n summands in the expected way. Given n time intervals $d_1 = [a_{11}, a_{12}], \ldots, d_n = [a_{n1}, a_{n2}]$, we have that $\sum d_i$ denotes the time interval $[\sum a_{i1}, \sum a_{i2}]$.

Given a set S, we consider that $|S|$ denotes the cardinal of S, $\mathcal{P}(S)$ denotes the powerset of S, and $\wp(S)$ denotes the powermultiset of S, that is, the set of multisets conformed from elements belonging to S. We will use the symbols $\{$ and $\}$ to denote multisets. Given a multiset $\mathcal{M}$, we write $r \in \mathcal{M}$ if r appears in $\mathcal{M}$ (that is, r has multiplicity greater than 0). We write $\|\mathcal{M}\|$ to denote the cardinal of $\mathcal{M}$ including multiplicity of its elements. For example, $\|\{1, 2, 3, 1, 2\}\| = 5$.   □

A temporal requirement such as $[t_1, t_2]$ indicates that the associated task should take at least t_1 time units and at most t_2 units to be performed. Intervals like $[0, t_2]$, $[t_1, \infty]$, or $[0, \infty]$ denote the absence of a temporal lower/upper bound and the absence of any bound, respectively. Let us note that in the case of $[t_1, \infty]$ and $[0, \infty]$ we are abusing the notation since these intervals represent, in fact, the intervals $[t_1, \infty)$ and $[0, \infty)$, respectively.

Definition 2. An *Interval Finite State Machine*, in the following IFSM, is a tuple $M = (S, I, O, Tr, s_{in})$ where S is a finite set of states, I is the set of input actions, O is the set of output actions, Tr is the set of transitions, and s_{in} is the initial state.

A transition belonging to Tr is a tuple (s, s', i, o, d) where $s, s' \in S$ are the initial and final states of the transition, $i \in I$ and $o \in O$ are the input and output actions, and $d \in \mathcal{I}_{\mathbb{R}_+}$ is the time interval associated with the transition.

We say that the IFSM M is *input-enabled* if for all state $s \in S$ and input $i \in I$, there exist s', o, and d such that $(s, s', i, o, d) \in Tr$. We say that the IFSM M is *observable* if there do not exist two different transitions (s, s_1, i, o, d_1) and (s, s_2, i, o, d_2).   □

Intuitively, a transition (s, s', i, o, d) indicates that if the machine is in state s and receives the input i then, after a time belonging to the interval d has passed, the machine emits the output o and moves to s'. In Figure 1 we give a graphical example of an IFSM.

Next, we introduce the notion of *trace*. As usual, a trace is a sequence of input/output pairs. In addition, we have to record the possible time values, that is a time interval, where the trace can be performed. An *evolution* is a trace starting at the initial state of the machine.

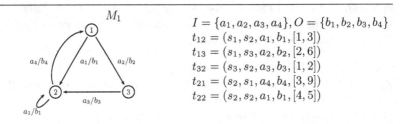

$$I = \{a_1, a_2, a_3, a_4\}, O = \{b_1, b_2, b_3, b_4\}$$
$$t_{12} = (s_1, s_2, a_1, b_1, [1, 3])$$
$$t_{13} = (s_1, s_3, a_2, b_2, [2, 6])$$
$$t_{32} = (s_3, s_2, a_3, b_3, [1, 2])$$
$$t_{21} = (s_2, s_1, a_4, b_4, [3, 9])$$
$$t_{22} = (s_2, s_2, a_1, b_1, [4, 5])$$

Fig. 1. Example of IFSM

Definition 3. Let $M = (S, I, O, Tr, s_{in})$ be an IFSM. A *timed trace*, or simply *trace*, of M is a tuple $(s, s', (i_1/o_1, \ldots, i_r/o_r), d)$ if we have that there exist transitions $(s, s_1, i_1, o_1, d_1), \ldots, (s_{r-1}, s', i_r, o_r, d_r) \in Tr$, such that $d = \sum d_i$. We say that $(i_1/o_1, \ldots, i_r/o_r)$ is a *non-timed evolution*, or simply *evolution*, of M if we have that $(s_{in}, s', (i_1/o_1, \ldots, i_r/o_r), d)$ is a trace of M for some $d \in \mathcal{I}_{\mathbb{R}_+}$ and $s' \in S$. We denote by $\text{NTEvol}(M)$ the set of non-timed evolutions of M.

We say that the pair $((i_1/o_1, \ldots, i_r/o_r), d)$ is a *timed evolution* of M if we have that $(s_{in}, s', (i_1/o_1, \ldots, i_r/o_r), d)$ is a trace of M. We denote by $\text{TEvol}(M)$ the set of timed evolutions of M. $\square$

Let us consider again the IFSM depicted in Figure 1 and its transitions t_{13}, t_{32}, and t_{21}. We can build the trace $(s_1, s_1, (a_2/b_2, a_3/b_3, a_4/b_4), [6, 17])$ based on these transitions. This trace represents that from state 1 the machine can accept the sequence of inputs (a_2, a_3, a_4) and it will emit the sequence of outputs (b_2, b_3, b_4) after a time belonging to the interval $[6, 17]$ has passed.

3   Implementation Relations

In this section we introduce our implementation relations. Following the classical pattern, we consider that an implementation *conforms* to a specification if for all possible sequence of inputs that the specification can perform, the outputs emitted by the implementation are a subset of those for the specification. Intuitively, this means that the implementation cannot *invent* a behavior (that is, an output) for those traces that the specification can perform. This pattern is borrowed from ioco [30] and was introduced in the context of finite state machines in [31].

A specification is an IFSM. Regarding implementations, we consider that they are also given by means of IFSMs. Besides, we assume that input actions are always enabled in any state of the implementation, that is, implementations are input-enabled according to Definition 2. This is a usual condition to assure that the implementation will react (somehow) to any input appearing in the specification. In order to simplify the presentation, we will consider that both specifications and implementations are given by observable IFSMs (see Definition 2). Let us note that even restricting to this kind of machines we may still

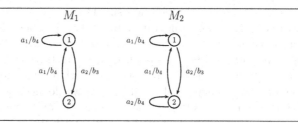

Fig. 2. Examples of non-timely conformance

have two transitions (s, s_1, i, o_1, d_1) and (s, s_2, i, o_2, d_2), as far as $o_1 \neq o_2$. Thus, we allow some degree of non-determinism.

Definition 4. Let S and I be two IFSMs. We say that I *non-timely conforms* to S, denoted by $I \operatorname{conf}_{nt} S$, if for all $e = (i_1/o_1, \ldots, i_{r-1}/o_{r-1}, i_r/o_r) \in \text{NTEvol}(S)$, with $r \geq 1$, we have that

$$e' = (i_1/o_1, \ldots, i_{r-1}/o_{r-1}, i_r/o'_r) \in \text{NTEvol}(I) \Longrightarrow e' \in \text{NTEvol}(S)$$

$\square$

In the previous definition, let us note that if the specification would have also the property of input-enabled then we may remove the condition "for all $e = (i_1/o_1, \ldots, i_{r-1}/o_{r-1}, i_r/o_r) \in \text{NTEvol}(S)$, with $r \geq 1$", so that we simply have to check trace inclusion.

Example 1. Let us consider the systems M_1 and M_2 depicted in Figure 2 where time information has been omitted. We have $M_2 \operatorname{conf}_{nt} M_1$. Let us note that the non-timed evolutions of M_2 having as prefix the sequence $(a_2/b_3, a_2/b_4)$ are not checked because M_1 (playing the role of specification) cannot perform those evolutions.

Let us now consider that M_1 is extended with the transition $(2, 2, a_2, \text{null}, d)$ so that M_1 is input-enabled. Then, M_1 does not conform to M_2. For example, M_2 may perform the non-timed evolution $e = (a_2/b_3, a_2/b_4)$, M_1 has the non-timed evolution $e' = (a_2/b_3, a_2/\text{null})$, but e' does not belong to the set of non-timed evolutions of M_2. Note that e and e' share the common prefix $a_2/b_3, a_2$. $\square$

Next we introduce our first timed implementation relation. In addition to the non-timed conformance of the implementation, we require a time condition to hold: The time intervals of the implementation correspond to those of the specification.

Definition 5. Let I and S be IFSMs. We say that I *conforms in time* to S, denoted by $I \operatorname{conf}_{int} S$, if $I \operatorname{conf}_{nt} S$ and for all $e \in \text{NTEvol}(I) \cap \text{NTEvol}(S)$ we have that for all time interval $d \in \mathcal{I}_{\mathbb{R}_+}$

$$(e, d) \in \text{TEvol}(S) \Longrightarrow (e, d) \in \text{TEvol}(S)$$

$\square$

Despite its neat definition, this relation suffers from practical problems due to our assumption that the implementation under test is a black box. Even though this is a very reasonable notion of conformance, the fact that we assume a black-box testing framework disallows us to check whether the corresponding intervals coincide indeed. In fact, since we are considering that time intervals are defined over the set of non-negative real numbers, we would need an infinite number of observations from a transition of the implementation (with an unknown time interval) to assure that its time interval coincides with the one from the specification (which it is accessible). Thus, we have to give more *realistic* implementation relations that are less accurate but are *checkable*. We only need to suppose that we can actually record the time that the implementation needs to perform a given sequence. In order to that, we introduce the concept of *timed execution*. They are simply input/output sequences together with the time that it took to perform the sequence. In a certain sense, timed executions can be seen as *instances* of the timed evolutions that the implementation can perform. Regarding the definition of observed time values, we just associate with each evolution the corresponding time values.

Definition 6. Let I be an IFSM. We say that $((i_1/o_1, \ldots, i_n/o_n), t)$ is an *observed timed execution* of I, or simply *timed execution*, if the observation of I shows that the sequence $(i_1/o_1, \ldots, i_n/o_n)$ is performed in time t.

Let $H = \{(e'_1, t_1), \ldots, (e'_n, t_n)\}$ be a multiset of observed timed executions and $\Phi = \{e \mid \exists t : (e, t) \in H\}$ be a set of input/output sequences. We say that $\texttt{Obs\_Time}_H : \Phi \longrightarrow \wp(\mathbb{R}^+)$ is the *multiset of observed time values* of H for Φ if for all $e \in \Phi$ we have $\texttt{Obs\_Time}_H(e) = \{t \mid (e, t) \in H\}$. □

Next, we introduce several conformance relations where we check that the observed time values fulfill, in each case, certain conditions with respect to the appropriate time intervals. The purpose of this paper is to introduce implementation relations where the time behavior of the implementation does not exactly correspond to what we expect, that is, it partially deviates from the behavior defined in the specification. In this case, we have to take into account this possible divergence. Intuitively, we will determine whether the amount of *incorrect* time values is relevant to ensure the possible conformance of the implementation to the specification. Moreover, we measure the degree of the deviation of the observed time values, with respect to the interval. So, by considering that there cannot be any error we test a hard deadline; soft deadlines will allow a certain error, as long as it is kept under a certain bound. First, we introduce some notation to relate a set of observed time values and a time interval.

Definition 7. Let $d = [a_1, a_2] \in \mathcal{I}_{\mathbb{R}_+}$ be a time interval, $\mathcal{R}$ be a non-empty multiset of non-negative real numbers, and $0 \leq \alpha \leq 1$.

- We write $\mathcal{R} \subseteq_\alpha d$ if we have

$$\frac{\|\{r \mid r \in \mathcal{R} \wedge (r < a_1 \vee r > a_2)\}\|}{\|\mathcal{R}\|} \leq 1 - \alpha$$

- We write $\mathcal{R} \preceq_\alpha d$ if we have

$$\frac{\|\{r \mid r \in \mathcal{R} \wedge r < a_1\}\|}{\|\mathcal{R}\|} \leq 1 - \alpha \text{ and } \|\{r \mid r \in \mathcal{R} \wedge r > a_2\}\| = 0$$

- We write $\mathcal{R} \ll_\alpha d$ if we have

$$\frac{\|\{r \mid r \in \mathcal{R} \wedge a_1 \leq r \leq a_2\}\|}{\|\mathcal{R}\|} \leq 1 - \alpha \text{ and } \|\{r \mid r \in \mathcal{R} \wedge r > a_2\}\| = 0$$

- We define three notions of *distance* of an observed time value $r \in \mathbb{R}^+$ to an interval $d = [a_1, a_2] \in \mathcal{I}_{\mathbb{R}_+}$, and their generalization to sets of values as

$$\mathtt{dist}(r, d) = \begin{cases} 0 & \text{if } r \in d \\ r - a_2 & \text{if } r > a_2 \\ a_1 - r & \text{if } r < a_1 \end{cases} \quad \mathtt{dist}(C, d) = \sum_{r \in C} \mathtt{dist}(r, d)^2$$

$$\mathtt{dist\_up}(r, d) = \begin{cases} 0 & \text{if } r \leq a_2 \\ r - a_2 & \text{if } r > a_2 \end{cases} \quad \mathtt{dist\_up}(C, d) = \sum_{r \in C} \mathtt{dist\_up}(r, d)^2$$

$$\mathtt{dist\_low}(r, d) = \begin{cases} 0 & \text{if } r < a_1 \\ r - a_1 & \text{if } r \geq a_1 \end{cases} \quad \mathtt{dist\_low}(C, d) = \sum_{r \in C} \mathtt{dist\_low}(r, d)^2$$

$\square$

Let us remark that bigger values of α denote smaller *tolerance* to have unexpected values. The first relation, $\subseteq_\alpha$, denotes that the number of values outside the considered interval is not big. There is no distinction between values being smaller/greater than the lower/upper bound of the interval. The second relation, $\preceq_\alpha$, can be used to indicate that we do not allow values greater than the upper bound and that the number of values smaller than the lower bound is acceptable. Finally, $\ll_\alpha$ is useful in situations where most of the values have to be smaller than the lower bound of the interval, while values greater than the upper bound are again not allowed. This last relation will be used to check that the system is fast. The previous relations count the number of errors but do not quantify how big the errors are. Regarding distance functions, they measure the error degree of wrong values. The first one, $\mathtt{dist}$, considers both time values greater and smaller than the bounds of the interval. The $\mathtt{dist\_up}$ function considers as wrong only values greater than the upper bound of the interval. Finally, we will use the $\mathtt{dist\_low}$ function for measuring the values that are not fast enough, that is, bigger than the lower bound of the interval. By combining inclusion relations and distance functions, we can evaluate the conformance of the implementation with respect to the specification in different ways.

Definition 8. Let I and S be two IFSMs, H be a multiset of timed executions of I, $\Phi = \{e \mid \exists t : (e, t) \in H\} \cap \mathtt{NTEvol}(S)$, $0 \leq \alpha \leq 1$, and $\beta \in \mathbb{R}^+$. We define the following implementation relations:

- I (H, α)-*timely conforms* to S, denoted by $I \operatorname{conf}_{int}^{(H,\alpha)} S$, if $I \operatorname{conf}_{nt} S$ and for all $e \in \Phi$ we have that for all time interval $d \in \mathcal{I}_{\mathbb{R}_+}$

$$(e, d) \in \operatorname{TEvol}(S) \Longrightarrow \operatorname{Obs\_Time}_H(e) \subseteq_\alpha d$$

- I (H, α)-*preferable timely conforms* to S, denoted by $I \operatorname{conf}_{intp}^{(H,\alpha)} S$, if $I \operatorname{conf}_{nt} S$ and for all $e \in \Phi$ we have that for all time interval $d \in \mathcal{I}_{\mathbb{R}_+}$

$$(e, d) \in \operatorname{TEvol}(S) \Longrightarrow \operatorname{Obs\_Time}_H(e) \preceq_\alpha d$$

- I (H, α)-*fast timely conforms* to S, denoted by $I \operatorname{conf}_{intf}^{(H,\alpha)} S$, if $I \operatorname{conf}_{nt} S$ and for all $e \in \Phi$ we have that for all time interval $d \in \mathcal{I}_{\mathbb{R}_+}$

$$(e, d) \in \operatorname{TEvol}(S) \Longrightarrow \operatorname{Obs\_Time}_H(e) \ll_\alpha d$$

- I (H, β)-*global timely conforms* to S, denoted by $I \operatorname{conf}_{intgb}^{(H,\beta)} S$, if $I \operatorname{conf}_{nt} S$ and for all $e \in \Phi$ we have that for all time interval $d \in \mathcal{I}_{\mathbb{R}_+}$

$$(e, d) \in \operatorname{TEvol}(S) \Longrightarrow \operatorname{dist}(\operatorname{Obs\_Time}_H(e), d) \leq \beta$$

- I (H, β)-*up-timely conforms* to S, denoted by $I \operatorname{conf}_{intup}^{(H,\beta)} S$, if $I \operatorname{conf}_{nt} S$ and for all $e \in \Phi$ we have that for all time interval $d \in \mathcal{I}_{\mathbb{R}_+}$

$$(e, d) \in \operatorname{TEvol}(S) \Longrightarrow \operatorname{dist\_up}(\operatorname{Obs\_Time}_H(e), d) \leq \beta$$

- I (H, β)-*low-timely conforms* to S, denoted by $I \operatorname{conf}_{intlw}^{(H,\beta)} S$, if $I \operatorname{conf}_{nt} S$ and for all $e \in \Phi$ we have that for all time interval $d \in \mathcal{I}_{\mathbb{R}_+}$

$$(e, d) \in \operatorname{TEvol}(S) \Longrightarrow \operatorname{dist\_low}(\operatorname{Obs\_Time}_H(e), d) \leq \beta$$

- I (H, α, β)-*timely conforms* to S, denoted by $I \operatorname{conf}_{int}^{(H,\alpha,\beta)} S$, if $I \operatorname{conf}_{nt} S$ and for all $e \in \Phi$ we have that for all time interval $d \in \mathcal{I}_{\mathbb{R}_+}$

$$(e, d) \in \operatorname{TEvol}(S) \Longrightarrow \left(\operatorname{Obs\_Time}_H(e) \subseteq_\alpha d \ \wedge \ \operatorname{dist}(\operatorname{Obs\_Time}_H(e), d) \leq \beta \right)$$

- I (H, α, β)-*preferable timely conforms* to S, denoted by $I \operatorname{conf}_{intp}^{(H,\alpha,\beta)} S$, if $I \operatorname{conf}_{nt} S$ and for all $e \in \Phi$ we have that for all time interval $d \in \mathcal{I}_{\mathbb{R}_+}$

$$(e, d) \in \operatorname{TEvol}(S) \Longrightarrow \left(\begin{array}{c} \operatorname{Obs\_Time}_H(e) \preceq_\alpha d \\ \wedge \\ \operatorname{dist\_low}(\operatorname{Obs\_Time}_H(e), d) \leq \beta \end{array} \right)$$

- I (H, α, β)-*fast timely conforms* to S, denoted by $I \operatorname{conf}_{intf}^{(H,\alpha,\beta)} S$, if $I \operatorname{conf}_{nt} S$ and for all $e \in \Phi$ we have that for all time interval $d \in \mathcal{I}_{\mathbb{R}_+}$

$$(e, d) \in \operatorname{TEvol}(S) \Longrightarrow \left(\begin{array}{c} \operatorname{Obs\_Time}_H(e) \ll_\alpha d \\ \wedge \\ \operatorname{dist\_low}(\operatorname{Obs\_Time}_H(e), d) \leq \beta \end{array} \right) \qquad \square$$

Intuitively, the new relations establish that the implementation must conform to the specification in the usual way (that is, I conf$_{nt}$ S). In addition, the observed execution time values corresponding to an evolution must *mostly* belong to the time interval indicated by the specification for that evolution (*timely conforms*), or be less than or equal to the lower/upper bound (*fast timely conforms/preferable timely conforms*) respectively. The relations *global timely, up-timely, and low-timely* require that the errors presented by the observed execution time values do not exceed a established threshold. Finally, in the last three relations, we consider both requests simultaneously, that is, the relations demand conditions both over the number of observed time values out of the interval and over the allowed deviation.

Let us remark that to have the previously defined relations parameterized by the set H is somehow similar to consider the, widely used, *fairness assumption* in formal testing: If we test a system enough, we can be sure that we go through all the possible paths of the tested machine. In the case of the fairness assumption, we would have something like $H = \texttt{TEvol}(I)$ while in our setting we have that an implementation is correct up to the submultiset of $\texttt{TEvol}(I)$ that we consider.

4   Definition and Application of Tests

A test represents a sequence of inputs applied to the implementation. After applying each input, we check whether the received output is expected or not. In the latter case, a fail signal is produced. In the former case, either a pass signal is emitted (indicating successful termination) or the testing process continues by applying another input. If we are testing an implementation with input and output sets I and O, respectively, tests are deterministic acyclic I/O labelled transition systems (i.e. trees) with a strict alternation between an input action and the set of output actions. After an output action we may find either a leaf (indicating either failure or successful termination) or another input action. Leaves are labelled either by *pass* or by *fail*. In the first case we add a *time stamp*. The time stamp will be a time interval. The idea is that we will record the time that the implementation takes to arrive to that point and compare it with the time stamp.

Definition 9. A *test* is a tuple $T = (S, I, O, Tr, s_0, S_I, S_O, S_F, S_P, C_T)$ where S is the set of states, I and O are disjoint sets of input and output actions, respectively, $Tr \subseteq S \times (I \cup O) \times S$ is the transition relation, $s_0 \in S$ is the initial state, and the sets $S_I, S_O, S_F, S_P \subseteq S$ are a partition of S. The transition relation and the sets of states fulfill the following conditions:

- S_I is the set of *input* states. We have that $s_0 \in S_I$. For all input state $s \in S_I$ there exists a unique outgoing transition $(s, a, s') \in Tr$. For this transition we have that $a \in I$ and $s' \in S_O$.
- S_O is the set of *output* states. For all output state $s \in S_O$ we have that for all $o \in O$ there exists a unique state s' such that $(s, o, s') \in Tr$. In this case, $s' \notin S_O$. Moreover, there do not exist $i \in I$ and $s' \in S$ such that $(s, i, s') \in Tr$.

- S_F and S_P are the sets of *fail* and *pass* states, respectively. We say that these states are *terminal*. That is, for all state $s \in S_F \cup S_P$ we have that there do not exist $a \in I \cup O$ and $s' \in S$ such that $(s, a, s') \in Tr$.

Finally, $C_T : S_P \longrightarrow \mathcal{I}_{\mathbb{R}_+}$ is a function associating time stamps, that is, a time intervals, with passing states.

Let $e = i_1/o_1, \ldots, i_r/o_r$. We write $T \overset{e}{\Longrightarrow} s$ if $s \in S_F \cup S_P$ and there exist states $s_{12}, s_{21}, s_{22}, \ldots s_{r1}, s_{r2} \in S$ such that $\{(s_0, i_1, s_{12}), (s_{r2}, o_r, s)\} \subseteq Tr$, for all $2 \leq j \leq r$ we have $(s_{j1}, i_j, s_{j2}) \in Tr$, and for all $1 \leq j \leq r-1$ we have $(s_{j2}, o_j, s_{(j+1)1}) \in Tr$.

We say that a test case T is *valid* if the graph induced by T is a tree with root at the initial state s_0. We say that a set of tests $\mathcal{T} = \{T_1, \ldots, T_n\}$ is a *test suite*.   □

From now on we will assume that when we talk about tests we refer only to valid tests. Next we define the application of a test to an implementation. We will say that the test suite $\mathcal{T}$ is *passed* if, for all test, the terminal states reached by the composition of implementation and test belong to the set of *passing* states. Let us remark that since we are assuming that implementations are input-enabled, the testing process will conclude only when the test reaches either a fail or a success state.

Definition 10. Let I be an implementation under test and T be a test. We denote the application of the test T to the implementation I by $I \parallel T$.

Let I be a IFSM, T be a test, and s be a state of T. We write $I \parallel T \overset{e}{\Longrightarrow} s$ if $T \overset{e}{\Longrightarrow} s$ and $e \in \texttt{NTEvol}(I)$.

We say that I *passes* the test suite $\mathcal{T}$, denoted by $\texttt{pass}(I, \mathcal{T})$, if for all test $T = (S, I, O, Tr, s, S_I, S_O, S_F, S_P, C_T) \in \mathcal{T}$ and $e \in \texttt{NTEvol}(I)$ there do not exist $s \in S_F$ such that $I \parallel T \overset{e}{\Longrightarrow} s$.   □

The previous definition of passing tests did not take into account the time values that will be collected during the application of tests. We apply time conditions to the set of *observed timed executions*. In fact, we need a set of test executions associated to each evolution in order to evaluate if they match, in a certain sense, the time interval associated to the corresponding state of the test. In order to increase the reliability degree, we will not take the classical approach where passing a test suite is defined according only to the results for each test. In our approach, we will put together all the observations, for each test, so that we have more samples for each evolution. In particular, some observations will be used several times. In other words, an observation from a given test may be used to check the validity of another test sharing the same observed sequence.

Definition 11. Let I be an IFSM, T be a test, and s be a state of T. We write $I \parallel T \overset{e}{\Longrightarrow}_t s$ if $T \overset{e}{\Longrightarrow} s$ and (e, t) is an observed timed execution of I. In this case we say that (e, t) is a *test execution* of I and T. Let I be an IFSM and $\mathcal{T} = \{T_1, \ldots, T_n\}$ be a test suite. Let $H_1, \ldots, H_n$ be sets of test executions of I and $T_1, \ldots, T_n$, respectively. Let $H = \bigcup_{i=1}^n H_i$, $\Phi = \{e \mid \exists t : (e, t) \in H\}$, $\beta \in \mathbb{R}^+$, and $0 \leq \alpha \leq 1$. We say that

- I (H, α)-*timely passes* the test suite $\mathcal{T}$ if $\mathbf{pass}(I, \mathcal{T})$ and for all $e \in \Phi$ and all $T \in \mathcal{T}$ such that $I \parallel T \stackrel{e}{\Longrightarrow} s$, we have that

$$\mathtt{Obs\_Time}_H(e) \subseteq_\alpha C_T(s)$$

- I (H, α)-*preferable passes* the test suite $\mathcal{T}$ if $\mathbf{pass}(I, \mathcal{T})$ and for all $e \in \Phi$ and all $T \in \mathcal{T}$ such that $I \parallel T \stackrel{e}{\Longrightarrow} s$, we have that

$$\mathtt{Obs\_Time}_H(e) \preceq_\alpha C_T(s)$$

- I (H, α)-*fast passes* the test suite $\mathcal{T}$ if $\mathbf{pass}(I, \mathcal{T})$ and for all $e \in \Phi$ and all $T \in \mathcal{T}$ such that $I \parallel T \stackrel{e}{\Longrightarrow} s$, we have that

$$\mathtt{Obs\_Time}_H(e) \ll_\alpha C_T(s)$$

- I (H, β)-*global timely passes* the test suite $\mathcal{T}$ if $\mathbf{pass}(I, \mathcal{T})$ and for all $e \in \Phi$ and all $T \in \mathcal{T}$ such that $I \parallel T \stackrel{e}{\Longrightarrow} s$, we have that

$$\mathtt{dist}(\mathtt{Obs\_Time}_H(e), C_T(s)) \le \beta$$

- I (H, β)-*up-timely passes* the test suite $\mathcal{T}$ if $\mathbf{pass}(I, \mathcal{T})$ and for all $e \in \Phi$ and all $T \in \mathcal{T}$ such that $I \parallel T \stackrel{e}{\Longrightarrow} s$, we have that

$$\mathtt{dist\_up}(\mathtt{Obs\_Time}_H(e), C_T(s)) \le \beta$$

- I (H, β)-*low-timely passes* the test suite $\mathcal{T}$ if $\mathbf{pass}(I, \mathcal{T})$ and for all $e \in \Phi$ and all $T \in \mathcal{T}$ such that $I \parallel T \stackrel{e}{\Longrightarrow} s$, we have that

$$\mathtt{dist\_low}(\mathtt{Obs\_Time}_H(e), C_T(s)) \le \beta$$

- I (H, α, β)-*timely passes* the test suite $\mathcal{T}$ if $\mathbf{pass}(I, \mathcal{T})$ and for all $e \in \Phi$ and all $T \in \mathcal{T}$ such that $I \parallel T \stackrel{e}{\Longrightarrow} s$, we have that

$$\mathtt{Obs\_Time}_H(e) \subseteq_\alpha C_T(s) \ \wedge \ \mathtt{dist}(\mathtt{Obs\_Time}_H(e), C_T(s)) \le \beta$$

- I (H, α, β)-*preferable passes* the test suite $\mathcal{T}$ if $\mathbf{pass}(I, \mathcal{T})$ and for all $e \in \Phi$ and all $T \in \mathcal{T}$ such that $I \parallel T \stackrel{e}{\Longrightarrow} s$, we have that

$$\mathtt{Obs\_Time}_H(e) \preceq_\alpha C_T(s) \ \wedge \ \mathtt{dist\_low}(\mathtt{Obs\_Time}_H(e), C_T(s)) \le \beta$$

- I (H, α, β)-*fast passes* the test suite $\mathcal{T}$ if $\mathbf{pass}(I, \mathcal{T})$ and for all $e \in \Phi$ and all $T \in \mathcal{T}$ such that $I \parallel T \stackrel{e}{\Longrightarrow} s$, we have that

$$\mathtt{Obs\_Time}_H(e) \ll_\alpha C_T(s) \ \wedge \ \mathtt{dist\_low}(\mathtt{Obs\_Time}_H(e), C_T(s)) \le \beta$$

$\square$

Let us remark that an observed timed execution does not return the time interval associated with performing the evolution (that is, the addition of all the intervals corresponding to each transition of the implementation) but the time that it took to perform the evolution. Let us also note that in a fix time values framework, these two notions (addition of time values corresponding to the transitions of the implementation and observed time) do in fact coincide.

Intuitively, an implementation passes a test if there does not exist an evolution leading to a fail state. Once we know that the functional behavior of the implementation is correct with respect to the test, we need to check time conditions. The set H corresponds to the observations of the (several) applications of the tests belonging to the test suite $\mathcal{T}$ to I. Thus, we have to decide whether, for each evolution e, the observed time values (that is, $\text{Obs\_Time}_H(e)$) *match* the definition of the time intervals appearing in the successful state of the tests corresponding to the execution of that evolution (that is, $C_T(s)$).

Due to space limitations, we cannot include in this paper the algorithm that we propose to derive tests from a specification. In spite of the differences, our algorithm is an adaptation of that in [32]. We get a test suite extracted from the specification S. We denote this test suite by $\text{tests}(S)$.

Next, we present a result to establish the application of the test suite $\text{tests}(S)$ for determining whether an implementation, for a sample H, conforms to a specification with respect to the relations given in Definition 8.

Theorem 1. (Soundness and Completeness) Let I and S be IFSMs. Given a multiset of timed executions H, $\beta \in \mathbb{R}_+$, and $0 \leq \alpha \leq 1$ we have

- $I \text{ conf}_{int}^{(H,\alpha)} S$ iff I (H, α)-*timely passes* $\text{tests}(S)$.
- $I \text{ conf}_{intf}^{(H,\alpha)} S$ iff I (H, α)-*fast passes* $\text{tests}(S)$.
- $I \text{ conf}_{intp}^{(H,\alpha)} S$ iff I (H, α)-*preferable passes* $\text{tests}(S)$.
- $I \text{ conf}_{intgb}^{(H,\beta)} S$ iff I (H, β)-*global timely passes* $\text{tests}(S)$.
- $I \text{ conf}_{intup}^{(H,\beta)} S$ iff I (H, β)-*up-timely passes* $\text{tests}(S)$.
- $I \text{ conf}_{intlw}^{(H,\beta)} S$ iff I (H, β)-*low-timely passes* $\text{tests}(S)$.
- $I \text{ conf}_{int}^{(H,\alpha,\beta)} S$ iff I (H, α, β)-*timely passes* $\text{tests}(S)$.
- $I \text{ conf}_{intf}^{(H,\alpha,\beta)} S$ iff I (H, α, β)-*fast passes* $\text{tests}(S)$.
- $I \text{ conf}_{intp}^{(H,\alpha,\beta)} S$ iff I (H, α, β)-*preferable passes* $\text{tests}(S)$.

$\square$

5   Conclusions and Future Work

In this paper we have presented a novel framework to specify and test timed systems showing both soft and hard deadlines. We have defined nine conformance relations that take into account the different considerations of what a *slightly* erroneous system is, that is, that soft deadlines are *almost* always met. We have also developed a testing theory by introducing a notion of test and by defining how tests are applied to implementations and what is the meaning of passing a test. Finally, we have stated that testing a system with the appropriate test suite is equivalent to establish that it is related with the specification from which the test suite was extracted.

There is still some room for future work. First, it would be interesting to study the precise relation between the different implementation relations that we define in this paper. Second, we would like to take this paper as a first step, together with [33], to define a testing theory for systems presenting both time and probabilistic information expressed by means of intervals.

References

1. Sifakis, J.: Use of Petri nets for performance evaluation. In: 3rd Int. Symposium on Measuring, Modelling and Evaluating Computer Systems, pp. 75–93. North-Holland, Amsterdam (1977)
2. Zuberek, W.: Timed Petri nets and preliminary performance evaluation. In: 7th Annual Symposium on Computer Architecture, pp. 88–96. ACM Press, New York (1980)
3. Reed, G., Roscoe, A.: A timed model for communicating sequential processes. Theoretical Computer Science 58, 249–261 (1988)
4. Nicollin, X., Sifakis, J.: An overview and synthesis on timed process algebras. In: Larsen, K.G., Skou, A. (eds.) CAV 1991. LNCS, vol. 575, pp. 376–398. Springer, Heidelberg (1992)
5. Glabbeek, R.v., Smolka, S., Steffen, B.: Reactive, generative and stratified models of probabilistic processes. Information and Computation 121(1), 59–80 (1995)
6. Baeten, J., Middelburg, C.: Process algebra with timing. EATCS Monograph. Springer, Heidelberg (2002)
7. Bravetti, M., Aldini, A.: Discrete time generative-reactive probabilistic processes with different advancing speeds. Theoretical Computer Science 290(1), 355–406 (2003)
8. Núñez, M.: Algebraic theory of probabilistic processes. Journal of Logic and Algebraic Programming 56(1–2), 117–177 (2003)
9. Higashino, T., Nakata, A., Taniguchi, K., Cavalli, A.: Generating test cases for a timed I/O automaton model. In: IWTCS 1999. 12th Int. Workshop on Testing of Communicating Systems, pp. 197–214. Kluwer Academic Publishers, Boston, MA (1999)
10. Springintveld, J., Vaandrager, F., D'Argenio, P.: Testing timed automata. Theoretical Computer Science 254(1-2), 225–257 (2001) Previously appeared as Technical Report CTIT-97-17, University of Twente (1997)
11. Fecko, M., Uyar, M., Duale, A., Amer, P.: A technique to generate feasible tests for communications systems with multiple timers. IEEE/ACM Transactions on Networking 11(5), 796–809 (2003)
12. En-Nouaary, A., Dssouli, R.: A guided method for testing timed input output automata. In: Hogrefe, D., Wiles, A. (eds.) TestCom 2003. LNCS, vol. 2644, pp. 211–225. Springer, Heidelberg (2003)
13. Núñez, M., Rodríguez, I.: Towards testing stochastic timed systems. In: König, H., Heiner, M., Wolisz, A. (eds.) FORTE 2003. LNCS, vol. 2767, pp. 335–350. Springer, Heidelberg (2003)
14. Stoelinga, M., Vaandrager, F.: A testing scenario for probabilistic automata. In: Baeten, J.C.M., Lenstra, J.K., Parrow, J., Woeginger, G.J. (eds.) ICALP 2003. LNCS, vol. 2719, pp. 464–477. Springer, Heidelberg (2003)
15. Brandán Briones, L., Brinksma, E.: Testing real-time multi input-output systems. In: Lau, K.-K., Banach, R. (eds.) ICFEM 2005. LNCS, vol. 3785, pp. 264–279. Springer, Heidelberg (2005)

16. Merayo, M., Núñez, M., Rodríguez, I.: Extending EFSMs to specify and test timed systems with action durations and timeouts. In: Najm, E., Pradat-Peyre, J.F., Donzeau-Gouge, V.V. (eds.) FORTE 2006. LNCS, vol. 4229, pp. 372–387. Springer, Heidelberg (2006)
17. Götz, N., Herzog, U., Rettelbach, M.: Multiprocessor and distributed system design: The integration of functional specification and performance analysis using stochastic process algebras. In: Donatiello, L., Nelson, R. (eds.) SIGMETRICS 1993 and Performance 1993. LNCS, vol. 729, pp. 121–146. Springer, Heidelberg (1993)
18. Hillston, J.: A Compositional Approach to Performance Modelling. Cambridge University Press, Cambridge (1996)
19. Bernardo, M., Gorrieri, R.: A tutorial on EMPA: A theory of concurrent processes with nondeterminism, priorities, probabilities and time. Theoretical Computer Science 202(1-2), 1–54 (1998)
20. Harrison, P., Strulo, B.: SPADES – a process algebra for discrete event simulation. Journal of Logic Computation 10(1), 3–42 (2000)
21. Hermanns, H., Herzog, U., Katoen, J.P.: Process algebra for performance evaluation. Theoretical Computer Science 274(1-2), 43–87 (2002)
22. Bravetti, M., Gorrieri, R.: The theory of interactive generalized semi-Markov processes. Theoretical Computer Science 282(1), 5–32 (2002)
23. López, N., Núñez, M., Rubio, F.: An integrated framework for the analysis of asynchronous communicating stochastic processes. Formal Aspects of Computing 16(3), 238–262 (2004)
24. Cleaveland, R., Lee, I., Lewis, P., Smolka, S.: A theory of testing for soft real-time processes. In: SEKE 1996. 8th Int. Conf. on Software Engineering and Knowledge Engineering, pp. 474–479 (1996)
25. de Nicola, R., Hennessy, M.: Testing equivalences for processes. Theoretical Computer Science 34, 83–133 (1984)
26. Hennessy, M.: Algebraic Theory of Processes. MIT Press, Cambridge (1988)
27. Yuen, S., Cleaveland, R., Dayar, Z., Smolka, S.: Fully abstract characterizations of testing preorders for probabilistic processes. In: Jonsson, B., Parrow, J. (eds.) CONCUR 1994. LNCS, vol. 836, pp. 497–512. Springer, Heidelberg (1994)
28. Bernardo, M., Cleaveland, W.: A theory of testing for markovian processes. In: Palamidessi, C. (ed.) CONCUR 2000. LNCS, vol. 1877, pp. 305–319. Springer, Heidelberg (2000)
29. López, N., Núñez, M.: A testing theory for generally distributed stochastic processes. In: Larsen, K.G., Nielsen, M. (eds.) CONCUR 2001. LNCS, vol. 2154, pp. 321–335. Springer, Heidelberg (2001)
30. Tretmans, J.: Test generation with inputs, outputs and repetitive quiescence. Software – Concepts and Tools 17(3), 103–120 (1996)
31. Núñez, M., Rodríguez, I.: Encoding PAMR into (timed) EFSMs. In: Peled, D.A., Vardi, M.Y. (eds.) FORTE 2002. LNCS, vol. 2529, pp. 1–16. Springer, Heidelberg (2002)
32. Núñez, M., Rodríguez, I.: Conformance testing relations for timed systems. In: Grieskamp, W., Weise, C. (eds.) FATES 2005. LNCS, vol. 3997, pp. 103–117. Springer, Heidelberg (2006)
33. López, N., Núñez, M., Rodríguez, I.: Specification, testing and implementation relations for symbolic-probabilistic systems. Theoretical Computer Science 353(1-3), 228–248 (2006)

Automatic Composition of Stateless Components: A Logical Reasoning Approach

Seyyed Vahid Hashemian and Farhad Mavaddat

David R. Cheriton School of Computer Science
University of Waterloo
Waterloo, Ontario, Canada
{svhashemian,fmavaddat}@cs.uwaterloo.ca

Abstract. Reusing available software components in developing new systems is always a priority, as it usually saves a considerable amount of time, money and human effort. An ideal scenario for software reuse is to build a new software system by composing existing components based on their behavioral properties. In this paper we take advantage of logical reasoning to find a solution for automatic composition of stateless components, which are components with a simple two step workflow: receiving inputs and then returning the corresponding outputs. We provide a concrete algorithm to find possible component compositions for a requested behavior. We then validate those compositions using a process algebra, which is specifically designed for this purpose.

Keywords: Software Reuse, Component Composition, Web Services Composition, Process Algebra.

1 Introduction

Software products are usually developed in such a way that, if necessary, they could be reused in future developments, as this usually saves a considerable amount of time, money and human effort. In building a software system based on components we usually break down the overall behavior of the system into smaller behavioral pieces for which we can build or find a component. Then by integrating all these components we develop the target system which performs according to that overall behavior. In other words, we take advantage of the divide-and-conquer method to build a complex software system. Nowadays, this approach is usually used in every software development attempt.

If there are only a few available components, manually searching for reuse options might be justifiable. However, if there are hundreds of these components this manual search would be impractical, if not impossible. That is why (semi-)automatic approaches have emerged to perform this search as efficient as possible. Finding reuse options becomes even more interesting, though more complicated, when we would also check the possibility of reusing compositions of available components. In other words, there might be situations, in which none of the single components provides the expected behavior, but a composition of some of them does so. This general version of the problem is studied in

F. Arbab and M. Sirjani (Eds.): FSEN 2007, LNCS 4767, pp. 175–190, 2007.

this paper. We can rephrase the problem, hereafter the *composition problem*, as follows:

A repository of available components specified by their behavior, and a request for a new component (or software system) are given. Is there any composition of some of the available components that provides the requested behavior? If so, what is that composition?

The *behavior* of a system is defined as actions that it performs, their order of execution, possible preconditions and effects, and possible nonfunctional aspects such as timing and probability. In this paper, we concentrate only on the actions and their order of execution as the observable behavior of a component. Moreover, we consider only stateless components. The behavior of a stateless component is a two step process: first it receives some inputs; and then it returns some outputs accordingly. In other words, in stateless components knowing the inputs and outputs is sufficient for figuring out the behavior. Most components that perform information retrieval tasks can be categorized as stateless components. For example, the web service *CityStateByZip* [1] as a software component is an information service with an input *zipCode* and two outputs *city* and *state*. It first receives the input *zipCode* and then returns the corresponding *city* and *state* as the result.

Stateless components are not limited to information components. As an example, the web service *EmailAddressValidator* [1] is a component which receives an *emailAddress* and returns a *boolean* value based on whether the given email address actually exists. Another example is the *CaesarCipher* service [1] which receives a *text* and a *shiftNo* and returns the ciphered text in its *cipher* output. We can imagine that stateless components form a large subset in any component based environment. For example, almost all the published web services in the repository http://www.xmethods.net/ are stateless.

As a solution to the composition problem, a composition plan is generated describing the available components that should be used, their order of execution, and possible data passings among them. In Figure 1, the role of a composition planner is shown in a typical component composition engine. The composition engine is used to extract and store specification of available components, finding composition plans for component requests, and finally providing appropriate facilities for executing the composite component according to the generated plan. This engine is comprised of four main parts:

- Component Specification Repository (or *repository*): It contains the necessary information about the available components. For example, in web services WSDL documents could be used for this purpose.
- Component Specification Extractor: From the specification of a component, it extracts the necessary information to be stored in the repository. In case there is no such document, the information can be entered manually.
- Component Composition Planner: Based on the specification of available components and the requested behavior it finds a composition plan to expose that behavior. This is the part that we focus on in this paper.

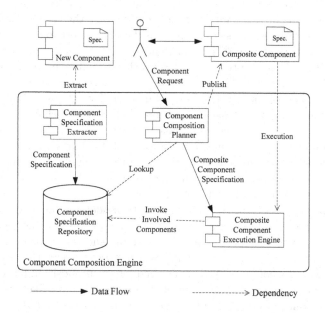

Fig. 1. The architecture of a typical component composition engine [2]

– Composite Component Execution Engine: It executes a given composition plan. In case it requires any information about the constituent components of the composition plan, it contacts the repository.

Note that the components outside the boundary of the composition engine in Figure 1 are the input and output of the engine. The input is a new component that is introduced to the engine, while the output is the composite component or the composition plan that is generated according to the given request.

In this paper we take advantage of logical reasoning to solve the composition problem for stateless components, i.e. to study how the composition planner should work. In Section 2 we address some of the related works on this subject. Section 3 contains necessary formalism for representing behavior of software components. In Section 4 we briefly review logical reasoning at an introductory level. Then, in Section 5 we use the logical reasoning techniques to solve the composition problem for the stateless components. Finally, we conclude the paper in Section 6 with a short summary and the future plans.

2   Related Works

Similar versions of the composition problem have been studied in a large number of academic and industrial research papers. They usually differ from one another in terms of the type of components they study, information they capture from each component, and the level of abstraction of their solution. In this section, we briefly review some of these works, that mostly study the composition problem in web services. Web services could be considered the best example of software components to fit the composition problem.

Benatallah et al. in [3] propose an approach for facilitating large-scale inter-operation of web services. They take advantage of service communities as the repositories of web services with similar functionality. The workflow, preconditions and effects of each web service are modeled by a statechart, in which each state is one of the constituting web services. They also introduce a specification language for web services interaction based on state-charts, and a peer-to-peer execution model for composite web services. They assume it is already known how the composite web service is built. In other words, they study the Composite Component Execution Engine (Figure 1).

Rao et al. in [4] use Linear Logic axioms to model the behavior of stateless services and their nonfunctional constraints. They consider the Linear Logic specification of available services as given axioms and try to prove a requested service, which is also a Linear Logic axiom, using proof trees. However, they do not explain how a proof tree can be converted into a composition plan. Although they do not discuss the performance of their approach, it most likely is dependent on the performance of possible automatic theorem provers that they would use.

Medjahed et al. in [5] propose an ontology-based framework for automatic composition of web services. Ontologies are simply different vocabularies that are used in specification of web services. Authors consider both syntactic and semantic attributes of web services to find a valid composition. To do so, they introduce a composability model and a matchmaking algorithm to search for composable operations and services. They mostly focus on matching algorithms for web services and their operations rather than finding a composition plan.

Laukkanen and Helin in [6] propose an approach for finding semantically similar web services to a specific service. This similarity search includes searching for a web service or a set of web services with similar inputs, outputs, preconditions and effects. The replacement may be a simple web service or a set of web services. In case there is a set of web services, the whole set as a single service should conform the required inputs, outputs, preconditions and effects. The steps taken to find this replacement include determining the functionality of the service to be replaced, finding semantically similar services from an available repository, and creating a workflow based on which the required functionality is provided. Authors do not represent any algorithm in this regard, especially for "how the discovery process is performed", "how semantic matching engine makes necessary reasonings" and also, "how the workflow composer works".

We studied a very simple version of composing stateless web services in [7], where we assumed that each service has only one input and one output. We introduced a dependency graph to capture dependencies among the input and output of available services. In this graph, nodes represent inputs and outputs of services, while edges stand for the input-output dependencies imposed by each web service. We used the dependency information to solve this simple version of the problem and explained how it can be solved in linear time in the size of the graph. Since this initial version of the dependency graph has some restrictions, we tried to extend the dependency graph in [2]. Apparently, generalizing the problem made the composition planner much more complex, i.e. exponential in the worst case. However, using some reasonable simplifying assumptions we could obtain a PTIME-Complete complexity.

In another paper [8], we introduced an algebra for process composition. We used this algebra and outlined how the composition problem in general could be solved. We use some of its results in this paper to solve the composition problem for stateless components.

3   Formal Representation of Components Behavior

In order to represent the behavior of components we use a specific process algebra, called *composition algebra*. It is based on the familiar algebras such as CSP [9] and CCS [10] with less operators and minor changes. We introduced this algebra in [8], and here we briefly review its main properties. In this paper, the behavior of a component is the observable actions that it performs, and their order of execution. In other words, a behavior is the underlying process through which a component is executed. That is why process algebras become helpful. We assume that associated with each component there is a process including some actions, where actions represent data types exchanged between components.

Operands of the composition algebra are actions and processes. Action names start with a lowercase letter, e.g. *emailAddress*, while process names start with an uppercase, e.g. *EmailAddressValidator*. Each action is an input or an output, and to distinguish them, outputs are identified by an overline, e.g. $\overline{boolean}$.

There are four main operators in the composition algebra. These operators are used to compose actions and processes and form more complex processes.

- Sequence (·): It represents the sequential execution of actions and processes.
- Choice (+): It is used to describe different branches of execution.
- Parallel ($\|$): It is used to represent a concurrent or unordered execution. Similar to other process algebras, concurrent executions are simulated with unordered executions; i.e. $(a \cdot P) \| (b \cdot Q) \equiv (a \cdot (P \| (b \cdot Q))) + (b \cdot ((a \cdot P) \| Q))$.
- Synchronization ⊙: It represents one or more synchronizations between two processes. There are two cases that two processes can be synchronized. In both cases as the result of the synchronization, the parts before synchronization points and the parts after in the two processes are executed in parallel.
  - Complimentary actions: When the output of one process is consumed by another process as an input, they become synchronized on that action. The result of synchronizing two complimentary actions is a *silent* action, represented by τ, which is not visible to the outside world. To calculate the result of such a synchronization the composition formulas of interface automata [11] can be used. For example, $(name \cdot \overline{emailAddress}) \odot (emailAddress \cdot \overline{boolean}) \equiv name \cdot \tau \cdot \overline{boolean} \equiv name \cdot \overline{boolean}$.

- Shared input: When two processes take the same input, they can be synchronized on that input. As an example, $(name \cdot \overline{emailAddress}) \odot (name \cdot \overline{phoneNo}) \equiv name \cdot \overline{(emailAddress \,||\, phoneNo)}$.

Two processes might have more than one pair of synchronizing actions, in which case they become synchronized on all those pairs, on the condition that the order of synchronizing actions in both processes is the same.

Among these operators, the binding power of the synchronization is the most, and then sequence, parallel and choice in order. We use σ-trace equivalence [10] as the equivalence semantics for processes. Specifically, two processes are equivalent ($\equiv$) if and only if every execution trace in one is an execution trace in the other. For example, two processes $a \cdot (b + c)$ and $a \cdot b + a \cdot (b + c)$ are σ-trace equivalent as their trace sets, $\{a \cdot b, a \cdot c\}$, are the same.

We finish this overview section with some of the important rules and axioms of the composition algebra.

- commutativity of all operators except the sequence
- associativity of all operators except the synchronization[1]
- $P \cdot \tau \equiv \tau \cdot P \equiv P$, $P + \tau \equiv \tau + P \not\equiv P$, $P \,||\, \tau \equiv \tau \,||\, P \equiv P$, $P \odot \tau \equiv \tau \odot P \equiv P$
- $\overline{P}$ is the inverse of P, and $P \odot \overline{P} \equiv \overline{P} \odot P \equiv \tau$
- $P = P_1 \cdot x \cdot P_2$ and $Q = Q_1 \cdot \overline{x} \cdot Q_2 \implies P \odot Q \equiv (P_1 \,||\, Q_1) \cdot (P_2 \odot Q_2)$, if x and $\overline{x}$ are the first synchronizing actions in P and Q.
- $P = P_1 \cdot x \cdot P_2$ and $Q = Q_1 \cdot x \cdot Q_2 \implies P \odot Q \equiv (P_1 \,||\, Q_1) \cdot x \cdot (P_2 \odot Q_2)$, if x is the first synchronizing action in P and Q.
- $P + P \equiv P$
- $P \cdot (Q + R) \equiv (P \cdot Q) + (P \cdot R)$, $(Q + R) \cdot P \equiv (Q \cdot P) + (R \cdot P)$
- $P \,||\, (Q + R) \equiv (P \,||\, Q) + (P \,||\, R)$, $(Q + R) \,||\, P \equiv (Q \,||\, P) + (R \,||\, P)$

4   Logical Reasoning

In simple terms, logical reasoning is defined as the formal manipulation of symbols representing a collection of believed propositions to produce representations of new ones. These symbols are used to represent the knowledge and also to infer it through some known rules. The collection of believed propositions is called the *knowledge base*. The type of logical reasoning we apply in composition planning is *logical inference*, in which the final result is considered to be a conclusion of the initial propositions. For example, if the knowledge base contains two propositions "patient x is allergic to medication m" and "anyone allergic to medication m is also allergic to medication m'" using logical inference we can conclude that "patient x is allergic to medication m'" [12].

In the reasoning problem we study in this paper there is a knowledge base S containing the known propositions and a goal proposition R. What we expect as the result is whether R can be inferred from the propositions in S, written

---

[1] The synchronization operator is associative if only one of the synchronization types, and not both, appears in an algebraic expression [11,9].

as $S \vDash R$. It is trivial that to prove $S \vDash R$ is equivalent to prove that $S \cup \{\neg R\}$ is unsatisfiable. In other words, if it turns out that $S \cup \{\neg R\}$ is satisfiable, we conclude that $S \nvDash R$; and if $S \cup \{\neg R\}$ is unsatisfiable, then $S \vDash R$. It is assumed that there is no contradicting propositions in S, which means $S \nvDash FALSE$. If $S \cup \{\neg R\}$ is unsatisfiable, or S entails R ($S \vDash R$), sometimes we might need to know how R is derived from S, i.e. which propositions from S and in what order have been applied to result in R.

The reasoning algorithm and its complexity is dependent on the expressivity of the underlying logic. Specifically, the way the knowledge is represented is a determinant factor in how we should reason about it. We would expect to reason simpler in propositional logic rather than in first-order predicate logic. Unfortunately, the logical reasoning even for propositional logic, as a non-parametric and simpler form of logic, is NP-Complete in the worst case. Therefore, trying to convert the composition problem into a propositional logic reasoning would not help much. However, there is a less expressive form of logic, i.e. Horn clauses, which comes with less reasoning complexity in special cases [12].

A Horn clause is a Disjunctive Normal Form clause in first order logic with at most one positive literal. For example, the clause $\neg child \lor \neg male \lor boy$ is a Horn clause with two negative and one positive literals. Since Horn clauses have no more than one positive literal they can be converted into a conditional clause, as the above clause is equivalent to $child \land male \implies boy$. Therefore, every such conditional clause in propositional logic is a Horn clause [12].

In order to reason about Horn clauses we need to see how we can infer a new clause from two Horn clauses. As the main inference rule, when a literal appears positive in one clause and negative in the other, the two clauses can be resolved; i.e. two clauses $\neg a_1 \lor \cdots \lor \neg a_m \lor b_1$ and $\neg b_1 \lor \cdots \lor \neg b_n \lor c_1$ result in $\neg a_1 \lor \cdots \lor \neg a_m \lor \neg b_2 \lor \cdots \lor \neg b_n \lor c_1$. In conditional format, $a_1 \land \cdots \land a_m \implies b_1$ and $b_1 \land \cdots \land b_n \implies c_1$ imply $a_1 \land \cdots \land a_m \land b_2 \land \cdots \land b_n \implies c_1$. This inference rule is used to solve the reasoning problem for Horn clauses. To do so, we start with a knowledge base S and, by resolving Horn clauses from S and the temporary clauses created through some steps, we try to prove a goal clause R. If this is successful, we say that R can be derived from S, and show it by $S \vdash R$.

A restricted but sufficient form of resolution is the SLD resolution. An SLD resolution starts with resolving two clauses from the knowledge base S and in every single intermediate step the result of the last step is resolved with another clause from S. Therefore, two resolution results can not be resolved in an SLD resolution. The derivation continues until R is proved to be either true or false.

There are two main SLD techniques for reasoning about propositional Horn clauses: *backward chaining* and *forward chaining*. The backward chaining procedure has two drawbacks; it might go into an infinite loop, or it might take exponential time to terminate. However, the forward chaining approach (the algorithm shown in Figure 2) is much more reliable and efficient as it always terminates and also performs the reasoning in linear time in the number of clauses. We use this procedure in the next section to provide a solution for the composition problem [12].

input: a finite list of literals $q_1, \cdots, q_n$
output: YES or NO according to whether a knowledge base S entails all q_i's

1. if all of the goals q_i are marked as solved, then return YES
2. check if there is a clause $p \vee \neg p_1 \vee \cdots \vee \neg p_m$ in S, such that all of its negative literals $p_1, \cdots, p_m$ are marked as solved, and its positive literal p is not marked as solved
3. if there is such a clause, mark p as solved and go to step (1)
4. otherwise, return NO

Fig. 2. The SLD forward chaining procedure [12]

5   The Composition Planning Approach

We described in Section 3 how actions in composition algebra are modeled by nonparametric names. Since we focus on stateless components in this paper, we can assume that in the composition algebra the underlying process of all these components is of the general form $P \equiv (i_1 \| \cdots \| i_m) \cdot (\overline{o_1} \| \cdots \| \overline{o_n})$, which correctly captures the intended behavior, i.e. receiving some inputs and then returning some outputs. In order to solve the composition problem using the reasoning techniques, in this section we discuss in more details our earlier procedure [8], its main drawback, and the improved approach.

5.1   The Old Procedure and Its Drawback

The algebraic representation of behavior mentioned above has an alternative representation in propositional logic, as it can be modeled by the conditional expression $P_k \equiv i_1^k \wedge \cdots \wedge i_{m_k}^k \implies o_1^k \wedge \cdots \wedge o_{n_k}^k$. For example, the web service *CityStateByZip* of Section 1 is specified in composition algebra by the algebraic expression *CityStateByZip* $\equiv zipCode \cdot (\overline{city} \| \overline{state})$. Alternatively, it can be described in propositional logic using the conditional expression *CityStateByZip* $\equiv zipCode \implies city \wedge state$. As the result the composition problem can be expressed as follows.

> There is a knowledge base S containing a set of propositional clauses in the form of $P_k \equiv I_k \implies O_k$, where $I_k \equiv i_1^k \wedge \cdots \wedge i_{m_k}^k$ and $O_k \equiv o_1^k \wedge \cdots \wedge o_{n_k}^k$. There is also a target clause $R \equiv I_R \implies O_R$, with $I_R \equiv i_1^R \wedge \cdots \wedge i_{m_R}^R$ and $O_R \equiv o_1^R \wedge \cdots \wedge o_{n_R}^R$. The question is whether $S \vDash R$. If so, the corresponding derivation is also required.

In [8] we provided a procedure based on the algorithm in Figure 2 to solve the above problem. To do so, we made a little change in the above composition problem so that we can apply the forward chaining algorithm. The idea was to add $i_1^R, \ldots, i_{m_R}^R$ as known facts to the knowledge base S, and try to prove that $o_1^R, \ldots, o_{n_R}^R$ hold. The algorithm shown in Figure 3 represents the proposed procedure. This algorithm runs in linear time as well, as it is quite similar to the forward chaining algorithm in terms of the steps taken. The composition

input: a finite set of literals $O_R = \{o_1^R, \cdots, o_{n_R}^R\}$
output: YES or NO according to whether $S \cup I_R$ entails all the literals in O_R

1. mark all the literals in I_R as true
2. if all of the literals in O_R are marked as true, then return YES
3. check if there is a clause in S such that all of its left-hand-side literals are marked as true, and there is at least one literal in its right-hand-side which is not marked as true
4. if there is such a clause, add it to the list of clauses used so far, and mark all the unmarked literals on its right-hand-side as true and go to step (2)
5. otherwise, return NO

Fig. 3. The modified version of the forward chaining algorithm [8]

plan can be obtained based on the order of using knowledge base clauses in the algorithm.

Example: Let us assume a repository of available components containing:

$P_1 \equiv address \cdot \overline{zipCode}$ $P_2 \equiv (name \,||\, birthDate) \cdot \overline{localMap}$
$P_3 \equiv (address \,||\, zipCode) \cdot \overline{localMap}$ $P_4 \equiv (name \,||\, birthDate) \cdot (\overline{zipCode} \,||\, \overline{birthPlace})$
$P_5 \equiv (sIN \,||\, name) \cdot \overline{address}$ $P_6 \equiv (sIN \,||\, birthDate \,||\, birthPlace) \cdot \overline{phoneNo}$
$P_7 \equiv (sIN \,||\, birthDate \,||\, zipCode) \cdot \overline{phoneNo}$

Given the target component $R \equiv (sIN \,||\, name \,||\, birthDate) \cdot (\overline{localMap} \,||\, \overline{phoneNo})$, we are interested to know whether R can be built by composing some of these components.

We convert the component specifications into the propositional logic format and apply the algorithm in Figure 3 in order to find a solution. To find a solution, we start by marking sIN, $name$ and $birthDate$ as true. If there are different choices from S to use in Step (3) of the algorithm, we can randomly pick one. Following the algorithm, we see that picking P_2, P_4 and P_6 in the same order is one solution[2]. To validate, we find the result of $(P_2 \odot P_4) \odot P_6$ in composition algebra:

$$P_2 \odot P_4 = ((name \,||\, birthDate) \cdot \overline{localMap}) \odot ((name \,||\, birthDate) \cdot (\overline{zipCode} \,||\, \overline{birthPlace}))$$
$$= (name \,||\, birthDate) \cdot (\overline{localMap} \,||\, \overline{zipCode} \,||\, \overline{birthPlace})$$
$$(P_2 \odot P_4) \odot P_6 = (name \,||\, birthDate) \cdot (\overline{localMap} \,||\, \overline{zipCode} \,||\, \overline{birthPlace})$$
$$\odot (sIN \,||\, birthDate \,||\, birthPlace) \cdot \overline{phoneNo}$$
$$= (sIN \,||\, name \,||\, birthDate) \cdot (\overline{localMap} \,||\, \overline{zipCode}) \cdot \overline{phoneNo}$$
$$=^2 (sIN \,||\, name \,||\, birthDate) \cdot \overline{localMap} \cdot \overline{phoneNo}$$

We realize that the result is slightly different from the specification of R; i.e. the outputs are not generated in parallel in the proposed composition. We explain this small difference as follows.

– Normally, the parallel operator in such requests means that the relative order of inputs and outputs is not important; and as long as inputs are taken and

---

[2] We assume that unwanted generated outputs can be ignored.

then outputs are produced based on them, the result is acceptable. This way, we can accept the composition $(P_2 \odot P_4) \odot P_6$ as an approximate solution[3]to the request $(sIN \| name \| birthDate) \cdot (\overline{localMap} \| \overline{phoneNo})$.

– If the above result is not acceptable, and we need to produce the exact parallel expression, we may assume that the published composite component of Figure 1 would take care of this ordering. In other words, it works as a wrapper around all the constituent components and can wait to receive both *localMap* and *phoneNo* and then return them to the user.

In case we needed to achieve a composition that is exactly equivalent to the request R and we found a solution leading to a non-equivalent expression, like the above example, we would have had to backtrack to the last choice we made and continue the algorithm with another alternative. This apparently would add to the complexity of the procedure, but we do not go into its details in this paper, as we assume that the approximate results are also acceptable.   □

Although the algorithm in Figure 3 takes linear time in the number of knowledge base clauses to find a solution, it does not work properly in all stateless cases. In particular, it fails to correctly capture the concept of *cardinality*. In other words, since there is no cardinality involved in propositional logic expressions, e.g. $a \wedge a \equiv a$, this algorithm would not be able to appropriately deal with multiple instances of literals.

Example: Let us add to the repository of the previous example a new component $P_8 \equiv (zipCode \| zipCode) \cdot \overline{distance}$, which has an input with cardinality 2. This expression can not be appropriately converted into a propositional logic formula, because following the above mapping we obtain $P_8 \equiv zipCode \wedge zipCode \implies distance \equiv zipCode \implies distance$ □

Therefore, the old logical representation for components behavior and the corresponding algorithm do not answer the composition problem in general. We show in the rest of this paper how they can be improved to capture the cardinality of literals as well.

---

[3] Formally speaking, two algebraic expressions $e_1 \equiv I_1 \cdot O_1$ and $e_2 \equiv I_2 \cdot O_2$, in which

- I_1 and I_2 contain only input actions, and moreover contain the same number of input actions of each type,
- O_1 and O_2 contain only output actions, and moreover contain the same number of output actions of each type,

are *approximately equivalent* if one or both of the followings hold:

- For some expression I_0, either $I_1 \equiv I_2 + I_0$ $(I_0 \not\equiv I_2)$ or $I_2 \equiv I_1 + I_0$ $(I_0 \not\equiv I_1)$.
- For some expression O_0, either $O_1 \equiv O_2 + O_0$ $(O_0 \not\equiv O_2)$ or $O_2 \equiv O_1 + O_0$ $(O_0 \not\equiv O_1)$.

For example, $e_1 \equiv a \cdot (\overline{b} \| \overline{c})$ is approximately equivalent to $e_2 \equiv a \cdot \overline{b} \cdot \overline{c}$, because

- $e_1 \equiv I_1 \cdot O_1$, where $I_1 \equiv a$ and $O_1 \equiv \overline{b} \| \overline{c}$,
- $e_2 \equiv I_2 \cdot O_2$, where $I_2 \equiv a$ and $O_2 \equiv \overline{b} \cdot \overline{c}$,
- I_1 and I_2 contain the same input actions, and O_1 and O_2 contain the same output actions,
- $I_1 \equiv I_2$ and $O_1 \equiv O_2 + \overline{c} \cdot \overline{b}$.

5.2   The New Procedure

The initial proposed composition procedure is promising enough that we try to apply the same ideas to capture cardinalities. In the old approach every component behavior could be seen as $P : I \rightarrow O$, in which I and O are sets containing the corresponding inputs and outputs identified by their data type names. Since sets are unable to represent duplicate members and cardinalities, in the new procedure we assume that inputs and outputs are multisets [13] of type names. To distinguish duplicate type names that might appear in these multisets, we use unique identifiers and we call them *data instances* or *instances*, where $type(m)$ is the data type of the instance identified by m.

In order to solve the more general version of the stateless composition problem there are some extra constraints that must be taken into account.

1. Each component might be used more than once in a composition. In algorithms shown in Figures 2 and 3 each clause is used at most once, because when its right hand side is marked as true, there is no need to use that clause again. Since cardinality of a data type can be more than one, a component might be needed more than once. Therefore, in the new procedure, when a component is selected to participate in a composition it should not be removed from the list of available components.

2. When some inputs are used by a component, they (exact same instances) can not be used by the same component again. This is because after the inputs are used by the component the expected result is generated, and there is no point in running the component on those inputs again, as it will produce the same result. Algorithms in Figures 2 and 3 automatically comply with this rule as they do not use the same clause more than once. To apply this constraint, we attach to each instance m, that is being processed, a set *usedBy* of identifiers of the form P^i specifying that the component P has been applied on m in the step i of the reasoning algorithm.

3. For every single piece of functionality, all the given input instances must be used to produce each of the corresponding output instances, unless otherwise is specified by the user. For example, for the request $(sIN \,\|\, name \,\|\, birthDate) \cdot (\overline{localMap} \,\|\, \overline{phoneNo})$, in producing the outputs *localMap* and *phoneNo* all the three inputs must be used. To comply with this constraint, which is not considered in the algorithm in Figure 3, in generating outputs through the composition algorithm we need to determine whether all the inputs have been used. Therefore, we attach to each instance m a multiset *uses* containing data types from I_R that have been used so far to generate m. If $uses(m) = I_R$ for some instance m, we conclude that all the inputs in I_R have participated in producing m.

4. In order to find the actual composition in case the algorithm returns a "YES", we keep a set *from* along with every instance m that contains the instances that have been used to produce m. This way we can find out the appropriate components from the repository that are used in each step.

The algorithm shown in Figure 4 contains the improved reasoning-based procedure for composition planning. In this algorithm, we define the set M to keep

---

input: a repository S of components of the form $C : I_C \rightarrow O_C$ where I_C and O_C are multisets of data types; and similarly, a request $R : I_R \rightarrow O_R$.
output: YES/NO according to whether there is a valid composition from S for R.

---

1. define M as the set of instances, and set $M = \emptyset$.
2. for each single data type i in I_R, create a new instance m in M, and set
   - $type(m) = i$,
   - $usedBy(m) = \emptyset$,
   - $uses(m) = \emptyset$,
   - $from(m) = \emptyset$.
3. use a step counter n, and set $n = 1$.
4. if there is a set $K \subseteq M$, such that
   - $TYPE(K) = O_R$, where $TYPE(K) = \{type(m)|m \in K\}$, and
   - for every instance $m \in K$, $uses(m) = I_R$,
   return YES.
5. check if there is a component $C : I_C \rightarrow O_C$ in S and a set $L \subseteq M$, such that
   - $TYPE(L) = I_C$, and
   - $C^k \notin \bigcap_{m \in L} usedBy(m)$ for some step k.
6. if there is such a component,
   - for every $m \in L$, $usedBy(m) = usedBy(m) \cup \{C^n\}$,
   - for every o in O_C, create a new instance m' in M, and set
     - $type(m') = o$,
     - $usedBy(m') = \emptyset$,
     - $uses(m') = (I_C \cap I_R) \cup (\bigcup_{m \in L} uses(m))$.
     - $from(m') = L$
   - $n = n + 1$,
   - go to step (4)
7. otherwise, return NO

Fig. 4. The improved procedure for composition planning

track of the instances that are already produced as the algorithm execution progresses (Step 1). To every instance m that is added to M we assign

- its data type $type(m)$,
- a set $usedBy(m)$ containing components that have used this instance so far,
- a multiset $uses(m)$ including data types I_R that have been used, either directly or indirectly, in producing m, and
- a set $from(m)$ which contains instances from M used directly to produce m.

In the beginning an instance is added to M for every single data type in I_R (Step 2). We also use a step counter to record the components used in each step (Step 3). In Step 4 a test is done to see if we have achieved a valid composition for the request R. A valid composition would produce an instance of the same type for every data type in O_R (to satisfy the cardinality constraint), where in producing each of them the whole I_R is used. If the test fails, we need to continue with a new component to produce more outputs (Step 5). We do so by finding some instances in M that can be used by a component C, and have not been used by that component before. If there is such a component (Step 6), C^n (component C at step n) is added to the set *usedBy* of each of those instances, and for each output o of C a new instance m' is added to M with the appropriate *type*, *usedBy*, *uses* and *from* values. In particular,

- *type*(m') would be o;
- *usedBy*(m') would be empty;
- *uses*(m') would contain all the data types from I_R that are in I_C too, plus all the data types from I_R that have participated in producing instances in L;
- *from*(m') would obviously contain the instances in L.

If there is no new component from the repository to use instances in M, the algorithm terminates with a negative result (Step 7).

We can consider the execution of the algorithm as a multi-level graph structure, in which nodes at each level represent a set of instances from M and edges represent components from the repository. In this structure, there is an edge with label C^n from an instance i at level l_i to an instance j at level l_j ($l_j > l_i$), if and only if there is a component $C : I_C \rightarrow O_C$ used in step n of the algorithm, such that $type(i) \in I_C$ and $type(j) \in O_C$ and for each other data type t in I_C there is an instance k at some level l ($l < l_j$) with $type(k) = t$. Moreover, at least one instance of one of the data types in I_C must have appeared at level $l_j - 1$. In other words, if the maximum level of instances in $from(m)$ is l, m would sit at level $l+1$. Let $min(n_l)$ and $max(n_l)$ denote the minimum and maximum of the set $\{n|$ there is an edge $i \xrightarrow{C^n} j$ such that $l_j = l\}$. In order to create the levels of this graph in a breadth-first order, we assume that $l_i < l_j \Leftrightarrow min(n_{l_j}) > max(n_{l_i})$. This assumption guarantees that all the possible instances at each level are created before creating instances at the next level. To start creating instances, we put instances corresponding to the initial inputs in I_R at level 0. Then intermediate instances generated by the algorithm sit at the next levels.

Theorem 1. *If there is a solution for a given composition problem, the algorithm in Figure 4 is able to find it; and if there is none, it terminates.*

Proof. According to the above breadth-first method in applying the components from the repository S and creating new instances, it is guaranteed that the algorithm will find a solution, if there is any, because all the instances leading to a valid composition would be at some levels of this graph and finally would be reached by the algorithm. Moreover, it is obvious that for every instance in the graph there is least one path from level 0 to that instance. Assuming that each repository component appears at most once in each such graph path, it is guaranteed that instances of all the possible data types (according to inputs and outputs of available components) would be created up to level $|S| = n$. This assumption is reasonable since we capture only syntactic information of available components and do not consider their behavioral semantics. Therefore, if there is no solution up to level n, there will not be any afterwards. □

As mentioned before, the algorithm in Figure 4 returns only a "YES/NO" answer, and does not return the actual composition in case the answer is a "YES".

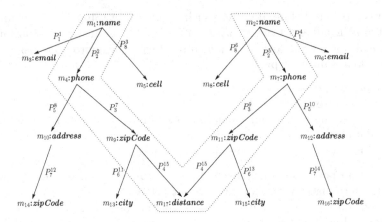

Fig. 5. The result of the algorithm shown in Figure 4 for the given example

In order to find the composition, we take advantage of the information stored along with instances in M and also the set K that was found right before the algorithm terminated (line 4). We can start by instances in K and go back step by step to the inputs and components that resulted them and so on, until we reach the original inputs, i.e. the instances corresponding to I_R. The above multi-level graph could be used to find the actual composition through its paths from level 0 to the desired outputs. We go through a brief example to clarify this graph structure and the whole approach in more details.

Example: Consider the following set of components:

$P_1 : name \rightarrow email,$ $P_2 : name \rightarrow phone, P_3 : phone \rightarrow zipCode,$ $P_4 : zipCode^2 \rightarrow distance,$

$P_5 : phone \rightarrow address, P_6 : zipCode \rightarrow city, P_7 : address \rightarrow zipCode, P_8 : name \rightarrow cell$

The superscript 2 in P_4 implies that this component takes two instances of $zipCode$ as inputs. We explain the algorithm using the multi-level graph in Figure 5. Given $R : name^2 \rightarrow distance$, the algorithm in Figure 4 starts by adding m_1 and m_2 of type $name$ to M. Each of these instances, can produce one instance of $email$, $phone$ and $cell$ in the next six steps (instances m_3 to m_8 by components P_1, P_2 and P_8). Since there is no solution yet, in the next four steps, each of the two $phone$ instances that are currently in M (m_4 and m_7) produce one instance of $zipCode$ and $address$ (instances m_9 to m_{12} by components P_3 and P_5). Again, there is no $distance$ instance in M up to this point. Continuing the algorithm, each $zipCode$ instance produces one $city$ instance (instances m_{13} and m_{15} by component P_6), and each $address$ instance creates one $zipCode$ instance (m_{14} and m_{16} by component P_7). Then, two initial $zipCode$ instances (m_9 and m_{11}) produce one $distance$ instance (m_{17} by component P_4). Since in producing m_{17} both $name$ instances in I_R have been used, the algorithm returns a "YES".

In the graph of Figure 5, the set $usedBy$ for each instance is the set of its outgoing edge labels. Also, the set $uses$ for each data instance is the multiset of the data types of all the instance at the top level of this graph which have a path to that specific instance. And finally, the set $from$ for each instance is the set of its parents in the graph. The section of the graph which is inside the dotted area represents the data instances leading to the "YES" response. Based on its structure and the components appearing on its edge labels we can find out the corresponding composition. In this specific example, we see two parallel paths that are merged using the component P_4. In other words, before the merge point, the two paths represent parallel execution of two instances of $P_2 \odot P_3$. Therefore, the proposed composition turns out to be $((P_2 \odot P_3) \| (P_2 \odot P_3)) \odot P_4$. To verify this solution, we use the composition algebraic rules:

$P_2 \odot P_3 \equiv (name \cdot \overline{phone}) \odot (phone \cdot \overline{zipCode}) \equiv name \cdot \overline{zipCode}$

$((P_2 \odot P_3) \| (P_2 \odot P_3)) \odot P_4 \equiv ((name \cdot \overline{zipCode}) \| (name \cdot \overline{zipCode})) \odot ((zipCode \| zipCode) \cdot \overline{distance}) \equiv (name \| name) \cdot \overline{distance}.$ □

Complexity

To discuss the complexity of the algorithm in Fugure 4, we assume that $|S| = n$; and further we assume that k is an upper bound for the number of inputs and outputs of each component and also the request, e.g. the number of instances in I_R and O_R is $O(k)$. It is not hard to see that at each level of the graph resulted from the algorithm, in the worst case each instance can be used by $O(n)$ components from the repository producing $O(kn)$ new instances in the next levels. Since a solution might not be found until level n of the graph is fully created, we conclude that, in the worst case, the algorithm runs exponentially in the number of components. However, we believe that this worst case situation is far from practice, as the more components are used in the first levels of the graph, the more is the possibility of finding a solution well before level n. On the other hand, if the graph is expanded up to level n, instances have been used by only a few (and not $O(n)$) components on average. These informal observations encourages us to believe that the real complexity of this algorithm is much less than the worst case above. Studying the complexity in more details and also possible improvements to the algorithm are parts of our future plan.

6   Summary and Future Work

In this paper we studied the composition problem for software components and, specifically, explained how a composition plan for stateless components can be found by presenting a reasoning approach. This approach is simpler than the one presented in [2] which takes advantage of dependency graphs. Compared to similar works on component composition, we believe that our algorithm is more concrete for implementation purposes, and its complexity is not worse, if not better. Although the algorithm has exponential time complexity in the worst case, we believe that a better complexity can be achieved in the real situations. As part of our future plan, we are going to study the algorithm in more details for possible improvements and also a more precise performance measure. Then, we will perform some evaluation by implementing the algorithm and running it against some test data to obtain a better understanding of its real complexity.

Acknowledgement

This work is supported by Natural Sciences and Engineering Research Council of Canada (NSERC) and the University of Waterloo which is gratefully acknowledged. Authors would also like to thank Solmaz Kolahi for her helpful comments.

References

1. StrikeIron, Inc.: StrikeIron, Extending Your SOA (2006),
   http://www.strikeiron.com
2. Hashemian, S.V., Mavaddat, F.: A graph-based framework for composition of stateless web services. In: ECOWS. Proceedings of the 4th European Conference on Web Services, pp. 75–86 (2006)
3. Benatallah, B., Dumas, M., Sheng, Q.Z., Ngu, A.H.: Declarative composition and peer-to-peer provisioning of dynamic web services. In: ICDE. Proceedings of the 18th International Conference on Data Engineering, pp. 297–308 (2002)
4. Rao, J., Küngas, P., Matskin, M.: Application of linear logic to web service composition. In: ICWS. Proceedings of the International Conference on Web Services, pp. 3–9 (2003)
5. Medjahed, B., Bouguettaya, A., Elmagarmid, A.: Composing web services on the semantic web. The VLDB Journal 12(4), 333–351 (2003)
6. Laukkanen, M., Helin, H.: Composing workflows of semantic web services. In: Proceedings of the Workshop on Web-Services and Agent-based Engineering (2003)
7. Hashemian, S.V., Mavaddat, F.: A graph-based approach to web services composition. In: SAINT. Proceedings of the 2005 IEEE/IPSJ International Symposium on Applications and the Internet, pp. 183–189 (2005)
8. Hashemian, S.V., Mavaddat, F.: Composition algebra: Process composition using algebraic rules. In: FACS. Preliminary Proceedings of the Third International Workshop on Formal Aspects of Component Software, pp. 247–264 (2006)
9. Hoare, C.A.R.: Communicating Sequential Processes. Prentice/Hall International, Englewood Cliffs (1985)
10. Milner, R.: Communication and Concurrency. Prentice-Hall, Englewood Cliffs (1989)
11. de Alfaro, L., Henzinger, T.: Interface automata. In: ESEC/SIGSOFT FSE. Proceedings of the 8th European Software Engineering Conference held jointly with 9th ACM SIGSOFT International Symposium on Foundations of Software Engineering, pp. 109–120. ACM Press, New York (2001)
12. Brachman, R., Levesque, H.: Knowledge Representation and Reasoning. Morgan Kaufmann, San Francisco (2004)
13. Weisstein, E.W.: Multiset; From MathWorld–A Wolfram Web Resource (2002),
    http://mathworld.wolfram.com/Multiset.html

A Model of Component-Based Programming

Xin Chen[1,4], Jifeng He[2], Zhiming Liu[1,*], and Naijun Zhan[1,3,**]

[1] International Institute for Software Technology, United Nations University, Macau
{chenxin,lzm}@iist.unu.edu
[2] Software Engineering Institute, East China Normal University, Shanghai, China
jifeng@sei.ecnu.edu.cn
[3] Lab. of Computer Science, Institute of Software, CAS, Beijing, China
znj@ios.ac.cn
[4] Department of Computer Science and Technology, Nanjing University, China

Abstract. Component-based programming is about how to create *application programs* from *prefabricated components* with *new software* that provides both *glue* between the components, and *new functionality*. Models of components are required to support *black-box compositionality* and *substitutability* by a third party as well as *interoperability*. However, the glue codes and programs designed by users of the components for new applications in general do not require these features, and they can be even designed in programming paradigms different from those of the components. In this paper, we extend the rCOS calculus of components with a model for glue programs and application programs that is different from that of components. We study the composition of a glue program with components and prove that the components glued by the glue program yield a new component.

Keywords: Components, Contracts, Protocols, Composition, Glue Codes, Application Programs, Refinement.

1 Introduction

Component-based development (CBD) is about how to create new software by combining *prefabricated components* with *new programs* that provide both glue between the components, and new functionality [1]. Furthermore, there seems to be no disagreement on the following interrelated properties that components enjoy.

1. *Black-box composability, substitutability and reusability:* there is no need to know the design and the implementation when composing a component with other parts of the system, substituting a component with another one or reusing it in another application.

---

[*] The author is partly supported by HighQSoftD and HTTS funded by Macao Science and Technology Development Fund, NSF Project 60573085 and 863 of China 2006AA01Z165.
[**] The author is partly supported by the projects NSFC-60493200, NSFC-60421001, NSFC-60573007 and NKBRPC-2002cb312200.

F. Arbab and M. Sirjani (Eds.): FSEN 2007, LNCS 4767, pp. 191–206, 2007.
© Springer-Verlag Berlin Heidelberg 2007

2. *Independent development:* components can be designed, implemented, verified, validated and deployed independently.
3. *Interoperability:* components can be implemented in different programming
languages and paradigms, but they can be composed, be glued together and
cooperate with each another.

These features require that a component has a black-box specification of what it
provides to and what it *requires* from its environment. In rCOS [2,3], the provided
services and required service of a component are given by the contract of the
provided interface and the contract of the *required interface* of the component,
respectively. Thus, the contracts together with the interfaces of a component
provide a black-box specification of the component. The model of contracts in
rCOS also defines the unified semantic model of implementations of interfaces
in different programming languages, and thus clearly supports interoperability
of components and analysis of the correctness of a component with respect to
its interface contract. The theory of refinements of contracts and components in
rCOS characterizes component substitutivity, as well as supporting independent
development of components. Compositions are defined in rCOS for chaining
the provided interface of one component to the required interface of another,
renaming and hiding interface operations of a component.

However, there is no precise characterization for the "new program" that
provides both "glue" between the components, and "new functionality". In this
paper, we introduce the notion of *processes* into rCOS. Like a component, a process has an interface declaring its local variables and methods, and its behavior
is specified by a process contract. Unlike a component that passively waits for
a client to call its provided services, a process is active and has its own control
on when to call out or to wait for a call to its provided services. For such an
active process, we cannot have separate contracts for its provided interface and
required interface, because we cannot have separate specifications of outgoing
calls and incoming calls [2]. For simplicity, but without losing expressiveness,
we assume a process like a Java thread does not provide services and only calls
operations provided by components. Therefore, processes can only communicate
via shared components. The composition of two processes will be by interleaving,
and produce a new process.

Let C be the parallel composition of a number of disjoint components C_i,
$i = 1, \ldots, k$. A glue program for C is a process P that makes calls to the operations in set X provided by C. The *synchronization composition* $P \parallel [X] C$ of C
and P is defined similarly to the alphabetized parallel in CSP [4,5]. The gluing
composition is defined by hiding the synchronized methods between the component C and the process P. We show that $(P \parallel [X] C)\backslash X$ is a component. We
will study the algebraic laws of the composition of processes and components as
well.

We also model an application program as a set of parallel processes that make
use of the services provided by components. As processes only interact with components via the provided interfaces of the components, interoperability is thus
supported as the contracts which define the semantics of the common interface

description language (IDL), even though components, glue programs and components are not implemented in the same language. Analysis and verification of an application program can be performed in the classical formal frameworks, but at the level of contracts of components instead of implementations of components. The analysis and verification can reuse any proved properties about the components, such as divergence freedom and deadlock freedom of the implementation of the components, without the need to reprove them.

Due to the limit of space, we omit all proofs in this paper, the interesting reader can be referred to [6] for the proofs.

The rest of this paper is organized as follows. Section 2 contains a brief summary of rCOS. In section 3, we define the model of process and gluing composition. As well, we prove that gluing components by a process indeed forms a new component and then present a method to calculate the contract of the resulted component. Section 4 presents a comparison between our work to the relative work. Section 5 draws a short conclusion and discusses the future work.

2 Interface, Contracts and Components

This section uses examples to briefly review the main modelling elements of the component model in rCOS. The read can be referred to [2] for details.

2.1 Preliminaries

For convenience, we first introduce some notions of traces. Given an alphabet Σ, Σ^* denotes all finite sequences generated from Σ, while Σ^∞ denotes all infinite sequences generated from Σ. Given a sequence s, we use $|s|$, $\mathbf{tail}(s)$, and $\mathbf{head}(s)$ to denote the length, tail, and head of s, respectively. $s_1 \bullet s_2$ denotes the concatenation of the sequences s_1 and s_2, and $s_1 \preceq s_2$ denotes that s_1 is a prefix of s_2. $s \restriction A$ stands for the sequence obtained by removing all events not in Σ from s. If A is a singleton $\{a\}$, $s \restriction A$ is abbreviated as $s \restriction a$. $s \downarrow b$ counts the number of occurrences of b in s.

2.2 Interface

An interface $I = \langle FDec, MDec \rangle$ declares a set of *fields* and a set of *operation signatures* without providing any semantic information of their designs and implementations. Here, for the sake of encapsulation, all fields declared in an interface are assumed to be *local* to the underpinning contract and component and therefore are not accessible to its environments. The environments can only access the declared fields via the declared methods[1]. Each field in *FDec* has the form $x : T$ of a variable with its type, and an operation $m(\mathbf{in}\ inx, \mathbf{out}\ outx) \in MDec$ declares a name for the operation and its input parameters and output parameters with their types. For simplicity, we do not deal with data types formally and assume

---

[1] In fact, such an assumption can be relaxed. In many cases, the relaxation will improve the ease in developing complex systems, typically, embedded systems.

that a method has at most one input parameter and one output parameter and is written in the form $m(\mathbf{in}\,u, \mathbf{out}\,v)$ in what follows.

Example 1. Consider a buffer of integers. It has an interface that enables the user to put data in and get data from the buffer:

$$B_1 = \langle buff{:}seq(int), \{put(\mathbf{in}\,x{:}int), get(\mathbf{out}\,y{:}int)\}\rangle,$$

where $seq(int)$ is the type of finite sequences of integers.

Interfaces can be *merged* and *extended* by adding new operations [2].

2.3   Contract

A contract of an interface of a component provides semantic information that specifies how the interface can be used and allows us to define the dynamic behavior of the component on the interface. Here, we are only concerned with components of concurrent and distributed software systems and thus only interested in the *functionality* and *interaction protocols* of components, leaving real-time and other non-functional quality of services (QoS) out of the scope of this paper. Formally, a **contract** is a tuple $Ctr(I, Init, MSpec, Prot)$, where

- I is an interface;
- *Init* is a predicate that defines the initial values of the fields in $I.FDec$;
- *MSPec* assigns each operation $m(x; y)$ a *static functionality specification* as pair of *pre* and *postconditions* of the form $p(x, I.FDec) \vdash R(x, I.FDec, y', I.FDec')$, where non-primed and primed variables represents the values of the variables in the pre and post state of the execution of the operation, respectively. If the precondition $p(x, I.FDec)$ is true, the pair will be abbreviated as $\vdash R(x, I.FDec, y', I.FDec')$;
- *Prot* is called the *protocol* of the interface, which is a set of finite sequences of method call events. Each sequence is of the form $m_1, \ldots, m_k$.

Example 2. For the buffer interface in Example 1, the following contract Ctr_B defines a one-place buffer:

$$Init \stackrel{def}{=} |buff| = 0$$
$$MSpec(put(\mathbf{in}\,x{:}int)) \stackrel{def}{=} (\vdash buff' = \langle x \rangle \bullet buff)$$
$$MSpec(get(\mathbf{out}\,y{:}int)) \stackrel{def}{=} (\vdash buff' = \mathbf{tail}(buff) \wedge y' = \mathbf{head}(buff))$$
$$Prot \stackrel{def}{=} (put; get)^* + (put; (get; put)^*)$$

In many applications, the protocols can be specified as regular expressions and in such a case protocol compatibility can be automatically checked.

A pair of pre and postconditions is called a *design* in [7]. It is proven there that designs are closed under all imperative programming constructors such as assignment, sequential composition, conditional choice, recursion and so on. These constructors are all monotonic with respect to the *refinement* order among designs. In [8], we showed how to define an object-oriented program as a design too. Therefore, the model of contracts of interfaces can be safely used as a common semantic model of different programming languages and paradigms to support interoperability of components.

For theoretical treatment of contracts and their refinement, the designs of operations and the interaction protocol can be combined by the notion of *guarded designs* [2].

A guarded design is a pair of a *guard* g and a design D, denoted by $g\&D$, and defined by $D \lhd g \rhd Idle^2$, meaning that the caller is forced to wait if the guard condition does not hold when invoking the method, otherwise it behaves as the design D. We have proven in [2] that guarded designs are closed under all programming constructors, and these constructors are all monotonic with respect to the *refinement* order.

A *reactive contract* is a triple $Ctr = (I, Init, MSpec)$, where $MSpec$ assigns each operation $m(x; y)$ in the interface I with a *guarded design*. In what follows, we use g_m to denote the guard part of $MSpec(m)$, for any $m \in MDec$.

Example 3. The contract in Example 2 can have an equivalent reactive version:

$$Init \stackrel{def}{=} |buff|=0$$
$$MSpec(put(\textbf{in}\,x{:}int)) \stackrel{def}{=} (|buff| = 0)\&(\vdash buff' = \langle x \rangle)$$
$$MSpec(get(\textbf{out}\,y{:}int)) \stackrel{def}{=} (|buff| = 1)\&(\vdash buff' = \langle\rangle \wedge y' = \textbf{head}(buff))$$

Given a reactive contract $Ctr = (I, Init, MSpec)$, its dynamic behavior is defined by its sets of failures and divergences $(\mathcal{F}(Ctr), \mathcal{D}(Ctr))$. Each method call $m(u, v)$ includes two events $?m(u)$ for receiving an invocation and $m(v)!$ for sending a return to the caller. Therefore, each trace in failures and divergences is of the form $?m_1(u_1), m_1(v_1)!, \ldots, ?m_n(u_n), m_n(v_n)!$ or $?m_1(u_1), m_1(v_1)!, \ldots, ?m_n(u_n)$. The failures and divergences are defined as:

- $\mathcal{D}(Ctr)$ consists of the sequences of interactions between Ctr and its environment which lead the contract to a divergent state.
- $\mathcal{F}(Ctr)$ is the set of pairs (s, X), where s is a sequence of interactions between Ctr and its environment, and X denotes a set of methods to which the contract may refuse to respond after executing s. A failure (s, X) should be one of the following cases:
  1. $s = \langle ?m_1(x_1), m_1(y_1)!, \ldots, ?m_k(x_k), m_k(y_k)! \rangle$ and $\forall m \in X.\neg g_m$, $k \geq 0$. If $k = 0$ then $s = \langle\rangle$. This corresponds to the case when the system reaches a state where none of the guards of the events in X is true, after executing s.
  2. $s = \langle ?m_1(x_1), m_1(y_1)!, \ldots, ?m_k(x_k) \rangle$ and $m_k! \notin X$. This corresponds to the case when the operation m_k is waiting to output its result, performing any of other operations will result in a failure, because it is assumed that the execution of a method is atomic in the sense that the method is either executed completely, or not at all, no other methods can interrupt its execution.
  3. $s = \langle ?m_1(x_1), m_1(y_1)!, \ldots, ?m_k(x_k) \rangle$ and X could be any set of methods, where the execution of m_k enters a waiting state.

---

^{2} This is the shorthand of **if** g **then** D **else** $Idle$.

4. Finally, $s \in \mathcal{D}(Ctr)$ and X can be any set of methods. That is, a divergent trace with any set of methods always forms a failure.

Example 4. The dynamic behaviour of the buffer of Example 3 can be described by the following *failure/divergence* model:

$$\mathcal{D} = \emptyset,$$
$$\mathcal{F} = \{(s, X) \mid \exists k \in \mathbb{N}.((s = \langle S(k)\rangle \wedge X \subseteq \overline{\{?put\}})$$
$$\vee (s = \langle S(k), ?put(x_{k+1})\rangle \wedge X \subseteq \overline{\{put!\}})$$
$$\vee (s = \langle S(k), ?put(x_{k+1}), !put()\rangle \wedge X \subseteq \overline{\{?get\}})$$
$$\vee (s = \langle S(k), ?put(x_{k+1}), put()!, ?get()\rangle \wedge X \subseteq \overline{\{get!\}}))\},$$

where

$$S(k) \stackrel{def}{=} ?put(x_1), put()!, ?get(), get(x_1)!, ...?put(x_k), put()!, ?get(), get(x_k)!,$$
$$\overline{Y} \stackrel{def}{=} \{?put, put!, ?get, get!\} - Y.$$

The following notion of *refinement* allows us to compare and substitute components according to their contracts.

Definition 1. *Let Ctr_1 and Ctr_2 be two contracts. We say that Ctr_1 is* refined *by Ctr_2, denoted by $Ctr_1 \sqsubseteq Ctr_2$, if*

1. *Ctr_2 provides the same services as Ctr_1, i.e. $Ctr_2.MDec = Ctr_1.MDec$,*
2. *Ctr_2 is not easier to diverge than Ctr_1, i.e. $\mathcal{D}(Ctr_2) \subseteq \mathcal{D}(Ctr_1)$, and*
3. *Ctr_2 is not easier to deadlock than Ctr_1, i.e. $\mathcal{F}(Ctr_2) \subseteq \mathcal{F}(Ctr_1)$.*

Ctr_1 *and* Ctr_2 *are* equivalent, *denoted by* $Ctr_1 \equiv Ctr_2$, *if they refine each other.*

For the full refinement calculus of components, we refer the reader to [3].

2.4 Component

A component is an implementation of a contract of its provided interface. To implement such a contract, the component may *use* services provided by other components. These services are called *required services* and are specified as a *contract* of an interface that is called the *required interface*.

Formally, a *component C* is a tuple $(I, Init, MCode, PriMDec, PriMCode, InMDec)$, where

1. *I and *Init* are its interface and initial condition, respectively;*
2. *PriMDec* is a set of method declarations that are internal to the component;
3. *MCode* (*PriMCode*) maps each method m in *I.MDec* (resp. *PriMDec*) to a program of a underlining programming language. However, according to the results of [7], any program can be abstracted as a *guarded command g&c*, further to a *guarded design*. W.l.o.g., we always assume that the two functions map each method to a guarded command from now on.
4. *InMDec* denotes a required interface which operations may be called in the implementations of the operations in *PriMCode* and *I.MDec*, but not declared there.

We use $C.I$, $C.Init$, $C.MCode$, $C.PriMDec$, $C.PriMCode$ and $C.InMDec$ to denote the corresponding parts of C.

According to [7], a guarded command $g\&c$ can always be defined as a guarded design $Dsn(g\&c)$. The command c may contain both invocations to methods in $PriMDec$ and $InMDec$. Once the code of the private commands are given, their semantics can be used for the calculation of $Dsn(g\&c)$. However, $Dsn(g\&c)$ also depends on the given contract of the required interface. Therefore, the semantics of component C is defined to be the contract function $[\![C]\!](\cdot)$ such that for any given contract $InCtr$ of the required interface $InMDec$, $[\![C]\!](InCtr)$ is the contract of the provided interface $I.MDec$ in which the guarded design of each operation m is calculated by $Dsn(MCode(m))$ from the code of $PriMDec$ and the given required contract. A component C is called *closed* if it does not require external services.

2.5 Chaining Components Together

It is a natural way to compose components by chaining the provided operations of one component to the required operation of the other.

Definition 2. *Let C_1 and C_2 be components such that $C_1.I.FDec \cap C_2.I.FDec = \emptyset$, $C_1.I.MDec \cap C_2.I.MDec = \emptyset$ and $C_1.PriMDec \cap C_2.PriMDec = \emptyset$. Then the chaining C_1 to C_2, denoted by $C_1\rangle\!\rangle C_2$, is the component with*

- $(C_1\rangle\!\rangle C_2).FDec \stackrel{def}{=} C_1.FDec \cup C_2.FDec,$
- $(C_1\rangle\!\rangle C_2).InMDec \stackrel{def}{=} (C_2.InMDec \cup C_1.InMDec) - (C_2.MDec \cup C_1.MDec),$
- $(C_1\rangle\!\rangle C_2).MDec \stackrel{def}{=} C_1.MDec \cup C_2.MDec,$
- $(C_1\rangle\!\rangle C_2).Init \stackrel{def}{=} C_1.Init \wedge C_2.Init,$
- $(C_1\rangle\!\rangle C_2).Code \stackrel{def}{=} C_1.Code \cup C_2.Code,$ *and*
- $(C_1\rangle\!\rangle C_2).PriCode \stackrel{def}{=} C_1.PriCode \cup C_2.PriCode.$

It is easy to show that the chaining operator is monotonic w.r.t. the refinement order of components [2]. In the special case when $(C_1.InMDec \cup C_2.InMDec) \cap (C_1.MDec \cup C_2.MDec) = \emptyset$, the chaining C_1 to C_2 is called *disjoint union* and denoted as $C_1 \| C_2$. Some other operators over components have also been defined in [2] such as *renaming, feedback* and *hiding*.

Example 5. Define two buffer components C_1 and C_2 as follows

$$
\begin{aligned}
C_1.FDec &= \{buff_1 : Seq(int)\} \\
C_1.MDec &= \{put(\mathbf{in}\ x{:}int), get_1(\mathbf{out}\ y{:}int)\} \\
C_1.Code(put) &= (buff_1 := \langle x \rangle) \lhd buff_1 = \langle \rangle \rhd (put_1(\mathbf{head}(buff_1)); buff_1 := \langle x \rangle) \\
C_1.Code(get_1) &= (buff_1 \neq \langle \rangle) \longrightarrow (y := \mathbf{head}(buff_1); buff_1 = \langle \rangle) \\
C_1.InMDec &= \{put_1(\mathbf{in}\ x{:}int)\}
\end{aligned}
$$

$$
\begin{aligned}
C_2.FDec &= \{buff_2 : Seq(int)\} \\
C_2.MDec &= \{put_1(\mathbf{in}\ x{:}int), get(\mathbf{out}\ y{:}int)\} \\
C_2.Code(put_1) &= (buff_2 = \langle \rangle) \longrightarrow buff_2 := \langle x \rangle \\
C_2.Code(get) &= (y := \mathbf{head}(buff_2); buff_2 := \langle \rangle) \lhd buff_2 \neq \langle \rangle \rhd get_1(y) \\
C_2.InMDec &= \{get_1(\mathbf{in}\ y{:}int)\}
\end{aligned}
$$

Then, $C_1\rangle\rangle C_2$ is shown in Fig.1 (a), hiding get_1 in $C_1\rangle\rangle C_2$, i.e. $(C_1\rangle\rangle C_2)\backslash\{get_1\}$ is shown in Fig.1 (b).

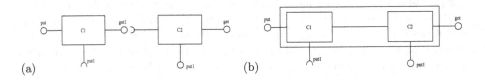

(a)   (b)

Fig. 1. (a) Chaining Composition, (b) Hiding After Chaining

3   Processes: A Model of Glue and Application Programs

In addition to building new components by applying the component operators defined in the previous section to existing components, we often need to *glue* existing components with a program to form a new component. Because in the most cases, we have to restrict the behaviour of the existing components and coordinate them in order to construct a new component from them. Thus, these component operators will not be applicable any more. For example, it is impossible to simply apply the chaining operator to two one-place buffers with the same contract defined in Example 3 to produce a two-place buffer as we did in Example 5.

Glue code in general has different characteristics from components and we model it as *a process*. Like a component, a process has an interface declaring its own local variables and methods and its behavior is specified by a process contract. Unlike a component which passively waits for a client to call its provided services, a process is active and has its own flow of control on when to call out or to wait for a call to its provided services. For such an active process, we cannot have separate contracts for the provided interface and required interface, because we cannot have separate specifications of outgoing calls and incoming calls [2].

Glue codes and application programs play different roles in component-based software development. However, their behavior shares common characteristics. Application programs have their own control flows, and carry out their own computation task by using services provided by components, interacting with components in the same way as a glue program.

In this section, we define the model of processes and the glue composition of a process and a component. For simplicity and predictability, we assume that processes do not provide methods to their environment and do not communicate directly with each other. They are loosely coupled and can only communicate via invoking methods of components. The composition of processes is defined by interleaving and yields a new process.

3.1   Processes

The interface of a process is the access point through which the process invokes the operations of components. The process also carries out local computation by changing its local variables.

Definition 3. *A process interface I is a pair $\langle FDec, MDec \rangle$, where FDec is a set of field declarations, and MDec is a set of method invocation signatures. Each of them is of the form $!m(\mathbf{in}\, u : U, \mathbf{out}\, v : V)$.*

A process contract Ctr is a triple $\langle I, Init, MSpec \rangle$, where I is a process interface, Init and MSpec are defined same as in a reactive contract.

We use the notation $\overline{I.MDec}$ to denote the set $\{m \mid !m(\mathbf{in}\, u : U, \mathbf{out}\, v : V) \in I.MDec\}$.

Example 6. As shown in Fig.2 (a), a three-place buffer is built by gluing two one-place buffers defined in Example 3. The contract of the glue process is

$$
\begin{aligned}
I.FDec &= \{tmp : seq(int)\} \\
I.MDec &= \{!put(\mathbf{in}\, u : int), !get(\mathbf{out}\, v : int)\} \\
Init &= |tmp| = 0 \\
MSpec(!put(u)) &= \{u, tmp\} : |tmp| > 0 \,\& \vdash u' = \mathbf{head}(tmp) \wedge tmp' = \langle\rangle \\
MSpec(!get(v)) &= \{v, tmp\} : |tmp| = 0 \,\& \vdash tmp' = \langle v \rangle
\end{aligned}
$$

As shown in the Fig.2 (b), to construct a two-place buffer, we need a new component that assures the execution of sequence $get_1(x), put_2(x)$ is not interrupted. Here, $M.Code(move) = \{get_1(u); put_2(u)\}$

The dynamic behavior of a process contract is defined on the basis of the observable events of the forms $!m(u)$ for making an invocation and $m(v)?$ for receiving a return from the invoked component. These are the *synchronization complementary events* of $?m(u)$ and $m(v)!$ in the behavior of a component contract.

$\mathcal{F}(Ctr)$ and $\mathcal{D}(Ctr)$ of a process contract Ctr are defined as:

- $\mathcal{D}(Ctr)$ consists of the sequences of interactions between Ctr and its environment which lead the contract to a divergent state. Each of such sequences is

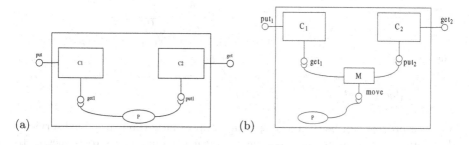

(a)   (b)

Fig. 2. (a) Gluing Two One-place Buffers Forms a Three-place Buffer, (b) Gluing Two One-place Buffers Forms a Two-place Buffer

of the form $\langle !m_1(x_1), m_1(y_1)?, \ldots, !m_k(x_k), m_k(y_k)?, !m_{k+1}(x_{k+1})\rangle \cdot s$, where s is any sequence of method calls and the execution of m_{k+1} diverges.

- $\mathcal{F}(Ctr)$ is the set of pairs (s, X) where s is a sequence of interactions between Ctr and its environment, and X denotes a set of methods that the contract may refuse to respond to after engaging all events in s. Any $(s, X) \in \mathcal{F}$ should be one of the following cases:

  1. $s = \langle !m_1(x_1), m_1(y_1)?, \ldots, !m_k(x_k), m_k(y_k)?\rangle$ and $\forall m \in X.\neg g_m$, $k \geq 0$. If $k = 0$ then $s =<>$. This case represents that each method in X cannot be engaged after executing the sequence of calls, because their guards do not hold in the state.
  2. $s = \langle !m_1(x_1), m_1(y_1)?, \ldots, !m_k(x_k)\rangle$ and $m_k? \notin X$. This corresponds to the case where the contract is waiting for the return.
  3. $s = \langle !m_1(x_1), m_1(y_1)?, \ldots, !m_k(x_k)\rangle$ and X could be any set of methods. Here the execution of m_k enters a waiting state.
  4. Finally, $s \in \mathcal{D}(Ctr)$ and X can be any set of methods. That is, a divergent trace with any set of methods always forms a failure.

For a divergence free contract, case (4) will disappear. We can combine $!m(x)$ and $m(y)?$ into $m(x, y)$ and describe the failures in terms of sequences over events $m(x, y)$ by removing $!m_k(x_k)$ from the traces in cases (2) and (3) and put the event $m(x, y)$ into the refusal set. Thus, $\mathcal{F}(Ctr)$ can be simply defined as:

1. $s = \langle m_1(x_1, y_1), \ldots, m_k(x_k, y_k)\rangle$ and $\forall m \in X.\neg g_m$; or
2. $s = \langle m_1(x_1, y_1), \ldots m_k(x_k, y_k)\rangle$ and $\forall m \in X$ if m is executed following s, then m must reach a waiting state.

It is worth noting that the difference of failures and divergences of processes and contracts lies in the forms of sequences of method calls, the former's is of the form $!m_1(x_1), m_1(y_1)?, \cdots, !m_k(x_k), m(y_k)?, \cdots$, while the latter's is of the form $?m_1(x_1), m_1(y_1)!, \cdots, ?m_k(x_k), m(y_k)!, \cdots$.

Example 7. The dynamic behaviour of the process given in the Example 6 can be described by the following *failure/divergence* model:

$$\mathcal{D} = \emptyset$$
$$\mathcal{F} = \{(s, X) \mid \exists k \in \mathbb{N}.((s = \langle S'(k)\rangle \wedge X \subseteq \overline{\{!get_1\}})$$
$$\vee\, (s = \langle S(k)', !get_1()\rangle \wedge X \subseteq \overline{\{get_1?\}})$$
$$\vee\, (s = \langle S'(k), !get_1(), get_1(x_{k+1})?\rangle \wedge X \subseteq \overline{\{!put_2\}})$$
$$\vee\, (s = \langle S'(k), !get_1(), get_1(x_{k+1})?, !put_2(x_{k+1})\rangle \wedge X \subseteq \overline{\{put_2?\}}))\}$$

where

$$S'(k) \overset{def}{=} !get_1(), get_1(x_1)?, !put_2(x_1), put_2()?, \ldots, !get_1(), get_1(x_k)?, !put_2(x_k), put_2()?$$
$$\overline{Y} \overset{def}{=} \{!get_1(), get_1()?, !put_2(), put_2()?\} - Y$$

In fact, a process can be seen as a special component without provided services. Therefore, we can apply the chaining operator of components to processes to produce new processes. However, all application of the operator to any two processes P_1 and P_2 will be degenerated to the *disjoint union* of P_1 and P_2, i.e.

$P_1 \parallel P_2$, as P_1 and P_2 both have no provided services. On the other hand, the other operators such as *renaming* and *hiding* can not apply to processes, because from a logical point of view, the names of the required services of a process are bound to the process.

3.2   Composing a Component with a Process

We consider the glue composition of a closed component and a process. If there are a number of closed components to be glued by a process, the disjoint union of these components forms another closed component.

Definition 4. *Let C be a closed component and P be a process that only calls methods provided by C, then the failures and divergences of the synchronization composition $C \parallel [X]P$, denoted as $\mathcal{F}(C \parallel [X]P)$ and $\mathcal{D}(C \parallel [X]P)$ respectively, similarly to [5], are defined as:*

$$\mathcal{D}(C \parallel [X]P)$$
$$= \{a \bullet b \mid \exists s \in T(C), t \in T(P).a \in (s \parallel [X]t) \cap \Sigma^* \wedge (s \in \mathcal{D}(C) \vee t \in \mathcal{D}(P))\}$$

$$\mathcal{F}(C \parallel [X]P)$$
$$= \{(a, Y \cup Z) \mid Y \setminus X = Z \setminus X \wedge \exists s \in T(C) \exists t \in T(P).((s, Y) \in \mathcal{F}(C) \wedge$$
$$(t, Z) \in \mathcal{F}(P) \wedge a \in (s \parallel [X]t))\} \cup \{(a, Y) \mid a \in \mathcal{D}(C \parallel [X]P)\}$$

where $T(Q)$ stands for the set of traces of Q, where Q is either a component or a process; X is the set of synchronized methods; $\Sigma = \{?m(x_i), m(y_i)! \mid m \in C.MDec\}$, $b \in \Sigma^*$ and $s \parallel [X]t$ denotes the parallel operation over traces, e.g. $abc \parallel [\{b,c\}]a'bcd = \{aa'bcd, a'abcd\}$.

We can also apply the hiding operator of CSP to a component C and make any action in X become internal and invisible, denoted as $C \backslash X$. Its dynamic behavior is defined as:

$$\mathcal{D}(C \setminus X) = \{(s \upharpoonright X) \bullet t \mid s \in \mathcal{D}(C) \wedge t \in T(C) \upharpoonright X\}$$
$$\cup \{(a \upharpoonright X) \bullet t \mid t \in T(C) \upharpoonright X \wedge a \in \Sigma^\infty \wedge |a \upharpoonright X| < \infty \wedge \forall s \preceq a.s \in T(C)\}$$
$$\mathcal{F}(C \upharpoonright X) = \{(s \upharpoonright X, Y - X) \mid (s, Y) \in \mathcal{F}(C)\} \cup \{(s, Y) \mid s \in \mathcal{D}(C \setminus X)\}$$

Definition 5. *Let C be a closed component, P a process s.t. $\overline{P.MDec} \subseteq C.MDec$, the gluing composition $C \odot P$ is defined as: $C \odot P \overset{def}{=} (C \parallel [\overline{P.MDec}]P) \setminus \overline{P.MDec}$.*

The following theorem gives an answer to what is the entity obtained by the glue composition.

Theorem 1. *Suppose a closed component C and a process P satisfying the condition $\overline{P.MDec} \subseteq C.MDec$, then $C \odot P$ is a closed component.*

Similarly, we can prove that the glue composition applying to an open component and a process produces an open component. That is,

Theorem 2. *If C is an open component with a required interface InMDec and P is a process that only calls the provided methods of C, then $(C \odot P)$ is an open component with the required interface InMDec.*

The semantics of the open component $(C \odot P)$ is defined as a function that given a contract of the required interface, returns a contract of the provided interface, denoted as $\lambda \, InCtr.(C \odot P)(InCtr)$. It is easy to see that $(C \odot P)(InCtr) = C(InCtr) \odot P$

Example 8. Consider the component given in Fig.2 (a). Its dynamic behaviour is given by the following failures since it is divergence free.

$$\mathcal{F} = \{(tr, X) \mid tr \in \{put_1, get_2\}^* \wedge X \in \mathbb{P}\{put_1, get_2\} \wedge \forall tr_1 \preceq tr.$$
$$(tr_1 \downarrow put_1 - tr_1 \downarrow get_2 \leq 3 \wedge vals(tr_1 \upharpoonright get_2) \preceq vals(tr_1 \upharpoonright put_1)) \wedge$$
$$((tr \downarrow put_1 = tr \downarrow get_2 \wedge X \subseteq \{get_2\}) \vee (tr \downarrow put_1 - tr \downarrow get_2 \leq 2 \wedge X = \emptyset) \vee$$
$$(tr \downarrow put_1 = tr \downarrow get_2 + 2 \wedge X \subseteq \{put_1\}))\}$$

where $vals(s)$ returns the parameters occuring in the sequence s, and $(tr \downarrow put_1 - tr \downarrow get_2)$ is used to compute the number of items stored in the buffer.

3.3   The State-Based Reactive Contract of a Glued Component

In this section, we study how to calculate the "state-based" reactive contract of a glued component in terms of the field variables of its subcomponent and process.

The approach is based on the observation that if there is a sequence of methods $s = \langle m, m_1, \ldots, m_k, n \rangle$ occurring in a trace of $C \parallel [\overline{P.MDec}]P$, where $m, n \notin \overline{P.MDec}$ and $m_1, \ldots, m_k \in \overline{P.MDec}$, the behaviour $[m]; [m_1]; \ldots; [m_n]$ can be considered as a possible behaviour of m in the glued component, where ";" means the sequential composition of guarded designs [7]. The reason is because $m_1, \ldots, m_k$ are hidden and therefore become invisible in the glued component. Thus, for an observable method $m \notin \overline{P.MDec}$, its guarded design is the *non-deterministic* choice [7] of all those possible behaviour. However, it is easy to see that this approach only works when the glued component does not diverge. The divergence freedom can be proved by the theory of CSP and the FDR model checking tool.

Whenever a divergence free trace of $C \parallel [\overline{P.MDec}]P$ has a prefix of the form $\langle m_1, \ldots, m_n, m \rangle$, where $m \notin \overline{P.MDec}$ and $m_1, \ldots, m_n \in \overline{P.MDec}$, we put the behaviour of the invisible sequence $\langle m_1, \ldots, m_n \rangle$ to be part of the initial condition.

Formally, we present our approach as follows: Let C be a closed component and P a process with $\overline{P.MDec} \subseteq C.MDec$. Then the contract for $(C \odot P)$ can be calculated as follows:

$$(C \odot P).FDec \stackrel{def}{=} C.FDec \cup P.FDec$$

$$(C \odot P).MDec \stackrel{def}{=} C.MDec - \{\overline{P.MDec}\}$$

$$(C \odot P).Init \stackrel{def}{=} (C.Init \wedge P.Init) \wedge \sqcap_{tr \in \mathcal{G}}(C.Init \wedge P.Init); [tr]$$

$$(C \odot P).MSpec(m) \stackrel{def}{=} C.MSpec(m) \sqcap_{tr \in \mathcal{Q}(m)} [tr], \quad \forall m \in (C \odot P).MDec$$

where

- $\mathcal{G} \stackrel{def}{=} \{h\tau \mid \exists s \in \Sigma^*, \exists n \in (C \odot P).MDec. (h\tau \in \overline{P.MDec}^+ \wedge h\tau \bullet \langle n \rangle \bullet s \in \mathcal{LT})\}$, which is the set of maximal invisible prefixes of legal traces.

- $\mathcal{Q}(m) \stackrel{def}{=} \{\langle m \rangle \bullet h\tau \mid \exists r, s \in \Sigma^*, \exists n \in (C \odot P).MDec.(h\tau \in \overline{P.MDec}^+ \wedge r \bullet \langle m \rangle \bullet h\tau \bullet \langle n \rangle \bullet s \in LT)\}$. $\mathcal{Q}(m)$ contains all the sequences of the form $\langle m, m_1, \ldots, m_n \rangle$ in each of the divergence free traces of $C \odot P$, where $m_1, \ldots, m_n \in \overline{P.MDec}$.
- $\mathcal{LT} \stackrel{def}{=} \{t \in \mathcal{T}(C) \mid \exists X \in \mathbb{P}(C.MDec). (t, X) \in \mathcal{F}(C \parallel [X]P) \wedge t \notin \mathcal{D}(C \parallel [X]P) \wedge (t \upharpoonright X) \notin \mathcal{D}((C \parallel [X]P) \setminus X)\}$. That is, the legal traces of $C \odot P$ are those that themselves and their projections on $\Sigma - X$ are not divergent .
- $[tr]$ maps each sequence tr to a guarded design which is calculated by sequentially composing the guarded design of each method of tr in turn. The guarded design of each method is defined by the following rules:
  1. $[m^g]$ is $C.MSpec(m)$ if $m \notin \overline{P.MDec}$, otherwise $C.MSpec(m) \wedge P.MSpec(\overline{m})$. It is easy to see that $[m^g]$ is a guarded design, for any $m \in C.MDec$;
  2. if $tr = \langle m_1, m_2, \ldots, m_n \rangle$, then $[tr] = [m_1^g]; [m_2^g]; \ldots; [m_n^g]$. Here, ";" means the sequential composition of (guarded) designs (see [7]).

Here, we have to point out that there may be different way to construct the possible behaviour of an observable method and the initial condition, it can therefore result in different contracts. For example, for the sequence $\langle m \rangle \bullet \tau_1 \bullet \tau_2 \bullet \langle n \rangle$, instead of defining their guarded design as $MSpec(m) \stackrel{def}{=} [m; \tau_1; \tau_2]$ and $MSpec(n) \stackrel{def}{=} [n]$, we can define them as $MSpec(m) \stackrel{def}{=} [m; \tau_1]$ and $MSpec(n) \stackrel{def}{=} [\tau_2; n]$. However, it is easy to prove that all these contracts should refine each other since they share the same failures and divergences as that of $(C \parallel [\overline{P.MDec}]P) \setminus \overline{P.MDec}$.

Example 9. Calculate the contract of the component given in Fig.2 (a) from its dynamic behaviour in Example 8, and the contract of the process and one place buffer given in Example 6 and Example 3 respectively.

$$I.FDec = \{tmp, buff_1, buff_2 : seq(int)\}$$
$$I.MDec = \{put_1(\mathbf{in}\, u : int;\,), get_2(\mathbf{out}\, v : int)\}$$
$$Init = tmp' = \langle \rangle \wedge buff_1' = \langle \rangle \wedge buff_2' = \langle \rangle$$
$$MSpec(put_1) = C_1.MSpec(put_1) \sqcap [put_1; get_1] \sqcap [put_1; get_1; put_2] \sqcap [put_1; put_2]$$
$$\sqcap [put_1; put_2; get_1] \sqcap [put_1; get_1]$$
$$= \{buff_1\} : |buff_1| = 0\& \vdash buff_1' = \langle u \rangle$$
$$\sqcap \{tmp\} : |buff_1| = 0 \wedge |tmp| = 0 \wedge |buff_2| = 0\& \vdash tmp' = \langle u \rangle$$
$$\sqcap \{buff_2\} : |buff_1| = 0 \wedge |tmp| = 0 \wedge |buff_2| = 0\& \vdash buff_2' = \langle u \rangle$$
$$\sqcap \{buff_1, tmp, buff_2\} : |buff_1| = 0 \wedge |tmp| \neq 0 \wedge |buff_2| = 0\&$$
$$\vdash buff_1' = \langle u \rangle \wedge tmp' = \langle \rangle \wedge buff_2' = tmp$$
$$\sqcap \{tmp, buff_2\} : |buff_1| = 0 \wedge |tmp| \neq 0 \wedge |buff_2| = 0\&$$
$$\vdash tmp' = \langle u \rangle \wedge buff_2' = tmp$$
$$\sqcap \{tmp, buff_2\} : |buff_1| = 0 \wedge |tmp| = 0 \wedge |buff_2| \neq 0\&$$
$$\vdash tmp' = \langle u \rangle \wedge buff_2' = tmp$$

Similarly, we can calculate $MSpec(get_2)$. Due to space, we omit it.

This example shows that the calculation of the failures and divergences is quite tedious. However it could be aided by the CSP tool FDR [5].

4   Relative Work

In CBD, how to construct composite components from existing ones is a challenging problem. In the object-oriented programming community, there has been extensive research on attacking this issue. For example, SuperGlue [9], Jiazzi [10], the calculus of assemblages [11] and so on. SuperGlue is a connection-based asynchronous programming model. In SuperGlue, a component is either SuperGlue code or Java code with a set of signals (possibly infinite many), and composing existing components is via connection rules over the signals of the subcomponents defined by SuperGlue Code. While Jiazzi [10] can be used to construct large-scale binary components in Java. Jiazzi components can be thought of as generalizations of Java packages with added support for external linking and separate compilation. Existing Java classes and Jiazzi components can be composed by Jiazzi linker to a new Jiazzi component. The linking is similar to the chaining operator in rCOS. Comparing with SuperGlue and Jiazzi, in our approach, each component is equipped with a provided interface and its contract, optionally as well as a required interface and its contract. Thus, components can be more easily reused across different applications, as the provided interfaces and contracts together with the required interfaces and contracts encapsulate their designs and implementations, as well as their data structures. Furthermore, the interoperability of components is well established in our model, since rCOS acts as the underlying theory of component designs which unifies semantic models of different programming languages and paradigms into the notion of interface contracts. What's more, our approach provides more means to compose new components from existing ones, either by component operators or by glue codes.

SuperGlue, Jiazzi and rCOS all cope with composing (gluing) components statically in the sense that all method names used for composing must be resolved in the moment these components are composed (glued). Whereas the calculus of assemblages [11] can handle the composing (gluing) dynamically. However, there is no the notion of contracts within it either.

[12] investigated the notions of components, composition of components and verification of composed components in an asynchronous interleaving event-based model, called Asynchronous Interleaving Message-passing computation model (AIM), with which the composition of components is interpreted as asynchronous parallel, analogous remark is applied to the composition of properties of components. In fact, we believe what was handled in [12] exactly corresponds to what the chaining operator can do in rCOS. However, rCOS is a combination of event-based model and state-based model, whose event-based model is a synchronous concurrent model in contrast to that of [12], an asynchronous concurrent model. So, rCOS allows different notations and methods for modelling and analysing different aspects of components and processes, such as pre and post conditions for functionality, traces of events for interaction protocols, failures and divergences for the denotational view of dynamic behavior and guarded designs for operational views of dynamic behavior. This supports the separation of concerns and gives the hope of integrating different verification techniques and tools via this common model. In fact, the assume-guarantee proof style

used in [12] can also be easily adopted in our framework. However, our work is not only about assume-guarantee verification in the original setting. When chaining components together, the verification and calculation of the composed components are different from the case when components are glued together. Using verified properties in our framework is more about substitution of proof obligations by theorems proved about services that are used in components or application programs.

There are also various approaches to handle the composition of components in the formal methods community. In [13], a component is defined as a stream process function which maps the input streams of actions to the output streams of actions. The refinement relation between components is defined over a pair of input streams and output streams. rCOS clearly divides the provided contract(input actions) and the required contract(output actions) and can treat them separately, which greatly ease the composition of components. Like rCOS, Reo[1] treats components and glue codes(connectors) as distinct types. The two types build on a common formal foundation, the Abstract Behaviour Types. The Abstract Behaviour Types is very expressive for specification, but it is hard to be linked to implementation language. The notion of guarded design in rCOS can link specifications and OO languages very smoothly.

5   Conclusions and Future Work

We have proposed a model supporting component-based programming. The model unifies the component model developed earlier in [2] and the process model defined here. Processes are introduced to model application programs and glue programs which help developers to build new components from existing ones.

In the proposed model, a typical component-based application consists of a family of components and a number of parallel application processes. Some of the components are reused from a component repository while others are newly built using gluing processes as well as component operators (chaining, service renaming, and service hiding).

As for future work, we need to investigate the following issues:

- In this paper, the method to calculate the resulted contract of the gluing of a component and a process is very complicated and difficult to track. Therefore, as a future work, on one hand, we need to simplify the procedure; on the other hand, we will look into automating the calculation.
- It will be interesting research topic to investigate how different verification techniques and tools can be applied to rCOS.
- We are also interested in investigating on how rCOS can be applied to web service systems, and to deal with quality of services (QoS) of components, such as time and resource constraints.
- Case studies of realistic component systems such as CORBA.

Acknowledgements

We are grateful to Prof. Anders P. Ravn for pointing out many features in the design of our model. We also thank Dr. Volker Stolz and Lu Yang for their comments. Special thanks are also due to the anonymous referees for their valuable suggestions and comments which help us to improve this paper including its contents as well as its presentation so much.

References

1. Arbab, F.: Abstract behavior types: A foundation model for components and their composition. In: de Boer, F.S., Bonsangue, M.M., Graf, S., de Roever, W.-P. (eds.) FMCO 2002. LNCS, vol. 2852, pp. 33–70. Springer, Heidelberg (2003)
2. He, J., Liu, Z., Li, X.: Component software engineering. In: Van Hung, D., Wirsing, M. (eds.) ICTAC 2005. LNCS, vol. 3722, pp. 269–276. Springer, Heidelberg (2005)
3. He, J., Li, X., Liu, Z.: A theory of reactive components. In: Proc. of FACS 2005. ENTCS, vol. 160, pp. 173–195. Elsevier, Amsterdam (2006)
4. Hoare, C.A.R.: Communicating Sequential Processes. Prentice-Hall, Englewood Cliffs (1985)
5. Roscoe, A.: The Theory and Practice of Concurrency. Prentice-Hall, Englewood Cliffs (1997)
6. Chen, X., He, J., Liu, Z., Zhan, N.: Component-based programming. Technical Report UNU-IIST Report No 350 (April 2007)
7. Hoare, C., He, J.: Unifying Theories of Programming. Prentice-Hall International, Englewood Cliffs (1998)
8. He, J., Li, X., Liu, Z.: rCOS: A refinement calculus of object systems. Theoretical Computer Science 365(1-2), 109–142 (2006)
9. McDirmid, S., Hsieh, W.: Superglue: Component programming with object-oriented signals. In: Thomas, D. (ed.) ECOOP 2006. LNCS, vol. 4067, pp. 206–229. Springer, Heidelberg (2006)
10. McDirmid, S., Flatt, M., Hsieh, W.: Jiazzi: New-age components for old-fashioned java. In: Proc. of OOPSLA 2001, pp. 211–222. ACM Press, New York (2001)
11. Liu, Y., Smith, S.: Modules with interfaces for dynamic linking and communication. In: Odersky, M. (ed.) ECOOP 2004. LNCS, vol. 3086, pp. 414–439. Springer, Heidelberg (2004)
12. Xie, F., Browne, J.: Verified systems by composition from verified components. In: FSE 2003, pp. 277–286. ACM, New York (2003)
13. Broy, M., Stølen, K.: Specification and Development of Interactive Systems: FOCUS on Streams, Interfaces, and Refinement. Springer, Heidelberg (2001)

Contract Based Multi-party Service Composition*

Mario Bravetti and Gianluigi Zavattaro

Department of Computer Science, University of Bologna, Italy
{bravetti,zavattar}@cs.unibo.it

Abstract. In the context of Service Oriented Computing, contracts are descriptions of the observable behaviour of services. Contracts have been already successfully exploited to solve the problem of client/service composition. In this paper we consider services where the choice to perform an output may not depend on the environment and we revisit the theory of contracts in order to tackle the problem of composition of multiple services (not only one client with one service). Moreover, we relate our theory of contracts with the theory of testing preorder (interpreted as a subcontract relation) and we show that a compliant group of contracts is still compliant if every contract is replaced by one of its subcontract.

1 Introduction

Service Oriented Computing (SOC) is a novel paradigm for distributed computing based on services intended as autonomous and heterogeneous components that can be published and discovered via standard interface languages and publish/discovery protocols. One of the peculiarities of Service Oriented Computing, distinguishing it from other distributed computing paradigms (such as component based software engineering), is that it is centered around the so-called *message oriented architectures*. This means that, given a set of collaborating services, the current state of their interaction is stored inside the exchanged messages and not only within the services. From a practical viewpoint, this means that it is necessary to include, in the exchanged messages, the so-called correlation information that permits to a service to associate a received message to the correct session of interaction (in fact, the same service could be contemporarily involved in different sessions at the same time).

Web Services is the most prominent service oriented technology: Web Services publish their interface expressed in WSDL, they are discovered through the UDDI protocol, and they are invoked using SOAP.

Even if one of the declared goal of Web Services is to support the automatic discovery of services, this is not yet practically achieved. Two main problems are still to be satisfactorily solved. The first one, investigated by the semantic web research community, is concerned with the lack of semantic information in the description of services. The second problem, addressed in this paper, is concerned

---

* Research partially funded by EU Integrated Project Sensoria, contract n. 016004.

F. Arbab and M. Sirjani (Eds.): FSEN 2007, LNCS 4767, pp. 207–222, 2007.

with the problem of guaranteeing that the interacting services are compliant in the sense that their behaviours are complementary. In particular, it is important to check whether a set of services, once combined in order to collaborate, are stuck-free.

In order to be able to check the compliance of the composed services, it is necessary that the services expose in their interface also the description of their expected behaviour. In the service oriented computing literature, this kind of information is referred to as the *service contract* [1]. More precisely, the service contract describes the sequence of input/output operations that the service intends to execute within a session of interaction with other services.

Contracts have been already investigated in the context of client-service interaction [2]. In this paper, we consider a different scenario: instead of analysing client-service architectures, we assume that several services interact according to a peer-to-peer architecture. Through the analysis of the service contracts we want to define a theory that, on the one hand, permits to formally verify whether the composed services are compliant (thus giving rise to a correct composition) and, on the other hand, permits to replace a service with another one without affecting the correctness of the overall system. In this case we say that the initially expected contract is replaced with one of its *subcontract*.

We foreseen at least two main applications for our theory of contracts. On the one hand, it can be exploited in the *service discovery* phase. Consider, for instance, a service system defined in terms of the contracts that should be exposed by each of the service components. The actual services to be combined could be retrieved independently one from the other (e.g. querying contemporarily different service registries) collecting that services that either exposes the expected contract, or one of its subcontract. On the other hand, the notion of subcontract could be useful in *service updates* in order to ensure backward compatibility. Consider, e.g., a service that should be updated in order to provide new functionalities; if the new version exposes a subcontract of the previous service, our theory ensures that the new service is a correct substitute for the previous one.

1.1 Technical Contribution

We define two process calculi, one for contracts and one for systems composed of contracts. The latter is an extension of the former. The calculus for contracts is a typical process calculus distinguishing between deadlock and successful termination. This distinction is necessary in order to model the fact that a service could internally deadlock due to its internal parallelism. Another peculiarity of the calculus is that the decision to execute output actions may not depend on the other services in the system. In more technical terms, we do not admit mixed choices $a + \overline{b}$ where a is an input action while $\overline{b}$ is an output. This reflects the fact that the current service oriented technologies (such as Web Services) are based on asynchronous communication and, as formally discussed in [3], mixed choice is not reasonably implementable in asynchronously communicating concurrent systems. We avoid mixed choices imposing that all output actions $\overline{b}$ are preceded by an internal τ action; in this way a service first decide to execute the output, and only subsequently the message becomes actually available.

The second calculus for systems permits to compose in parallel contracts that interact within a session, and to add restrictions in order to model local channel names, that can be used only inside subsessions involving a proper subset of the composed contracts.

The calculus is used to define our notion of correct composed system; a system is correct if all the composed contracts are ensured to reach successful completion. Then, we introduce contract refinement as the possibility to independently replace each contract with a subcontract without breaking correctness. In general, this notion of refinement is rather complex to be checked mainly because it is defined in order to permit the contemporary and independent refinement of the contracts. Our main result is that in our calculus this notion of refinement coincides with a more treatable subcontract relation in which only one contract is replaced and the other ones are left unchanged. This new notion characterizes refinement in a testing scenario, thus giving us the possibility to resort to the theory of testing [4,5]. In particular, we show how to use the theory of *should-testing* [5] to prove that one contract is a subcontract of another one.

1.2   Related Work

As stated above, we resort to the theory of testing. There are some relevant differences between our form of testing and the traditional one proposed by De Nicola-Hennessy [4]. The most relevant difference is that, besides requiring the success of the test, we impose also that the tested process should successfully complete its execution. This further requirement has important consequences; for instance, we do not distinguish between the always unsuccessful process $\mathbf{0}$ and other processes, such as $a.\mathbf{1} + a.b.\mathbf{1}$,[1] for which there are no guarantees of successful completion in any possible context. Another relevant difference is in the treatment of divergence: we do not follow the traditional catastrophic approach, but the fair approach introduced by the theory of should-testing of Rensink-Vogler [5]. In fact, we do not impose that all computations must succeed, but that all computations can always be extended in order to reach success.

Contracts have been investigated also by Fournet et al. [6] and Carpineti et al. [2].

In [6] contracts are CCS-like processes; a generic process P is defined as compliant to a contract C if, for every tuple of names $\tilde{a}$ and process Q, whenever $(\nu\tilde{a})(C|Q)$ is stuck-free then also $(\nu\tilde{a})(P|Q)$ is. Our notion of contract refinement differs from stuck-free conformance mainly because we consider a different notion of stuckness. In [6] a process state is stuck (on a tuple of channel names $\tilde{a}$) if it has no internal moves (but it can execute at least one action on one of the channels in $\tilde{a}$). In our approach, an end-states different from successful termination is stuck (independently of any tuple $\tilde{a}$). Thus, we distinguish between internal deadlock and successful completion while this is not the case in [6]. Another difference follows from the exploitation of the restriction $(\nu\tilde{a})$; this is used

---

[1] We use $\mathbf{0}$ to denote unsuccessful termination and $\mathbf{1}$ for successful completion.

in [6] to explicitly indicate the local channels of communication used between the contract C and the process Q. In our context we can make a stronger *closed-world* assumption (corresponding to a restriction on all channel names) because service contracts do not describe the entire behaviour of a service, but the flow of execution of its operations inside one session of communication.

The closed-world assumption is considered also in [2] where, as in our case, a service oriented scenario is considered. In particular, in [2] a theory of contracts is defined for investigating the compatibility between one client and one service. Our paper consider multi-party composition where several services are composed in a peer-to-peer manner. Moreover, we impose service substitutability as a mandatory property for our notion of refinement; this does not hold in [2] where it is not in general possible to substitute a service exposing one contract with another one exposing a subcontract. Another relevant difference is that the contracts in [2] comprises also mixed choices.

Structure of the paper. Section 2 reports syntax and semantics of the process calculi. In Section 3 we describe our theory of contracts and we prove our main results. Finally, Section 4 reports some conclusive remarks.

2   Syntax and Semantics of the Process Calculi

In this Section we introduce incrementally the two calculi. The first one is the calculus for contracts; it is a typical calculus comprising two possible final states (failure or success), input and output prefixes, sequencing, choice, parallel composition, restriction and repetition.

2.1   Definition of Contracts

We assume a denumerable set of names $\mathcal{N} = \{a, b, c, ...\}$. The set $\mathcal{N}_{loc} = \{a_* \mid a \in \mathcal{N}\}$ is the set of local names. We take α to range over the set of all names $\mathcal{N}_{all} = \mathcal{N} \cup \mathcal{N}_{loc}$. The set $\mathcal{A} = \mathcal{N} \cup \{\overline{a} \mid a \in \mathcal{N}\}$ is the set of input and output actions. The set $\mathcal{A}_{loc} = \mathcal{N}_{loc} \cup \{\overline{a}_* \mid a_* \in \mathcal{N}_{loc}\}$ is the set of input and output local actions. We take β to range over the set of all actions $Act = \mathcal{A}_{loc} \cup \mathcal{A} \cup \{\tau\}$, where τ denotes an internal computation.

Definition 1 (Contracts). *The syntax of contracts is defined by the following grammar*

$$C ::= \mathbf{0} \mid \mathbf{1} \mid \tau \mid \alpha \mid \tau;\overline{\alpha} \mid$$
$$C;C \mid C+C \mid C|C \mid C\backslash M \mid C^*$$

where $M \subseteq \mathcal{N}_{loc}$. The set of all contracts C is denoted by $\mathcal{P}_{con}$.

We consider four possible atoms: unsuccessful termination $\mathbf{0}$, successful termination $\mathbf{1}$, input action a, and silent move τ. Output actions always appear after an internal move τ. The operators are: sequencing $\_;\_$, choice $\_+\_$, parallel $\_|\_$, restriction $\_ \backslash M$, and repetition $\_^*$.

In the following we will omit trailing "1" when writing contracts and, given a set of names M, with $\overline{M} = \{\overline{a} \mid a \in M\}$ we denote the set output actions performable on those names.

The operational semantics of contracts is defined by the rules in Table 1 (plus the omitted symmetric rules). We take λ to range over the set of labels $\mathcal{L} = Act \cup \{\surd\}$, where $\surd$ denotes successful termination.

Table 1. Semantic rules for contracts (symmetric rules omitted)

$$1 \xrightarrow{\surd} 0 \qquad \beta \xrightarrow{\beta} 1$$

$$\frac{C \xrightarrow{\lambda} C'}{C+D \xrightarrow{\lambda} C'} \qquad \frac{C \xrightarrow{\lambda} C' \quad \lambda \neq \surd}{C;D \xrightarrow{\lambda} C';D} \qquad \frac{C \xrightarrow{\surd} C' \quad D \xrightarrow{\lambda} D'}{C;D \xrightarrow{\lambda} D'}$$

$$\frac{C \xrightarrow{a_*} C' \quad D \xrightarrow{\overline{a}_*} D'}{C|D \xrightarrow{\tau} C'|D'} \qquad \frac{C \xrightarrow{\surd} C' \quad D \xrightarrow{\surd} D'}{C|D \xrightarrow{\surd} C'|D'} \qquad \frac{C \xrightarrow{\lambda} C' \quad \lambda \neq \surd}{C|D \xrightarrow{\lambda} C'|D}$$

$$\frac{C \xrightarrow{\lambda} C' \quad \lambda \notin M \cup \overline{M}}{C\backslash M \xrightarrow{\lambda} C'\backslash M} \qquad C^* \xrightarrow{\surd} 0 \qquad \frac{C \xrightarrow{\lambda} C'}{C^* \xrightarrow{\lambda} C';C^*}$$

The operational semantics is rather standard for process calculi with sequential composition, where the $\surd$ label is used to explicitly denote completion. The unique relevant remark is that synchronization within a contract is permitted only on local names a_*; the synchronization on global names between different contracts will be considered in the next calculus used to model the composition of contracts.

In the remainder of the paper we use the following notations: $C \xrightarrow{\lambda}$ to mean that there exists C' such that $C \xrightarrow{\lambda} C'$ and, given a sequence of labels $w = \lambda_1\lambda_2\cdots\lambda_{n-1}\lambda_n$ (possibly empty, i.e., $w = \varepsilon$), we use $C \xrightarrow{w} C'$ to denote the sequence of transitions $C \xrightarrow{\lambda_1} C_1 \xrightarrow{\lambda_2} \cdots \xrightarrow{\lambda_{n-1}} C_{n-1} \xrightarrow{\lambda_n} C'$ (in case of $w = \varepsilon$ we have $C' = C$, i.e., $C \xrightarrow{\varepsilon} C$).

The main results reported in this paper are consequences of a property of contracts that we call *output persistency*. This property states that once a contract decides to execute an output, its actual execution is mandatory in order to successfully complete the execution of the contract. In order to formally prove this property we need to formalize two (easy to prove) preliminary lemmata.

Lemma 1. *Let $C \in \mathcal{P}_{con}$ s.t. $C \xrightarrow{\overline{a}}$ and $C \xrightarrow{\lambda} C'$, then $\lambda \neq \surd$.*

Lemma 2. *Let $C \in \mathcal{P}_{con}$ s.t. $C \xrightarrow{\overline{a}}$ and $C \xrightarrow{\beta} C'$ with $\beta \neq \overline{a}$, then $C' \xrightarrow{\overline{a}}$.*

Output persistency is a trivial consequence of these two lemmata.

Proposition 1 (Output persistency). *Let* $C \in \mathcal{P}_{con}$ *be a contract such that* $C \xrightarrow{w} C' \xrightarrow{\bar{a}}$. *We have that, for every* C'' *such that* $C' \xrightarrow{w'} C''$ *and* $C'' \xrightarrow{\surd}$, *the string* w' *must include* $\bar{a}$.

2.2 Composing Contracts

We now introduce the calculus for modeling systems of composed contracts. This is an extension of the previous calculus; the basic terms are contracts under execution denoted with $[C]$.

Besides the parallel composition operator $\|$, we consider also restriction $\backslash\backslash$ in order to model the possibility to open local channels of interaction among contracts. This operator of restriction distinguishes between input and output operations; this allows us, e.g., to model a system composed of two contracts C_1 and C_2 such that channel a is used for communications from C_1 to C_2 and channel b is used for communications along the opposite directions:

$$([C_1]\backslash\backslash\{a,\bar{b}\}) \parallel ([C_2]\backslash\backslash\{\bar{a},b\})$$

Definition 2 (Contract composition). *The syntax of contract compositions is defined by the following grammar*

$$P \quad ::= \quad [C] \quad | \quad P\|P \quad | \quad P\backslash\backslash L$$

where $L \subseteq \mathcal{A}$.

In the following we will sometimes omit parenthesis "[ ]" when writing contract compositions and we will call *system* a composition of contracts.

The operational semantics of systems is defined by the rules in Table 2 (plus the omitted symmetric rules).

Table 2. Semantic rules for contract compositions (symmetric rules omitted)

$$\frac{C \xrightarrow{\lambda} C' \quad \lambda \notin \mathcal{A}_{loc}}{[C] \xrightarrow{\lambda} [C']} \qquad \frac{P \xrightarrow{\lambda} P' \quad \lambda \neq \surd}{P\|Q \xrightarrow{\lambda} P'\|Q}$$

$$\frac{P \xrightarrow{a} P' \quad Q \xrightarrow{\bar{a}} Q'}{P\|Q \xrightarrow{\tau} P'\|Q'} \qquad \frac{P \xrightarrow{\surd} P' \quad Q \xrightarrow{\surd} Q'}{P\|Q \xrightarrow{\surd} P'\|Q'} \qquad \frac{P \xrightarrow{\lambda} P' \quad \lambda \notin L}{P\backslash\backslash L \xrightarrow{\lambda} P'\backslash\backslash L}$$

Note that, due to the absence of internal communication of actions of $\mathcal{A}$ inside contracts, when we apply external restriction directly to a contract C, i.e. we consider $[C]\backslash\backslash L$ for some $L \subseteq \mathcal{A}$, we obtain a transition system isomorphic to that of the contract $C\{\mathbf{0}/\beta|\beta \in L\} \backslash \mathcal{N}_{loc}$ or, equivalently, to that of $[C\{\mathbf{0}/\beta|\beta \in L\}]$, where $C\{\mathbf{0}/\beta|\beta \in L\}$ represents the syntactical substitution of $\mathbf{0}$ for every occurence of any subterm β such that $\beta \in L$.

We are now ready to define our notion of correct composition of contracts. Intuitively, a system composed of contracts is correct if all possible computations may guarantee completion; this means that the system is both deadlock and livelock free (there could be an infinite computation, but given any possible prefix of this infinite computation, it can be extended to reach a successfully completed computation).

Definition 3 (Correct contract composition). *A system P is a correct contract composition, denoted $P\downarrow$, if for every P' such that $P \xrightarrow{\tau}^* P'$ there exists P'' such that $P' \xrightarrow{\tau}^* P'' \xrightarrow{\sqrt{}}$.*

As examples of correct contract compositions, you can consider $C_1 \| C_2$ with

$$C_1 = a + b \qquad\qquad C_2 = (\tau; \overline{a}) + (\tau; \overline{b})$$
$$C_1 = a; b \qquad\qquad C_2 = \tau; \overline{a}; \tau; \overline{b}$$
$$C_1 = a + b + c \qquad\qquad C_2 = (\tau; \overline{a}) + (\tau; \overline{b})$$
$$C_1 = (a; b) + (b; a) \qquad\qquad C_2 = (\tau; \overline{a}) \,|\, (\tau; \overline{b})$$
$$C_1 = (a; \tau; \overline{b})^* \qquad\qquad C_2 = \tau; \overline{a}; (b; \tau; \overline{a})^*; b$$

3   Contract Refinement

In this Section we introduce our theory of contracts. The basic idea is to have a notion of refinement of contracts such that, given a system composed of the contracts $C_1, \cdots, C_n$, we can replace each contract C_i with one of its refinements C_i' without breaking the correctness of the system.

Some simple example of refinement follows. Consider the correct system $C_1 \| C_2$ with

$$C_1 = a + b \qquad C_2 = (\tau; \overline{a}) + (\tau; \overline{b})$$

We can replace C_1 with $C_1' = a + b + c$ or C_2 with $C_2' = \tau; \overline{a}$ without breaking the correctness of the system. This example shows a first important intuition: a contract could be replaced with another one that has more external nondeterminism and/or less internal nondeterminism.

Consider now

$$D_1 = a + b + c \qquad D_2 = (\tau; \overline{a}) + (\tau; \overline{b})$$

where we can refine D_1 with $D_1' = a + b + d$. Clearly, this refinement does not hold in general because we could have another correct system

$$D_1 = a + b + c \qquad D_2' = (\tau; \overline{a}) + (\tau; \overline{b}) + (\tau; \overline{c})$$

where such a refinement does not hold. This second example shows that refinement is influenced by the potential actions that could be executed by the other contracts in the system. Indeed, D_1' is not a correct substitute for D_1 because D_2' has the possibility to produce $\overline{c}$.

Based on this intuition, we parameterize our notion of subcontract relation $C' \leq_{I,O} C$ on the set I of inputs, and the set O of outputs, that could be potentilly executed by the other contracts in the system. We will see that $D_1' \leq_{\emptyset,\{a,b\}} D_1$ but $D_1' \not\leq_{\emptyset,\{a,b,c\}} D_1$.

3.1   Subcontract Pre-order

We first define two auxiliary functions that extract from contracts and systems the set of names used in input and output actions, respectively.

Definition 4 (Input and Output sets). *Given the contract $C \in \mathcal{P}_{con}$, we define $I(C)$ (resp. $O(C)$) as the subset of $\mathcal{N}$ of the potential input (resp. ouput) actions of C. Formally, we define $I(C)$ as follows ($O(C)$ is defined similarly):*

$$I(0) = I(1) = I(\tau) = I(\tau; \overline{\alpha}) = \emptyset \qquad\qquad I(\alpha) = \text{if } \alpha \in \mathcal{N} \text{ then } \{\alpha\} \text{ else } \emptyset$$
$$I(C;C') = I(C+C') = I(C|C') = I(C) \cup I(C') \quad I(C \backslash M) = I(C^*) = I(C)$$

Note that the set M in $C \backslash M$ does not influence $I(C \backslash M)$ because it contains only local names outside $\mathcal{N}$. Given the system P, we define $I(P)$ (resp. $O(P)$) as the subset of $\mathcal{N}$ of the potential input (resp. ouput) actions of P. Formally, we define $I(P)$ as follows ($O(P)$ is defined similarly):

$$I([C]) = I(C) \qquad I(P \| P') = I(P) \cup I(P') \qquad I(P \backslash L) = I(P) - L$$

We are now ready to define the notion of subcontract pre-order $C'_i \leq_{I,O} C_i$ in which the substitutability of contract C_i with C'_i is parameterized in the possible input and output actions I and O of the other contracts in the considered system.

More precisely, we consider a correct system $C_1 \backslash I_1 \cup \overline{O}_1 \| \ldots \| C_n \backslash I_n \cup \overline{O}_n$ composed of the contracts $C_1, \cdots, C_n$ following a particular name discipline: the names in I_i (resp. O_i) cannot be used in input (resp. output) actions by the contract C_i. This discipline is guaranteed restricting each contract C_i on the set of actions $I_i \cup \overline{O}_i$. In this particular system, we want to be able to subtitute each of the contract C_i with any contract C'_i such that $C'_i \leq_{I,O} C_i$ where I and O comprise the possible input and output actions that can be executed by the other contracts C_j with $j \neq i$. This last condition can be ensured imposing that

$$\left(\bigcup_{j \neq i} I(C_j) - I_j\right) - O_i \subseteq I \quad \wedge \quad \left(\bigcup_{j \neq i} O(C_j) - O_j\right) - I_i \subseteq O$$

This kind of formula is considered in the subsequent definition that formalizes the notion of subcontract pre-order family.

Definition 5 (Subcontract pre-order family). *A family $\{\leq_{I,O} | I, O \subseteq \mathcal{N}\}$ of pre-orders over $\mathcal{P}_{con}$ is a subcontract pre-order family if, for any $n \geq 1$, contracts $C_1, \ldots, C_n \in \mathcal{P}_{con}$ and $C'_1, \ldots, C'_n \in \mathcal{P}_{con}$ and input and output names $I_1, \ldots, I_n \subseteq \mathcal{N}$ and $O_1, \ldots, O_n \subseteq \mathcal{N}$, we have*

$$(C_1 \backslash I_1 \cup \overline{O}_1 \| \ldots \| C_n \backslash I_n \cup \overline{O}_n) \downarrow \wedge$$
$$\forall i. C'_i \leq_{I'_i, O'_i} C_i \wedge \left(\bigcup_{j \neq i} I(C_j) - I_j\right) - O_i \subseteq I'_i \wedge \left(\bigcup_{j \neq i} O(C_j) - O_j\right) - I_i \subseteq O'_i$$
$$\Rightarrow (C'_1 \backslash I_1 \cup \overline{O}_1 \| \ldots \| C'_n \backslash I_n \cup \overline{O}_n) \downarrow$$

We will prove that there exists a maximal subcontract pre-order family; this is a direct consequence of the output persistency property. In fact, if we consider mixed choice it is easy to prove that there exists no maximal subcontract pre-order family. Consider, e.g., the trivially correct system $C_1 \| C_2$ with $C_1 = a$ and $C_2 = \overline{a}$; we could have two subcontract pre-order families $\leq^1_{I,O}$ and $\leq^2_{I,O}$ such that

$$a + c.\mathbf{0} \leq^1_{\emptyset,\{a\}} a \quad \text{and} \quad \overline{a} + c.\mathbf{0} \leq^1_{\{a\},\emptyset} \overline{a}$$

and

$$a + \overline{c}.\mathbf{0} \leq^2_{\emptyset,\{a\}} a \quad \text{and} \quad \overline{a} + \overline{c}.\mathbf{0} \leq^2_{\{a\},\emptyset} \overline{a}$$

but no subcontract pre-order family $\leq$ could have

$$a + c.\mathbf{0} \leq_{\emptyset,\{a\}} a \quad \text{and} \quad \overline{a} + \overline{c}.\mathbf{0} \leq_{\{a\},\emptyset} \overline{a}$$

because if we refine C_1 with $a + c.\mathbf{0}$ and C_2 with $\overline{a} + \overline{c}.\mathbf{0}$ we achieve the incorrect system $a + c.\mathbf{0} \| \overline{a} + \overline{c}.\mathbf{0}$ that can deadlock after synchronization on channel c.

We will show that the maximal subcontract pre-order family can be achieved defining a coarser form of refinement in which, given any system composed of a set of contracts, refinement is applied to one contract only (thus leaving the other unchanged). We call this form of refinement *singular subcontract pre-order*.

Intuitively a family of pre-orders $\{\leq_{I,O} | I, O \subseteq \mathcal{N}\}$ is a singular subcontract pre-order family whenever the correctness of systems is preserved by refining just one of the contracts. More precisely, for any $n \geq 1$, $C_1, \ldots, C_n \in \mathcal{P}_{con}$, $I_1, \ldots, I_n \subseteq \mathcal{N}$, $O_1, \ldots, O_n \subseteq \mathcal{N}$, $1 \leq i \leq n$ and $C'_i \in \mathcal{P}_{con}$ we require

$$(C_1 \backslash I_1 \cup \overline{O}_1 \| \ldots \| C_i \backslash I_i \cup \overline{O}_i \| \ldots \| C_n \backslash I_n \cup \overline{O}_n) \downarrow \wedge$$
$$C'_i \leq_{I,O} C_i \wedge (\textstyle\bigcup_{j \neq i} I(C_j) - I_j) - O_i \subseteq I \wedge (\textstyle\bigcup_{j \neq i} O(C_j) - O_j) - I_i \subseteq O$$
$$\Rightarrow \quad (C_1 \backslash I_1 \cup \overline{O}_1 \| \ldots \| C'_i \backslash I_i \cup \overline{O}_i \| \ldots \| C_n \backslash I_n \cup \overline{O}_n) \downarrow$$

By exploiting commutativity and associativity of parallel composition, and the fact that the internal behavior of $C_1 \backslash I_1 \cup \overline{O}_1 \| \ldots \| C_n \backslash I_n \cup \overline{O}_n$ is the same as that of $C_1 \| ((C_2 \{\mathbf{0}/\beta | \beta \in I_2 \cup \overline{O}_2\} \| \ldots \| C_n \{\mathbf{0}/\beta | \beta \in I_n \cup \overline{O}_n\}) \backslash O_1 \cup \overline{I}_1)$ we can group the contracts which are not being refined and denote them with a generic term P taken from $\mathcal{P}_{conpar}$, the set of the systems of the form $(C_1 \| \ldots \| C_n) \backslash I \cup \overline{O}$, with $C_i \in \mathcal{P}_{con}$ for all $i \in \{1, \ldots, n\}$ and $I, O \subseteq \mathcal{N}$. Moreover we note that, given $P = (C_1 \| \ldots \| C_n) \backslash I \cup \overline{O} \in \mathcal{P}_{conpar}$, we have $I(P) = (\bigcup_{1 \leq i \leq n} I([C_i])) - I$ and $O(P) = (\bigcup_{1 \leq i \leq n} O([C_i])) - O$.

Definition 6 (Singular subcontract pre-order family). *A family of pre-orders* $\{\leq_{I,O} | I, O \subseteq \mathcal{N}\}$ *is a singular subcontract pre-order family if, for any* $C, C' \in \mathcal{P}_{con}$, $P \in \mathcal{P}_{conpar}$ *we have*

$$(C \| P) \downarrow \wedge C' \leq_{I,O} C \wedge I(P) \subseteq I \wedge O(P) \subseteq O \quad \Rightarrow \quad (C' \| P) \downarrow$$

In order to prove the existence of the maximal subcontract pre-order family, we prove that every family of pre-orders that is a subcontract family is also a singular subcontract family (Theorem 1). Moreover we show that there exists a maximal singular subcontract family and we prove that it also a subcontract family (Theorem 2).

Theorem 1. *If a family of pre-orders $\{\leq_{I,O} |\ I, O \subseteq \mathcal{N}\ \}$ is a subcontract pre-order family then it is also a singular subcontract pre-order family.*

Proof. *Suppose that $\{\leq_{I,O} |\ I, O \subseteq \mathcal{N}\ \}$ is a subcontract pre-order family. Consider $n \geq 1$, $P \in \mathcal{P}_{conpar}$, $C, C' \in \mathcal{P}_{con}$. From $(C\|P)\downarrow$ and $C' \leq_{I,O} C$, where $I(P) \subseteq I$ and $O(P) \subseteq O$, we can derive $(C'\|P)\downarrow$ by just taking in the definition of subcontract pre-order family, $C_1 = C$, $C_1' = C'$, $C_2 \ldots C_n$ and I_1 and O_1 to be such that $P = (C_2\| \ldots \|C_n)\backslash O_1 \cup \bar{I}_1$; $I_2 \ldots I_n$ and $O_2 \ldots O_n$ to be the emptyset; and finally C_i' to be C_i for every $i \geq 2$ (since $\leq_{I,O}$ are pre-orders we have $C \leq_{I,O} C$ for every I, O and C).*

From the simple structure of their definition we can easily deduce that singular subcontract pre-order families have maximum, i.e. there exists a singular subcontract pre-order family such that every pre-order $\leq_{I,O}$ in the family includes all the corresponding pre-order $\leq_{I,O}$ of the other singular subcontract pre-order families. In the following we let $\mathcal{P}_{conpar,I,O}$ denote the subset of processes of $\mathcal{P}_{conpar}$ such that $I(P) \subseteq I$ and $O(P) \subseteq O$.

Definition 7 (Input-Output Subcontract relation). *A contract C' is a subcontract of a contract C with respect to a set of input channel names $I \subseteq \mathcal{N}$ and output channel names $O \subseteq \mathcal{N}$, denoted $C' \preceq_{I,O} C$, if*

$$\forall P \in \mathcal{P}_{conpar,I,O}. \quad (C\|P)\downarrow \quad \Rightarrow \quad (C'\|P)\downarrow$$

It is trivial to verify that the family of pre-orders $\{\preceq_{I,O} |\ I, O \subseteq \mathcal{N}\ \}$ is a singular subcontract pre-order family and is the maximum of all the singular subcontract pre-order families.

The following Proposition states an intuitive contravariant property: given $\preceq_{I',O'}$, and the greater sets I and O (i.e. $I' \subseteq I$ and $O' \subseteq O$) we obtain a smaller pre-order $\preceq_{I,O}$ (i.e. $\preceq_{I,O} \subseteq \preceq_{I',O'}$). This follows from the fact that extending the sets of input and output actions means considering a greater set of discriminating contexts.

Proposition 2. *Let $C, C' \in \mathcal{P}_{con}$ be two contracts, $I, I' \subseteq \mathcal{N}$ be two sets of input channel names such that $I' \subseteq I$ and $O, O' \subseteq \mathcal{N}$ be two sets of output channel names such that $O' \subseteq O$. We have:*

$$C' \preceq_{I,O} C \quad \Rightarrow \quad C' \preceq_{I',O'} C$$

The following Proposititon states that a subcontract is still a subcontract even if we restrict its actions in order to consider only the inputs and outputs already available in the supercontract. The result about the possibility to restrict the outputs will be extensively used in the remainder of the paper.

Proposition 3. *Let $C, C' \in \mathcal{P}_{con}$ be contracts and $I, O \subseteq \mathcal{N}$ be sets of input and output names. We have*

$$C' \preceq_{I,O} C \quad \Rightarrow \quad C'\backslash(I(C') - I(C)) \preceq_{I,O} C$$
$$C' \preceq_{I,O} C \quad \Rightarrow \quad C'\backslash\overline{(O(C') - O(C))} \preceq_{I,O} C$$

Proof. We discuss the result concerned with restriction of outputs (the proof for the restriction of inputs is symmetrical). Let $C' \preceq_{I,O} C$. Given any $P \in \mathcal{P}_{conpar,I,O}$ such that $(C\|P)\downarrow$, we will show that $(C'\backslash\overline{(O(C') - O(C))} \parallel P)\downarrow$. We first observe that $(C \parallel P\backslash(O(C') - O(C)))\downarrow$. Since $C' \preceq_{I,O} C$, we derive $(C' \parallel P\backslash(O(C')-O(C)))\downarrow$. As a consequence $(C'\backslash\overline{(O(C') - O(C))} \parallel P\backslash(O(C')-O(C)))\downarrow$. We can conclude $(C'\backslash\overline{(O(C') - O(C))} \parallel P)\downarrow$.

All the results discussed so far do not depend on the output persistency property. The first relevant result depending on this peculiarity is reported in the following Proposition. It states that if we substitute a contract with one of its subcontract, the latter cannot activate outputs that were not included in the potential outputs of the supercontract.

Proposition 4. *Let $C, C' \in \mathcal{P}_{con}$ be contracts and $I, O \subseteq \mathcal{N}$ be sets of input and output names. If $C' \preceq_{I,O} C$ we have that, for every $P \in \mathcal{P}_{conpar,I,O}$ such that $(C\|P)\downarrow$,*

$$(C'\|P) \xrightarrow{\tau}^{*} (C'_{der}\|P_{der}) \quad \Rightarrow \quad \forall a \in O(C') - O(C). C'_{der} \xrightarrow{\bar{a}}\!\!\!\!/$$

Proof. We proceed by contradiction. Suppose that there exist C'_{der}, P_{der} such that $(C'\|P) \xrightarrow{\tau}^{*} (C'_{der}\|P_{der})$ and $C'_{der} \xrightarrow{\bar{a}}$ for some $a \in O(C') - O(C)$. We further suppose (without loss of generality) that such a path is minimal, i.e. no intermediate state $(C'_{der2}\|P_{der2})$ is traversed, such that $C'_{der2} \xrightarrow{\bar{a}}$ for some $a \in O(C') - O(C)$. This implies that the same path must be performable by $(C'\backslash\overline{(O(C') - O(C))} \parallel P)$, thus reaching the state $(C'_{der}\backslash\overline{(O(C') - O(C))} \|P_{der})$. However, since in the state C'_{der} of contract C' we have $C'_{der} \xrightarrow{\bar{a}}$ for some $a \in O(C') - O(C)$ and the execution of $\bar{a}$ is disallowed by restriction, due to output persistency, the contract will never be able to reach success (no matter what contracts in P will do). Therefore $(C'\backslash\overline{(O(C') - O(C))} \parallel P) \not\downarrow$ and (due to Proposition 3) we reached a contradiction.

The following Proposition permits to conclude that the set of potential inputs of the other contracts in the system is an information that does not influence the subcontract relation.

Proposition 5. *Let $C \in \mathcal{P}_{con}$ be contracts, $O \subseteq \mathcal{N}$ be a set of output names and $I, I' \subseteq \mathcal{N}$ be two sets of input names such that $O(C) \subseteq I, I'$. We have that for every contract $C' \in \mathcal{P}_{con}$,*

$$C' \preceq_{I,O} C \quad \Longleftrightarrow \quad C' \preceq_{I',O} C$$

Proof. Let us suppose $C' \preceq_{I',O} C$ (the opposite direction is symmetric). Given any $P \in \mathcal{P}_{conpar,I,O}$ such that $(C\|P)\downarrow$, we will show that $(C'\|P)\downarrow$. We first observe that $(C \parallel P\backslash(I - O(C)))\downarrow$. Since $C' \preceq_{I',O} C$ and $O(C) \subseteq I'$, we derive $(C' \parallel P\backslash(I - O(C)))\downarrow$. Due to Proposition 4 we have that $(C' \parallel P\backslash(I - O(C)))$ can never reach by τ transitions a state where outputs in $O(C') - O(C)$ are executable by some derivative of C', so we conclude $(C' \parallel P)\downarrow$.

We are now in place to prove the main result of this paper, i.e. that the *Input-Output Subcontract relation* defined in the Definition 7 is also a subcontract pre-order family.

Theorem 2. *The family of pre-orders* $\{\preceq_{I,O}| I, O \subseteq \mathcal{N}\}$ *is a subcontract pre-order family.*

Proof. Consider $n \geq 1$, $C_1, \ldots, C_n \in \mathcal{P}_{con}$, $C_1', \ldots, C_n' \in \mathcal{P}_{con}$, $I_1, \ldots, I_n \subseteq \mathcal{N}$ *and* $O_1, \ldots, O_n \subseteq \mathcal{N}$. *For any* i *we let* $P_i = C_i \backslash\backslash I_i \cup \overline{O}_i$ *and* $P_i' = C_i' \backslash\backslash I_i \cup \overline{O}_i$. *If* $(P_1 \| \ldots \| P_n) \downarrow$ *and for all* i *we have that* $C_i' \preceq_{I_i', O_i'} C_i$, *with* I_i' *and* O_i' *satisfying the constraint on names as specified in Definition 5, we can derive* $(P_1' \| \ldots \| P_n') \downarrow$ *as follows. For every* i *from 1 to* n *we show that*

$$(P_1' \backslash\backslash \overline{(O(C_1') - O(C_1))} \| \ldots \| P_i \| \ldots \| P_n' \backslash\backslash \overline{(O(C_n') - O(C_n))}) \downarrow$$

by multiply applying the definition of singular subcontract pre-order family to any C_j *with* $j \neq i$. *For instance if* i *is 1, from* $(P_1 \| \ldots \| P_n) \downarrow$ *we derive*

$$(P_1 \| P_2' \backslash\backslash \overline{(O(C_2') - O(C_2))} \| P_3 \| \ldots \| P_n) \downarrow$$

by applying the definition of singular subcontract pre-order to refine C_2 *and by using Proposition 3. We then use this intermadiate result to re-apply the definition of singular subcontract pre-order family for refining* C_3 *and we derive*

$$(P_1 \| P_2' \backslash\backslash \overline{(O(P_2') - O(P_2))} \| P_3' \backslash\backslash \overline{(O(C_3') - O(C_3))} \| P_4 \| \ldots \| P_n) \downarrow$$

We proceed in this way until we yield

$$(P_1 \| P_2' \backslash\backslash \overline{(O(C_2') - O(C_2))} \| \ldots \| P_n' \backslash\backslash \overline{(O(C_n') - O(C_n))}) \downarrow$$

For $i \in \{2 \ldots n\}$ *we proceed in a similar way to obtain*

$$(P_1' \backslash\backslash \overline{(O(C_1') - O(C_1))} \| \ldots \| P_i \| \ldots \| P_n' \backslash\backslash \overline{(O(C_n') - O(C_n))}) \downarrow$$

We conclude the proof as follows. For any i, *since* $C_i' \preceq_{I,O} C_i$, *by Proposition 4 we have that* $(P_1' \backslash\backslash \overline{(O(C_1') - O(C_1))} \| \ldots \| P_i' \| \ldots \| P_n' \backslash\backslash \overline{(O(C_n') - O(C_n))})$ *can never reach by* τ *transitions a state where outputs in* $O(C_1') - O(C_1)$ *are executable by the derivative* $C_{i,der}'$ *of* C_i' *that is syntactically included in the derivative* $P_{i,der}'$ *of* P_i'. *If now we consider the behavior of*

$$(P_1' \backslash\backslash \overline{(O(C_1') - O(C_1))} \| \ldots \| P_n' \backslash\backslash \overline{(O(C_n') - O(C_n))})$$

we derive that, for any i, *we cannot reach by* τ *transitions a state*

$$(P_{1,der}' \backslash\backslash \overline{(O(C_1') - O(C_1))} \| \ldots \| (P_{i,der}' \backslash\backslash \overline{(O(C_i') - O(C_i))} \| \ldots$$
$$\| P_{n,der}' \backslash\backslash \overline{(O(C_n') - O(C_n))})$$

where $C_{i,der}'$ *(the derivative of* C_i' *syntactically included in* $P_{i,der}'$*) can execute outputs in* $O(C_i') - O(C_i)$. *Hence the presence of the restriction operators does not*

affect the internal behavior of $(P_1'\backslash\overline{(O(C_1') - O(C_1))}\| \ldots \|P_n'\backslash\overline{(O(C_n') - O(C_n))})$
with respect to $(P_1'\| \ldots \|P_n')$. *Therefore, we can finally derive* $(P_1'\| \ldots \|P_n')\downarrow$ *from*
$(P_1'\backslash\overline{(O(C_1') - O(C_1))}\| \ldots \|P_n'\backslash\overline{(O(C_n') - O(C_n))})\downarrow$, *that is obtained by furher*
applying the definition of singular subcontract pre-order to refine C_i *in any of*
the i-indexed statement in the first part of the proof.

This last Theorem proves that the maximal singular subcontract pre-order family
is also a subcontract preorder family; since we proved that every subcontract
preorder family is also a singular subcontract pre-order family (see Theorem 1),
we can conclude that there exists a maximal subcontract pre-order family and
it corresponds to the family $\{\preceq_{I,O} \,|I, O \subseteq \mathcal{N}\}$.

Moreover, the Proposition 5 permits to abstract away from the index I of $\preceq_{I,O}$
assuming always $I = \mathcal{N}$; formally, let $\preceq_O = \preceq_{\mathcal{N},\mathcal{O}}$. Similarly, we use $\mathcal{P}_{conpar,O}$ to
denote the set of processes $\mathcal{P}_{conpar,\mathcal{N},\mathcal{O}}$. Hence, we can characterize the maximal
subcontract pre-order family with the following *subcontract relation*.

Definition 8 (Subcontract relation). *A contract* C' *is a subcontract of a*
contract C *with respect to a set of output channel names* $O \subseteq \mathcal{N}$, *denoted* $C' \preceq_O$
C, *if*

$$\forall P \in \mathcal{P}_{conpar,O}. \quad (C\|P)\downarrow \;\Rightarrow\; (C'\|P)\downarrow$$

The remainder of this Section is devoted to the definition of an actual way for
proving that two contracts are in subcontract relation. This is achieved resorting
to the theory of *should-testing* [5]. The main difference of should-testing with
respect to the standard must-testing [4] is that fairness is taken into account;
an (unfair) infinite computation that never gives rise to success is observed in
the standard must-testing scenario, while this is not the case in the should-
testing scenario. The formal definition of should-testing is reported in the proof
of Theorem 3.

We need a preliminary result that essentially proves that $C' \preceq_O C$ if and only
if $C'\backslash\mathcal{N}-O \preceq_\mathcal{N} C\backslash\mathcal{N}-O$.

Lemma 3. *Let* C, C' *be two contracts and* $O \subseteq \mathcal{N}$ *be a set of output names.*
We have $C' \preceq_O C$ *iff*

$$\forall P \in \mathcal{P}_{conpar}. \quad (C\backslash\mathcal{N}-O \| P)\downarrow \;\Rightarrow\; (C'\backslash\mathcal{N}-O \| P)\downarrow$$

Proof. Given $P \in \mathcal{P}_{conpar}$, *we have* $(C\backslash\mathcal{N}-O \| P)\downarrow \Longleftrightarrow (C\backslash\mathcal{N}-O \| P\overline{\mathcal{N}-O})\downarrow$
$\Longleftrightarrow (C \| P\overline{\mathcal{N}-O})\downarrow$ *and* $(C'\backslash\mathcal{N}-O \| P)\downarrow \Longleftrightarrow (C'\backslash\mathcal{N}-O \| P\overline{\mathcal{N}-O})\downarrow \Longleftrightarrow$
$(C' \| P\overline{\mathcal{N}-O})\downarrow$. *In the particular case of* $P \in \mathcal{P}_{conpar,O}$ *we have that* $P\overline{\mathcal{N}-O}$
is isomorphic to P.

In the following we denote with $\preceq_{test}$ the *should-testing* preorder defined in [5]
where we consider the set of actions used by terms as being $\mathcal{L}$ (i.e. $\sqrt{}$ is included
in the set of actions of terms under testing as any other action). We denote here
with $\sqrt{}'$ the special action for the success of the test (denoted by $\sqrt{}$ in [5]).

In order to resort to the theory defined in [5], we define a normal form for
contracts of our calculus that corresponds to terms of the language in [5]. The

normal form of the system P (denoted with $\mathcal{NF}(\mathcal{P})$) is defined as follows, by using the operator $rec_X\theta$ (defined in [5]) that represents the value of X in the solution of the minimum fixpoint of the finite set of equations θ,

$$\mathcal{NF}(\mathcal{P}) = rec_{X_1}\theta \quad \text{where } \theta \text{ is the set of equations}$$
$$X_i = \sum_j \lambda_{i,j}; X_{der(i,j)}$$

where, assuming to enumerate the states in the labeled transition system of P starting from X_1, each variable X_i corresponds to the i-th state of the labeled transition system of P, $\lambda_{i,j}$ is the label of the j-th outgoing transition from X_i, and $der(i,j)$ is the index of the state reached with the j-th outgoing transition from X_i. We assume empty sums to be equal to $\mathbf{0}$, i.e. if there are no outgoing transitions from X_i, we have $X_i = \mathbf{0}$.

Theorem 3. *Let C, C' be two contracts and $O \subseteq \mathcal{N}$ be a set of output names. We have*

$$\mathcal{NF}(C' \backslash\!\backslash (\mathcal{N}-O)) \preceq_{test} \mathcal{NF}(C \backslash\!\backslash (\mathcal{N}-O)) \quad \Rightarrow \quad C' \preceq_O C$$

Proof. According to the definition of should-testing of [5], since

$$\mathcal{NF}(C' \backslash\!\backslash (\mathcal{N}-O)) \preceq_{test} \mathcal{NF}(C \backslash\!\backslash (\mathcal{N}-O))$$

we have that, for every test t, if $\mathcal{NF}(C \backslash\!\backslash (\mathcal{N}\!-\!O))$ shd t, then also $\mathcal{NF}(C' \backslash\!\backslash (\mathcal{N}\!-\!O))$ shd t, where Q shd t iff

$$\forall w \in \mathcal{L}^*, Q'. \quad Q \|_{\mathcal{L}} t \xrightarrow{w} Q' \quad \Rightarrow \quad \exists v \in \mathcal{L}^*, Q'' : Q' \xrightarrow{v} Q'' \xrightarrow{\sqrt{'}}$$

where $\|_{\mathcal{L}}$ is the CSP parallel operator: in $R \|_{\mathcal{L}} R'$ transitions of R and R' with the same label λ (with $\lambda \neq \tau, \sqrt{'}$) are required to synchronize and yield a transition with label λ.

Let us now suppose $P \in \mathcal{P}_{conpar}$ with $(C \backslash\!\backslash \mathcal{N} - O \| P) \downarrow$. We consider $t = \mathcal{NF}(P)\{\sqrt{}/\sqrt{}; \sqrt{'}\}$, i.e., the normal form of P where we replace each occurrence of $\sqrt{}$ with the sequence $\sqrt{}; \sqrt{'}$. We denote with $\bar{t}$ the term obtained by turning each a occurring in t into $\bar{a}$, and each $\bar{a}$ into a. From the definition of shd it immediately follows that $\mathcal{NF}(C \backslash\!\backslash (\mathcal{N}-O))$ shd $\bar{t}$. Since $\mathcal{NF}(C' \backslash\!\backslash (\mathcal{N}-O)) \preceq_{test} \mathcal{NF}(C \backslash\!\backslash (\mathcal{N}-O))$, we have that also $\mathcal{NF}(C' \backslash\!\backslash (\mathcal{N}-O))$ shd $\bar{t}$. From the definition of shd we can conclude that $(C' \backslash\!\backslash \mathcal{N} - O \| P) \downarrow$. The thesis directly follows from Lemma 3.

Note that the opposite implication

$$C' \preceq_O C \Rightarrow \mathcal{NF}(C' \backslash\!\backslash (\mathcal{N}-O)) \preceq_{test} \mathcal{NF}(C \backslash\!\backslash (\mathcal{N}-O))$$

does not hold in general. For example if we take contracts $C = a + a; c$ and $C' = b + b; c$ we have that $C' \preceq_O C$ (and $C \preceq_O C'$) for any O (there is no contract P such that $(C\|P)\downarrow$ or $(C'\|P)\downarrow$), but obviously $\mathcal{NF}(C' \backslash\!\backslash (\mathcal{N}-O)) \preceq_{test} \mathcal{NF}(C \backslash\!\backslash (\mathcal{N}-O))$ (and $\mathcal{NF}(C \backslash\!\backslash (\mathcal{N}-O)) \preceq_{test} \mathcal{NF}(C' \backslash\!\backslash (\mathcal{N}-O))$) does not hold for any O that includes $\{a, b, c\}$. As another example, consider contracts $C = \tau; \mathbf{0}+a$ and $C' = \tau; \mathbf{0} + b$. We have that $C' \preceq_O C$ (and $C \preceq_O C'$) for any O (there is no contract P such that $(C\|P) \downarrow$ or $(C'\|P) \downarrow$), but $\mathcal{NF}(C'\backslash\!\backslash(\mathcal{N}-O)) \preceq_{test} \mathcal{NF}(C\backslash\!\backslash(\mathcal{N}-O))$ (and $\mathcal{NF}(C\backslash\!\backslash(\mathcal{N}-O)) \preceq_{test} \mathcal{NF}(C'\backslash\!\backslash(\mathcal{N}-O))$)) does not hold for any O that includes $\{a, b\}$: this can be seen by considering the test $t = \sqrt{}' + b; \mathbf{0}$ ($t = \sqrt{}' + a; \mathbf{0}$).

Finally, we observe that the labeled transition system of each contract C is finite state as we consider the Kleene-star repetition operator and not general recursion. This implies that also $\mathcal{NF}(C\backslash\!\backslash \mathcal{N} - O)$ is finite state for any O. In [5] it is proved that for finite state terms *should-testing* preorder is decidable and an actual verification algorithm is presented. This algorithm, in the light of our Theorem 3, represents a sound approach to prove also our subcontract relation.

4   Conclusion and Future Work

We have introduced a notion of subcontract relation useful for service oriented computing, where services are to be composed in such a way that deadlocks and livelocks are avoided. In order to be as much flexible as possible, we want to relate with our subcontract relation all those services that could safely replace their supercontracts. In the Introduction we have already discussed the practical impact of our notion of subcontract and we have compared our theory with the related literature.

Here, we simply add some comments about future plans. We intend to investigate the connection between the calculi used in this paper and calculi for service choreography such as those presented in [7] and [8]. In particular, in [8] an end-point calculus similar to our contract calculus is considered where external choices must be guarded on input operations. Moreover, a subtyping relation is used in [8] to formalize similar aspects: the addition of input guarded branches in external choices is safe as well as the cancellation of output guarded branches in internal choices. Differently from [8] we consider a weaker *should-testing* semantics instead of the more restrictive (bi)simulation approach of [8]. This permits us, for instance, to abstract away from branching information that reveals not significant for contract composition.

References

1. Carpineti, S., Laneve, C.: A basic contract language for web services. In: Sestoft, P. (ed.) ESOP 2006 and ETAPS 2006. LNCS, vol. 3924, pp. 197–213. Springer, Heidelberg (2006)
2. Carpineti, S., Castagna, G., Laneve, C., Padovani, L.: A formal account of contracts for web services. In: Bravetti, M., Núñez, M., Zavattaro, G. (eds.) WS-FM 2006. LNCS, vol. 4184, pp. 148–162. Springer, Heidelberg (2006)
3. Nestmann, U.: What is a "good" encoding of guarded choice? Inf. Comput. 156(1-2), 287–319 (2000)
4. De Nicola, R., Hennessy, M.: Testing equivalences for processes. Theor. Comput. Sci. 34, 83–133 (1984)

5. Rensink, A., Vogler, W.: Fair testing. Technical Report TR-CTIT-05-64, Department of Computer Science, University of Twente (2005)
6. Fournet, C., Hoare, C.A.R., Rajamani, S.K., Rehof, J.: Stuck-free conformance. In: Alur, R., Peled, D.A. (eds.) CAV 2004. LNCS, vol. 3114, pp. 242–254. Springer, Heidelberg (2004)
7. Busi, N., Gorrieri, R., Guidi, C., Lucchi, R., Zavattaro, G.: Choreography and orchestration: A synergic approach for system design. In: Benatallah, B., Casati, F., Traverso, P. (eds.) ICSOC 2005. LNCS, vol. 3826, pp. 228–240. Springer, Heidelberg (2005)
8. Carbone, M., Honda, K., Yoshida, N.: Structured communication-centred programming for web services. In: Proc. of ESOP 2007. LNCS, vol. 4421, pp. 2–17. Springer, Heidelberg (2007)

Regulating Data Exchange in Service Oriented Applications*

Alessandro Lapadula, Rosario Pugliese, and Francesco Tiezzi

Dipartimento di Sistemi e Informatica Università degli Studi di Firenze
{lapadula,pugliese,tiezzi}@dsi.unifi.it

Abstract. We define a type system for COWS, a formalism for specifying and combining services, while modelling their dynamic behaviour. Our types permit to express policies constraining data exchanges in terms of sets of service partner names attachable to each single datum. Service programmers explicitly write only the annotations necessary to specify the wanted policies for communicable data, while a type inference system (statically) derives the minimal additional annotations that ensure consistency of services initial configuration. Then, the language dynamic semantics only performs very simple checks to authorize or block communication. We prove that the type system and the operational semantics are sound. As a consequence, we have the following data protection property: services always comply with the policies regulating the exchange of data among interacting services. We illustrate our approach through a simplified but realistic scenario for a service-based electronic marketplace.

1 Introduction

Service-oriented computing (SOC) is an emerging paradigm for developing loosely coupled, interoperable, evolvable applications which exploits the pervasiveness of the Internet and its related technologies. SOC systems deliver application functionality as services to either end-user applications or other services. Current software engineering technologies for SOC, however, remain at the descriptive level and do not support analytical tools for checking that SOC applications enjoy desirable properties and do not manifest unexpected behaviors. To reason about and guarantee such properties, one must also be able to specify and enforce some security policies. Indeed, programming service oriented middlewares and the applications running on them without putting data at risk or compromising robustness of the whole platform requires services to be checked and their resource usage to be strictly put in relation to their capabilities.

Great efforts have been recently devoted to embed security mechanisms within standard programming features (some of these techniques are surveyed in [1]). Language-based mechanisms are a scalable way to provide evidence that a large number of applications enjoy some given properties. For example, by using type systems, one can prove the type soundness of the language as a whole, from which it follows that all well-typed applications do comply with the policies stated by their types. To facilitate the task of designing such a sound language for SOC, one can initially focus only on

---

* This work has been supported by the EU project SENSORIA, IST-2005-016004.

F. Arbab and M. Sirjani (Eds.): FSEN 2007, LNCS 4767, pp. 223–239, 2007.

the mechanisms at the basis of SOC. Afterwards, this core formalism could hopefully be expanded into a full-fledged language by adding the high level, often redundant, constructs typical of effective programming languages.

Many researchers have hence put forward exploiting the studies on *process calculi*, a cornerstone of current foundational research on specification and analysis of concurrent, distributed and mobile systems through mathematical — mainly algebraic and logical — tools. Indeed, due to their algebraic nature, process calculi convey in a distilled form the compositional programming style of SOC. This is witnessed by the several process calculi like formalisms for SOC proposed in the literature by now (see, e.g., [2,3,4,5,6,7,8,9]). However, although capable of describing complex systems and applications, such proposals still lack those reasoning mechanisms and analytical tools, e.g. type systems and behavioural equivalences, that process calculi usually hand down.

In this paper, we tailor the type-based approach for protecting data in global computing applications put forward in [10] to COWS, a formalism for specifying service-based applications that we introduce in [9]. We thus define a typed variant of COWS that permits expressing and forcing policies regulating the exchange of data among interacting services. Programmers can indeed settle the partners usable to exchange any given datum (and, then, the services that can share it), thus avoiding the datum be accessed (by unwanted services) through unauthorized partners. The language (static and dynamic) semantics then guarantees that well-typed services always comply with the constraints expressed by the type associated to each single datum.

The rest of the paper is organized as follows. Section 2 introduces syntax, type inference and operational semantics of (our typed variant of) COWS, while Section 3 presents our main results. Section 4 demonstrates our approach through a simplified but realistic scenario for a service-based electronic marketplace. Finally, Section 5 touches upon comparisons with more strictly related work and directions for future work.

2 COWS: Calculus for Orchestration of Web Services

Before formally defining our language, we provide some insights on its main features. We refer the interested reader to [9] for further motivations on the design of COWS, for many examples illustrating its peculiarities and expressiveness, and for comparisons with other process-based and orchestration formalisms.

The design of COWS has been influenced by the principles underlying WS-BPEL [11], the *de facto* standard language for orchestration of web services. Similarly to WS-BPEL, COWS supports service instances with shared states, allows a same process to play more than one partner role and permits programming stateful sessions by correlating different service interactions. However, COWS intends to be a foundational model not specifically tight to web services' current technology. Thus, some WS-BPEL constructs, such as e.g. fault and compensation handlers and flow graphs, do not have a precise counterpart in COWS, rather they are expressed in terms of more primitive operators (see [12], Sect. 3). The design of COWS has also taken advantage of previous work on process calculi. In fact, it combines in an original way constructs and features borrowed from well-known process calculi, e.g. asynchronous communication, polyadic synchronization, pattern matching, protection, delimited receiving and killing activities, while however resulting different from any of them.

The basic elements of COWS are *partners* and *operations*. They can be combined to designate *communication endpoints* and can be exchanged in communication, but dynamically received names cannot form endpoints used to receive further invocations. Endpoints naming mechanism is very flexible, e.g. it permits identifying a same service by means of different logic names and separately dealing with the names composing an endpoint. This is, e.g., exploited in request-response interaction, where usually the service provider knows the name of the response operation, but not the partner name of the service it has to reply to.

COWS computational entities are called *services*. Typically, a service creates one specific instance to serve each received request. Instances may run concurrently. Each instance can be composed of concurrent threads that may offer a choice among alternative receive activities. Services could be able to receive multiple messages in a statically unpredictable order and in such a way that the first incoming message triggers creation of a service instance which subsequent messages are routed to. *Pattern matching* is the mechanism used for correlating messages logically forming a same interaction 'session' by means of their same contents. It permits locating those data that are important to identify service instances and is flexible enough for allowing a single message to participate in multiple interaction sessions, each identified by separate correlation values.

Inter-service communication give rise to substitutions of variables with values. However, to enable concurrent instances or threads within an instance to share the state (or part of it), receive activities in COWS do *not* bind variables. The range of application of the substitution generated by a communication is then regulated by the *delimitation* operator, that is the only binder of the calculus. Delimitation, additionally, can be used to generate fresh private names (as the restriction operator of the π-calculus) and to delimit the field of action of the *kill* activity, a powerful orchestration construct that can be used to force termination of whole service instances. Sensitive code can however be protected from the effect of a forced termination by using the *protection* operator.

The type system we present in this paper permits to express and enforce policies for regulating the exchange of data among services. To implement such policies, programmers can annotate data with sets of partner names characterizing the services authorized to use and exchange them; these sets are called *regions*. The language operational semantics uses these annotations to guarantee that computations proceed according to them. This property, called *soundness*, can be stated as follows

A service s is *sound* if, for any datum v in s associated to region r and for all evolutions of s, it holds that v can be exchanged only by using partners in r.

To facilitate the task of decorating COWS terms with type annotations, we let the type system partially infer such annotations *à la* ML: service programmers explicitly write only the annotations necessary to specify the wanted policies for communicable data; then, a type inference system (statically) performs some coherence checks (e.g. the partner used by an invoke must belong to the regions of all data occurring in the argument of the activity) and derives the minimal region annotations for variable declarations that ensure consistency of services initial configuration. This allows us to define an *operational semantics with types* [13] which is simpler than a full-fledged *typed operational semantics*, because it only performs simple checks (i.e. subset inclusion) using region

Table 1. COWS syntax

$s ::= \mathbf{kill}(k) \mid u \cdot u'!\overline{\{e(\bar{x})\}_r} \mid g \mid s\mid s \mid \{\!\|s\!\|\} \mid [d]\,s \mid *\,s$	(services)
$g ::= \mathbf{0} \mid p \cdot o?\bar{w}.s \mid g+g$	(receive-guarded choice)

annotations to authorize or block transitions. Our main results prove that the type system and the operational semantics are sound. As a consequence, we have that services always comply with the constraints expressed by the type of each single datum.

Syntax. COWS syntax is parameterized by three countable and pairwise disjoint sets: the set of *(killer) labels* (ranged over by $k, k', \ldots$), the set of *values* (ranged over by v, v', $\ldots$) and the set of 'write once' *variables* (ranged over by $x, y, \ldots$). The set of values is left unspecified; however, we assume that it includes the set of *names*, ranged over by n, $m, \ldots$, mainly used to represent partners and operations. COWS is also parameterized by a set of *expressions*, ranged over by e, whose exact syntax is deliberately omitted; we just assume that expressions contain, at least, values and variables. Notably, killer labels are *not* (communicable) values. Notationally, we prefer letters $p, p', \ldots$ when we want to stress the use of a name as a partner, $o, o', \ldots$ when we want to stress the use of a name as an operation. We will use w to range over values and variables, u to range over names and variables, and d to range over killer labels, names and variables.

Regions can be either finite subsets of partners and variables or the distinct element $\top$ (denoting the universe of partners). The set of all regions, ranged over by r, is partially ordered by the subset inclusion relation $\subseteq$, and has $\top$ as top element.

Notation $\bar{}$ stands for tuples of objects, e.g. $\bar{x}$ is a compact notation for denoting the tuple of variables $\langle x_1, \ldots, x_n \rangle$ (with $n \geq 0$). We assume that variables in the same tuple are pairwise distinct. All notations shall extend to tuples component-wise. An expression e tagged with region r will be written as $\{e\}_r$; an untagged e will stand for $\{e\}_\top$. We will write $e(\bar{x})$ to make explicit all the variables $\bar{x}$ occurring in e (we still write e when this information is not needed), and $\bar{e}$ (resp. $\bar{r}$) to denote the tuple of the expressions (resp. regions) occurring in $\{e\}_r$.

We will call *raw* services those COWS services written according to the syntax in Table 1. Intuitively, raw services only contain those region annotations that implement the policies for data exchange settled by the programmers. *Services* are structured activities built from basic activities, i.e. the empty activity $\mathbf{0}$, the kill activity $\mathbf{kill}(\_)$, the invoke activity $\_ \cdot \_!\_$ and the receive activity $\_ \cdot \_?\_$, by means of (receive) prefixing $\_.\_$, guarded choice $\_ + \_$, parallel composition $\_ \mid \_$, protection $\{\!\|\_\!\|\}$, delimitation $[\_]\_$ and replication $* \_$. Notably, as in the Lπ [14], communication endpoints of receive activities are identified statically because their syntax only allows using names and not variables. We adopt the following conventions about the operators precedence: monadic operators bind more tightly than parallel composition, and prefixing more tightly than choice. We shall omit a trailing $\mathbf{0}$ and use $[d_1, \ldots, d_n]\,s$ to denote $[d_1] \ldots [d_n]\,s$.

The only *binding* construct is delimitation: $[d]\,s$ binds d in the scope s. The occurrence of a name/variable/label is *free* if it is not under the scope of a binder. We denote by $\mathrm{fd}(t)$ (resp. $\mathrm{bd}(t)$) the set of names, variables and killer labels that occur free

Table 2. Type inference system

$\Gamma \vdash \mathbf{0} > \Gamma \vdash \mathbf{0}$ *(t-nil)* $\Gamma \vdash \mathbf{kill}(k) > \Gamma \vdash \mathbf{kill}(k)$ *(t-kill)*

$$\frac{\forall\, r' \in \{r_i\}_{i \in \{1,\dots,n\}} \quad u_1 \in r'}{\begin{array}{c}\Gamma \vdash u_1 \bullet u_2 !\langle \{e_1(\bar{y}_1)\}_{r_1}, \dots, \{e_n(\bar{y}_n)\}_{r_n}\rangle >\\[2pt] (\Gamma + \{x : r_1\}_{x \in \bar{y}_1} + \dots + \{x : r_n\}_{x \in \bar{y}_n}) \vdash u_1 \bullet u_2 !\langle \{e_1(\bar{y}_1)\}_{r_1}, \dots, \{e_n(\bar{y}_n)\}_{r_n}\rangle\end{array}} \;\; \text{(t-inv)}$$

$$\frac{\Gamma + \{x : \{p\}\}_{x \in \mathrm{fv}(\bar{w})} \vdash s > \Gamma' \vdash s'}{\Gamma \vdash p \bullet o ? \bar{w}.s > \Gamma' \vdash p \bullet o ? \bar{w}.s'} \;\; \text{(t-rec)}$$

$$\frac{\Gamma \vdash g_1 > \Gamma_1 \vdash g_1' \qquad \Gamma \vdash g_2 > \Gamma_2 \vdash g_2'}{\Gamma \vdash g_1 + g_2 > \Gamma_1 + \Gamma_2 \vdash g_1' + g_2'} \;\; \text{(t-sum)}$$

$$\frac{\Gamma \vdash s > \Gamma' \vdash s'}{\Gamma \vdash \{|s|\} > \Gamma' \vdash \{|s'|\}} \;\; \text{(t-prot)} \qquad\qquad \frac{\Gamma \vdash s > \Gamma' \vdash s'}{\Gamma \vdash {*}s > \Gamma' \vdash {*}s'} \;\; \text{(t-repl)}$$

$$\frac{\Gamma \vdash s > \Gamma' \vdash s' \qquad n \notin \mathrm{reg}(\Gamma')}{\Gamma \vdash [n]\, s > \Gamma' \vdash [n]\, s'} \;\; \text{(t-del}_{name}) \qquad \frac{\Gamma \vdash s > \Gamma' \vdash s'}{\Gamma \vdash [k]\, s > \Gamma' \vdash [k]\, s'} \;\; \text{(t-del}_{lab})$$

$$\frac{\Gamma, \{x : \emptyset\} \vdash s > \Gamma', \{x : r\} \vdash s' \qquad x \notin \mathrm{reg}(\Gamma')}{\Gamma \vdash [x]\, s > \Gamma' \vdash [\{x\}^{r - \{x\}}]\, s'} \;\; \text{(t-del}_{var})$$

$$\frac{\Gamma \vdash s_1 > \Gamma_1 \vdash s_1' \qquad \Gamma \vdash s_2 > \Gamma_2 \vdash s_2'}{\Gamma \vdash s_1 \mid s_2 > \Gamma_1 + \Gamma_2 \vdash s_1' \mid s_2'} \;\; \text{(t-par)}$$

(resp. bound) in a term t, by $\mathrm{fv}(t)$ (resp. $\mathrm{bv}(t)$) the set of free (resp. bound) variables in t, and by $\mathrm{fk}(t)$ the set of free killer labels in t. Two terms are *alpha-equivalent* if one can be obtained from the other by consistently renaming bound names/variables/labels. As usual, we identify terms up to alpha-equivalence. For simplicity sake, in the sequel we assume that bound variables in services are pairwise distinct (of course, this condition is not restrictive and can always be fulfilled by possibly using alpha-conversion).

A type inference system. The annotations put by the type inference are written as superscripts, to better distinguish them from those put by the programmers. Thus, the syntax of variable delimitation becomes $[\{x\}^r]\, s$, which means that the datum that dynamically will replace x will be used at most by the partners in r. *Typed* COWS services are then generated by the syntax in Table 1 where, differently from the previous section, d ranges over killer labels, names and annotated variables as $\{x\}^r$. Notably, types may *depend* on partner variables, i.e. on parameters of receiving activities; during computation, they are therefore affected by application of substitutions that replace partner variables with partner names. We assume that the region of a partner name always contains, at least implicitly, such partner.

The type inference system is presented in Table 2. Typing judgements are written $\Gamma \vdash s > \Gamma' \vdash s'$, where the type environment Γ is a finite function from variables to regions such that $fv(s) \subseteq dom(\Gamma)$ and $bv(s) \cap dom(\Gamma) = \emptyset$ (the same holds for Γ' and s'). Type environments are written as sets of pairs of the form $x : r$, where x is a partner variable and r is its assumed region annotation. The domain of an environment is defined as usual: $dom(\emptyset) = \emptyset$ and $dom(\Gamma, \{x : r\}) = dom(\Gamma) \cup \{x\}$, where ',' denotes union between environments with disjoint domains. The *region* of Γ is the union of the regions in Γ, i.e. $reg(\emptyset) = \emptyset$ and $reg(\Gamma, \{x : r\}) = r \cup reg(\Gamma)$. We will write $\Gamma + \Gamma'$ to denote the environment obtained by extending Γ with Γ'; $+$ is inductively defined by

$$\Gamma + \emptyset = \Gamma$$

$$\Gamma + \{x : r\} = \begin{cases} \Gamma', \{x : r \cup r'\} & \text{if } \Gamma = \Gamma', \{x : r'\} \\ \Gamma, \{x : r\} & \text{otherwise} \end{cases}$$

$$\Gamma + (\{x : r\}, \Gamma') = (\Gamma + \{x : r\}) + \Gamma'$$

Hence, the judgement $\emptyset \vdash s > \emptyset \vdash s'$ can be derived only if s is a closed raw service (because the initial environment is empty); if it is derivable, then s' is the typed service obtained by decorating s with the region annotations describing the use of each variable of s in its scope. Type inference determines such regions by considering the invoking and receiving partners where the variables occur.

We now comment on the most significant typing rules. Rule *(t-inv)* checks if the invoked partner u_1 belongs to the regions of the communicated data. If it succeeds, the type environment Γ is extended by associating a proper region to each variable used in the expressions argument of the invoke activity. Rule *(t-rec)* tries to type s in the type environment Γ extended by adding the receiving partner to the regions of the variables in $\bar{w}$. Rules *(t-sum)* and *(t-par)* yield the same typing; this is due to the sharing of variables. For instance, service $[x] (p \cdot o?\langle x \rangle \mid p' \cdot o'!\langle\{x\}_r\rangle)$ with $p' \in r$ is annotated as $[\{x\}^{r'}] (p \cdot o?\langle x \rangle \mid p' \cdot o'!\langle\{x\}_r\rangle)$ with $r' = (\{p\} \cup r - \{x\})$. In rule *(t-del_name)*, premise $n \notin reg(\Gamma')$ prevents a new name n to escape from its binder $[n]$ in the inference. As an example, consider the closed raw service

$$[z]\, p \cdot o?\langle z \rangle \,.\, [p']\, p'' \cdot o''!\langle\{z\}_{\{p'',p'\}}\rangle \qquad (*)$$

Without the premise $n \notin reg(\Gamma')$, the service resulting from the type inference would be $[\{z\}^{\{p'',p',p\}}]\, p \cdot o?\langle z \rangle \,.\, [p']\, p'' \cdot o''!\langle\{z\}_{\{p'',p'\}}\rangle$. The problem with this service is that the name p' occurring in the annotation associated to z by the inference system escapes from the scope of its binder and, thus, represents a completely different name. Although, service $(*)$ is not typable, by a simple semantics preserving manipulation one can get a typable service as, e.g., the following one $[p']\, [z]\, p \cdot o?\langle z \rangle \,.\, p'' \cdot o''!\langle\{z\}_{\{p'',p'\}}\rangle$.

Similarly, in rule *(t-del_var)*, premise $x \notin reg(\Gamma')$ prevents initially closed services to become open at the end of the inference. Otherwise, e.g., the type inference would transform the closed raw service

$$[x]\, p \cdot o?\langle x \rangle \,.\, [y]\, p' \cdot o'?\langle y \rangle \,.\, p'' \cdot o''!\langle\{x\}_{\{p'',y\}}\rangle \qquad (**)$$

into the open service $[\{x\}^{\{p,p'',y\}}]\, p \cdot o?\langle x \rangle \,.\, [\{y\}^{\{p'\}}]\, p' \cdot o'?\langle y \rangle \,.\, p'' \cdot o''!\langle\{x\}_{\{p'',y\}}\rangle$. Also in this case, we can easily modify the untypable service $(**)$ to get a typable one with a similar semantics like, e.g., the service $[y]\, [x]\, p \cdot o?\langle x \rangle \,.\, p' \cdot o'?\langle y \rangle \,.\, p'' \cdot o''!\langle\{x\}_{\{p'',y\}}\rangle$.

Table 3. Structural congruence

$$
\begin{array}{lll}
*\mathbf{0} \equiv \mathbf{0} & *s \equiv s \mid *s & \{\mathbf{0}\} \equiv \mathbf{0} \\
\{\{s\}\} \equiv \{s\} & \{[d]\,s\} \equiv [d]\,\{s\} & [d]\,\mathbf{0} \equiv \mathbf{0} \\
[d_1]\,[d_2]\,s \equiv [d_2]\,[d_1]\,s & \text{if } d_1 \neq \{x\}^{r_1} \text{ and } d_2 \neq \{y\}^{r_2} \\
[n]\,[\{x\}^r]\,s \equiv [\{x\}^r]\,[n]\,s & \text{if } n \notin r \\
[\{x\}^{r_1}]\,[\{y\}^{r_2}]\,s \equiv [\{y\}^{r_2}]\,[\{x\}^{r_1}]\,s & \text{if } y \notin r_1 \text{ and } x \notin r_2 \\
s_1 \mid [d]\,s_2 \equiv [d]\,(s_1 \mid s_2) & \text{if } d \notin \mathrm{fd}(s_1) \cup \mathrm{fk}(s_2)
\end{array}
$$

Table 4. Matching rules

$$
M(v, \{v\}_r) = \emptyset \qquad M(x, \{v\}_r) = \{x \mapsto \{v\}_r\} \qquad \dfrac{M(w_1, \{v_1\}_{r_1}) = \sigma_1 \qquad M(\bar{w}_2, \overline{\{v_2\}_{r_2}}) = \sigma_2}{M((w_1, \bar{w}_2), (\{v_1\}_{r_1}, \overline{\{v_2\}_{r_2}})) = \sigma_1 \uplus \sigma_2}
$$

Furthermore, in *(t-del$_{var}$)*, x is annotated with $r - \{x\}$, rather than with r, otherwise initially closed services could become open. E.g., the closed raw service $[x]\,p \cdot o?\langle x \rangle .$ $p' \cdot o'!\langle\{x\}_{\{p',x\}}\rangle$ would be transformed into the open service $[\{x\}^{\{p,p',x\}}]\,p \cdot o?\langle x \rangle .$ $p' \cdot o'!\langle\{x\}_{\{p',x\}}\rangle$ (indeed, x occurs in the annotation associated to its declaration). Notice that, although the region associated to x by the inference does never record that a service possibly transmits x with regions containing x, rule *(t-del$_{var}$)* is sound because we assumed that the region of a partner name, at least implicitly, contains the partner name.

Definition 1. *A service s is* well-typed *if $\emptyset \vdash s' > \emptyset \vdash s$ for some raw service s'.*

Operational semantics. COWS operational semantics is defined only for *closed* services, i.e. services without free variables/labels (similarly to many real compilers, we consider terms with free variables/labels as programming errors), but of course the rules also involve non-closed services (see e.g. the premises of rules *(del_)*). Formally, the semantics is given in terms of a structural congruence and of a labelled transition relation.

The structural congruence $\equiv$ identifies syntactically different services that intuitively represent the same service. It is defined as the least congruence relation induced by a given set of equational laws. We explicitly show in Table 3 the laws for replication, protection and delimitation, while omit the (standard) laws for the other operators stating that parallel composition is commutative, associative and has $\mathbf{0}$ as identity element, and that guarded choice enjoys the same properties and, additionally, is idempotent. All the presented laws are straightforward. Only notice that the last law can be used to extend the scope of names (like a similar law in the π-calculus), thus enabling communication of restricted names, except when the argument d of the delimitation is a free killer label of s_2 (this avoids involving s_1 in the effect of a kill activity inside s_2).

To define the labelled transition relation, we need a few auxiliary functions. First, we exploit a function $[\![\_]\!]$ for evaluating *closed* expressions (i.e. expressions without variables): it takes a closed expression and returns a value. However, $[\![\_]\!]$ cannot be explicitly defined because the exact syntax of expressions is deliberately not specified.

Table 5. Is there an active $\mathbf{kill}(k)$? / Are there conflicting receives along $p \cdot o$ matching $\overline{\{v\}_r}$?

$$
\mathbf{kill}(k) \downarrow_{kill} \qquad \frac{s \downarrow_{kill} \ \vee \ s' \downarrow_{kill}}{s \mid s' \downarrow_{kill}} \qquad \frac{s \downarrow_{kill}}{\{|s|\} \downarrow_{kill}} \qquad \frac{s \downarrow_{kill}}{[d]\, s \downarrow_{kill}} \qquad \frac{s \downarrow_{kill}}{* s \downarrow_{kill}}
$$

$$
\frac{|\mathcal{M}(\bar{w}, \overline{\{v\}_r})| < \ell}{p \cdot o?\bar{w}.s \downarrow^{\ell}_{p \cdot o, \overline{\{v\}_r}}} \qquad \frac{s \downarrow^{\ell}_{p \cdot o, \overline{\{v\}_r}} \quad d \notin \{p, o\}}{[d]\, s \downarrow^{\ell}_{p \cdot o, \overline{\{v\}_r}}} \qquad \frac{s \downarrow^{\ell}_{p \cdot o, \overline{\{v\}_r}}}{\{|s|\} \downarrow^{\ell}_{p \cdot o, \overline{\{v\}_r}}}
$$

$$
\frac{g \downarrow^{\ell}_{p \cdot o, \overline{\{v\}_r}} \ \vee \ g' \downarrow^{\ell}_{p \cdot o, \overline{\{v\}_r}}}{g + g' \downarrow^{\ell}_{p \cdot o, \overline{\{v\}_r}}} \qquad \frac{s \downarrow^{\ell}_{p \cdot o, \overline{\{v\}_r}} \ \vee \ s' \downarrow^{\ell}_{p \cdot o, \overline{\{v\}_r}}}{s \mid s' \downarrow^{\ell}_{p \cdot o, \overline{\{v\}_r}}} \qquad \frac{s \downarrow^{\ell}_{p \cdot o, \overline{\{v\}_r}}}{* s \downarrow^{\ell}_{p \cdot o, \overline{\{v\}_r}}}
$$

Then, through the rules in Table 4, we define the partial function $\mathcal{M}(\_, \_)$ that permits performing *pattern-matching* on semi-structured data thus determining if a receive and an invoke over the same endpoint can synchronize. The rules state that two tuples match if they have the same number of fields and corresponding fields have matching values/variables. Variables match any annotated value, and a value matches an annotated value only if, apart for the region annotation, they are identical. When tuples $\bar{w}$ and $\overline{\{v\}_r}$ do match, $\mathcal{M}(\bar{w}, \overline{\{v\}_r})$ returns a substitution, that also records region annotations of values exchanged in communication, for the variables in $\bar{w}$; otherwise, it is undefined. *Substitutions* (ranged over by σ) are functions mapping variables to annotated values and are written as collections of pairs of the form $x \mapsto \{v\}_r$. Application of substitution σ to s, written $s \cdot \sigma$, has the effect of replacing every free occurrence of x in s with v, for each $x \mapsto \{v\}_r \in \sigma$, by possibly using alpha-conversion for avoiding v to be captured by name delimitations within s. We use $|\sigma|$ to denote the number of pairs in σ and $\sigma_1 \uplus \sigma_2$ to denote the union of σ_1 and σ_2 when they have disjoint domains.

We also define a function, named $halt(\_)$, that takes a service s as an argument and returns the service obtained by only retaining the protected activities inside s. $halt(\_)$ is defined inductively on the syntax of services. The most significant case is $halt(\{|s|\}) = \{|s|\}$. In the other cases, $halt(\_)$ returns $\mathbf{0}$, except for parallel composition, delimitation and replication operators, for which it acts as an homomorphism.

Finally, in Table 5, we inductively define two predicates: $s \downarrow_{kill}$ checks if s can immediately perform a $\mathbf{kill}(k)$; $s \downarrow^{\ell}_{p \cdot o, \overline{\{v\}_r}}$, with ℓ natural number, checks existence of potential communication conflicts, i.e. the ability of s of performing a receive activity matching $\overline{\{v\}_r}$ over the endpoint $p \cdot o$ that generates a substitution with fewer pairs than ℓ.

The labelled transition relation $\xrightarrow{\alpha}$ is the least relation over services induced by the rules in Table 6, where α is generated by the following grammar:

$$
\alpha ::= \dagger k \quad | \quad (p \cdot o) \triangleleft \overline{\{v\}_r} \quad | \quad (p \cdot o) \triangleright \bar{w} \quad | \quad p \cdot o \lfloor \sigma \rfloor \bar{w} \, \overline{\{v\}_r} \quad | \quad \dagger
$$

In the sequel we use $d(\alpha)$ to denote the set of names, variables and killer labels occurring in α, except for $\alpha = p \cdot o \lfloor \sigma \rfloor \bar{w} \, \overline{\{v\}_r}$ for which we let $d(p \cdot o \lfloor \sigma \rfloor \bar{w} \, \overline{\{v\}_r}) = d(\sigma)$, where $d(\{x \mapsto \{v\}_r\}) = \{x, v\} \cup r$ and $d(\sigma_1 \uplus \sigma_2) = d(\sigma_1) \cup d(\sigma_2)$. The meaning of labels is as follows: $\dagger k$ denotes execution of a request for terminating a term from within the

Table 6. Operational semantics

$$\mathbf{kill}(k) \xrightarrow{\dagger k} \mathbf{0} \quad (kill)$$

$$p \cdot o?\bar{w}.s \xrightarrow{(p \cdot o) \triangleright \bar{w}} s \quad (rec)$$

$$\frac{[\![\bar{e}]\!] = \bar{v} \qquad fv(\bar{r}) = \emptyset}{p \cdot o!\{e\}_r \xrightarrow{(p \cdot o) \triangleleft \overline{\{v\}}_r} \mathbf{0}} \quad (inv)$$

$$\frac{g_1 \xrightarrow{\alpha} s}{g_1 + g_2 \xrightarrow{\alpha} s} \quad (choice)$$

$$\frac{s \xrightarrow{p \cdot o \lfloor \sigma \uplus \{x \mapsto \{v\}_r\} \rfloor \bar{w} \overline{\{v'\}}_{r'}} s' \qquad r'' \cdot \sigma \subseteq r}{[\{x\}^{r''}] \, s \xrightarrow{p \cdot o \lfloor \sigma \rfloor \bar{w} \overline{\{v'\}}_{r'}} s' \cdot \{x \mapsto \{v\}_r\}} \quad (del_{sub})$$

$$\frac{s \xrightarrow{\dagger k} s'}{[k] \, s \xrightarrow{\dagger} [k] \, s'} \quad (del_{kill})$$

$$\frac{s \xrightarrow{\alpha} s' \quad d \ne \{x\}^r \quad d \notin d(\alpha) \quad s \downarrow_{kill} \Rightarrow \alpha = \dagger, \dagger k}{[d] \, s \xrightarrow{\alpha} [d] \, s'} \quad (del_{pass})$$

$$\frac{s \xrightarrow{\alpha} s' \quad x \notin d(\alpha)}{[\{x\}^r] \, s \xrightarrow{\alpha} [\{x\}^r] \, s'} \quad (x_{pass})$$

$$\frac{s_1 \xrightarrow{(p \cdot o) \triangleright \bar{w}} s_1' \quad s_2 \xrightarrow{(p \cdot o) \triangleleft \overline{\{v\}}_r} s_2' \quad M(\bar{w}, \overline{\{v\}}_r) = \sigma \quad \neg(s_1 \mid s_2 \downarrow^{|\sigma|}_{p \cdot o, \overline{\{v\}}_r})}{s_1 \mid s_2 \xrightarrow{p \cdot o \lfloor \sigma \rfloor \bar{w} \overline{\{v\}}_r} s_1' \mid s_2'} \quad (com)$$

$$\frac{s_1 \xrightarrow{p \cdot o \lfloor \sigma \rfloor \bar{w} \overline{\{v\}}_r} s_1' \quad \neg(s_2 \downarrow^{|M(\bar{w}, \overline{\{v\}}_r)|}_{p \cdot o, \overline{\{v\}}_r})}{s_1 \mid s_2 \xrightarrow{p \cdot o \lfloor \sigma \rfloor \bar{w} \overline{\{v\}}_r} s_1' \mid s_2} \quad (par_{conf})$$

$$\frac{s_1 \xrightarrow{\dagger k} s_1'}{s_1 \mid s_2 \xrightarrow{\dagger k} s_1' \mid halt(s_2)} \quad (par_{kill})$$

$$\frac{s_1 \xrightarrow{\alpha} s_1' \quad \alpha \ne (p \cdot o \lfloor \sigma \rfloor \bar{w} \overline{\{v\}}_r), \dagger k}{s_1 \mid s_2 \xrightarrow{\alpha} s_1' \mid s_2} \quad (par_{pass})$$

$$\frac{s \xrightarrow{\alpha} s'}{\{\!|s|\!\} \xrightarrow{\alpha} \{\!|s'|\!\}} \quad (prot)$$

$$\frac{s \equiv s_1 \quad s_1 \xrightarrow{\alpha} s_2 \quad s_2 \equiv s'}{s \xrightarrow{\alpha} s'} \quad (cong)$$

delimitation $[k]$, $(p \cdot o) \triangleleft \overline{\{v\}}_r$ and $(p \cdot o) \triangleright \bar{w}$ denote execution of invoke and receive activities over the endpoint $p \cdot o$, respectively, $p \cdot o \lfloor \sigma \rfloor \bar{w} \overline{\{v\}}_r$ (if $\sigma \ne \emptyset$) denotes execution of a communication over $p \cdot o$ with receive parameters $\bar{w}$ and matching values $\overline{\{v\}}_r$ and with substitution σ to be still applied, $\dagger$ and $p \cdot o \lfloor \emptyset \rfloor \bar{w} \overline{\{v\}}_r$ denote *computational steps* corresponding to taking place of forced termination and communication (without pending substitutions), respectively. Hence, a *computation* from a closed service s_0 is a sequence of connected transitions of the form

$$s_0 \xrightarrow{\alpha_1} s_1 \xrightarrow{\alpha_2} s_2 \xrightarrow{\alpha_3} s_3 \dots$$

where, for each i, α_i is either $p \cdot o \lfloor \emptyset \rfloor \bar{w} \overline{\{v\}}_r$ or $\dagger$, and s_i is called *reduct* of s_0.

We comment on salient points. Activity $\mathbf{kill}(k)$ forces termination of all unprotected parallel activities (rules *(kill)* and *(par$_{kill}$)*) inside an enclosing $[k]$, that stops the killing effect by turning the transition label $\dagger k$ into $\dagger$ (rule *(del$_{kill}$)*). Existence of such delimitation is ensured by the assumption that the semantics is only defined for closed services.

Sensitive code can be protected from killing by putting it into a protection $\{\_\}$; this way, $\{\!\{s\}\!\}$ behaves like s (rule *(prot)*). Similarly, $[d]\,s$ behaves like s, except when the transition label α contains d or when a kill activity is active in s and α does not correspond to a kill activity (rules *(del$_{pass}$)* and *(x$_{pass}$)*): in such cases the transition should be derived by using rules *(del$_{kill}$)* or *(del$_{sub}$)*. In other words, kill activities are executed *eagerly*. A service invocation can proceed only if the expressions in the argument can be evaluated and their regions do not contain variables (rule *(inv)*). A receive activity offers an invocable operation along a given partner name (rule *(rec)*). The execution of a receive permits to take a decision between alternative behaviours (rule *(choice)*). Communication can take place when two parallel services perform matching receive and invoke activities (rules *(com)*). Communication generates a substitution that is recorded in the transition label (for subsequent application), rather than a silent transition as in most process calculi. If more then one matching is possible the receive that needs fewer substitutions is selected to progress (rules *(com)* and *(par$_{conf}$)*). This mechanism permits to correlate different service communications thus implicitly creating interaction sessions and can be exploited to model the precedence of a service instance over the corresponding service specification when both can process the same request. A substitution $\{x \mapsto \{v\}_r\}$ for a variable x is applied to a term (rule *(del$_{sub}$)*) when the delimitation for x is encountered, i.e. the whole scope s of x is determined, provided that the region annotations of the variable declaration and of the substituent datum v do comply i.e. $r' \cdot \sigma \subseteq r$. This condition also means that as a value is received it gets annotated with a smaller region. The substitution for x is then applied to s and x disappears from the term and cannot be reassigned a value. Execution of parallel services is interleaved (rule *(par$_{pass}$)*), but when a kill activity or a communication is performed. Indeed, the former must trigger termination of all parallel services (according to rule *(par$_{kill}$)*), while the latter must ensure that the receive activity with greater priority progresses (rule *(com)* and *(par$_{conf}$)*). The last rule states that structurally congruent services have the same transitions.

3   Main Results

Our main results are standard and state that well-typedness is preserved along computations (*subject reduction*) and that well-typed services do respect region annotations (*type safety*). Together, these results imply the *soundness* of our theory, i.e. no violation of data regions will ever occur during the evolution of well-typed services. The formal account of these results follow. To save space, we only outline the techniques used in the proofs and refer the interested reader to [15] for a full account.

For the proof of subject reduction, we need some standard lemmata concerning substitution and weakening. The substitution lemma handles the substitution of partner variables with partner names. Application of a substitution σ to a type environment Γ, written $\Gamma \cdot \sigma$, is defined only when $\text{dom}(\sigma) \cap \text{dom}(\Gamma) = \emptyset$ and, for each $x \mapsto \{v\}_r \in \sigma$, has the effect of replacing every occurrence of x in the regions of Γ with v, i.e.

$$\emptyset \cdot \{x \mapsto \{v\}_r\} = \emptyset \quad \text{and} \quad (\Gamma, \{y : r'\}) \cdot \{x \mapsto \{v\}_r\} = \Gamma \cdot \{x \mapsto \{v\}_r\}, \{y : (r' \cdot \{x \mapsto \{v\}_r\})\}.$$

Lemma 1 (Substitution Lemma). *If* $\Gamma, \{x : r\} \vdash s > \Gamma', \{x : r'\} \vdash s'$ *and* $\sigma = \{x \mapsto \{v\}_{r''}\}$, *then* $\Gamma \cdot \sigma \vdash s \cdot \sigma > \Gamma' \cdot \sigma \vdash s' \cdot \sigma$.

Proof. By induction on the length of the type derivation, with a case analysis on the last rule used in the derivation.   □

Lemma 2 (Weakening Lemma). *Let* $\Gamma' \vdash s' > \Gamma \vdash s$ *and* $x \notin bd(s)$, *then* $\Gamma' + \{x : r\} \vdash s' > \Gamma + \{x : r\} \vdash s$.

Proof. By a straightforward induction on the length of the type derivation, with a case analysis on the last used rule, and by exploiting the fact that extending Γ by adding $\{x : r\}$ does not affect the premise of rule *(t-inv)*.   □

We also need a few auxiliary results. The first one states that function *halt(_)* preserves well-typedness and can be easily proved by induction on the definition of *halt(_)*.

Lemma 3. *If* s *is well-typed then* $halt(s)$ *is well-typed.*

The next results establish well-typedness preservation by the structural congruence and by the labelled transition relation, respectively. We use the following preorder $\sqsubseteq$ on type environments: we write $\Gamma \sqsubseteq \Gamma'$ if there exists a Γ'' such that $\Gamma + \Gamma'' = \Gamma'$.

Lemma 4. *If* $\Gamma' \vdash s_1' > \Gamma \vdash s_1$ *and* $s_1 \equiv s_2$ *then there exists a raw service* s_2' *such that* $\Gamma' \vdash s_2' > \Gamma \vdash s_2$.

Proof. By a straightforward induction on the derivation of $s_1 \equiv s_2$.   □

Theorem 1. *If* $\Gamma_1' \vdash s_1' > \Gamma_1 \vdash s_1$ *and* $s_1 \xrightarrow{\alpha} s_2$ *then there exist a raw service* s_2' *and two type environments* Γ_2 *and* Γ_2' *such that* $\Gamma_2 \sqsubseteq \Gamma_1$, $\Gamma_1' \sqsubseteq \Gamma_2'$ *and* $\Gamma_2' \vdash s_2' > \Gamma_2 \vdash s_2$.

Proof. By induction on the length of the inference of $s_1 \xrightarrow{\alpha} s_2$, with a case analysis on the last used rule.   □

We can now easily prove that well-typedness is preserved along computations.

Corollary 1 (Subject Reduction). *If service* s *is well-typed and* $s \xrightarrow{\alpha} s'$ *with* $\alpha \in \{\dagger, \hat{n} \lfloor \emptyset \rfloor \bar{w} \{v\}_r\}$, *then* s' *is well-typed.*

To characterize the errors that our type system can capture we use predicate $\Uparrow$: $s \Uparrow$ holds true when s can immediately generate a runtime error. This happens when in an active context there is an invoke activity on a partner not included in the region annotation of some of the expressions argument of the activity. Formally, $\Uparrow$ is defined as the least predicate closed under the following rules

$$\frac{\exists r' \in \bar{r}. \ p \notin r'}{p \cdot o!\{e\}_r \ \Uparrow} \qquad \frac{s \Uparrow}{A[\![s]\!] \ \Uparrow} \qquad \frac{s \equiv s' \quad s \Uparrow}{s' \ \Uparrow}$$

We remark that the runtime errors that our type discipline can capture are related to the policies for the exchange of data. We skip such runtime errors as 'unproper use of variables' (e.g. in $x \cdot o!\bar{v}$ the variable x is not replaced by a partner name) that can be easily dealt with standard type systems.

We can now prove that well-typed services do respect region annotations, from which it follows that the type system and the operational semantics are *sound*.

Theorem 2 (Type Safety). *If s is a well-typed service then s* $\Uparrow$ *holds false.*

Proof. By induction on the derivation of $s \Uparrow$, with a case analysis on the last used rule, we prove that if $s \Uparrow$ then s is not well-typed, from which the thesis follows. $\square$

Corollary 2 (Type Soundness). *Let s be a well-typed service. Then s'* $\Uparrow$ *holds false for every reduct s' of s.*

Proof. Corollary 1 can be repeatedly applied to prove that s' is well-typed, then Theorem 2 permits to conclude. $\square$

4   A Case Study by W3C

In this section we illustrate an application of our framework to a simplified but realistic electronic marketplace scenario inspired by [16]. To show usefulness of our approach, we focus on the central part of the protocol where sensitive data are exchanged, i.e. we omit the initial bartering and the concluding interactions, and expand the part relative to the payment process. We will write $Z \triangleq s$ to assign a symbolic name Z to service s.

Suppose a service *buyer* invokes a service *seller* to purchase some goods. Once *seller* has received an order request, it sends back the partner name of the service *credit_agency* to be used for the payment. *buyer* can then check the information on *credit_agency* and, possibly, confirm the payment by sending its credit card data to *seller*. In this case, *seller* forwards the received data to *credit_agency* and passes the order to the service *shipper*. In the end, the whole system is

$$EMP \triangleq buyer \mid credit\_agency \mid [p_{sh}] \, (seller \mid shipper)$$

When fixing the policies for data exchange, services can (safely) assume that, at the outset, partner names p_s, p_{ca} and p_b are publicly available for invoking *seller*, *credit_agency* and *buyer*, respectively. Instead, the partner name p_{sh} for invoking *shipper* is private and only shared with *seller*. Of course, due to the syntactical restrictions, the 'locality' condition for partner names is preserved by the semantics. Thus, the initials assumptions remain true forever.

The *buyer* service is defined as

$$buyer \triangleq [id] \, (\, p_s \cdot o_{ord}! \langle \{id\}_{\{p_s, p_b\}}, p_b, order \rangle$$
$$\mid [x_{ca}] \, p_b \cdot o_{ca\_info}? \langle id, x_{ca} \rangle.$$
$$[p, o] \, (\, p \cdot o! \langle \rangle \mid p \cdot o? \langle \rangle.p_s \cdot o_{pay}! \langle \{id\}_{\{p_s, p_b\}}, \{cc\_data\}_{\{p_s, x_{ca}\}} \rangle$$
$$+ \, p \cdot o? \langle \rangle.p_s \cdot o_{canc}! \langle \{id\}_{\{p_s, p_b\}} \rangle \,) \,)$$

The endpoint $p_s \cdot o_{ord}$ is used for invoking the seller service and transmitting the order together with the *buyer*'s partner name p_b. The (restricted) name *id* represents the order identifier and is used for correlating all those service interactions that logically form a same session relative to the processing of *order*. For example, the specification of *buyer* could be slightly modified to allow the service to simultaneously make multiple orders: of course, although all such parallel threads must use the same partner p_s to interact with *seller*, they can exploit different order identifiers as a means to correlate messages belonging to different interaction sessions. The type attached to *id* only allows *buyer* and *seller* to exchange and use it, since they are the only services that can receive along p_s and p_b. Instead, p_b comes without an attached policy, since it is publicly known (it is transmitted to indicate the service making the invocation for the call-back operation). For simplicity, also *order* has no attached policy; thus, it could be later on communicated to any other service. Variable x_{ca} is used to store the partner name of the credit agency service to be used to possibly finalize the purchase and also to implement the policy for *buyer*'s credit card data. After the information on the credit agency service are verified, *buyer* sends a message to *seller* either to confirm or to cancel the order. This is simply modelled as an internal non-deterministic choice, by exploiting the private endpoint $p \cdot o$ (a more precise model can be obtained by exploiting the encodings shown in [9]).

The *seller* service is defined as

$$seller \triangleq * [x_b, x_{id}, x_{ord}, k] \, p_s \cdot o_{ord}?\langle x_{id}, x_b, x_{ord} \rangle.$$
$$(\, x_b \cdot o_{ca\_info}!\langle \{x_{id}\}_{\{x_b\}}, p_{ca} \rangle$$
$$| \, [x_{cc}] \, p_s \cdot o_{pay}?\langle x_{id}, x_{cc} \rangle.(\, p_{ca} \cdot o_{cr\_req}!\langle x_{ord}, \{x_{cc}\}_{\{p_{ca}\}} \rangle$$
$$| \, p_{sh} \cdot o_{sh\_req}!\langle x_{ord} \rangle \,)$$
$$| \, p_s \cdot o_{canc}?\langle x_{id} \rangle.\mathbf{kill}(k) \,)$$

Once *seller* receives an order along $p_s \cdot o_{ord}$, it creates one specific instance that sends back to *buyer* (via x_b) the partner name p_{ca} of the credit agency service where the payment will be made. Whenever the seller instance receives the credit card data correlated to x_{id}, it forwards them to *credit_agency* and passes the order to the (internal) shipper service. Instead, if *buyer* demands cancellation of the order, the corresponding instance of *seller* is immediately terminated. Name k is used to delimit the effect of the kill activity only to the relevant instance.

The remaining two services are defined as

$$credit\_agency \triangleq * [x, y] \, p_{ca} \cdot o_{cr\_req}?\langle x, y \rangle. < \texttt{execute\_the\_payment} >$$
$$shipper \triangleq * [z] \, p_{sh} \cdot o_{sh\_req}?\langle z \rangle. < \texttt{process\_the\_order} >$$

Let now consider the type inference phase. Service *seller* gets annotated as follows:

$$seller' \triangleq * [\{x_b\}^{\{p_s\}}] [\{x_{id}\}^{\{p_s, x_b\}}, \{x_{ord}\}^{\top}, k] \, p_s \cdot o_{ord}?\langle x_{id}, x_b, x_{ord} \rangle.$$
$$(\, x_b \cdot o_{ca\_info}!\langle \{x_{id}\}_{\{x_b\}}, p_{ca} \rangle$$
$$| \, [\{x_{cc}\}^{\{p_s, p_{ca}\}}] \, p_s \cdot o_{pay}?\langle x_{id}, x_{cc} \rangle.(\, p_{ca} \cdot o_{cr\_req}!\langle x_{ord}, \{x_{cc}\}_{\{p_{ca}\}} \rangle$$
$$| \, p_{sh} \cdot o_{sh\_req}!\langle x_{ord} \rangle \,)$$
$$| \, p_s \cdot o_{canc}?\langle x_{id} \rangle.\mathbf{kill}(k) \,)$$

The type inference has the task of checking consistency of region annotations of the arguments occurring within invoke activities and that of deriving the annotations for variable declarations. As regards consistency, there are only two explicitly typed expressions used as arguments of invoke activities, i.e. x_{id} and x_{cc}, and their types $\{x_b\}$ and $\{p_{ca}\}$ satisfy the consistency constraint (see rule *(t-inv)*). The remaining expressions occurring as arguments of invoke activities, i.e. the only x_{ord}, have implicitly assigned type $\top$ (indeed, recall that we assumed that an untagged e stands for $\{e\}_{\top}$) and are thus trivially consistent. As regards type derivation, when a variable is put in the environment (rule *(t-del$_{var}$)*), it is assigned type $\emptyset$. Later on, when a variable is used as an argument of an invoke or receive, its type can possibly be enriched (rules *(t-inv)* and *(t-rec)*). Thus, at the end of the inference, declaration of variable x_b, that is only used in $p_s \cdot o_{ord}?\langle x_{id}, x_b, x_{ord}\rangle$, will have assigned region $\{p_s\}$ (application of rule *(t-rec)*). Instead, declaration of x_{ord} has assigned type $\top$ (rule *(t-inv)* is used) while that of x_{cc} has assigned type $\{p_s, p_{ca}\}$ and, similarly, declaration of x_{id} gets annotated with $\{p_s, x_b\}$ (in both cases rules *(t-inv)* and *(t-rec)* are used). Notably, in *seller'*, delimitation $[\{x_b\}^{p_s}]$ does not commute any longer with delimitations $[\{x_{id}\}^{\{p_s, x_b\}}, \{x_{ord}\}^\top, k]$ (otherwise the service would become opened).

The variable declarations of the other services are annotated in a trivial way: x_{ca} with $\{p_b\}$, x and y with $\{p_{ca}\}$, and z with $\{p_{sh}\}$ (we assume that *credit_agency* and *shipper* do not re-transmit the received data). Thus, if we call *buyer'*, *credit_agency'* and *shipper'* the other typed services, then the system resulting from the type inference is

$$buyer' \mid credit\_agency' \mid [p_{sh}]\,(seller' \mid shipper')$$

After some computation steps, the system can become

$$[id]\,(\;p_s \cdot o_{pay}!\langle\{id\}_{\{p_s, p_b\}}, \{cc\_data\}_{\{p_s, p_{ca}\}}\rangle \mid [p_{sh}]\,(seller' \mid$$
$$[k, \{x_{cc}\}^{\{p_s, p_{ca}\}}]\,(\;p_s \cdot o_{pay}?\langle id, x_{cc}\rangle.(\,p_{ca} \cdot o_{cr\_req}!\langle order, \{x_{cc}\}_{\{p_{ca}\}}\rangle$$
$$\mid p_{sh} \cdot o_{sh\_req}!\langle order\rangle\,)$$
$$\mid p_s \cdot o_{canc}?\langle id\rangle.\mathbf{kill}(k)\,)$$
$$\mid *[\{x\}^{\{p_{ca}\}}, \{y\}^{\{p_{ca}\}}]\,p_{ca} \cdot o_{cr\_req}?\langle x, y\rangle.< \texttt{execute\_the\_payment} >$$
$$\mid *[\{z\}^{\{p_{sh}\}}]\,p_{sh} \cdot o_{sh\_req}?\langle z\rangle.< \texttt{process\_the\_order} >))$$

Thus, after *buyer'* sends the credit card data, we get

$$[id, p_{sh}]\,(\;seller'$$
$$\mid [k]\,(\,p_{ca} \cdot o_{cr\_req}!\langle order, \{cc\_data\}_{\{p_{ca}\}}\rangle \mid p_{sh} \cdot o_{sh\_req}!\langle order\rangle$$
$$\mid p_s \cdot o_{canc}?\langle id\rangle.\mathbf{kill}(k)\,)$$
$$\mid *[\{x\}^{\{p_{ca}\}}, \{y\}^{\{p_{ca}\}}]\,p_{ca} \cdot o_{cr\_req}?\langle x, y\rangle.< \texttt{execute\_the\_payment} >$$
$$\mid *[\{z\}^{\{p_{sh}\}}]\,p_{sh} \cdot o_{sh\_req}?\langle z\rangle.< \texttt{process\_the\_order} >)$$

At this point, *seller'* can safely communicate credit card data of *buyer'* to *credit_agency'* and, then, forward the order to *shipper'*.

Suppose now that service *seller'* also contains such a malicious invocation as $p_{sh} \cdot o!\langle\ldots, \{x_{cc}\}_r, \ldots\rangle$. In order to successfully pass the type inference phase, it should be that $p_{sh} \in r$ (otherwise rule *(t-inv)* could not be applied). Therefore, in the resulting typed service we would have the variable declaration $[\{x_{cc}\}^{r'}]$, with $r \subseteq r'$. Now, communication with *buyer'* would be blocked by the runtime checks because the datum is tagged as $\{cc\_data\}_{\{p_s, p_{ca}\}}$, and $p_{sh} \in r \subseteq r'$ implies that $r' \nsubseteq \{p_s, p_{ca}\}$.

5   Concluding Remarks

We have introduced a first analytical tool for checking that COWS specifications enjoy some desirable properties concerning the partners, and hence the services, that can safely access any given datum and, in that respect, do not manifest unexpected behaviors. Our type system is quite simple: types are just sets and operations on types are union, intersection, subset inclusion, etc. The language operational semantics only involves types in efficiently implementable checks, i.e. subset inclusions. While implementation of our framework is currently in progress, we are also working on the definition of a completely static variant where all dynamic checks have been moved to the static phase.

The types used in this paper are essentially inspired by the 'region types' for Confined-λ of [17] and for global computing calculi of [10]. There are however some noticeable differences. In fact, COWS permits describing not necessarily distributed systems and exchanging heterogeneous data along endpoints, which calls for a more dynamic typing mechanism than communication channels. Moreover, COWS permits annotating only the relevant data while Confined-λ requires typing any constant, function and channel. The group types, originally proposed for the Ambients calculus [18] and then recast to the π-calculus [19], have purposes similar to our region annotations, albeit they are only used for constraining the exchanges of ambient and channel names. Confinement has been also explored in the context of Java, and related calculi, for confining classes and objects within specific packages [20,21].

More expressive type disciplines based, e.g., on session types and behavioural types are emerging as powerful tools for taking into account behavioural and non-functional properties of computing systems. In the case of services, they could permit to express and enforce many relevant policies for, e.g., regulating resources usage, constraining the sequences of messages accepted by services, ensuring service interoperability and compositionality, guaranteeing absence of deadlock in service composition, checking that interaction obeys a given protocol. Some of the studies developed for the π-calculus (see e.g. [22,23,24,25,26]) are promising starting points, but they need non trivial adaptations to deal with all COWS peculiar features. For example, one of the major problems we envisage concerns the treatment of killing and protection activities, that are not commonly used in process calculi.

Many efforts have been devoted to develop analytical tools for SOC foundational languages. Some works study mechanisms for comparing global descriptions (i.e. choreographies) and local descriptions (i.e. orchestrations) of a same system. Means to check conformance of these different views have been defined in [5] and, by relying on session types, in [22]. COWS, instead, only considers service orchestration and focuses on modelling the dynamic behaviour of services without the limitations possibly introduced by a layer of choreography. Some other works [27,28] have concentrated on modelling web transactions and on studying their properties in programming languages based on the π-calculus, while [29,30] formalize long running transactions with special care for the *Sagas* mechanism [31]. A type system specifying security policies for orchestration has been introduced in [32] for a very basic formalism based on the λ-calculus. Finally, a type system for checking compliance between (simplified) WS-BPEL terms and the associated WSDL documents has been defined in [7].

Acknowledgements. We thank the anonymous referees for their useful comments.

References

1. Schneider, F.B., Morrisett, G., Harper, R.: A language-based approach to security. In: Wilhelm, R. (ed.) Informatics. LNCS, vol. 2000, pp. 86–101. Springer, Heidelberg (2001)
2. Brogi, A., Canal, C., Pimentel, E., Vallecillo, A.: Formalizing web service choreographies. ENTCS 105, 73–94 (2004)
3. Viroli, M.: Towards a formal foundational to orchestration languages. ENTCS 105, 51–71 (2004)
4. Geguang, P., Xiangpeng, Z., Shuling, W., Zongyan, Q.: Towards the semantics and verification of bpel4ws. In: WLFM, Elsevier, Amsterdam (2005)
5. Busi, N., Gorrieri, R., Guidi, C., Lucchi, R., Zavattaro, G.: Choreography and orchestration conformance for system design. In: Ciancarini, P., Wiklicky, H. (eds.) COORDINATION 2006. LNCS, vol. 4038, pp. 63–81. Springer, Heidelberg (2006)
6. Laneve, C., Padovani, L.: Smooth orchestrators. In: Aceto, L., Ingólfsdóttir, A. (eds.) FOSSACS 2006 and ETAPS 2006. LNCS, vol. 3921, pp. 32–46. Springer, Heidelberg (2006)
7. Lapadula, A., Pugliese, R., Tiezzi, F.: A WSDL-based type system for WS-BPEL. In: Ciancarini, P., Wiklicky, H. (eds.) COORDINATION 2006. LNCS, vol. 4038, pp. 145–163. Springer, Heidelberg (2006)
8. Guidi, C., Lucchi, R., Gorrieri, R., Busi, N., Zavattaro, G.: SOCK: a calculus for service oriented computing. In: Dan, A., Lamersdorf, W. (eds.) ICSOC 2006. LNCS, vol. 4294, pp. 327–338. Springer, Heidelberg (2006)
9. Lapadula, A., Pugliese, R., Tiezzi, F.: A Calculus for Orchestration of Web Services. In: ESOP. LNCS, vol. 4421, pp. 33–47. Springer, Heidelberg (2007)
10. De Nicola, R., Gorla, D., Pugliese, R.: Confining data and processes in global computing applications. Science of Computer Programming 63, 57–87 (2006)
11. OASIS. Web Services Business Process Execution Language Version 2.0. Technical report, WS-BPEL TC OASIS (August 2006), http://www.oasis-open.org/
12. Lapadula, A., Pugliese, R., Tiezzi, F.: A Calculus for Orchestration of Web Services (full version). Technical report, Dipartimento di Sistemi e Informatica, Univ. Firenze (2007), http://rap.dsi.unifi.it/cows
13. Goguen, H.: Typed operational semantics. In: Dezani-Ciancaglini, M., Plotkin, G. (eds.) TLCA 1995. LNCS, vol. 902, pp. 186–200. Springer, Heidelberg (1995)
14. Merro, M., Sangiorgi, D.: On asynchrony in name-passing calculi. Mathematical Structures in Computer Science 14(5), 715–767 (2004)
15. Lapadula, A., Pugliese, R., Tiezzi, F.: Regulating data exchange in service oriented applications (full version). Technical report, Dipartimento di Sistemi e Informatica, Univ. Firenze (2007), http://rap.dsi.unifi.it/cows
16. Ross-Talbot, S., Fletcher, T.: Web services choreography description language: Primer (working draft). Technical report, W3C (June 2006)
17. Kirli, Z.D.: Confined mobile functions. In: CSFW, pp. 283–294. IEEE, Los Alamitos (2001)
18. Cardelli, L., Ghelli, G., Gordon, A.D.: Types for the ambient calculus. Inf. Comput. 177(2), 160–194 (2002)
19. Cardelli, L., Ghelli, G., Gordon, A.D.: Secrecy and group creation. Inf. Comput. 196(2), 127–155 (2005)
20. Vitek, J., Bokowski, B.: Confined types in java. SPE 31(6), 507–532 (2001)
21. Zhao, T., Palsber, J., Vitek, J.: Lightweight confinement for featherweight java. In: OOPSLA, pp. 135–148. ACM Press, New York (2003)
22. Carbone, M., Honda, K., Yoshida, N.: A calculus of global interaction based on session types. In: DCM, Elsevier, Amsterdam (2006) (to appear as ENTCS)

23. Yoshida, N., Vasconcelos, V.T.: Language primitives and type discipline for structured communication-based programming revisited: Two systems for higher-order session communication. In: SecReT. ENTCS, Elsevier, Amsterdam (2006)
24. Kobayashi, N.: Type systems for concurrent programs. In: Aichernig, B.K., Maibaum, T.S.E. (eds.) Formal Methods at the Crossroads. From Panacea to Foundational Support. LNCS, vol. 2757, pp. 439–453. Springer, Heidelberg (2003)
25. Igarashi, A., Kobayashi, N.: A generic type system for the pi-calculus. Theor. Comput. Sci. 311(1-3), 121–163 (2004)
26. Kobayashi, N., Suenaga, K., Wischik, L.: Resource usage analysis for the π-calculus. In: Emerson, E.A., Namjoshi, K.S. (eds.) VMCAI 2006. LNCS, vol. 3855, pp. 298–312. Springer, Heidelberg (2005)
27. Laneve, C., Zavattaro, G.: Foundations of web transactions. In: Sassone, V. (ed.) FOSSACS 2005. LNCS, vol. 3441, pp. 282–298. Springer, Heidelberg (2005)
28. Mazzara, M., Lucchi, R.: A pi-calculus based semantics for WS-BPEL. Journal of Logic and Algebraic Programming 70(1), 96–118 (2006)
29. Bruni, R., Melgratti, H.C., Montanari, U.: Theoretical foundations for compensations in flow composition languages. In: POPL, pp. 209–220. ACM Press, New York (2005)
30. Bruni, R., Butler, M., Ferreira, C., Hoare, T., Melgratti, H.C., Montanari, U.: Comparing two approaches to compensable flow composition. In: Abadi, M., de Alfaro, L. (eds.) CONCUR 2005. LNCS, vol. 3653, pp. 383–397. Springer, Heidelberg (2005)
31. Garcia-Molina, H., Salem, K.: Sagas. In: SIGMOD, pp. 249–259. ACM Press, New York (1987)
32. Bartoletti, M., Degano, P., Ferrari, G.: Security Issues in Service Composition. In: Gorrieri, R., Wehrheim, H. (eds.) FMOODS 2006. LNCS, vol. 4037, pp. 1–16. Springer, Heidelberg (2006)

A Behavioural Congruence for Web Services*

Filippo Bonchi, Antonio Brogi, Sara Corfini, and Fabio Gadducci

Department of Computer Science, University of Pisa, Pisa, Italy
{fibonchi,brogi,corfini,gadducci}@di.unipi.it

Abstract. Web services are emerging as a promising technology for the development of next generation distributed heterogeneous software systems. We define a new behavioural equivalence for Web services, based on bisimilarity and inspired by recent advances in the theory of reactive systems. The proposed equivalence is compositional and decidable, and it provides a firm ground for enhanced behaviour-aware discovery and for a sound incremental development of services and service compositions.

1 Introduction

Web services are emerging as a promising technology for the development of next generation distributed heterogeneous software systems [1]. Roughly, a Web service is any piece of software that makes itself available over the Internet. A Web service is identified by a URI, it is universally accessible by means of standard protocols (WSDL, UDDI, SOAP), and it self-describes its functionalities by exposing a public interface.

WSDL [2] is the currently employed standard for describing services. A WSDL description details what a service provides, by listing its operations in terms of input and output messages, and how a service can be invoked, by specifying one or more network locations where it can be accessed. WSDL descriptions do not include any information on the interaction *behaviour* of services, that is, on the order with which messages can be received or sent by each service. Unfortunately, the lack of behavioural information inhibits the possibility of *a priori* determining whether two services have the same behaviour as well as the possibility of verifying properties of service compositions, such as deadlock-freedom.

Various proposals have been put forward to feature service descriptions that include both semantics (viz., ontology-based) and behaviour information about services. One of the major efforts in this direction is OWL-S [3], a high-level ontology-based language for describing services, proposed by the OWL-S coalition. Since OWL-S is a computer-interpretable semantic mark-up language providing all the needed information for describing services, OWL-S paves the way for the full automation of service discovery, invocation and composition. In particular, OWL-S service descriptions include a declaration of the interaction

* Research partially supported by the EU FP6-IST IP 16004 SENSORIA and STREP 033563 SMEPP, and the MIUR FIRB TOCAI.IT and PRIN 2005015824 ART.

F. Arbab and M. Sirjani (Eds.): FSEN 2007, LNCS 4767, pp. 240–256, 2007.

behaviour of services (the *process model*), which provides the needed information for the *a priori* analysis and verification of service invocations and compositions.

The objective of this paper is to define a notion of *behavioural equivalence* for Web services. An immediate application of such a notion is the possibility of establishing whether syntactically different services feature the same behaviour, and hence for instance of verifying whether the upgrade of a service S with a new version S' may affect the interoperability with existing clients of S. The availability of a well-founded notion of behavioural equivalence can also be exploited to develop enhanced service discovery techniques so as to go beyond functional matching and determine whether a given service (or service composition) features a desired interaction behaviour. According to these aims, two fundamental properties of any equivalence relation are *computability* and *compositionality*. Computability is a key requirement in ensuring the viability of an equivalence relation, that is, in allowing the development of automated software capable of determining whether two services are behaviourally equivalent or not. Compositionality permits to exploit the equivalence relation for a disciplined incremental development of services, by means of sound compositions and replacements.

In this paper we first show how the behaviour of a Web service can be suitably described by means of a *Petri net*. Petri nets [4] are one of the best known and most widely adopted formalisms to express the concurrent behaviour of (software) systems: besides providing a clear and precise semantics, they feature an intuitive graphical notation, and a number of techniques and tools for their analysis, simulation and execution are available. Petri nets have also been already employed to model Web services (e.g., see [5,6,7]). We introduce a simple variant of standard condition/event Petri nets (viz., CPR nets for Consume-Produce-Read nets) to naturally model the behaviour of Web services, and in particular the persistence of data. We then show how OWL-S process models can be directly mapped into CPR nets, borrowing from the translation from OWL-S to place-transition nets (P/T for short) described in [8].

Our next step is the identification of a suitable behavioural equivalence for our class of nets. Indeed, the dynamics of a Petri net, as well as those of most functional and process calculi, is usually defined in terms of reduction relations among its markings (i.e., the states of a system). Despite its simplicity, the main drawback of reduction semantics is poor compositionality, in the sense that the dynamic behaviour of an arbitrary stand alone net may become unpredictable whenever it becomes a part of a larger net. Recently, Leifer and Milner [9] deviced a methodology for distilling from a reduction relation a set of labels satisfying suitable requirements of minimality, in order to build a *labelled* reduction relation, such that the associated behavioural notion of *bisimilarity* is a compositional equivalence. The methodology has been later applied to P/T nets [10] as well as to their condition/event variant [11] (C/E for short). Thus, after discussing a motivating example, we define a novel notion of net equivalence, based on bisimilarity and inspired by the recent theoretical advances we just mentioned above. We show that this new equivalence relation is indeed compositional (i.e., that is a *congruence*), and that it is also decidable.

The main contribution of this paper is therefore the definition of a decidable behavioural congruence for Web services, which paves the way for the deployment of behaviour-aware discovery mechanisms and for a sound incremental development of services and service compositions.

2   Modeling Web Services with Petri Nets

Before describing how Petri nets can be employed to model Web services, we recall the essence of OWL-S, a high-level ontology-based language for describing Web services. An OWL-S service advertisement consists of three documents: the *service profile*, providing a high-level specification of the service by describing its functional (i.e., inputs and outputs) and extra-functional attributes; the *process model*, describing the service behaviour by providing a view of the service in terms of process composition; and the *service grounding*, stating how to interact with the service by specifying protocol and message format information.

In the paper we focus on the OWL-S process model, as it details the behavioural information needed to represent a service as a Petri net. More precisely, the process model describes a service as a composite process which consists, in turn, of composite processes and/or atomic processes. An atomic process can not be decomposed further and it has associated inputs and outputs, while a composite process is built up by using a few control constructs: `sequence` (i.e., sequential execution), `choice` (conditional execution), `split` (parallel execution), `split+join` (parallel execution with synchronization), `any-order` (unordered sequential execution), `repeat-while` and `repeat-until` (iterative execution).

In [8] the second and third author proposed a mapping from OWL-S service descriptions to P/T nets with the objective to exploit the Petri net representation of services for a behaviour-aware service discovery. Given a query specifying the inputs and outputs of the service to be found, first the functional attributes of the available services are considered, in order to discover a composition capable of satisfying the query functionally. Next, the found composition is translated into a P/T net and analysed in order to verify properties such as deadlock-freedom.

The mapping presented in [8] takes into account the fact that an OWL-S atomic operation can be executed only if all its inputs are available and all the operations that must occur before its execution have been completed. Hence, atomic operations are mapped into transitions, and places and transition firing rules are employed to model both the availability of data (i.e., the *data flow*) and the executability of atomic operations (i.e., the *control flow*). Indeed, an atomic operation T is modelled as a transition t having an input/output *data place* for each input/output of T, an *input control place* to denote that t is executable as well as an *output control place* to denote that t has completed its execution.

However, the specific features concerning the Web service framework (already emphasised in [8]) suggest more specific nets. In this paper we introduce a simple variant of standard Petri nets [4] as a tool for properly modelling Web services. Given a net N modelling a Web service, we first of all noted that the portion of N restricted to transitions and control places should behave as a classical C/E net, that is, only one token should occur at most for each place. Furthermore, we opted for a model stressing the persistence of data, meaning that, once a data has been produced by some service operation, it has to be kept available for all the service operations that input it. In other words, whilst control places can be produced and consumed, data places can be read, produced but not consumed. Hence, the portion of N restricted to data places behaves as a *contextual* net [12].

To encompass into the same structure the different net behaviour determined by data and control places, we introduce our own particular flavour of contextual C/E nets, which is going to be formally introduced in the following subsection.

2.1   Consume-Produce-Read Nets

This subsection introduces *consume-produce-read* nets. These are a slight extension of standard Petri nets, since they are equipped with two disjoint sets of places, namely, the *control* places (to be consumed and produced) and the *data* places (to be produced and read) .

Definition 1 (CPR net). *A* consume-produce-read *net (simply,* CPR net*) N is a five-tuple $(C_N, D_N, T_N, F_N, I_N)$ where*

- C_N *is a finite set of* control places,
- D_N *is a finite set of* data places *(disjoint from C_N),*
- T_N *is a finite set of* transitions,
- $F_N \subseteq (C_N \times T_N) \cup (T_N \times C_N)$ *is the* control flow relation,
- $I_N \subseteq (D_N \times T_N) \cup (T_N \times D_N)$ *is the* data flow relation.

Our nets behave as standard C/E nets with respect to control places; while, as we are going to see, data places are never emptied, once they are inhabited.

As for standard nets, we associate a *pre-set* and a *post-set* with each transition t, together with two additional sets, called *read-* and *produce-set*.

Definition 2 (pre-, post-, read-, and produce-set). *Given a CPR net N, we define for each $t \in T_N$ the sets*

$$^{\circ}t = \{s \in C_N \mid (s,t) \in F_N\} \qquad t^{\circ} = \{s \in C_N \mid (t,s) \in F_N\}$$

$$^{\bullet}t = \{s \in D_N \mid (s,t) \in I_N\} \qquad t^{\bullet} = \{s \in D_N \mid (t,s) \in I_N\}$$

which denote respectively the pre-set, post-set, read-set *and* produce-set *of t.*

Fig. 1 depicts our chosen graphical notation. Diamonds represent control places, while circles and rectangles represent data places and transitions, respectively. For instance, the transition shown in Fig. 1 *reads* the data places labelled $I_1, I_2, \ldots, I_n$ (this is represented by a straight line) and *produces* the data places labelled $O_1, \ldots, O_m$ (this is represented by a pointed arrow). In doing so, the control flow passes from the left-most to the right-most control place.

Definition 3 (marking). *Given a CPR net N, a marking M for N is a finite set of places in $P_N = C_N \cup D_N$.*

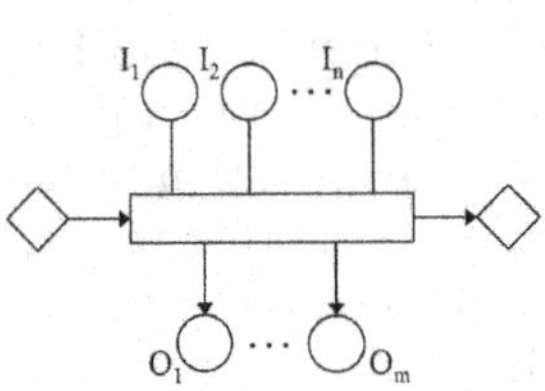

Fig. 1. Modelling atomic operations as CPR net transitions

A marking of the net N coincides with a subset of its set P_N of *places*, since each place can contain at most one token. The evolution of a net is given by a relation over markings. A transitions t is *enabled* by a marking M if the control places which belong to the pre-set of t as well as the data places which belong to the read-set of t are contained in M, and no overlap (as defined later) between M and the post-set of t occurs. In this case a *firing step* may take place: t removes the tokens from the control places which belong to the pre-set of t and adds a token to each place which belongs to the post- and produce-set of t.

Definition 4 (firing step). *Let N be a CPR net. Given a transition $t \in T_N$ and a marking M for N, a firing step is a triple $M[t\rangle M'$ such that $(^\circ t \cup {}^\bullet t) \subseteq M$ and $(M \cap t^\circ) \subseteq {}^\circ t$ (M enables t), and moreover $M' = (M \setminus {}^\circ t) \cup t^\circ \cup t^\bullet$.*
We write $M[\rangle M'$ if there exists some t such that $M[t\rangle M'$.

The enabling condition states that (i) all the tokens of the pre-set of a transition have to be contained in the marking, and (ii) that the marking does not contain any token in the post-set of the transition, unless it is consumed and regenerated. The second condition usually characterizes C/E nets. Note instead that data places act as sinks, hence, any token can be added and only the occurrence of a token is checked. The read-only feature of data places is reminiscent of the work on so-called *contextual* C/E nets by Montanari and Rossi [12].

2.2 From OWL-S to CPR Nets

After formally defining CPR nets, we can show how OWL-S service descriptions can be mapped into CPR nets.

Let us define a service as a triple (i, P, f) where P denotes the CPR (sub)net representing the service and i and f denote the initial and the final control places of P, respectively. To define compositional operators is sufficient to properly coordinate the initial and final control places of the employed services. For instance, let us consider the *sequential composition* of two services $(i_1, P1, f_1)$ and $(i_2, P2, f_2)$. This is a CPR net consisting of the two services and a transition whose starting control place is f_1 and the final control place is i_2. By doing so, $P1$ has to be completed before $P2$ can start.

For lack of space, we do not give a formal semantics of the sequence operator and of the other OWL-S control constructs. Anyway, the reader can intuitively understand how OWL-S composite operations can be mapped into CPR nets by observing Fig. 2. The PX-labelled boxes represent (i_x, PX, f_x) services, the dark gray rectangles identify empty transitions, and the light gray diamonds denote the starting and final control places of the resulting nets. To simplify reading we omitted data places from the nets of Fig. 2. Yet, it is important to note that the PX-boxes can share data places to simulate the exchange of data amongst services, as we will formally define in Section 4.1.

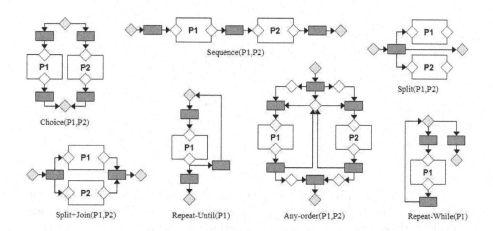

Fig. 2. Modelling OWL-S composite operations as CPR nets

3   Motivating Examples

The ultimate objective of this paper is to introduce a decidable notion of equivalence between Web services represented as CPR nets. This notion establishes whether two service behaviours are equivalent and it can be employed to suitably address the following issues:

1) *incremental development of services* — to check whether two different versions of a service are equivalent;
2) *matching services* — to check whether a (composition of) service(s) matches a query that specifies the behaviour of the desired service (composition) to be found (viz., the notion of equivalence needed by [8]);
3) *replaceability of services* — to check whether a service s which takes part in a composition $C[s]$ can be replaced with a different service r without changing the behaviour of C, i.e., guaranteeing the equivalence between $C[s]$ and $C[r]$.

We can hence outline the main features that a suitable notion of equivalence should have, that is, *weakness* and *compositionality*. It has to be weak as it must equate services with respect to their externally observable behaviour. Indeed, it is reasonable that two versions of a service differently implement the same operations (1), as well as we can imagine that a simple query can be satisfied by a complex service composition (2). Therefore, this notion of equivalence has

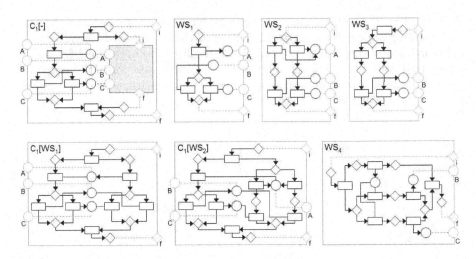

Fig. 3. Example of (non-)equivalent services

to be abstract enough to equate services that differ only on internal transition steps. Furthermore, (3) also asks for compositionality, and if two services are equivalent, then they can be always used interchangeably.

Let us now consider some examples (inspired by [13]). Fig. 3 illustrates the CPR nets of seven services, where rectangles, circles and diamonds represent transitions, data places and control places, respectively. Note the boxes that limit each service. As we will formalise in the following section, a box represents the *outer* interface of a service, that is, the set of places which can interact with the environment. Hence, those places that in Fig. 3 lie on the box are the ones that can be observed externally. Consider the services WS_1 and WS_2 of Fig. 3. As one may note, WS_1 and WS_2 have the same behaviour with respect to the notion of *trace equivalence*. Indeed, they have identical sets of traces, since after producing A they may alternatively read either B or C. Consider now the context $C_1[-]$, depicted in Fig. 3, which represents a possible environment in which WS_1 and WS_2 can be embedded. Note the gray area contained in $C_1[-]$. Its border is the *inner* interface of $C_1[-]$. As formalised in Section 4.1, a service WS can be inserted inside a context $C[-]$ if the outer interface of WS and the inner interface of $C[-]$ coincide. The resulting composition $C[WS]$ consists of the fusion of such interfaces, as well as of the fusion of the data places and the union of the transitions of WS and $C[-]$. We note that $C_1[-]$ inputs A, produced by WS_1, and yields B or C, taken as input by WS_1. Hence, the composition $C_1[WS_1]$ works and finishes properly. Now, in order to test if the trace equivalence is the notion suitable for our purpose, we replace WS_1 with the trace equivalent service WS_2 and we check whether the composition $C_1[WS_2]$ works properly as well. Yet, $C_1[WS_2]$ produces a possibly deadlocking system.

Let us now describe a second example arguing the need of weakness. Consider the services WS_3 and WS_4. For instance, WS_4 could be a composition candidate to satisfy the query represented by WS_3. Although WS_3 and WS_4 appear different as they perform a different number of transitions, they both produce B or C. Namely, WS_3 and WS_4 have identical externally observable behaviour, and they indeed should be considered equivalent.

By taking into account the requirements briefly outlined in this motivating section, we define a novel notion of equivalence based on bisimilarity which features weakness, compositionality and decidability.

4   A Congruence for Open CPR Nets

In the previous section we argued about the relevance of a behavioural equivalence, formally characterizing the notion of replaceability, and we motivated why such an equivalence should be both compositional and weak.

A first step for defining compositionality is to equip nets with a notion of interface and context. Next, we introduce two notions of equivalence: the first is conceptually the correct one, even if it turns out to be quite hard to reason about, while the second provides a simple, decidable characterization of the former.

4.1   Open CPR Nets and CPR Contexts

For the sake of presentation, a chosen net $N = (C_N, D_N, T_N, F_N, I_N)$ is assumed.

Definition 5 (Open CPR net). *Let N be a CPR net. An* interface *for N is a triple $\langle i, f, OD \rangle$ such that $i \neq f$ and*

- *i is a control place (i.e., $i \in C_N$), the* initial *place;*
- *f is a control place (i.e., $f \in C_N$), the* final *place; and*
- *OD is a set of data places (i.e, $OD \subseteq D_N$), the* open *data places.*

An interface is an outer *interface O for N if there exists no transition $t \in T_N$ such that either $i \in t^\diamond$ or $f \in {}^\diamond t$. An* open *CPR net $\mathcal{N}$ (OCPR for short) is a pair $\langle N, O \rangle$, for N a CPR net and O an outer interface for N.*

The condition characterizing outer interfaces requires that the initial place has no incoming transition and the final place has no outgoing transition. Hence, OCPR nets recall the Work-Flow (WF) nets[1] proposed by van der Aalst [14].

The components of a specific interface or open net are often denoted by adding them a subscript. Given an open net $\mathcal{N}$, $Op(\mathcal{N})$ denotes the set of *open places*, which consists of those places occurring on the interface, initial and final places included. Furthermore, the places of $\mathcal{N}$ not belonging to $Op(\mathcal{N})$ constitute the *closed places*. It is important to note that open places are crucial for the definition of observational equivalence that we propose in the next subsection.

Fig. 4 shows the graphical notation used to represent OCPR nets. The bounding box of the OCPR net WS_1 represents the outer interface of the net. Note the initial and final places used to compose the control of services (as suggested

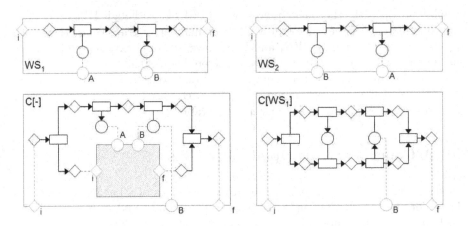

Fig. 4. Two open nets, a context and a composite net

in Fig. 2) as well as the open data places employed to share data. Next, we symmetrically define an *inner interface* for N as an interface such that there is no transition $t \in T_N$ verifying either $f \in t^\diamond$ or $i \in {}^\diamond t$.

Definition 6 (CPR context). *A CPR context $C[-]$ is a triple $\langle N, O, I \rangle$ such that N is a CPR net, $I = \langle i_I, f_I, OD_I \rangle$ and $O = \langle i_O, f_O, OD_O \rangle$ are an inner and an outer interface for N, respectively, and $i_I \neq f_O$, $i_O \neq f_I$.*

A context $C[-]$ is shown in Fig. 4. Substantially, it is an open net with an hole, represented there by a gray area. The border of the hole denotes the inner interface of the context. As for open nets, the bounding box is the outer interface. The only difference between inner and outer interfaces is that the initial place of the former has no outgoing transitions (and vice versa for final places).

Contexts represent environments in which services can be embedded, i.e., possible ways they can be used by other services. An OCPR net can be inserted in a context if the net outer interface and the context inner interface coincide.

Definition 7 (CPR composition). *Let $\mathcal{N} = \langle N, O \rangle$ be an OCPR net and $C[-] = \langle N_C, O_C, I_C \rangle$ a CPR context, such that $O = I_C$. Then, the composite net $C[\mathcal{N}]$ is the OCPR net $(C_N \uplus_O C_{N_C}, D_N \uplus_O D_{N_C}, T_N \uplus T_{N_C}, F_N \uplus F_{N_C}, I_N \uplus I_{N_C})$ with outer interface O_C.*

In other words, the disjoint union of the two nets is performed, except for those places occurring in O, which are coalesced: this is denoted by the symbol $\uplus_O$. Moreover, O_C becomes the set of open places of the resulting net.

Consider e.g. the net WS_1, the context $C[-]$ and their composition, denoted by $C[WS_1]$, as illustrated in Fig. 4. The places on the outer interface of $WS1$ are

---

[1] More precisely, our nets lack the connectiveness requirement, see e.g. [14, Sect. 2.2]. Note however that, even if this is not made explicit, the property holds for all the nets obtained by modeling OWL-S composite operations.

coalesced with the ones on the inner interface of $C[-]$. The output interface of $C[WS_1]$ is the outer interface of $C[-]$. Note that the data place A is open in WS_1 and closed in $C[WS_1]$: this example highlights the capability of hiding places, removing them from the outer interface of an open net. Indeed, this feature is reminiscent of the restriction operator of process calculi, such as CCS [15].

It is worth observing that contexts can be composed with contexts as well: CPR contexts form a category where interfaces are objects and contexts are arrows going from the inner interface to the outer interface[2] (and OCPR nets are arrows whose source is the empty interface and target is the outer interface).

4.2 Saturated Bisimilarity for OCPR Nets

This section addresses the question of the equivalence between nets. Our answer relies on an observational approach, equating two systems if they can not be told apart from an external observer. More precisely, the observer can only examine the open places of a net, which is otherwise a black box, and those places may be checked for verifying if they are actually inhabited or if they are empty.

For the sake of presentation, a chosen OCPR net $\mathcal{N} = \langle N, O \rangle$ is assumed.

Definition 8 (observation). *Let $\mathcal{N}$ be an OCPR net, and M a marking of N. The* observation *on $\mathcal{N}$ at M is the set of places $Obs(\mathcal{N}, M) = Op(\mathcal{N}) \cap M$.*

Thus, an observer looks at the evolution of the system by observing if tokens are produced or consumed in the open places. Accordingly, two OCPR nets $\mathcal{N}$ and $\mathcal{N}'$ with the same outer interface and with initial markings M and M' are considered equivalent if $Obs(\mathcal{N}, M) = Obs(\mathcal{N}', M')$ and if every state reachable from M in N is equivalent to a state reachable from M' in N' (and vice versa).

The previous remark is formalized by the definition below, where $\mathcal{MN}$ denotes the set of all OCPR nets with markings and $\twoheadrightarrow_N$ denotes the reflexive and transitive closure of the firing relation $[\rangle$ for the net N underlying $\mathcal{N}$.

Definition 9 (naive bisimulation). *A symmetric relation $\mathfrak{R} \subseteq \mathcal{MN} \times \mathcal{MN}$ is a* naive bisimulation *if whenever $(\mathcal{N}, M) \mathfrak{R} (\mathcal{N}', M')$ then*

- $O_{\mathcal{N}} = O'_{\mathcal{N}'}$ *and $Obs(\mathcal{N}, M) = Obs(\mathcal{N}', M')$, and*
- $M \twoheadrightarrow_N M_1$ *implies $M' \twoheadrightarrow_{N'} M_1'$ & $(\mathcal{N}, M_1) \mathfrak{R} (\mathcal{N}', M_1')$.*

The union of all naive bisimulations is called naive bisimilarity.

The equivalence above is "naive" in the sense that it clearly fails to be compositional. Indeed, consider the OCPR nets WS_1 and WS_2 in Fig. 4. They are trivially equivalent since none of them can fire. However, they are not equivalent anymore whenever they are inserted into a context (such as the one on that same

---

[2] CPR nets and their morphisms (not defined here) form an *adhesive category* [16]. The category of CPR contexts is the *cospan bicategory* over such category [17], thus it is amenable to the borrowed context technique [18] for distilling a set of labels from a reduction relation. That technique is implicitly exploited in the next section.

Fig. 4) containing a transition that generates a token in the initial place and in the data place A. Indeed the former can now produce a token on B reaching the final state f, while the latter can not move.

The solution out of the impasse, which is quite standard both in functional languages and process calculi, is to allow the observer to perform more complex experiments, inserting a net into any possible context.

Definition 10 (saturated bisimulation). *A symmetric relation* $\mathfrak{R} \subseteq \mathcal{MN} \times \mathcal{MN}$ *is a* saturated bisimulation *if whenever* $(\mathcal{N}, M)\, \mathfrak{R}\, (\mathcal{N}', M')$ *then*

- $O_{\mathcal{N}} = O_{\mathcal{N}'}$ *and* $Obs(\mathcal{N}, M) = Obs(\mathcal{N}', M')$, *and*
- $\forall C[-].M \twoheadrightarrow_{C[\mathcal{N}]} M_1$ *implies* $M' \twoheadrightarrow_{C[\mathcal{N}']} M_1'$ *&* $(C[\mathcal{N}], M_1)\, \mathfrak{R}\, (C[\mathcal{N}'], M_1')$.

The union of all saturated bisimulations is called saturated bisimilarity *($\approx_S$).*

Clearly, $\approx_S$ is by definition a congruence. Indeed, it is the largest bisimulation that preserves compositionality, as stated below.

Proposition 1. $\approx_S$ *is the largest bisimulation that is also a congruence.*

The above proposition ensures the compositionality of the equivalence, hence, the possibility of replacing one service by an equivalent one without changing the behaviour of the whole composite service. Moreover, the equivalence is "weak" in the sense that, differently from most of the current proposals, no explicit occurrence of a transition is observed. The previous definition leads to the following notion of equivalence between OCPR nets, hence, between services.

Definition 11 (bisimilar nets). *Let* $\mathcal{N}, \mathcal{N}'$ *be OCPR nets. They are* bisimilar, *denoted by* $\mathcal{N} \approx \mathcal{N}'$, *if* $(\mathcal{N}, \emptyset) \approx_S (\mathcal{N}', \emptyset)$.

The choice of the empty marking guarantees that the equivalence is as general as possible. Indeed, the presence of a token in an open place can be simulated by closing the net with respect to a transition adding a token in that place, and if any two nets are saturated bisimilar with respect to the empty marking, they are so also with respect to any marking with tokens in the open places.

The negative side of $\approx$ is that this equivalence seems quite hard to be automatically decided because of the quantification over all possible contexts. In the following subsection we introduce an alternative equivalence, easier to reason about and to automatically verify, and we prove that it coincides with $\approx_S$.

4.3   An Equivalent Decidable Bisimilarity

Saturated bisimulation seems conceptually the right notion, and this is further argued in the following section. However, it seems quite hard to analyze (or automatically verify), due to the universal quantification over contexts. In this section we thus introduce *semi-saturated* bisimilarity, based on a simple *labelled transition system* (LTS) distilled from the firing semantics of an OCPR net.

The introduction of an LTS is inspired to the theory of *reactive systems* [9]. This meta-theory suggests guidelines for deriving a LTS from an unlabelled one, choosing a set of labels with suitable requirements of minimality. In the setting of OCPR nets, the reduction relation is given by $[\rangle$, and a firing is allowed if all the preconditions of a transition are satisfied. Thus, intuitively, the minimal context that allows a firing just adds the tokens needed for that firing.

Definition 12 (labelled transition system). *Let $\mathcal{N}$ be an OCPR net, and let $\Lambda = \{\tau\} \cup (\{+\} \times P_N) \cup (\{-\} \times C_N)$ be a set of labels, ranged over by l. The transition relation for $\mathcal{N}$ is the relation $R_{\mathcal{N}}$ inductively generated by the set of inference rules below*

$$\frac{o \in Op(\mathcal{N}) \setminus (M \cup \{f\})}{M \xrightarrow{+o}_{\mathcal{N}} M \cup \{o\}} \qquad \frac{f \in M}{M \xrightarrow{-f}_{\mathcal{N}} M \setminus \{f\}} \qquad \frac{M[\rangle M'}{M \xrightarrow{\tau}_{\mathcal{N}} M'}$$

where $M \xrightarrow{l}_{\mathcal{N}} M'$ means that $\langle M, l, M' \rangle \in R_{\mathcal{N}}$, and i, f denote the initial and the final place of $\mathcal{N}$, respectively.

Thus, a context may add tokens in open places in order to perform a firing, as represented by the transition $\xrightarrow{+o}_{\mathcal{N}}$. Similarly, a context may consume tokens from the final place f. A context can not interact with the net in any other observable way, as the initial place i can be used by the context only as a post condition, and all the other open places are data places whose tokens can be read but not consumed. Likewise, τ transitions represent internal firing steps, i.e., steps that do not need any additional token from the environment.

The theory of reactive systems ensures that, for a suitable choice of labels, the bisimilarity on the derived LTS is a congruence [9]. However, often that bisimilarity does not coincide with the saturated one. In [19] the first author, together with König and Montanari, discusses this problem and introduces the notion of semi-saturated bisimilarity that coincides with the saturated one.

Definition 13 (semi-saturated bisimulation). *A symmetric relation $\mathfrak{R} \subseteq \mathcal{MN} \times \mathcal{MN}$ is a semi saturated bisimulation if whenever $(\mathcal{N}, M) \, \mathfrak{R} \, (\mathcal{N}', M')$*

- $O_{\mathcal{N}} = O'_{\mathcal{N}'}$ and $Obs(\mathcal{N}, M) = Obs(\mathcal{N}', M')$,
- $M \xrightarrow{+o}_{\mathcal{N}} M_1$ implies $M' \cup \{o\} \twoheadrightarrow_{\mathcal{N}'} M'_1$ and $(\mathcal{N}, M_1) \, \mathfrak{R} \, (\mathcal{N}', M'_1)$,
- $M \xrightarrow{-f}_{\mathcal{N}} M_1$ implies $M' \setminus \{f\} \twoheadrightarrow_{\mathcal{N}'} M'_1$ and $(\mathcal{N}, M_1) \, \mathfrak{R} \, (\mathcal{N}', M'_1)$,
- $M \xrightarrow{\tau}_{\mathcal{N}} M_1$ implies $M' \twoheadrightarrow_{\mathcal{N}'} M'_1$ and $(\mathcal{N}, M_1) \, \mathfrak{R} \, (\mathcal{N}', M'_1)$.

The union of all semi-saturated bisimulations is called semi-saturated bisimilarity $(\approx_{SS})$.

The key theorem of the paper is stated below.

Theorem 1. $\approx_S = \approx_{SS}$.

Thus, in order to prove that two OCPR nets are bisimilar, it suffices to exhibit a semi-saturated bisimulation between the states of the two nets that includes the pair of empty markings. Most importantly, though, this search can be automatically performed, since the set of possible states of an OCPR net are finite. Hence, the result below immediately follows.

Corollary 1. $\approx_S$ *is decidable.*

5   Related Works

The successful introduction of observational equivalences for process calculi in the early 1980s spawned similar researches on nets, as witnessed[3] by the survey [20]. According to the taxonomy there, saturated bisimilarity is a state-based equivalence, since it encompasses a notion of interface (a set of observable places) and it is dictated by the way the firing relation crosses the interfaces. Indeed, our bisimilarity is reminiscent of *ST-equivalence*, as in [20, Def. 4.2.6].

This section does not try to survey the field: first of all, the literature is very large, and its retelling is not suitable for a conference paper. Moreover, our CPR nets have distinctive features, since data places act as sinks, thus any comparison should take that fact into account, putting an additional layer of complexity. Furthermore, our main interest is in a *compositional* equivalence, thus restricting the area of possible intersection with former works.

In the rest of the section we then focus on two issues that are closely related to the novelties introduced in our framework: the use of the theory of reactive systems for obtaining a tractable equivalence; and the use of (equivalences on) nets for dealing with the specification of Web services and of their composition.

5.1   Nets, Open Places and Labels

Most current-day formalisms for system specification come equipped with a reduction semantics: a suitable algebra of states is defined, and system evolution is represented by a relation between states. However, the lack of observable actions (either associated to the states, or to the reductions) forbids the development of observational equivalences, which are often handier and more tractable.

Concerning Petri nets, the need of primitives for expressing the interaction with an environment was recognized early on, and notions of "net interface", intended as a subset of the items of the net, are already reported in [20]. Interfaces are key ingredients for defining an observation, as well as for expressing net operators: along this line, a classical approach is the Box Algebra [21]. The main difference with our proposal is in the use of a set of labels for obtaining a labelled reduction relation, on top of which to define the semi-saturated semantics.

Indeed, mostly related to our solution are *open nets*: place/transitions nets where two distinguished sets of input and output places (where tokens may be added or removed, respectively) are identified, and then used to compose nets by place coalescing [22]. A comparison among the derived equivalences is in order, even if it is left for future work: note however that the authors stick to P/T nets; and the dichotomy between input and output places, that is reflected on net composition, is missing in our approach. We refer to [22], and the references therein, for a survey and comparison with other interface-based techniques, mostly important the *net components* proposed by Kindler [23].

The most important source of inspiration for our work is the theory of reactive systems [9], introducing a technique for the synthesis of labels with suitable

---

[3] The analysis there is restricted to *contact-free* C/E nets, i.e., such that the second requirement of the enabling condition in Definition 4 is never verified.

minimality requirements from a reduction relation: the main advantage of the tecnique is that it guarantees that the bisimilarity on the derived labelled relation is a congruence. Indeed, our approach benefits from the general definition of interface deriving from the theory. Concerning Petri nets, the technique was first applied by Milner in [10], after implementing nets into a more complex graphical structure, namely *bigraphs*. And later by Sassone and Sobociński [11]: the labelled relation of the latter work largely coincides with ours. The main difference, besides the use of our flavour of C/E nets, is the introduction of saturated bisimilarity and the corresponding characterisation by semi-saturated bisimilarity. Moreover, our equivalence is weak (the number of transitions is not observed) and interleaving (parallelism is reduced to non-determinism). To the best of our knowledge, the treatment of such a bisimilarity for nets, and its decidable characterisation, is original to our paper, and it exploits the results by the first author, König and Montanari reported in [19].

5.2 Nets for Service Equivalence

The application of Petri nets to the specification and the modelling of distributed systems has been around since their inception. Concerning Web services, the use of nets has been strongly advocated in the works by van der Aalst, see e.g. [14] and the position paper [7]. More specifically, he and his coauthors address the issue of equivalences for nets in [24]: they propose a trace-based, probabilistic equivalence for nets which is quite far from our proposal.

Tightly related to us is the work of Martens, which actually inspired some of our examples in Section 3. More precisely, we refer to [6], where van der Aalst's WF Petri nets (with disjoint sets of input, output and internal places) are analysed for checking structural properties of Web services. The author introduces there the notions of net module and net composition: these recall the open nets formalism mentioned above, and roughly coincide with our own solution.

Martens introduces in [6] the notion of net soundness and net usability, basically related to state reachability with respect to composition with suitable modules. We sketch here a solution for recasting those notions in terms of saturated bisimilarity. Let us start considering the OCPR net **1** depicted in Fig. 5; moreover, let $\nu_O[-]$ be the OCPR context that close all the elements in the set O of open data places of an OCPR net $\mathcal{N}$. According to [6], we say that a net $\mathcal{N}$ is *weakly sound* if and only if $\nu_O[\mathcal{N}] \approx \mathbf{1}$; a context $C[-]$ *utilizes* a net $\mathcal{N}$ if $\nu_O[C[\mathcal{N}]] \approx \mathbf{1}$; and a net $\mathcal{N}$ is *usable* if there exists a context $C[-]$ utilizing it.

Next, the author considers there a few notions of observational equivalence for his flavour of WF nets, discussing in turn trace, bisimulation and simulation equivalences. He identifies the weakness of trace equivalence with respect to deadlock, as we echoed in Section 3. He further argues on bisimulation, reaching

Fig. 5. The OCPR net **1**

the conclusion of simulation as the most adequate equivalence. Note that Martens' notion of simulation (denoted here by $\equiv$) can be expressed by saturated bisimilarity. Indeed, $\mathcal{N} \equiv \mathcal{N}'$ if and only if $\nu_O[C[\mathcal{N}]] \approx 1 \Leftrightarrow \nu_O[C[\mathcal{N}']] \approx 1$ for all possible contexts $C[-]$: intuitively, this means that the two nets are usable by exactly the same environments. Note that our solution is stricter, since $\approx \subseteq \equiv$, while the converse does not hold. In fact, M_3 and M_4 of Fig. 4 of [13] are equivalent according to Martens, even if they are not saturated bisimilar.

6 Concluding Remarks

We introduced *Open Consume-Produce-Read* (OCPR) nets to naturally model the behaviour of OWL-S Web services (although our approach could tackle WS-BPEL services, in the line of [25]). We also defined the notion of *saturated bisimilarity* for OCPR nets, relying on the concepts of interface and CPR context: An interface is a set of places which interact with the environment, while a CPR context represents a possible environment where a service can be embedded in.

To the best of our knowledge, the proposed bisimilarity is the first equivalence employing Petri nets for Web services that features:

- *weakness* – It abstracts from internal transition steps by equating structurally different, yet externally indistinguishable services. An obvious application of such a notion is for checking whether a (complex) service implements a given specification. Indeed, it is often the case that a service provider publishes simple service specifications by hiding unnecessary and/or confidential details of their implementations, as well as, similarly, a matchmaking system verifies whether a (composition of) service(s) matches a client query.
- *compositionality* – It is the largest bisimulation that is also a congruence. Thus, two equivalent services can be always used interchangeably. Consider, for instance, a complex application where a component service S fails (e.g., it becomes unavailable). S can be replaced with an equivalent service S' without changing the behaviour of the whole application.
- *decidability* – As the set of the states of an OCPR net is finite, the saturated bisimilarity is decidable. It can hence be employed by automated software tools in order to check whether two services are behaviourally equivalent.

We leave to future work a throughout analysis of the connection between our saturated bisimilarity and Martens' simulation. We just note here that our relying on a standard notion of observational equivalence allows the reuse of existing theoretical techniques and practical tools, such as e.g. the characterizations of minimal equivalent nets and the algorithms for calculating them.

References

1. Newcomer, E.: Understanding Web Services: XML, WSDL, SOAP, and UDDI. Addison-Wesley, Reading (2002)
2. W3C: WSDL 1.1 (2001), http://www.w3.org/TR/wsdl

3. OWL-S Coalition: OWL-S 1.1 (2004), http://www.daml.org/services/owl-s/1.1/
4. Reisig, W.: Petri Nets: An Introduction. EATCS Monographs in Theoretical Computer Science, vol. 4. Springer, Heidelberg (1985)
5. Hamadi, R., Benatallah, B.: A petri net-based model for web service composition. In: Schewe, K.D., Zhou, X. (eds.) Australasian Database Conference in Research and Practice in Information Technology, vol. 17, pp. 191–200. Australian Computer Society (2003)
6. Martens, A.: Analyzing Web service based business processes. In: Cerioli, M. (ed.) FASE 2005. LNCS, vol. 3442, pp. 19–33. Springer, Heidelberg (2005)
7. van der Aalst, W.: Pi calculus versus Petri nets: Let us eat "humble pie" rather than further inflate the "Pi hype". BPTrends 3(5), 1–11 (2005)
8. Brogi, A., Corfini, S.: Behaviour-aware discovery of Web service compositions. International Journal of Web Services Research 4(3), 1–25 (2007)
9. Leifer, J., Milner, R.: Deriving bisimulation congruences for reactive systems. In: Palamidessi, C. (ed.) CONCUR 2000. LNCS, vol. 1877, pp. 243–258. Springer, Heidelberg (2000)
10. Milner, R.: Bigraphs for Petri nets. In: Desel, J., Reisig, W., Rozenberg, G. (eds.) Lectures on Concurrency and Petri Nets. LNCS, vol. 3098, pp. 686–701. Springer, Heidelberg (2004)
11. Sassone, V., Sobociński, S.: A congruence for Petri nets. In: Ehrig, H., Padberg, J., Rozenberg, G. (eds.) Petri Nets and Graph Transformation. Electr. Notes in Theor. Comp. Sci, vol. 127, pp. 107–120. Elsevier, Amsterdam (2005)
12. Montanari, U., Rossi, F.: Contextual nets. Acta Informatica 32(6), 545–596 (1995)
13. Martens, A.: Consistency between executable and abstract processes. In: e-Technology, e-Commerce, and e-Services, pp. 60–67. IEEE Computer Society, Los Alamitos (2005)
14. Verbeek, H., van der Aalst, W.: Analyzing BPEL processes using Petri nets. In: Marinescu, D. (ed.) Applications of Petri Nets to Coordination, Workflow and Business Process Management, pp. 59–78 (2005)
15. Milner, R.: A Calculus of Communication Systems. LNCS, vol. 92. Springer, Heidelberg (1980)
16. Lack, S., Sobociński, P.: Adhesive categories. In: Walukiewicz, I. (ed.) FOSSACS 2004. LNCS, vol. 2987, pp. 273–288. Springer, Heidelberg (2004)
17. Sassone, V., Sobociński, P.: Reactive systems over cospans. In: Logic in Computer Science, pp. 311–320. IEEE Computer Society, Los Alamitos (2005)
18. Ehrig, H., König, B.: Deriving bisimulation congruences in the DPO approach to graph rewriting. In: Walukiewicz, I. (ed.) FOSSACS 2004. LNCS, vol. 2987, pp. 151–166. Springer, Heidelberg (2004)
19. Bonchi, F., König, B., Montanari, U.: Saturated semantics for reactive systems. In: Logic in Computer Science, pp. 69–80. IEEE Computer Society, Los Alamitos (2006)
20. Pomello, L., Rozenberg, G., Simone, C.: A survey of equivalence notions for net based systems. In: Rozenberg, G. (ed.) Advances in Petri Nets 1992. LNCS, vol. 609, pp. 410–472. Springer, Heidelberg (1992)
21. Best, E., Devillers, R., Koutny, M.: The Box Algebra = Petri nets + process expressions. Information and Computation 178(1), 44–100 (2002)

22. Baldan, P., Corradini, A., Ehrig, H., Heckel, R.: Compositional semantics for open Petri nets based on deterministic processes. Mathematical Structures in Computer Science 15(1), 1–35 (2005)

23. Kindler, E.: A compositional partial order semantics for Petri net components. In: Azéma, P., Balbo, G. (eds.) ICATPN 1997. LNCS, vol. 1248, pp. 235–252. Springer, Heidelberg (1997)

24. van der Aalst, W., de Medeiros, A.A., Weijters, A.: Process equivalence: Comparing two process models based on observed behavior. In: Dustdar, S., Fiadeiro, J.L., Sheth, A. (eds.) BPM 2006. LNCS, vol. 4102, Springer, Heidelberg (2006)

25. Ouyang, C., Verbeek, E., van der Aalst, W., Breutel, S., Dumas, M., ter Hofstede, A.: Formal semantics and analysis of control flow in WS-BPEL. Technical Report BPM-05-15, BPM Center (2005)

Logic–Based Detection of Conflicts in APPEL Policies

Carlo Montangero[1], Stephan Reiff-Marganiec[2], and Laura Semini[1]

[1] Dipartimento di Informatica, Università di Pisa
{monta,semini}@di.unipi.it
[2] Department of Computer Science, University of Leicester
srm13@le.ac.uk

Abstract. APPEL is a general language for expressing policies in a variety of application domains with a clear separation between the core language and its specialisation for concrete domains. Policies can conflict, thus leading to undesired behaviour. We present a novel formal semantics for the APPEL language based on ΔDSTL(x) (so far APPEL only had an informal semantics). ΔDSTL(x) is an extension of temporal logic to deal with global applications: it includes modalities to localize properties to system components, an operator to deal with events, and temporal modalities à la Unity. A further contribution of the paper is the development of techniques based on the semantics to reason about conflicts.

1 Motivation

In general the idea of policies is to adapt the behaviour of an existing system. Policies are high-level statements to support personal, organisational or system goals. Policies have been defined as *information which can be used to modify the behaviour of a system* [1]. Policies have been studied in applications such as distributed systems management, network management, Quality of Service, and access control [2,3].

More recently policies have been studied as means for end-users to express how they want for a system to behave. The work has mostly concentrated on telecommunications systems [4], but there have also been initial attempts at transferring this to service oriented systems [5]. Notably these approaches have been more operational in nature, that is they use a general purpose policy language with an informal semantics.

In general policies are not singular entities, they are generally arranged in groups to collectively express overall goals. However, when several policies are composed (or applied simultaneously) they might contradict each other: a phenomenon referred to as policy conflict. Policy conflict has been recognised as a problem [6] and there have been some attempts to address this, mostly in

F. Arbab and M. Sirjani (Eds.): FSEN 2007, LNCS 4767, pp. 257–271, 2007.
© Springer-Verlag Berlin Heidelberg 2007

the domain of access or resource control. In the case of end-user policies the problem is significantly increased by a number of factors. To name a few: the application domains are much more open and hence increase difficulty in modelling them, there will be many more end-user policies than there are system policies (sheer number of policies) and end-users are not necessarily aware of the wider consequences of a policy that they formulate. However, policy conflict hinders maximum gain when using policies and hence it is important to tackle the problem. Both, detection and resolution are important aspects – resolution at design-time means redesign of the policies.

We propose a logic based reasoning approach to detect policy conflict in the APPEL policy language [7,4]. As APPEL has so far only been presented with an informal semantics, we must first formalise this in a suitable logic. This paper presents the novel formal semantics for APPEL which is based on ΔDSTL(x) (distributed state temporal logic [8,9]) and then shows how this helps with the rigorous detection of conflicts.

Policy conflicts need to be first detected and then resolved. In this paper we concentrate on detecting conflicts in APPEL policies that for simplicity are assumed to be co-located (i.e. not distributed). The paper is structured as follows: In the next section we introduce the policy language and the logic we use for reasoning. In Section 3 we introduce the formal semantics for APPEL. Section 4 considers reasoning about conflict. Section 5 discusses the results and achievements. After highlighting related work in Section 6, the paper is rounded up with a brief summary and pointers to further work.

2   Background

2.1   APPEL

Policies have been used for some time to adapt the behaviour of systems at runtime. Mostly they have been used in the context of Quality of Service and Access Control. There are a number of policy languages specific to these domains. The APPEL policy language [7,4] has been developed in the context of telecommunication systems, to express end-user policies. A detailed discussion why this language was required can be found in [10].

APPEL is a general language for expressing policies in a variety of application domains with a clear separation between the core language and its specialisation for concrete domains (e.g. telecommunications). Here we concentrate on the core language; the semantics developed later maintains the separation between core and application domain. As APPEL is designed for end users rather than administrators the style of APPEL is closer to natural language allowing policies to be more readily formulated and understood by ordinary users. To aid this, a wizard has been presented to allow users to formulate policies [4].

So far, there has not been a formal semantics for APPEL – one aspect that this work is addressing. Let us consider the following syntax:

policy	::= pol_rule_group | pol_rule_group policy
pol_rule_group	::= polrule | pol_rule_group op pol_rule_group
op	::= **g**(conditions) | **u** | **par** | **seq**
polrule	::= [triggers] [conditions] actions
triggers	::= trigger | triggers **or** triggers
conditions	::= condition | **not** conditions |
	conditions **or** conditions | conditions **and** conditions
actions	::= action | actions actionop actions
actionop	::= **and** | **or** | **andthen** | **orelse**

Trigger and action are domain specific atoms. Condition is either a domain specific or a more generic (e.g. time) predicate.

A policy consists of a number of policy rules. The applicability of a rule depends on whether its trigger has occurred and whether its conditions are satisfied. Policy rules may be grouped using a number of operators (**sequential**, **parallel**, **guarded** and **unguarded** choice) – we will discuss details when formalising their semantics.

A policy rule consists of an optional trigger, an optional condition, and an action. The core language defines the structure but not the details of these, these are defined in specific application domains. This allows the core language to be used for different purposes.

Triggers are caused by external events. Triggers may be combined using and and or, with the obvious meaning that both or either must occur. Conditions may be combined with and, or and not with the expected meaning. A condition expresses properties of the state and of the trigger parameters. Finally, actions have an effect on the system in which the policies are applied. A few operators have been defined to create composite actions (again, we discuss details when considering the formal semantics).

2.2 A Fragment of the Distributed States Temporal Logic

ΔDSTL(x) is an extension of temporal logic to deal with global applications: it includes modalities to localize properties to system components, an operator to deal with events, and temporal modalities à la Unity [8,9]. For instance, one may say that event Δq (q becomes true) occurring in component m when property p holds, entails that properties q and r hold in future states of components n and m, respectively: m $(p \land \Delta q)$ LEADS_TO n $r \land$ m s.

In this paper we need the following fragment of the logic:

$$F ::= A \mid false \mid \Delta A \mid \sim F \mid F \land F' \mid mF$$
$$\phi ::= \exists_{\bar{x}} F \mid F \text{ LEADS\_TO } F' \mid F \text{ BECAUSE } F'$$

where: A is an atom, ΔA is an event, and mF is a located formula[1]. A formula ϕ can be an invariant, a formula constraining the future, or a formula constraining the past: operator LEADS_TO expresses a liveness condition, F is eventually

---

[1] Here we consider only one component, m. The spatial features will be helpful when considering "full APPEL" that distributes policies to several sites.

followed by F'; BECAUSE expresses a safety condition, and says that F has been preceded by F'.

For the sake of readability, we leave universal quantification implicit, and make explicit existential quantifiers, when needed, i.e. in the case of invariants $\exists_{\bar{x}}F$. The intended meaning of a temporal formula is that a formula is universally quantified over all values of the variables appearing in its premises, and existentially quantified on the remaining variables.

We now show the semantics. Let $\mathcal{C}$ be a computation, i.e. a sequence of states. Let S be the set of $\mathcal{C}$'s states: s, s' are states in S and ds, ds' are distributed states in 2^S [2]. Moreover, let S be totally ordered by $\geq$, the reflexive and transitive closure of the *next* state relation. These relations are extended as follows to $2^S \times 2^S$: ds *follows (precedes)* ds' iff for each $s \in ds$ there exists $s' \in ds'$ with $s \geq s'$ ($\leq$), and for each $s' \in ds'$ there exists $s \in ds$ with $s' \leq s$ ($\geq$); ds *i–precedes (immediately precedes)* ds' iff for each $s \in ds$ there exists $s' \in ds'$ with $next(s, s')$ and for each $s' \in ds'$ there exists $s \in ds$ with $next(s, s')$. Let $\vartheta_{\bar{x}}$ be a grounding substitution for the (tuple of) variables $\bar{x}$, ϑ_F for the variables in F, and $F\vartheta$ the application of substitution ϑ to F. We say:

$$\mathcal{C} \models \exists_{\bar{x}}F \text{ iff } \forall \vartheta_{F \backslash \bar{x}} \text{ each } ds \models F\vartheta_{F \backslash \bar{x}}\vartheta_{\bar{x}} \text{ for some } \vartheta_{\bar{x}}$$

$$\mathcal{C} \models F \text{ LEADS\_TO } G \text{ iff } \forall \vartheta_F \text{each } ds \models F\vartheta_F \text{ is followed by a } ds' \models G\vartheta_F\vartheta_{G \backslash F}$$
$$\text{for some } \vartheta_{G \backslash F}$$

$$\mathcal{C} \models F \text{ BECAUSE } G \text{ iff } \forall \vartheta_F \text{each } ds \models F\vartheta_F \text{ is preceded by a } ds' \models G\vartheta_F\vartheta_{G \backslash F}$$
$$\text{for some } \vartheta_{G \backslash F}$$

$$ds \models A \text{ iff } \text{each } s \in ds \models A$$
$$ds \not\models \text{false}$$
$$ds \models \sim F \text{ iff } ds \not\models F$$
$$ds \models F \wedge F' \text{ iff } ds \models F \text{ and } ds \models F'$$
$$ds \models \Delta A \text{ iff } ds \models A \text{ and for } ds' \text{ i–preceding } ds, ds' \models \sim A$$
$$ds \models mF \text{ iff } \text{there exists } s \in ds \text{ such that } \{s\} \models F$$

For instance, the following computation fragment satisfies p LEADS_TO q:

$$\rightarrow . \rightarrow p \rightarrow . \rightarrow . \rightarrow q \rightarrow . \rightarrow p \rightarrow q \rightarrow . \rightarrow . \rightarrow . \rightarrow p \wedge q \rightarrow .$$

and $\rightarrow . \rightarrow p \wedge q \rightarrow . \rightarrow . \rightarrow r \wedge s \rightarrow . \rightarrow .$ satisfies both $m(p \wedge q)$ LEADS_TO $m(r \wedge s)$ and $mp \wedge mq$ LEADS_TO $mr \wedge ms$. Only the latter formula is also satisfied by any of the following:

$$\rightarrow . \rightarrow p \wedge q \rightarrow . \rightarrow . \rightarrow r \rightarrow s \rightarrow . \rightarrow .$$
$$\rightarrow . \rightarrow p \rightarrow . \rightarrow q \rightarrow . \rightarrow . \rightarrow r \rightarrow s \rightarrow . \rightarrow . \rightarrow .$$
$$\rightarrow . p \rightarrow . \rightarrow r \rightarrow . \rightarrow q \rightarrow . \rightarrow s \rightarrow . \rightarrow .$$

---

[2] In the full logic, these subset can contain states of several components, hence the name.

since a distributed state can be composed of distinguished and possibly non adjacent states. As a further example, the formulae $m(p \wedge \sim p)$ and $p \wedge \sim p$ are false, while any ds containing at least a state satisfying p and a state satisfying $\sim p$ satisfies $mp \wedge m(\sim p)$. On the contrary, $m(p \vee q)$ is equivalent to $mp \vee mq$.

Some rules of the logic follows. All rules hold both for LEADS_TO and for BECAUSE: we abstract the operator by OP. Rule CC applies when formulae G and G' are located, i.e. prefixed by m, or composed of located formulae.

$$\text{CC} \frac{F \text{ OP } G \quad F' \text{ OP } G'}{F \wedge F' \text{ OP } G \wedge G'} \qquad \text{PD} \frac{F \text{ OP } G \quad F' \text{ OP } G}{F \vee F' \text{ OP } G} \quad \text{E} \frac{F \text{ OP } false}{\sim F}$$

$$\text{SW} \frac{F' \to F \quad F \text{ OP } G \quad G \to G'}{F' \text{ OP } G'} \quad \text{TR} \frac{F \text{ OP } G \quad G \text{ OP } H}{F \text{ OP } H} \quad \text{I: } F \text{ OP } F$$

The logic comes with MaRK, a proof assistant that partially automates the verification process and is a valuable tool supporting the proof process, making it feasible to avoid error prone "by hand" arguments [11].

3 ΔDSTL(x) Semantics for APPEL

The semantics will be developed in two steps: first of all we define rules for the interpretation of a policy rule, then we consider combining policy rules.

3.1   Semantics for a Policy Rule

Let us recall that a policy rule is essentially a triple $(triggers, conditions, actions)$, where triggers is either a single trigger or a combination of a number of them. The same holds for conditions and actions. Also recall that triggers and actions are optional.

Let us define functions $\mathcal{M}$, $\mathcal{C}$ and $\mathcal{T}$, which will map (elements of) a policy rule into a set of ΔDSTL(x) formulae in 2^ϕ.

What is a trigger? Assume $t \in trigger$ and $ts \in triggers$.

$\mathcal{T}[\![\epsilon]\!] = true$
$\mathcal{T}[\![t]\!] = \Delta t$
$\mathcal{T}[\![ts \text{ or } ts']\!] = \mathcal{T}[\![ts]\!] \vee \mathcal{T}[\![ts']\!]$

What is a condition? Assume $c \in condition$ and $cs \in conditions$.

$\mathcal{C}[\![\epsilon]\!] = true$
$\mathcal{C}[\![c]\!] = c$
$\mathcal{C}[\![cs \text{ or } cs']\!] = \mathcal{C}[\![cs]\!] \vee \mathcal{C}[\![cs']\!]$
$\mathcal{C}[\![cs \text{ and } cs']\!] = \mathcal{C}[\![cs]\!] \wedge \mathcal{C}[\![cs']\!]$

More complicated, what is the meaning of an action? And furthermore what does it mean to compose actions? We note that actions can succeed and fail, which is important in the context of composing operations. Of course what exactly it means for an action to succeed or fail is dependent on the domain and specifics of the operation. As we are considering the semantics for the core language, we strive to stay clear of the domain specifics here. In order to capture the difference of success and failure we define two functions:

$$\mathcal{S}, \mathcal{F} : actions \rightarrow \phi \times 2^\phi$$

The first element in the resulting pair is a formula describing the success or failure of the action, the second element is a (possibly empty) set of side conditions that are imposing further restrictions on the first element. These extra formulae capture the rather intricate dependencies of executing an action depending on success/failure of a previous one that arise with some of the operators. Hence, for a simple action $a \in action$ we gain:

$$\mathcal{S}[\![a]\!] = \langle ms(a), \emptyset \rangle \text{ and } \mathcal{F}[\![a]\!] = \langle mf(a), \emptyset \rangle$$

Irrespective of the domain, it seems sensible to expect that an action either succeeds or fails, but never does both: $s(a) \oplus f(a)$. Let us postpone discussion of the details of $\mathcal{S}$ and $\mathcal{F}$ for a moment. In the following, assume $a \in action$ and $as \in actions$. We now have all the parts to define the meaning of a policy rule as a function $\mathcal{M} : triggers \times conditions \times actions \rightarrow 2^\phi$. Let $\mathcal{S}[\![as]\!] = \langle h_{sa}, sc_{sa} \rangle$ and $\mathcal{F}[\![as]\!] = \langle h_{fa}, sc_{fa} \rangle$, then:

$$\mathcal{M}[\![ts\ cs\ as]\!] = \{m(\mathcal{T}[\![ts]\!] \wedge \mathcal{C}[\![cs]\!]) \text{ LEADS\_TO } h_{sa} \vee h_{fa}\} \cup \{sc_{sa}\} \cup \{sc_{fa}\}$$

The informal semantics for the action operators is as follows [7]:

and: This specifies that the policy should lead to the execution of both actions in either order. This can be implemented by executing the actions in a specific order or in parallel.

andthen: This is a stronger version of **and**, since the first action must precede the second in any execution.

or: This specifies that either one of the actions should be taken.

orelse: This is the **or** operator with a prescribed order. It means that a user feels more strongly about the first action specified.

Let $\mathcal{S}[\![As]\!] = \langle h_{sa}, sc_{sa} \rangle$, $\mathcal{S}[\![Bs]\!] = \langle h_{sb}, sc_{sb} \rangle$, $\mathcal{F}[\![As]\!] = \langle h_{fa}, sc_{fa} \rangle$, $\mathcal{F}[\![Bs]\!] = \langle h_{fb}, sc_{fb} \rangle$, then

$\mathcal{S}[\![As \text{ and } Bs]\!] = \langle h_{sa} \wedge h_{sb}, sc_{sa} \cup sc_{sb} \rangle$

$\mathcal{S}[\![As \text{ or } Bs]\!] = \langle h_{sa} \vee h_{sb}, sc_{sa} \cup sc_{sb} \rangle$

$\mathcal{S}[\![As \text{ andthen } Bs]\!] = \langle h_{sa} \wedge h_{sb}, h_{sb} \text{ BECAUSE } h_{sa} \cup sc_{sa} \cup sc_{sb} \rangle$

$\mathcal{S}[\![As \text{ orelse } Bs]\!] = \langle h_{sa} \vee h_{sb}, h_{sb} \text{ BECAUSE } h_{fa} \cup sc_{sa} \cup sc_{sb} \cup sc_{fa} \rangle$

and

$\mathcal{F}[\![As \text{ and } Bs]\!] = \langle h_{fa} \vee h_{fb}, sc_{fa} \cup sc_{fb} \rangle$

$\mathcal{F}[\![As \text{ or } Bs]\!] = \langle h_{fa} \wedge h_{fb}, sc_{fa} \cup sc_{fb} \rangle$

$\mathcal{F}[\![As \text{ andthen } Bs]\!] = \langle h_{fa} \vee h_{fb}, h_{fb} \text{ BECAUSE } h_{sa} \cup sc_{fa} \cup sc_{fb} \cup sc_{sa} \rangle$

$\mathcal{F}[\![As \text{ orelse } Bs]\!] = \langle h_{fa} \wedge h_{fb}, h_{fb} \text{ BECAUSE } h_{fa} \cup sc_{fa} \cup sc_{fb} \rangle$

Let us consider an example, $\mathcal{S}[\![(a \text{ orelse } b) \text{ orelse } c]\!]$, with $a, b, c \in action$.

$\mathcal{S}[\![(a \text{ orelse } b) \text{ orelse } c]\!]$

$\qquad \mathcal{S}[\![a \text{ orelse } b]\!]$

$\qquad\qquad \mathcal{S}[\![a]\!] = \langle ms(a), \emptyset \rangle$

$$\mathcal{S}[\![b]\!] = \langle \mathsf{m}s(b), \emptyset \rangle$$
$$\mathcal{F}[\![a]\!] = \langle \mathsf{m}f(a), \emptyset \rangle$$
$$= \langle \mathsf{m}s(a) \vee \mathsf{m}s(b), \mathsf{m}s(b) \text{ BECAUSE } \mathsf{m}f(a) \rangle$$
$$\mathcal{S}[\![c]\!] = \langle s(c), \emptyset \rangle$$
$$\mathcal{F}[\![a \text{ orelse } b]\!]$$
$$\mathcal{F}[\![a]\!] = \langle \mathsf{m}f(a), \emptyset \rangle$$
$$\mathcal{F}[\![b]\!] = \langle \mathsf{m}f(b), \emptyset \rangle$$
$$= \langle \mathsf{m}f(a) \wedge \mathsf{m}f(b), \mathsf{m}f(b) \text{ BECAUSE } \mathsf{m}f(a) \rangle$$
$$= \langle \mathsf{m}s(a) \vee \mathsf{m}s(b) \vee \mathsf{m}s(c),$$
$$\{\mathsf{m}s(b)\text{BECAUSE } \mathsf{m}f(a), \mathsf{m}s(c) \text{ BECAUSE } \mathsf{m}f(a) \wedge \mathsf{m}f(b), \mathsf{m}f(b) \text{ BECAUSE } \mathsf{m}f(a)\} \rangle$$

3.2   Semantics for a Policy Rule Group

A policy rule group is the composition of a number of policy rules. The AP-PEL language provides a number of operators to compose policy rules with the following informal semantics [7]:

g(condition): When two policy rules are joined by the *guarded choice* operator, the execution engine will first evaluate the nested condition. If the guard evaluates to true, the first of the two rules will be applied, otherwise the second. Clearly once the guard has been evaluated it is necessary to decide whether the individual rule is applicable. Once a guarded choice has been made, it is not undone even if the resulting rule is not followed.

u: *Unguarded choice* provides more flexibility, as both parts will be tested for applicability. If only one of the two policy rules is applicable, this will be chosen. If both are applicable, the system can choose one at random.

seq: *Sequential composition* allows the rules to be enforced in the specified order. That is we traverse the structure, determining whether the first rule is applicable. If so we apply the first rule, otherwise we check the second rule. Note that the second rule will only be checked if the first rule is not applicable.

par: *Parallel composition* of two rules allows for a user to express an indifference with respect to the order of two rules. Both rules are applied, but the order in which this is done is not important.

To define function $\mathcal{G}$, giving semantics to a policy group, we need two auxiliary functions. The first one expresses the weakest precondition for a policy rule group to be applicable. Let $(t, c, a) \in polrule$ and $ps \in pol\_rule\_group$:

$$\mathcal{WP}[\![(t, c, a)]\!] = c$$
$$\mathcal{WP}[\![ps_1 \text{ seq } ps_2]\!] = \mathcal{WP}[\![ps_1]\!] \vee \mathcal{WP}[\![ps_2]\!]$$
$$\mathcal{WP}[\![ps_1 \text{ par } ps_2]\!] = \mathcal{WP}[\![ps_1]\!] \vee \mathcal{WP}[\![ps_2]\!]$$
$$\mathcal{WP}[\![ps_1 \text{ g}(c) \ ps_2]\!] = (c \wedge \mathcal{WP}[\![ps_1]\!]) \vee (\sim c \wedge \mathcal{WP}[\![ps_2]\!])$$
$$\mathcal{WP}[\![ps_1 \text{ u } ps_2]\!] = \mathcal{WP}[\![ps_1]\!] \vee \mathcal{WP}[\![ps_2]\!]$$

The second auxiliary function is a syntactic transformation to substitute the conditions in the policies:

$$d((t, c, a), x) = (t, x, a)$$
$$d(ps_1 \text{ op } ps_2, x) = d(ps_1, x) \text{ op } d(ps_2, x)$$

We can now define $\mathcal{G}$: $policy\_rule\_group \rightarrow 2^{\phi}$. Here $first$, $second$ and $either$ are fresh predicates. Predicate $pick$ is randomly set.

$$\mathcal{G}[\![(t, c, a)]\!] = \mathcal{M}[\![(t, c, a)]\!]$$

$\mathcal{G}[\![ps_1 \text{ seq } ps_2]\!] =$
$\qquad \mathcal{WP}[\![ps_1]\!] \longleftrightarrow first$
$\qquad \sim \mathcal{WP}[\![ps_1]\!] \wedge \mathcal{WP}[\![ps_2]\!] \longleftrightarrow second$
$\qquad \mathcal{G}[\![d(ps_1, first)]\!]$
$\qquad \mathcal{G}[\![d(ps_2, second)]\!]$

$\mathcal{G}[\![ps_1 \text{ par } ps_2]\!] =$
$\qquad \mathcal{G}[\![ps_1]\!]$
$\qquad \mathcal{G}[\![ps_2]\!]$

$\mathcal{G}[\![ps_1 \text{ g(c) } ps_2]\!] =$
$\qquad c \wedge \mathcal{WP}[\![ps_1]\!] \longleftrightarrow first$
$\qquad \sim c \wedge \mathcal{WP}[\![ps_2]\!] \longleftrightarrow second$
$\qquad \mathcal{G}[\![d(ps_1, first)]\!]$
$\qquad \mathcal{G}[\![d(ps_2, second)]\!]$

$\mathcal{G}[\![ps_1 \text{ u } ps_2]\!] =$
$\qquad \mathcal{WP}[\![ps_1]\!] \wedge \sim \mathcal{WP}[\![ps_2]\!] \longleftrightarrow first$
$\qquad \mathcal{WP}[\![ps_2]\!] \wedge \sim \mathcal{WP}[\![ps_1]\!] \longleftrightarrow second$
$\qquad \mathcal{WP}[\![ps_1]\!] \wedge \mathcal{WP}[\![ps_2]\!] \longleftrightarrow either$
$\qquad \mathcal{G}[\![d(ps_1, first \vee (either \wedge pick))]\!]$
$\qquad \mathcal{G}[\![d(ps_2, second \vee (either \wedge \sim pick))]\!]$

3.3   The Else Operator

The example in the following section originally made use of the **else** operator in P_2 and P_3. Since it is only syntactic sugar, we are not adding it to the language presented earlier, but rather show how it can be rewritten into the considered fragment.

The informal description of **else** is that it behaves like **or** unless it occurs at the top level. So if it occurs at the top level, *if trigger and condition then a_1 else a_2* is equivalent to two rules combined with a guarded choice where the condition is acting as guard, i.e. *trigger then a_1 g(condition) trigger then a_2*.

If the condition is empty or **else** occurs below the top level it can simply be replaced with **or**.

3.4   A Non–trivial Example

We will here study Example 5.7 from [7] with the purpose of showing the formal semantics at work. The purpose of the policies is to forward an incoming call when the recipient is busy. Otherwise, if not answered within 5 seconds, the call should be forwarded in a way that depends on the caller: calls from "acme" or "tom" should be forwarded to the office. If once more unanswered, the call goes to the recipient's mobile. Any other call should be forwarded home. In any case, business calls during office hours should be logged as such, and other calls as "out of hours" calls.

The policy is expressed by the policy group P_1 seq $(P_2$ par $P_3)$, where:

```
P_1 = when call
         if busy
         do forward_to(vm)
```

$P_2 = P_{2a} \; g(c_2) \; P_{2b}$ with:

```
c_2  = if not caller(acme) and not caller(tom)
P_2a = when not_answered(5)
          do forward_to(home)
P_2b = when not_answered(5)
          do forward_to(office)
       orelse
          do forward_to(mobile)
```

$P_3 = P_{3a} \; g(c_3) \; P_{3b}$ with:

```
c_3  = if call_type(business) and calltime(h) and inbusinesshours(h)
P_3a = when call
          do log(office_hours_call)
P_3b = when call
          do log(out_of_hours_call)
```

So, following the definitions[3] , we get

$\mathcal{G}[\![P_1 \; seq \; ((P_{2a} \; g(c_2) \; P_{2b}) \; par \; (P_{3a} \; g(c_3) \; P_{3b}))]\!] =$

> $busy \longleftrightarrow first$
>
> $\sim busy \longleftrightarrow second$
>
> $m(\Delta call \wedge first)$ LEADS_TO $ms(forward\_to(vm)) \vee mf(forward\_to(vm))$
>
> $\sim caller(acme) \wedge \sim caller(tom) \wedge second \longleftrightarrow first'$
>
> $(caller(acme) \vee caller(tom)) \wedge second \longleftrightarrow second'$
>
> $m(\Delta not\_answered(5) \wedge first')$ LEADS_TO $ms(forward\_to(home)) \vee mf(forward\_to(home))$
>
> $m(\Delta not\_answered(5) \wedge second')$ LEADS_TO
> $\quad (ms(forward\_to(office)) \vee ms(forward\_to(mobile)))$
> $\quad \vee (mf(forward\_to(office)) \wedge mf(forward\_to(mobile)))$
>
> $ms(forward\_to(mobile))$ BECAUSE $mf(forward\_to(office))$
>
> $call\_type(business) \wedge calltime(h) \wedge inbusinesshours(h) \wedge second \longleftrightarrow first''$
>
> $\sim (call\_type(business) \wedge calltime(h) \wedge inbusinesshours(h)) \wedge second \longleftrightarrow second''$
>
> $m(\Delta call \wedge first'')$ LEADS_TO $ms(log(office\_hours\_call)) \vee mf(log(office\_hours\_call))$
>
> $m(\Delta call \wedge second'')$ LEADS_TO $ms(log(out\_of\_hours\_call)) \vee mf(log(out\_of\_hours\_call))$

Remark 1. We model the application of two or more policies as an atomic step, independently of the fact that the policies are applied concurrently or in sequence. We only distinguish between *before* and *after* their application. To this purpose, we consider all predicates to be stable, including those describing the success and failure of an action. Stability means that once a predicate becomes true it stays so, and is related to the following rule: $\dfrac{F \text{ LEADS\_TO } mG \wedge mG'}{F \text{ LEADS\_TO } m(G \wedge G')}$

---

[3] From now on, we will represent sets of formulae as lists, without brackets.

This rule holds only when G and G' are stable. Since we are only interested in detecting conflict between actions, the stability assumption is reasonable. Indeed, the execution of an action does not cancel the fact that another action has been executed. Moreover, stability does not hinder the detection of situations where an action is executed when some conflicting conditions hold in the domain. In other words, we do not need to define the semantics of the actions and look at the state transformation caused by their execution. Finally, note that stability is preserved by conjunction and disjunction.

4   Dealing with Policy Conflicts

A conflict arises when, as a result of the policy application, two actions are executed, and they are defined to be conflicting in the domain description. A conflict arises also when a state is reached where a pair of conflicting predicates hold (these can be a predicate and its negation, or predicates defined to be conflicting in the domain description).

We can distinguish two types of conflict:

- actual conflict: from the policy theory and the domain description, we derive *true* LEADS_TO *conflict*. This means that the policy as it is gives raise to a conflict.
- possible conflict: from the policy theory and the domain description, we derive *true* LEADS_TO *disjunction*, and one of the disjuncts is a conflict. A typical case is when the disjunction arises from two actions, like $m((s(a) \lor f(a)) \land (s(b) \lor f(b)))$. Distributing, one sees immediately that the conflict $s(a) \land s(b)$ may be avoided because one of the actions fails.

To introduce a further kind of conflict, we look at the policies in Example 5.1 of [6]:

P1 = if user(x) and if admin(x) do allow(x)
P2 = if user(Joe) do deny(Joe)

There is also a piece of domain information: $admin(Joe)$. Also, we know from the domain description that actions allow and deny are conflicting, i.e., $s(allow(x)) \land s(deny(x)) \rightarrow conflict$. To detect conflicts, we first express the rules in the logic:

$\mathcal{G}[\![P1]\!] = m(user(x) \land admin(x))$ LEADS_TO $ms(allow(x)) \lor mf(allow(x))$
$\mathcal{G}[\![P2]\!] = m\,user(Joe)$ LEADS_TO $ms(deny(Joe)) \lor mf(deny(Joe))$

and then we develop the following proof:

$$\frac{\dfrac{\mathcal{G}[\![P1]\!] \quad admin(Joe)}{m\,user(Joe) \text{ LEADS\_TO } ms(allow(Joe)) \lor mf(allow(Joe))} \quad \mathcal{G}[\![P2]\!]}{\begin{array}{l} m\,user(Joe) \text{ LEADS\_TO} \\ \quad m(s(allow(Joe)) \lor f(allow(Joe))) \land m(s(deny(Joe)) \lor f(deny(Joe))) \end{array}}$$

We cannot go further. That is, we have not actually found a possible conflict, but we have discovered a *potential* one: only if the domain description is extended to satisfy the premise, i.e. if *user(Joe)* is stated, the conflict arises.

A systematic way to find all the interesting facts that might be added to the domain description and possibly generate (potential) conflicts, is to take finite consistent subsets of the Herbrand Base ($\mathcal{HB}$) of the theory obtained from the policies and the domain description. The $\mathcal{HB}$ of a theory is the set of all ground atoms which can be constructed using the ground terms and the predicate symbols from the language fragment used to define the theory itself[4]. Since triggers and actions are not interesting extensions of the domain description, we restrict the $\mathcal{HB}$ to the atoms built using the predicates symbols in the conditions.

In our example, we have
$$\mathcal{HB} = \{admin(Joe), user(Joe)\}$$
Hence we can go a step further:

$$\frac{\mathsf{m}(user(Joe) \wedge admin(Joe)) \ \text{LEADS\_TO}}{\mathsf{m}(s(allow(Joe)) \vee f(allow(Joe))) \wedge \mathsf{m}(s(deny(Joe)) \vee f(deny(Joe)))} \quad \mathcal{HB}}{true \ \text{LEADS\_TO} \ \mathsf{m}((s(allow(Joe)) \vee f(allow(Joe))) \wedge (s(deny(Joe)) \vee f(deny(Joe))))}$$

Distributing the conjunction we get a typical case of possible conflict. Since the conflict is derived in the theory extended with $\mathcal{HB}$, we consider it to be potential.

In the following example, we consider a slight variant on the previous:

$$\mathcal{G}[\![P3]\!] = \mathsf{m}(user(x) \wedge admin(x) \wedge daytime) \ \text{LEADS\_TO} \ \mathsf{m}s(allow(x)) \vee \mathsf{m}f(allow(x))$$
$$\mathcal{G}[\![P4]\!] = \mathsf{m}(user(Joe) \wedge nighttime) \ \text{LEADS\_TO} \ \mathsf{m}s(deny(Joe)) \vee \mathsf{m}f(deny(Joe))$$

and apply the same the proof pattern:

$$\frac{user(Joe) \wedge admin(Joe) \quad \mathcal{G}[\![P3]\!]}{\mathsf{m}\,daytime \ \text{LEADS\_TO}} \qquad \frac{user(Joe) \quad \mathcal{G}[\![P4]\!]}{\mathsf{m}\,nighttime \ \text{LEADS\_TO}}$$
$$\frac{\mathsf{m}\,s(allow(Joe)) \vee \mathsf{m}\,f(allow(Joe)) \qquad \qquad \mathsf{m}\,s(deny(Joe)) \vee \mathsf{m}\,f(deny(Joe))}{\mathsf{m}\,daytime \wedge \mathsf{m}\,nighttime \ \text{LEADS\_TO}}$$
$$\mathsf{m}(s(allow(Joe)) \vee f(allow(Joe))) \wedge \mathsf{m}(s(deny(Joe)) \vee f(deny(Joe)))$$

One could factorize m, but this is not the point. To detect a potential conflict we would need to reduce the premise to *true*, by exploiting the $\mathcal{HB}$. However, any consistent subset of $\mathcal{HB}$ contains either *daytime* or *nighttime*, but not both of them. Hence it is not possible to simplify to *true*.

5 Discussion

The above method allows to detect conflicts. However, which conflict exactly is being detected depends on the definitions of the conflict 'rules'. In particular we can distinguish between two types of conflict rules that allow to detect two distinct types of conflict: conflicts between two or more policies and conflict between a policy and the system (in the absence of other policies).

---

[4] The formal definition of $\mathcal{HB}$, in particular for the temporal case, states a set of requirements on the form of the theory (e.g. clausal, skolemized). This form is equivalent to that of the theories obtained from APPEL policies.

Considering the relation between feature interaction and policy conflict, we can draw parallels with features. When considering features we can also find problems when a feature interacts with the system (that is in the absence of other features) – traditionally these have been considered as bugs. Feature interaction work is always based on the assumption that the individual features on their own (of course the base system is always present) work as expected and problems occur when more than one feature is added to the system simultaneously.

Let us consider the following example:

$[\![P_1]\!] = daytime$ LEADS_TO $s(allow)$

$[\![P_2]\!] = lunchtime$ LEADS_TO $s(blacklist)$

$daytime$ and $lunchtime$ are overlapping, that is they can both hold at the same time; $blacklist$ is an action.

In the light of the previous, we could say that a policy conflict is clearly a conflict between a number of policies and the problem does not occur if only one policy is present. Let us first investigate this in more detail. To detect this type of conflict, we do not require a partial specification of the actions. It is sufficient to say that $s(a)$ and $s(b)$ lead to a conflict, as we have indeed done in the previous section.

If we consider the blacklisting example at hand, the definition of conflict here would be $s(allow) \wedge s(blacklist) \rightarrow conflict$. Adding the domain dependent information $lunchtime \rightarrow daytime$, we detect the potential conflict.

In this case we do not model the fact that an action might change the value of a predicate, say $blacklisted$; we also do not model the fact that predicates might change "miracleously" (that is by other actions in the system or spontaneously). In the light of this we can see predicates in the precondition as stable.

On the other hand, a policy interacting in an undesired way with the system (in the absence of other policies) is also an interesting case to consider. It might make less sense to speak about a bug here, after all policies are not implementations of system components, but rather high level descriptions of how the system should behave. Our method allows also to detect these, however more detail and a different definition of the conflict rules is required. The conflict rules will include a notion of state variables and the actions need to be specified somewhat. For the example on blacklisting, this means that we know that $s(blacklist) \rightarrow blacklisted$, that is the action leads to a change of the predicate. Our definition of conflict then is $blacklisted \wedge s(allow) \rightarrow conflict$. It should be obvious that this conflict exists in the absence of P_2, and indeed we can detect it.

In this latter case each action comes with a (possibly empty) list of conflicting states, while in the former each action comes with a list of conflicting actions.

One further aspect to consider, and this is again based on experience in feature interaction, is the question as to how many policies are required to generate a conflict. In feature interaction there is only one example for a true three-way interaction, and that is quite contrived.

In some sense this question is important, as the definition of conflict could be done considering only conflicting pairs if the same holds for policies. Note that it only influences the definition of conflict rules, and thus is more important as a design guideline.

6   Related Work

Of particular relevance is the work on policy conflict: policies may contradict since they may be set by different organisations or at different levels in the same organisation. Surprisingly, there does not appear to have been much work on policy conflicts. [12] recognises but does not address conflicts that arise in policy-driven adaptation mechanisms. [13] aims to define hierarchical policies such that, by definition, the subordinate policies cannot conflict. Conflicts are still possible if one policy in the hierarchy is changed. The use of meta-policies (policies about policies) is proposed as a solution, e.g. in [1], where meta-policy checks are applied when policies are specified and when they are executed. Similar ideas, where predefined rules and good understanding of the domain allow resolution of conflicts, are presented in [14]. In [15], it is anticipated that authorisation policies may lead to conflict. This is resolved by providing a function to compare policies and decide which should take precedence.

Further discussion on policy conflicts exist in the area of access control policies, often using logics to model policies. A formal model that permits the enforcement of complex access policies through composition is presented in [16]. Policies are expressed as safety conditions in Interval Temporal Logic, and they can be checked at run-time by the simulation tool Tempura. A fragment of first order logic, more expressive than Datalog, is used in [17]. The restrictions are such that no conflicts can arise. The logic permits to query the policy set for permissible/prohibited actions, via a friendly interface for naive users. UCON, a recent model of usage control that extends the concepts of access control has been formalized in [18], using an extension of Lamport's Temporal Logic of Actions.

Policy have also been applied to resource management in distributed system. [19] discusses the need for both static and dynamic conflict detection and resolution, and introduces computationally feasible algorithms to this purpose. The underlying model exploits a deontic logic of permission, prohibition, and obligation, coupled with temporal classifiers that indicate the span of the mode. Our approach is more flexible in expressing policies (it is not restricted to resource management and OPI type rules) and broader in scope (the conflict detection considers conflicting actions and not conflicting permissions applied to the same action).

We have made comparisons to features and feature interaction in the discussion; features stem from the telecommunications industry, but similar concepts exist in other areas such as component-based systems. In general a feature is new functionality to enhance a base system. Features are often developed in isolation and each feature's operation is tested with respect to the base system, and also with common known features.

Unfortunately, when two or more features are added to a base system, unexpected behaviour might occur. This is caused by the features influencing each other, and is referred to as feature interaction. Feature interaction shows many similarities to policy conflict, the main difference being the detail to which it has been studied. A general discussion of the problem appears in [20]. The literature on feature interaction is large [21,22].

7   Conclusion and Further Work

In this paper we have presented a formal semantics for a slightly reduced subset of the APPEL policy language, which sofar benefited only from an informal semantics. We also presented a novel method to reason about policy conflict in APPEL policies based on the developed semantics.

The semantics is a temporal logic theory, and a conflict is found if we derive, from the semantics of the policies, the formula *true* LEADS_TO *conflict*, a liveness formula stating that a conflict will surely arise.

As stated earlier, policies that are being used in software systems will be created and maintained by different parties, ranging from system administrators to lay users. Clearly this scope of authors and their respective interest means that inevitably policies will conflict with each other. An automatisation of our approach, using the proof assistant MaRK [11], will lead to tool support for detecting conflicts when policies are created or changed. Note that, due to the basic structure of APPEL terms, the size of the $\mathcal{HB}$ is not an issue.

To prove the absence of a conflict, we need to derive *conflict* BECAUSE *false*, which is a safety formula. To do so, we have to augment the semantic translation with safety conditions. This is left to further investigation.

As APPEL policies can be distributed in the networked system, we will enhance our conflict detection technique to deal with the distributed situation. ΔDSTL(x) lends itself naturally to this as the logic as concepts of location. For this it will be required to model the location information provided in policies in the logic. A further aspect is the enhancement of the formal semantics to include APPEL's user preferences.

Acknowledgements

This work has been conducted while Stephan Reiff-Marganiec was on leave at the University of Pisa, supported by the Royal Society International Outgoing Short Visit – 2006/R2 programme. The authors are all partially supported by the EU project SENSORIA IST-2005-16004.

References

1. Lupu, E., Sloman, M.: Conflicts in policy based distributed systems management. IEEE Transactions on Software Engineering 25(6) (1999)
2. Michael, J.B., Lobo, J., Dulay, N. (eds.): Proc. 3rd. International Workshop on Policies for Distributed Systems and Networks. IEEE Computer Society, Los Alamitos, California, USA (2002)

3. Sloman, M., Lobo, J., Lupu, E.C. (eds.): POLICY 2001. LNCS, vol. 1995. Springer, Heidelberg (2001)
4. Turner, K.J., Reiff-Marganiec, S., Blair, L., Pang, J., Gray, T., Perry, P., Ireland, J.: Policy support for call control. Computer Standards and Interfaces 28(6), 635–649 (2006)
5. Gorton, S., Reiff-Marganiec, S.: Policy support for business-oriented web service management. la-web 0, 199–202 (2006)
6. Reiff-Marganiec, S., Turner, K.J.: Feature interaction in policies. Comput. Networks 45(5), 569–584 (2004)
7. Reiff-Marganiec, S., Turner, K., Blair, L.: Appel: The accent project policy environment/language. Technical Report TR-161, University of Stirling (2005)
8. Montangero, C., Semini, L.: Distributed states logic. In: TIME 2002. 9th International Symposium on Temporal Representation and Reasoning, Manchester, UK, IEEE CS Press, Los Alamitos (2002)
9. Montangero, C., Semini, L., Semprini, S.: Logic Based Coordination for Event–Driven Self–Healing Distributed Systems. In: De Nicola, R., Ferrari, G.L., Meredith, G. (eds.) COORDINATION 2004. LNCS, vol. 2949, pp. 248–262. Springer, Heidelberg (2004)
10. Reiff-Marganiec, S., Turner, K.J.: Use of logic to describe enhanced communication services. In: Peled, D.A., Vardi, M.Y. (eds.) FORTE 2002. LNCS, vol. 2529, Springer, Heidelberg (2002)
11. Ferrari, G., Montangero, C., Semini, L., Semprini, S.: Mark, a reasoning kit for mobility. Automated Software Engineering 9(2), 137–150 (2002)
12. Efstratiou, C., Friday, A., Davies, N., Cheverst, K.: Utilising the event calculus for policy driven adaptation on mobile systems. [2], 13–24 (2002)
13. Amer, M., Karmouch, A., Gray, T., Mankovskii, S.: Feature interaction resolution using fuzzy policies. [23], 94–112 (2000)
14. Moffett, J.D., Sloman, M.S.: Policy conflict analysis in distributed systems management. Journal of Organizational Computing 4(1), 1–22 (1994)
15. Bertino, E., Catania, B., Ferrari, E., Perlasca, P.: A system to specify and manage multipolicy access control models. [2], 116–127 (2002)
16. Siewe, F., Cau, A., Zedan, H.: A compositional framework for access control policies enforcement. In: FMSE 2003. Proceedings of the 2003 ACM workshop on Formal methods in security engineering, pp. 32–42. ACM Press, New York, NY, USA (2003)
17. Halpern, J.Y., Weissman, V.: Using first-order logic to reason about policies. csfw 00, 187 (2003)
18. Zhang, X., Parisi-Presicce, F., Sandhu, R., Park, J.: Formal model and policy specification of usage control. ACM Trans. Inf. Syst. Secur. 8(4), 351–387 (2005)
19. Dunlop, N., Indulska, J., Raymond, K.: Methods for conflict resolution in policy-based management systems. In: Enterprise Distributed Object Computing Conference, IEEE Computer Society, pp. 15–26. IEEE Computer Society, Los Alamitos (2002)
20. Calder, M., Kolberg, M., Magill, E.H., Reiff-Marganiec, S.: Feature interaction: A critical review and considered forecast. Computer Networks 41, 115–141 (2001)
21. Amyot, D., Logrippo, L. (eds.): Feature Interactions in Telecommunications and Software Systems VII. IOS Press, Amsterdam (2003)
22. Reiff-Marganiec, S., Ryan, M. (eds.): Feature Interactions in Telecommunications and Software Systems VIII. IOS Press, Amsterdam (2005)
23. Calder, M., Magill, E. (eds.): Feature Interactions in Telecommunications and Software Systems VI. IOS Press, Amsterdam (2000)

Hoare Logic for ARM Machine Code

Magnus O. Myreen, Anthony C.J. Fox, and Michael J.C. Gordon

Computer Laboratory, University of Cambridge, Cambridge, UK
{magnus.myreen,anthony.fox,mike.gordon}@cl.cam.ac.uk

Abstract. This paper shows how a machine-code Hoare logic is used
to lift reasoning from the tedious operational model of a machine language to a manageable level of abstraction without making simplifying
assumptions. A Hoare logic is placed on top of a high-fidelity model of
the ARM instruction set. We show how the generality of ARM instructions is captured by specifications in the logic and how the logic can
be used to prove loops and procedures that traverse pointer-based data
structures. The presented work has been mechanised in the HOL4 theorem prover and is currently being used to verify ARM machine code
implementations of arithmetic and cryptographic operations.

1 Introduction

Although software runs on real machines like Intel, AMD, Sun, IBM, HP and
ARM processors, most current verification activity is performed using highly
simplified abstract models. For bug finding this is sensible, as simple models are
much more tractable than realistic models. However, the use of unrealistically
simple models is unsatisfactory for assurance of correctness, since correctness-
critical low level details will not have been taken into account. Details that are
frequently overlooked at the low levels include: finiteness of stacks and integers,
whether or not addresses need to be aligned and details of status bits.

Recently software verification based on realistically modelled software has received an increasing amount of attention as tools become able to cope with
tedious operational models. Boyer and Yu [1] have done some impressive pio-
neering work on verification of programs for the Motorola MC68020, Tan and
Appel [2] verified memory safety of Sun's SPARC machine code, and Hardin
et al. [3] verified machine code written for Rockwell Collins AAMP7G.

Curiously these efforts have made little use of advances in programming logics, while efforts for proving programs written in realistically modelled low-level
programming languages such as C have [4]. The work of Tan and Appel is –
to the best of our knowledge – the only significant effort that places a general
programming logic on top of a realistically modelled machine language. Their
approach requires substantial effort to prove the soundness of applying the logic
to their SPARC model. Hardin *et al.* and Boyer and Yu verify machine-code
programs using a form of symbolic simulation of the bare operational semantics
of their respective processor models.

In an earlier paper we developed a general Hoare logic for realistically modelled machine code [5]. In this paper the general logic is specialised to a detailed

F. Arbab and M. Sirjani (Eds.): FSEN 2007, LNCS 4767, pp. 272–286, 2007.

model of ARM machine code. This paper shows how the logic captures the details of ARM instructions and uses examples to illustrate how programs can be proved using the logic. The examples present proofs of loops and procedures that traverse recursive data structures.

This paper avoids a lengthy proof of soundness by simply instantiating abbreviating definitions for which sound proof rules have been proved in an earlier paper [5]. All specifications and proofs presented in this paper have been mechanically checked using the HOL4 system [6]. The detailed ARM model at the base of this work has been extracted from a proof of correctness of the instruction set architecture of an ARM processor [7].

The remainder of this paper is organised as follows. Section 2 gives a brief overview of the ARM machine language and specialises a Hoare logic to reason about ARM machine code. Section 3 presents how the details of ARM instructions are captured by specifications in the new logic. Section 4 illustrates the use of the logic through examples. Section 5 presents the ARM model and Section 6 concludes with a summary.

2   Hoare Triples for ARM

This section instantiates a Hoare logic to ARM machine code. We start with a brief overview of ARM machine code and then describe how a general Hoare logic is specialised to reason about ARM code.

2.1   ARM Machine Code

ARM machine code runs on ARM processors. These are widely used commercial RISC processors often found in mobile phones. The resources that ARM instructions access are, from a birds-eye-view, the following:

1. 16 registers are visible at any time: register 15 is the program counter and the others are general purpose registers each holding a 32-bit value (by convention register 13 is the stack pointer and register 14 is the link register);

2. 4 status bits: negative, zero, carry and overflow;

3. a 32-bit addressable memory with entries of 8 bits (or equivalently, a 30-bit addressable memory with 32-bit entries).

This high-level view is sufficient for all 32-bit ARM instructions that do not require interaction between operation modes. In some sense these are the instructions of the "programmer's model" of ARM. The Hoare logic presented in this paper is restricted to the subset of 32-bit ARM instructions that can execute equally regardless of operation mode (user, supervisor, etc). However the operational model at the base of this work considers also the instructions that do depend on the operation mode, for more details see Section 5.

Some interesting features of the 32-bit ARM instructions that have required special attention are listed below.

1. All instructions can be executed conditionally, i.e. instructions can be con-
   figured to have no effect when the status bits fail to satisfy some condition.
2. All "data processing" instructions can update the status bits.
3. During execution, undefined instruction encodings or forbidden instruction
   arguments can be encountered, in which case the subsequent behaviour is
   implementation specific (modelled as *unpredictable* behaviour).

2.2   ARM Hoare Logic

This section specialises a general machine-code Hoare logic, presented earlier [5],
to ARM machine code. The general logic specifies the behaviour of collections of
code segments using Hoare triples that allow multiple entry points and multiple
exit points. In this paper we will mainly use specifications with a single entry
point and a single sequence of code:

$$\{P\}\ \ cs\ \ \{Q_1\}^{h_1} \cdots \{Q_k\}^{h_k}$$

Such specifications are to be read informally as follows: whenever P holds for the
current state and code sequence cs is executed, a state will be reached where one
of the postconditions Q_i holds and the program counter will have been updated
by function h_i.

Models of states usually consist of tuples of components. However, when defining the semantics of our general Hoare logic, we have found it more convenient to
represent states as sets of *basic state elements* that separately specify the values
of single pieces of the state. This allows states to be split and partitioned using
elementary set operations (e.g. $\cup$, $\cap$, $-$). The elements we need for ARM are:
Reg i x (specifies register i has value x), Mem j y (specifies memory location j
has value y), Status (s_n, s_z, s_c, s_v) (specifies the values of the four status flags),
Undef b (specifies whether an 'undefined' instruction has been encountered) and
Rest z (specifies the remainder of the state). Thus for ARM, each state will be
a set of the form[1]:

$$\{ \text{Reg } 0\ x_0,\ \text{Reg } 1\ x_1,\ \text{Reg } 2\ x_2,\ \cdots,\ \text{Reg } 15\ x_{15},$$
$$\text{Mem } 0\ y_0,\ \text{Mem } 1\ y_1,\ \text{Mem } 2\ y_2,\ \cdots,\ \text{Mem } (2^{30}-1)\ y_{(2^{30}-1)},$$
$$\text{Status } (s_n, s_z, s_c, s_v),\ \text{Undef } b,\ \text{Rest } z \}$$

Fox's ARM model uses a tuple-like state representation, thus in order to spe-
cialise our general Hoare logic to his ARM model, we need a translation function
from Fox's state representation to our set-based representation. Such a translation is defined as follows. Let *reg a s* extract the value of register a from
state s, *mem a s* extract the value of memory location a from s and *status*
extract the value of the four status bits from s. Also let *s.undefined* indicate
whether s is considered as a state from which *unpredictable* behavior may occur

---

[1] Numerals denote both bit strings and natural numbers. Type annotations in the
syntax of HOL4: Reg $(i:\texttt{word4})$ $(x:\texttt{word32})$ and Mem $(j:\texttt{word30})$ $(y:\texttt{word32})$.

and let *hidden* project the remaining part of an ARM state, i.e. the part that is not observable by *reg*, *mem*, *status* and *undefined*. We can then define:

$$arm2set(s) = \{ \text{ Reg } a \ (reg \ a \ s) \mid \text{any } a \ \} \cup$$
$$\{ \text{ Mem } a \ (mem \ a \ s) \mid \text{any } a \ \} \cup$$
$$\{ \text{ Status } (status \ s), \text{ Undef } s.undefined, \text{ Rest } (hidden \ s) \ \}$$

The translation does not loose any information and therefore has an inverse *set2arm* such that $\forall s. \ set2arm(arm2set(s)) = s$.

The general theory is formally specialised to reason about ARM machine code by instantiating a 6-tuple $(\Sigma, \alpha, \beta, next, pc, inst)$ that parametrises the general theory. Here Σ is the set of states, *next* is a next-state function $next : \Sigma \rightarrow \Sigma$, and $pc : \alpha \rightarrow \Sigma \rightarrow \mathbb{B}$ and $inst : \alpha \times \beta \rightarrow \Sigma \rightarrow \mathbb{B}$ are elementary assertions over states. The general theory is instantiated to the ARM model by setting Σ to be the range of *arm2set*, α to be the set of 30-bit addresses and β to be the set of 32-bit words. The next-state function is defined using the next-state function for the ARM model (*next_arm*) and translations *arm2set* and *set2arm*.

$$next(s) = arm2set(next\_arm(set2arm(s)))$$

In what follows *addr* is a function that transforms a 30-bit address to a 32-bit (word-aligned) address by appending two zeros as new least significant bits. The program-counter assertion $pc(p)$ is defined to check that a subset of a state implies that the program counter is set to p and that the state is well-defined. The instruction assertion $inst(p, c)$ makes sure that instruction c is stored in the location which is executed when the program counter has value p. These assertions are predicates on sets of basic state elements: $pc(p)$ is true of a set if it is $\{ \text{ Reg } 15 \ (addr(p)), \text{ Undef } F \ \}$ and $inst(p, c)$ is true of a set if it is $\{ \text{ Mem } p \ x \ \}$. Thus:

$$pc(p) = \lambda s. \ s = \{ \text{ Reg } 15 \ (addr(p)), \text{ Undef } F \ \}$$
$$inst(p, x) = \lambda s. \ s = \{ \text{ Mem } p \ x \ \}$$

3   Instruction Specifications

The previous section discussed how we instantiate our abstract Hoare logic to ARM machine code. This section shows how the new Hoare triples capture the behaviour of basic ARM instructions. We start by explaining how a simple specification relates to the ARM model and then go on to show how the full generality of ARM instructions is captured by the new Hoare triples.

Consider the following specification of SUB $a,a,$#1 (subtract by one).

$$\{R \ a \ x\}$$
$$\text{SUB } a,a,\text{#1}$$
$$\{R \ a \ (x{-}1)\}^{+1}$$

This specification states that register a is decremented by one and that the program counter is incremented by one. Let $R \ r \ x = \lambda s. \ (s = \{\text{Reg } r \ x\})$. In terms of the set-based state representation the specification ought to be read as follows: whenever SUB a,a,#1 is executed, the part of the state corresponding to {Reg a x} is updated to {Reg a $(x-1)$} and simultaneously the part corresponding to the program counter is updated by function $+1$ (abbreviates $\lambda n.\ n+1$), i.e. the subset corresponding to {Reg 15 $(addr(p))$, Undef F}, for some value p, becomes {Reg 15 $(addr(p+1))$, Undef F}.

In terms of the ARM model, the above specification is formally equivalent to the following. Let $run(k, s)$ be a function that applies $next\_arm$ k times to state s, and let $\lfloor \cdot \rfloor$ be a function that produces the 32-bit encoding of a given ARM instruction. Also let FRAME $=$ { Reg a x | any x } $\cup$ { Reg 15 x | any x }.

$$\forall s\ p.\ (reg\ a\ s = x) \wedge (reg\ 15\ s = addr(p)) \wedge (a \neq 15) \wedge$$
$$(mem\ p\ s = \lfloor \text{SUB}\ a,a,\text{\#1} \rfloor) \wedge \neg s.undefined \Rightarrow$$
$$\exists k.\ \text{let}\ s' = run(k, s)\ \text{in}$$
$$(reg\ a\ s' = x-1) \wedge (reg\ 15\ s' = addr(p+1)) \wedge (a \neq 15) \wedge$$
$$(mem\ p\ s' = \lfloor \text{SUB}\ a,a,\text{\#1} \rfloor) \wedge \neg s'.undefined \wedge$$
$$(arm2set(s) - \text{FRAME} = arm2set(s') - \text{FRAME})$$

For most part this expansion contains no surprises: whenever registers a is x, the program counter points at an encoding of SUB a,a,#1 and the state is well-defined, then register a is decremented, the program counter is updated by function $+1$ and the state remains well-defined. The interesting part of the above specification is the last line. The last line states that the initial state is the same as the result state, if one removes registers a and 15 from both states. The last line specifies what is left unchanged, i.e. the scope of the operation.

The Hoare triples satisfy a frame rule similar to that of separation logic [8]. The frame rule uses a separating conjunction ($*$), which we define as follows: Define $split\ s\ (u, v)$ to mean that the pair of sets (u, v) partitions set s, i.e. $split\ s\ (u, v) = (u \cup v = s) \wedge (u \cap v = \emptyset)$, and then define $P * Q$ to be true for states that can be split such that P and Q are true for disjoint parts of the state: $P * Q = \lambda s.\ \exists u\ v.\ split\ s\ (u, v) \wedge P\ u \wedge Q\ v$. The frame rule:

$$\frac{\{P\}\ c\ \{Q\}^h}{\forall F.\ \{P * F\}\ c\ \{Q * F\}^h}$$

The frame rule can be used to expand the basic specification of SUB a,a,#1 to say that the value of register b stays constant, if b is distinct from a:

$$\{R\ a\ x * R\ b\ y\}$$
$$\text{SUB}\ a,a,\text{\#1}$$
$$\{R\ a\ (x-1) * R\ b\ y\}^{+1}$$

The expansion of the extended specification is equal to the above expansion with the inclusion of $(reg\ b\ s = y) \wedge (a \neq b) \wedge (b \neq 15)$ for both s and s'. The separating conjunction implies necessary inequalities as a result of its requirement of disjointness. We use $*$ as a basic building block in all our specifications.

The remainder of this section describes the generalisations that are made in order to accommodate the full features of real ARM instructions.

3.1   Conditional Execution

Every 32-bit ARM instruction can execute conditionally according to a condition code that is encoded in each instruction. The instruction is executed if the condition associated with the given condition code is satisfied by the status bits. If the condition is not satisfied then the instruction has no effect (other than incrementing the program counter). The behavior of conditional execution is captured by giving each instruction two specifications, one for the case when it has an effect and one for the case when it has no effect. Let $\text{PASS}(c, z)$ assert that bits z satisfy condition code c. Let $\neg\text{PASS}(c, z)$ be its negation. Let $S\ z = \lambda s.\ (s = \{\text{Status } z\})$.

$$\{R\ a\ x * S\ z * \text{PASS}(c, z)\} \qquad \{S\ z * \neg\text{PASS}(c, z)\}$$
$$\text{SUB}c\ \ a,a,\#1 \qquad\qquad \text{SUB}c\ \ a,a,\#1$$
$$\{R\ a\ (x{-}1) * S\ z\}^{+1} \qquad\qquad \{S\ z\}^{+1}$$

3.2   Status Bits

Most ARM instructions have a flag called the s-flag. When this flag is set, executing the command will update the status bits. Let $sub\_status(x, y)$ calculate the value of the four status bits for the subtraction $x{-}y$.

$$\{R\ a\ x * S\ z * \text{PASS}(c, z)\}$$
$$\text{SUB}cs\ \ a,a,\#1$$
$$\{R\ a\ (x{-}1) * S\ (\text{if } s \text{ then } sub\_status(x, 1) \text{ else } z)\}^{+1}$$

3.3   Addressing Modes

The SUB instruction, used above, can of course do more than subtract by one. It can subtract by any small (shifted/rotated) constant or a (shifted/rotated) register value. The form of the second term in a subtraction is specified by an *addressing mode* (for SUB: ARM Addressing Mode 1). Our specifications parametrise the addressing mode as a variable m. The functions $encode\_am_1$ and $value\_am_1$ construct, respectively, the instruction encoding and second argument of an arithmetic operation for a given instance m of ARM Addressing Mode 1. Examples:

$$\{R\ a\ x\} \qquad\qquad \{R\ a\ x * R\ b\ y\}$$
$$\text{SUB}\ \ a,a,encode\_am_1(m, a) \qquad \text{SUB}\ \ b,b,encode\_am_1(m, a)$$
$$\{R\ b\ (x{-}value\_am_1(m, x))\}^{+1} \qquad \{R\ a\ x * R\ b\ (y{-}value\_am_1(m, x))\}^{+1}$$

Specifications, such as those shown below, can be produced, if we instantiate m appropriately and rewrite using the definitions of $encode\_am_1$ and $value\_am_1$.

$$\{R\ a\ x\} \qquad \{R\ a\ x * R\ b\ y\} \qquad \{R\ a\ x * R\ b\ y\}$$
$$\text{SUB}\ \ a,a,\#1 \qquad \text{SUB}\ \ b,b,a \qquad\qquad \text{SUB}\ \ b,b,a,\text{LSL }\#5$$
$$\{R\ a\ (x{-}1)\}^{+1} \qquad \{R\ a\ x * R\ b\ (y{-}x)\}^{+1} \qquad \{R\ a\ x * R\ b\ (y{-}(x \ll 5))\}^{+1}$$

3.4   Aligned Addresses

A 32-bit address is word aligned if it is divisible by four. On ARM, memory accesses to word-sized entities generally result in rotations of the accessed words, if the accessed address is not word aligned. In order to avoid cluttering specifications with details of word rotations, we specify word-aligned memory accesses separately from the general case. The specification for aligned load-word LDR requires no rotations. Let $R'\ r\ x$ assert that register r holds a word-aligned address x, i.e. $R'\ r\ x = R\ r\ (addr(x))$, and let $M\ a\ x = \lambda s.\ (s = \{\mathsf{Mem}\ a\ x\})$.

$$\{R\ a\ z * R'\ b\ x * M\ (address\_am_2(m, x))\ y\}$$
$$\text{LDR } a, encode\_am_2(m, b)$$
$$\{R\ a\ y * R'\ b\ (writeback\_am_2(m, x)) * M\ (address\_am_2(m, x))\ y\}^{+1}$$

The above can be specialised to the following by instantiation of m:

$$\{R\ a\ z * R'\ b\ x * M\ x\ y\}$$
$$\text{LDR } a, \text{[}b\text{]}$$
$$\{R\ a\ y * R'\ b\ x * M\ x\ y\}^{+1}$$

$$\{R\ a\ z * R'\ b\ x * M\ (x-1)\ y\}$$
$$\text{LDR } a, \text{[}b, \text{\#-4]} !$$
$$\{R\ a\ y * R'\ b\ (x-1) * M\ (x-1)\ y\}^{+1}$$

3.5   Branch Instructions

Branch instructions are given one postcondition for each exit point. The specification of a conditional relative branch:

$$\{S\ z\}$$
$$\text{B } c\ \#k$$
$$\{S\ z * \text{PASS}(c, z)\}^{+(k+2)}$$
$$\{S\ z * \neg\text{PASS}(c, z)\}^{+1}$$

The intuition for multiple postconditions is that one of the postconditions will be reached. Whenever B c #k is executed, there will either be a jump of $k + 2$ instructions or a jump to the next instruction. The formal semantics is based on disjunction, for details see our earlier paper [5].

3.6   Automation

The above specifications are rather hard to use in practice if addressing modes and condition codes have to be instantiated by hand. We found it useful to write an ML function that maps string representations of the instructions to their respective instantiations of the general specifications. The instantiating ML function was connected to an ML function that calculates the composition of a given list of instruction specifications using the composition rule from our earlier paper [5], e.g. the input ["LDR a,[b],#16","SUBS a,a,#1","BNE k"] gives:

$$\{R\ a\ z * R'\ b\ x * M\ x\ y * S\ \_\}$$
$$\text{LDR } a, \text{[}b\text{]}, \text{\#16; SUBS } a, a, \text{\#1; BNE } \#k$$
$$\{R\ a\ (y-1) * R'\ b\ (x+4) * M\ x\ y * S\ \_ * \langle y-1 \neq 0\rangle\}^{+(k+2)}$$
$$\{R\ a\ (y-1) * R'\ b\ (x+4) * M\ x\ y * S\ \_ * \langle y-1 = 0\rangle\}^{+3}$$

Here the ML function treats x as a word-aligned address and hides the initial and final value of the status bits using an underscore (_) which denotes 'some-value' (formally _ is a postfix function: P _ $= \lambda s.\ \exists x.\ P\ x$).

4 Case Studies

This section demonstrates how specifications from the previous section can be reformulated and combined in order to prove specifications for ARM code with loops, procedures and pointer-based data structures.

4.1 Factorial Program

As an initial example, we will show how loop rules can be proved and used. A loop rule will be proved for a count-down loop and then used in the proof of the following factorial program:

```
      MOV  b, #1     ; b := 1
   L: MUL  b, a, b   ; b := a × b
      SUBS a, a, #1  ; decrement a and update status bits
      BNE  L         ; if a is nonzero then jump to L
```

This program stores the factorial of register a (modulo 2^{32}) in register b, if a is initially non-zero. It calculates the factorial by executing a count-down loop:

$$b := 1;\ \mathtt{repeat}\ \{\ b := a \times b;\ a := a-1\ \}\ \mathtt{until}\ (a{=}0)$$

Loop. A specification for a loop of the form "L: *body*; SUBS $a,a,\#1$; BNE L" can be devised using the specification of the combined effect of SUBS and BNE. For the proof we will require that *body* has a specification of the following form. Let m be the length of the code sequence *body*.

$$\{Inv(x) * R\ a\ x * S\ \_ * \langle x \neq 0 \rangle\}$$
$$body \tag{1}$$
$$\{Inv(x{-}1) * R\ a\ x * S\ \_\}^{+m}$$

The technique described in Section 3.6 can be used to construct a specification for "SUBS $a,a,\#1$; BNE $\#k$", which can be composed with (1) to give:

$$\{Inv(x) * R\ a\ x * S\ \_ * \langle x \neq 0 \rangle\}$$
$$body;\ \mathtt{SUBS}\ a,a,\#1;\ \mathtt{BNE}\ \#k$$
$$\{Inv(x{-}1) * R\ a\ (x{-}1) * S\ \_ * \langle x{-}1 \neq 0 \rangle\}^{+(m+k+3)}$$
$$\{Inv(x{-}1) * R\ a\ (x{-}1) * S\ \_ * \langle x{-}1 = 0 \rangle\}^{+(m+2)}$$

A loop is constructed if k is assigned value $-(m{+}3)$, since the program counter update is then $+0$, i.e. the program counter returns to its original value. With a few other simplifications we can reveal that the precondition is satisfied by each jump to the top of the loop. Let $<$ denote less-than over unsigned 32-bit words.

$$\{Inv(x) * R\,a\,x * S\,_- * \langle x \neq 0 \rangle\}$$
$$body;\ \text{SUBS}\ a,a,\#1;\ \text{BNE}\ \#\text{-}(m\text{+}3)$$
$$\{\exists z.\ Inv(z) * R\,a\,z * S\,_- * \langle z \neq 0 \rangle * \langle z < x \rangle\}^{+0}$$
$$\{Inv(0) * R\,a\,0 * S\,_-\}^{+(m+2)}$$

Postconditions that describe a jump to a precondition, with some bounded variant that decreases at each jump, can be removed since the loops they describe will terminate and thus a different postconditions will eventually be reached [5]. The postcondition with update $+0$ is removed:

$$\{Inv(x) * R\,a\,x * S\,_- * \langle x \neq 0 \rangle\}$$
$$body;\ \text{SUBS}\ a,a,\#1;\ \text{BNE}\ \#\text{-}(m\text{+}3) \tag{2}$$
$$\{Inv(0) * R\,a\,0 * S\,_-\}^{+(m+2)}$$

We have proved a loop rule: any code $body$ and invariant Inv that satisfies specification (1) will also satisfy specification (2).

Factorial. The factorial program is easily proved in case we can find a specification of MUL that fits specification (1) from above. Notions of factorials and partial factorials are needed in order to create a suitable specification for MUL. Let fac be the factorial function over natural numbers:

$$fac(n)\ =\ \begin{cases} 1 & \text{if } n = 0 \\ n \times fac(n{-}1) & \text{if } n > 0 \end{cases}$$

Let factorial and partial factorial (e.g. $5 \times 4 \times 3 = fac(5)/fac(2)$) over 32-bit words be defined using conversion to and from the natural numbers, $w2n$: $\texttt{word32->num}$ and $n2w$: $\texttt{num->word32}$.

$$x!\ =\ n2w(fac(w2n(x)))$$
$$y \cdot\cdot\, x\ =\ n2w(fac(w2n(y))/fac(w2n(x)))$$

Notable features of the partial factorial ($\cdot\cdot$) are that $x \cdot\cdot 0 = x!$ and $y \cdot\cdot y = 1$ and $(z \cdot\cdot y) \times y = z \cdot\cdot (y{-}1)$, if $y \leq z$ and $y \neq 0$.

A specification for MUL can now be molded into the required form:

$$\{R\,a\,x * R\,b\,(z \cdot\cdot x) * S\,_- * \langle x \neq 0 \rangle\}$$
$$\text{MUL}\ b,a,b$$
$$\{R\,a\,x * R\,b\,(z \cdot\cdot (x{-}1)) * S\,_-\}^{+1}$$

The loop rule from the previous section then gives the following result:

$$\{R\,a\,x * R\,b\,(z \cdot\cdot x) * S\,_- * \langle x \neq 0 \rangle\}$$
$$\text{MUL}\ b,a,b;\ \text{SUBS}\ a,a,\#1;\ \text{BNE}\ \#\text{-}4$$
$$\{R\,a\,0 * R\,b\,(z \cdot\cdot 0) * S\,_-\}^{+3}$$

```
sum:    CMP     a,#0             ; compare a with 0
        MOVEQ   r15,r14          ; return, if a = 0
        STR     a,[r13,#-4]!     ; push a
        STR     r14,[r13,#-4]!   ; push link-register
        LDR     r14,[a]          ; temp := node value
        ADD     s,s,r14          ; s := s + temp
        LDR     a,[a,#4]         ; a := address of left
        BL      sum              ; s := s + sum of a
        LDR     a,[r13,#4]       ; a := original a
        LDR     a,[a,#8]         ; a := address of right
        BL      sum              ; s := s + sum of a
        LDR     r15,[r13],#8     ; pop two and return
```

Fig. 1. BINARY_SUM: ARM code to sum the values at the nodes of a binary tree

Instantiating z to x and composing a specification for MOV at the front yields a specification for the factorial program:

$$\{R\, a\, x * R\, b\, \_ * S\, \_ * \langle x \neq 0 \rangle\}$$
MOV b,#1; MUL b,a,b; SUBS a,a,#1; BNE #-4
$$\{R\, a\, 0 * R\, b\, x! * S\, \_\}^{+4}$$

The final specification states that the program stores the factorial of register a (modulo 2^{32}) in register b, if the initial value of register a was non-zero.

4.2 Sum of Nodes in Binary Tree

Next we illustrate the proof of a recursive procedure that sums the values stored at the nodes of a binary tree. The implementation we prove is called BINARY_SUM. Its code is shown in Figure 1. BINARY_SUM makes a depth-first pass through a binary tree, where nodes are stored as blocks of three consecutive memory elements: one 32-bit value and two aligned addresses pointing to the root of the subtrees (called left and right). The procedure adds the sum of the tree with root at address a into register s. When executing BINARY_SUM on the tree depicted below, it adds the values 5, 2, 6, 1, 3, 8 to register s. The recursive calls are realised by the BL instruction.

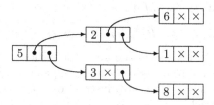

Binary Tree. The trees BINARY_SUM traverses are modelled as trees that are either empty (Leaf) or a branch (Node(x, l, r)). Each branch holds a 32-bit value x and two subtrees l and r. The sum of such a tree is defined as follows:

$$sum(\mathsf{Leaf}) = 0$$
$$sum(\mathsf{Node}(x,l,r)) = x + sum(l) + sum(r)$$

A predicate $tree(x,t)$ is defined to assert that tree t is stored in memory with its root at address x. For ease of presentation we require that subtrees are stored in disjoint parts of the memory (which is implied by the occurrence of $*$ between the recursive assertions of $tree$). Here and throughout M' a x asserts that memory location a holds aligned address x, i.e. M' a $x = M$ a $(addr(x))$.

$$tree(a,\mathsf{Leaf}) = \langle a = 0 \rangle$$
$$tree(a,\mathsf{Node}(x,l,r)) = \exists a_1\,a_2.\ M\,a\,x * M'\,(a{+}1)\,a_1 * M'\,(a{+}2)\,a_2 * \\ tree(a_1,l) * tree(a_2,r) * \langle a \neq 0 \rangle$$

The $tree$ assertion allows us to prove that "LDR b,[a]; ADD s,s,b" adds the value of a node, addressed by register a, to register s. Notice that the specification must mention register b, since the value of register b is updated by this operation.

$$\{R'\,a\,x * R\,s\,z * tree(x,\mathsf{Node}(y,l,r)) * R\,b\,\_\}$$
$$\text{LDR } b,[a];\ \text{ADD } s,s,b$$
$$\{R'\,a\,x * R\,s\,(z{+}y) * tree(x,\mathsf{Node}(y,l,r)) * R\,b\,\_\}^{+2}$$

The above specification is a result of a composition of the specifications for LDR and ADD, an application of the frame rule, and a reformulation that introduces the existential quantifier hidden in $tree(x,\mathsf{Node}(y,l,r))$.

Stack. BINARY_SUM uses the stack to store local variables. In order to specify the stack operations, a notion of a stack segment is formalised. On ARM processors the stack is by convention descending, i.e. it grows towards lower addresses. The stack pointer, register 13, holds the address of the top element of the stack.

A stack predicate is defined using two auxiliary definitions: $ms(a,[x_0;\cdots;x_m])$ specifies that the 32-bit words $x_0,\cdots,x_n$ are stored in sequence from address a upwards in memory and $blank(a,n)$ asserts that n memory locations from address a downwards have 'some value'. The stack predicate $stack(sp,xs,n)$ is defined to assert that the aligned address sp is stored in register 13, that xs is the sequence of elements pushed onto the stack (above sp) and that there are n unused slots on top of the descending stack (immediately beneath sp).

$$ms(a,[x_0;x_1;\cdots;x_m]) = M\,a\,x_0 * M\,(a{+}1)\,x_1 * \cdots * M\,(a{+}m)\,x_m$$
$$blank(a,n) = M\,a\,\_ * M\,(a{-}1)\,\_ * \cdots * M\,(a{-}(n{-}1))\,\_$$
$$stack(sp,xs,n) = R'\,13\,sp * ms(sp,xs) * blank(sp{-}1,n)$$

The predicate $blank$ is needed in the above definition in order to state how much stack space is allowed to be used. As an example, consider the specification for a stack push given below. The push instruction consumes one slot of stack space. Here cons is defined by cons x_0 $[x_1;\cdots;x_n] = [x_0;x_1;\cdots;x_n]$.

$$\{R\,a\,x * stack(sp,xs,n{+}1)\}$$
$$\text{STR } a,[\text{r13},\#{-}4]\,!$$
$$\{R\,a\,x * stack(sp{-}1,\mathsf{cons}\,x\,xs,n)\}^{+1}$$

The verification of BINARY_SUM requires the pushed elements to be separated from the stack predicate at one point. The pushed elements can be extracted using the following equivalence. Let [] denote an empty list.

$$stack(sp, xs, n) \;=\; ms(sp, xs) * stack(sp, [], n)$$

Procedures. On ARM, procedures are by convention passed a return address in register 14 to which they must jump on exit. The control-flow contract of a procedure is enforced by a specification that requires the code to have a single exit point that updates the program counter to the address passed in register 14. If the program counter is initially p then the function $\lambda x.y$ updates the program counter to y, since $(\lambda x.y)\, p = y$.

$$\{P * R' \, 14 \, y\} \; code \; \{Q * R \, 14 \, \_\}^{\lambda x.y}$$

BINARY_SUM has the following procedure specification:

$$\{R' \, a \, x * R \, b \, \_ * R \, s \, z * S \, \_ *$$
$$tree(x,t) * stack(sp, [\,], 2 \times depth(t)) * R' \, 14 \, y\}$$
$$\text{BINARY\_SUM}$$
$$\{R \, a \, \_ * R \, b \, \_ * R \, s \, (z + sum(t)) * S \, \_ *$$
$$tree(x,t) * stack(sp, [\,], 2 \times depth(t)) * R \, 14 \, \_\}^{\lambda x.y}$$

Let $pre \; x \; t \; z \; y$ and $post \; x \; t \; z$ be the pre- and postcondition from above.

Procedure Calls and Recursion. The specification for BINARY_SUM is proved using induction. We induct on $depth(t)$ and assume that there is some code C that executes recursive calls correctly for any t' such that $depth(t') < depth(t)$.

$$\forall t'. \; depth(t') < depth(t) \;\Rightarrow\; \forall x \; z \; y. \; \{\, pre \; x \; t' \; z \; y \,\} \, C \, \{\, post \; x \; t' \; z \,\}^{\lambda x.y}$$

With this assumption we can derive specifications for the BL instruction which perform the recursive calls in BINARY_SUM. The specifications are constructed using the proof rule derived in our earlier paper [5]. The code in these specifications is the union of the assumed code and the BL instruction:

$$\{\, pre \; x \; t' \; z \; \_ \,\} \, \text{BL \#}k \;\cup\; C \, \{\, post \; x \; t' \; z \,\}^{+1}$$

The rest of the verification is simple: compose the specifications for each instruction of BINARY_SUM in order to produce:

$$\{\, pre \; x \; t \; z \; y \,\} \, \text{BINARY\_SUM} \;\cup\; C \, \{\, post \; x \; t \; z \,\}^{\lambda x.y}$$

An application of the following instance of complete induction over the natural numbers removes the imaginary code C and the assumption on t'.

$$\frac{\forall t \, C. \; (\forall t'. \; depth(t') < depth(t) \Rightarrow \psi(t', C)) \Rightarrow \psi(t, code \cup C)}{\forall t. \; \psi(t, code)}$$

Tail-Recursion. BINARY_SUM, proved above, was constructed with clarity of presentation in mind. A good implementation would make use of the fact that the second recursive call can be made into a tail-recursive call. The last two instructions of BINARY_SUM are the following.

```
BL    sum              ; s := s + sum of a
LDR   r15,[r13],#8     ; pop two and return
```

These are turned tail-recursive by reversing the order as follows:

```
LDR   r14,[r13],#8     ; restore stack and link register
B     sum              ; s := s + sum of a
```

The new code copies the return address of the stack into the link register (register 14) rather than the program counter (register 15). It then performs a normal branch to the top of the procedure.

The optimised variant of BINARY_SUM is no harder to prove than the original version, normal composition is used instead of the rule for procedure calls. One can prove that the tail-recursive version requires only $2 \times ldepth(t)$ slots of stack space during execution. $ldepth$ is defined as follows.

$$ldepth(\mathsf{Leaf}) \quad = \quad 0$$
$$ldepth(\mathsf{Node}(x, l, r)) \quad = \quad \max(ldepth(l)+1, ldepth(r))$$

5   ARM Model

In Section 2.2, a Hoare logic for ARM machine code was constructed by placing a general Hoare logic on top of an operational model of the ARM instruction set. This section gives a brief overview of the ARM model that was used.

In the model underlying the Hoare triples, the state space is represented as a concrete HOL type (as opposed to a set of sets). The HOL type is a record type with four fields: *registers* (a mapping from register names to 32-bit words), *psrs* (a mapping from names of program status registers to 32-bit words), *memory* (a mapping from 30-bit words to 32-bit words) and *undefined* (a boolean indicating whether implementation specific behaviour follows from the current state).

The ARM Hoare triples only have access to 16 registers. However, the underlying model includes all 37 registers of an ARM processor. System modes have their own copies of some of the general purpose registers, thus the large number of register in total. The conceptual layout of the actual register bank is illustrated in Figure 2. The ARM Hoare triples convey the image of only 16 registers by presenting only the registers usable by the instructions of the current operation mode (for any mode, in case the Rest element is not mentioned in the precondition). This view of the registers is achieved by defining the functions *reg*, *status* and *hidden* (used in the definition of *arm2set*) to project the values of registers and status bits as viewed by the current operation mode, e.g. when operating in supervisor mode (svc), *reg* 14 *s* denotes the value of register r14_svc, *reg* 2 *s* is the value of register r2 and *reg* 8 *s* is the value of register r8_fiq.

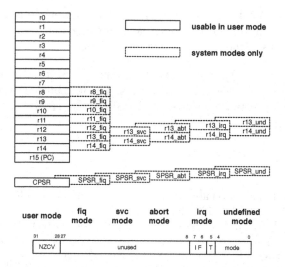

Fig. 2. ARM register banks and format of the Program Status Registers (PSRs)

The memory model deserves a comment, since a simple memory model is adopted: it is assumed that only data transfer instructions (memory stores) can alter the state of the memory i.e. the memory cannot be updated by the *environment*; when loading an instruction from memory, instruction pre-fetching (pipelining) is not considered; pre-fetch and data aborts are never raised i.e. it is assumed that one can always successfully access any memory address. Furthermore, input from the environment is not modelled i.e. it is assumed that there are no hardware interrupts. The Hoare logic that was instantiated in Section 2.2 can handle a more realistic model of memory, provided that it behaves as described above, for the part of memory mentioned in the precondition.

The ARM model used here is a conservative extension of a previously reported ARM model [7]. A well-understood path (by virtue of HOL theorems) exists between the ARM Hoare triples and a detailed register-transfer-level model of the hardware of an ARM processor. The path can be depicted as follows.

6 Summary

In this paper we have placed a general machine-code Hoare logic on top of a detailed model of the ARM machine language. By doing this we have constructed a framework that lifts reasoning from the tedious operational model to a manageable level. We have illustrated how specifications capture the generality of ARM instructions and demonstrated the use of the framework on examples that include loops, stacks, pointer data structures, procedures, procedural recursion and tail recursion. We have not yet applied the framework to large case studies, but we believe we have a methodology and implemented tools that will scale. Demonstrating this is the next phase of our research.

Acknowledgments. We would like to thank Joe Hurd, Konrad Slind and Thomas Tuerk for discussions and comments. The first author, Magnus Myreen, is funded by Osk.Huttusen Säätiö and EPSRC. The second author, Anthony Fox, is also funded by EPSRC.

References

1. Boyer, R.S., Yu, Y.: Automated proofs of object code for a widely used microprocessor. J. ACM 43(1), 166–192 (1996)
2. Tan, G., Appel, A.W.: A compositional logic for control flow. In: Emerson, E.A., Namjoshi, K.S. (eds.) VMCAI 2006. LNCS, vol. 3855, Springer, Heidelberg (2005)
3. Hardin, D.S., Smith, E.W., Young, W.D.: A robust machine code proof framework for highly secure applications. In: Manolios, P., Wilding, M. (eds.) ACL2, pp. 11–20. ACM Press, New York (2006)
4. Tuch, H., Klein, G., Norrish, M.: Types, bytes, and separation logic. In: Hofmann, M., Felleisen, M. (eds.) POPL. Proc. 34th ACM SIGPLAN-SIGACT Symposium on Principles of Programming Languages, pp. 97–108. ACM Press, New York (2007)
5. Myreen, M.O., Gordon, M.J.: Hoare logic for realistically modelled machine code. In: TACAS. LNCS, pp. 568–582. Springer, Heidelberg (2007)
6. Gordon, M.J.C., Melham, T.F. (eds.): Introduction to HOL (A theorem-proving environment for higher-order logic). Cambridge University Press, Cambridge (1993)
7. Fox, A.: Formal specification and verification of ARM6. In: Basin, D., Wolff, B. (eds.) TPHOLs 2003. LNCS, vol. 2758, Springer, Heidelberg (2003)
8. Reynolds, J.: Separation logic: A logic for shared mutable data structures. In: LICS. Proceedings of Logic in Computer Science, IEEE Computer Society, Los Alamitos (2002)

Action Abstraction in Timed Process Algebra
The Case for an Untimed Silent Step

Michel A. Reniers and Muck van Weerdenburg

Technical University Eindhoven (TU/e)
P.O. Box 513, NL-5600 MB Eindhoven, The Netherlands
M.A.Reniers@tue.nl, M.J.van.Weerdenburg@tue.nl

Abstract. This paper discusses action abstraction in timed process algebras. It is observed that the leading approaches to action abstraction in timed process algebra all maintain the timing of actions, even if these actions are abstracted from.

This paper presents a novel approach to action abstraction in timed process algebras. Characteristic for this approach is that in abstracting from an action, also its timing is abstracted from. We define an abstraction operator and a timed variant of rooted branching bisimilarity and establish that this notion is an equivalence relation and a congruence.

1 Introduction

One of the main tools in analysing processes in a process-algebraic setting is abstraction. Abstraction allows for the removal of information that is regarded as unobservable (or irrelevant) for the verification purpose at hand. Abstraction is introduced in the form of an action abstraction operator, called hiding, or in the form of data abstraction through abstract interpretations. In action hiding, certain action names are made anonymous and/or unobservable by replacing them by a predefined *silent step* (also called internal action) denoted by τ.

In the field of untimed process algebra, there is reasonable consensus about the properties of the silent step. In ACP-style process algebras [1] the notion of (rooted) branching bisimilarity, as put forward by Van Glabbeek and Weijland in [2,3], is mostly adopted. The few timed versions of rooted branching bisimilarity found in the literature (see [4,5,6]) and of weak bisimilarity (see [7,8,9,10]) all agree on maintaining the timing of actions, even if these actions are abstracted from. In all of these approaches the passing of time by itself (i.e., without subsequent action execution or termination) can be observed. As a consequence, not as many identifications between processes can be made as is desirable for verification purposes. This hinders the verification of correctness of real-time systems and therefore this situation needs to be improved.

In this paper, we study an action abstraction mechanism that not only abstracts from an action, but also from its timing. We introduce an *untimed silent step* into a timed process algebra. We define a timed version of rooted branching bisimilarity based on this untimed silent step, show that it is an equivalence and

F. Arbab and M. Sirjani (Eds.): FSEN 2007, LNCS 4767, pp. 287–301, 2007.

a congruence, and present a remarkably straightforward axiomatisation for this notion of equivalence. We give a short account of the identifications between processes that can be obtained using this equivalence. This is done by showing simplifications of the PAR protocol using the notions of equivalence from the literature and the notion introduced in this paper.

It should be mentioned that when studying timed process algebras (or timed automata for that matter), one encounters a number of different interpretations of the interaction between actions and time. There are the so-called two-phase models, where the progress of time is modeled separately from action execution, and there is the time-stamped setting, where time progress and action execution are modeled together. Two-phase models are used in [11], and time-stamped models are found in timed μCRL [12], for example. In this paper, we study timed rooted branching bisimilarity in the context of an absolute time, time-stamped model.

Structure. First, we introduce a simple timed process algebra with absolute timing and a time-stamped model (Sect. 2). This process algebra serves as a vehicle for our discussions on abstraction and equality of processes. It contains primitives that are fundamental to virtually every timed process algebra. In Sect. 3, we discuss the notions of timed rooted branching bisimilarity as they are encountered in the literature. In Sect. 4, we adapt the timed process algebra to incorporate our ideas for abstraction and equality for timed processes interpreted in a time-stamped model. In Sect. 5, we illustrate the consequences of our definitions on the PAR protocol. In Sect. 6, we present axioms for timed strong bisimilarity and timed rooted branching bisimilarity. In Sect. 7, we discuss the possibilities and impossibilities of adapting our notions to other settings in timed process algebra from the literature. Section 8 wraps up the paper.

2   The Universe of Discourse

In this section, we introduce a simple time-stamped process algebra without abstraction. This process algebra serves well for a more formal exposition of our discomfort with the existing ways of dealing with abstraction in timed process algebra and for a discussion of the possible solutions. Also, this process algebra will be used for the treatment of the chosen solution.

The timed process algebra presented in this section, $\mathrm{BSP}^{@}_{\mathrm{abs}}$ (for *Basic Sequential Processes* with *absolute time* and *time-stamping*), is an extension of the process theory BSP from [13] with absolute-timing and time-stamping (both syntactically and semantically) inspired by the process algebra *timed* μCRL [12][1].

We first present the starting point of our deliberations. We assume a set Time that is totally ordered by $\leq$ with smallest element 0 that represents the time domain[2]. We also assume a set Act of actions, *not* containing τ.

---

[1] Note that in the original semantics of timed μCRL [14], a two-phase model is used with states consisting of a closed process term and a moment in time, and separate action transitions $\xrightarrow{a}$ and a time transition $\xrightarrow{\iota}$.

[2] It does not matter for the treatment whether this time domain is discrete or dense.

The signature of the process algebra $\mathrm{BSP}^{@}_{\mathrm{abs}}$ consists of the following constants and operators:

- for each $t \in$ Time, a timed deadlock constant $0^{@t}$. The process $0^{@t}$ idles up to time t and then deadlocks.
- for each $t \in$ Time, a timed termination constant $1^{@t}$. The process $1^{@t}$ idles up to time t and then terminates successfully.
- for each $a \in$ Act and $t \in$ Time, an action prefix operator $a^{@t}.\_$. The process $a^{@t}.p$ represents the process that idles up to time t, executes action a at that time and after that behaves as process p insofar time allows.
- the alternative-composition operator $\_ + \_$. The process $p + q$ represents the nondeterministic choice between the processes p and q. The choice is resolved by the execution of an action or an occurrence of a termination.
- for each $t \in$ Time, a time-initialisation operator $t \gg \_$. The process $t \gg p$ is p limited to those alternatives that execute their first action not before time t.

Terms can be constructed using variables and the elements from the signature. Closed terms are terms in which no variables occur. We decide to allow the execution of more than one action at the same moment of time (in some order). There are no fundamental reasons for this choice: we could equally well have adopted the choice to disallow such *urgent* actions.

Next, we provide a structured operational semantics for the closed terms from this process algebra. We define the following transition relations and predicates:

- a time-stamped action-transition relation $\_ \xrightarrow{a}_t \_$ (with $a \in$ Act and $t \in$ Time), representing the execution of an action a at time t.
- a time-stamped termination predicate $\_ \downarrow_t$ (with $t \in$ Time), representing successful termination at time t.
- a time-parameterised delay predicate $\_ \rightsquigarrow_t$ (with $t \in$ Time), representing that a process can idle until time t (at least).

The reason for including the delay predicate is to discriminate between differently timed deadlocks: $0^{@3} \rightsquigarrow_3$, whereas $0^{@2} \not\rightsquigarrow_3$. These transition relations and predicate are defined by means of a so-called term deduction system [15]. The deduction rules are presented in Table 1. In this table and others in the rest of this paper, x, x', y and y' are variables representing arbitrary process terms, $a \in$ Act is an action name, $I \subseteq$ Act and $t, u \in$ Time.

Note that the time-initialisation operator is used in the structured operational semantics to impose upon a process the absolute time point that has been reached by previous activity.

Timed strong bisimilarity (as defined in [12], for example) is a congruence for all operators from this process algebra. One can quite easily obtain a sound and complete axiomatisation of timed strong bisimilarity. The details are omitted as they are of no importance to the goal of this paper.

Table 1. Structured Operational Semantics of $BSP^@_{abs}$

$$\frac{}{0^{@t} \leadsto_u} [u \le t] \qquad \frac{}{1^{@t} \downarrow_t} \qquad \frac{}{1^{@t} \leadsto_u} [u \le t] \qquad \frac{}{a^{@t}.x \xrightarrow{a}_t t \gg x}$$

$$\frac{}{a^{@t}.x \leadsto_u} [u \le t] \qquad \frac{x \xrightarrow{a}_t x'}{\begin{array}{c} x + y \xrightarrow{a}_t x' \\ y + x \xrightarrow{a}_t x' \end{array}} \qquad \frac{x \downarrow_t}{\begin{array}{c} x + y \downarrow_t \\ y + x \downarrow_t \end{array}} \qquad \frac{x \leadsto_t}{\begin{array}{c} x + y \leadsto_t \\ y + x \leadsto_t \end{array}}$$

$$\frac{x \xrightarrow{a}_u x'}{t \gg x \xrightarrow{a}_u x'} [t \le u] \qquad \frac{x \downarrow_u}{t \gg x \downarrow_u} [t \le u] \qquad \frac{}{t \gg x \leadsto_u} [u \le t] \qquad \frac{x \leadsto_u}{t \gg x \leadsto_u}$$

3   Abstraction and the Timed Silent Step

In order to facilitate abstraction of actions, usually a special atomic action $\tau \notin Act$ is assumed that represents an *internal action* or *silent step*. Also, an abstraction operator τ_I (for $I \subseteq Act$) is used for specifying which actions need to be considered internal. This leads to the following extensions to the signature of the process algebra:

- for each $t \in Time$, a silent step prefix operator $\tau^{@t}._-$. The process $\tau^{@t}.p$ represents the process that idles up to time t, executes silent step τ at that time and after that behaves as process p insofar time allows.
- for each $I \subseteq Act$, an abstraction operator τ_I. The process $\tau_I(p)$ represents process p in which all actions from the set I are made invisible (i.e., replaced by silent step τ).

To express execution of a silent step at a certain time t the predicate $\_ \xrightarrow{\tau}_t \_$ is used. The silent step prefix operator has precisely the same deduction rules as the action prefix operator (with a replaced by τ). The deduction rules for the abstraction operator are given below.

$$\frac{x \xrightarrow{a}_t x'}{\tau_I(x) \xrightarrow{a}_t \tau_I(x')} [a \notin I] \qquad \frac{x \xrightarrow{a}_t x'}{\tau_I(x) \xrightarrow{\tau}_t \tau_I(x')} [a \in I]$$

$$\frac{x \xrightarrow{\tau}_t x'}{\tau_I(x) \xrightarrow{\tau}_t \tau_I(x')} \qquad \frac{x \downarrow_t}{\tau_I(x) \downarrow_t} \qquad \frac{x \leadsto_t}{\tau_I(x) \leadsto_t}$$

Again, congruence of timed strong bisimilarity is obvious and obtaining a sound and complete axiomatisation of timed strong bisimilarity is not difficult either.

Timed Rooted Branching Bisimilarity. In the rest of this section, we discuss several timed versions of the well-known notion of rooted branching bisimilarity [2,3]. We refer to the relevant literature for definitions of these notions. We only present some characteristic equalities and inequalities between processes to illustrate the notions.

In [4, Chapter 6], Klusener defines notions of timed rooted branching bisimilarity for a timed process algebra in a setting that does not allow for consecutive actions at the same moment in time, i.e., non-urgent actions. Two semantics and equivalences are defined, both in a setting with time-stamped action transitions. The first semantics, the so-called *idle* semantics employs idle transitions to model time passing. The second, called the *term* semantics, uses an ultimate delay predicate instead. Characteristic for the equivalences is that an action transition a at time t in one process may be mimicked in another process by a well-timed sequence (i.e., a sequence in which the timing of the subsequent actions does not decrease) of silent steps that is ultimately followed by an a-transition at time t. The intermediate states need to be related with the original state (at the right moment in time). Klusener shows that in his setting these two semantics and equivalences coincide. In almost the same setting[3], using the term semantics, Fokkink proves a completeness result for the algebra of regular processes [16,17]. By means of the following examples we will discuss the equivalences of Klusener. For these examples it is possible to eliminate the abstraction operator from the process terms. We have not done so in order to be able to use these examples again in their current form in the next section (where we have a slightly different syntax).

Example 1 (No-Choice Silent Step). The three processes $\tau_{\{b\}}(a^{@1}.b^{@2}.c^{@4}.0^{@5})$, $\tau_{\{b\}}(a^{@1}.b^{@3}.c^{@4}.0^{@5})$ and $a^{@1}.c^{@4}.0^{@5}$ are obviously considered equal. Thus, the timing of the action that is hidden is of no importance insofar it does not disallow other actions from occurring (due to ill-timedness).

Example 2 (Time-Observed Silent Step). The processes $\tau_{\{b\}}(a^{@1}.(b^{@2}.(c^{@3}.0^{@4}+d^{@3}.0^{@4})+d^{@3}.0^{@4}))$ and $a^{@1}.(c^{@3}.0^{@4}+d^{@3}.0^{@4})$ are distinguished by the notion of timed rooted branching bisimilarity from [4, Chapter 6]. The reason is that in the first process at time 2 it may be determined that the d will be executed at time 3, while in the latter process term the choice between the c and the d at 3 can not be done earlier than at time 3.

Example 3 (Swapping). The processes $\tau_{\{b\}}(a^{@1}.(b^{@2}.c^{@3}.0^{@4} + d^{@3}.0^{@4}))$ and $\tau_{\{b\}}(a^{@1}.(c^{@3}.0^{@4}+b^{@2}.d^{@3}.0^{@4}))$ are considered equal with respect to Klusener's notion of equality, since in both processes it is decided at time 2 whether the c or the d will be executed at time 3.

It is interesting to note that, if one considers Klusener's definition of timed rooted idle branching bisimilarity in a setting in which urgent actions are allowed, the swapping of silent steps as portrayed in this example does not hold anymore. With timed rooted branching bisimilarity as defined for the term semantics though, it remains valid. This is due to the fact that the latter notion explicitly limits the behaviour of processes.

---

[3] Fokkink uses a relative-time syntax and semantics and defines the ultimate delay predicate slightly different.

Example 4 (Time-Choice). According to [4] the processes $\tau_{\{b\}}(a^{@1} \cdot (b^{@3}.0^{@4} + c^{@2}.0^{@4}))$ and $a^{@1}.(0^{@4} + c^{@2}.0^{@4})$ are equal, since the passage of time already decides at time point 2 whether or not the alternative $c^{@2}.0^{@4}$ occurs or not.

Baeten and Bergstra introduce the silent step to relative time, absolute time and parametric time (i.e., a mixture of both relative and absolute time) versions of ACP with discrete time in [5]. A difference with the work of Klusener is that time steps are represented explicitly in the syntax in [5]. In [18], a complete axiomatisation for timed rooted branching bisimilarity is provided, for a variant of this theory. With respect to the four examples presented before, the only difference between Klusener's notion and Baeten and Bergstra's notion is that the latter does *not* consider the processes from Example 3 (Swapping) equal.

In [6], Van der Zwaag defines a notion of timed branching bisimilarity for a process algebra that has almost the same syntax and semantics as ours. In the setting studied by Van der Zwaag there is no successful termination. In [19], Fokkink et al. show that the notion of timed branching bisimilarity as put forward by Van der Zwaag is not an equivalence for dense time domains and therefore they present a stronger notion of timed branching bisimilarity that is an equivalence indeed. Also, the definitions are extended to include successful termination. These notions of timed rooted branching bisimilarity are similar to that of Baeten and Bergstra for the examples presented before.

The way in which abstraction of actions leads to very precisely timed silent steps can be considered problematic (from a practical point of view). This was also recognised by Baeten, Middelburg and Reniers in [20] in the context of a relative-time discrete-time process algebra with two-phase time specifications. The equivalences as described above are not coarse enough in practical cases such as the PAR protocol. An attempt is made to establish a coarser equivalence (called abstract branching bisimilarity) that "treats an internal action always as redundant if it is followed by a process that is only capable of idling till the next time slice." This leads to an axiom (named DRTB4) of the form $\tau_{\{a\}}(a^{@t}.x) = \tau_{\{a\}}(t \gg x)$ (in a different syntax).

Although we support the observation of the authors from [20] that a coarser notion of equivalence is needed, we have a major problem with the treatment of this issue in [20]. The authors have sincere difficulties in defining the equivalence on the structured operational semantics. This difficulty is ultimately solved by using the (standard) definition of rooted branching (tail) bisimilarity from [18] in combination with a structured operational semantics that is a silent-step-saturated version of the original semantics.

4   Untimed Silent Step

In this section, we present a novel abstraction mechanism in timed process algebra that is inspired by the opinion that *the timing of a silent step as such is not observable.* Therefore, one might consider defining an abstraction operator that abstracts from an action *and* from its timing. One should be careful though, that abstraction from the timing of action a may not result in an abstraction of the consequences of this timing of a for the rest of the process!

In the next section, we formally present our novel approach to action abstraction in timed process algebras. First we give the consequences of our intuition about the equality (called timed rooted branching bisimilarity, denoted by $\underline{\leftrightarrow}_{\mathrm{rb}}$, see Sect. 4.2 for a definition) of the example processes from the previous section.

The timing of the action that is hidden is of no importance insofar it does not disallow other actions from occurring (due to ill-timedness). Therefore, the processes from Example 1 (No-Choice) should be considered equal:

$$\tau_{\{b\}}(a^{@1}.b^{@2}.c^{@4}.0^{@5}) \quad \underline{\leftrightarrow}_{\mathrm{rb}} \quad \tau_{\{b\}}(a^{@1}.b^{@3}.c^{@4}.0^{@5}) \quad \underline{\leftrightarrow}_{\mathrm{rb}} \quad a^{@1}.c^{@4}.0^{@5}$$

The processes from Example 2 (Time-Observed Silent Step) are equal in our setting since we do not wish to consider the timing of the internal step relevant:

$$\tau_{\{b\}}(a^{@1}.(b^{@2}.(c^{@3}.0^{@4}+d^{@3}.0^{@4})+d^{@3}.0^{@4})) \quad \underline{\leftrightarrow}_{\mathrm{rb}} \quad a^{@1}.(c^{@3}.0^{@4}+d^{@3}.0^{@4})$$

The processes from Example 3 (Swapping) are different processes, since by executing the silent step, an option that was there before has disappeared:

$$\tau_{\{b\}}(a^{@1}.(b^{@2}.c^{@3}.0^{@4}+d^{@3}.0^{@4})) \quad \underline{\not\leftrightarrow}_{\mathrm{rb}} \quad \tau_{\{b\}}(a^{@1}.(c^{@3}.0^{@4}+b^{@2}.d^{@3}.0^{@4}))$$

Since we do not allow to take the timing of the abstracted action into account, we cannot have the equality of the processes from Example 4 (Time-Choice):

$$\tau_{\{b\}}(a^{@1}.(b^{@3}.0^{@4}+c^{@2}.0^{@4})) \quad \underline{\not\leftrightarrow}_{\mathrm{rb}} \quad a^{@1}.(0^{@4}+c^{@2}.0^{@4})$$

In contrast with the other equivalences discussed in this paper, the process $\tau_{\{b\}}(a^{@1}.(b^{@3}.0^{@4}+c^{@2}.0^{@4}))$ can only be 'simplified' to $a^{@1}.(\tau.0^{@4}+c^{@2}.0^{@4})$. Thus the silent step remains.

In our opinion, in [20] too many silent steps can be omitted. Consider for example the process $\tau_{\{a\}}(a^{@1}.0^{@2}+b^{@3}.0^{@4})$. In [20], it is considered to be equal to $b^{@3}.0^{@4}$. In our opinion, the execution of the internal step disables the execution of action b altogether.

4.1 Abstraction Using the Untimed Silent Step

We propose to extend the process algebra from Sect. 2 with the following primitives instead of the timed silent action prefix operators and abstraction operator from Sect. 3:

- the silent step prefix operator $\tau.\_$. The process $\tau.p$ performs an internal action (not at any specific time) and thereafter behaves as p. Note that the occurrence of such an internal action cannot result in disabling an action from p.
- for each $I \subseteq \mathrm{Act}$, the abstraction operator τ_I. The process $\tau_I(p)$ represents process p where all actions from the set I are made invisible (replaced by the untimed silent step τ). It should be noted that the consequences of the timing of the abstracted action are not abstracted from.

In the structured operational semantics, we add a relation $\_ \xrightarrow{\tau} \_$ that represents the execution of an untimed silent step. For alternative composition and time initialisation we add deduction rules for this new transition relation (the first two deduction rules in Table 2). In the second deduction rule for the abstraction operator one can see that a timed action is replaced by an untimed silent step

Table 2. Structured Operational Semantics of untimed silent step and abstraction operator

$$\frac{x \xrightarrow{\tau} x'}{x + y \xrightarrow{\tau} x' \quad y + x \xrightarrow{\tau} x'} \qquad \frac{x \xrightarrow{\tau} x'}{t \gg x \xrightarrow{\tau} t \gg x'} \qquad \overline{\tau.x \xrightarrow{\tau} x} \qquad \frac{x \rightsquigarrow_t}{\tau.x \rightsquigarrow_t}$$

$$\frac{x \xrightarrow{a}_t x'}{\tau_I(x) \xrightarrow{a}_t \tau_I(x')} \, [a \notin I] \qquad \frac{x \xrightarrow{a}_t x'}{\tau_I(x) \xrightarrow{\tau} \tau_I(x')} \, [a \in I] \qquad \frac{x \xrightarrow{\tau} x'}{\tau_I(x) \xrightarrow{\tau} \tau_I(x')}$$

$$\frac{x \downarrow_t}{\tau_I(x) \downarrow_t} \qquad \frac{x \rightsquigarrow_t}{\tau_I(x) \rightsquigarrow_t}$$

in case the action is to be abstracted from. Also note that the consequences of the timing of the action are imposed on the rest of the process by means of the time-initialisation operator in the deduction rule for action-transitions of the action prefix operator (in Table 1). This means that the process x' incorporates the fact that time t has been reached.

Example 5. Somewhat surprisingly, the process $p = a^{@2}.\tau_{\{b\}}(b^{@1}.0^{@4})$ is not ill-timed. This is a consequence of our decision that the timing of abstracted actions is not observable. Thus the process p is equal to $a^{@2}.0^{@4}$ and of course also to $a^{@2}.\tau_{\{b\}}(b^{@3}.0^{@4})$ (which can hardly be considered ill-timed).

4.2   Timed Rooted Branching Bisimilarity

In the following definition we use the notation $p \Rightarrow q$ to denote that q can be reached from p by executing an arbitrary number (possibly zero) of τ-transitions. The notation $p \xrightarrow{(\tau)} q$ means $p \xrightarrow{\tau} q$ or $p = q$.

Definition 1 (Timed Rooted Branching Bisimilarity). *Two closed terms p and q are timed branching bisimilar, notation $p \underline{\leftrightarrow}_b q$, if there exists a symmetric binary relation R on closed terms, called a timed branching bisimulation relation, relating p and q such that for all closed terms r and s with $(r, s) \in R$:*

1. *if $r \xrightarrow{a}_t r'$ for some $a \in$ Act, $t \in$ Time and closed term r', then there exist closed terms s^* and s' such that $s \Rightarrow s^* \xrightarrow{a}_t s'$, $(r, s^*) \in R$ and $(r', s') \in R$;*

2. *if* $r \xrightarrow{\tau} r'$ *for some closed term* r', *then there exist closed terms* s^* *and* s' *such that* $s \Rightarrow s^* \xrightarrow{(\tau)} s'$, $(r, s^*) \in R$ *and* $(r', s') \in R$;

3. *if* $r \downarrow_t$ *for some* $t \in$ Time, *then there exists a closed term* s^* *such that* $s \Rightarrow s^* \downarrow_t$ *and* $(r, s^*) \in R$;

4. *if* $r \leadsto_t$ *for some* $t \in$ Time, *then there exists a closed term* s^* *such that* $s \Rightarrow s^* \leadsto_t$ *and* $(r, s^*) \in R$.

If R is a timed branching bisimulation relation, we say that the pair (p, q) satisfies the root condition *with respect to R if*

1. *if* $p \xrightarrow{a}_t p'$ *for some* $a \in$ Act, $t \in$ Time *and closed term* p', *then there exists a closed term* q' *such that* $q \xrightarrow{a}_t q'$ *and* $(p', q') \in R$;

2. *if* $p \xrightarrow{\tau} p'$ *for some closed term* p', *then there exists a closed term* q' *such that* $q \xrightarrow{\tau} q'$ *and* $(p', q') \in R$;

3. *if* $p \downarrow_t$ *for some* $t \in$ Time, *then* $q \downarrow_t$;

4. *if* $p \leadsto_t$ *for some* $t \in$ Time, *then* $q \leadsto_t$.

Two closed terms p and q are called timed rooted branching bisimilar, *notation $p \underline{\leftrightarrow}_{\text{rb}} q$, if there is a timed branching bisimulation relation R relating p and q such that the pairs (p, q) and (q, p) satisfy the root condition with respect to R.*

Note that we have actually defined a timed version of the notion of semi-branching bisimilarity of [21].

4.3 Properties of Timed Rooted Branching Bisimilarity

In this section, we show that timed rooted branching bisimilarity as defined in the previous section is indeed an equivalence. Moreover we show that it is a congruence for the rather restricted set of operators introduced. Proofs of the theorems given in this section can be found in [22].

Theorem 1. *Timed rooted branching bisimilarity is an equivalence relation.*

Theorem 2. *Timed strong bisimilarity and timed rooted branching bisimilarity are congruences for all operators from the signature of the process algebra* $\text{BSP}^{@}_{\text{abs}}$.

Furthermore, obviously timed rooted branching bisimilarity identifies strictly more processes than timed strong bisimilarity does.

Theorem 3. *Timed strongly bisimilar processes are timed rooted branching bisimilar: i.e.,* $\underline{\leftrightarrow} \subset \underline{\leftrightarrow}_{\text{rb}}$.

From the examples presented in the previous sections, we can easily conclude that our notion of equality is incomparable with the notions from Klusener [4], Baeten and Bergstra [5] and Van der Zwaag [6]. We claim that the notion of abstract branching bisimilarity from [20] is coarser than ours.

5 Case Study: PAR Protocol

In [20] the Positive Acknowledgement Retransmission protocol is used to illustrate the need for a coarser equivalence. In this paper, we will use the same protocol to illustrate our notion of timed rooted branching bisimilarity. An informal description of the protocol can be found in [20]. For comparison, we present a linearised version of the protocol in which the internal communications are abstracted from and as many silent steps as possible have been removed/omitted using the notion of abstraction and timed rooted branching bisimilarity from [5]. This result is obtained by translating the result from [20] to our setting. Note that we have used notations such as $\sum_{t'} p$ that describe a potentially infinite alternative composition consisting of one alternative of p for each t'. We refrain from giving operational semantics for this operator, called summation [12] or alternative quantification [23].

$$X_{b,t} = \sum_{t'} \sum_{d \in D} r_1(d)^{@t+t'}.Y_{d,b,t+t'+t_S}$$

$$Y_{d,b,t} = \tau^{@t+t_K}.s_2(d)^{@t+t_K+t_R}.Z_{d,b,t+t_K+t_R+t'_R} + \sum_{k \leq t_K} \tau^{@t+k}.Y_{d,b,t+t'_S}$$

$$Z_{d,b,t} = \tau^{@t+t_L}.X_{\bar{b},t+t_L} + \sum_{l \leq t_L} \tau^{@t+l}.U_{d,b,t+t'_S-t_K-t_R-t'_R}$$

$$U_{d,b,t} = \tau^{@t+t_K}.V_{d,b,t+t_K+t'_R} + \sum_{k \leq t_K} \tau^{@t+k}.U_{d,b,t+t'_S}$$

$$V_{d,b,t} = \tau^{@t+t_L}.X_{\bar{b},t+t_L} + \sum_{l \leq t_L} \tau^{@t+l}.U_{d,b,t+t'_S-t_K-t'_R}$$

Below, we present a linearised version based on the notion of abstraction and timed rooted branching bisimilarity as proposed in this paper:

$$X_{b,t} = \sum_{t'} \sum_{d \in D} r_1(d)^{@t+t'}.Y_{d,b,t+t'+t_S}$$

$$Y_{d,b,t} = \tau.s_2(d)^{@t+t_k+t_R}.U'_{d,b,t,t_R} + \tau.Y_{d,b,t+t'_S}$$

$$U'_{d,b,t,u} = \tau.X_{\bar{b},t+t_K+u+t'_R+t_L} + \tau.U'_{d,b,t+t'_S,0}$$

The silent steps that are left are essential. The silent steps in Y determine whether or not an error occurred in channel K and those in U' determine the same for channel L. As these errors result in an additional delay before the next action occurs, they are not redundant. In [22] a more detailed discussion of this case study can be found.

6   Axioms for Timed Rooted Branching Bisimilarity

In Table 3 we present axioms for timed strong bisimilarity. The axioms (A1)-(A3) express some standard properties of alternative composition. Axiom (WT) (for well-timedness) describes that the time that is reached by executing an action is passed on to the subsequent process. The axioms (A6a)-(A6d) describe the properties of timed deadlocks, especially the circumstances under which they can be removed from the process description. An important equality that can be derived for closed terms p is $p + 0^{@0} = p$.

Axioms (I1)-(I7) describe how the time-initialisation operator can be eliminated from terms. Note that the silent step neglects this operator (axiom (I6)). Axioms (H1)-(H6) describe how the abstraction operator can be eliminated. Note that the timing of an action that is abstracted from is passed on to the rest of the process (axiom (H4)). The time-initialisation operator in the right-hand side of axiom (H3) is needed in order to enforce the timing restriction from the action prefix before applying further abstractions.

Table 3. Axioms for timed strong bisimilarity and timed rooted branching bisimilarity

(A1) $x + y = y + x$	(A6a) $0^{@t} + 0^{@u} = 0^{@\max(t,u)}$
(A2) $(x + y) + z = x + (y + z)$	(A6b) $u \le t \Rightarrow 1^{@t} + 0^{@u} = 1^{@t}$
(A3) $x + x = x$	(A6c) $u \le t \Rightarrow a^{@t}.x + 0^{@u} = a^{@t}.x$
(WT) $a^{@t}.x = a^{@t}.t \gg x$	(A6d) $u \le t \Rightarrow \tau.(x + 0^{@t}) + 0^{@u} = \tau.(x + 0^{@t})$

(I1) $t \gg 0^{@u} = 0^{@\max(t,u)}$	(H1) $\tau_I(0^{@t}) = 0^{@t}$
(I2) $u < t \Rightarrow t \gg 1^{@u} = 0^{@t}$	(H2) $\tau_I(1^{@t}) = 1^{@t}$
(I3) $u \ge t \Rightarrow t \gg 1^{@u} = 1^{@u}$	
(I4) $u < t \Rightarrow t \gg a^{@u}.x = 0^{@t}$	(H3) $a \notin I \Rightarrow \tau_I(a^{@t}.x) = a^{@t}.\tau_I(t \gg x)$
(I5) $u \ge t \Rightarrow t \gg a^{@u}.x = a^{@u}.x$	(H4) $a \in I \Rightarrow \tau_I(a^{@t}.x) = \tau.\tau_I(t \gg x)$
(I6) $t \gg \tau.x = \tau.t \gg x$	(H5) $\tau_I(\tau.x) = \tau.\tau_I(x)$
(I7) $t \gg (x + y) = t \gg x + t \gg y$	(H6) $\tau_I(x + y) = \tau_I(x) + \tau_I(y)$

We claim that the axioms from Table 3 are sound and complete for timed strong bisimilarity on closed terms. These axioms are (of course; see Theorem 3) also valid for timed rooted branching bisimilarity. In Table 4, one additional axiom is presented for timed rooted branching bisimilarity. The reader should notice that this axiom resembles the untimed axiom for rooted branching bisimilarity $a.(\tau.(x + y) + x) = a.(x + y)$ meticulously. Also, it is expected that the axioms from both tables provide a sound and complete axiomatisation of timed rooted branching bisimilarity on closed terms.

Table 4. Axiom for timed rooted branching bisimilarity

$$(\text{B})\ a^{@t}.(\tau.(x+y)+x) = a^{@t}.(x+y)$$

---

7 Other Timed Process Algebra Settings

The process algebra that we have chosen as our universe of discourse can be classified (both syntactically and semantically) as an absolute-time time-stamped process algebra. As mentioned before, in the literature there are some other versions available, with respect to both the syntax used and the semantics adopted. In this section, we discuss, with respect to the semantics, how the abstraction technique presented here for an absolute-time time-stamped process algebra can be carried over to other types of timed process algebras and what problems are expected to arise in doing so.

In a setting where the time-stamping mechanism uses relative time the treatment becomes even simpler. In such a setting $a^{@t}.p$ means that a is to be executed t time after the execution of the previous action (or after the conception of the process). As a consequence of this relative-timing the problem of ill-timedness is avoided. Therefore, the time-initialisation operator can be left out. Instead, one needs to have a mechanism for updating the relative time-stamp of the initial actions of the subsequent process due to abstraction:

$$\frac{x \xrightarrow{a}_t x' \quad a \in I}{\tau_I(x) \xrightarrow{\tau} t \circledast \tau_I(x')}$$

where $t \circledast p$ means that t time has to be added to the time-stamp of the first visible action from p. For example $3 \circledast a^{@5}.p$ behaves as $a^{@8}.p$. An example of such an operator is the time shift operator $(t)\_$ (also with negative t!) that has been used by Fokkink for defining timed branching bisimilarity in [16].

We have chosen to carry out our deliberations in a time-stamped setting because this setting allows for a very natural definition of the abstraction operator since the timing of the action (before abstraction) and the action itself are tightly coupled in the model. To illustrate the difficulties that arise in defining abstraction in a two-phase model, we look at the following processes (in the syntax of [24,25]). Note that $\sigma.\_$ is a time step prefix operator and $\underline{a}.\_$ is an immediate action prefix operator.

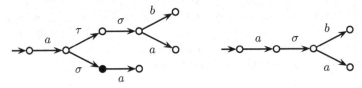

Fig. 1. Processes $\underline{a}.(\sigma.\underline{a}.\underline{0} + \underline{\tau}.\sigma.(\underline{a}.\underline{0} + \underline{b}.\underline{0}))$ and $\underline{a}.\sigma.(\underline{a}.\underline{0} + \underline{b}.\underline{0})$

As we have discussed in Sect. 4, we consider these processes equivalent. However, to express this in an equivalence, we need to be able to relate the states of both processes. In the diagram above one can see that the first process can make a time transition that results in a state (the black one) that has no corresponding state in the second process. The essence of this problem is that one tries to relate states that are reached solely by time steps such as the black one. We thus believe the solution is to not necessarily relate such states, even if they exist.

8   Concluding Remarks

In this paper, we have introduced a notion of abstraction that abstracts from the identity of an action as well as its timing, resulting in an untimed silent step. We have developed an accompanying notion of equality of processes, also called timed rooted branching bisimilarity. We have shown that this notion is an equivalence relation and a congruence for all operators considered in this paper and as such may be a meaningful tool in analysing and verifying systems. A first experiment, on the PAR protocol, indicates that our notions allow for a much clearer and smaller representation of the abstract system than the standard notions do. An axiomatisation of timed rooted branching bisimilarity for closed process terms is given with an axiom for the removal of untimed silent steps that resembles the well-known axiom from untimed process algebra.

In this paper, we have made many claims about the timed process algebra with untimed silent steps. Of course, these claims need to be substantiated further. Also, it is worthwhile to study our notion of abstraction in other timed settings, most notably those with relative timing and where timing is described by separate timing primitives (decoupled from actions) as in [11] and most other mainstream timed process algebras.

We have illustrated the differences and similarities between the different definitions of timed rooted branching bisimilarity from literature and the version introduced in this paper by means of examples only. A more thorough comparison is needed. Also, a comparison with timed versions of weak bisimilarity (e.g., [7,8,9,10]) should be performed.

In order to illustrate that our restriction to the limited set of operators is not inspired by fundamental limitations, in [22], we have extended the timed process algebra with sequential composition and parallel composition as these operators are frequently encountered in timed process algebras in the ACP community. It turns out that the deduction rules are standard. Also it is shown that timed rooted branching bisimilarity as defined in this paper in a congruence for those operators.

The success of an abstraction mechanism and notion of equality not depend only on the theoretical properties (though important) of these notions, but much more so on the practical suitability of these notions. Therefore, we need to perform more case studies to observe whether these notions contribute to a better/easier verification of correctness and/or properties of relevant systems. In this direction, we are also interested in a weaker version of the notion of equivalence presented in this paper that additionally considers the processes from Example 4 (Time-Choice) equal.

We are, in line with our previous work ([24,25]), very interested in obtaining a collection of theories that are nicely related by means of conservativity results and embeddings. Therefore, it is interesting to extend the rather limited timed process algebra from this paper with untimed action prefix operators $a._{-}$ in order to formally study, in one framework, the relationship between rooted branching bisimilarity on untimed processes and our timed version.

A complementary way of specifying a timed system is by means of a timed (modal) logic. It is worthwhile to get a deeper understanding of our notion of action abstraction and timed rooted branching bisimilarity by considering the relationship with modal logics for timed systems as has been done for strong bisimilarity [26] and Hennessy-Milner logic [27]. We have good hope that the majority of the logics that are used for the specification of properties of timed systems are preserved by our notion of timed rooted branching bisimilarity.

Acknowledgements. We acknowledge useful comments from Jos Baeten, Pieter Cuijpers, Wan Fokkink, Jan Friso Groote, Bas Luttik, Bas Ploeger, Yaroslav Usenko and Tim Willemse.

References

1. Bergstra, J., Klop, J.: Process algebra for synchronous communication. Information and Control 60(1/3), 109–137 (1984)
2. van Glabbeek, R., Weijland, W.: Branching time and abstraction in bisimulation semantics (extended abstract). In: Ritter, G. (ed.) Information Processing 1989, pp. 613–618. North-Holland, Amsterdam (1989)
3. van Glabbeek, R., Weijland, W.: Branching time and abstraction in bisimulation semantics. Journal of the ACM 43(3), 555–600 (1996)
4. Klusener, A.: Models and Axioms for a Fragment of Real Time Process Algebra. PhD thesis, Eindhoven University of Technology (1993)
5. Baeten, J., Bergstra, J.: Discrete time process algebra with abstraction. In: Reichel, H. (ed.) FCT 1995. LNCS, vol. 965, pp. 1–15. Springer, Heidelberg (1995)
6. van der Zwaag, M.B.: The cones and foci proof technique for timed transition systems. Information Processing Letters 80(1), 33–40 (2001)
7. Moller, F., Tofts, C.: Behavioural abstraction in TCCS. In: Kuich, W. (ed.) Automata, Languages and Programming. LNCS, vol. 623, pp. 559–570. Springer, Heidelberg (1992)
8. Chen, L.: A model for real-time process algebras (extended abstract). In: Borzyszkowski, A.M., Sokolowski, S. (eds.) MFCS 1993. LNCS, vol. 711, pp. 372–381. Springer, Heidelberg (1993)
9. Quemada, J., de Frutos, D., Azcorra, A.: TIC: A TImed calculus. Formal Aspects of Computing 5(3), 224–252 (1993)
10. Ho-Stuart, C., Zedan, H., Fang, M.: Congruent weak bisimulation with dense real-time. Information Processing Letters 46(2), 55–61 (1993)
11. Baeten, J.C.M., Middelburg, C.A.: Process Algebra with Timing. EATCS Monographs. Springer, Heidelberg (2002)

12. Reniers, M., Groote, J., van der Zwaag, M., van Wamel, J.: Completeness of timed μCRL. Fundamenta Informaticae 50(3-4), 361–402 (2002)
13. Baeten, J., Basten, T., Reniers, M.: Process algebra: Equational theories of communicating processes (2007)
14. Groote, J.: The syntax and semantics of timed μCRL. Technical Report SEN-R9709, CWI, Amsterdam (1997)
15. Aceto, L., Fokkink, W., Verhoef, C.: Structural operational semantics. In: Bergstra, J., Ponse, A., Smolka, S. (eds.) Handbook of Process Algebra, pp. 197–292. Elsevier, Amsterdam (2001)
16. Fokkink, W.: Clock, Trees and Stars in Process Theory. PhD thesis, University of Amsterdam (1994)
17. Fokkink, W.: An axiomatization for regular processes in timed branching bisimulation. Fundamenta Informaticae 32, 329–340 (1997)
18. Baeten, J., Bergstra, J., Reniers, M.: Discrete time process algebra with silent step. In: Plotkin, G., Stirling, C., Tofte, M. (eds.) Proof, Language, and Interaction: Essays in Honour of Robin Milner. Foundations of Computing Series, pp. 535–569. MIT Press, Cambridge (2000)
19. Fokkink, W., Pang, J., Wijs, A.: Is timed branching bisimilarity an equivalence indeed? In: Pettersson, P., Yi, W. (eds.) FORMATS 2005. LNCS, vol. 3829, pp. 258–272. Springer, Heidelberg (2005)
20. Baeten, J., Middelburg, C., Reniers, M.: A new equivalence for processes with timing: With an application to protocol verification. Technical Report CSR 02-10, Eindhoven University of Technology, Department of Computer Science (2002)
21. Basten, T.: Branching bisimilarity is an equivalence indeed! Information Processing Letters 58(3), 141–147 (1996)
22. Reniers, M., van Weerdenburg, M.: Action abstraction in timed process algebra: The case for an untimed silent step. Technical Report CSR 06-32, Eindhoven University of Technology, Department of Computer Science (2006)
23. Luttik, S.: Choice Quantification in Process Algebra. PhD thesis, University of Amsterdam (April 2002)
24. Baeten, J., Mousavi, M., Reniers, M.: Timing the untimed: Terminating successfully while being conservative. In: Middeldorp, A., van Oostrom, V., van Raamsdonk, F., de Vrijer, R. (eds.) Processes, Terms and Cycles: Steps on the Road to Infinity. LNCS, vol. 3838, pp. 251–279. Springer, Heidelberg (2005)
25. Baeten, J., Reniers, M.: Duplication of constants in process algebra. Journal of Logic and Algebraic Programming 70(2), 151–171 (2007)
26. Park, D.: Concurrency and automata on infinite sequences. In: Deussen, P. (ed.) Theoretical Computer Science. LNCS, vol. 104, pp. 167–183. Springer, Heidelberg (1981)
27. Hennessy, M., Milner, R.: Algebraic laws for nondeterminism and concurrency. Journal of the ACM 32, 137–161 (1985)

Type Abstractions of Name-Passing Processes*

Lucia Acciai[1] and Michele Boreale[2]

[1] Laboratoire d'Informatique Fondamentale de Marseille, Université de Provence
[2] Dipartimento di Sistemi e Informatica, Università di Firenze
lucia.acciai@lif.univ-mrs.fr, boreale@dsi.unifi.it

Abstract. We study methods to statically approximate "first-order" process calculi (Pi, Join) by "propositional" models (CCS, BPP, Petri nets). We consider both open and closed behavior of processes. In the case of open behavior, we propose a type system to associate pi-calculus processes with restriction-free CCS types. A process is shown to be in simulation relation with each of its types, hence safety properties that hold of the types also hold of the process. We refine this approach in the case of closed behavior: in this case, types are BPP processes. Sufficient conditions are given under which a minimal BPP type can be computed that is bisimilar to a given process. These results are extended to the Join calculus using place/transition Petri nets as types.

1 Introduction

The behavior of large, possibly distributed programs that heavily rely on reference-passing is generally difficult to comprehend, both intuitively and formally. Process calculi like Pi [1] and Join [2] posses "first-order" features, like value passing and dynamic name creation, difficult to recast into well-analyzable operational formats. This situation should be contrasted with that found in "propositional" formalisms like CCS and Petri nets, that enjoy simpler and more tractable operational models, studied and utilized for decades (the terminology "first order" and "propositional" is not standard in the present context, and should be taken with a grain of salt.)

For many purposes it may be sufficient to take an abstract view of name-passing processes, hopefully easy to recast into propositional terms. Imagine one specifies a context Γ associating values and free names of a pi-process P with *tags* drawn from a finite set. Tags might represent particular events an external observer is interested in. Different names/values can possibly be collapsed onto the same tag (e.g., different values could be mapped to a unique tag representing their type). Imagine further that P's code specifies how to make such associations at run-time for newly generated names. If one observes P "through" Γ, that is, dynamically maps values/names to tags in transition labels as prescribed, one obtains an abstract process P_Γ. The latter is operationally described by a possibly infinite, yet simpler propositional transition system. In many cases, it may be sufficient to further limit one's attention to the *closed* behavior of P_Γ, that is, to communication actions suitably decorated with tags, such as the identity of

---

* The first author is supported by the French government research grant ACI TRALALA. The second author is supported by the EU within the FET-GC2 initiative, project SENSORIA.

F. Arbab and M. Sirjani (Eds.): FSEN 2007, LNCS 4767, pp. 302–317, 2007.

the service that is called, types of the passed parameters and so on. In other words, P_Γ provides a bird's eye view of the system under observation, which is often sufficient to establish interesting properties of the system, typically safety ones.

The goal of this paper is to study means to *statically* computing finitary representations of P_Γ, or at least suitable approximations of P_Γ. The proposed methods will take the form of behavioral type systems for process calculi. Such systems can be used to assign a process P a propositional type T that, in general, over-approximates the behavior of P_Γ. This technique should in principle allow one to verify certain properties of T, being assured that the same properties also hold for P_Γ. In each of the considered type systems, the emphasis will be on keeping the class of types tractable. In particular, (bi)similarity and model-checking for interesting modal logics should be decidable for the given class. In other words, the aim here is laying a basis for property verification by a combination of type-checking and model-checking techniques. This approach is along the lines of the work on behavioral types by Igarashi and Kobayashi [3] .

More specifically, we start by introducing an asynchronous, "tagged" version of the pi-calculus and the notion of abstract process P_Γ (Section 2). In the first type system (Section 3), types are a class of asynchronous, restriction-less CCS processes, which we name CCS$^-$. Both bisimulation and model checking for interesting logics are decidable for CCS$^-$ (e.g., by translation into Petri nets [4]). Our main result here shows that P_Γ is in simulation relation with the types inhabited by P; hence safety properties that hold for the types also holds for the abstract process P_Γ. The absence of restriction causes an obvious loss of precision in types; note however that in practice this can be remedied by hiding certain actions at the level of modal logic formulae. In the second system (Section 4), we focus on closed behavior. The goal is to obtain simpler and hopefully more efficient behavioral approximations, by getting rid of synchronization in types. We achieve this goal by directly associating each output action with an *effect* corresponding to the observable behavior that that output can trigger. Input actions have no associated effect, thus an inert type is associated to input processes. Types we obtain in this way are precisely *Basic Parallel Processes* (BPP, [5]): these are infinite-state processes for which, however, a wealth of decidability results exists [6,7]. We show that if we restrict ourselves to a class of pi-processes satisfying a generalized version of uniform receptiveness [8], a type can be computed that is bisimilar to P_Γ. These techniques will be illustrated using a concrete example (Section 5). We finally move to the Join calculus (Section 6) and generalize some of the results obtained for the pi-calculus. At the level of types, the main step is moving from BPP to the more general class of place/transition Petri nets, for which again interesting decidability results are known [6,7]. We end the paper with some remarks on related and further work (Section 7).

2   The Asynchronous Pi-Calculus

2.1   Processes

Let $\mathcal{N}$, ranged over by $a, b, c, \ldots, x, y, \ldots$, be a countable set of *names* and $\mathcal{T}ag$, ranged over by $\alpha, \beta, \ldots$, be a set of *tags* disjoint from $\mathcal{N}$; we assume $\mathcal{T}ag$ also contains a distinct "unit" tag (). The set $\mathcal{P}$ of processes $P, Q, \ldots$ is defined as the set of terms generated by the following grammar:

$$P, Q ::= \overline{a}\langle b\rangle \mid \sum_{i \in I} a_i(b).P_i \mid \sum_{i \in I} \tau.P_i \mid \text{if } a = b \text{ then } P \text{ else } P \mid {!}a(b).P \mid (va : \alpha)P \mid P|P .$$

This language is a variation on the asynchronous π-calculus. A non-blocking *output* of a name b along a is written $\overline{a}\langle b\rangle$. *Nondeterministic guarded summation* $\sum_{i \in I} a_i(b).P_i$ waits for a communication on a_i, for $i \in I$. An *internal choice* $\sum_{i \in I} \tau.P_i$ can choose to behave like any of the P_i via an invisible τ transition. *Conditional* if $a = b$ then P else Q behaves as P if a equals b, as Q otherwise. *Replication* $!a(b).P$ provides an unbounded number of copies of $a(b).P$. *Restriction* $(va : \alpha)P$ creates (and assigns a tag α to) a new restricted name a with initial scope P. As usual, the *parallel composition* $P|Q$ represents concurrent execution of P and Q.

In an output action $\overline{a}\langle b\rangle$, name a is the *subject* and b the *object* of the action. Similarly, in a replicated input prefix $!a(b).P$ and in $\sum_{i \in I} a_i(b).P_i$, the names a and a_i for $i \in I$ are said to occur in *input subject position*. Binders and alpha-equivalence arise as expected and processes are identified up to alpha-equivalence. Substitution of a with b in an expression e is denoted by $e[b/a]$. In what follows, **0** stands for the empty summation $\sum_{i \in \emptyset} a_i(x).P_i$. We shall sometimes omit the object parts of input and output actions, when not relevant for the discussion; e.g. $\overline{a}$ stands for an output action with subject a and an object left unspecified. Similarly, we shall omit tag annotations, writing e.g. $(va)P$ instead of $(va : \alpha)P$, when the identity of the tag is not relevant.

2.2 Operational Semantics

The (early) semantics of processes is given by the labelled transition system in Tab. 1. We let $\ell, \ell', \ldots$ represent generic elements of $\mathcal{N} \cup \mathit{Tag}$. A transitions label μ can be a free output, $\overline{a}\langle b\rangle$, a bound output, $(vb : \alpha)\overline{a}\langle b\rangle$, an input, $a(b)$, or a silent move, $\tau\langle\ell, \ell'\rangle$. We assume a distinct tag ι for decorating *internal* transitions (arising from conditional and internal chioce; see Table 1) and often abbreviate $\tau\langle\iota, \iota\rangle$ simply as τ. In the following we indicate by $n(\mu)$ the set of all names in μ and by $fn(\mu)$, the set of free names of μ, defined as expected. The rules are standard, except for the extra book-keeping required by tag annotation of bound output and internal actions. In particular, in (RES-TAU) bound names involved in a synchronization are hidden from the observer and replaced by the corresponding tags. Note that if we erase the tag annotation from labels we get exactly the usual labelled semantics of asynchronous pi-calculus.

2.3 Γ-Abstractions of Processes

A *context* Γ is a finite partial function from names to tags, written $\Gamma = \{a_1 : \alpha_1, \cdots, a_n : \alpha_n\}$, with distinct a_i. In what follows $\Gamma \vdash a : \alpha$ means that $a : \alpha \in \Gamma$. A *tag sorting system* $\mathcal{E}$ is a finite subset of $\{\alpha[\beta] \mid \alpha, \beta \text{ are tags and } \alpha \neq ()\}$. Informally, $\alpha[\beta] \in \mathcal{E}$ means that subject names associated with tag α can carry object names associated with tag β. In what follows, if $\alpha[\beta_1], \cdots, \alpha[\beta_n]$ are the only elements of $\mathcal{E}$ with subject α, we write $\alpha[\beta_1, \cdots, \beta_n] \in \mathcal{E}$.

A triple $(P, \Gamma, \mathcal{E})$, written $P_{\Gamma;\mathcal{E}}$, is called Γ-*abstraction* of P under $\mathcal{E}$. In what follows, we shall consider a fixed sorting system $\mathcal{E}$, and keep $\mathcal{E}$ implicit by writing P_Γ instead of $P_{\Gamma;\mathcal{E}}$. Next, we define a labeled transition system with process abstractions as states and

Table 1. Operational semantics of pi-calculus processes

$$(\text{OUT}) \ \overline{a}\langle b\rangle \xrightarrow{\overline{a}\langle b\rangle} \mathbf{0}$$

$$(\text{I-SUM}) \ \textstyle\sum_{i\in I}\tau.P_i \xrightarrow{\tau} P_j, \quad j\in I \qquad (\text{G-SUM}) \ \textstyle\sum_{i\in I}a_i(b_i).P_i \xrightarrow{a_j\langle c\rangle} P_j[c/b_j], \quad j\in I$$

$$(\text{REP}) \ !a(c).P \xrightarrow{a\langle b\rangle} P[b/c]\,|\,!a(c).P \qquad (\text{OPEN}) \ \dfrac{P \xrightarrow{\overline{b}\langle a\rangle} P' \quad b\neq a}{(va:\alpha)P \xrightarrow{(va:\alpha)\overline{b}\langle a\rangle} P'}$$

$$(\text{COM}) \ \dfrac{P \xrightarrow{\overline{a}\langle b\rangle} P' \quad Q \xrightarrow{a\langle b\rangle} Q'}{P\,|\,Q \xrightarrow{\tau\langle a,b\rangle} P'\,|\,Q'} \qquad (\text{CLOSE}) \ \dfrac{P \xrightarrow{(vb:\beta)\overline{a}\langle b\rangle} P' \quad Q \xrightarrow{a\langle b\rangle} Q'}{P\,|\,Q \xrightarrow{\tau\langle a,\beta\rangle} (vb:\beta)(P'\,|\,Q')}$$

$$(\text{IF-T}) \ \text{if } a=a \text{ then } P \text{ else } Q \xrightarrow{\tau} P \qquad (\text{IF-F}) \ \text{if } a=b \text{ then } P \text{ else } Q \xrightarrow{\tau} Q, \quad a\neq b$$

$$(\text{PAR}) \ \dfrac{P \xrightarrow{\mu} P'}{P\,|\,Q \xrightarrow{\mu} P'\,|\,Q} \qquad (\text{RES}) \ \dfrac{P \xrightarrow{\mu} P' \quad a\notin n(\mu)}{(va:\alpha)P \xrightarrow{\mu} (va:\alpha)P'}$$

$$(\text{RES-TAU}) \ \dfrac{P \xrightarrow{\tau\langle \ell_1,\ell_2\rangle} P' \quad a\in\{\ell_1,\ell_2\} \quad \ell=\ell_1[\alpha/a] \quad \ell'=\ell_2[\alpha/a]}{(va:\alpha)P \xrightarrow{\tau\langle \ell,\ell'\rangle} (va:\alpha)P'}$$

Symmetric rules not shown.

transition labels λ, which can be output, $\overline{\alpha}\langle\beta\rangle$, input, $\alpha\langle\beta\rangle$ or annotated silent action, $\tau\langle\alpha,\beta\rangle$. The set of labels generated by this grammar is denoted by Λ. The labeled transition system is defined by the rules below. Here, μ_Γ denotes the result of substituting each $a\in \text{fn}(\mu)\cap\text{dom}(\Gamma)$ by $\Gamma(a)$ in μ. Informally, P_Γ represents the abstract behavior of P, once each concrete action μ has been mapped to an abstract action λ. Note that in both rule (A-OUT$_N$) and rule (A-INP$_N$) the context Γ grows with a new association $b:\beta$. In rule (A-INP$_N$), a tag for b is chosen among the possible tags specified in $\mathcal{E}$. Note that no type checking is performed by these rules, in particular (A-OUT$_N$) does not look up $\mathcal{E}$ to check that β can be carried by α.

$$(\text{A-OLD}) \ \dfrac{P \xrightarrow{\mu} P' \quad \mu::=\tau\langle \ell,\ell'\rangle\,|\,a(b)\,|\,\overline{a}\langle b\rangle \quad n(\mu)\subseteq\text{dom}(\Gamma) \quad \lambda=\mu_\Gamma}{P_\Gamma \xrightarrow{\lambda} P'_\Gamma}$$

$$(\text{A-OUT}_N) \ \dfrac{P \xrightarrow{(vb:\beta)\overline{a}\langle b\rangle} P' \quad \Gamma\vdash a:\alpha}{P_\Gamma \xrightarrow{\overline{\alpha}\langle\beta\rangle} P'_{\Gamma,b:\beta}} \quad (\text{A-INP}_N) \ \dfrac{P \xrightarrow{a\langle b\rangle} P' \quad \Gamma\vdash a:\alpha \quad \alpha[\beta]\in\mathcal{E} \quad b\notin\text{dom}(\Gamma)}{P_\Gamma \xrightarrow{\alpha\langle\beta\rangle} P'_{\Gamma,b:\beta}}$$

2.4 Simulation, Bisimulation and Modal Logic

Let T any labelled transition system with labels in Λ. As usual, the *(strong) simulation* relation over T, written $\lesssim$, is the largest binary relation over states of T such that whenever $s_1 \lesssim s_2$ and $s_1 \xrightarrow{\lambda} s_1'$ then there is a transition $s_2 \xrightarrow{\lambda} s_2'$ such that $s_1' \lesssim s_2'$. The relation $\lesssim$ is easily seen to be a preorder. *(Strong) Bisimulation* over T, written $\sim$, is the largest binary relation over states of T such that both $\sim$ and $\sim^{-1}$ are simulations. The *closed* versions of simulation and bisimulation, written $\lesssim^c$ and $\sim^c$, respectively, are defined in a similar manner, but limited to silent transitions.

Next, we introduce a simple action-based modal logic that will help us to formulate concisely properties of processes and types. The logic is very simple and only serves to illustrate the approach presented in the paper. More precisely, we let $\mathcal{L}$ be given by $\phi ::= \text{true} \mid \langle A \rangle \phi \mid \langle\langle A \rangle\rangle \phi \mid \neg \phi \mid \phi \wedge \phi$, where $\emptyset \neq A \subseteq \Lambda$. These formulae are interpreted in the expected manner, in particular, a state s satisfies $\langle A \rangle \phi$, written $s \vDash \langle A \rangle \phi$, if there is a transition $s \xrightarrow{\lambda} s'$ with $\lambda \in A$ and $s' \vDash \phi$. The interpretation of modality $\langle\langle A \rangle\rangle \phi$ is similar, but the phrase "a transition $s \xrightarrow{\lambda} s'$ with $\lambda \in A$" is changed into "a sequence of transitions $s \xrightarrow{\sigma} s'$ with $\sigma \in A^*$". We shall make use of standard notational conventions, like abbreviating $\neg \langle A \rangle \neg \phi$ as $[A]\phi$, omitting a trailing "true", and so on. Note that $\mathcal{L}$ can be regarded as a fragment of the modal mu-calculus [9].

3 CCS⁻ Types for Open Behavior

In the first type system we propose, types are essentially CCS expressions whose behavior over-approximate the (abstract) process behavior.

3.1 CCS⁻ Types

The set $\mathcal{T}_{\text{CCS}}$ of types, ranged over by $T, S, \ldots$, is defined by the following syntax:

$$T ::= \overline{\alpha}\langle\beta\rangle \mid \sum_{i \in I} \alpha_i \langle\beta_i\rangle.T_i \mid \sum_{i \in I} \tau.T_i \mid !\alpha\langle\beta\rangle.T \mid T|T$$

where $\alpha, \alpha_i \neq ()$. The empty summation $\sum_{i \in \emptyset} \alpha_i \langle\beta_i\rangle.T_i$ will be often denoted by nil, and $T_1 \mid \cdots \mid T_n$ will be often written as $\prod_{i \in \{1, \cdots, n\}} T_i$. As usual, we shall sometimes omit the object part of actions when not relevant for the discussion or equal to the unit tag $()$, writing e.g. $\overline{\alpha}$ and $\tau\langle\alpha\rangle$ instead of $\overline{\alpha}\langle\beta\rangle$ and $\tau\langle\alpha, \beta\rangle$. Types are essentially asynchronous, restriction-free CCS processes over the alphabet of actions Λ. The standard operational semantics of CCS, giving rise to a labelled transition system with labels in Λ, is assumed (Table 2).

Table 2. Operational semantics of CCS⁻ types

$$
\begin{array}{ll}
(\text{C-OUT}) \ \overline{\alpha}\langle\beta\rangle \xrightarrow{\overline{\alpha}\langle\beta\rangle} \text{nil} & (\text{C-GSUM}) \ \sum_{i \in I} \alpha_i \langle\beta_i\rangle.T_i \xrightarrow{\alpha_j\langle\beta_j\rangle} T_j, \quad j \in I \\[2ex]
(\text{C-ISUM}) \ \sum_{i \in I} \tau.T_i \xrightarrow{\tau} T_j, \quad j \in I & (\text{C-REP}) \ !\alpha\langle\beta\rangle.T \xrightarrow{\alpha\langle\beta\rangle} T \,|\, !\alpha\langle\beta\rangle.T \\[2ex]
(\text{C-COM}) \ \dfrac{T \xrightarrow{\overline{\alpha}\langle\beta\rangle} T' \quad S \xrightarrow{\alpha\langle\beta\rangle} S'}{T|S \xrightarrow{\tau\langle\alpha,\beta\rangle} T'|S'} & (\text{C-PAR}) \ \dfrac{T \xrightarrow{\lambda} T'}{T|S \xrightarrow{\lambda} T'|S}
\end{array}
$$

Symmetric rules for $|$ not shown.

3.2 The Typing Rules

Let $\mathcal{E}$ be a fixed tag sorting system and Γ a context. Judgements of the type system are of the form $\Gamma \vdash_{\mathcal{E}} P : \mathsf{T}$. The rules of the type system are presented in Tab. 3.

A brief explanation of some typing rules follows. In rule (T-OUT), the output process $\bar{a}\langle b \rangle$ gives rise to the action $\bar{a}\langle b \rangle_\Gamma = \bar{\alpha}\langle\beta\rangle$, provided this action is expected by the tag sorting system $\mathcal{E}$. The type T of an input process depends on $\mathcal{E}$: in (T-INP) all tags which can be carried by α, the tag associated with the action's subject, contribute to the definition of the summation in T as expected. In the case of (T-REP), summation is replaced by a parallel composition of replicated types, which is behaviorally – up to strong bisimulation – the same as a replicated summation. Note that, concerning guarded summation, the case with a single input $|I| = 1$, (T-INP), is kept separate from the case with $|I| \neq 1$, (T-GSUM), only for ease of presentation. In (T-IF), the behavior of a conditional process is approximated by a type that subsumes both branches of the if-then-else into an internal choice. The subtyping relation $\lesssim$ is the simulation preorder over $\mathcal{E}$, (T-SUB). The rest of the rules should be self-explanatory.

Table 3. Typing rules for CCS$^-$ types

$$(\text{T-OUT}) \quad \frac{\Gamma \vdash a : \alpha \quad \alpha[\beta] \in \mathcal{E} \quad \Gamma \vdash b : \beta}{\Gamma \vdash_{\mathcal{E}} \bar{a}\langle b \rangle : \bar{\alpha}\langle\beta\rangle}$$

$$(\text{T-INP}) \quad \frac{\Gamma \vdash a : \alpha \quad \alpha[\beta_1, \cdots, \beta_n] \in \mathcal{E} \quad \forall i \in \{1, \cdots, n\} : \Gamma, b : \beta_i \vdash_{\mathcal{E}} P : \mathsf{T}_i}{\Gamma \vdash_{\mathcal{E}} a(b).P : \sum_{i \in \{1, \cdots, n\}} \alpha\langle\beta_i\rangle.\mathsf{T}_i}$$

$$(\text{T-REP}) \quad \frac{\Gamma \vdash a : \alpha \quad \alpha[\beta_1, \cdots, \beta_n] \in \mathcal{E} \quad \forall i \in \{1, \cdots, n\} : \Gamma, b : \beta_i \vdash_{\mathcal{E}} P : \mathsf{T}_i}{\Gamma \vdash_{\mathcal{E}} !a(b).P : \prod_{i \in \{1, \cdots, n\}} !\alpha\langle\beta_i\rangle.\mathsf{T}_i}$$

$$(\text{T-GSUM}) \quad \frac{|I| \neq 1 \quad \forall i \in I : \Gamma \vdash_{\mathcal{E}} a_i(b_i).P_i : \sum_{j \in J_i} \alpha_i\langle\beta_j\rangle.\mathsf{T}_{ij}}{\Gamma \vdash_{\mathcal{E}} \sum_{i \in I} a_i(b_i).P_i : \sum_{i \in I, j \in J_i} \alpha_i\langle\beta_j\rangle \mathsf{T}_{ij}} \qquad (\text{T-ISUM}) \quad \frac{\forall i \in I : \Gamma \vdash_{\mathcal{E}} P_i : \mathsf{T}_i}{\Gamma \vdash_{\mathcal{E}} \sum_{i \in I} \tau.P_i : \sum_{i \in I} \tau.\mathsf{T}_i}$$

$$(\text{T-PAR}) \quad \frac{\Gamma \vdash_{\mathcal{E}} P : \mathsf{T} \quad \Gamma \vdash_{\mathcal{E}} Q : \mathsf{S}}{\Gamma \vdash_{\mathcal{E}} P|Q : \mathsf{T}|\mathsf{S}} \qquad\qquad (\text{T-RES}) \quad \frac{\Gamma, a : \alpha \vdash_{\mathcal{E}} P : \mathsf{T}}{\Gamma \vdash_{\mathcal{E}} (\nu a : \alpha)P : \mathsf{T}}$$

$$(\text{T-IF}) \quad \frac{\Gamma \vdash_{\mathcal{E}} P : \mathsf{T} \quad \Gamma \vdash_{\mathcal{E}} Q : \mathsf{S}}{\Gamma \vdash_{\mathcal{E}} \text{if } a = b \text{ then } P \text{ else } Q : \tau.\mathsf{T} + \tau.\mathsf{S}} \qquad (\text{T-SUB}) \quad \frac{\Gamma \vdash_{\mathcal{E}} P : \mathsf{T} \quad \mathsf{T} \lesssim \mathsf{S}}{\Gamma \vdash_{\mathcal{E}} P : \mathsf{S}}$$

3.3 Results

The subject reduction theorem establishes an operational correspondence between the abstract behavior P_Γ and any type T that can be assigned to P under Γ.

Theorem 1 (subject reduction). $\Gamma \vdash_{\mathcal{E}} P : \mathsf{T}$ and $P_\Gamma \xrightarrow{\lambda} P'_{\Gamma'}$ imply that there is T' such that $\mathsf{T} \xrightarrow{\lambda} \mathsf{T}'$ and $\Gamma' \vdash_{\mathcal{E}} P' : \mathsf{T}'$.

As a corollary, we obtain that T simulates P_Γ; thanks to Theorem 1, it is easy to see that the relation $\mathcal{R} = \{(P_\Gamma, \mathsf{T}) \mid \Gamma \vdash_{\mathcal{E}} P : \mathsf{T}\}$ is a simulation relation.

Corollary 1. *Suppose* $\Gamma \vdash_{\mathcal{E}} P : \mathsf{T}$. *Then* $P_\Gamma \lesssim \mathsf{T}$.

A consequence of the previous result is that safety properties satisfied by a type are also satisfied by the processes that inhabit that type – or, more precisely, by their Γ-abstract versions. Consider the small logic defined in Section 2.4: let us say that $\phi \in L$ is a *safety* formula if every occurrence of $\langle A \rangle$ and $\langle\langle A \rangle\rangle$ in ϕ is underneath an odd number of negations. The following proposition, follows from Corollary 1 and first principles.

Proposition 1. *Suppose* $\Gamma \vdash_{\mathcal{E}} P : \mathsf{T}$ *and* ϕ *is a safety formula, with* $\mathsf{T} \vDash \phi$. *Then* $P_\Gamma \vDash \phi$.

As a final remark on the type system, consider taking out rule (T-SUB): the new system can be viewed as a (partial) function that for any P computes a minimal type for P, that is, a subtype of all types of P (just read the rules bottom-up).

In the examples we describe below, we shall consider a calculus enriched with polyadic communication and values: these extensions are easy to accommodate. Polyadic communications are written as $\tau \langle \alpha_1, \alpha_2, \cdots, \alpha_n \rangle$, where α_1 is the subject and $\alpha_2, \cdots, \alpha_n$ are the objects; we omit objects that correspond to the unit tag.

Example 1 (factorial). Consider the process F defined below, which is the usual RPC encoding of the factorial function, and the system S, where F is called with an actual parameter n, a result is received on a private channel r and then the received value is printed.

$$F \triangleq \ !f(n,r).\text{if } n = 0 \text{ then } \bar{r}\langle n \rangle \text{ else } (\nu r' : ret)\big(\bar{f}\langle n-1, r'\rangle \mid r'(m).\bar{r}\langle n * m \rangle\big)$$

$$S \triangleq (\nu r : ret)\big(\bar{f}\langle n, r \rangle \mid r(m).\overline{print}\langle m \rangle\big) \mid F \ .$$

Let $\mathcal{E} = \{fact[ret], ret[()], pr[()]\}$ and $\Gamma = \{f : fact, print : pr, n : ()\}$. It is not difficult to check that $\Gamma \vdash_{\mathcal{E}} F : \mathsf{T}_F$ and $\Gamma \vdash_{\mathcal{E}} S : \mathsf{T}_S$, where:

$$\mathsf{T}_F \triangleq \ !fact\langle ret \rangle.\big(\ \tau.\overline{ret} + \tau.(\overline{fact}\langle ret \rangle \mid ret.\overline{ret})\ \big) \qquad \mathsf{T}_S \triangleq \overline{fact}\langle ret \rangle \mid ret.\overline{pr} \mid \mathsf{T}_F$$

and that

$$\mathsf{T}_S \vDash \phi_1 \triangleq \neg \langle\langle \Lambda - \{fact\langle ret \rangle, ret\} \rangle\rangle \langle \overline{ret} \rangle \langle\langle \Lambda - \{fact\langle ret \rangle\} \rangle\rangle \langle \overline{fact}\langle ret \rangle \rangle$$

$$\mathsf{T}_S \vDash \phi_2 \triangleq \neg \langle\langle \Lambda - \{fact\langle ret \rangle, ret\} \rangle\rangle \langle \overline{pr} \rangle \langle\langle \Lambda - \{fact\langle ret \rangle\} \rangle\rangle \langle \overline{fact}\langle ret \rangle \rangle$$

meaning that no call at f can be observed after observing a return (ϕ_1) or a print (ϕ_2), that is, as expected, after receipt of 0 as argument, no other calls to f can be produced. Note that in both formulas we are forced to restrict certain actions so as to avoid interaction with the environment (e.g. in the first case we disallow action $fact\langle ret \rangle$): this is the price to pay for getting rid of restriction in types. Formulas ϕ_1 and ϕ_2 express safety properties, thus thanks to Proposition 1, we can conclude that $S_\Gamma \vDash \phi_1 \wedge \phi_2$.

4   BPP Types for Closed Behavior

We focus here on the closed behavior of abstract processes. Although the system in the previous section already takes into account closed behavior, it is possible in this case to obtain a "direct style" behavioral type system by getting rid of synchronization in types. This is achieved by directly associating each output action with an *effect*, corresponding to the observable behavior that that output can trigger. Input actions have no associated effect, thus an inert type is associated to input guarded processes. The types we obtain in this way are precisely Basic Parallel Processes (BPP, [5]). We show that if we restrict ourselves to a particular class of processes, notably to (a generalization of) uniform receptive processes [8], a bisimulation relation relates processes and their types.

4.1   BPP Types

The set $\mathcal{T}_{\mathrm{BPP}}$ of BPP types, ranged over by $\mathsf{T}, \mathsf{S}, \ldots$, is defined by the following syntax:

$$\mathsf{T} ::= \alpha[\beta] \ (Invocation) \ \Big| \ \sum_{i \in I} \tau.\mathsf{T}_i \ (Internal \ Choice) \ \Big| \ \mathsf{T} \parallel \mathsf{T} \ (Interleaving)$$

where $\alpha \neq ()$. We consider an extended tag sorting system where each element $\alpha[\beta]$ is enriched with an effect T, written $\alpha[\beta] \rightarrow \mathsf{T}$. More precisely, we let $\mathcal{E}$ be a set of rules of the form $\{\alpha_i[\beta_i] \rightarrow \mathsf{T}_i \mid 1 \leq i \leq n\}$. This can be viewed as a set of rules defining a set of BPP processes. In particular, a process invocation $\alpha[\beta]$ activates the corresponding rule in $\mathcal{E}$; the rest of the syntax and operational semantics should be self-explanatory (Table 4). In what follows we write nil for $\sum_{i \in \emptyset} \tau.\mathsf{T}_i$, and often omit dummy nil's, writing e.g. $\mathsf{T}|$nil simply as T.

Table 4. Operational semantics of BPP types

$$(\text{BPP-INV}) \ \frac{\alpha[\beta] \rightarrow \mathsf{T} \in \mathcal{E}}{\alpha[\beta] \xrightarrow{\tau\langle\alpha,\beta\rangle}_{\mathcal{E}} \mathsf{T}} \qquad\qquad (\text{BPP-INT}) \sum_{i \in I} \tau.\mathsf{T}_i \xrightarrow{\tau}_{\mathcal{E}} \mathsf{T}_j \ (j \in I)$$

$$(\text{BPP-PAR}_{\mathrm{L}}) \ \frac{\mathsf{T} \xrightarrow{\lambda}_{\mathcal{E}} \mathsf{T}'}{\mathsf{T} \parallel \mathsf{S} \xrightarrow{\lambda}_{\mathcal{E}} \mathsf{T}' \parallel \mathsf{S}} \qquad (\text{BPP-PAR}_{\mathrm{R}}) \ \frac{\mathsf{T} \xrightarrow{\lambda}_{\mathcal{E}} \mathsf{T}'}{\mathsf{S} \parallel \mathsf{T} \xrightarrow{\lambda}_{\mathcal{E}} \mathsf{S} \parallel \mathsf{T}'}$$

4.2   Typing Rules

Again, we consider contexts Γ of the form $\{a_1 : \alpha_1, \ldots, a_n : \alpha_n\}$. The new type system is defined in Tab. 5. Derivable statements take now the form $\Gamma \vdash_{\mathcal{E};\mathcal{E}'} P : \mathsf{T}$, where Γ and $\mathcal{E}$ are respectively a fixed context and extended tag sorting system. The parameter $\mathcal{E}'$ is used to keep track of rules of $\mathcal{E}$ actually used in the derivation: this extra parameter will be useful to formulate a condition under which a bisimulation relation, rather than simply a simulation, can be established between a type and its inhabiting processes.

A brief explanation of the typing rules follows. Rule (T-BPP-O) ensures that there are some effects associated to the output action. In (T-BPP-INP) and (T-BPP-REP), dom($\mathcal{E}$)

denotes the set of all elements $\alpha[\beta]$'s occurring in $\mathcal{E}$: hence all object tags β_i associated with the subject tag α are taken into account. For each of them, it is checked that the effects produced by the continuation process P are those expected by the corresponding rule in $\mathcal{E}$. As previously mentioned, input has no associated effect, hence the resulting type is nil. In (T-BPP-SUB), note that the subtyping relation is now the closed simulation preorder $\lesssim^c$. The other rules are standard. In what follows we write $\Gamma \vdash_{\mathcal{E}} P$ if there exist $\mathcal{E}'$ and T such that $\Gamma \vdash_{\mathcal{E};\mathcal{E}'} P : \mathsf{T}$.

Table 5. Typing rules for BPP

$$\text{(T-BPP-INP)} \quad \frac{\Gamma \vdash a : \alpha \quad \forall \beta_i \text{ s.t. } \alpha[\beta_i] \in \text{dom}(\mathcal{E}) \quad \exists \mathsf{T}_i \text{ s.t. } \alpha[\beta_i] \to \mathsf{T}_i \in \mathcal{E} \text{ and:}}{\Gamma \vdash_{\mathcal{E};\mathcal{E}'} a(b).P : \text{nil}}$$
$$\frac{\Gamma, b : \beta_i \vdash_{\mathcal{E};\mathcal{E}_i} P : \mathsf{T}_i \quad \mathcal{E}' = \bigcup_i (\mathcal{E}_i \cup \{\alpha[\beta_i] \to \mathsf{T}_i\})}{}$$

$$\text{(T-BPP-REP)} \quad \frac{\Gamma \vdash a : \alpha \quad \forall \beta_i \text{ s.t. } \alpha[\beta_i] \in \text{dom}(\mathcal{E}) \quad \exists \mathsf{T}_i \text{ s.t. } \alpha[\beta_i] \to \mathsf{T}_i \in \mathcal{E} \text{ and:}}{\Gamma \vdash_{\mathcal{E};\mathcal{E}'} !a(b).P : \text{nil}}$$
$$\frac{\Gamma, b : \beta_i \vdash_{\mathcal{E};\mathcal{E}_i} P : \mathsf{T}_i \quad \mathcal{E}' = \bigcup_i (\mathcal{E}_i \cup \{\alpha[\beta_i] \to \mathsf{T}_i\})}{}$$

$$\text{(T-BPP-O)} \quad \frac{\Gamma \vdash a : \alpha \quad \Gamma \vdash b : \beta \quad \exists \mathsf{T} : \alpha[\beta] \to \mathsf{T} \in \mathcal{E}}{\Gamma \vdash_{\mathcal{E};0} \bar{a}\langle b \rangle : \alpha[\beta]} \qquad \text{(T-BPP-RES)} \quad \frac{\Gamma, a : \alpha \vdash_{\mathcal{E};\mathcal{E}'} P : \mathsf{T}}{\Gamma \vdash_{\mathcal{E};\mathcal{E}'} (va : \alpha)P : \mathsf{T}}$$

$$\text{(T-BPP-GSUM)} \quad \frac{|I| \neq 1 \quad \forall i \in I : \Gamma \vdash_{\mathcal{E};\mathcal{E}_i} a_i(b_i).P_i : \text{nil} \quad \mathcal{E}' = \bigcup_i \mathcal{E}_i}{\Gamma \vdash_{\mathcal{E};\mathcal{E}'} \sum_{i \in I} a_i(b_i).P_i : \text{nil}}$$

$$\text{(T-BPP-ISUM)} \quad \frac{\forall i \in I : \Gamma \vdash_{\mathcal{E};\mathcal{E}_i} P_i : \mathsf{T}_i \quad \mathcal{E}' = \bigcup_i \mathcal{E}_i}{\Gamma \vdash_{\mathcal{E};\mathcal{E}'} \sum_{i \in I} \tau.P_i : \sum_{i \in I} \tau.\mathsf{T}_i} \qquad \text{(T-BPP-SUB)} \quad \frac{\Gamma \vdash_{\mathcal{E};\mathcal{E}'} P : \mathsf{T} \quad \mathsf{T} \lesssim^c \mathsf{S}}{\Gamma \vdash_{\mathcal{E};\mathcal{E}'} P : \mathsf{S}}$$

$$\text{(T-BPP-PAR)} \quad \frac{\Gamma \vdash_{\mathcal{E};\mathcal{E}_1} P : \mathsf{T} \quad \Gamma \vdash_{\mathcal{E};\mathcal{E}_2} Q : \mathsf{S} \quad \mathcal{E}' = \mathcal{E}_1 \cup \mathcal{E}_2}{\Gamma \vdash_{\mathcal{E};\mathcal{E}'} P | Q : \mathsf{T} \| \mathsf{S}}$$

$$\text{(T-BPP-IF)} \quad \frac{\Gamma \vdash_{\mathcal{E};\mathcal{E}_1} P : \mathsf{T} \quad \Gamma \vdash_{\mathcal{E};\mathcal{E}_2} Q : \mathsf{S} \quad \mathcal{E}' = \mathcal{E}_1 \cup \mathcal{E}_2}{\Gamma \vdash_{\mathcal{E};\mathcal{E}'} \text{if } a = b \text{ then } P \text{ else } Q : \tau.\mathsf{T} + \tau.\mathsf{S}}$$

4.3 Results

The results obtained in Section 3.3 can be extended to the new system.

Theorem 2 (main results on $\vdash_{\mathcal{E};\mathcal{E}'}$). *Suppose* $\Gamma \vdash_{\mathcal{E};\mathcal{E}'} P : \mathsf{T}$. *Then: (a)* $P_\Gamma \xrightarrow{\lambda} P'_{\Gamma'}$ *implies that there are a* T' *and* $\mathcal{E}'' \subseteq \mathcal{E}'$ *such that* $\mathsf{T} \xrightarrow{\lambda}_{\mathcal{E}} \mathsf{T}'$ *and* $\Gamma \vdash_{\mathcal{E};\mathcal{E}''} P' : \mathsf{T}'$; *(b)* $P_\Gamma \lesssim^c \mathsf{T}$; *(c) safety formulas satisfied by* T *are also satisfied by* P_Γ.

Example 2 (factorial). Consider the processes defined in Example 1, the same context Γ and a new system augmented with a (stub) printing service: $S' = S \,|\, !print(d)$. In what follows, we omit the unit tag and write e.g. $\alpha \to \beta$ for $\alpha[()] \to \beta[()]$ Consider the following extended tag sorting system

$$\mathcal{E} = \{fact[ret] \to (\tau.ret + \tau.fact[ret]),\ ret \to ret,\ ret \to pr,\ pr \to \mathsf{nil}\}\ .$$

Let $\Lambda^\tau \subseteq \Lambda$ be the set of communication labels (all labels of the form $\tau\langle\alpha,\tilde{\beta}\rangle$). It is not difficult to prove that $\Gamma \vdash_{\mathcal{E}} S' : fact[ret]$ (note that subtyping plays an essential role in this derivation). Moreover, it holds that $fact[ret] \models \phi_1', \phi_2'$, where ϕ_1' and ϕ_2' are the versions of ϕ_1 and ϕ_2 defined in Example 1 with visible actions replaced by silent ones:

$$\phi_1' \overset{\triangle}{=} \neg\langle\!\langle\Lambda^\tau\rangle\!\rangle\,\langle\tau\langle ret\rangle\rangle\,\langle\!\langle\Lambda^\tau\rangle\!\rangle\,\langle\tau\langle fact, ret\rangle\rangle \qquad \phi_2' \overset{\triangle}{=} \neg\langle\!\langle\Lambda^\tau\rangle\!\rangle\,\langle\tau\langle pr\rangle\rangle\,\langle\!\langle\Lambda^\tau\rangle\!\rangle\,\langle\tau\langle fact, ret\rangle\rangle\ .$$

Formulas ϕ_1' and ϕ_2' express safety properties, hence thanks to Theorem 2, we can conclude the analog of what shown in Example 1: $S'_\Gamma \models \phi_1' \wedge \phi_2'$.

In several cases, the simulation preorder relating processes and their types is unnecessarily over-approximating. The rules for conditional and subtyping are obvious source of over-approximation, as well as the presence in $\mathcal{E}$ of dummy rules that are not actually used in type-checking the process: these are sources of "fake" transitions in types, that is, transitions with no correspondence in processes. A subtler problem is raised by input prefixes. Input prefixes correspond to rules in $\mathcal{E}$: but while an input prefix may never become available, and a (non-replicated) input disappears upon synchronization, the corresponding rules in $\mathcal{E}$ are always available and may give rise to fake transitions in types. In the rest of the section we show that, for processes enjoying a certain "uniform receptiveness" condition with respect to Γ (Definition 1), a bisimilarity relation between processes and types can be established. In this case, the abstract process and its type satisfy the same properties.

Let us introduce some extra notation and terminology first. In what follows, $\equiv$ will denote the standard structural congruence in pi-calculus (see e.g. [1]), while $out(P)$ (resp. $inp(P)$) will denote the set of free names occurring in some output (resp. input) action in P. Moreover, we define $\Gamma^{-1}(\alpha)$ as the set $\{a\,|\,\Gamma \vdash a : \alpha\}$ and define contexts as $C ::= (\nu a : \alpha)C \mid P|C \mid a(b).C \mid [\,]$. A process P is *input-local* if for every action prefix $a(x).Q$ in P, replicated or not, it holds $x \notin inp(Q)$. Finally, a *receptor* is a process of the form $(\nu a)\big(\sum_{i \in I} a_i(x).P_i \mid \prod_{j \in J} !a(x).Q_j\big)$ such that $a \notin inp(P_i, Q_j)$ for each i, j.

The definition below has a simple explanation: each tag should correspond to a unique receptor, and the latter should be immediately available to any potential sender. This somehow generalizes Sangiorgi's uniform receptiveness [8]. In particular, it is straightforward to modify the type system in [8] so that well-typed processes are uniform receptive in our sense. A more general technique for proving Γ-uniform receptiveness in concrete cases is given by its co-inductive definition: that is, finding a relation that satisfies the conditions listed in the definition and contains the given Γ and P. Below, we use $\to$ as an abbreviation of $\xrightarrow{\tau\langle\alpha,\beta\rangle}$ for some α and β.

Definition 1 (Γ-uniform receptiveness). *Let $\theta : \alpha \mapsto R_\alpha$ be a function from tags to receptors. We let $\rhd_\theta$ be the largest relation over contexts and input-local processes such that whenever $\Gamma \rhd_\theta P$ then:*

1. *for each α such that $\Gamma^{-1}(\alpha) \cap \text{out}(P) \neq \emptyset$ it holds that*
   (a) *$\forall a \in \Gamma^{-1}(\alpha)$ there are R and Q such that $(\nu a)P \equiv (\nu a)(R|Q)$ with $a \notin \text{inp}(Q)$ and $(\nu a)R = R_\alpha$;*
   (b) *whenever $P \equiv C[(\nu a : \alpha)P']$ there are R' and Q' such that $P' \equiv R'|Q'$ with $a \notin \text{inp}(Q')$ and $(\nu a)R' = R_\alpha$;*
2. *whenever $P \equiv (\nu a : \alpha)P'$ with $a \in \text{out}(P')$ then $\Gamma, a : \alpha \rhd_\theta P'$;*
3. *whenever $P \to P'$ then $\Gamma \rhd_\theta P'$.*

We write $\Gamma \rhd P$, and say P is Γ-uniform receptive, if $\Gamma \rhd_\theta P$ for some θ.

In what follows, we write $\Gamma \vdash^-_{\mathcal{E}} P : \mathsf{T}$ if $\Gamma \vdash_{\mathcal{E};\mathcal{E}'} P : \mathsf{T}$ is derived without using rules (T-BPP-SUB) and (T-BPP-IF), and $\mathcal{E} = \mathcal{E}'$.

Theorem 3. *Suppose P is Γ-uniform receptive and that $\Gamma \vdash^-_{\mathcal{E}} P : \mathsf{T}$. Then $P_\Gamma \sim^c \mathsf{T}$.*

5   An Extended Example

A simple printing system is defined where users are required to authenticate for being allowed to print. Users are grouped into trusted and untrusted, which are distinguished by two groups of credentials: $\{c_i \mid i \in I\}$ (also written $\tilde{c}_i$) for trusted and $\{c_j \mid j \in J\}$ (also written $\tilde{c}_j$) for untrusted, with $\tilde{c}_i \cap \tilde{c}_j = \emptyset$. Process A is an authentication server that receives from a client its credential c, a return channel r and an error channel e and then sends both r and e to a credential-handling process T. If the client is untrusted, T produces an error, otherwise a private connection between the client and the printer is established, by creating a new communication link k and passing it to C. C simulates the cumulative behavior of all clients: nondeterministically, it tries to authenticate by using credential c_l, for an $l \in I \cup J$, and waits for the communication link with the printer, on the private channel r, and for an error, on the private channel e. After printing, or receiving an error, C's execution restarts.

We expect that every printing request accompanied by trusted credentials will be satisfied, and that every print is preceded by an authentication request.

$$Sys \overset{\triangle}{=} (\nu a : aut, \tilde{c}_i : ok, \tilde{c}_j : nok, M : (), print : pr)\big(T \mid C \mid A \mid !print(d)\big)$$

$$T \overset{\triangle}{=} \prod_{i \in I} !c_i(x,e).(\nu k : key)\big(\bar{x}\langle k\rangle \mid k(d).\overline{print}\langle d\rangle\big) \mid \prod_{j \in J} !c_j(x,e).\bar{e}$$

$$A \overset{\triangle}{=} !a(c,r,e).\bar{c}\langle r,e\rangle$$

$$C \overset{\triangle}{=} (\nu i : iter)\big(\bar{i} \mid !i.(\nu r : ret, e : err)\big(\textstyle\sum_{l \in I \cup J} \tau.\bar{a}\langle c_l,r,e\rangle \mid r(z).((\bar{z}\langle M\rangle \mid \bar{i}) + e.\bar{i})\big)\big)$$

Example 3 (CCS$^-$ types). Consider the tag sorting system

$$\mathcal{E} = \{aut[ok, ret, err], aut[nok, ret, err], ok[ret, err],$$
$$nok[ret, err], ret[key], pr[()], err[], key[()], iter[]\}.$$

It is easy to prove that $\emptyset \vdash_{\mathcal{E}} Sys : \mathsf{T}_T \mid \mathsf{T}_A \mid \mathsf{T}_C \mid !pr = \mathsf{T}$, where

$$\mathsf{T}_T \overset{\triangle}{=} !ok\langle ret, err\rangle.\big(\overline{ret}\langle key\rangle \mid key.\overline{pr}\big) \mid !nok\langle ret, err\rangle.\overline{err}$$

$$\mathsf{T}_A \overset{\triangle}{=} !aut\langle ok, ret, err\rangle.\overline{ok}\langle ret, err\rangle \mid !aut\langle nok, ret, err\rangle.\overline{nok}\langle ret, err\rangle$$

$T_C \stackrel{\triangle}{=} \overline{iter} \mid !iter. \left(\left(\tau.\overline{aut}\langle ok,ret,err \rangle + \tau.\overline{aut}\langle nok,ret,err \rangle \right) \mid \left(ret\langle key \rangle . \left(\overline{key} \mid \overline{iter} \right) + err.\overline{iter} \right) \right).$

Furthermore, it holds that

$$T \vDash \varphi_3 \stackrel{\triangle}{=} \neg \langle\langle \Lambda - \{ nok\langle ret,err \rangle, aut\langle nok,ret,err \rangle, \tau\langle aut,nok,ret,err \rangle \} \rangle\rangle \langle \overline{err} \rangle$$

$$T \vDash \varphi_4 \stackrel{\triangle}{=} \neg \langle\langle \Lambda - \{ ok\langle ret,err \rangle, aut\langle ok,ret,err \rangle, \tau\langle aut,ok,ret,err \rangle \} \rangle\rangle \langle \overline{pr} \rangle$$

that is, *error* is always generated by an authentication request containing untrusted credentials, and every *pr* action is preceded by a successful authentication request. Both formulas express safety properties, hence Proposition 1 ensures that are both satisfied by the abstract process Sys_0.

Example 4 (BPP types). Consider the system *Sys* previously defined; in this example we show that a BPP type for *Sys*, which allow a more precise analysis of the system can be obtained. Consider the following extended tag sorting system

$$\mathcal{E} = \{ \quad aut[ok,ret,err] \rightarrow ok[ret,err], \quad ok[ret,err] \rightarrow ret[key], \quad err \rightarrow iter,$$

$$aut[nok,ret,err] \rightarrow nok[ret,err], \quad nok[ret,err] \rightarrow err, \quad key \rightarrow pr, \quad pr \rightarrow nil,$$

$$ret[key] \rightarrow (key \mid iter), \quad iter \rightarrow \tau.aut[ok,ret,err] + \tau.aut[nok,ret,err]) \}.$$

First, it is easy to see that $\emptyset \vdash_{\mathcal{E}} Sys : iter$. Moreover it is not difficult to prove, by coinduction, that *Sys* is 0-uniform receptive. Hence from

$$iter \vDash \varphi'_3 \stackrel{\triangle}{=} [\![\Lambda^\tau]\!] \, [\tau\langle aut,ok,ret,err \rangle] \, \langle\langle \Lambda^\tau \rangle\rangle \, \langle \tau\langle pr \rangle \rangle$$

$$iter \vDash \varphi'_4 \stackrel{\triangle}{=} [\![\Lambda^\tau]\!] \, [\tau\langle aut,nok,ret,err \rangle] \, \langle\langle \Lambda^\tau \rangle\rangle \, \langle \tau\langle err \rangle \rangle$$

and Theorem 3, $Sys_0 \vDash \varphi'_3 \wedge \varphi'_4$, that is, every authentication request accompanied by trusted credentials will be followed by a *pr*, while every untrusted request will be followed by an *err*.

6   Join Calculus and Petri Nets Types

We extend the treatment of the previous section to the Join calculus [2]. We shall only consider the case of *closed* behavior; the open case requires some more notational burden and we leave it for an extended version of the paper. The essential step we have to take, at the level of types, is now moving from BPP to Petri nets. Technically, this leap is somehow forced by the presence of the join pattern construct in the calculus. In the context of infinite states transition systems [7,6], the leap corresponds precisely to moving from rewrite rules with a single nonterminal on the LHS (BPP) to rules with multisets of nonterminals on the LHS (PN).

6.1   Processes and Types

The syntax of the calculus is given in Tab. 6. Note that we consider a "pure" version of the calculus without conditionals. Adding if-then-else is possible, but again implies some notational burden at the level of types (notably, simulating an internal choice operator with Petri nets), which we prefer to avoid. Over this language, we presuppose the standard notions of binding, alpha-equivalence, structural congruence $\equiv$ and (tag-annotated) reduction semantics $\xrightarrow{\mu}$, where $\mu ::= \tau\langle(\ell_1,\ell'_1),\ldots,(\ell_n,\ell'_n)\rangle$. Here $(\ell_1,\ell'_1),\ldots,(\ell_n,\ell'_n)$ must be regarded as a *multiset* of pairs (subject, object). For a context Γ, the transitional semantics $\xrightarrow{\lambda}$ of the abstract processes P_Γ is defined as expected, where $\lambda = \tau\langle(\alpha_1,\beta_1),\ldots,(\alpha_n,\beta_n)\rangle$. A type is a multiset $\mathsf{T} ::= \alpha_1[\beta_1],\ldots,\alpha_n[\beta_n]$ that is, "," is an associative and commutative operator with the empty multiset as unit. Types will play the role of markings in a Petri net. We consider a tag sorting system $\mathcal{E}$ containing elements of the form $\mathsf{T} \to \mathsf{S}$, to be interpreted as transitions of a Petri net. More precisely, we shall fix a set of rules $\mathcal{E} = \{\mathsf{T}_i \to \mathsf{S}_i \mid 1 \le i \le n\}$, where the following *uniformity* condition is satisfied by $\mathcal{E}$: let $\mathrm{dom}(\mathcal{E})$ be the set of all $\alpha[\beta]$'s occurring in $\mathcal{E}$; then for every α, β and β' such that $\alpha[\beta], \alpha[\beta'] \in \mathrm{dom}(\mathcal{E})$, if $\alpha[\beta], \mathsf{T} \to \mathsf{S} \in \mathcal{E}$ then also $\alpha[\beta'], \mathsf{T} \to \mathsf{S}' \in \mathcal{E}$ for some S'. The operational semantics of types is then defined by the rules below, which make it clear that $\mathcal{E}$ is a Petri net, and a type T is a marking of this net.

$$(\text{J-T-COM}) \quad \frac{\alpha_1[\beta_1],\ldots,\alpha_n[\beta_n] \to \mathsf{T} \in \mathcal{E}}{\alpha_1[\beta_1],\cdots,\alpha_n[\beta_n] \xrightarrow{\tau\langle(\alpha_1,\beta_1),\ldots,(\alpha_n,\beta_n)\rangle} \mathsf{T}} \qquad (\text{J-T-PAR}) \quad \frac{\mathsf{T} \xrightarrow{\lambda} \mathsf{T}'}{\mathsf{T},\mathsf{S} \xrightarrow{\lambda} \mathsf{T}',\mathsf{S}}$$

Table 6. Syntax of the Join calculus

Processes	$P,Q ::=$	$\overline{a}\langle b\rangle$	*Output*
		$\mid$ def D in P	*Definition*
		$\mid P\mid P$	*Parallel*
Definitions	$D ::=$	$J \rhd P$	*Pattern*
		$\mid D \wedge D$	*Conjunction*
Patterns	$J ::=$	$a^\alpha(b)$	*Input pattern*
		$\mid J \parallel J$	*Join pattern*

6.2 Typing Rules and Results

The typing rules are defined in Tab. 7. The rules generalizes as expected those of Section 4. In the rules, we use a function $\mathrm{tags}(D)$ that extracts tags associated with definitions, as follows:

$$\mathrm{tags}(D_1 \wedge \cdots \wedge D_n) = \bigcup_{i=1,\ldots,n} \mathrm{tags}(D_i) \qquad \mathrm{tags}(J \rhd P) = \mathrm{tags}(J)$$
$$\mathrm{tags}(J_1 \parallel \cdots \parallel J_n) = \bigcup_{i=1,\ldots,n} \mathrm{tags}(J_i) \qquad \mathrm{tags}(a^\alpha(c)) = \{a : \alpha\}$$

We have the following result.

Table 7. Typing rules for the Join calculus and Petri nets

$$
\text{(T-J-DEF)} \quad \frac{\Gamma \vdash_{\mathcal{E}} D : \text{nil} \quad \Gamma, \text{tags}(D) \vdash_{\mathcal{E}} P : \mathsf{T}}{\Gamma \vdash_{\mathcal{E}} \text{def } D \text{ in } P : \mathsf{T}} \qquad \text{(T-J-PAR)} \quad \frac{\Gamma \vdash_{\mathcal{E}} P : \mathsf{T} \quad \Gamma \vdash_{\mathcal{E}} Q : \mathsf{S}}{\Gamma \vdash_{\mathcal{E}} P|Q : \mathsf{T}, \mathsf{S}}
$$

$$
\text{(T-J-CON)} \quad \frac{\Gamma \vdash_{\mathcal{E}} D_i : \text{nil} \quad i = 1, \ldots, n}{\Gamma \vdash_{\mathcal{E}} D_1 \wedge \cdots \wedge D_n : \text{nil}} \qquad \text{(T-J-SUB)} \quad \frac{\Gamma \vdash_{\mathcal{E}} P : \mathsf{T} \quad \mathsf{T} \lesssim^c \mathsf{S}}{\Gamma \vdash_{\mathcal{E}} P : \mathsf{S}}
$$

$$
\text{(T-J-OUT)} \quad \frac{\Gamma \vdash a : \alpha \quad \Gamma \vdash b : \beta \quad \alpha[\beta] \in \text{dom}(\mathcal{E})}{\Gamma \vdash_{\mathcal{E}} \overline{a}\langle b \rangle : \alpha[\beta]}
$$

$$
J = a_1{}^{\alpha_1}(c_1) \parallel \cdots \parallel a_n{}^{\alpha_n}(c_n) \quad \forall \beta_{k_1}, \ldots, \beta_{k_n} \text{ s.t. } \alpha_i[\beta_{k_i}] \in \text{dom}(\mathcal{E}) \quad \exists \mathsf{T}_k \text{ s.t.}
$$

$$
\alpha_1[\beta_{k_1}], \ldots, \alpha_n[\beta_{k_n}] \rightarrow \mathsf{T}_k \in \mathcal{E} \wedge \Gamma, \text{tags}(D), c_1 : \beta_{k_1}, \ldots, c_n : \beta_{k_n} \vdash_{\mathcal{E}} P : \mathsf{T}_k
$$

$$
\text{(T-J-PAT)} \quad \frac{\mathcal{E}' = \bigcup_k \{\alpha_1[\beta_{k_1}], \ldots, \alpha_n[\beta_{k_n}] \rightarrow \mathsf{T}_k\}}{\Gamma \vdash_{\mathcal{E}} J \triangleright P : \text{nil}}
$$

Theorem 4. *Suppose* $\Gamma \vdash_{\mathcal{E}} P : \mathsf{T}$. *Then: (a) if* $P_\Gamma \xrightarrow{\lambda} P'_{\Gamma'}$ *then there exists a* T' *such that* $\mathsf{T} \xrightarrow{\lambda}_{\mathcal{E}} \mathsf{T}'$ *and* $\Gamma' \vdash_{\mathcal{E}} P' : \mathsf{T}'$; *and (b)* $P_\Gamma \lesssim^c \mathsf{T}$.

7 Conclusions and Related Works

We have proposed methods for statically abstracting propositional approximations of first-order process calculi (pi-calculus and Join). These methods take the form of behavioral type systems. Correspondingly, three classes of types have been considered: restriction-free CCS, BPP and Petri nets. Concerning type reconstruction, we give methods to compute minimal types under certain assumptions on processes, but leave the development of explicit type inference algorithms for future work.

In Igarashi and Kobayashi's work [3], types are restriction-free CCS processes and output prefixes are allowed. Roughly, types are obtained from pi-processes by replacing any bound subject with the corresponding tag, and turning each object into a CCS-annotation describing the behavior of the prefix continuation. Depending on the actual instantiation of this framework, the type checking algorithm of [3] may need to call analysis procedures that check run-time properties of types (well-formedness). Our work is mostly inspired by [3], but we try to simplify its approach by considering an asynchronous version of the calculus and by extracting a tag-wise, rather than channel-wise, behavior of processes. On one hand, this simplification leads to some loss of information, which prevents us from capturing certain liveness properties such as race- and deadlock-freedom. On the other hand, it allows us to make the connection between different kinds of behavior (open/closed) and different type models (CCS/BPP) direct and explicit. As an example, in the case of BPP we can spell out reasonably simple conditions under which the type analysis is "precise" (Γ-uniform receptiveness). Also, our approach naturally carries over to the Join calculus, by moving to Petri nets types.

The papers [10,11] present type systems inspired by [3]. The main difference between these works and Igarashi and Kobayashi's, is that behavioral types here are more precise than in [3], because described by using full CCS. An open (in the sense of [12]) version of simulation is used as a subtyping relation. Undecidability of (bi)simulation on CCS with restriction is somehow bypassed by providing an ad-hoc assume-guarantee principle to discharge safety checks at name restriction in a modular way.

Igarashi and Kobayashi' type system was inspired by work on the analysis of various properties of concurrent programs, notably linearity [13] and deadlock-freedom [14,15,16]. Nowadays, the list of such properties has grown, so as to include several forms of refined lock-freedom and resource usage analyses [17,18,19].

Concerning the Join calculus, previous work on type systems [20,21] proposed a functional typing à la ML and a type system à la Hindley/Milner. The analogy between Join and Petri nets was first noticed in [22] and then in [23]. In [24], Buscemi and Sassone classify join processes by comparison with different classes of Petri nets. Four distinct type systems are proposed, that give rise to a hierarchy comprising four classes of join processes. These classes are shown to be encodable respectively into place/transition Petri nets, Colored nets, Reconfigurable nets and Dynamic nets. While only the last class contains all join terms, note that only place/transition Petri nets are actually "propositional" and enjoy effective analysis techniques. In other words, the emphasis of [24] is on assessing expressiveness of Join rather than on computing tractable approximations of processes.

More loosely related to our work, there is a strong body of research on behavioral types for object calculi. Notably, [25,26] put forward behavioral types for object interfaces; these types are based on labelled transition systems that specify the possible sequences of calls at available methods (services). Our extended tag sorting systems are reminiscent of this mechanism. Similarly, in [27], a behavioral typing discipline for TyCO, a name-passing calculus of concurrent objects, is introduced. Types are defined by using graphs and the type compatibility relation is a bisimulation. This work is related to Yoshida's paper [28], where *graph types* are used for proving full abstraction of translations from sorted polyadic pi-terms into monadic ones.

References

1. Milner, R.: The polyadic π-calculus: a tutorial. In: Logic and Algebra of Specification, pp. 203–246. Springer, Heidelberg (1993)
2. Fournet, C., Gonthier, G.: The reflexive chemical abstract machine and the join calculus. In: POPL, pp. 372–385. ACM Press, New York (1996)
3. Igarashi, A., Kobayashi, N.: A generic type system for the pi-calculus. TCS 311(1-3), 121–163 (2004)
4. Christensen, S., Hirshfeld, Y., Moller, F.: Decidable subsets of CCS. The Computer Journal 37(4), 233–242 (1994)
5. Christensen, S., Hishfeld, Y., Moller, F.: Bisimulation equivalence is decidable for basic parallel processes. In: Best, E. (ed.) CONCUR 1993. LNCS, vol. 715, pp. 143–157. Springer, Heidelberg (1993)
6. Hirshfeld, Y., Moller, F.: Decidability results in automata and process theory. In: Moller, F., Birtwistle, G. (eds.) Logics for Concurrency. LNCS, vol. 1043, pp. 102–148. Springer, Heidelberg (1996)
7. Burkart, O., Esparza, J.: More infinite results. In: Current Trends in Theoretical Computer Science: entering the 21st centuary, pp. 480–503. World Scientific Publishing Co., Inc., Singapore (2001)

8. Sangiorgi, D.: The name discipline of uniform receptiveness. TCS 221(1-2), 457–493 (1999)
9. Stirling, C.: Modal logics for communicating systems. TCS 49(2-3), 311–347 (1987)
10. Rajamani, S.K., Rehof, J.: A behavioral module system for the pi-calculus. In: Cousot, P. (ed.) SAS 2001. LNCS, vol. 2126, pp. 375–394. Springer, Heidelberg (2001)
11. Chaki, S., Rajamani, S.K., Rehof, J.: Types as models: Model checking message-passing programs. In: POPL, pp. 45–57. ACM Press, New York (2002)
12. Sangiorgi, D.: A theory of bisimulation for π-calculus. Acta Informartica 33 (1996)
13. Kobayashi, N., Pierce, B.C., Turner, D.N.: Linearity and the Pi-Calculus. ACM Transactions on Programming Languages and Systems 21(5), 914–947 (1999)
14. Kobayashi, N.: A partially deadlock-free typed process calculus. ACM Transactions on Programming Languages and Systems 20(2), 436–482 (1998)
15. Kobayashi, N., Saito, S., Sumii, E.: An implicitly-typed deadlock-free process calculus. In: Palamidessi, C. (ed.) CONCUR 2000. LNCS, vol. 1877, pp. 489–503. Springer, Heidelberg (2000)
16. Kobayashi, N.: A type system for lock-free processes. Information and Computation 177(2), 122–159 (2002)
17. Kobayashi, N.: Type-based information flow analysis for the pi-calculus. Acta Informartica 42(4-5), 291–347 (2005)
18. Kobayashi, N.: A new type system for deadlock-free processes. In: Baier, C., Hermanns, H. (eds.) CONCUR 2006. LNCS, vol. 4137, pp. 233–247. Springer, Heidelberg (2006)
19. Kobayashi, N., Suenaga, K., Wischik, L.: Resource usage analysis for the pi-calculus. In: Emerson, E.A., Namjoshi, K.S. (eds.) VMCAI 2006. LNCS, vol. 3855, pp. 298–312. Springer, Heidelberg (2005)
20. Fournet, C., Laneve, C., Maranget, L., Rémy, D.: Implicit typing à la ML for the join-calculus. In: Mazurkiewicz, A., Winkowski, J. (eds.) CONCUR 1997. LNCS, vol. 1243, pp. 196–212. Springer, Heidelberg (1997)
21. Odersky, M., Zenger, C., Zenger, M., Chen, G.: A functional view of join. Technical Report ACRC-99-016, University of South Australia (1999)
22. Asperti, A., Busi, N.: Mobile petri nets. Technical Report UBLCS 96-10, Università di Bologna (1996)
23. Odersky, M.: Functional nets. In: Smolka, G. (ed.) ESOP 2000 and ETAPS 2000. LNCS, vol. 1782, pp. 1–25. Springer, Heidelberg (2000)
24. Buscemi, M.G., Sassone, V.: High-level petri nets as type theories in the join calculus. In: Honsell, F., Miculan, M. (eds.) ETAPS 2001 and FOSSACS 2001. LNCS, vol. 2030, pp. 104–120. Springer, Heidelberg (2001)
25. Najm, E., Nimour, A.: Explicit behavioral typing for object interfaces. In: Moreira, A.M.D., Demeyer, S. (eds.) Object-Oriented Technology. ECOOP 1999 Workshop Reader. LNCS, vol. 1743, p. 321. Springer, Heidelberg (1999)
26. Najm, E., Nimour, A., Stefani, J.B.: Infinite types for distributed object interfaces. In: FMOODS of IFIP Conference Proceedings, vol. 139, p. 450 (1999)
27. Ravara, A., Vasconcelos, V.T.: Behavioral types for a calculus of concurrent objects. In: Lengauer, C., Griebl, M., Gorlatch, S. (eds.) Euro-Par 1997. LNCS, vol. 1300, pp. 554–561. Springer, Heidelberg (1997)
28. Yoshida, N.: Graph types for monadic mobile processes. In: Chandru, V., Vinay, V. (eds.) Foundations of Software Technology and Theoretical Computer Science. LNCS, vol. 1180, pp. 371–386. Springer, Heidelberg (1996)

Formal Specification of Multi-agent Systems by Using EUSMs*

Mercedes G. Merayo, Manuel Núñez, and Ismael Rodríguez

Dept. Sistemas Informáticos y Programación
Universidad Complutense de Madrid, E-28040 Madrid. Spain
mgmerayo@fdi.ucm.es, {mn,isrodrig}@sip.ucm.es

Abstract. The behavior of e-commerce agents can be defined at different levels of abstraction. A formalism allowing to define them in terms of their *economic* activities, *Utility State Machines*, has been proposed. Due to its high level of abstraction, this formalism focuses on describing the economic *goals* rather on *how* they are achieved. Though this approach is suitable to *specify* the objectives of e-commerce agents, as well as to construct formal analysis methodologies, this framework is not suitable to define the *strategic* behavior of agents. In this paper we develop a new formalism to explicitly define the strategic behavior of agents in a modular way. In particular, we reinterpret the role of *utility functions*, already used in USMs in a more restrictive manner, so that they define strategic preferences and activities of agents. We apply the formalism to define the agents in a benchmark e-commerce agent environment, the *Supply Chain Management Game*. Since the strategic behavior of agents is located in a specific part of the formalism, different strategies can be easily considered, which enhances the reusability of the proposed specification.

Keywords: Formal specification of multi-agent systems, autonomous agents, e-commerce.

1 Introduction

One of the most interesting applications of agent-oriented computation is the area of *agent-mediated e-commerce* [1,2,3,4,5]. These agents can look for profitable offers, recommend products, negotiate with other agents, or, even autonomously, perform transactions on behalf of their respective users. However, users may be reluctant to delegate activities that dramatically affect their possessions. On the one hand, they may think that agents are biased by the manufacturer for commercial reasons. On the other hand, some users would never (voluntarily) delegate critical activities to *intelligent* entities.

---

* This research was partially supported by the Spanish MEC projects MASTER/TERMAS TIC2003-07848-C02-01 and WEST/FAST TIN2006-15578-C02-01, the Junta de Castilla-La Mancha project PAC06-0008, the Comunidad de Madrid project to fund research groups CAM-910606,‘ and the Marie Curie project MRTN-CT-2003-505121/TAROT.

F. Arbab and M. Sirjani (Eds.): FSEN 2007, LNCS 4767, pp. 318–333, 2007.

The use of *formal methods* through the different stages of a system development increases the chance of finding and isolating mistakes in early phases of the system creation. Formal languages are used to define the critical aspects of the system under consideration, that is, to create a *model* of the system. Formal specification languages and formal semantics have been already used in the field of agent-oriented systems (see e.g. [6,7,8]). Then, some theoretical machinery allows to analyze the model and extract some relevant properties concerning the aspects included in the model. In this line we can mention *model checking* [9] and its application to agent systems [10]. We can also consider that the model is the *specification* of the system under construction. Thus, we can compare its behavior with that of a real system and *test* whether it correctly implements the model [11]. Such approach is taken in the agents field, for instance, in [12]. Regarding agent-mediated e-commerce, formal methods can be used to analyze the *high-level* requirements of agents. These requirements can be defined in economic terms. Basically, the high-level objective of an e-commerce agent is *"get what the user said he wants and when he wants it"*. Let us note that *what the user wants* might include not only what goods or services he wants (e.g., DVD movies) but also other conditions (e.g., he wants to keep his information private, he wants to perform only legal transactions, etc).

Following these ideas, a formalism allowing to *specify* the high-level behavior of autonomous e-commerce agents, as well as to test agents with respect to their specifications, is proposed in [13,14,15]. Users objectives are defined in terms of their preferences, denoted in turn by means of *utility functions*. A utility function associates a numerical value with each basket of resources, where a *resource* is any scarce good that can be traded in the market. Preferences may change as long as the time passes and objectives are fulfilled. Regarding the former, time is used as a parameter in utility functions, that is, if $\bar{x}$ and $\bar{y}$ are baskets of resources and f is a utility function, $f(\bar{x}, t) > f(\bar{y}, t)$ means that, at time t, $\bar{x}$ is preferred to $\bar{y}$. Concerning the latter, the formalism allows agents to behave according to different utility functions depending on the current *state* of the agent. We called *Utility State Machines* to our formalism. A USM is inspired in the notion of *finite state machine* but it is more powerful. A set of variables denote the current possessions of the user (i.e., the resources it can exchange with other agents) and each state is provided with a utility function denoting the objectives in the state. USMs evolve by changing their state, by performing an exchange with other USMs, or by waiting for some time. By performing these activities, they represent the economic behavior of an autonomous e-commerce agent. The work in USMs has also been supported by the specification of small case studies such as the specification of all the entities involved in the Kasbah system [16].

Even though there is a well-founded theory underlying USMs, the application of this formalism to the specification of complex agents has not been as successful as expected. In fact, our experimentation has detected some features of the original formalism that are almost not needed when specifying a wide range of different agents. In contrast, although USMs have a big expressive power, this experimentation has also revealed that there are several agents character-istics that can be expressed only in a very difficult and intricate way. Thus, we have decided to create a new formalism based on USMs but overcoming most of its drawbacks. We call this new specification language *extended utility state machines*, in short, EUSM. The term *extended* indicates not only that these new machines are an *extension* of the previous formalism; it also shows that these new machines are more powerful since the specification of some agent properties can be done in a more straight way. Among the several modifications and additions, we can remark the following structural contributions. First, utility functions al-low now to specify not only short-term behavior but also strategic behavior. Second, EUSMs allow to create general patterns to build agents; by modifying some utility functions located in specific places, it is easy to define agents that, following the same behavior, present completely different characteristics.

In order to illustrate the features of our formalism, we apply it to the specifi-cation of a system that can be considered as a *benchmark* in the agent-mediated e-commerce community: The *Supply Chain Management Game* [17]. In a few words, in this system, agents face a simulated environment where they interact with suppliers and customers to stock up with components and sell constructed products, respectively. Next we briefly introduce the main components in the *Supply Chain Management Game*. We restrict ourselves to the most relevant as-pects of the system. The system simulates an environment where PCs are traded. Thus, the system contains final consumers, vendors, and component providers. The global behavior is very simple: Clients buy PCs to vendors, which in turn buy the needed components to providers, ensemble them, and sell the final PCs to clients. While consumers and providers are simulated by the system, vendors have to be implemented by the different teams taking part in the game. As ex-pected, the goal of these agents is to earn as much money as possible. Once these agents simulating vendors are added to the system, they have to take autonomous decisions. Each agent communicates with clients and component providers by following a simple protocol. Agents receive *requests for quotes* from the clients. Then, the agent sends quotes to the chosen clients (each agent can decide with which clients it wants to make business). Next, the clients accept the quotes that they like. Finally, the last communication is the transaction itself. It is worth to point out that each quote contains not only the price and the number of desired pieces, but also the reception date as well as the penalty to be paid in case of late delivery. The communication of agents with providers is similar, but exchanging in the previous dialogue the role of agent by the role of provider and the role of client by the role of agent. That is, an agent sends a request for quotes to the providers, and so on. In each game turn, the agents send to their *factories* the requests for assembling some PCs by using the available components that they bought in previous turns. The production capacity of each factory is not unlimited. Moreover, to store both components and PCs has an associated cost.

The rest of the paper is structured as follows. In the next section we relate the approach presented in this paper with some previous work. In Section 3, we introduce the language constructions to define EUSMs. We will use the Supply

Chain Management Game to show, along this section, the main EUSMs characteristics. In Section 4 we define the operational behavior of EUSMs in terms of
their transitions. In Section 5 we show how to extend the concepts underlying
EUSMs to deal with multi-agent systems. In Section 6 we present some general
guidelines to define EUSMs. Finally, in Section 7 we present our conclusions and
some lines for future work.

2   Related Work

Several approaches have been proposed to formally define the behavior of e-
commerce systems. Most of them focus on providing models for checking the
validity of *communications* in these systems (see e.g.[18,19]). Clearly, these aspects are critical for the reliability of these systems. For instance, features such as
authentication, *non-repudiation*, *integrity*, and *privacy* are required in this kind
of systems [20]. These requirements are critical in other system domains as well,
so they are not *specific* to the e-commerce domain. Moreover, in these formal approaches entities are defined in terms of low level activities (e.g. messages), not in
terms of their high level behavior (which, in this case, is the *economic* behavior).
Thus, considering their behavior in terms of economic concepts such as *preferences*, *utilities*, *profit* or *Pareto equilibria* might be tricky or cumbersome. Similarly, other formalisms allowing to formally define the behavior of autonomous
agents have been proposed (see e.g. AgentSpeak(L) [21] or 3APL [22]). Since they
are generic and do not focus on any specific agent-oriented application domain,
the decision-making procedures of entities are not defined in economic terms
either. Some formalisms for defining and analyzing decision-making scenarios
have been proposed. For example, we may consider *Markov Decision Processes*
(MDP) [23] and *Partially Observable Markov Decision Processes* (POMDP) [24].
In these formalisms, the specifier totally or partially defines the consequences of
the agent decisions. For example, we may specify that, in a given state s, the
decision a will lead us to either a state s_1 with *profit* 2 or to a state s_2 with *profit*
3, with probabilities 0.25 and 0.75, respectively. Given this kind of information,
optimal sequences of decisions can be computed in some cases. Let us note that
composing these specifications requires to (partially or totally) know the actual
(probabilistic) consequences of taking each decision. Such a condition may be
unfeasible in several scenarios where the uncertainty about the environment is
too high to approximately define its behavior. However, providing entities with a
strategy is also required in these cases. In the approach presented in this paper,
we consider that models are provided with a strategy, but we are not concerned
with the data or the method followed to *choose* this strategy. On the contrary,
the formalism will focus on analyzing the behaviors of systems where each entity
is provided with a *given* strategy, regardless of its origin. That is, we will focus
on checking the *consequences* of taking these strategies (though this feedback
could be useful to choose them).

As we said before, the formalism presented in this paper, *extended utility
state machines* (EUSMs), are constructed from a previous formalism presented

in [13,14,15], *utility state machines* (USMs). One could think that, in order to consider the strategic behavior of agents, it is enough to reinterpret the meaning of the *utility functions* associated to states in EUSMs so that they denote *strategic* preferences rather than *true* preferences. For instance, let us suppose that I have two apples and that, according to my *true* preferences, I assign the same utility to one apple and to two oranges. Besides, let us suppose that, according to my knowledge, I suspect that the relative price of apples is raising. In this case, perhaps I should not accept *now* an exchange where I give one apple and I receive two oranges, despite of the fact that it is acceptable for my true preferences (note that my true utility would not decrease). Instead, I should act according to some *strategic* preferences. For example, strategic preferences could denote that now I give the same value to one apple and to *five* oranges.

Reinterpreting utility functions in this way in USMs is necessary but not sufficient to properly denote agents with strategic behaviors. USMs have other characteristics that have to be modified in order to provide a formalism allowing to denote strategic behaviors. First, USMs require that agents have a positive utility outcome before a given deadline is reached. Since utility functions will not denote *true* preferences in the new formalism, this is not suitable. Besides, in USMs variables only denote the amounts of *resources* owned by the agent and the *time*. However, in order to take strategic decisions, other variables (e.g., a historic file of last transactions) are required. In USMs, utility functions are used only to enable/disable exchanges of resources. However, in order to define strategies in the long term, utility functions should also be able to affect other decisions not directly involving transactions. In USMs, the only available kind of communication between agents is the *exchange of resources*, but it is not suitable for defining strategic scenarios where a transaction could be just the last step of a long term negotiation process. Actually, since in USMs only resource variables are modified in exchanges, it is not possible to affect other variables that could be relevant for the future strategy (e.g., the historic file). Finally, in USMs actions associated to transitions do not depend on the actual values that are taken to make conditions to hold, though registering these values could be useful for the strategy. As we will see in the next section, the new formalism, EUSMs, will overcome these problems by providing new constructions that enhance the expressivity in these cases.

3   Introducing Extended Utility State Machines

In this section we formally define the state machines that we propose as an appropriate formalism to define agents that incur in e-commerce activities. We put a special emphasis in the novelties with respect to USMs. Essentially, an *extended utility state machine* is a state machine where we introduce some additional features to help in defining e-commerce autonomous agents. Thus, we have several *states* and *transitions* among them. Transitions have an associated *condition*, that is, a transition can be performed only if the condition holds. Each transition also contains an *action*. This action can be either to change the value of some variables that the agent is controlling or to send a message to another agent. A particular case of action is associated with *exchanges of resources*, that is, two agents exchange messages, inducing a common transaction. The *configuration* of a EUSM is given by the current state and the current value of the variables. Finally, the *operational semantics* of our machines, indicating how such a machine evolves, is defined as follows:

- If there exists a transition from the current state where the condition holds then this transition can be performed.
- If there is more than one transition with the condition holding then there is a non-deterministic choice among all the possibilities.
- If there does not exist such a transition then the machine can let the time pass until one of the conditions hold.

The previous description of our state machines coincides with the classical notion. The important difference so far comes from the introduction of utility functions. In our framework, each EUSM has a function associating a utility function with each state. These functions have three parameters (the value of the variables V, an agent identifier id, and a time t) and return a real number indicating the *utility* of having the values of the variables V, at time t, after interacting with agent id. Thus, one of the main roles of utility functions consists in deciding whether a future exchange of resources with a certain agent will be *good* according to the current available information. So, utility functions are used to guide both current and future exchanges. However, we can give more sophisticated uses. For example, since the utility function takes as parameter all the available variables, we can decide to refuse a purchase at a low price because our record indicates that the prices are decreasing very fast. In this line, utility functions will be used to decide whether a vendor purchases components, at a given price, by taking into account the requests previously received. So, utility functions can be used to define complex strategies. This is a big advantage with respect to USMs [13,15]. In particular, in order to define agents as EUSMs, their strategies will be codified in the utility functions. Thus, by leaving the utility functions undefined, we are providing a *reusable pattern* to create new agents having a similar behavior but taking decisions in completely different ways.

We have already mentioned that utility functions will be taking as parameter a set of variables. Next, we describe the different types of variables as well as their roles in the framework of EUSMs. A distinguished set of variables will represent *resources*. The idea is that all the agents participating in a multi-agent system denote a specific resource with the same name; the rest of the variables will be considered *private* and they can have arbitrary names. A distinguished variable will be associated with the *buffer* (organized as a fifo queue) storing *incoming messages*. Symmetrically, another variable will refer to the *port* for *outgoing messages*. Any message sent to this port will be received in the buffer associated to the destination agent. The last distinguished variable is *time*.

In order to perform operations, agents will communicate with each other via *messages*. A special kind of message are *exchange* messages. We consider two types of exchange messages: *Proposal* (denoted by *expr*) and *acceptance* (denoted by *exac*). The agent sending a proposal does not modify its resources until it receives an acceptance from the partner. In both cases, these messages include the exchanged resources as well as the *id* of the agent proposing the exchange. This identifier is useful to keep a record of transactions and, in particular, to refer to deals that were reached but not concluded yet (e.g. the goods or the payment were not received yet). For example, if an agent receives the message $(id_4, expr(\{oranges =_\diamond 6, money =_\diamond -3\}))$, this means that the id_4 agent is offering 3 euros to purchase 6 oranges. Similarly, if the agent has as identifier id_7 and, after evaluating the exchange with the utility function corresponding to its current state, the deal is acceptable then the agent will send the message $(id_7, exac(\{oranges =_\diamond -6, money =_\diamond 3\}))$, indicating that it accepts the exchange.

Definition 1. Let M be a data type. A data type L is a *list data type for M* if it is defined as follows: $[\ ] \in L$; if $l \in L$ and $m \in M$ then $m \cdot l \in L$.

Let $l \in L$. We consider that l_i denotes the i-th element of l. Besides, $tail(l)$ represents the result of eliminating l_1 in l, while $enqueue(l, m)$ represents the result of inserting m as the new last element of l.

Let $v_1, \ldots, v_n$ be different identifiers and $t_1, \ldots, t_n$ be data types. We say that $V = \{v_1 : t_1, \ldots, v_n : t_n\}$ is a *set of variables*.

Let R and A be disjoint sets of identifier names. We consider

$$S = \left\{ \{r_1 =_\diamond x_1, \ldots, r_k =_\diamond x_k\} \ \middle| \ \begin{array}{l} \forall\, 1 \leq i \leq k : (r_i \in R \ \wedge \ x_i \in \mathbb{R}) \ \wedge \\ \forall\, 1 \leq i, j \leq k, i \neq j : r_i \neq r_j \end{array} \right\}$$

Let `ExchProposal` $= \{expr(s) | s \in S\}$ and `ExchAccept` $= \{exac(s) | s \in S\}$. We say that $M = A \times$ `Info`, for some type `Info` such that `ExchProposal` $\cup$ `ExchAccept` $\subseteq$ `Info`, is a *messages data type* for *resources* R and *agents* A.   □

Example 1. Let us consider the set of agents $A = \{Jimmy, Mary, Johnny\}$ and the set of resources $R = \{oranges, apples\}$. Any messages data type for R and A includes, e.g., the messages $(Johnny, expr(\{oranges =_\diamond 3, apples =_\diamond -2\}))$ and $(Mary, exac(\{apples =_\diamond 4\}))$. Moreover, depending on the definition of the type `Info` considered in the previous definition, other messages not involving an exchange proposal (*expr*) or an exchange acceptance (*exac*) could be included as well. For example, if $hello \in$ `Info` then $(Jimmy, hello)$ is also a message included in the messages data type.   □

Next we introduce some concepts related to variables in `EUSMs`. An *extended set of variables* includes some special variables that must be present in the machine (time, buffer of incoming messages, port for outgoing messages). In this set, variable representing resources are explicitly marked. An *assignment* associates each variable identifier with its current value.

Definition 2. Let $V = \{v_1 : t_1, \ldots, v_n : t_n\}$ a set of variables. Let R and A be disjoint sets of identifier names, `Messages` be a messages data type for resources

R and agents A, and `MessagesList` be a list data type for `Messages`. We say that (V, R) is an *extended set of variables* if the following conditions hold:

- $\{v : \mathbb{R} | v \in R\} \subseteq V$. Each resource is represented by a variable in the set.
- $t : \mathbb{R}^+ \in V$ represents the *time*.
- $ib : \texttt{MessagesList} \in V$ represents the *input buffer*.
- $op : \texttt{Messages} \cup \{\perp\} \in V$ represents the message to be sent through the *output port*. The symbol $\perp$ indicates that no message is waiting to be sent.

Let us consider an extended set of variables $E = (V, R)$. We say that a set $\mathcal{V} = \{v_1 =_\diamond a_1, \ldots, v_p =_\diamond a_p\}$ is an *assignment* for E if for all $1 \leq i \leq p$ we have $v_i \in V$ and $a_i \in t_i$. The set of all assignments is denoted by `Assign`.

Let $\mathcal{V} \in \texttt{Assign}$ and v be an identifier such that $v \in \{v' | \exists y' : v' =_\diamond y' \in \mathcal{V}\}$. The *update* of the variable v with the value x in V, denoted by $\mathcal{V}[v := x]$, is the substitution of the former value of v by x. Formally,

$$\mathcal{V}[v := x] = \{v' =_\diamond y' | v' =_\diamond y' \in \mathcal{V} \wedge v' \neq v\} \cup \{v =_\diamond x\}$$

We extend this operation to update k variables in the expected way:

$$\mathcal{V}[v_1 := x_1, v_2 := x_2, \ldots v_k := x_k] = (\ldots ((\mathcal{V}[v_1 := x_1])[v_2 := x_2]) \ldots [v_k := x_k])$$

Let $\mathcal{V}, \mathcal{V}' \in \texttt{Assign}$ be assignments. The *addition* of $\mathcal{V}$ and $\mathcal{V}'$, denoted by $\mathcal{V} + \mathcal{V}'$, is defined as

$$\{v' =_\diamond x' | v' =_\diamond x' \in \mathcal{V} \wedge \not\exists y' : v' =_\diamond y' \in \mathcal{V}'\}$$
$$\cup$$
$$\{v' =_\diamond x' | v' =_\diamond x' \in \mathcal{V}' \wedge \not\exists y' : v' =_\diamond y' \in \mathcal{V}\}$$
$$\cup$$
$$\{v' =_\diamond x' + y' | v' =_\diamond x' \in \mathcal{V} \wedge v' =_\diamond y' \in \mathcal{V}'\}$$

Let A be a set of agent identifier names. A *utility function* is any function $f : A \times \texttt{Assign} \to \mathbb{R}^+$. The set of all utility functions is denoted by `UtilFuncs`. □

Example 2. The EUSM representing a vendor in the Supply Chain Management Game communicates with clients and suppliers by using some messages. Besides, they will keep some variables to control their interactions. Figure 1 shows the messages agents can send/receive to/from customers and suppliers, as well as the set of variables that agents keep. Vendors use some variables to register past interactions with clients and suppliers (requests for quotes to be attended, proposed quotes, actual commitments, and historical transactions). In this way, they know what to expect from them in subsequent turns. These variables are *sets* where each element keeps the corresponding interaction message as well as the sender/receiver of the message and other relevant data. Other variables represent resources, the time consumed in the current state, the remaining capacity of the factory in this turn, and all mandatory variables previously introduced. □

Types of messages:

$ClientRFQ$: Client requests a quote to agent
  $crfq(pcModel, units)$

$AgentRFQ$: Agent requests a quote to supplier
  $arfq(compModel, units)$

$AgentQ$: An agent sends a quote to a client
  $aq(pcModel, units, price, deadline, penalty)$

$SupplierQ$: A supplier sends a quote to an agent
  $sq(compModel, units, price, deadline, penalty)$

$AcceptAgentQ$: Client accepts quote from agent
  $aaq(pcModel, units, price, deadline, penalty)$

$AcceptSupplierQ$: Agent accepts quote from sup.
  $asq(compModel, units, price, deadline, penalty)$

$expr(E)$: The exchange E is proposed
  $E \in$ Assign

$exac(E)$: The exchange E is accepted
  $E \in$ Assign

Variables:

Resources:
  $money$: money units
  $pcModel_x$: units of model x PC
  $compModel_y$: units of component y
Mandatory variables: t, ib, op
st: Time EUSM moved to the current state
$factoryCap$: # PCs the EUSM can still build
- Registering interactions with clients:
$RFQfromClients$: received RFQs
  $(client, clientRFQ)$
$QtoClients$: quotes sent to clients
  $(client, agentQ)$
$CwithClients$: commitments with clients
  $(client, agentQ)$
$HwithClients$: past transactions with clients
  $(client, agentQ, delay, finalPrice)$
- Registering interact. with suppliers:
$RFQtoSuppliers$: RFQs asked to suppliers
  $(supplier, agentRFQ)$
$QfromSuppliers$: Qs from suppliers
  $(supplier, supplierQ)$
$CwithSuppliers$: commitments with sup.
  $(supplier, supplierQ)$
$HwithSuppliers$: past transactions with sup.
  $(supplier, supplierQ, delay, finalPrice)$

Fig. 1. Messages and variables managed by vendors

Next we introduce our notion of state machine. In the next definition we use the term *explicit transition* to denote all the transitions contained in the set of transitions. The idea is that there are other transitions that are not included in that set: Time transitions.

Definition 3. An *Extended Utility State Machine*, in the following EUSM, is a tuple $M = (id, S, E, U, s_0, \mathcal{V}_0, \mathcal{T})$ where:

- id is the (unique) *agent identifier* of M.
- S is the *set of states* and s_0 is the *initial state*.
- E is the *extended set of variables* and $\mathcal{V}_0$ is the *initial assignment*.
- $U : S \longrightarrow$ UtilFuncs is a function associating a utility function with each state.
- $\mathcal{T}$ is the set of *explicit transitions*. For all transition $\gamma = (s_1, C, Z, s_2) \in \mathcal{T}$ we have
  - $s_1, s_2 \in S$ denote the initial and final states of the transition, respectively.
  - $C :$ Assign $\times$ Extra $\longrightarrow$ Bool is the transition *condition*, where Extra is a data type.
  - $Z :$ Assign $\times$ Extra $\to$ Assign is the transition *transformation*.

A *configuration* of M is a tuple $(s, \mathcal{V})$ where $s \in S$ and $\mathcal{V}$ is an assignment for E. □

We consider that all the variables belonging to the extended set of variables appear in the *initial assignment*. As we will see later in Definition 4 the C and

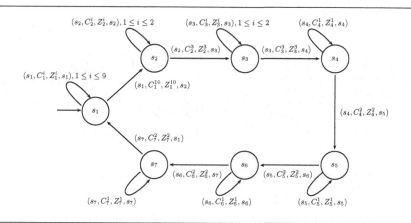

Fig. 2. EUSM denoting an agent

Z functions work as follows: If there exists e such that $C(\mathcal{V}, e)$ holds then $\mathcal{V}$ is substituted by $Z(\mathcal{V}, e)$. Let us note that there may exist several values of e such that $C(\mathcal{V}, e)$ holds. In these cases, the EUSM will be provided with different nondeterministic choices. Next we introduce the EUSM defining the behavior of a vendor in our case study. In particular, we show how C and Z can coordinate to find/use the extra parameter e.

Example 3. We consider that the interactions of the vendor with the environment are defined by using several states. Exchange proposals, on the basis of the utility function of the agent associated with the current state, are accepted/rejected. The objective of each state conforming the EUSM consists in dealing with a kind of messages or agent activities. The resulting EUSM will be denoted by $\mathcal{A}$. The graphical presentation of $\mathcal{A}$ is given in Figure 2.

In order to illustrate the behavior of the C and Z functions, let us consider the agent transition $tran_2^1 = (s_2, C_2^1, Z_2^1, s_2)$, which links the state s_2 with itself. This transition defines how the agent takes a client RFQ from its set $RFQfromClients$ and composes a quote q to be sent back to the client. For the sake of simplicity, in this approach the quote *penalty* (i.e., the price reduction due to a delayed delivery per time unit) will be 0. The transition condition C_2^1 requires that a client RFQ of the form $(client, crfq(pcModel_z, units))$ is found in $RFQfromClients$. Besides, C_2^1 requires finding a quote that is profitable for the agent, that is, a quote that would improve the utility in s_2. In order to do that, it searches for some values *price* and *deadline* such that exchanging *units* PCs of model $pcModel_z$ by *price* at time *deadline* would improve the utility of the agent, given by $U(s_2)$. If such values of *price* and *deadline* are found then C_2^1 returns True and these parameters are passed to function Z_2^1. The function Z_2^1 removes the concerned client RFQ to avoid processing it again. Besides, it composes a quote q with the considered parameters *price* and *deadline*. The quote is inserted in the set of quotes $QtoClients$ and it is written in the output port op so that it is sent to the client. Formally, we have

$$C_2^1 \begin{pmatrix} \mathcal{V}, \\ (price, \\ deadline) \end{pmatrix} = \begin{cases} \textbf{True} & \text{if } (client, crfq(pcModel_z, units)) \in RFQfromClients \\ & \qquad\qquad\qquad \wedge \\ & U(s_2)\left(client, \mathcal{V} + \begin{cases} pcModel_z =_\diamond -units, \\ t =_\diamond deadline, \\ money =_\diamond price \end{cases} \right) \\ & \qquad\qquad\qquad > \\ & U(s_2)(client, \mathcal{V} + \{t =_\diamond deadline\}) \\ \textbf{False} & \text{otherwise} \end{cases}$$

$$Z_2^1 \begin{pmatrix} \mathcal{V}, \\ (price, \\ deadline) \end{pmatrix} = \mathcal{V} \begin{bmatrix} RFQfromClients := \\ RFQfromClients \backslash (client, crfq(pcModel_z, units)), \\ QtoClients := QtoClients \cup \{(client, q)\}, \\ op := (client, q) \end{bmatrix}$$

where q is defined as $aq(pcModel_z, units, deadline, price, 0)$.

Next we show a possible utility function to analyze the suitability of transactions in s_2. In the next expression, $prodCost_i$ denotes the estimated production cost of a model i PC. It can be calculated by taking into account $CwithClients$, $CwithSuppliers$, $HwithClients$, and $HwithSuppliers$. Besides, the utility function will discourage sending quotes that are clearly *unacceptable* for the other part, which would be a waste of time. A value $maxAcceptablePrice_{id,z}$ denotes the maximal price the agent estimates the client id would pay for a PC of model z. This value can be computed from $HwithClients$ by considering previous interactions with this or other clients. Let us note that sending a quote to an entity or accepting a quote from one of them (in our system, a supplier) are very different activities in terms of strategy. In the latter case, which is considered in the next state s_3, we would actually accept excessively profitable (low) prices, because the other part implicitly accepted the transaction by sending the quote.

$$U(s_2)(id, \mathcal{V}) = money + \sum_z min(maxAcceptablePrice_{id,z}, (prodCost_z + \delta)) \cdot pcModel_z$$

□

Let us comment on the previous expression. It is the addition of some terms. The first term denotes the value given to money, while the rest ones denote the value given to PCs of each model. The relation between the value of money and the value of a given PC model is the key to decide whether an exchange (in this case, a sale) involving this model is acceptable or not. Let us note that the number of PCs of each model is multiplied by a factor. This multiplicative factor implicitly denotes the *exchange ratio* that is acceptable for the agent when PCs of this model are sold. For example, if this factor is equal to 1500, then 1500 units of the resource *money* (that is, $1500) receive the same value than one PC of the model where this factor is applied. Thus, selling this PC at any price higher than or equal to this value will be acceptable, because in this case the value returned by the utility function will be at least the same as before. Finally, let us note that the multiplicative factor is the minimum between the maximal price the agent thinks the buyer would pay for a PC of this model and the cost of producing it (plus a small amount δ).

4   Evolutions in EUSMs

In order to define the operational behavior of a EUSM, as we said before, we consider two types of evolutions: *Explicit evolutions* (labelled by exp) and *temporal evolutions* (labelled by tm). An evolution is denoted by a tuple $(c, c')_K$, with $K \in \{exp, tm\}$, where c is the former configuration and c' is the new configuration. Let us note that, for a given c and K, there might exist several configurations c' such that $(c, c')_K$ is an evolution. Single evolutions of a EUSM can be concatenated to conform a *trace*.

Definition 4. Let $M = (id, S, E, U, s_0, \mathcal{V}_0, \mathcal{T})$ be a EUSM and $c = (s, \mathcal{V})$ be a configuration of M. Let us consider that $t =_\diamond time \in \mathcal{V}$. An *evolution* of M from c is a pair $(c, c')_K$, where $c' = (s', \mathcal{V}')$ and $K \in \{exp, tm\}$ are defined in such a way that one of the following conditions holds:

(1) (*Explicit evolution*) If there exists $(s, C, Z, s'') \in \mathcal{T}$ and e such that $C(\mathcal{V}, e) =$ **True** then $K = exp$, $s' = s''$, and $\mathcal{V}' = Z(\mathcal{V}, e)$.
(2) (*Passing of time*) If the condition of (1) does not hold then $K = tm$, $s' = s$, and $\mathcal{V}' = \mathcal{V}[t := \beta]$, where

$$\beta \leq min\{\beta' | \beta' > time \,\wedge\, \exists\, (s, C, Z, s'') \in \mathcal{T}, e : C(\mathcal{V}[t := \beta'], e) = \text{True}\}$$

We denote by Evolutions(M, c) the set of evolutions of M from c.

Let $M = (id, S, E, U, s_0, \mathcal{V}_0, \mathcal{T})$ be a EUSM and $c_1, \dots, c_n$ be configurations such that $c_1 = (s_0, \mathcal{V}_0)$ and for all $1 \leq i \leq n - 1$ we have $(c_i, c_{i+1})_{K_i} \in$ Evolutions(M, c_i). Then, we say that $c_1 \Longrightarrow c_n$ is a *trace* of M. The set of traces of M is denoted by Traces(M, c_1).   □

Example 4. Next we show an evolution in the context of our running example. We will suppose that the variable t denotes the time in days, and *money* denotes the amount of dollars owned by the agent. Let $c = (s_2, \mathcal{V})$ be a configuration where $pcModel_8 =_\diamond 10$, $money =_\diamond 200$, $t =_\diamond 5$, and $QtoClients =_\diamond \emptyset$ are in $\mathcal{V}$, that is, the agent owns 10 PCs of model 8 and \$200, it is day 5, and the set of quotes sent to clients is empty. Besides, let us consider $RFQfromClients =_\diamond \{(client_{15}, crfq(pcModel_8, 1))\} \in \mathcal{V}$, that is, client 15 requested a quote to buy one PC of model 8.

Besides, let $U(s_2)(client_{15}, \mathcal{V} + \{t =_\diamond 2, pcModel_8 =_\diamond -1, money =_\diamond 999\}) > U(s_2)(client_{15}, \mathcal{V} + \{t =_\diamond 2\})$, that is, the agent would accept to sell a PC of model 8 to client 15 by \$999 in day $5 + 2 = 7$. In this case, $tran_2^1$ can be taken: By setting the parameters *price* and *deadline* to 999 and 7, respectively, C_2^1 holds.

Let $\mathcal{V}' = Z_2^1(\mathcal{V}, (999, 7))$, i.e., the only variations between $\mathcal{V}$ and $\mathcal{V}'$ are that $RFQfromClients =_\diamond \emptyset$, $QtoClients =_\diamond \{(client_{15}, aq(pcModel_8, 1, 7, 999, 0))\}$, and $op =_\diamond (client_{15}, aq(pcModel_8, 1, 7, 999, 0))$. Let $c' = (s', \mathcal{V}')$. Then, we have $(c, c')_{exp} \in$ Evolutions$(\mathcal{A}, c)$ and $c \Longrightarrow c' \in$ Traces$(\mathcal{A}, c)$, being $\mathcal{A}$ the EUSM of our running example.   □

5   Defining Multi-agent Systems with EUSMs

In our formalism, a *system* is just a tuple of agents. The evolutions of a system are defined from the ones corresponding to the individual agents by taking into account the following: If an agent can perform an explicit transition (that is, the condition of a transition from the current state holds) then the transition is performed. If the transition creates a message in the port of outgoing messages then the message is enqueued in the buffer of incoming messages of the corresponding agent. Afterwards, the message must be removed from the port of outgoing messages (this is simulated by setting the message to the $\perp$ value). Finally, if no condition holds then all the agents idle an amount of time less than or equal to the time needed for a condition to hold.

Definition 5. Let $M_1, \ldots, M_n$ be EUSMs such that for all $1 \leq i \leq n$ we have $M_i = (id_i, S_i, E_i, U_i, s_{0i}, \mathcal{V}_{0i}, \mathcal{T}_i)$ and $E_i = (V_i, R_i)$. If $R_1 = \ldots = R_n$ then we say that the tuple $S = (M_1, \ldots, M_n)$ is a *system* of EUSMs. A *configuration* of S is a tuple $(c_1, \ldots, c_n)$, where for all $1 \leq i \leq n$ we have that c_i is a configuration of M_i.

Let $S = (M_1, \ldots, M_n)$ be a system. Let $c = (c_1, \ldots, c_n)$ be a configuration of S, where for all $1 \leq i \leq n$ we have $c_i = (s_i, \mathcal{V}_i)$. An *evolution* of S from c is a pair $(c, c')_K$, where $c' = (c'_1, \ldots, c'_n)$ and $K \in \{exp, tm\}$ are defined in such a way that one of the following conditions hold:

(1) (*Explicit evolution*) If there exist $1 \leq i \leq n$ and $d = (s', \mathcal{V}')$ such that $(c_i, d)_{exp} \in \texttt{Evolutions}(M_i, c_i)$, then $K = exp$ and we consider the following possibilities:
   (1.a) (*No communication*) If $op =_\diamond \perp \in \mathcal{V}'$ then we have $c'_i = d$ and for all $1 \leq j \leq n$ with $j \neq i$ we have $c'_j = c_j$.
   (1.b) (*The agent communicates*) If $op =_\diamond (id_j, m) \in \mathcal{V}'$, for some $1 \leq j \leq n$, then $c'_i = (s', \mathcal{V}'[op := \perp])$, $c'_j = (s_j, \mathcal{V}_j[ib := enqueue(ib, (id_i, m))])$ and for all $1 \leq k \leq n$, with $k \neq i, j$, we have $c'_k = c_k$.
(2) (*Passing of time*) If there exists $newtime \in \mathbb{R}^+$ such that for all $1 \leq i \leq n$ we have $(c_i, c''_i)_{tm} \in \texttt{Evolutions}(M_i, c_i)$, with $c''_i = (s_i, \mathcal{V}_i[t := newtime])$, then for all $1 \leq i \leq n$ we have $c'_i = c''_i$ and $K = tm$.

We denote by $\texttt{Evolutions}(S, c)$ the set of evolutions of S from c.

Let $S = (M_1, \ldots, M_n)$ be a system with $M_i = (id_i, S_i, E_i, U_i, s_{i0}, \mathcal{V}_{i0}, \mathcal{T}_i)$ for all $1 \leq i \leq n$. Besides, let $c_1, \ldots, c_n$ be configurations such that we have $c_1 = ((s_{10}, \mathcal{V}_{10}), \ldots, (s_{n0}, \mathcal{V}_{n0})$ and for all $1 \leq i \leq n-1$ we have $(c_i, c_{i+1})_{K_i} \in \texttt{Evolutions}(S, c_i)$. We say that $c_1 \Longrightarrow c_n$ is a *trace* of S. The set of traces of S is denoted by $\texttt{Traces}(S, c_1)$.   □

6   Defining EUSMs: General Guidelines

In this section we provide some general guidelines to properly define agents by means of EUSMs. First, let us note that our language focuses on splitting the behavior of each agent in two separate parts:

(a) *Tasks*: They are the actions the agent must perform. In order to properly define their behavior, *states*, *transitions*, and *variables* of the EUSM can be used.

(b) *Strategic decisions*: They refer to all the situations where the agent must choose among some choices in such a way that its decision may affect the future chances of success. This part of the agent should be defined by means of *utility functions* associated to states of the EUSM.

In general, the *strategy* of an agent is defined by the utility functions governing each state. Thus, the selection of suitable utility functions dramatically depends on the kind of strategic behavior we want to provide the agent with. In fact, if we leave undefined the utility functions associated to states, an EUSM provides a reusable framework to design agents with different strategy choices. For example, if we consider the specification described in the previous section and we remove utility functions, we obtain a generic reusable framework for defining vendor agents in the Supply Chain Management Game. In particular, the same specification allows to consider different strategies by just associating different suites of utility functions to states.

Tasks involving decision-making, optimization, etc. should be abstracted by means of the utility functions. Let us note that utility functions provide an implicit definition of what is preferable: In any situation where some choices are available, the best choice is, by definition, the one returning the highest utility. Sometimes, finding the values that maximize a utility function may be a hard task, specially if the form of utility functions is not constrained to a given form (in general, if the searching space is finite, it is an NP-hard problem). Hence, given a specification defined by means of an EUSM, an implementation should not be required to find the *optimal* choices in general. Depending on the time/optimality necessities, the method followed by an implementation to find *good enough* suboptimal choices should be based on a suitable tradeoff. Let us note that these issues do not concern the EUSM because they are *implementation* details.

Due to space limitations we cannot include the remaining parts of the case study that we are using along the paper. The objective of each state consists in dealing with a certain kind of messages by considering the agent preferences established by means of utility functions.

7 Conclusions and Future Work

In this paper we have presented a formalism called extended utility state machines, in short EUSMs. We have illustrated the behavior of these machines with a medium-size example: The specification of vendors in the Supply Chain Management Game. EUSMs are a big improvement with respect to the original USM formalism. In particular, strategic behavior can be now defined in an easier and more direct way. In this paper we tried to keep a balance between theory (by introducing a formal language) and practice (by applying the language to the specification of a benchmark in e-commerce agents). Our work needs a natural continuation in both directions. Regarding the more theoretical component, our previous results for USMs should be adapted to the new framework. Regarding the more practical component, we are assessing the formalism with other case studies that are not related to e-commerce. Specifically, we are continuing the work initiated in [25] by specifying in our formalism not only the *Interactive Driving System*, but the next layer of the system containing it.

References

1. Guttman, R., Moukas, A., Maes, P.: Agent-mediated electronic commerce: A survey. The Knowledge Engineering Review 13(2), 147–159 (1998)
2. Sandholm, T.: Agents in electronic commerce: Component technologies for automated negotiation and coalition formation. In: Klusch, M., Weiss, G. (eds.) CIA 1998. LNCS (LNAI), vol. 1435, pp. 113–134. Springer, Heidelberg (1998)
3. Ma, M.: Agents in e-commerce. Communications of the ACM 42(3), 79–80 (1999)
4. He, M., Jennings, N., Leung, H.: On agent-mediated electronic commerce. IEEE Trans. on Knowledge and Data Engineering 15(4), 985–1003 (2003)
5. Sierra, C.: Agent-mediated electronic commerce. Autonomous Agents and Multi-Agent Systems 9(3), 285–301 (2004)
6. Gruer, P., Hilaire, V., Koukam, A., Cetnarowicz, K.: A formal framework for multi-agent systems analysis and design. Expert Systems and Applications 23, 349–355 (2002)
7. Hilaire, V., Simonin, O., Koukam, A., Ferber, J.: A formal approach to design and reuse agent and multiagent models. In: Odell, J.J., Giorgini, P., Müller, J.P. (eds.) AOSE 2004. LNCS, vol. 3382, pp. 142–157. Springer, Heidelberg (2005)
8. Cabac, L., Moldt, D.: Formal semantics for AUML agent interaction protocol diagrams. In: Odell, J.J., Giorgini, P., Müller, J.P. (eds.) AOSE 2004. LNCS, vol. 3382, pp. 47–61. Springer, Heidelberg (2005)
9. Clarke, E., Grumberg, O., Peled, D.: Model Checking. MIT Press, Cambridge (2000)
10. Benerecetti, M., Cimatti, A.: Validation of multiagent systems by symbolic model checking. In: Giunchiglia, F., Odell, J.J., Weiss, G. (eds.) AOSE 2002. LNCS, vol. 2585, pp. 32–46. Springer, Heidelberg (2003)
11. Myers, G.: The Art of Software Testing, 2nd edn. John Wiley and Sons, West Sussex, England (2004)
12. Núñez, M., Rodríguez, I., Rubio, F.: Testing of autonomous agents described as utility state machines. In: Núñez, M., Maamar, Z., Pelayo, F.L., Pousttchi, K., Rubio, F. (eds.) FORTE 2004. LNCS, vol. 3236, pp. 322–336. Springer, Heidelberg (2004)
13. Rodríguez, I.: Formal specification of autonomous commerce agents. In: SAC 2004, pp. 774–778. ACM Press, New York (2004)
14. Rodríguez, I., Núñez, M., Rubio, F.: Specification of autonomous agents in e-commerce systems. In: Núñez, M., Maamar, Z., Pelayo, F.L., Pousttchi, K., Rubio, F. (eds.) FORTE 2004. LNCS, vol. 3236, pp. 30–43. Springer, Heidelberg (2004)
15. Núñez, M., Rodríguez, I., Rubio, F.: Specification and testing of autonomous agents in e-commerce systems. Software Testing, Verification and Reliability 15(4), 211–233 (2005)

16. Chavez, A., Maes, P.: Kasbah: An agent marketplace for buying and selling goods. In: PAAM 1996. 1st Int. Conf. on the Practical Application of Intelligent Agents and Multi-Agent Technology, pp. 75–90 (1996)

17. Collins, J., Arunachalam, R., Sadeh, N., Eriksson, J., Finne, N., Janson, S.: The supply chain management game for 2005 trading agent competition. Technical Report CMU-ISRI-04-139, Carnegie Mellon University (2004)

18. Padget, J., Bradford, R.: A pi-calculus model of a spanish fish market - preliminary report. In: Noriega, P., Sierra, C. (eds.) AMET 1998 and AMEC 1998. LNCS (LNAI), vol. 1571, pp. 166–188. Springer, Heidelberg (1999)

19. Adi, K., Debbabi, M., Mejri, M.: A new logic for electronic commerce protocols. Theoretical Computer Science 291(3), 223–283 (2003)

20. Bhimani, A.: Securing the commercial Internet. Communications of the ACM 39(6), 29–35 (1996)

21. Rao, A.: AgentSpeak(L): BDI agents speak out in a logical computable language. In: Perram, J., Van de Velde, W. (eds.) MAAMAW 1996. LNCS (LNAI), vol. 1038, pp. 42–55. Springer, Heidelberg (1996)

22. Hindriks, K., de Boer, F., van der Hoek, W., Meyer, J.J.: Formal semantics for an abstract agent programming language. In: Rao, A., Singh, M.P., Wooldridge, M.J. (eds.) ATAL 1997. LNCS (LNAI), vol. 1365, pp. 215–229. Springer, Heidelberg (1998)

23. Feinberg, E., Shwartz, A.: Handbook of Markov Decision Processes, Methods and Applications. Kluwer Academic Publishers, Boston, MA (2002)

24. Cassandra, A., Kaelbling, L., Littman, M.: Acting optimally in partially observable stochastic domains. In: 12th National Conf. on Artificial Intelligence (1994)

25. Núñez, M., Pelayo, F., Rodríguez, I.: A formal methodology to test complex embedded systems: Application to interactive driving system. In: IESS 2005. IFIP TC10 Working Conf.: International Embedded Systems Symposium, pp. 125–136. Springer, Heidelberg (2005)

Strong Safe Realizability of Message Sequence Chart Specifications

Abdolmajid Mousavi[1], Behrouz Far[1], Armin Eberlein[2], and Behrouz Heidari[3]

[1]Department of Electrical and Computer Engineering,
University of Calgary,
2500 University Drive N.W., Calgary, AB, T2N1N4, Canada
[2]Computer Engineering Department,
American University of Sharjah,
Sharjah, P.O. Box 26666, UEA
[3]Department of Electrical and Computer Engineering,
Islamic Azad University of Arak,
Arak, P.C., 6813844967, Iran
{amousavi, far, eberlein}@ucalgary.ca, B-HEIDARI@iau-arak.ac.ir

Abstract. We study the notion of safe realizability and implied scenarios for Message Sequence Chart (MSC) specifications with the following contributions: (1) We investigate the cause of implied scenarios and show that even though implied scenarios are an artifact of the distributed and global system behaviour, nevertheless, they are the result of the nondeterminism in the local behaviour of processes, (2) Instead of deadlock states and safe realizability for MSC specifications, we introduce the notions of *stuck* states and *strong* safe realizability. Moreover, we use emergent scenarios to name both implied scenarios and those anomalies of MSC specifications that are captured by the notion of strong safe realizability, (3) We give an algorithm that reduces strong safe realizability (or safe realizability) of MSC specifications to strong safe realizability (or safe realizability) of a set of MSCs.

Keywords: Strong safe realizability, stuck states, emergent scenarios.

1 Introduction

Message Sequence Chart (MSC) specifications ([1]) are one of the popular approaches for representing requirements specifications for concurrent systems that consist of multiple autonomous agents or processes. In an MSC (see Fig. 1) vertical lines correspond to asynchronous processes or autonomous agents. Arrows are used to represent messages that are communicated between processes. The tail of each arrow corresponds to the event of sending a message, while the head corresponds to the event of receiving a message. An MSC depicts exchange of messages among communicating processes in a distributed system and corresponds to a single execution of the system.

One of the problems that is usually encountered for an MSC specification is whether there exists a distributed implementation (also called a realization)

F. Arbab and M. Sirjani (Eds.): FSEN 2007, LNCS 4767, pp. 334–349, 2007.

for it that covers the behaviours described by the specification, where a distributed implementation is the concurrent execution of the automata models of the processes. If there exists such a realization whatsoever that is deadlock free and shows exactly the behaviours specified by an MSC specification, it is said that the specification is safely realizable [2]. If on the other hand, there is no such realization, there would be some implied scenarios that are not part of the specification but part of the behaviour of any concurrent automata covering the specification [2], [3], [4].

Our motivation in this work derives from multiple problems related to realizability and implied scenarios for MSC specifications. First, even though some methods have been developed for detecting implied scenarios both in a set of MSCs and high-level MSCs (hMSCs allows sequential, alternative and iterative compositions of MSCs) [2], [3], [4], [5], however, the exact cause of implied scenarios has remained as a debate causing confusion and some errors in the current works (see [3] and [6] for the practical consequences of having the exact cause of implied scenarios undefined).

Second, because usually the same semantics is assumed for MSC specifications and automata, the current definition for realizability is based on the concept of deadlock defined in automata machinery [2], [7]. While this assumption helps to detect deadlocks caused by an MSC specification, it will overlook some anomalies that cannot be captured by the definition of deadlocks in automata theory.

Third, although there are some methods that address complexity of safe realizability problem [8], [9], there exists no specific algorithm for checking safe realizability in the presence of hMSCs. The methods and the relevant algorithms in [4] and [3] work only for detecting implied scenarios in the synchronous setting and in fact check for a weaker notion of realizability called weak realizability that ignores deadlocks.

Fourth, methods for detecting implied scenarios are divided between those that work on a set of MSCs in one hand [2], and on the other hand, those that work in the presence of hMSCs [3], [4]. In other words, there is not a unique method that can explain and address implied scenarios for a set of MSCs as well as for hMSCs.

Our work in this paper is an attempt to address the above problems with the following contributions. First, we give a localized cause for implied scenarios in terms of non-determinism in the local behaviour of individual processes. In fact, we prove that whenever an implied scenario happens for an MSC specification with autonomous processes, some processes show non-deterministic behaviours in the sense that a non-deterministic behaviour will be defined in this paper. This will provide the first step to devise a common way of addressing implied scenarios in a set of MSCs and hMSCs.

Second, instead of deadlock states, we introduce a stronger condition developed by MSC specifications called *stuck* states and reformalize safe realizability in terms of this condition such that it captures such anomalies for MSC specifications that cannot be addressed by the current definitions of implied scenarios and deadlock states. We call this new notion *strong* safe realizability because whenever an MSC specification is *Strongly Safe Realizable*, it will be safely re-alizable as well. Also, to stick to the current definition for implied scenarios we use *emergent scenarios* to name both implied scenarios and those misbehaviours that are captured by our definition of stuck states.

Third, we give an approach that reduces strong safe realizability in the presence of hMSCs to strong safe realizability of a set of MSCs (see [10] for more details and the proofs for theorems, propositions and lemmas presented in this paper).

2   Background

The MSC syntax and semantics that we use in the sequel are both subsets of ITU definition for MSCs [1]. Let P be a finite set of processes (with the total number of processes $|P| \geq 2$) and C be a finite set of message contents. Denote $\Sigma_i = \{i!j(c), i?j(c)|j \in P \setminus \{i\}, c \in C\}$ to be the alphabet of process $i \in P$, where $i!j(c)$ denotes an event that sends a message from process i with content c to process j, whereas $i?j(c)$ denotes an event that receives on process i a message with content c from process j. Also, the alphabet (of all processes $i \in P$) will be $\Sigma = \bigcup_{i \in P} \Sigma_i$.

Definition 1. *(partial Message Sequence Chart): A partial Message Sequence Chart (pMSC) over P and C is defined to be a tuple $m = (E, \alpha, \beta, \prec)$ where:*

- *E is a finite set of events.*
- *$\alpha : E \to \Sigma$ maps each event to its label. The set of events located on process i is $E_i = \alpha^{-1}(\Sigma_i)$. The set of all send events in the event set E is denoted by $E! = \{e \in E | \exists i, j \in P, c \in C : \alpha(e) = i!j(c)\}$ and the set of receive events as $E? = E \setminus E!$.*
- *$\beta : F! \to E?$, $F! \subseteq E!$, is a bijection mapping between send and receive events such that whenever $\beta(e_1) = e_2$ and $\alpha(e_1) = i!j(c)$, then $\alpha(e_2) = j?i(c)$.*
- *$\prec$ is a partial order on E such that for every process $i \in P$, the restriction of $\prec$ to E_i is a total order, and $\prec$ is equal to the transitive closure of $\{(e_1, e_2)|e_1 \prec e_2, \exists i \in P : e_1, e_2 \in E_i\} \cup \{(e, \beta(e))|e \in F!\}$.*

Usually pMSCs are restricted to a FIFO condition, which means that for all $e_1, e_2 \in E!$, if $e_1 \prec e_2$, $\alpha(e_1) = i!j(c)$, $\alpha(e_2) = i!j(d)$, and $e_2 \in F!$, then also $e_1 \in F!$ and $\beta(e_1) \prec \beta(e_2)$. In the rest of this paper, we assume the FIFO restriction. Moreover, if for a pMSC m there exist no unmatched send events, which means $F! = E!$, then m is called a *Message Sequence Chart (MSC)* over P and C.

Definition 2. *(Syntactical causality between events): For a pMSC $m = (E, \alpha, \beta, \prec)$ and $e' \in E$, define the set $S_{e'} = \{e | e' \prec e : e \in E\}$ to be the set of events in m that must occur after e' as defined by $\prec$. Then, we say e' is a syntactical cause for $S_{e'}$ and denote it by $e' \xrightarrow{C}_{sy} S_{e'}$. If $e \notin S_{e'}$, we write $e' \xrightarrow{NC}_{sy} e$.*

For example, the event of receiving of message b in MSC1 in Fig. 1 is a syntactical cause for the events of sending of message c, receiving of message c, sending of message d, and receiving of message d.

Definition 3. *(Process's projection): The projection $m|_i$ for process i in pMSC m is the ordered sequence of messages that corresponds to the events occurring on process i in the pMSC m. For $m|_i$, $\|m|_i\|$ indicates its length, which equals to the total number of events of m on process i, and $m|_i[k]$ refers to k^{th} element of $m|_i$, so that if e_k is the kth event on process i according to the total order of the events of i in m, then $\alpha_m(e_k) = m|_i[k-1]$, $0 < k < \|m|_i\|$.*

For example, the projection for process $C1$ in MSC1 of Fig. 1 will be "$C1!C2(a)$ $C1?C2(b)$ $C1!C2(c)$ $C1?C2(d)$". In the rest of this section, we recall some concepts from [2].

2.1 Scenarios as Words in a Formal Language

In [2], scenarios are treated as words in a formal language, which is defined over the alphabet Σ. To account for the definition of an MSC, well-formed and complete words are defined. A well-formed word captures the definition of a pMSC and defined to be a word over the alphabet Σ that for every receive event its corresponding send event exists in it. A complete word over the alphabet Σ is the one that for every send event, its corresponding receive event also exists in it. Therefore a complete and well-formed word addresses an MSC.

For any MSC m in a set of MSCs M, any word ω over Σ obtained by first considering a sequence of events of m that respects the partial order $\prec$, and then replacing each event by its label (as defined by the mapping α in the definition of a pMSC) is called a linearization of m. The language $L(M)$ of M consists of all the words ω over Σ such that ω is a linearization of m, $\forall m \in M$. Furthermore, similar to Definition 3, for a word $\omega \in L(M)$ its projection $\omega|_i$ on process i is defined to be the subsequence of ω that involves the send and receive events of process i.

2.2 Concurrent Automata

With asynchronous message setting and FIFO buffers between processes, the behaviour of process i can be specified by an automaton A_i over the alphabet Σ_i with the following components: 1) a set Q_i of states, 2) a transition relation $\delta_i \subseteq Q_i \times \Sigma_i \times Q_i$, 3) an initial state $q_0 \in Q_i$, and 4) a set $F_i \subseteq Q_i$ of accepting states. Then, the joint behaviour of automata A_i is defined as their asynchronous product $\prod_{i \in P} A_i$.

In order to define $\prod_{i \in P} A_i$, for each ordered pair (i,j) of processes, two message buffers $B_{i,j}^s$ and $B_{i,j}^r$ are defined. $B_{i,j}^s$ is a pending buffer which stores the messages that have been sent by process i but are still in transit and not yet accessible by process j. On the other hand, $B_{i,j}^r$ stores messages that have already reached process j but are not accessed and removed from the buffer by process j. All the buffers are words over the set of message contents C. Then, the product automaton $A = \prod_{i \in P} A_i$ over the alphabet Σ is given by:

States. A state q of A consists of the local states q_i of component processes A_i, along with the contents of the buffers $B_{i,j}^s$ and $B_{i,j}^r$.

Initial state. The initial state q_0 of A is given by having the component for each process i be in the start state q_i^0, and by having every buffer be empty.

Transitions. The transition relation $\delta \subseteq Q \times (\Sigma \cup \{\tau\}) \times Q$ (the τ transitions model the transfer of messages from the sender to the receiver) is defined as:

1. For $x \in \Sigma_i$, $(q, x, q') \in \delta$ iff (a) the local states of processes $k \neq i$ are identical in q and q', (b) the local state of process i in q is q_i and in q' is q_i' such that $(q_i, x, q_i') \in \delta_i$, (c) for $x = j?i(c)$, the buffer $B_{i,j}^r$ in state q contains the message c in the front, and the corresponding buffer in state q' is obtained by deleting c, (d) for $x = i!j(c)$, the buffer $B_{i,j}^s$ in state q' is obtained by appending the message c to the corresponding buffer in state q, and (e) all other buffers are identical in states q and q'.
2. There is a τ-labeled transition from state q to q', iff states q and q' are identical except that for one pair (i, j), the buffer $B_{i,j}^s$ in state q' is obtained from that in q by deleting the first message c, and the buffer $B_{i,j}^r$ in state q' is obtained from that in q by adding that message c at its end.

Accepting states. A state q of A is accepting if for all processes i, the local states q_i of process i in q is accepting, and all the buffers in q are empty.

The language $L(A)$ over the alphabet Σ of the product automaton A is defined as all possible execution of A where τ transitions are interpreted as ϵ transitions in the usual automata theory.

2.3   Safe Realizability as Defined in [2]

In [2], a set of MSCs M is said to be safely realizable if there exists a concurrent automata $A = \prod_{i \in P} A_i$ such that A is deadlock free and $L(M) = L(A)$, where a deadlock is defined as follows:

Deadlock: A reachable state q of the product $A = \prod_{i \in P} A_i$ is said to be a deadlock state if no accepting state of A is reachable from q.

A path in A that leads to a deadlock is an *implied partial scenario (implied pMSC)* and a closure condition is used to capture implied pMSCs as follows. For a language L, let $pref(L)$ denotes the set of all prefixes of the words in L.

Closure condition CC3: A language L over the alphabet Σ is said to satisfy closure condition CC3 iff for all well-formed words ω: if for each process i there is a word $\nu^i \in pref(L)$ such that $\omega|_i = \nu^i|_i$, then ω is in $pref(L)$.

Those words that have the condition described in CC3 and falsify the closure of the language of the set of MSCs M under this closure condition are called implied partial scenarios for the set M. A straightforward check for CC3 has exponential complexity. So, an equivalent condition, which can be checked by a polynomial time algorithm is defined.

Closure condition CC3': A language L over the alphabet Σ is said to satisfy closure condition CC3' iff for all $\omega, \nu \in pref(L)$ and all processes i: if $\omega|_i = \nu|_i$, and $\omega x \in pref(L)$ and νx is well-formed for some $x \in \Sigma_i$, then νx is also in $pref(L)$.

On the other hand, closure condition CC3 as it is shown in [9] cannot completely address safe realizability. Thus, safe realizability is given as a combination of CC3 and another closure condition CC2$'$ given below:

Closure condition CC2$'$: A language L over the alphabet Σ satisfies closure condition CC2$'$ iff for all well-formed and complete words ω over Σ such that $\omega \in pref(L)$: if for all processes i there exists a word ν^i in L such that $\omega|_i = \nu^i|_i$, then ω is in L.

Then, a language L is proved to be safely realizable iff it satisfies both CC3$'$ (equivalent to CC3) and CC2$'$.

3 Safe Realizability Revisited

3.1 Non-determinism and Implied Scenarios

In this section, we (informally) explain how implied scenarios are related to a local property of process's behaviour. Fig. 1 shows two scenarios for a system in MSC notation with three processes C1, C2 and C3. In these scenarios, process C1 has the same sequence of messages before message d in MSC1 and message e in MSC2. Every Finite State Machine (FSM) for describing the behaviour of process C1 would have this common sequence, which can be better seen in Figs. 2 and 3 (to simplify the presentation, we only use the message content instead of the whole message in terms of Definition 1, i.e. instead of the complete message $C1!C2(a)$, we only use its content a). Fig. 2 shows two FSMs for describing the behaviour of process C1 in MSC1 and MSC2 and Fig. 3 shows the combination of two FSMs of Fig. 2 in a single deterministic FSM. In Fig. 3 and from C1's

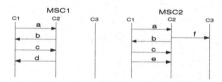

Fig. 1. Two scenarios for a system

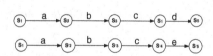

Fig. 2. Two FSMs for description of the behaviour of process C1 in two scenarios of Fig. 1

perspective, after sending message c, there exists no rule to tell the next event that must happen on process C1. The immediate consequence of this lack of rule for process C1 is that starting by MSC1 and after message c, C1 can send message e instead of what it is supposed to do in MSC1, which is receiving of message d. This choice of action for a process is what we call *non-deterministic behaviour* for the process. Because of this non-deterministic behaviour in the specification, we get an implied partial scenario depicted in Fig. 4 (see closure condition CC3). The circle at the head of an arrow indicates that the receive part of that message may not exist (resulting in a partial scenario or a pMSC).

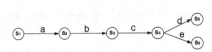

Fig. 3. The combination of two FSMs of Fig. 1

Fig. 4. An implied partial scenario from two scenarios of Fig. 1

As another case for non-deterministic behaviour of processes consider Fig. 5. Again, from C1's perspective and based on MSC3 and MSC4, after sending message c there exists no rule to tell the next event that must happen on this process. Therefore, the rule that says whether to receive message e or f will be determined by the processes that are sending these messages. Consider message f. By looking into MSC3, there is no rule for sending message f by process C2 after receiving of message e by process C1 (there is no order between them). In other words, the receive event of message e is not a syntactical cause for the send event of message f. Thus, in MSC3 message f can be sent by process C2 without waiting for the receive of the message e by process C1 and the behaviour of process C1 in MSC4 gives the required *certificate* to process C1 to receive f instead of e. So, we can get a new behaviour shown in Fig. 6 that is a partial implied scenario with respect to MSC3 and MSC4 (see closure condition CC3).

Formally, non-deterministic behaviour of a process in a pMSC m is defined as follows.

Definition 4. *(Non-deterministic behaviour of a process): In a pMSC $m = (E, \alpha, \beta, \prec)$, we say process $i \in P$ has a non-deterministic behaviour because of pMSC n, if one of the followings holds:*

i) For the smallest index k that $m|_i[k] \neq n|_i[k]$: $n|_i[k] = i!j(c)$, $0 \leq k \prec \|n|_i\|$, $j \in P$, $c \in C$

ii) For the smallest index k that $m|_i[k] \neq n|_i[k]$: $n|_i[k] = i?j(c)$, $0 \leq k \prec \|n|_i\|$, $j \in P$, $c \in C$, and for $\alpha(e) = m|_i[k]$, $e \in E$, $\exists e' \in E$ such that $\alpha(e') = j!i(c)$, $e' \notin S_e$ and $\beta(e') \in S_e$

iii) $n|_i$ is a prefix of $m|_i$ and $m|_i[\|n|_i\|] = i!j(c)$, $j \in P$, $c \in C$

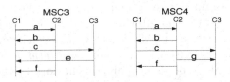

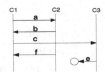

Fig. 5. Two scenarios for a system

Fig. 6. An implied partial scenario from two scenarios in Fig. 5

If a FIFO architecture is assumed for the communication between processes and $m|_i[k]$ is a receive message, then for Case ii) of Definition 4, it is also required that $m|_i[k]$ is sent by a process other than j. Essentially, Definition 4 is saying that a process i in pMSC m shows non-deterministic behaviour because of another pMSC n, if one of the followings holds: i) for the first events e and e' on process i respectively in m and n that have different message contents, e' is a send event (see Figs. 1 and 4); ii) e' is a receive event like $i?j(c)$, $j \in P$, $c \in C$, and a message $j!i(c)$ exists in m such that event e is not a cause for it (so that by removing e, $j!i(c)$ still can happen) and this message does not have a corresponding receive event before e (see Figs. 5 and 6); iii) $n|_i$ is a prefix of $m|_i$ and the immediate event after the sequence $n|_i$ in $m|_i$ is a send event (see the next section and Figs. 7 and 8).

Note that, *non-deterministic behaviour of processes* that captures the choice of local actions for a process is different from *non-determinism* defined for non-deterministic automata ([11]) and Definition 4 is only meaningful in the context of MSCs. Furthermore, although the choice of local actions for a process that is captured by the Definition 4 is not in the first look problematic for the process, nevertheless, when the process is collaborating with other processes to fulfill a scenario, it might hinder the completion of the intended scenario.

3.2   Strong Safe Realizability and Emergent Scenarios

Case iii) of Definition 4 can result in new behaviours that cannot be captured by the closure conditions CC3 and CC2$'$. Consider MSC5 and MSC6 in Fig. 7. Based on these two MSCs, process C1 in MSC6 will be able to stop sending message e because MSC5 provides the required *certificate* for process C1 to stop after sending message c. This is the intuition behind Case iii) of Definition 4 by which the choice of a process to send a message or stop at a final state can result in unwanted scenarios for a system. Note how in the scenario of Fig. 8 processes C1 and C3 have reached their final states and stopped there, while process C2 is waiting to receive message e, which might never receive.

To see how Case iii) of Definition 4 can be problematic, observe that based on the MSCs of Fig. 7 there is no mechanism (in terms of some synchronizing messages) to force process C1 to send message e in Fig. 8, because according to MSC5 the behaviour of process C1 is already a valid behaviour in Fig. 8. However, Fig. 8 is a prefix of MSC6, and therefore, it fulfills the closure condition CC3. On the other hand, since the projection of process C2 in Fig. 8 is neither the same as its projection in MSC5 nor in MSC6, the MSC of Fig. 8 does not have the condition of the words specified in the closure condition CC2$'$, and so, it is not addressed by CC2$'$. This situation is similar to a property defined under the notion of *stuck* in the context of Communicating Sequential Processes (CSP) [12]. Informally, stuck-freeness means that a message sent by a sender will not get stuck without some receiver ever receiving it, and a receiver waiting for a message will not get stuck without some sender ever sending it. Analogously, we define stuck states in the context of MSC specifications and in terms of the product automata $A = \prod_{i \in P} A_i$, as follows.

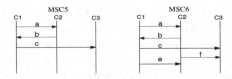

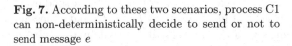

Fig. 7. According to these two scenarios, process C1 can non-deterministically decide to send or not to send message e

Fig. 8. An emergent scenario from two scenarios of Fig. 7

Definition 5. *(Stuck state): A reachable state q in $A = \prod_{i \in P} A_i$, is called a stuck state either if q is a deadlock state or if for every process $i \in P$ for which its local state q_i in the state q is an accepting state of A_i we remove all outgoing transitions $i!j(c)$ from q (for some $j \in P$ and $c \in C$), none of the accepting states of A is reachable from q.*

Then, because of the definition of stuck states (that also covers the definition of deadlock states), instead of safe realizability, we define the notion of *strong* safe realizability that captures stuck states in the concurrent automata of processes. However, first we define the closure condition CC_{ss} that captures stuck states in the concurrent automata.

Closure condition CC_{ss}: A language L over the alphabet Σ satisfies closure condition CC_{ss} iff for all well-formed words ω over Σ such that $\omega \in pref(L)$, there exists an x in L such that ω is a prefix of x and for all processes $i \in P$, for which $\omega|_i = \nu^i|_i$ for some $\nu^i \in L$, either $x|_i = \omega|_i$ or $x|_i[|||\omega|_i|||]$ is a receive event.

Note that CC_{ss} is a stronger condition than $CC2'$. This fact is stated by the following proposition.

Proposition 1. *A language L satisfies $CC2'$ if it satisfies CC_{ss}.*

Now, we define the notion of *strong* safe realizability of a set of MSCs M, and then relates it to the closure conditions $CC3$ and CC_{ss} by Theorem 1.

Definition 6. *A set of MSCs M is said to be Strongly Safe Realizable (SSR) iff there exists a concurrent automata $A = \prod_{i \in P} A_i$ such that A is stuck free and $L(M) = L(A)$.*

Theorem 1. *A set of MSCs M is SSR iff it is closed under both $CC3$ and CC_{ss}.*

It is easy to see that based on Theorem 1 and Proposition 1, strong safe realizability implies safe realizability.

In [2], those words that falsify the closure of language L under closure conditions $CC3$ or $CC2'$ are called implied (partial) scenarios. Analogously, we call those words that falsify the closure of language L under closure conditions $CC3$ or CC_{ss}, *emergent (partial) scenarios* or *emergent pMSCs*. In this way, emergent pMSCs include implied (partial) scenarios, together with the new scenarios developed by stuck states.

Now, we show how emergent pMSCs are related to the non-deterministic behaviour of processes. If we look at the closure conditions CC3 and CC_{ss} and the words that might falsify them, it comes out that we need to check the set of MSCs against those words that their projections on processes are the same as or a prefix of the projections of some of the current MSCs on the processes. Alternatively, we can define a *candidate emergent pMSC* for every MSC in the set of MSCs M to account for those words that have the conditions of the closure conditions CC3 and CC_{ss}. More specifically, a kth order candidate emergent pMSC m^k for the MSC m has $|P| - k$ process's projections from m, and the rest k process's projections $(0 \leq k < |P|)$ from other MSCs different from m. In m^k, if there exists an MSC $n \in M$, such that $m^k|_i$ is a prefix of $n|_i$ for some $i \in P$ and either $m^k|_i$ is not a prefix of $m|_i$, or $n|_i$ is a prefix of $m|_i$ and $m|_i[\|n|_i\|] = i!j(c)$, $j \in P$, $c \in C$ (see Definition 4), then we say the projection of process i in m^k is from n. Otherwise, the projection of process i in m^k is from m.

In a kth order candidate emergent pMSC m^k, we call those process's projections that are not from m, *the replaceable process's projections* for m. For example, in Figure 3, the projection of MSC5 on process C1 is a replaceable process's projection for MSC4. It is not hard to see that for all MSCs m in the set of MSCs M, when k varies from 0 to $|P| - 1$, candidate emergent pMSCs are the same words that have the conditions of the closure conditions CC3 and CC_{ss}. Thus, a kth order *emergent pMSC* (including implied pMSCs) for M is a kth order *candidate emergent pMSC* for an MSC $m \in M$ that falsifies the closure of $L(M)$ under CC3 or CC_{ss}. On the other hand, candidate emergent pMSCs have a close relation to the non-deterministic behaviour of processes expressed in the following proposition.

Proposition 2. *For any k^{th} order $(1 \leq k \leq |P| - 1)$ candidate emergent pMSC m^k for the MSC $m \in M$, there exists a $k - 1^{th}$ order candidate emergent pMSC m^{k-1} for the MSC m such that there is a non-deterministic behaviours for a process $i \in P$ in m^{k-1} because of an MSC $n \in M$, and m^k can be obtained from m^{k-1} by replacing $m^{k-1}|_i$ by a prefix of $n|_i$.*

Then, an implication of Proposition 2 is the following corollary.

Corollary 1. *A set of MSCs M is SSR iff there exist no 1st order emergent pMSCs for all $m \in M$.*

As the result of Corollary 1, checking strong safe realizability for M is equivalent to finding a 1st order candidate emergent pMSC for some $m \in M$ that falsifies the closure of M under CC3 or CC_{ss}.

4   Strong Safe Realizability of MSC Specifications

4.1   High-Level Message Sequence Charts

A high-level Message Sequence Chart (hMSC) is a way to structure multiple scenarios. An hMSC $h = (V, \rightarrow, \nu_0, V_t, \mu)$ is a graph with a set of nodes V, a binary relation $\rightarrow$ over V, an initial node ν_0, an optional set of terminal nodes $V_t \subseteq V$, and a labeling function μ that maps each node to an MSC in a set of MSCs M or another hMSC (resulting in hierarchy). An hMSC h together with its set of MSCs M defines an MSC specification $Spec = (h, M)$. Any sequence of nodes $\nu_0\nu_1\cdots\nu_k\cdots$ of h that starts at initial node ν_0 and $\nu_l\rightarrow\nu_{l+1}$, for $0 \leq l < k$, is an execution of h. An execution of h that is not a prefix of other executions is called a *maximal execution*. An *acceptable execution* of h either is a finite execution that terminates at a terminal node or is a maximal execution (which could be an infinite execution).

To associate a language with $Spec = (h, M)$ we need to define concatenation of two MSCs m and m'. The concatenation of MSCs $m = (E, \alpha, \beta, \prec)$ and $m' = (E', \alpha', \beta', \prec')$ defines the MSC $m.m' = (E\cup E', \alpha\cup\alpha', \beta\cup\beta', \prec'')$, where $\prec''$ is the transitive closure of: $\prec \cup \prec' \cup \{(e, e') \in E_i \times E'_i,$ for some $i \in P\}$. Then, the language $L(Spec)$ of $Spec = (h, M)$ is all the MSCs (or words over the alphabet Σ) of the form $\mu(\nu_0).\mu(\nu_1).\cdots.\mu(\nu_k).\cdots$, $\nu_0, \nu_1, \cdots, \nu_k \in V$, in which the sequence $\nu_0\nu_1\cdots\nu_k\cdots$ is an acceptable execution of h.

Analogous to concurrent automata, a distributed implementation $T = \prod_{i\in P} T_i$ of an MSC specification with asynchronous messages and FIFO buffers between processes is defined where T_i is a Labeled Transition System (LTS) over alphabet Σ_i that specifies the behaviour of process i (see also [4]). An LTS is defined similar to an automaton except that having accepting states that is a part of the definition of an automaton is optional for an LTS. In fact, for $Spec = (h, M)$, an LTS T_i can be obtained for each process i in this way (see also [4]):

1. Obtain an automaton A_i^m that accepts $m|_i$ for all the MSCs $m \in M$
2. For each node $\nu_l \in V$ for which $\mu(\nu_l) = m$, $m \in M$, obtain all the nodes $\nu_k \in V$, $\mu(\nu_k) = n$, $n \in M$, that are reachable from ν_l through one edge
3. Beginning with the initial node ν_0 and for all $\nu_l \in V$, connect the accepting state of A_i^m to the initial state of each A_i^n with an ϵ transition to obtain a non-deterministic LTS T_i' with ϵ transitions. If ν_l is a terminal node of h, then mark the accepting state of A_i^m as an accepting state of T_i'
4. Remove ϵ transitions of T_i' and use the minimization and the deterministic operators on T_i' to obtain T_i

Like an automaton, any word ω over the alphabet Σ_i that brings an LTS T_i from its initial state to any state in T_i is an execution of T_i. A path in T_i is a sequence of states and transitions developed by an execution of T_i. A maximal execution of T_i is an execution of T_i that is not a prefix of other executions. The language $L(T_i)$ consists of all the words ω over the alphabet Σ_i such that ω either is a finite execution of T_i that ends in an accepting state or is a maximal execution of T_i (which can be infinite). Some examples for process's LTS are given in Section 4.3.

4.2 Algorithm

In this section, we give an algorithm that reduces strong safe realizability of an MSC specification strong safe realizability for a set of MSCs. We fix our setting to asynchronous message passing, FIFO buffers, and bounded hMSCs. In a bounded hMSC h, communication between processes in every loop in h is performed in such a way that prevents flooding a process by the messages sent by another one (see [8] or [9] for a precise definition).

Let $T = \prod_{i \in P} T_i$ be a distributed implementation of $Spec = (h, M)$ obtained through parallel execution of the process's LTSs T_i, $i \in P$. Then, a stuck state (or a deadlock state) q in the concurrent LTSs T is defined similar to a stuck state (or a deadlock state) in the concurrent automata A, except that instead of unreachability of accepting states from q, we require that starting from q only finite executions are possible that none of them ends in an accepting state of T. Apparently, $L(Spec) \subseteq L(T)$, meaning that all the words in $L(Spec)$ are included in $L(T)$. Furthermore, T is minimal in the sense that all the executions of T starting from its initial state, including $L(T)$ and those that end at a stuck state are included in any other distributed implementation T' of $Spec$ in the form of prefixes of some execution of T' (see [4] for the proof). Thus, if $L(Spec) \neq L(T)$ or T has a stuck state it means that $Spec$ is not SSR. To check these two conditions, the bottom line of our approach is to characterize those paths that their length (in terms of the transitions of T) is as short as possible and guarantee to capture emergent (partial) scenarios (if there is any) of $Spec$. First, we define basic words and basic paths.

Definition 7. *(Basic words of an LTS): Let $\omega = \omega_0\omega_1 \cdots \omega_k$ be a word over the alphabet Σ_i that brings the LTS T_i to a state q_k through a path $r = q_0\omega_0q_j\omega_1 \cdots \omega_k q_k$ in T_i (q_0 is the initial state of T_i) such that r goes through loops at most once and skips self loops. Then, x is called a basic word of T_i either if $x = \omega$ and q_k is an accepting state of T_i or x is obtained from ω with the following conditions:*
- For all reachable nodes q_{k+1} from q_k, q_{k+1} is a state in the path r
- $x = \omega_0\omega_1 \cdots \omega_u$, where starting from the end of ω every ω_v for which $q_t\omega_vq_s$ is a repeated sequence in r is deleted, $0 \leq u \leq k$, $0 < v \leq k$

Then, a *basic execution* of T_i is a basic word of T_i that is not a prefix of other basic words.

Definition 8. *(Basic paths of an hMSC): Let $s = \nu_0\nu_1 \cdots \nu_k$, $\nu_l \rightarrow \nu_{l+1}$, $0 \leq l < k$ be an execution of h that goes through loops at most once and skips self loops. Then, b is called a basic path of h either if $b = s$ and ν_k is a terminal node of h or b is obtained from s with the following conditions:*
- For all reachable nodes ν_{k+1} from ν_k, $\nu_{k+1} \in \{\nu_0, \nu_1, \cdots, \nu_k\}$
- $b = \nu_0\nu_1 \cdots \nu_u$, where starting from the end of s all the nodes ν_z for which $\nu_{z-1}\nu_z$ is a repeated sequence (or edge in the graph representation of h) in s is deleted, $0 \leq u \leq k$, $0 < z \leq k$

A *basic execution* of h is an execution $\nu_0\nu_1 \cdots \nu_k$ of h such that for $m = \mu(\nu_0)\mu(\nu_1) \cdots \mu(\nu_k)$, $m|_i$ is a basic execution of T_i for some $i \in P$. Since loops of LTSs T_i are the projections of loops in h, projections of a basic path of h that is not a prefix of another basic path of h results in basic executions for local

LTSs T_i, $\forall i \in P$. Thus, a basic path of h that is not a prefix of other basic paths will be a basic execution for h.

The first condition in the definition of a basic path (word) ensures that the path is extended to include as much as reachable nodes or states. After it is found that the path cannot be extended further, the second condition removes repeated nodes (in h) or transitions (in T_i) that have been traversed by the path before and their inclusion in the path only increases its length without exploring new nodes or transitions. Finally, since when a basic word x' is a prefix of another basic word x, all the transitions and their sequencing in x' are included in x, we only keep x and call it a basic execution for T_i. Thus, when all the basic executions of an LTS (or an hMSC) are executed, all the states and transitions in that LTS (or nodes and edges in that hMSC) are traversed at least once.

Now, we relate strong safe realizability of an MSC specification $Spec = (h, M)$ to strong safe realizability of the set B where members of B are the MSCs obtained from basic executions of h. Note that, this result also holds for safe realizability of $Spec = (h, M)$.

Lemma 1. *The language $L(Spec)$ of an MSC specification $Spec = (h, M)$ is SSR iff the language $L(B)$ is SSR where members of B are all the MSCs $\mu(\nu_0)\mu(\nu_1)\cdots\mu(\nu_k)$ such that $\nu_0\nu_1\cdots\nu_k$ is a basic execution of h.*

Based on Lemma 1, the following algorithm checks whether a given MSC specification is SSR or not.

Algorithm 1. Checking strong safe realizability for an MSC specification $Spec = (h, M)$.

1. Compute all the basic executions of h
2. For each basic execution obtained in Step 1 construct an MSC that corresponds to the concatenation of the MSCs of its nodes to obtain a set B of finite MSCs
3. Check whether there exists any 1st order emergent pMSC for B. If there exists no 1st order emergent pMSC (B is SSR), *output Spec* is SSR; otherwise, *output Spec* is not SSR

In the worst case, the algorithm terminates in time $O(K^6 2^{4K^2+2K} K'^3 K''^3)$ where for $Spec = (h, M)$, K is the number of nodes in h, K' is the number of events in the set of MSCs M, and $K'' = |P|$ is the number of processes [10]. Also, completeness and correctness of the algorithm is provided by Lemma 1 (for Steps 1 and 2) and Corollary 1 (for Step 3).

4.3   Application of the Algorithm

To illustrate the algorithm, consider an MSC specification for the Boiler Control system shown in Fig. 9 [4]. The LTS models for the processes in this system are also shown in Fig. 10. Because the hMSC of Fig. 9 is not bounded for asynchronous message passing (see the self loop of ν_1), we assume synchronous (or hand-shake) message passing between processes. However, in general the

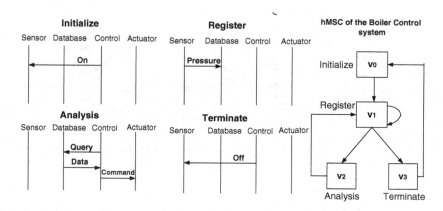

Fig. 9. MSC specification for a Boiler Control system

algorithm can be applied to asynchronous setting as long as the hMSCs are bounded.

As shown in Fig. 9, mapping between nodes and MSCs are: $\mu(\nu_0) = Initialize$, $\mu(\nu_1) = Register$, $\mu(\nu_2) = Analysis$, and $\mu(\nu_3) = Terminate$. To compute basic executions of the hMSC of Fig. 9, note that most of the time computing basic paths of h gives all the basic executions of h and there is no need to compute other paths in h that goes through loops more than once or goes through self loops. For instance, basic executions of the hMSC of Fig. 9 are only the basic paths $s_1 = \nu_0. \nu_1. \nu_3. \nu_0. \nu_1. \nu_2. \nu_1$ and $s_2 = \nu_0. \nu_1. \nu_2. \nu_1. \nu_3. \nu_0$ (Step 1). The reason is that the projections of s_1 and s_2 on each of the processes Control, Actuator, Sensor, and Database gives all the basic executions of the LTS's of these processes (in other words, non-deterministic LTS T_i' obtained for each process i is the same as its deterministic LTS T_i).

The corresponding MSCs resulting from concatenating of the MSCs in the basic executions s_1 and s_2 are respectively: $m_1 = Initialize. Register. Terminate. Initialize. Register. Analysis. Register$ and $m_2 = Initialize. Register. Analysis. Register. Terminate. Initialize$, which are shown in Fig. 11 (Step 2).

For the MSCs of Fig. 11, the Sensor process in m_2 has a non-deterministic behaviour because of the MSC m_1, which makes it possible to replace the second *Pressure* message for this process in m_2 with the message *Off* and get the emergent scenario of Fig. 12 (Step 3). Fig. 12 is an emergent scenario since while the

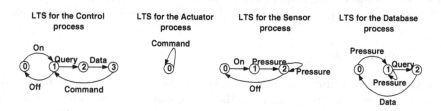

Fig. 10. LTS models of the processes in the Boiler Control system

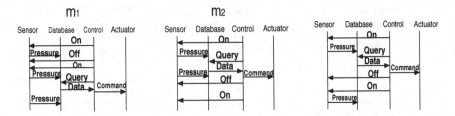

Fig. 11. Two MSCs obtained from two basic executions of the hMSC of Fig. 9

Fig. 12. An emergent scenario obtained from two MSCs of Fig. 11

Database, the Actuator, and the Control processes are acting according to the path $\nu_0.\ \nu_1.\ \nu_2.\ \nu_1.\ \nu_3.\ \nu_0$ (path s_2), the Sensor process is acting according to the path $\nu_0.\ \nu_1.\ \nu_3.\ \nu_0.\ \nu_1$ (a prefix of path s_1). As the result, the set of MSCs m_1 and m_2 obtained from the basic executions of the hMSC of Fig. 9 has a 1st order emergent MSC m_2^1 (it is not closed under CC3 and CC_{ss}). Thus, the algorithm outputs that the specification shown in Fig. 9 is not SSR.

5   Related Work

Our work for a set of MSCs is different from [2] in the following. First, we localized the cause of implied scenarios in the non-deterministic behaviour of processes, which provides a better insight for studying implied scenarios. Second, we characterized and defined stuck states that captures such anomalies for MSC specifications that are not addressed by the current definitions of deadlock states and implied scenarios. Third, based on the definition of stuck states we introduced a new notion of realizability for MSC specifications called strong safe realizability.

On the other hand, our work is different from [3] and [4] in the following. First, in order to detect implied scenarios, [4] builds a distributed implementation from the specification in terms of parallel execution of process's LTSs and checks this model against another behavioural model that represents the exact behaviour of the specification. Second, [3] and [4] assume synchronous message passing while we assume asynchronous setting, which from a practical point of view is more realistic. Third, [3] and [4] only detect implied scenarios and in fact checks for a weaker notion of realizability (weak realizability) that ignores deadlocks while our method checks for (strong) safe realizability that implies weak realizability.

6   Conclusions

We localized the cause of implied scenarios in the non-deterministic behaviour of processes in a concurrent system. Also, the notions of stuck states and strong safe realizability are introduced that capture such anomalies for MSC specifications that are not covered by safe realizability. Furthermore, an algorithm was given that reduces (strong) safe realizability of MSC specifications to (strong) safe realizability of a set of MSCs. Finally, our work bridges the gap between realizability for a set of MSCs studied in [2], and realizability in the presence of hMSCs studied in [3] and [4].

References

1. ITU: Recommendation Z.120: Message Sequence Chart(MSC), Geneva (1996)
2. Alur, R., Etessami, K., Yannakakis, M.: Inference of Message Sequence Charts. IEEE Transaction on Software Engineering 29(7), 623–633 (2003)
3. Muccini, H.: Detecting implied scenarios analyzing non-local branching choice. In: Pezzé, M. (ed.) ETAPS 2003 and FASE 2003. LNCS, vol. 2621, pp. 1–15. Springer, Heidelberg (2003)
4. Uchitel, S.: Incremental Elaboration of Scenario-Based Specifications and Behaviour Models Using Implied Scenarios. PhD thesis, PhD Thesis, Imperial College, London (2003)
5. Uchitel, S., Kramer, J., Magee, J.: Negative scenarios for implied scenario elicitation. In: FSE 2002. 10th ACM SIGSOFT International Symposium on the Foundations of Software Engineering, pp. 109–118. ACM Press, New York (2002)
6. Mooij, A., Goga, N., Romijn, J.: Non-local choice and beyond: Intricacies of MSC choice nodes. In: Cerioli, M. (ed.) FASE 2005. LNCS, vol. 3442, pp. 273–288. Springer, Heidelberg (2005)
7. Ben-Abdhallah, H., Leue, S.: Syntactic detection of process divergence and non-local choice in Message Sequence Charts. In: Brinksma, E. (ed.) TACAS 1997. LNCS, vol. 1217, pp. 259–274. Springer, Heidelberg (1997)
8. Alur, R., Etessami, K., Yannakakis, M.: Realizability and verification of MSC graphs. Theoretical Computer Science 331(1), 97–114 (2005)
9. Lohery, M.: Safe realizability of high-Level Message Sequence Charts. In: Brim, L., Jančar, P., Křetínský, M., Kucera, A. (eds.) CONCUR 2002. LNCS, vol. 2421, pp. 177–192. Springer, Heidelberg (2002)
10. Mousavi, A., Far, B., Eberlein, A.: The Problematic Property of Choice Nodes in high-level Message Sequence Charts. Technical report, Laboratory for Agent-Based Software Engineering, University of Calgary (2006), http://www.enel.ucalgary.ca/~amousavi/reports/choice_nodes.pdf
11. Hopcroft, J., Motwani, R., Ullman, J.: Introduction to Automata Theory, Languages, and Computation, 2nd edn. Addison-Wesley Publishing Company, Reading (2001)
12. Fournet, C., Hoare, C., Rajamani, S., Rehof, J.: Stuck-free conformance. In: Alur, R., Peled, D.A. (eds.) CAV 2004. LNCS, vol. 3114, Springer, Heidelberg (2004)

Implication-Based Approximating Bounded Model Checking*

Zhenyu Chen[1], Zhihong Tao[2], Baowen Xu[1], and Lifu Wang[2]

[1] School of Computer Science and Engineering, Southeast University, Nanjing, China
[2] School of Software and Microelectronics, Peking University, Beijing, China
zychen@seu.edu.cn

Abstract. This paper presents an iterative framework based on over-approximation and under-approximation for traditional bounded model checking (BMC). A novel feature of our approach is the approximations are defined based on "implication" instead of "simulation". As a common partial order relation of logic formulas, implication is suitable for the satisfiability checking of BMC for debugging. Our approach could generate the implication-based approximations efficiently with necessary accuracy, thus it potentially enables BMC to go deeper and the output counterexamples with fewer variables are easier to understand. An experiment on a suite of Petri nets shows the effectiveness of implication-based approximating BMC.

Keywords: Implication, Abstraction, Approximation, Bounded Model Checking.

1 Introduction

In the past years, SAT solvers have been found to be quite efficient at producing counterexamples for systems that are too large to allow standard model checking. Bounded model checking (BMC) [1] [2] based on SAT is rapidly gaining popularity as a debugging technique, that is, as a technique for refuting properties with shallow counterexamples, if they exist. BMC iteratively deepens the search for counterexamples until either a bug is found or the problem becomes too hard to solve in a given time limit. The motivation for making this technique more powerful is to enable it to go deeper in a given time limit.

Abstraction [3] may be one of the most successful techniques for handling the state explosion problem. Abstraction techniques can be classified as over-approximation and under-approximation. Over-approximation techniques, systematically release constraints, and thus add more behaviors to the system. In

---

* This work was supported in part by the National Natural Science Foundation of China (60425206, 60373066, 60403016), Natural Science Foundation of Jiangsu Province (BK2005060), High Technology Research Project of Jiangsu Province (BG2005032), Excellent Talent Foundation on Teaching and Research of Southeast University, and Open Foundation of State Key Laboratory of Software Engineering in Wuhan University.

F. Arbab and M. Sirjani (Eds.): FSEN 2007, LNCS 4767, pp. 350–363, 2007.

contrast, under-approximation techniques systematically remove irrelevant behaviors from the system. Intuitively, abstraction could be regarded as an approximation of the original system by hiding "irrelevant" details. Verifying the simplified approximations is in general more efficient than verifying the original models. Therefore, abstraction could enable BMC to go deeper in a given time limit.

In this paper, we introduce an iterative framework called approximating bounded model checking (ABMC). We use a set of *visible* variables V^i to construct approximations of the original system for bounded model checking. V^i corresponds to the part of the system that is currently believed to be important for verifying the desired property. Along BMC iteratively deepens the search for counterexamples, $BMC(M, f, k)$ may become too large to solve in a limit time. We construct two approximations of M over V^i: an over-approximation M^o and an under-approximation M^u. M^o guides to search deep counterexamples. M^u establish the counterexamples' existence in the original model.

Related Work: One common feature of many existing work on approximation (abstraction) is the application of a BDD-based model checker to the approximate models, and of SAT solvers to the original ones. In [4,5], BMC is used to check whether counterexamples found in over-approximations are real. A new SAT-based approach of model checking using approximations has been proposed in [6]. Given an unsatisfiable problem, and a proof of unsatisfiability derived by a SAT solver, a *Craig interpolant* can be efficiently computed to characterize the interface between two partitions of the problem. The interpolant serves directly as an over-approximation. Thus the state space exploration could potentially be deep. Recently, a new approach on abstraction refinement for bounded model checking is present in [7]. Their work is related because they also suggest using the approximations to perform deeper searches with BMC.

Contribution: Applying approximation (abstraction) in bounded model checking is not a new idea. Almost all approaches to generate approximations must balance the efficient construction against the necessary accuracy. Most existing efforts define the approximations based on simulation relation [8]. Usually, generating such an accurate approximation requires exponential number calls to a deduction tool. Simulation relation is not suitable for bounded model checking, because the unrolled path is represented as a propositional formula with the satisfiability checking instead of state space exploration.

In this paper, we introduce implication as a partial order relation to define approximations. The implication-based approximation could be generated in linear time without calls to deduction tools, although it may loss some accuracy in general. For some particular structures of transition relations, such as conjunctive normal form (CNF) and disjunctive normal form (DNF), we prove that implication-based approximations are as accurate as simulation-based ones. Furthermore, through an experiment on a suite of Petri nets, we show the effectiveness of implication-based BMC.

On the other hand, most existing efforts [6,7] only use over-approximation in BMC. However, it is a tedious task to understand the complex counterexamples generated by BMC [9]. It is valuable to eliminate irrelevant variables from counterexamples. Combined with under-approximation, the output counterexamples always contain fewer variables, thus it is easier to understand.

Overview: This paper is organized as follows. In the next section, we introduce some basic concepts of SAT and bounded model checking. Section 3 presents the framework of approximating bounded model checking. In section 4 and section 5, we start with a sound mathematical definitions and reason about the proposed method in a rigorous way. Practical experience for Petri nets is described in section 6. The conclusion is drawn in the last section.

2   Preliminaries

2.1   SAT Notations

A propositional formula is said to be satisfiable if there is at least one satisfying assignment. If a formula has no satisfying assignment then the formula is called unsatisfiable. $F \models F'$ if any satisfying assignment of F satisfies F'. $F \approx F'$ if $F \models F'$ and $F' \models F$, i.e., F' is equivalent to F.

A literal l is an atomic Boolean variable x or its negation $\neg x$. A clause C_i is a disjunction of literals $(l_1 \vee \cdots \vee l_m)$. A cube D_i is a conjunction of literals $(l_1 \wedge \cdots \wedge l_m)$. A formula is in Negation Normal Form (NNF) if the only connectives in it are $\wedge$, $\vee$, and $\neg$, where $\neg$ is only applied to atomic variables. A formula is in Conjunctive Normal Form (CNF) if it has the conjunction form of clauses $C_1 \wedge \cdots \wedge C_n$. A formula is in Disjunctive Normal Form (DNF) if it has the disjunction form of cubes $D_1 \vee \cdots \vee D_n$. A clause and a cube could be regarded as a set of literals. A CNF formula could be regarded as a set of clauses. A DNF formula could be regarded as a set of cubes.

In this paper, SAT is the class of all satisfiable formulas, $UNSAT$ is the class of all unsatisfiable formulas. $F \Rightarrow F'$ means that if $F \in SAT$ then $F' \in SAT$. $var(F)$ is the set of variables in F. $F[x/i]$ is the resulting formula by replacing each x in F where $i \in \{0, 1\}$.

2.2   Bounded Model Checking

Definition 1. *Considering a system with a set of boolean variables V over $\{true, false\}$. The system model is 3-tuple $M := (S, T, I)$, where:*

1. *S is a set of states.*
2. *$T \subseteq S \times S$ is a transition relation.*
3. *I is a set of initial states.*

Without loss of generality, we can assume that S, T and I are in NNF and there is only one initial state. In particular, each state s is represented as a cube $(l_1 \wedge \cdots \wedge l_n)$ or considered as a set $\{l_1, ..., l_n\}$. The transition relation $T(s, s')$

can be represented as a propositional formula. We say that the current state of system is s if the values (assignments) of system variables satisfies s. There is a transition from s to s' if and only if $(s \land s') \models T$.

Given a model M, a property f, and a positive integer k representing the depth of search, a bounded model checker generates a propositional formula $BMC(M, f, k)$ that is satisfiable if and only if there is a counterexample of length k or less to f in M. The basic idea is to iteratively deepen the search for counterexamples until either a bug is found or the problem becomes too hard to solve in a given time limit. $BMC(M, f, k)$ is in general represented as follows.

$$BMC(M, f, k) := I(s_0) \land T(s_0, s_1) \land ... \land T(s_{k-1}, s_k) \land F(f, k) \qquad (1)$$

$I(s_0)$ and $T(s_i, s_{i+1})$ is described above. $F(f, k)$ is a translation of property f, and it could be regarded as a small CNF formula with variables in f. More details could be found in [1].

3   Approximating Bounded Model Checking

For a realistic system, the number of variables is usually more than hundreds even thousands. The number of all potential states would be astronomical. In order to reduce the state space, we extract a set of variables from V (called *visible* variables), denoted by V^i. V^i corresponds to the part of the system that is currently believed to be important for verifying the desired property. We use V^i to generate approximations to enable BMC to find deeper counterexamples, namely approximating bounded model checking (ABMC). The underlying principles behind the ABMC framework are the following:

1. It needs to generate an over-approximation M^o and an under-approximation M^u, such that

$$BMC(M^u, f, k) \Rightarrow BMC(M, f, k) \Rightarrow BMC(M^o, f, k)$$

   That is, if $BMC(M^u, f, k)$ is satisfiable then $BMC(M, f, k)$ is satisfiable; If $BMC(M^o, f, k)$ is unsatisfiable then $BMC(M, f, k)$ is unsatisfiable. M^o guides to search deep counterexamples. M^u establish the counterexamples' existence in the original system.
2. M^o and M^u should be much simpler than M, i.e., they always contain much fewer variables than M. Therefore solving M^o and M^u is much efficient than solving M, special for deep search (large k).
3. If $BMC(M^o, f, k)$ is satisfiable and $BMC(M^u, f, k)$ is unsatisfiable, i.e. it does not prove the property, then a variable minimal unsatisfiable (VMU) [10] sub-formula is extracted form $BMC(M^o, f, k)$. The refined approximate model based on the VMU sub-formula would rule out all spurious counterexamples of maximum length k.

We apply these principles to guide the SAT-solvers. The pseudo-code of Approximating Bounded Model Checking is shown in algorithm 1.

Algorithm 1. ABMC

ABMC(M,f)

1: $k = 0$; $V^i = var(f)$;

2:    $k = k + 1$;

3: **if** $BMC(M^o, f, k) \in UNSAT$ **then**

4:    **goto** line 2;

5: **else if** $BMC(M^u, f, k) \in SAT$ **then**

6:    **return** "bug found in length k";

7: **else** Enlarge V^i, such that

8:    **case** $BMC(M^o, f, k) \in UNSAT$:

9:       **goto** line 2;

10:    **case** $BMC(M^u, f, k) \in SAT$:

11:       **return** "bug found in length k";

We start with an initial approximate model based on $V^i = var(f)$ and an initial search depth $k = 1$. In each iteration of the ABMC loop, we first try to find a counterexample in the over-approximate model M^o (line 3). If there is no counterexample in M^o, we make a deeper search (line 4). Otherwise, we check it in the under-approximate model M^u (line 5). If it is "true", then it reports a bug and exits (line 6). Otherwise, we try to find a new subset V^i to rule out the spurious counterexamples (line 7), and make a deeper search (line 8-9). Otherwise, i.e., $BMC(M^u, f, k) \in SAT$, we report a bug and finish the verification (line 10-11).

Following the above description, the performance of ABMC largely depends on efficient construction and necessary accuracy of approximations. In the following subsections, we introduce two different types of approximations. One is based on simulation for exact accuracy, the other is based on implication for efficient construction.

3.1   Simulation-Based Approximations

Firstly, we introduce simulation $\preceq$ [8] as a partial order to define approximations. Given two models $M = (S, T, I)$ over V and $M' = (S', T', I')$ over $V' \subseteq V$, a relation $H \subseteq S \times S'$ is a simulation relation if and only if for all s and s', if $H(s, s')$ then the following conditions hold [8]:

1. $s \lceil V' = s'$. $\lceil V'$ could be considered as a sub-cube which is projected on V'. (The details could be found in section 5.)
2. For every state s_1 such that $T(s, s_1)$, there is a state s'_1 satisfying $T'(s', s'_1)$ and $H(s_1, s'_1)$.

For two states s from M and s' from M', (M', s') simulates (M, s), denoted by $(M, s) \preceq (M', s')$, if there is a simulation relation $H(s, s')$. If for each initial state $s \in I$, there exists $s' \in I'$, $(M, s) \preceq (M', s')$, then M' simulates M, denoted by $M \preceq M'$.

Definition 2 (Simulation Approximation [3]). *Given a model M over V and a set $V' \subseteq V$, a model M' over V' is an over-approximation (resp. to under-approximation) of M w.r.t. V' if and only if $M \preceq M'$ (resp. to $M' \preceq M$).*

Given a system model $M = (S, T, I)$ over V and a set of visible variables $V^i \subseteq V$, let S^a be the set of approximate states, in which each approximate state s^a is a sub-cube of s by hiding variables not in V^i (details in definition 10). s^a could be regarded as a set of original states, i.e. a subset of S. Similarly, I^a is a sub-cube of I by hiding variables not in V^i (details in definition 10). In order to reason about the approximations for model checking, we describe two transition relation of the approximations, $T^{\exists\exists}$ and $T^{\forall\exists}$.

Definition 3 (Approximate Relation [3]). *Let S be a set of states, $T \subseteq S \times S$ and $S^a \subseteq \mathcal{P}(S)$ be a set of approximate states. The approximate relations $T^{\exists\exists}$, $T^{\forall\exists} \subseteq S^a \times S^a$ are defined as follows.*

- $T^{\exists\exists}(s^a, s'^a) \iff \exists s \in s^a \exists s' \in s'^a : T(s, s')$
- $T^{\forall\exists}(s^a, s'^a) \iff \forall s \in s^a \exists s' \in s'^a : T(s, s')$

$T^{\exists\exists}(s^a, s'^a)$ if and only if there exists a original state s represented by s^a and there exists a original state s' represented by s'^a such that $T(s, s')$. $T^{\forall\exists}(s^a, s'^a)$ if and only if for each original state s represented by s^a and there exists a original state s' represented by s'^a such that $T(s, s')$. Furthermore, we draw the following theorem. Let $M^{\exists\exists} := (S^a, R^{\exists\exists}, I^a)$ and $M^{\forall\exists} := (S^a, R^{\forall\exists}, I^a)$. It is not difficult see that $M^{\exists\exists}$ is an over-approximation of M and $M^{\forall\exists}$ is an under-approximation of M.

Theorem 1 (Preservation Theorem [3])

$$M^{\forall\exists} \preceq M \preceq M^{\exists\exists} \tag{2}$$

For two set of variables $V \subset V'$, one would expect that the approximation over V' is more accurate than the one over V, i.e., it is monotonic. Unfortunately, $M^{\exists\exists}$ is monotonic but $M^{\forall\exists}$ is non-monotonic [11], that is, $M'^{\forall\exists}$ over V' may not simulate $M^{\forall\exists}$ over V. In [11], *must hyper-transition* is introduced to overcome the non-monotonic problem. However, this definition is not intuitive and hard to implement. We aim at simple and monotonic approximate relations.

On the other hand, the exact computation of $T^{\exists\exists}$ and $T^{\forall\exists}$ is problematic, requiring in the worst case an exponential number of calls to a deduction tool. For this reason, model checkers typically use weak approximations, which could be constructed efficiently.

3.2   Implication-Based Approximations

Many typical tasks of system design could be formulated as an instances of Boolean satisfiability. The satisfying assignment could be regarded as a behavior of system. In this section, we introduce implication, "$\models$", as a partial order for propositional formulas.

Definition 4 (Implication Approximation). *Given a formula F and a sub-set of variables $V \subseteq var(F)$, a formula F' over V is an over-approximation (resp. to under-approximation) of F w.r.t. V if and only if $F \models F'$ (resp. to $F' \models F$).*

F' is called a minimal over-approximation of F w.r.t. V if and only if (1) F' is an over-approximation of F w.r.t. V. (2) for any over-approximation F'' of F w.r.t. V, $F' \models F''$. Similarly, F' is called a maximal under-approximation of F w.r.t. V if and only if (1) F' is an under-approximation of F w.r.t. V. (2) for any under-approximation F'' of F w.r.t. V, $F'' \models F'$.

An interesting problem is how to generate a minimal over-approximation and a maximal under-approximation for a given formula. Please notice that $F[x/0]$ remains the satisfying assignments with $x = 0$ of F, $F[x/1]$ remains the satisfying assignments with $x = 1$ of F. We use $F[x/0]$ and $F[x/1]$ to generate the minimal over-approximation and maximal under-approximation.

Lemma 1. *Given a formula F and a variable x, $F[x/0] \vee F[x/1]$ is a minimal over-approximation of F w.r.t. $var(F) - \{x\}$; $F[x/0] \wedge F[x/1]$ is a maximal under-approximation of F w.r.t. $var(F) - \{x\}$.*

Proof. (1) For any satisfying assignment $\mathcal{A}$ of F, x is assigned either 0 or 1, then $\mathcal{A}$ satisfies $F[x/0]$ or $F[x/1]$, thus $\mathcal{A}$ satisfies $F[x/0] \vee F[x/1]$. Therefore, $F \models F[x/0] \vee F[x/1]$, $F[x/0] \vee F[x/1]$ is an over-approximation of F.

For any formula $F \models F'(var(F') \subseteq var(F) - \{x\})$, if $\mathcal{A}$ is a satisfying assignment of $F[x/0] \vee F[x/1]$, then $\mathcal{A} \cup \{x = 0\}$ or $\mathcal{A} \cup \{x = 1\}$ is a satisfying assignment of F. Since $F \models F'$, $\mathcal{A} \cup \{x = 0\}$ or $\mathcal{A} \cup \{x = 1\}$ is a satisfying assignment of F'. Since $x \notin var(F')$, $\mathcal{A}$ is a satisfying assignment of F'. Therefore, $F[x/0] \vee F[x/1]$ is a minimal over-approximation of F w.r.t. $var(F) - \{x\}$.

(2) For any satisfying assignment $\mathcal{A}$ of $F[x/0] \wedge F[x/1]$, i.e. $\mathcal{A}$ satisfies $F[x/0]$ and $F[x/1]$. Both $\mathcal{A} \cup \{x = 0\}$ and $\mathcal{A} \cup \{x = 1\}$ satisfy F, thus $\mathcal{A}$ satisfies F. $F[x/0] \wedge F[x/1]$ is an under-approximation of F.

For any formula $F' \models F(var(F') \subseteq var(F) - \{x\})$, if $\mathcal{A}$ is a satisfying assignment of F', then both $\mathcal{A} \cup \{x = 0\}$ and $\mathcal{A} \cup \{x = 1\}$ satisfy F', because $x \notin var(F')$. Since $F' \models F$, both $\mathcal{A} \cup \{x = 0\}$ and $\mathcal{A} \cup \{x = 1\}$ satisfy F, thus $\mathcal{A}$ satisfies $F[x/0]$ and $F[x/1]$, that is it satisfies $F[x/0] \wedge F[x/1]$. Therefore, $F[x/0] \wedge F[x/1]$ is a maximal under-approximation of F w.r.t. $var(F) - \{x\}$.

Please notice that $F[x/k_1][y/k_2] = F[y/k_1][x/k_2]$ for any x, y and $k_1, k_2 \in \{0, 1\}$. Suppose that it need to hide the variables $x_1, \cdots, x_n$ in F, let $F_0^\vee = F$, $F_i^\vee = F_{i-1}^\vee[x_i/0] \vee F_{i-1}^\vee[x_i/1]$, $1 \leq i \leq n$. If we exchange x_i and x_j for any i, j, then it does not affect the resulting formula $F_n^\vee$. That is, the replacement of variable, $F[x/i]$, is order-independent. Therefore, we could use $F[V]^\vee$ and $F[V]^\wedge$ to denote the resulting formula by replacing each variable which is not in V.

Theorem 2. *Given a formula F and a subset of variables V, $F[V]^\vee$ is a minimal over-approximation of F w.r.t. V; $F[V]^\wedge$ is a maximal under-approximation of F w.r.t. V.*

The sizes of $F[V]^\vee$ and $F[V]^\wedge$ would grow exponential in the size of $var(F) - V$ in the worst case. However, for CNF and DNF formula, there may be some simple constructions.

Given a CNF(DNF) formula F and a variable x, the formula can be divided into three sets: (1) Clauses(Cubes) that contain x in positive phase will be denoted as the set $F^+(x)$. (2) Clauses(Cubes) that contain x in negative phase will be denoted as the set $F^-(x)$. (3) Clauses(Cubes) that do not contain x will be denoted as the set F/x.

$F_*^+(x)$ denotes the resulting set by removing the positive occurrences of x from $F^+(x)$ and $F_*^-(x)$ denotes the resulting set by removing the negative occurrences of x from $F^-(x)$. For a CNF formula F, $F[x/0] = F_*^+(x) \wedge F/x$, $F[x/1] = F_*^-(x) \wedge F/x$. $F[x/0] \vee F[x/1] = (F_*^+(x) \vee F_*^-(x)) \wedge F/x$, which is the resulting formula of Davis-Putnam Resolution [12] w.r.t. x. $F[x/0] \wedge F[x/1] = F_*^+(x) \wedge F_*^-(x) \wedge F/x$, which is the resulting formula by removing all occurrences of x from F. It is similar to DNF formulas. A generalization approximation operations for NNF formulas is defined as follows.

Definition 5 (Approximation Operations). *Given an NNF formula F and a set of variables V, $F\lceil V$ (resp. to $F\lfloor V$) is a formula obtained from F by substituting each literal l, where $var(l) \notin V$, by 1 (resp. to 0).*

Please notice that $\wedge$ and $\vee$ are monotonic connectives, that is, if $F_1 \models F_1'$ and $F_2 \models F_2'$, then $F_1 \wedge F_2 \models F_1' \wedge F_2'$ and $F_1 \vee F_2 \models F_1' \vee F_2'$. For any literal l, $0 \models l$ and $l \models 1$. $F\lceil V$ has more satisfying assignments than F, thus $F\lceil V$ is an over-approximation of F w.r.t. V. $F\lfloor V$ has fewer satisfying assignments than F, thus $F\lfloor V$ is an under-approximation of F w.r.t. V.

For a CNF formula F, $F\lceil V$ is obtained from F by removing all clauses which contain variables not in V; $F\lfloor V$ is obtained from F by removing all occurrences of literals whose variables not in V, i.e. $F[V]^\wedge$. For a DNF formula F, $F\lfloor V$ is obtained from F by removing all cubes which contain variables not in V; $F\lceil V$ is obtained from F by removing all occurrences of literals whose variables not in V, i.e. $F[V]^\vee$. It is not difficult to see that $F\lfloor V$ and $F\lceil V$ could be generated in linear time for a CNF or DNF formula F.

Corollary 1. *For a DNF formula F, $F\lceil V$ is a minimal over-approximation of F w.r.t. V. For a CNF formula F, $F\lfloor V$ is a maximal under-approximation of F w.r.t. V.*

Proof. (1) For a DNF formula F and $x \in var(F)$, $F[x/0] \vee F[x/1]=F_*^+(x) \vee F_*^-(x) \vee F/x=F\lceil(var(F) - x)$. Thus $F[V]^\vee = F\lceil V$.
(2) For a CNF formula F and $x \in var(F)$, $F[x/0] \wedge F[x/1]=F_*^+(x) \wedge F_*^-(x) \wedge F/x=F\lfloor(var(F) - x)$. Thus $F[V]^\wedge = F\lceil V$.

Please recall that, for a system model $M = (S, T, I)$, s is in DNF; I is in DNF; T could be represented in NNF. Following by operations $\lceil$ and $\lfloor$, we could hide some variables to generate approximations.

Definition 6 (Implication-based Approximate Model). *Given a model $M = (S, T, I)$ over a set of boolean variables V and a set of visible variables*

$V^i \subseteq V$, *the over-approximate model $M^\lceil$ and under-approximate model $M^\lfloor$ of M w.r.t. V^i is 3-tuples $M^\lceil := (S^a, T^\lceil, I^a)$ and $M^\lfloor := (S^a, T^\lfloor, I^a)$ defined as follows:*

1. *S^a is a set of approximate states, in which $s^a := s \lceil V^i$.*
2. *$T^\lceil := T \lceil V^i$ is an over-approximate transition relation.*
3. *$T^\lfloor := T \lfloor V^i$ is an under-approximate transition relation.*
4. *$I^a := I \lceil V^i$ is a set of approximate initial states.*

$M^\lceil$ and $M^\lfloor$ could be generated much more efficiently than $M^{\forall\exists}$ and $M^{\exists\exists}$, because $\lceil$ and $\lfloor$ are linear time operations. As we know, for existential LTL formula f [13], if $M_1 \preceq M_2$, then $BMC(M_1, f, k) \Rightarrow BMC(M_2, f, k)$. $M^\lceil$ and $M^\lfloor$ could be regarded as weak approximations of $M^{\exists\exists}$ and $M^{\forall\exists}$, respectively. Formally, we draw the following conclusion.

Theorem 3 (Preservation Theorem)

$$BMC(M^\lfloor, f, k) \Rightarrow BMC(M^{\forall\exists}, f, k) \Rightarrow BMC(M, f, k) \Rightarrow$$

$$BMC(M^{\exists\exists}, f, k) \Rightarrow BMC(M^\lceil, f, k) \tag{3}$$

Proof. It is shown that $M^{\forall\exists} \preceq M \preceq M^{\exists\exists}$ in [3]. Therefore, $BMC(M^{\forall\exists}, f, k) \Rightarrow BMC(M, f, k) \Rightarrow BMC(M^{\exists\exists}, f, k)$.

(1) For $BMC(M^\lfloor, f, k) \Rightarrow BMC(M^{\forall\exists}, f, k)$, notice that S^a and I^a in $M^\lfloor$ are the same ones in $M^{\forall\exists}$. It just need to compare $T^\lfloor$ and $T^{\forall\exists}$. Suppose $T^\lfloor(s^a, s'^a)$, for any two states (i.e. assignment) s and s', if $s \in s^a$ and $s' \in s'^a$, then $T(s, s')$. That is, $T^\lfloor(s^a, s'^a) \Leftrightarrow \forall s \in s^a \forall s' \in s'^a : T(s, s') \Rightarrow \forall s \in s^a \exists s' \in s'^a : T(s, s') \Leftrightarrow T^{\forall\exists}(s^a, s'^a)$. Thus $T^\lfloor(s^a, s'^a) \Rightarrow T^{\forall\exists}(s^a, s'^a)$. Therefore, $BMC(M^\lfloor, f, k) \Rightarrow BMC(M^{\forall\exists}, f, k)$.

(2) For $BMC(M^{\exists\exists}, f, k) \Rightarrow BMC(M^\lceil, f, k)$, it just need to compare $T^\lceil$ and $T^{\exists\exists}$. $\wedge$ and $\vee$ are monotonic connectives. The resulting formula by replacing some literals l with 1 will contain more satisfying assignments. Thus $T^{\exists\exists}(s^a, s'^a) \Rightarrow T^\lceil(s^a, s'^a)$. Therefore $BMC(M^{\exists\exists}, f, k) \Rightarrow BMC(M^\lceil, f, k)$.

From the above theorem, we could find that $M^\lfloor$ and $M^\lceil$ are not the exact accurate approximations. However, profiting from the simpleness of approximation operations $\lceil$ and $\lfloor$, the approximate models $M^\lfloor$ and $M^\lceil$ could be generated efficiently.

4   Practical Experience

In many cases, BMC does not work well for asynchronous systems like Petri nets, because the encoding scheme into propositional formulas is not suited for such systems [14]. In this section, we discuss how to exploit the results of the previous sections in practice through a suite of Petri nets [14,15]. The primary experimental evaluation is to demonstrate the effectiveness of implication-based ABMC.

4.1   Encoding of Petri Nets

A Petri net [16] is a 4-tuple $PN = (P, T, F, I)$, where $P = \{p_1, ..., p_m\}$ is a finite set of places, $T = \{t_1, ..., t_n\}$ is a finite set of transitions $(P \cap T = \emptyset)$, $F \subseteq (P \times T) \cup (T \times P)$ is a set of arcs (flow relation), $I : P \to \mathcal{N}$ is the initial marking. The marking is also called state. A place p is called an input place of a transition t iff there exists a directed arc from p to t. Place p is called an output place of transition t iff there exists a directed arc from t to p. We use $\bullet t$ to denote the set of input places for a transition t. The notations $t\bullet$, $\bullet p$ and $p\bullet$ have similar meanings.

A pair of a place p and a transition t is called a self-loop if p is both an input and output place of t. In this paper, we consider pure Petri nets, i.e., without self-loop. A Petri net is said to be 1-bounded or safe if the number of tokens in each place does not exceed one for any state reachable from the initial state. For a safe Petri net, a state s can be viewed as a cube(Boolean vector) $s = (l_1, \cdots, l_m)$ of length m such that $l_i = p_i$ iff place p_i is marked with a token, $l_i = \neg p_i$ otherwise. This section describes how a safe Petri net can be represented symbolically.

For Petri nets, I is the only initial state. Thus we have:

$$I(s) := \bigwedge_{p_i \in I} p_i \wedge \bigwedge_{p_i \in P-I} \neg p_i \qquad (4)$$

Any relation over states can be similarly encoded since a relation is simply a set of tuples. We denote by $En_t(s)$ the characteristic function of the set of states in which transition t is enabled, i.e., $\bigwedge_{p_i \in \bullet t} p_i$. For simplicity, we assume that there is no deadlock in Petri nets, that is, for each state s, at least one transition is enabled. Let $T_t(s, s')$ be the characteristic function for the transition t. $T_t(s, s')$ is represented as follows:

$$T_t(s, s') := \bigwedge_{p_i \in \bullet t} p_i \wedge \bigwedge_{p_i \in \bullet t} \neg p'_i \wedge \bigwedge_{p_i \in t\bullet} p'_i \wedge \bigwedge_{p_i \in P-(\bullet t \cup t\bullet)} (p_i \leftrightarrow p'_i) \qquad (5)$$

$$T(s, s') := \bigvee_{t \in T} T_t(s, s') \qquad (6)$$

4.2   Encoding of Approximation

Given a Petri net $PN = (P, T, F, I)$ and a set of visible variables $V \subseteq P$, the approximations project states on V, that is, hide the variables(places) not in V, denoted by $s^a = s\lceil V$. For approximate initial states, we have

$$I^a(s^a) := \bigwedge_{p_i \in I \cap V} p_i \wedge \bigwedge_{p_i \in (P-I) \cap V} \neg p_i \qquad (7)$$

For Petri nets, T could be regarded as a DNF formula, because $p_i \leftrightarrow p'_i$ contains only one variable. For implication-based over-approximate relation $T\lceil V$, the literals, whose variables are not in V, are replaced with *true*, i.e., removed from T. The expression is formalized as follows.

$$T\lceil V(s^a, s'^a) := \bigvee_{t \in T} T_t \lceil V(s^a, s'^a) \tag{8}$$

$$T_t\lceil V(s^a, s'^a) := \bigwedge_{p_i \in \bullet t \cap V} p_i \wedge \bigwedge_{p_i \in \bullet t \cap V} \neg p'_i \wedge \bigwedge_{p_i \in t \bullet \cap V} p'_i \wedge \bigwedge_{p_i \in (P \cap V) - (\bullet t \cup t \bullet)} (p_i \leftrightarrow p'_i) \tag{9}$$

It is not difficult to see that if $T_t\lceil V(s^a, s'^a)$, then there exists $x \in s^a$ and $y \in s'^a$, such that $T(x, y)$. It is similar to simulation-based over-approximate relation $T^{\exists\exists}(s^a, s'^a)$. However, we could not guarantee that x and y are original states, i.e., reachable states from I.

For implication-based under-approximation $T\lfloor V$, the literals, whose variables are not in V, are replaced with *false*. That is, if there is an input place or output place of transition t not in V, T_t is removed from $T\lfloor V$. The expression is formalized as follows.

$$T\lfloor V(s^a, s'^a) := \bigvee_{(\bullet t \cup t \bullet) \subseteq V} T_t \lfloor V(s^a, s'^a) \tag{10}$$

$$T_t\lfloor V(s^a, s'^a) := \bigwedge_{p_i \in \bullet t} p_i \wedge \bigwedge_{p_i \in \bullet t} \neg p'_i \wedge \bigwedge_{p_i \in t \bullet} p'_i \wedge \bigwedge_{p_i \in (P \cap V) - (\bullet t \cup t \bullet)} (p_i \leftrightarrow p'_i) \tag{11}$$

In particular, we could generate an efficient and more precise under-approximation T^u. In T^u, the input place not in V is replaced with *false*, the output place not in V is replaced with *true*. The formal expression is described as follows.

$$T^u(V)(s^a, s'^a) := \bigvee_{(\bullet t) \subseteq V} T_t^u(V)(s^a, s'^a) \tag{12}$$

$$T_t^u(V)(s^a, s'^a) := \bigwedge_{p_i \in \bullet t} p_i \wedge \bigwedge_{p_i \in \bullet t} \neg p'_i \wedge \bigwedge_{p_i \in t \bullet \cap V} p'_i \wedge \bigwedge_{p_i \in (P \cap V) - (\bullet t \cup t \bullet)} (p_i \leftrightarrow p'_i) \tag{13}$$

Obviously, $T^{\lfloor} \models T^u \models T$. Let $M^u := (S^a, T^u, I^a)$, then, a corollary of ABMC could be drawn as follows.

Corollary 2 (Improved Under-approximation)

$$BMC(M^{\lfloor}, f, k) \Rightarrow BMC(M^u, f, k) \Rightarrow BMC(M, f, k) \tag{14}$$

4.3   Experimental Results

In this subsection, we conducted experimental evaluation on safe Petri nets, which are taken from [14,15]. We implemented our techniques on top of the Petri net tool PEP [17] and the model checker NuSMV [18]. All experiments

Table 1. Experimental Results

Problem	$|P|$	$|T|$	k	Time BMC	ABMC	CNF-var M	$M^\lceil$	M^u	CNF-cla M	$M^\lceil$	M^u
ELEV(1)	63	99	7	12.056	5.341	47774	1665	1683	141436	4414	4603
ELEV(2)	146	299	5	65.866	1.900	225953	945	980	674359	2503	2608
ELEV(3)	327	783	11	NA	208.05	NA	4792	4924	NA	13372	13768
MMGT(2)	86	114	8	36.041	8.632	84599	2279	2343	250963	6181	6373
MMGT(3)	122	172	5	27.518	2.850	110707	1559	1604	329197	4201	4336
MMGT(4)	158	232	4	43.765	1.668	152847	1203	1239	455227	3214	3322

were run on a Windows 2000 server with a 2.6GHz Pentium IV processor and 1024MByte memory. Table 1 shows the experimental results. The columns are:

- Problem: The problem name with the size of the instance in parenthesis.
- $|P|$: The number of places in Petri net.
- $|T|$: The number of transitions in Petri net.
- k: The depth of search.
- Time: The running time in seconds.
- CNF-var: The number of variables of resulting CNF formula.
- CNF-cla: The number of clauses of resulting CNF formula.

For comparison purposes, the standard BMC of NuSMV [18] was tested. We used the PEP tool [17] to generate the input programs to NuSMV from the Petri nets. For each problem instance, we select one safety property, of the form $G(!p_i)$. p_i is a place selected randomly form Petri nets. All the properties are inconsistent in the system model, thus it could report counterexamples. In each refinement cycle, we select the new variables depending on the transition relation of Petri net manually. Therefore, the "Time" of ABMC mentioned in table 1 includes verification time and approximation time, but it is not the whole verification period.

From the results in table 1, it can be seen that ABMC outperformed BMC in both execution time and the size of CNF formulas. The results of our experiment are very encouraging, although the set of benchmarks we used is too small to say anything conclusive about the performance of the method.

5 Conclusion

In this paper, we have present a framework of implicant-based approximating bounded model checking (ABMC). ABMC combines over-approximation and under-approximation to iteratively enable BMC to search deeper counterexamples. In order to generate suitable approximations efficiently, implication is introduced as a partial order relation to define approximations $M^\lceil$ and $M^\lfloor$. They are weak approximations but could be generated efficiently and monotonously. The experimental results for Petri nets show the effectiveness of our approach.

Acknowledgement

The authors would like to thank Prof. Decheng Ding and Prof. Hans Kleine Büning for their valuable discussions. The authors are also grateful to the referees for their helpful comments and suggestions.

References

1. Biere, A., Cimatti, A., Clarke, E.M., Strichman, O., Zhu, Y.: Bounded Model Checking. Advances in Cpmputers 58 (2003)
2. Tao, Z.H., Zhou, C.H., Chen, Z., Wang, L.F.: Bounded Model Checking of CTL*. Journal of Computer Science and Technology 22(1), 39–43 (2007)
3. Clarke, E.M., Grumberg, O., Long, D.E.: Model checking and abstraction. ACM Transactions on Programming Languages and Systems 16(5), 1512–1542 (1994)
4. Chauhan, P., Clarke, E., Kukula, J., Sapra, S., Veith, H., Wang, D.: Automated Abstraction Refinement for Model Checking Large State Spaces Using SAT based Conflict Analysis. In: Aagaard, M.D., O'Leary, J.W. (eds.) FMCAD 2002. LNCS, vol. 2517, pp. 33–51. Springer, Heidelberg (2002)
5. Chen, Z.Y., Zhou, C.H., Ding, D.C.: Automatic abstraction refinement for Petri nets verification. In: Proceedings of the 10th IEEE International High-Level Design Validation and Test Workshop, pp. 168–174. IEEE, Los Alamitos (2005)
6. McMillan, K.L.: Interpolation and SAT-based model checking. In: Hunt Jr., W.A., Somenzi, F. (eds.) CAV 2003. LNCS, vol. 2725, pp. 1–13. Springer, Heidelberg (2003)
7. Gupta, A., Strichman, O.: Abstraction refinement for bounded model checking. In: Etessami, K., Rajamani, S.K. (eds.) CAV 2005. LNCS, vol. 3576, pp. 112–124. Springer, Heidelberg (2005)
8. Milner, R.: An algebraic definition of simulation between programs. In: Proceedings of the 2nd international Joint Conference on Artificial Intelligence, pp. 481–489 (1971)
9. Ravi, K., Somenzi, F.: Minimal assignments for bounded model checking. In: Jensen, K., Podelski, A. (eds.) TACAS 2004. LNCS, vol. 2988, pp. 31–45. Springer, Heidelberg (2004)
10. Chen, Z.Y., Ding, D.C.: Variable Minimal Unsatisfiability. In: Cai, J.-Y., Cooper, S.B., Li, A. (eds.) TAMC 2006. LNCS, vol. 3959, pp. 262–273. Springer, Heidelberg (2006)
11. Shoham, S., Grumberg, O.: Monotonic Abstraction-Refinement for CTL. In: Garavel, H., Hatcliff, J. (eds.) ETAPS 2003 and TACAS 2003. LNCS, vol. 2619, pp. 546–560. Springer, Heidelberg (2003)
12. Davis, M., Putnam, H.: A computing procedure for quantification theory. Journal of the ACM 7(3), 201–215 (1960)
13. Clarke, E.M., Grumberg, O., Peled, D.A.: Model Checking. MIT Press, Cambridge (1999)
14. Ogata, S., Tsuchiya, T., Kikuno, T.: SAT-based Verification of Safe Petri Nets. In: Wang, F. (ed.) ATVA 2004. LNCS, vol. 3299, pp. 79–92. Springer, Heidelberg (2004)

15. Heljanko, K.: Bounded Reachability Checking with Process Semantics. In: Larsen, K.G., Nielsen, M. (eds.) CONCUR 2001. LNCS, vol. 2154, pp. 218–232. Springer, Heidelberg (2001)
16. Murata, T.: Petri nets: Properties, Analysis and Applications. IEEE 77(4), 541–580 (1989)
17. Grahlmann, B.: The PEP Tool. In: Grumberg, O. (ed.) CAV 1997. LNCS, vol. 1254, pp. 440–443. Springer, Heidelberg (1997)
18. Cimatti, A., Clarke, E.M., Giunchiglia, F., Roveri, M.: NUSMV: A New Symbolic Model Checker. International Journal on Software Tools for Technology Transfer 2(4), 410–425 (2000)

Logical Bisimulations and Functional Languages*

Davide Sangiorgi[1], Naoki Kobayashi[2], and Eijiro Sumii[2]

[1] University of Bologna, Italy
Davide.Sangiorgi@cs.unibo.it
[2] Tohoku University, Japan
{koba,sumii}@ecei.tohoku.ac.jp

Abstract. Developing a theory of bisimulation in higher-order languages can be hard. Particularly challenging can be the proof of congruence and, related to this, enhancements of the bisimulation proof method with "up-to context" techniques.

We present *logical bisimulations*, a form of bisimulation for higher-order languages, in which the bisimulation clause is somehow reminiscent of logical relations. We consider purely functional languages, in particular untyped call-by-name and call-by-value lambda-calculi, and, in each case: we present the basic properties of logical bisimilarity, including congruence; we show that it coincides with contextual equivalence; we develop some up-to techniques, including up-to context, as examples of possible enhancements of the associated bisimulation method.

1 Introduction

Applicative bisimulations and behavioral equivalence in higher-order languages. Equivalence proof of computer programs is an important but challenging problem. Equivalence between two programs means that the programs should behave "in the same manner" under any context [1]. Finding effective methods for equivalence proofs is particularly challenging in higher-order languages (i.e., languages where program code can be passed around like other data).

Bisimulation has emerged as a very powerful operational method for proving equivalence of programs in various kinds of languages, due to the associated co-inductive proof method. Further, a number of enhancements of the bisimulation method have been studied, usually called *up-to techniques*. To be useful, the behavioral relation resulting from bisimulation—*bisimilarity*—should be a *congruence*. Bisimulation has been transplanted onto (sequential) higher-order languages by Abramsky [2]. This version of bisimulation, called *applicative bisimulations*, and variants of it, have received considerable attention [3,4,5,6,7]. In short, two functions P and Q are applicatively bisimilar when their applications $P(M)$ and $Q(M)$ are applicatively bisimilar for any argument M.

---

* Sangiorgi's research was partially supported by european FET project SENSORIA and italian MIUR Project n. 2005015785, "Logical Foundations of Distributed Systems and Mobile Code".

F. Arbab and M. Sirjani (Eds.): FSEN 2007, LNCS 4767, pp. 364–379, 2007.

Applicative bisimulations have two significant limitations. First, they do not scale very well to languages richer than pure λ-calculus. For instance, they are unsound under the presence of generative names [8] or data abstraction [9] because they apply bisimilar functions to an *identical* argument. Secondly, congruence proofs of applicative bisimulations are notoriously hard. Such proofs usually rely on Howe's method [10]. The method appears however rather subtle and fragile, for instance under the presence of generative names [8], non-determinism [10], or concurrency (e.g., [11,12]). Also, the method is very syntactical and lacks good intuition about when and why it works. Related to the problems with congruence are also the difficulties of applicative bisimulations with "up-to context" techniques (the usefulness of these techniques in higher-order languages and its problems with applicative bisimulations have been extensively studied by Lassen [7]; see also [6,13]).

Congruence proofs for bisimulations usually exploit the bisimulation method itself to establish that the closure of the bisimilarity under contexts is again a bisimulation. To see why, intuitively, this proof does not work for applicative bisimulation, consider a pair of bisimilar functions P_1, Q_1 and another pair of bisimilar terms P_2, Q_2. In an application context they yield the terms $P_1 P_2$ and $Q_1 Q_2$ which, if bisimilarity is a congruence, should be bisimilar. However the arguments for the functions P_1 and Q_1 are bisimilar, but not necessarily identical: hence we are unable to apply the bisimulation hypothesis on the functions.

The above congruence argument would work if the bisimulation were required to apply bisimilar functions to *bisimilar* arguments. This definition of bisimulation, that in this discussion we call BA-bisimulation[1], breaks the monotonicity of the generating functional (the function from relations to relations that represents the clauses of bisimulation). Indeed, BA-bisimulations in general are unsound. For instance, take the identity function $I = \lambda x. x$ and $\Sigma = EE$ where $E = \lambda x. \lambda y. xx$. Term Σ is a "purely convergent term" because it always reduces to itself when applied to any argument, regardless of the input received. Of course I and Σ should not be regarded as bisimilar, yet $\{(I, \Sigma)\}$ would be a BA-bisimulation (the only related input is the pair (I, Σ) itself, and the result of the application is again the pair) according to the definition above.

Logical bisimulations. In this paper we investigate a different approach to defining bisimilarity on functions. The main feature of our bisimulations, that we call *logical bisimulations*, is to apply related functions (i.e., functions in the bisimulation relation) P and Q to arguments in the context closure of the bisimulation, that is, arguments of the forms $C[V_1, \ldots, V_n]$ and $C[W_1, \ldots, W_n]$ for a context C and related values $(V_1, W_1), \ldots, (V_n, W_n)$. Thus the arguments can be identical terms, as for applicative bisimilarity, or related terms, as in BA-bisimulation, or combinations of these. As in BA-bisimulation, so in logical bisimulations the generating functional is non-monotone. However, as in applicative bisimilarity—and in contrast with BA-bisimulations—logical bisimulations are sound and the corresponding functional has a greatest fixed-point which coincides with contextual equivalence.

---

[1] BA indicates that the bisimilarity uses "Bisimilar Arguments".

The intuition behind the bisimulation requirement of logical bisimulations is the following. Consider an observer that is playing the bisimulation game, testing related terms. Values produced by related terms are like outputs towards the observer, who can use them at will: they have become part of the observer's *knowledge*. Thus the observer can check the consistency of such values (for instance, the outermost construct should be same). In addition, however, the observer can use them to build more complex terms (such as $C[V_1, \ldots, V_n]$ and $C[W_1, \ldots, W_n]$ above) and use them as arguments when testing pairs of related functions. Of course this power is useless if the values are first-order, since related values must then be identical. But it is relevant in a higher-order language and yields the bisimulation requirement described above.

A possible drawback of logical bisimulations over applicative bisimulations is that the set of arguments to related functions that have to be considered in the bisimulation clause is larger (since it includes also non-identical arguments). As a remedy to this, we propose the use of up-to techniques, as enhancements to the bisimulation proof method. We consider a number of such enhancements in the paper, including forms of up-to context and up-to expansion.

Another difference of logical bisimulations over applicative bisimulations (as well as most definitions of bisimulation for functions in the literature) is that we use a small-step, rather than big-step, semantics. For this reason, logical bisimulations are defined on arbitrary closed terms, rather than values. The use of small-step semantics may seem cumbersome—in particular for languages without non-determinism—because it seems to require more elements in bisimulations than big-step semantics. However, again, this disadvantage disappears by means of up-to techniques. In fact, the extension to small-step semantics often *simplifies* an equivalence proof, because we can now compare terms in the middle of evaluations without reducing them to values. Further, big-step versions of logical bisimulations will be derived as a corollary of the soundness of certain up-to techniques (precisely "up-to reduction"). Another reason for choosing a small-step semantics is that this is often required for non-determinism or concurrency.

In summary, with logical bisimulations we aim at (1) maintaining the definition of the bisimulation as simple as possible, so to facilitate proofs of its basic properties (in particular congruence and up-to-context techniques, which are notoriously hard in higher-order languages); and (2) separately developing enhancements of the bisimulation method, so as to have simple bisimilarity proofs between terms.

The bisimulation clause on functions of logical bisimulations is somehow reminiscent of logical relations, see, e.g., [14, Chapter 8] and [15]. (The analogy is stronger for the BA-bisimulations discussed earlier; we recall that in logical relations two functions are related if they map related arguments to related results.) However, logical relations represent a type-directed technique and as such remain quite different from bisimulations, which can be untyped. Logical relations work well in pure simply-typed or polymorphic λ-calculus, but they tend to become incomplete and/or require more advanced meta theory in languages with recursive types [16,17,18,19], existential types [15,17,20,19], store [20], or encryption [21], to give just a few examples.

The idea of logical bisimulations stems from bisimulations for higher-order calculi with information hiding mechanisms (such as encryption [22], data abstraction [9], and store [13]), where the use of context closures of function arguments was *necessary* because of the information hiding. In this respect, our contribution in this paper is to isolate this idea and propose it as a general method for higher-order languages. Moreover, we simplify and strengthen the method and develop its basic theory.

In this paper we consider purely functional languages, in particular untyped call-by-name and call-by-value lambda-calculi. It seems difficult to adapt logical bisimulation, at least in the form presented here, to non-functional languages; for instance, languages with information hiding constructs (e.g., for store, encryption, data abstraction) or with parallelism. To treat these languages we have added an explicit notion of environment to the bisimulations. The technical details become rather different, and can be found in [23].

2 Preliminaries

In this section, we introduce general notations and terminologies used throughout the paper. Familiarity with standard terminologies (such as free/bound variables, and α-conversion) for the λ-calculus is assumed.

We use meta-variables $M, N, P, Q, \ldots$ for terms, and $V, W, \ldots$ for values (in untyped λ-calculus the only closed values are the abstractions). We identify α-convertible terms. We write $M\{N/x\}$ for the capture-avoiding substitution of N for x in M. A term is *closed* if it contains no free variables. The set of free variables of a term M is $\mathsf{fv}(M)$. A *context* C is an expression obtained from a term by replacing some sub-terms with *holes* of the form $[\cdot]_i$. We write $C[M_1, \ldots, M_n]$ for the term obtained by replacing each occurrence of $[\cdot]_i$ in C with M_i. Note that a context may contain no holes, and therefore any term is a context. A context may bind variables in $M_1, \ldots, M_n$; for example, if $C = \lambda x. [\cdot]_1$ and $M = x$, then $C[M]$ is $\lambda x. x$, not $\lambda y. x$. The set Λ of λ-terms is defined by:

$$M, N ::= x \mid \lambda x. M \mid MN$$

We write $\Lambda^\bullet$ for the subset of closed terms.

We use meta-variables $\mathcal{R}, \mathcal{S}, \ldots$ for binary relations; $\mathcal{R}\mathcal{S}$ is the composition of $\mathcal{R}$ and $\mathcal{S}$, whereas $\mathcal{R}^\star$ is the *closure of relation $\mathcal{R}$ under contexts*, i.e.

$$\{(C[M_1, \ldots, M_n], C[N_1, \ldots, N_n]) \mid M_i \mathcal{R} N_i \text{ for each } i\}$$

By definition $\mathcal{R}^\star$ contains both R and the identity relation. By default, we restrict $\mathcal{R}^\star$ to closed terms unless noted otherwise.

Sequences $M_1, \ldots, M_n$ are often abbreviated to $\widetilde{M}$, and notations are extended to tuples componentwise. Hence, we often write $C[\widetilde{M}]$ for $C[M_1, \ldots, M_n]$, and $\widetilde{M}\mathcal{R}\widetilde{N}$ for $(M_1 \mathcal{R} N_1) \wedge \cdots \wedge (M_n \mathcal{R} N_n)$.

We have some remarks on the results in the remainder of this paper:

- Although the results are often stated for closed values only, they can be generalized to open terms in a common way. This can be done by defining an ad hoc relation—the least congruence containing $(M, (\lambda x. M)x)$ for every M—and proving its preservation under evaluation, as in Sumii-Pierce [22] and Koutavas-Wand [13]. (Alternatively, we may also consider a bisimulation between M and $(\lambda x. M)x$. The proof is straightforward in either case.) Thus properties between open terms M and N can be derived from the corresponding properties between the closed terms $\lambda \widetilde{x}. M$ and $\lambda \widetilde{x}. N$, for $\{\widetilde{x}\} \supseteq \mathsf{fv}(M) \cup \mathsf{fv}(N)$.
- The results in this paper are stated for untyped languages. Adapting them to languages with a simply-typed discipline is straightforward. (We will use a simply-typed calculus in an example.)

3   Call-by-Name λ-Calculus

The *call-by-name reduction relation* $\longrightarrow$ is the least relation over $\Lambda^\bullet$ closed under the following rules.

$$\beta: \quad (\lambda x. M)N \longrightarrow M\{N/x\} \qquad \mu: \quad \frac{M \longrightarrow M'}{MN \longrightarrow M'N}$$

We write $\Longrightarrow$ for the reflexive and transitive closure of $\longrightarrow$. The values are the terms of the form $\lambda x. M$.

3.1   Logical Bisimulations

If $\mathcal{R}$ is a relation on closed terms, then we extend it to open terms thus: if $\mathsf{fv}(M, N) = \{\widetilde{x}\}$, then $M \mathcal{R}^\circ N$ holds if for all $\widetilde{M}, \widetilde{N} \in \Lambda^\bullet$ with $\widetilde{M} \mathcal{R}^\star \widetilde{N}$ we have $M\{\widetilde{M}/\widetilde{x}\} \mathcal{R} N\{\widetilde{N}/\widetilde{x}\}$.

Definition 1 (logical bisimulation). *A relation* $\mathcal{R} \subseteq \Lambda^\bullet \times \Lambda^\bullet$ *is a* logical bisimulation *if whenever* $M \mathcal{R} N$,

1. *if* $M \longrightarrow M'$ *then* $N \Longrightarrow N'$ *and* $M' \mathcal{R} N'$;
2. *if* $M = \lambda x. M'$ *then* $N \Longrightarrow \lambda x. N'$ *and* $M' \mathcal{R}^\circ N'$;
3. *the converse of (1) and (2) above, on* N.

We write $\approx$ *for the union of all logical bisimulations, and call it* logical bisimilarity.

As $\mathcal{R}$ occurs in negative position in the definition of logical bisimulation, the existence of the *largest* bisimulation is unclear. Indeed the union of two logical bisimulations is not necessarily a logical bisimulation. We however prove below that $\approx$ itself is a bisimulation, so that it is also the largest bisimulation. We often omit "logical" in the remainder of the paper.

Remark 1. The negative occurrence of $\mathcal{R}$ in the definition of logical bisimulation breaks the monotonicity of the generating functional (the function from relations to relations that represents the clauses of bisimulation). Therefore we cannot appeal to the Knaster-Tarski's fixed point theorem for the existence of a largest bisimulation. (Such a theorem guarantees the existence of the greatest fixed point for a monotone function on a complete lattice; moreover this point coincides with the greatest post-fixed point of the function; see [24] for discussions on the theorem and on coinduction). Thus, if we take Knaster-Tarski as the justification of coinduction, then we could not call *coinductive* the proof method for logical bisimulations. However we can show that the largest logical bisimulation exists, and therefore the proof method given by logical bisimulations is sound and complete. We call the method coinductive because it has the form of standard coinductive proof methods. We thus take coinduction with a meaning broader than that given by Knaster-Tarski's theorem, namely as a notion for reasoning about functions on complete lattices that have a greatest post-fixed point.

First we prove that $\approx$ is an equivalence relation; the only non-trivial case is transitivity.

Lemma 1. *Suppose $\mathcal{R}$ is a bisimulation, $M \mathrel{\mathcal{R}} N$, and $M \Longrightarrow M'$. Then there is N' such that $N \Longrightarrow N'$ and $M' \mathrel{\mathcal{R}} N'$.*

Proof. Induction on the length of $M \Longrightarrow M'$.

Lemma 2. *Suppose $\mathcal{R}_1$ and $\mathcal{R}_2$ are bisimulations. Then also $\mathcal{R}_1 \mathcal{R}_2$ (the relational composition between them) is a bisimulation.*

Proof. We prove that $\mathcal{R}_1 \mathcal{R}_2$ is a bisimulation. As an example, consider clause (2) of the bisimulation. Thus, suppose $M \mathrel{\mathcal{R}_1 \mathcal{R}_2} N$ because $M \mathrel{\mathcal{R}_1} L \mathrel{\mathcal{R}_2} N$, and $M = \lambda x. M'$.

Since $\mathcal{R}_1$ is a bisimulation, there is L' such that $L \Longrightarrow \lambda x. L'$ and $M' \mathrel{\mathcal{R}_1^{\circ}} L'$. Using Lemma 1, since also $\mathcal{R}_2$ is a bisimulation, there is N' such that $N \Longrightarrow \lambda x. N'$ and $L' \mathrel{\mathcal{R}_2^{\circ}} N'$.

We have to prove that for all $(M_1, N_1) \in (\mathcal{R}_1 \mathcal{R}_2)^{\star}$, we have $M'\{M_1/x\} \mathrel{\mathcal{R}_1 \mathcal{R}_2} N'\{N_1/x\}$. If $(M_1, N_1) \in (\mathcal{R}_1 \mathcal{R}_2)^{\star}$, then there is a context C and terms $\widetilde{M_1'}, \widetilde{N_1'}$ with $\widetilde{M_1'} \mathrel{\mathcal{R}_1 \mathcal{R}_2} \widetilde{N_1'}$ such that $M_1 = C[\widetilde{M_1'}]$ and $N_1 = C[\widetilde{N_1'}]$. By definition of relational composition, there are $\widetilde{L_1'}$ such that $\widetilde{M_1'} \mathcal{R}_1 \widetilde{L_1'} \mathcal{R}_2 \widetilde{N_1'}$. Hence, since $\mathcal{R}_1$ and $\mathcal{R}_2$ are bisimulations, we have

$$M'\{C[\widetilde{M_1'}]/x\} \mathrel{\mathcal{R}_1} L'\{C[\widetilde{L_1'}]/x\} \text{ and } L'\{C[\widetilde{L_1'}]/x\} \mathrel{\mathcal{R}_2} N'\{C[\widetilde{N_1'}]/x\}.$$

We can therefore conclude $M'\{C[\widetilde{M_1'}]/x\} \mathrel{\mathcal{R}_1 \mathcal{R}_2} N'\{C[\widetilde{N_1'}]/x\}$.

Next we prove that $\approx$ is preserved by contexts, which allows us to conclude that $\approx$ is a congruence relation. In bisimilarities for higher-order languages, the congruence properties are usually the most delicate basic properties to establish. In contrast with proofs for applicative bisimilarity, which usually involve sophisticated techniques such as Howe's, for logical bisimilarity simple inductive reasoning on contexts suffices.

Lemma 3. *If $\mathcal{R}$ is a bisimulation, then also $\mathcal{R}^\star$ is a bisimulation.*

Proof. We prove that $\mathcal{R}^\star$ is a bisimulation. Suppose $(C[\widetilde{M}], C[\widetilde{N}]) \in \mathcal{R}^\star$ with $\widetilde{M} \mathcal{R} \widetilde{N}$. We prove clauses (1) and (2) of the bisimulation by induction on the size of C. There are three cases to consider.

The case $C = [\cdot]_i$ is immediate, using the fact that $(\mathcal{R}^\star)^\star = \mathcal{R}^\star$.

In the case $C = \lambda x.\, C'$, only clause (2) of bisimulation applies: let M_1, N_1 be the arguments of the functions, with $M_1 \mathcal{R}^\star N_1$; we have also $C'[\widetilde{M}]\{M_1/x\} \mathcal{R}^\star C'[\widetilde{N}]\{N_1/x\}$, and we are done.

It remains the case $C = C_1 C_2$, where only clause (1) of bisimulation applies. There are two possibilities of reduction for $C_1[\widetilde{M}]C_2[\widetilde{M}]$: the left-hand side $C_1[\widetilde{M}]$ reduces alone; the left-hand side is a function, say $\lambda x.\, P$, and the final derivative is $P\{C_2[\widetilde{M}]/y\}$. The first possibility is dealt with using induction. In the second one, by the induction hypothesis, we infer: $C_1[\widetilde{N}] \implies \lambda y.\, Q$ and $P (\mathcal{R}^\star)^\circ Q$. Hence $P\{C_2[\widetilde{M}]/y\}\mathcal{R}^\star Q\{C_2[\widetilde{N}]/y\}$, and we are done.

Corollary 1. $\approx$ *is a congruence relation.*

Finally, we prove that $\approx$ itself is a bisimulation, exploiting the previous results.

Lemma 4. $\approx$ *is a bisimulation.*

Proof. In the proof that $\approx$ is a bisimulation, clause (1) of Definition 1 is straightforward to handle.

We consider clause (2). Thus, suppose $\lambda x.\, M \approx N$. By definition of $\approx$, there is a bisimulation $\mathcal{R}$ such that $\lambda x.\, M \mathcal{R} N$; hence there is N' such that $N \implies \lambda x.\, N'$ and $M \mathcal{R}^\circ N'$. We have to prove that also $M \approx^\circ N'$ holds.

Take $M_1 \approx^\star N_1$; we want to show $M\{M_1/x\} \approx N'\{N_1/x\}$. If $M_1 \approx^\star N_1$, then there is a context C and terms $M_1', \ldots, M_n', N_1', \ldots, N_n'$ with $M_i' \mathcal{S}_i N_i'$ for some bisimulation $\mathcal{S}_i$ such that $M_1 = C[M_1', \ldots, M_n']$ and $N_1 = C[N_1', \ldots, N_n']$. We have:

$$M\{C[M_1', \ldots, M_n']/x\} \; \mathcal{R} \; N'\{C[M_1', \ldots, M_n']/x\} \qquad \text{(since } M \mathcal{R}^\circ N')$$
$$\mathcal{S}_1^\star \; N'\{C[N_1', M_2', \ldots, M_n']/x\}$$
$$\cdots$$
$$\mathcal{S}_n^\star \; N'\{C[N_1', , \ldots, N_{n-1}', N_n']/x\}$$

This closes the proof, because each $\mathcal{S}_i^\star$ is a bisimulation (Lemma 3) and because bisimulations are closed under composition (Lemma 2).

Example 1. We have $I_1 \approx I_2$ for $I_1 \overset{\text{def}}{=} \lambda x.\, x$ and $I_2 \overset{\text{def}}{=} \lambda x.\, (\lambda y.\, y)x$, by taking $\mathcal{R} \overset{\text{def}}{=} \{(M, N), (M, (\lambda y.\, y)N) \mid M \, S^\star \, N\}$, for $S \overset{\text{def}}{=} \{(I_1, I_2)\}$. Note that the singleton relation $\{(I_1, I_2)\}$ by itself is not a logical bisimulation because of the implicit use of $\mathcal{R}^\star$ in clause (2) of bisimulation. Burdens like this are frequent in bisimulation proofs, and will be removed by the up-to techniques described later in this section. Specifically, the singleton relation $\{(I_1, I_2)\}$ will be a logical bisimulation "up to reduction and contexts".

3.2 Up-to Techniques

We show a few "up-to" techniques, as enhancements of the bisimulation proof method. They allow us to prove bisimulation results using relations that in general are not themselves bisimulations, but are contained in a bisimulation. Rather than presenting complete definitions, we indicate the modifications to the bisimulation clauses (Definition 1). For this, it is however convenient to expand the abbreviation $M' \mathcal{R}^\circ N'$ in clause (2) of the definition, which thus becomes "for all $(M_1, N_1) \in \mathcal{R}^\star$ it holds that $M'\{M_1/x\} \mathcal{R} N'\{N_1/x\}$", and to describe the modifications with respect to this expanded clause.

We also omit the statements of soundness of the techniques.

Up-to bisimilarity. This technique introduces a (limited) use of $\approx$ on tested terms. This can allow us to avoid bisimulations with elements that, behaviorally, are the same. In clause (1), we replace "$M' \mathcal{R} N'$" with "$M' \mathcal{R} \approx N'$"; in (2), we replace "$M'\{M_1/x\} \mathcal{R} N'\{N_1/x\}$" with "$M'\{M_1/x\} \approx \mathcal{R} \approx N'\{N_1/x\}$". We cannot strengthen up-to bisimilarity by using $\approx$ also on the left-hand side of $\mathcal{R}$ in clause (1), for the technique would be unsound; this is reminiscent of the problems of up-to bisimilarity in standard small-step bisimilarity for concurrency. [25].

Up-to reduction. This technique exploits the confluent property of reduction so to replace tested terms with derivatives of them. When reduction is confluent this technique avoids the main disadvantage of small-step bisimulations over the big-step ones, namely the need of considering each single derivative of a tested term.

In clause (1), we replace "$M' \mathcal{R} N'$" with "there are M'', N'' with $M' \Longrightarrow M''$ and $N' \Longrightarrow N''$ such that $M'' \mathcal{R} N''$"; similarly, in (2) we replace "$M'\{M_1/x\} \mathcal{R} N'\{N_1/x\}$" with "there are M'', N'' with $M'\{M_1/x\} \Longrightarrow M''$ and $N'\{N_1/x\} \Longrightarrow N''$ such that $M'' \mathcal{R} N''$".

The technique allows us to derive the soundness of the "big-step" version of logical bisimulation, in which clauses (1) and (2) are unified by requiring that

– if $M \Longrightarrow \lambda x. M'$ then $N \Longrightarrow \lambda x. N'$ and $M' \mathcal{R}^\circ N'$.

Up-to expansion. In concurrency, a useful auxiliary relation for up-to techniques is the *expansion relation*. (A similar relation is Sands' improvement for functional languages [6]). We adapt here the concept of expansion to the λ-calculus. We write $M \Longrightarrow_n M'$ if M reduces to M' in n steps. We present the big-step version of expansion, since we will use it in examples. As for bisimilarity, so for expansion the small-step version is equally possible. Similarly, the up-to techniques described for bisimilarity can also be used to enhance expansion proofs, and then the big-step version of expansion below can be derived from the small-step version plus a "weighted" version of up-to reduction.

Definition 2. *A relation $\mathcal{R}$ is an* expansion relation *if whenever $M \mathcal{R} N$,*

1. $M \Longrightarrow_m \lambda x. M'$ implies $N \Longrightarrow_n \lambda x. N'$ with $m \leq n$, and $M' \mathcal{R}^\circ N'$;

2. The converse, i.e., $N \Longrightarrow_n \lambda x. N'$ *implies* $M \Longrightarrow_m \lambda x. M'$ *with* $m \leq n$ *and* $M' \mathcal{R}^\circ N'$;

Expansion, *written* $\preceq$, *is the union of all expansion relations.*

Thus if $M \longrightarrow M'$ then $M \succeq M'$ holds, but not necessarily $M' \succeq M$.

Lemma 5. $\preceq$ *is a pre-congruence and is an expansion relation itself.*

Proof. Similar to the proofs for $\approx$.

In the *bisimulation up-to expansion* technique, in Definition 1, we replace the occurrence of $\mathcal{R}$ in clause (1), and that in clause (2), with $\succeq \mathcal{R} \preceq$.

Since $\longrightarrow \subseteq \preceq$, the up-to expansion technique subsumes, and is more powerful than, up-to reduction. Still, up-to reduction is interesting because it can be simpler to combine with other techniques and to adapt to richer languages.

Up-to values. Using up-to expansion, and exploiting the basic properties of expansion (notably pre-congruence, and the fact that any pair of closed divergent terms is in the expansion relation) we can prove that the quantification over $\mathcal{R}^\star$ in clause (2) can be restricted to $\widehat{\mathcal{R}}^\star$, where $\widehat{\mathcal{R}}$ indicates the subset of $\mathcal{R}$ with only pairs of values.

Up-to contexts. This technique allows us to cancel a common context in tested terms, requiring instead that only the arguments of such context be pairwise related. Thus in clauses (1) and (2) the final occurrence of $\mathcal{R}$ is replaced by $R^\star$.

Up-to full contexts. The difference between "up-to contexts" and "up-to full contexts" is that in the latter the contexts that are cancelled can also bind variables of the arguments. As a consequence, however, a relation for the "up-to full contexts" is on open terms. Clauses (1) and (2) of Definition 1 are used only on closed terms, but with the last occurrence of $\mathcal{R}$ in each clause replaced by $\mathcal{R}^\star$. We add a new clause for open terms:

– If $M \mathcal{R} N$ then also $M \mathcal{R}^\circ N$ (i.e., if $\widetilde{x} = \mathsf{fv}(M, N)$, then for all $(\widetilde{M_1}, \widetilde{N_1}) \in \mathcal{R}^\star$, it holds that $M\{\widetilde{M_1}/\widetilde{x}\} \mathcal{R}^\star N\{\widetilde{N_1}/\widetilde{x}\}$).

Again, the up-to full contexts subsumes, and is more powerful than, up-to contexts, but the latter is simpler to establish and use.

Remark 2. An up-to-full-contexts technique similar to the one above has been proposed by Lassen [26, Lemma 7] and proved sound with respect to applicative bisimilarity. (Lassen was actually hoping to prove the soundness of the up-to-full-contexts technique for applicative bisimilarity itself, but failed; indeed forms of up-to contexts for applicative bisimilarities are notoriously hard). Further, Lassen's paper contains a number of interesting examples, such as least-fixed point properties of recursion and a syntactic minimal invariance property, that are proved for applicative bisimilarity by making use of up-to techniques. Similar proofs can be given for logical bisimilarity.

Big-step versions and combinations of up-to. The previous techniques can be combined together, in the expected manner. Further, for each technique both the small-step and the big-step versions are possible. We give two examples. The (small-step) *"up-to expansion and full contexts"* is defined as "up-to full contexts", but expansion appears in the conclusions. Thus clause (1) becomes:

– if $M, N \in \Lambda^\bullet$ and $M \longrightarrow M'$ then $N \Longrightarrow N'$ and $M' \succeq \mathcal{R}^\star \preceq N'$

Clause (2) is modified similarly; and in the clause for open terms, "$M\{\widetilde{M_1}/\widetilde{x}\} \, \mathcal{R}^\star$ $N\{\widetilde{N_1}/\widetilde{x}\}$" is replaced by "$M\{\widetilde{M_1}/\widetilde{x}\} \succeq \mathcal{R}^\star \preceq N\{\widetilde{N_1}/\widetilde{x}\}$".

In the *big-step up-to expansion and context*, the bisimulation clause becomes:

– if $M \Longrightarrow \lambda x. M'$ then $N \Longrightarrow \lambda x. N'$ and for all $(M_1, N_1) \in \mathcal{R}^\star$ it holds that $M'\{M_1/x\} \succeq \mathcal{R}^\star \preceq N'\{N_1/x\}$.
$$(*)$$

Of course, in general the more powerful the up-to is, the more work is required in its proof of soundness.

3.3   Contextual Equivalence

Definition 3 (contextual equivalence). *Terms M and N are contextually equivalent, written $M \equiv N$, if, for any context C such that $C[M]$ and $C[N]$ are closed, $C[M] \Downarrow$ iff $C[N] \Downarrow$.*

Theorem 1 (soundness and completeness of bisimulation). *Relations $\equiv$ and $\approx$ coincide.*

Proof. For closed terms, we prove that $M \equiv N$ implies $M \approx N$ by showing that $\equiv$ is a bisimulation; the proof is simple, proving first that $\equiv$ is an equivalence, that $\equiv^\star \, = \, \equiv$ and that reduction is included in $\equiv$. The converse implication ($M \approx N$ implies $M \equiv N$) immediately follows from the congruence of $\approx$. The result for open terms is obtained as discussed in Section 2.

3.4   Example 1

This example gives the proof of the equivalence between the two fixed-point combinators:

$$Y \stackrel{\text{def}}{=} \lambda y. y(Dy(Dy))$$
$$\Theta \stackrel{\text{def}}{=} \Delta\Delta$$

where

$$\Delta \stackrel{\text{def}}{=} \lambda x. \lambda y. (y(xxy))$$
$$D \stackrel{\text{def}}{=} \lambda y. \lambda x. y(xx)$$

We establish $Y \approx \Theta$ using a relation $\mathcal{R}$ that has just one pair, namely (Y, Θ), and proving that $\mathcal{R}$ is a big-step logical bisimulation up to expansion and context. First, we note that, for any term M,

$$DM(DM) \succeq YM \tag{1}$$

This holds because $DM(DM) \Longrightarrow_2 M(DM(DM))$ and $YM \Longrightarrow_1 M(DM(DM))$. We now check the bisimilarity clause (*) on the pair (Y, Θ). Term Y is a function; the other term, Θ, becomes a function as follows:

$$\Theta \longrightarrow \lambda y. (y(\Delta\Delta y)) \overset{\text{def}}{=} \Theta_1$$

Consider now any argument $M \; \mathcal{R}^\star \; N$ for Y and Θ_1. The results are $M(DM(DM))$ and $N(\Delta\Delta N)$, respectively. Now, by (1), it holds that

$$M(DM(DM)) \succeq M(YM)$$

and we are done, since $M(YM) \; \mathcal{R}^\star \; N(\Delta\Delta N) = N(\Theta N)$.

4   Call-by-Value λ-Calculus

The *one-step call-by-value reduction relation* $\longrightarrow \; \subseteq \Lambda^\bullet \times \Lambda^\bullet$ is defined by these rules:

$$\beta_{\mathrm{v}} : \; (\lambda x. M)V \longrightarrow M\{V/x\}$$

$$\mu : \; \frac{M \longrightarrow M'}{MN \longrightarrow M'N} \qquad \nu_{\mathrm{v}} : \; \frac{N \longrightarrow N'}{VN \longrightarrow VN'}$$

We highlight what changes in the theory for call-by-name of the previous sections. For a relation $\mathcal{R}$ we write $\mathcal{R}^{\widehat{\star}}$ for the subset of $\mathcal{R}^\star$ that only relate pairs of values.

- The input for two functions must be values. Therefore, in the definition of bisimulation, the input terms M_1 and N_1 should be in $\mathcal{R}^{\widehat{\star}}$ (rather than $\mathcal{R}^\star$). A similar modification on the quantification over inputs of functions is needed in all definitions of bisimulations and up-to techniques.
- In clause (2) of bisimilarity we add the requirement that the two functions themselves are related, i.e., $\lambda x. M' \; \mathcal{R} \; \lambda x. N'$. Roughly, this is needed because, in call-by-value, by definition, function arguments are evaluated before applications. The proof of congruence itself for bisimilarity requires this addition. We will nevertheless be able to remove the requirement later, exploiting appropriate up-to techniques.

Remark 3. To make the definition of logical bisimulation uniform for call-by-name and call-by-value, the requirement "$\lambda x. M' \; \mathcal{R} \; \lambda x. N'$" could also be added in call-by-name. This would not affect the proofs of the result presented. As in call-by-value, the requirement could then be removed by means of appropriate up-to techniques.

For ease of reference, we report the complete definition of bisimulation. If $\mathcal{R}$ is a relation on closed terms, and $\mathsf{fv}(M, N) = \widetilde{x}$, then $M \; \mathcal{R}^{\widehat{\circ}} \; N$ holds if for all $\widetilde{V}, \widetilde{W}$ with $\widetilde{V} \; \mathcal{R}^{\widehat{\star}} \; \widetilde{W}$ it holds that $M\{\widetilde{V}/\widetilde{x}\} \; \mathcal{R} \; N\{\widetilde{W}/\widetilde{x}\}$.

Definition 4. *A relation* $\mathcal{R} \subseteq \Lambda^\bullet \times \Lambda^\bullet$ *is a* logical bisimulation *if whenever* $M \; \mathcal{R} \; N,$

1. *if $M \longrightarrow M'$ then $N \Longrightarrow N'$ and $M' \mathcal{R} N'$*
2. *if $M = \lambda x.\, M'$ then $N \Longrightarrow \lambda x.\, N'$ and*
   (a) $\lambda x.\, M' \mathcal{R} \lambda x.\, N'$
   (b) $M' \mathcal{R}^{\hat{\circ}} N'$
3. *the converse of (1) and (2) above.*

With these modifications, all definitions and results in Section 3 are valid for call-by-value. The structure of the proof also remains the same, with the expected differences in technical details due to the change in reduction strategy. It is however worth revisiting the proof of Lemma 3; although the structure of the proof is the same, the few differences are important, in particular to understand the requirement (2.a) in Definition 4.

Lemma 6. *If $\mathcal{R}$ is a bisimulation, then also $\mathcal{R}^{\star}$ is a bisimulation.*

Proof. As before we prove that $\mathcal{R}^{\star}$ is a bisimulation reasoning by induction on the size of the common contexts of terms $(C[\widetilde{M}], C[\widetilde{N}]) \in \mathcal{R}^{\star}$ with $\widetilde{M} \mathcal{R} \widetilde{N}$. In the case $C = [\cdot]_i$ we use the fact that $(\mathcal{R}^{\star})^{\hat{\star}} = \mathcal{R}^{\hat{\star}}$.

The interesting case is $C = C_1 C_2$ when both $C_1[\widetilde{M}]$ and $C_2[\widetilde{M}]$ are values, say $\lambda x.\, P$ and V, respectively. By the induction hypothesis, we infer:

$$C_2[\widetilde{N}] \Longrightarrow W,$$

for some W with $V \mathcal{R}^{\hat{\star}} W$. (Note that here we exploit the requirement (2.a) of Definition 4.) Similarly we infer $C_1[\widetilde{N}] \Longrightarrow \lambda x.\, Q$, for some Q with $P (\mathcal{R}^{\star})^{\hat{\circ}} Q$. This implies, since $V \mathcal{R}^{\hat{\star}} W$, that $P\{V/x\} \mathcal{R}^{\star} Q\{W/x\}$.

4.1   Up-to Techniques

All up-to techniques described for call-by-name are valid also for call-by-value, modulo the technical differences in definitions that we have discussed in the previous subsection. In addition, however, we can also derive the soundness (and completeness) of a form of logical bisimulation with big-step restricted to values (in call-by-value, applicative bisimulation is normally defined this way) and that we call *value big-step logical bisimulation.*

Definition 5. *A relation $\mathcal{E}$ on closed values is a* value big-step logical bisimulation *if for all $V \mathcal{E} W$ and $V_1 \mathcal{E}^{\hat{\star}} W_1$, if $V V_1 \Longrightarrow V'$ then there is W' such that $W W_1 \Longrightarrow W'$ and $V'\mathcal{E} W'$; and the converse, on the reductions from W.*

We also provide a further up-to technique, that we call *up-to environment* whereby clause (2.a) of bisimilarity (the requirement $\lambda x.\, M' \mathcal{R} \lambda x.\, N'$) is removed. Its soundness is proved as follows. If $\mathcal{R}$ is a bisimulation up-to environment, define

$$\mathcal{R}_1 \stackrel{\text{def}}{=} \{(\lambda x.\, M, \lambda x.\, N) \mid \exists M', N'.\, M'\mathcal{R}N' \text{ and } M' \Longrightarrow \lambda x.\, M, N' \Longrightarrow \lambda x.\, N\}$$

and then take

$$\mathcal{R}_2 \stackrel{\text{def}}{=} \mathcal{R} \cup \mathcal{R}_1$$

We then show that $\mathcal{R}_2$ is a bisimulation up-to bisimilarity.

4.2   Example 2

This example uses a simply-typed call-by-value extended with integers, an operator for subtraction ($\hat{-}$), a conditional, and a fixed-point operator Y. The reduction rule for Y is $YV \longrightarrow V(\lambda x. YVx)$. As mentioned in Section 2, it is straightforward to accommodate such additions in the theory developed. (We could also encode arithmetic into the untyped calculus and adapt the example, but it would become harder to read.) Let P, Q be the terms

$$P \stackrel{\text{def}}{=} \lambda f. \lambda g. \lambda x. \lambda y. \text{ if } x = 0 \text{ then } y \text{ else } g(f\, g\,(x \hat{-} 1)\, y)$$
$$Q \stackrel{\text{def}}{=} \lambda f. \lambda g. \lambda x. \lambda y. \text{ if } x = 0 \text{ then } y \text{ else } f\, g\,(x \hat{-} 1)\,(g\, y)$$

Let $F_1 \stackrel{\text{def}}{=} \lambda z. Y\, P\, z$ and $F_2 \stackrel{\text{def}}{=} \lambda z. Y\, Q\, z$.

The terms $F_1\, g\, n\, m$ and $F_2\, g\, n\, m$ (where g is a function value from integers to integers and n, m are integers) computes $g^n(m)$ if $n \geq 0$, diverge otherwise. In both cases, however, the computations made are different. We show $F_1\, g\, n\, m \approx F_2\, g\, n\, m$ using an up-to technique for logical bisimulations. For this, we use the following relation $\mathcal{R}$:

$$\{(g^r(F_1\, g\, n\, m), F_2\, g\, n\, (g^r(m))) \mid$$
$$r, m, n \in \mathbf{Z}, r \geq 0, \text{ and } g \text{ is a closed value of type int} \to \text{int}\}.$$

We show that $\mathcal{R}$ is a bisimulation up-to expansion and context.

Let us consider the pair $(g^r(F_1\, g\, n\, m), F_2\, g\, n\, (g^r(m)))$. If $n = 0$, then we have:

$$g^r(F_1\, g\, 0\, m) \longrightarrow \Longrightarrow g^r(m)$$
$$\mathcal{R}^*$$
$$F_2\, g\, 0\, (g^r(m)) \longrightarrow \succeq\ g^r(m)$$

So, the required condition holds. If $n \neq 0$, then we have

$$g^r(F_1\, g\, n\, m) \longrightarrow \Longrightarrow g^r(g(F_1\, g\, (n \hat{-} 1)\, m))$$
$$\succeq\quad g^{r+1}(F_1\, g\, (n-1)\, m).$$

and

$$F_2\, g\, n\, (g^r(m)) \longrightarrow \succeq F_2\, g\, (n \hat{-} 1)\, (g(g^r(m)))$$
$$\succeq\quad F_2\, g\, (n-1)\, (g^{r+1}(m)).$$

Here, the first $\succeq$ comes from the fact that y is not copied inside the function F_2. We are done, since

$$(g^{r+1}(F_1\, g\, (n-1)\, m), F_2\, g\, (n-1)\, (g^{r+1}(m))) \in \mathcal{R}.$$

The example above makes use of key features of logical bisimulations: the ability to compare terms in the middle of evaluations, and (some of) its up-to techniques.

5 Data Hiding and Concurrency

To handle higher-order calculi with information hiding mechanisms, such as store, encryption, data abstraction, we have to enrich logical bisimulations with environments, which roughly collect the partial knowledge on the transmitted values, acquired by an observer interacting with the terms. The same happens in concurrency, where bisimulations with forms of environment have been first proposed, for instance to handle information hiding due to types [27,28] and encryption [29] (this in π-calculus-like languages; information hiding in higher-order concurrency remains largely unexplored). Bisimulations with environments have also been used in λ-calculi with information hiding mechanisms (such as encryption [22], data abstraction [9], and store [13]); as pointed out in the introductions, these works have motivated and inspired ours. The resulting form of bisimulation, that we have called *environmental bisimulation*, seems robust. The technical details—which are non-trivial—are presented in [23].

6 Conclusions

In this paper we have developed the basic theory of logical bisimulations and tested it on a few representative higher-order calculi.

Bisimulation and co-inductive techniques are known to represent a hard problem in higher-order languages. While we certainly would not claim that logical bisimulations are definitely better than applicative bisimulations or other co-inductive techniques in the literature (indeed, probably a single *best* bisimulation for this does not exist), we believe it is important to explore different approaches and understand their relative merits. This paper reports our initial experiments with logical bisimulations. More experiments, both with concrete examples and with a broader spectrum of languages, are needed.

Acknowledgment

We would like to thank Søren B. Lassen for comments.

References

1. Morris, Jr., J.H.: Lambda-Calculus Models of Programming Languages. PhD thesis, Massachusetts Institute of Technology (1968)
2. Abramsky, S.: The lazy lambda calculus. In: Turner, D.A. (ed.) Research Topics in Functional Programming, pp. 65–117. Addison-Wesley, Reading (1990)
3. Gordon, A.D.: Functional Programming and Input/Output. PhD thesis, University of Cambridge (1993)
4. Gordon, A.D., Rees, G.D.: Bisimilarity for a first-order calculus of objects with subtyping. In: Proceedings of the 23rd ACM SIGPLAN-SIGACT Symposium on Principles of Programming Languages, pp. 386–395. ACM Press, New York (1996)

5. Pitts, A.: Operationally-based theories of program equivalence. In: Pitts, A.M., Dybjer, P. (eds.) Semantics and Logics of Computation. Publications of the Newton Institute, pp. 241–298. Cambridge University Press, Cambridge (1997)
6. Sands, D.: Improvement theory and its applications. In: Gordon, A.D., Pitts, A.M. (eds.) Higher Order Operational Techniques in Semantics. Publications of the Newton Institute, pp. 275–306. Cambridge University Press, Cambridge (1998)
7. Lassen, S.B.: Relational Reasoning about Functions and Nondeterminism. PhD thesis, Department of Computer Science, University of Aarhus (1998)
8. Jeffrey, A., Rathke, J.: Towards a theory of bisimulation for local names. In: 14th Annual IEEE Symposium on Logic in Computer Science, pp. 56–66. IEEE Computer Society Press, Los Alamitos (1999)
9. Sumii, E., Pierce, B.C.: A bisimulation for type abstraction and recursion. In: Proceedings of the 32nd ACM SIGPLAN-SIGACT Symposium on Principles of Programming Languages, pp. 63–74. ACM Press, New York (2005)
10. Howe, D.J.: Proving congruence of bisimulation in functional programming languages. Information and Computation 124(2), 103–112 (1996)
11. Ferreira, W., Hennessy, M., Jeffrey, A.: A theory of weak bisimulation for core CML. Journal of Functional Programming 8(5), 447–491 (1998)
12. Godskesen, J.C., Hildebrandt, T.: Extending Howe's method to early bisimulations for typed mobile embedded resources with local names. In: Ramanujam, R., Sen, S. (eds.) FSTTCS 2005. LNCS, vol. 3821, pp. 140–151. Springer, Heidelberg (2005)
13. Koutavas, V., Wand, M.: Small bisimulations for reasoning about higher-order imperative programs. In: Proceedings of the 33rd ACM SIGPLAN-SIGACT Symposium on Principles of Programming Languages, pp. 141–152. ACM Press, New York (2006)
14. Mitchell, J.C.: Foundations for Programming Languages. MIT Press, Cambridge (1996)
15. Pitts, A.: Typed operational reasoning. In: Pierce, B.C. (ed.) Advanced Topics in Types and Programming Languages, pp. 245–289. MIT Press, Cambridge (2005)
16. Birkedal, L., Harper, R.: Relational interpretations of recursive types in an operational setting. Information and Computation 155(1–2), 3–63 (1999) Summary appeared in TACS 1997, LNCS, vol. 1281, pp. 458–490. Springer, Heidelberg (1997)
17. Crary, K., Harper, R.: Syntactic logical relations for polymorphic and recursive types. In: Computation, Meaning, and Logic: Articles dedicated to Gordon Plotkin. ENTCS, vol. 172, pp. 259–299. Elsevier Science, Amsterdam (2007)
18. Appel, A.W., McAllester, D.: An indexed model of recursive types for foundational proof-carrying code. ACM Transactions on Programming Languages and Systems 23(5), 657–683 (2001)
19. Ahmed, A.: Step-indexed syntactic logical relations for recursive and quantified types. In: 15th European Symposium on Programming, pp. 69–83 (2006)
20. Ahmed, A., Appel, A.W., Virga, R.: An indexed model of impredicative polymorphism and mutable references (2003), http://www.cs.princeton.edu/~amal/papers/impred.pdf
21. Sumii, E., Pierce, B.C.: Logical relations for encryption. Journal of Computer Security 11(4), 521–554 (2003) (extended abstract appeared) In: 14th IEEE Computer Security Foundations Workshop, pp. 256–269 (2001)
22. Sumii, E., Pierce, B.C.: A bisimulation for dynamic sealing. Theoretical Computer Science 375(1–3), 169–192 (2007) (extended abstract appeared) In: Proceedings of the 31st ACM SIGPLAN-SIGACT Symposium on Principles of Programming Languages, pp. 161–172 (2004)

23. Sangiorgi, D., Kobayashi, N., Sumii, E.: Environmental bisimulations for higher-order languages. In: 22nd Annual IEEE Symposium on Logic in Computer Science, IEEE Computer Society Press, Los Alamitos (2007)
24. Sangiorgi, D.: On the origins of bisimulation, coinduction, and fixed points. Draft (May 2007)
25. Milner, R.: Communication and Concurrency. Prentice-Hall, Englewood Cliffs (1989)
26. Lassen, S.B.: Relational reasoning about contexts. In: Gordon, A.D., Pitts, A.M. (eds.) Higher Order Operational Techniques in Semantics. Publications of the Newton Institute, pp. 91–135. Cambridge University Press, Cambridge (1998)
27. Boreale, M., Sangiorgi, D.: Bisimulation in name-passing calculi without matching. In: 13th Annual IEEE Symposium on Logic in Computer Science, pp. 165–175. IEEE Computer Society Press, Los Alamitos (1998)
28. Pierce, B.C., Sangiorgi, D.: Behavioral equivalence in the polymorphic pi-calculus. Journal of the ACM 47(3), 531–586 (2000) (extended abstract appeared) In: Proceedings of the 24th ACM SIGPLAN-SIGACT Symposium on Principles of Programming Languages, pp. 531–584 (1997)
29. Boreale, M., De Nicola, R., Pugliese, R.: Proof techniques for cryptographic processes. SIAM Journal on Computing 31(3), 947–986(2002) (preliminary version appeared) In: 14th Annual IEEE Symposium on Logic in Computer Science, pp. 157–166 (1999)

Efficient State Space Reduction for Automata by Fair Simulation[*]

Jin Yi[1,2] and Wenhui Zhang[1]

[1] Laboratory of Computer Science,
Institute of Software, Chinese Academy of Sciences, Beijing, China
[2] Graduate University of the Chinese Academy of Sciences, Beijing, China
{yijin,zwh}@ios.ac.cn

Abstract. State space reduction for automata is important to automata-theoretic model checking. Optimizing automata by simulation relation is a practical method. We propose an approach to simplify Büchi automata by fair simulation, which is based on integrating the method of [6] and conditions of [7]. The approach can optimize an automaton without changing the language of each state and apply the optimization immediately after finding one pair of states with fair simulation equivalence. The experimental result shows our approach needs less time than that of [6].

1 Introduction

State space reduction for automata is important to automata-theoretic model checking. For LTL model checking, there are two possibilities, one is to simplify the property automaton transformed from a formula or provided by an user, the other is to optimize the transformation procedure from an LTL formula to an automaton [1]. Simulation relation is a pre-order relation of states and can be computed in polynomial time, therefore most of automata optimizations use the simulation method.

The general simulation notion for LTS (Label Transition System) in [2] has been studied thoroughly. Considering the automaton's accepting condition, we get the following simulation concepts: direct simulation [3], delayed simulation [4] and fair simulation [5]. These simulations can be used to reduce state space of Büchi automata [4,6,7], generalized Büchi automata [8], and alternating automata. Fair simulation has the least restriction on the acceptance condition in the above simulation concepts for automata. Although fair simulation by itself is not a sufficient condition for collapsing two states or deleting one transition without affecting the original language, the experimental result in [6] shows that given a Büchi automata, there are more pairs of states with fair simulation than that of direct or delayed simulation, and according to it, we can reduce states and transitions safely.

---

[*] Supported by the National Natural Science Foundation of China under Grant No. 60573012 and 60421001, and the National Grand Fundamental Research 973 Program of China under Grant No. 2002cb312200.

F. Arbab and M. Sirjani (Eds.): FSEN 2007, LNCS 4767, pp. 380–387, 2007.

In our paper, we also use fair simulation to minimize Büchi automata, the goal is to efficiently reduce the number of states and transitions by fair simulation. We propose an approach based on integrating the method of [6] and conditions of [7], such that each state in the reduced automaton has the same language as that of the corresponding state in the original. Moreover, we can apply the optimization technique immediately after finding a pair of states with fair simulation equivalence. Since we find each pair with fair simulation from the reduced automaton thus our approach requires less time than the method which needs finding all candidates before applying optimization.

Section 2 is the background knowledge. Section 3 gives theoretical basis for our approach. Section 4 describes the whole optimization procedure. In Section 5, the experimental result shows the efficiency of our approach. Concluding remarks are given in Section 6.

2   Preliminaries

Definition 1. *A Büchi automaton is a tuple* $A = \langle Q, \Sigma, s_0, \Delta, F \rangle$ *where* Q *is a finite set of states,* Σ *is the input alphabet,* $s_0 \in Q$ *is the initial state,* $F \subseteq Q$ *is the set of accepting states,* $\Delta \subseteq Q \times \Sigma \times Q$ *is the transition relation.*

A run of A on an infinite word $\alpha = \alpha(0)\alpha(1) \cdots$ is a sequence $r = r(0)r(1) \cdots$ such that $r(0) = s_0$, and for every $i \geq 0$, $(r(i), \alpha(i), r(i+1)) \in \Delta$. Let $inf(r)$ be the set of states that r visits infinitely often. If $inf(r) \cap F \neq \emptyset$, then the run r is an *accepting run* and α is in the language of A. The language of A is denoted by $L(A)$. For convenience, we write $q \in A$ for q being a reachable state of A. We write Q^A, Δ^A, F^A for respectively the set of states of A, the set of transition relations of A, and the set of accepting states of A. If $A = \langle Q, \Sigma, s_0, \Delta, F \rangle$ is an automaton and $q \in Q$, then $A[q]$ denotes the modified automaton $\langle Q, \Sigma, q, \Delta, F \rangle$. In our paper, the language of q of A means the language of $A[q]$.

Now we give the definition of fair simulation from the game perspective [4]. Let $q_0 \in A$ and $q'_0 \in A'$, fair simulation game $G^f_{A,A'}(q_0, q'_0)$ is played by two players: Spoiler and Duplicator. At the first round, Spoiler puts a red pebble on q_0 while Duplicator puts a blue pebble on q'_0. Suppose in the ith round, Spoiler is in q_i, and moves the pebble to q_{i+1} according to $(q_i, \alpha_i, q_{i+1}) \in \Delta^A$, Duplicator must have a matching transition $(q'_i, \alpha_i, q'_{i+1}) \in \Delta^{A'}$ to move the pebble from q'_i to q'_{i+1}. If someone cannot move, then the game halts and the one who cannot move loses. Otherwise, there are two infinite paths $\pi = q_0...q_i...$ and $\pi' = q'_0...q'_i...$, we call (π, π') an outcome of the game. Then the outcome is winning for Duplicator iff there are infinitely many j in π' such that $q'_j \in F^{A'}$, or there are finitely many i in π such that $q_i \in F^A$.

A strategy for Duplicator is a partial function $f : Q(Q'\Sigma Q)^* \to Q'$. It determines the next move of Duplicator according to the history of the play. That is, $f(q_0) = q'_0$ and $q'_j = f(q_0 q'_0 a_0 q_1 q'_1 a_1 \cdots a_{j-1} q_j)$ where $(q_i, a_i, q_{i+1}) \in \Delta^A$ and $(q'_i, a_i, q'_{i+1}) \in \Delta^{A'}$ for $i < j$. A strategy for Duplicator is a winning strategy if whenever $\pi = q_0 a_0 q_1 \cdots$ is a run of A and $\pi' = q'_0 a_0 q'_1 \cdots$ is a run defined by $q'_{i+1} = f(q_0 q'_0 a_0 q_1 q'_1 \cdots a_i q_{i+1})$, then (π, π') is winning for Duplicator.

Definition 2. *[4] Let $q \in A$ and $q' \in A'$, q' fair simulates q if there is a winning strategy for Duplicator in $G^f_{A,A'}(q,q')$. We denote such relation by $q \leq^f q'$.*

For convenience, we use $q \sim^f q'$ to denote $q' \leq^f q'$ and $q' \leq^f q$.

Proposition 1. *[4] Let $q \in A$, $q_1 \in A_1$ and $q' \in A'$ (1)if $q \leq^f q_1$ and $q_1 \leq^f q'$, then $q \leq^f q'$ (2)if $q \leq^f q'$, then $L(A[q]) \subseteq L(A'[q'])$*

Now we give the definition of parity game which can be used to represent fair simulation.

Definition 3. *[9] A parity game graph is a tuple $G = \langle V, V_0, V_1, E, p \rangle$, where V is the set of vertexes, V_0 and V_1 are two disjoint sets such that $V = V_0 \cup V_1$, $E \subseteq V \times V$ is the set of edges, and p is a priority function that maps V to $\{0, ..., d-1\}$, $d \in \mathbf{N}$.*

There are two players: One and Zero in G. At the beginning, Zero puts a pebble on v_0, then the players play the game according to the following rule: if the pebble is currently on v_i, and $v_i \in V_0(V_1)$, Zero(One) moves the pebble to the next position v_{i+1}, where $(v_i, v_{i+1}) \in E$. The *winning conditions* which judge the winner of a play are: (1) If a player cannot move the pebble, then this player loses and this is a finite play in G. (2) Otherwise, there is an infinite path $\pi = v_0 v_1 \cdots$ in G. We denote by $inf(\pi)$ the set of vertexes that appear infinitely in π, and $\forall v_i \in inf(\pi)$, $p(v_i)$ is the priority of v_i. Let k_π be the minimal number of all $p(v_i)$. Then Zero wins the play if k_π is even, whereas One wins if k_π is odd.

Given two Büchi automata A_1, A_2, we can represent fair simulation by a parity game with three priorities [4]. Thus the game between One and Zero on G_{A_1,A_2} represents the fair simulation game between Spoiler and Duplicator on $G^f_{A_1,A_2}$. Therefore One represents Spoiler, and Zero represents Duplicator.

3   Reduction of States and Transitions

[6] provided an approach to reduce state space of Büchi automata by fair simulation. First it finds all pairs of states with fair simulation, which are candidates for merging states and deleting transitions. Second according to each candidate, it optimizes the automaton and checks whether this optimization is correct, i.e. whether there exists a fair simulation equivalence between the initial state of the reduced automaton A' and that of the original automaton A. One of important contributions of this approach is that it does not create a parity game graph $G_{A,A'}$ or $G_{A'A}$ for each candidate when checking the correctness of the optimization, $G_{A,A'}$ or $G_{A'A}$ is implemented by adding or deleting the edges from the game graph $G_{A,A}$. Therefore it is an efficient approach.

However, there exist two disadvantages in this approach. The first one is that after each optimization, it only guarantees that the language of the initial state of A' is the same as that of A, the language of other states of A' may not be the same as that of the states of A. Then we can't use this method to reduce the state space of a Büchi automaton as a model of some system, because we may need to verify the system from any given state, therefore we must preserve the langauge of every state after optimization.

The second is that it must find all candidates in advance. However, the method that simplifies the automaton as soon as a candidate is detected is more efficient, because if merging or deleting successes at this time, then at the next time, we can find a candidate from a new Büchi automaton with fewer states or transitions.

3.1   Merging and Deleting States

In this subsection, we first introduce a criterion to judge the correctness of merging two states, base on this criterion, we prove the language of each state in the reduced automaton keeps unchanged. Then we prove that deleting one state directly by the condition in [7] also has this property. Additionally, the new reduced automaton constructed by above two methods preserves the fair simulation relation of the original automaton.

Merging Two States.   For convenience, we use $[s_1, s_2]$ to denote a new state in A_m which is an automaton created by merging s_1 and s_2, where (s_1, s_2) is a pair in the fair simulation equivalence relation of A. Since there may form some new cycles in A_m when s_1 reaches s_2 or s_2 reaches s_1 in A. So if there exists an accepting state in these new cycles, then $L(A[s_2]) = L(A[s_1]) \subset L(A_m[[s_1, s_2]])$. Thus the language of some state in A_m which reaches $[s_1, s_2]$ may be changed even $L(A_m) = L(A)$. The following proposition shows that in order to keep the language of remaining state unchanged, we require $[s_1, s_2]$ be fair simulated by s_1.

Since a state s may belong to A, A_m and A_d(built by deleting states or transitions from A) at the same time, for convenience, we use s_A, s_{A_m} and s_{A_d} to denote $s \in A$, $s \in A_m$ and $s \in A_d$ respectively.

Proposition 2.   *If $[s_1, s_2]_{A_m}$ is fair simulated by s_1 of A, then $s_{A_m} \sim^f s_A$.*

The proof of the above proposition is to construct a winning strategy f such that the state chosen by Duplicator is identical with the state chosen by Spoiler or is decided by the winning strategy f' which decides $[s_1, s_2] \leq^f s_1$.

Therefore, $[s_1, s_2]_{A_m}$ is fair simulated by s_1 of A guarantees the correctness to merge s_1 and s_2. While [6] judges the correctness by whether the initial state of A_m is fair simulated by that of A. Since there may be a situation that two states is merged in [6] but not in our approach, so the condition we use to merge states is more restrictive.

According to Proposition 2 and item 1 of Proposition 1, we get an important property of A_m, it shows that A_m preserves the fair simulation relation of A.

Proposition 3.   *If $[s_1, s_2]_{A_m}$ is fair simulated by s_1 of A, then $s_A \leq^f q_A$ iff $s_{A_m} \leq^f q_{A_m}$.*

Deleting One State.   Given two states with the same language, if they do not reach each other, then we can get a reduced automaton A_d by deleting one state and it's transitions [7]. Since fair simulation equivalence implies language equivalence, thus given a candidate with fair simulation equivalence, we may delete one state and it' transitions. Therefore using the condition in [7] is efficient for it does not need to check the correctness and deletes states and transitions at the same time. Note that [7] just proved that $L(A_d) = L(A)$. Now we show that if two states with the same language is judged by fair simulation equivalence, then A_d has two important properties: (1) s_{A_d} and s_A fair simulate each other, therefore any state of A_d has the same language as that of the corresponding state in A. (2) A_d preserves the fair simulation relation of A.

Proposition 4. $s_{A_d} \sim^f s_A$

Proposition 5. $s_A \leq^f q_A$ iff $s_{A_d} \leq^f q_{A_d}$.

Note that the detail proof of each proposition of this paper is in [10].

3.2   Deleting Transitions

Given A and a pair of states (s, s') with $L(A[s]) \subseteq L(A[s'])$, if $\exists p \in A$ such that $(p, a, s), (p, a, s') \in \Delta^A$ and s' cannot reach p, we can construct A_d by deleting the transition (p, a, s) directly [7]. Since fair simulation implies language containment, so we can use the method of [7] to delete transitions.

Now we strengthen the conclusion $L(A_d) = L(A)$ of [7] by the following proposition which shows that each state of A_d has the same language as that of A.

Proposition 6. *Given A and $s \leq^f s'$, let p be a state such that $(p, a, s), (p, a, s') \in \Delta^A$, if s' cannot reach p, then $t_{A_d} \sim^f t_A$, where A_d is constructed by deleting (p, a, s) from A.*

However, if s' can reach p, we need check the correctness, like the method in [6]. In order to make the reduced automaton preserve the language of each state of A, the following proposition shows a more restricted criterion than that in [6]. That is, we require p_{A_d} fair simulate p_A, while [6] require the initial state of A_d fair simulate the initial state of A.

Proposition 7. *Given A and $s \leq^f s'$, let p be a state such that $(p, a, s), (p, a, s') \in \Delta^A$, if $p_A \leq^f p_{A_d}$, then $t_{A_d} \sim^f t_A$, where A_d is constructed by deleting (p, a, s) from A.*

So Proposition 6 and 7 help us overcome the first disadvantage of [6].

3.3   Efficiently Finding Candidates

The approach of [6] finds all candidates before applying any optimization. Our approach aims to delete one state or merge two states immediately after finding one successful candidate. Thus in the next time, we find new candidates on the reduced automaton A_d or A_m, which needs less time than that on A.

Since we do not find all candidates from one parity game $G_{A,A}$, we have to build and resolve the parity game for each time to find new candidates on the reduced automaton. In order to improve the efficiency of the whole optimization procedure, we reuse the information.

We describe how to reuse information in detail. Given a pair (s_1, s_2) and a Büchi automaton A^i which is built from A^{i-1} by merging states or deleting states according to the method in the section 3.1 (let $A^0 = A$). In order to check whether a pair of states with fair simulation(i.e., whether the pair is a new candidate to be reduced), we create game G. By Propositions 1, 3 and 5, for any $0 \leq j < i$, A^i preserves the fair simulation relation of A^j. So if $s \leq^f s'$ is true in A^j, then $s \leq^f s'$ is true in A^i. Therefore, if $v = v_{(s,s')}$ is one of vertexes of G, then v is the winning state for One in G. Thus we need not compute v when resolving G, for we can reuse the information from some game which computes $s \leq^f s'$ before building A^i. Therefore we save the time to computing fair simulation on G when we check the pair on A^i.

4 Algorithm

The whole optimization procedure has two phases:

- Remove states based on fair simulation equivalence.
- Remove transitions based on fair simulation.

In first stage, we will check all pairs of states in A. Suppose the current pair is (s_1, s_2). If we do not know whether $s_1 \sim^f s_2$, we need construct and resolve two parity game graphs $G_{A[s_1],A[s_2]}$ and $G_{A[s_2],A[s_1]}$. If $s_1 \sim^f s_2$, we first check whether s_1 and s_2 can reach each other, if it is not, then we delete one of states and its transitions from A directly. Otherwise, we construct A_m from A by merging s_1 and s_2, and build a parity game $G_{A_m[[s_1,s_2]],A[s_1]}$ to check whether $[s_1,s_2]$ is fair simulated by s_1. If the candidate (s_1, s_2) is safe, replace A by A_m. So in this stage, we do optimization immediately after finding one suitable candidate. After this stage, we find all pairs of states in the fair simulation relation of the current A, which is the basis of the next stage.

Before beginning the second stage, we construct a parity game $G_{A,A}$. Then for each pair of A with fair simulation, we do the following. Suppose the current pair is (s, s'). If $\exists p \in A$ such that $(p, a, s) \in \Delta^A$ and $(p, a, s') \in \Delta^A$, then we first check whether s' reaches p, if it is not, we delete the transition (p, a, s) from A directly. Otherwise, we delete some edges (v, v') from $G_{A,A}$ where $v = v_{(t,p,a)} \in V_0, v' = v_{(t,s)} \in V_1, t \in A$. In fact, now $G_{A,A}$ becomes G_{A,A_d}. Therefore, if the vertex $v = v_{(p,p)}$ of the new $G_{A,A}$ is a winning state for Zero, then we delete (p, a, s) from A. Otherwise, we must restore the game $G_{A,A}$.

Although our algorithm has the same worst time complexity as that of [6], since we use the conditions [7] which delete states and transitions without any additional checking, and we find candidates on the reduced automaton which has smaller and smaller state space in the optimizing procedure, thus our algorithm needs less time than that of [6].

5   Experiment

We have implemented our algorithm in C which runs on a PC with 3.2 GHz Intel Pentium 4 and 1G RAM. Büchi automata to be optimized are transformed from LTL formulae based on lbtt [11] and LTL2BA [1].We use lbtt to create random LTL formulae and LTL2BA to transform LTL formulae to transition-labeled Büchi automata.

We also have implemented the algorithm [6], because the original implementation is based on Wring [7] by Perl, which translates a random LTL formula to a generalized state-labeled Büchi automaton, but the algorithm in [6] can only optimize Büchi automata but not the generalized Büchi automata.

We use *ERSS*(Efficiently Reduce State Space) to denote our algorithm. We have tested three groups of automata, each group has 200 Büchi automata. In the following table, the column marked by *state* and *trans* shows the average number of states and transitions respectively. The column *Original* is the data obtained using the original Büchi automaton without any optimization.

Table 1 shows ERSS and GBS02 have the similar abilities to reduce state space of Büchi automata. Moreover, ERSS needs less computing time than that of GBS02, and these advantages become more obvious when increasing the number of states and transitions.

Table 1. Compare ERSS with GBS02

Original		Reduced		ERSS	GBS02
state	transition	state	transition	time	time
69.865	652.33	50.62	441.615	49.686	71.936
140.115	1897.35	93.065	1215.235	370.955	574.948
241.84	3849.315	140.715	2197.2	1312.083	3026.622

6   Conclusion

In our paper, based on [6], we provide the restricted criteria to check the correctness of the optimization. At the same time, we use the conditions in [7] to delete states and transitions without any additional checking. In the whole optimization procedure, the language of each state of the reduced automaton is same as that of the corresponding state of the original one. According to this property, we reduce states without waiting for finding all candidates, thus we find each candidate in a new reduced automaton with fewer states and transitions. We have implemented our algorithm (ERSS) described in Section 3. The experimental result shows that ERSS needs less optimization time than that of [6].

References

1. Gastin, P., Oddoux, D.: Fast LTL to Büchi Automata Translation. In: Vardi, M.Y., Alur, R. (eds.) CAV 2001. LNCS, vol. 2102, pp. 53–65. Springer, Heidelberg (2001)
2. Milner, R.: Communication and Concurrency. Prentice-Hall, Englewood Cliffs (1989)
3. Dill, D.L., Hu, A.J., Wong-Toi, H.: Checking for language inclusion using simulation preorders. In: Larsen, K.G., SkouLecture, A. (eds.) CAV 1991. LNCS, vol. 575, pp. 255–265. Springer, Heidelberg (1991)
4. Etessami, K., Wilke, Th., Schuller, R.: Fair simulation relations, parity games, and state space reduction for Büchi automata. SIAM Journal of Computing 34(5), 1159–1175 (2005)
5. Henzinger, T.A., Kupferman, O., Rajamani, S.K.: Fair simulation. In: Mazurkiewicz, A., Winkowski, J. (eds.) CONCUR 1997. LNCS, vol. 1243, pp. 273–287. Springer, Heidelberg (1997)
6. Gurumurthy, S., Bloem, R., Somenzi, F.: Fair Simulation Minimization. In: Brinksma, E., Larsen, K.G. (eds.) CAV 2002. LNCS, vol. 2404, pp. 610–624. Springer, Heidelberg (2002)
7. Somenzi, F., Bloem, R.: Efficient Büchi automata from LTL formulae. In: Emerson, E.A., Sistla, A.P. (eds.) CAV 2000. LNCS, vol. 1855, pp. 248–263. Springer, Heidelberg (2000)
8. Juvekar, S., Piterman, N.: Minimizing Generalized Buchi Automata. In: Ball, T., Jones, R.B. (eds.) CAV 2001. LNCS, vol. 2102, pp. 53–65. Springer, Heidelberg (2001)
9. Grädel, E., Thomas, W., Wilke, T. (eds.): Automata, Logics, and Infinite Games. LNCS, vol. 2500. Springer, Heidelberg (2002)
10. Yi, J., Zhang, W.: Efficient State Space Reduction for Automata by Fair Simulation. Technical Report ISCAS-LCS-07-01, Institute of Software, Chinese Academy of Sciences
11. Tauriainen, H., Heljanko, K.: Testing LTL formula translation into Büchi automata. International Journal on Software Tools for Technology Transfer 4(1), 57–70 (2002)

Model Checking Temporal Metric Specifications with Trio2Promela[*]

Domenico Bianculli[1], Paola Spoletini[2], Angelo Morzenti[2], Matteo Pradella[3], and Pierluigi San Pietro[2]

[1] Faculty of Informatics, University of Lugano, Switzerland
domenico.bianculli@lu.unisi.ch
[2] Dipartimento di Elettronica e Informazione, Politecnico di Milano, Italy
[3] CNR IEIIT-MI, Italy
{spoleti,morzenti,pradella,sanpietr}@elet.polimi.it

Abstract. We present Trio2Promela, a tool for model checking TRIO specifications by means of Spin. TRIO is a linear-time temporal logic with both future and past operators and a quantitative metric on time. Our approach is based on the translation of TRIO formulae into Promela programs guided by equivalence between TRIO and alternating Büchi automata. Trio2Promela may be used to check both purely descriptive TRIO specifications, a distinguishing difference with other model checking tools, and usual Promela programs for which the user needs to verify complex temporal properties. Then, we report on extensive and encouraging experimentation results, and compare Trio2Promela with similar tools.

Keywords: temporal logic, model checking, Spin.

1   Introduction and Background

TRIO is a first order, linear-time temporal logic with both future and past operators and a quantitative metric on time, which has been extensively applied to the specification, validation and verification of large, critical, real-time systems [1,2]. TRIO formulae are built much in the same way as in traditional mathematical logic, starting from variables, functions, predicates, predicate symbols, and quantifiers over finite or infinite, dense or discrete, domains (a detailed and formal definition of TRIO can be found in [3]). Besides the usual propositional operators and the quantifiers, one may compose TRIO formulae by using a pair of basic modal operators, called *Futr* and *Past*, that relate the *current time*, which is left implicit in the formula, with another time instant: the formula $Futr(F, t)$, where F is a formula and t a term indicating a time distance, specifies that F holds at a time instant at t time units in the future from the current instant (symmetrically for past). Notice that the usage of both past and future modalities in TRIO is widely recognized to make specifications simpler and more concise than using either only future or only past operators.

---

[*] Work partially supported by the MIUR project "FIRB: Applicazioni della Teoria degli Automi all'Analisi, alla Compilazione e alla Verifica di Sistemi Critici e in Tempo Reale", and the IST EU project "PLASTIC", contract number. 026955.

F. Arbab and M. Sirjani (Eds.): FSEN 2007, LNCS 4767, pp. 388–395, 2007.

Many derived temporal operators can be defined from the basic operator through propositional composition and first order quantification on variables representing a time distance. The traditional operators *Since* and *Until* of linear temporal logics, as well as many other operators, can easily be obtained as TRIO derived operators. For instance, $SomF(F)$ (Sometimes in the Future) is $Until(\text{true}, F)$ and corresponds to the "Eventually" operator of temporal logic; $AlwF(F)$ (Always in the Future) is $\neg SomF(\neg F)$ (F will always hold), that is the "Globally" operator. Moreover, TRIO adds another level of succinctness because of the metric operators *Lasts* and *Lasted* and their duals *WithinF* and *WithinP*. $Lasts(F, c)$ means that F will hold for c instants in the future and $WithinF(F, c)$ means that F will hold within c instants in the future. For instance, a TRIO formula such as: $WithinF(Lasts(B, h), k)$ for some $h, k > 0$, may be expressed in LTL only with a formula of length proportional to $h \cdot k$.

Over the years a variety of methods and tools have been defined to support typical validation and verification activities in TRIO, such as: 1) testing, by generation of execution traces or checking of such simulations for consistency against the TRIO specification [4], 2) derivation of system properties in the form of theorems, based on the definition of a suitable axiomatization of the logic and on its encoding in the notation of a general purpose theorem prover, such as PVS [5].

In the present paper, we present another tool, called Trio2Promela, for the mechanical verification of a decidable subset[1] of TRIO specifications, by using a well-known model checker such as Spin [6] to perform proof of properties and simulation. The approach and background theory upon which Trio2Promela is constructed was originally presented in [7,8]. The main aim of the present paper is to report on our experience of actually using the tool, now fully implemented and publicly available, together with examples and the experiments summarized in the paper (at `http://www.elet.polimi.it/upload/sanpietr/Trio2Promela.zip`.

Trio2Promela can be used, at various levels of generality, to support satisfiability checking of generic TRIO formulae (and hence property proof) and model checking. In the former activity, every possible interpretation structure for the formula is potentially enumerated (but great care is of course taken to allow Spin to determine, during a verification, that many structures can be safely ignored as early as possible). In the latter activity, Trio2Promela translates the property to be checked from TRIO into Promela, combining the resulting code with a pure-Promela model to perform verification. When the desired property is fairly complex or contains several bounded temporal statements, which is typical e.g. of real-time systems, the traditional approach of generating a so-called *never claim* for Spin, i.e., an automaton specifying the negation of a temporal logic property over the already available state-transition system, becomes unfeasible. Both the internal LTL to Büchi automata translator, and other more recent tools, like LTL2BA [9] and Wring [10], simply cannot manage a complex real-time statement with metric operators, as we report in Sect. 3. For instance, the LTL version of a statement of the form "every occurrence of event A must be followed within 20 time units by an occurrence of event B", which in TRIO can be modeled as simply as $AlwF(A \rightarrow WithinF(B, 20))$ cannot be translated by LTL2BA or Wring (the system

---

[1] Essentially, a concise (thanks to metric operators) version of LTL with past operators. For instance, $Lasts(A, 3)$ corresponds to $X(A \wedge X(A \wedge X(A)))$ in LTL.

was stopped after waiting for 24 hours), even if it actually corresponds (if one time unit is taken to correspond to one transition) to a Büchi automaton with only 21 states. Trio2Promela is able to translate the above statement into a short Promela program almost instantaneously.

The Trio2Promela tool is ideally based on the translation of TRIO formulae into a set of Promela processes, derived from a well known correlation between temporal logic and alternating automata [11]. As opposed to previous approaches, however, the Promela code generated from TRIO formulae performs an actual simulation of an alternating automaton, rather than simulating a Büchi automaton equivalent to the alternating one, resulting in a Promela code whose size is essentially proportional to the length of the TRIO specification (although of course the state space may not be affected in either way). This is by itself a remarkable result since TRIO, which contains metric and past operators, is quite concise compared with propositional, future-time temporal logics like LTL. Our approach can be naturally compared with recent works appeared in the literature (such as those on LTL2BA and Wring) that aim at the translation of LTL properties into Büchi automata and then Promela programs). We point out, however, that the result of those tools is usually the construction, as in the traditional model-checking scenario, of a *never claim*. In our approach, instead, the Promela processes obtained from the translation of the TRIO specification define an acceptor of a language over the alphabet of the specification, and therefore it must be coupled with some additional Promela program fragments generating the values, over time, for the logical variables that constitute the specification alphabet. Our translation techniques, combined with other optimizations, related for example with the management of TRIO past-time operators, allowed us to perform efficiently the verification in Spin of some significant benchmarks.

2   Trio2Promela

Trio2Promela translates a TRIO specification, i.e., a complex TRIO formula, into Promela code. The translation is based on a correspondence between TRIO and *Alternating Modulo Counting Automata* (AMCA) described in [8]. The main idea is based on the well-known correspondence between Linear Temporal Logic and Alternating Automata (which are a generalization of non-deterministic automata: see for instance [12]), together with *counters*, associated with states of the AMCA, that are used to express TRIO's metric temporal operators in a natural and concise manner.

Each temporal subformula, i.e., one of the form $Z(\_)$ for a temporal operator Z, of the original specification is translated into a single state of the AMCA. Then, an AMCA is *directly* translated into a Promela program: every state of the automaton will correspond to a single type of process (i.e., a Promela proctype), to be instantiated when needed. An or-combination of states $s_1 \lor s_2$ in the transition function corresponds to a non-deterministic choice (if ::s1; ::s2; fi), while an and-combination $s_1 \land s_2$ corresponds to the starting of two new Promela process instances, having type s1 and s2, respectively. Hence, the produced code consists of a network of processes, each corresponding to a temporal subformula of the original specification. Each Promela process receives as input a chronological sequence of values taken by the propositional letters that constitute the alphabet of the associated TRIO formula, and then it returns its computed truth value to the network. When the process representing the whole TRIO formula being analyzed returns `false`, every process in the network is stopped, and the analysis terminates.

When Trio2Promela is used to translate a complex TRIO property in the context of traditional model-checking, the input values to the processes come from a Promela program that encodes the operational model under analysis. On the other hand, when Trio2Promela is used to check satisfiability of a TRIO specification, the input values come from a purely generative Promela component that exhaustively enumerates all possible values over time of the propositional letters.

Notice that in the translation we encode time (integer-valued) constants of TRIO formulae into int variables, so the size of the resulting Promela code is linear in the size of the AMCA, and therefore also in the size of the original TRIO specification. Here our approach differs substantially from others (such as LTL2BA and Wring): these translate LTL formulae (which in the first place are less compact than TRIO formulae, as they cannot include integer values representing time constants, and therefore must use long chains of nested X operators), into Spin *never claims* or Büchi automata whose size can grow to become unmanageable even for relatively simple specifications, as it will be shown in Sect. 3 on experimental results.

As TRIO past operators are concerned, we take advantage of the fact that time is unlimited only towards the future (there is a *start* time instant) to treat past operators differently, using a technique illustrated in our paper [7] that stores a bounded amount of information derived from the past portion of the sequence of input values.

Our approach becomes practically feasible in Spin by adopting a set of optimizations, such as:

- Processes representing future operators are in general, with the only exception of *Futr*, grouped in a unique process.
- Process instances for *Futr* are reused (since every new process is very costly for verification).
- Various kinds of TRIO subformulae are simplified (e.g., the nesting of a bounded future and a bounded past operator is replaced by one equivalent operator).
- Communication channels are used to abort related processes when a process produces a `false` result.

Tool Description. The translator front-end, implemented in Java with ANTLR[2], takes a TRIO file in input, containing the declarations of variables, constants and the logic formulae of the specification; each variable is associated with an integer domain. The output of the parsing phase is an array of abstract syntax trees, one for each formula in the specification. Each tree in the array is processed by a chain of tree walkers that perform optimizations on the propositional connectives of the TRIO formula and nested operators (such as $Futr(WithinF(\_,\_),\_)$ or $Past(WithinP(\_,\_),\_)$, apply derivation rules for derived operators as defined in TRIO (e.g., the formula $NextTime(A, t)$ becomes $Futr(A, t) \wedge Lasts(\neg A, t)$, push inward in the formula all the negations, taking into account the definition of TRIO operators (e.g., $\neg Lasts(A, t)$ is equivalent to

---

[2] http://www.antlr.org

WithinF$(\neg A, t)$). The back-end is composed of a set of translation procedures, each one implementing the translation schema for a TRIO operator; they produce: the temporal constant characterizing the metric operator, the local variables needed in the main Promela process, the body code for an autonomous Promela process and the associated launching and error propagation code, the additional code for formula evaluation, and the logic expression corresponding to the truth value of the formula. The code resulting from the translation of each operator is then composed with the generative component to produce the final Promela program.

3 Experimental Results and Comparisons

We extensively experimented with the tool and compared it with the main toolkits available for translating from temporal logic to Büchi automata. In particular, we compared Trio2Promela with LTL2BA, which is probably one of the most efficient LTL-to-Büchi automata translators. We also experimented with Wring, but we do not report the results here because its translation times were always worse than those of LTL2BA. The same happens for other translators, such as LTL→NBA [13] (which may lead to slightly smaller automata than LTL2BA, but it is significantly slower).

The setup for all experiments was the following: we used a laptop with an Intel Pentium M 1.2 GHz, and 632 Mb RAM. Spin's version was 4.2.3, LTL2BA's was 1.0.

The comparison was conducted with reference to two case studies: the Kernel Railroad Crossing Problem (KRC, see [14]) and a version of Fischer's protocol (FP, [15]). KRC and FP are two fairly good representatives of very different problems: the former is a typical real-time system, with a limited number of reachable configurations but with quantitative timing requirements; Fischer's protocol instead has basically very weak quantitative timing requirements, but it has strong combinatorial aspects, making the number of possible configurations grow quickly with the number of processes.

Satisfiability Checking and Model Checking. It is well-known that LTL model checking, while being PSPACE-complete, is linear in the number of the states of the automaton and exponential in the size of the LTL formula to be checked. On the other hand, LTL satisfiability checking is exponential in the size of the formula. Hence, our first set of experiments has studied the unavoidable loss in efficiency of going from model checking to satisfiability checking. Hence, we developed one logic model, defined in TRIO assuming an underlying discrete time model, and one automaton model of both KRC and FP, which were coded in Promela. Table 1 shows the experimental results. The KRC models used various integer values for the time constants of the problem, with KRC1 having the smaller constants and KRC3 the highest. The property proved was a safety property. Also, the results on Fischer's protocol FP are shown, with a number of processes going from 2 to 5, for checking a simple mutual exclusion property.

Clearly, the comparison of satisfiability checking and model checking may be affected by the choice of the two different, although equivalent, models for the same system: one could have defined a "smart" logic model and a "sloppy" automaton, or viceversa. The results are nonetheless of some interest. The exponential blow-up for

Table 1. Comparison of satisfiability checking and model checking using KRC and FP

	Satisfiability checking (Trio2Promela)[a][b]			Model checking of a Promela model against a safety formula translated with Trio2Promela[c]			Model checking of a Promela model against a safety formula translated with LTL2BA[c]		
	Mem (MB)	States	Time (s)	Mem (MB)	States	Time (s)	Mem (MB)	States	Time (s)
KRC1	8.2	105151	2	2.6	298	1	2.6	909	1
KRC2	31.8	361627	8	2.6	674	1	2.6	2233	1
KRC3	171.0	1371870	46	2.6	1390	1	2.7	3658	1
FP2	3.0	13179	1	2.6	345	1	2.6	326	1
FP3	13.3	304047	2	2.7	3355	1	2.6	3240	1
FP4	241.1	6321520	59	3.5	27977	1	3.3	41694	1
FP5	EX[d]	NC[e]	NC[e]	9.7	215886	1	9.8	222940	1

[a] A temporal logic model has been translated into Promela, along with a safety property.

[b] Satisfiability checking with LTL2BA is infeasible (i.e. no translation can be generated) for every example shown in the table.

[c] Only the safety property has been translated into Promela.

[d] Memory exhausted (>400 MB).

[e] Not completed.

satisfiability checking against model checking tends to show up, but still the tool can manage with fairly large time constants in the KRC model (case KRC3). With Fischer's protocol, instead, the state explosion is more substantial. These data show also a large improvement over our previous work [8], where, for instance, the case KRC1 required four times the number of states and the case KRC3 could not be dealt with.

Satisfiability checking of KRC and FP temporal logic models is infeasible in LTL2-BA, i.e., LTL2BA ran for more than 24 hours without providing a translation, while the translation time of both examples with Trio2Promela is negligible (under one second). When Trio2Promela is used for model checking (hence, only a short TRIO formula is translated into Promela), the performance of the verification does not appear substantially different from the case when LTL2BA is used for checking the same Promela program. Hence, even though Trio2Promela is geared towards translation of large metric-temporal logic formulae, rather than applying sophisticated optimizations to small LTL formulae as LTL2BA does, it appears that in practice Trio2Promela works at least as well (or even better) than LTL2BA even on small LTL formulae, at least when used for model checking.

Translation of Short Formulae. To better understand the relative strength of LTL2BA and Trio2Promela, we also ran both tools on a set of short formulae. The comparison could be done only on formulae without past operators, since, while the theory underlying LTL2BA has been extended to deal with past formulae [16], the toolkit publicly available for LTL2BA can only deal with the future fragment LTL. Purely past formulae are anyway translated by Trio2Promela into very small Promela programs with only one process (e.g., the formula $AlwF(A \rightarrow WithinP(B, 20))$ is translated into one single Promela process with 21 states).

In Table 2 we give translation times and also a measure of the size of the Promela code. For LTL2BA, we give the number of states of the corresponding Büchi automaton (since every state is explicitly listed), while for Trio2Promela we give the sum of the states of each Promela process defined by the translation, and also the total number of

Table 2. Comparison of translation times and size

	Translation time (s)		Size	
	LTL2BA	Trio2Promela	LTL2BA[a]	Trio2Promela[b]
Safety-KRC	< 1	< 1	2	9–1
Mutex-Fischer	< 1	< 1	2	8–1
$AlwF(A \rightarrow WithinF(B,10))$	< 1	< 1	11	218–11
$AlwF(A \rightarrow WithinF(B,15))$	222	< 1	16	308–16
$AlwF(A \rightarrow WithinF(B,17))$	3127	< 1	18	308–18
$AlwF(A \rightarrow WithinF(B,20))$	infeasible	< 1	21[c]	398–21
$AlwF(A \wedge SomF(B))$	< 1	< 1	1	20–1
$AlwF(A \wedge SomF(B) \wedge Lasts(C,5))$	< 1	< 1	5	26–1

[a] Number of states of the corresponding Büchi automaton.
[b] Sum of states of each Promela process – total number of processes.
[c] Estimated.

processes. For Trio2Promela, this is a very indirect measure of the number of states of the corresponding Büchi automaton, which can only be determined dynamically.

The results show that LTL2BA's translation times grow quickly also on very small formulae with metric temporal operators, even though the resulting Büchi automaton is small. For instance, a formula like $AlwF(A \rightarrow WithinF(B,c))$, where c is a constant, corresponds to a Büchi automaton with $c+1$ states, and it is translated by Trio2Promela into c processes of 18 states each, and one process of 38 states. However, LTL2BA fails to translate the formula within 24 hours for c greater than 19. The reason for LTL2BA's failure is that on this (and other) kind of formulae, the construction method of LTLBA must pass through a stage where a (generalized) Büchi automaton is built, describing all possible configurations of the original alternating automaton. LTL2BA then performs an optimization phase that may, at least for this kind of formulae, lead to an optimal Buchi automaton. However, the number of states of the intermediate automaton may be so large that it cannot be handled, causing the tool's failure.

4   Conclusions

We presented experimental evidence that, when dealing with metric temporal logic, the Trio2Promela toolkit has many advantages over existing toolkits that address the same goal. In fact, Trio2Promela always derives a Promela code whose size is linear in the size of the original TRIO formula (which may be substantially smaller than an equivalent LTL formula). This is obtained by avoiding, at least at translation time, the state explosion problem, thanks to the fact that we generate a Promela program that will simulate (at verification time) the alternating automaton. The alternation removal is then left to the model checker, allowing the verification of many temporal logic formulae which could not be translated into Promela by means of other techniques. In fact, if the alternation is removed during the translation phase, as all techniques we know of do, then there are many cases where a translator cannot even build the resulting automaton (where all states are explicitly enumerated). This happens, for instance, when specifications are very large, or use metric temporal operators, or mix past and future temporal operators.

Our experiments also support the conclusion that, even when the translation of an LTL formula is possible with other tools, the performance of model checking in Trio2Promela leads to comparable performance results. Hence, current experimental evidence shows that Trio2Promela could be used also for LTL model checking. Future work will be devoted to further optimization of the translation, trying to incorporate other techniques into Trio2Promela.

We have also shown that Trio2Promela can be used for satisfiability checking of large TRIO formulae. Therefore, we plan to assess the merit of satisfiability checking by means of a translation into Spin's Promela (as currently done by Trio2Promela) against the translation into the language of boolean satisfiability solvers, which are well-known for their efficiency in many practical cases.

References

1. Ghezzi, C., Mandrioli, D., Morzenti, A.: TRIO, a logic language for executable specifications of real-time systems. The Journal of Systems and Software 12, 107–123 (1990)
2. Morzenti, A., San Pietro, P.: Object-oriented logical specification of time-critical systems. ACM Trans. Softw. Eng. Methodol. 3, 56–98 (1994)
3. Morzenti, A., Mandrioli, D., Ghezzi, C.: A model parametric real-time logic. ACM Trans. Program. Lang. Syst. 14, 521–573 (1992)
4. Felder, M., Morzenti, A.: Validating real-time systems by history-checking TRIO specifications. ACM Trans. Softw. Eng. Methodol. 3, 308–339 (1994)
5. Gargantini, A., Morzenti, A.: Automated deductive requirements analysis of critical systems. ACM Trans. Softw. Eng. Methodol. 10, 255–307 (2001)
6. Holzmann, G.J.: The model checker SPIN. IEEE Trans. Softw. Eng. 23, 279–295 (1997)
7. Pradella, M., San Pietro, P., Spoletini, P., Morzenti, A.: Practical model checking of LTL with past. In: ATVA 2003 (2003)
8. Morzenti, A., Pradella, M., San Pietro, P., Spoletini, P.: Model checking TRIO specifications in Spin. In: Araki, K., Gnesi, S., Mandrioli, D. (eds.) FME 2003. LNCS, vol. 2805, pp. 542–561. Springer, Heidelberg (2003)
9. Gastin, P., Oddoux, D.: Fast LTL to Büchi automata translation. In: Berry, G., Comon, H., Finkel, A. (eds.) CAV 2001. LNCS, vol. 2102, pp. 53–65. Springer, Heidelberg (2001)
10. Somenzi, F., Bloem, R.: Efficient Büchi automata from LTL formulae. In: Emerson, E.A., Sistla, A.P. (eds.) CAV 2000. LNCS, vol. 1855, pp. 248–263. Springer, Heidelberg (2000)
11. Vardi, M.Y.: An automata-theoretic approach to linear temporal logic. In: Moller, F., Birtwistle, G. (eds.) Logics for Concurrency. LNCS, vol. 1043, pp. 238–266. Springer, Heidelberg (1996)
12. Chandra, A.K., Kozen, D.C., Stockmeyer, L.J.: Alternation. J. ACM 28, 114–133 (1981)
13. Fritz, C.: Constructing Büchi automata from linear temporal logic using simulation relations for alternating Büchi automata. In: Ibarra, O.H., Dang, Z. (eds.) CIAA 2003. LNCS, vol. 2759, pp. 35–48. Springer, Heidelberg (2003)
14. Heitmeyer, C., Mandrioli, D. (eds.): Formal Methods for Real-Time Computing. Trends in Software, vol. 5. Wiley, Chichester (1996)
15. Lamport, L.: A fast mutual exclusion algorithm. ACM Trans. Comput. Syst. 5, 1–11 (1987)
16. Gastin, P., Oddoux, D.: LTL with past and two-way very-weak alternating automata. In: Rovan, B., Vojtáš, P. (eds.) MFCS 2003. LNCS, vol. 2747, pp. 439–448. Springer, Heidelberg (2003)

Design and Implementation of a Dynamic-Reconfigurable Architecture for Protocol Stack

Mahdi Niamanesh[1], Sirwah Sabetghadam[2], Reza Yousefzadeh Rahaghi[3], and Rasool Jalili[1]

[1] Department of Computer Engineering
Sharif University of Technology
[2] Computer Engineering Department
Shahid Beheshti University
[3] Computer Engineering Department
Tehran University
Tehran, Iran
{niamanesh@mehr.,jalili@}sharif.edu, s_sabetghadam@std.sbu.ac.ir,
ryousefz@sms.sharif.edu

Abstract. Future communication and computation devices require mechanisms for on-the-fly reconfiguration in their protocol stack to operate in different situations and networks. This paper proposes a component-based framework for dynamic-reconfigurable protocol stack. Considering that every running protocol component communicates with at least one peer component, unlike related work our framework supports synchronous reconfiguration of two peer protocol components in two communicating protocol stacks.

1 Introduction

Future communication and computation world, known as pervasive computing environment, includes a lot of wireless networks, networked systems and devices with heterogeneous standards and protocols for different contexts and situations[1]. Protocol stacks of such systems and devices can dynamically be reconfigured to present applications like changing the network of a device due to its mobility, changing routing algorithms of switches, and adding or changing the security module in protocol stacks for better performance.

In general, dynamic reconfiguration process for a software component includes some phases, namely, freezing (to stop the current execution of the component), changing (to add and bind a new component to as well as unbind and remove unnecessary old component from the system), state transferring (find a proper state in the new component and valuate its parameters in order to resume the execution) and re-execution (resuming the execution from a non-initial state in the new component) [2].

For reconfiguration in protocol stack context, since every protocol is defined at least between two peer components, reconfiguring a running component of

F. Arbab and M. Sirjani (Eds.): FSEN 2007, LNCS 4767, pp. 396–403, 2007.

a protocol stack may require corresponding reconfiguration in the peer components in the other systems. For example, consider a running networked system
with Internet protocol stack and a reconfiguration that changes TCP component
in the stack into SCTP component [3]. In order to ensure the reconfiguration
correctness, not only SCTP component should be "compatible" with its upper
and lower layers, it should preserve the protocol stack "compatibility" with the
peer protocol stacks. For this purpose, it is necessary to change the TCP components in two stacks into SCTP components at the same time (synchronously).
Unlike related work (e.g. [4,5] among others), we do not suppose a running protocol stack as a stand-alone system. We propose a framework that can change
the protocol components of two communicating protocol stacks.

In this paper, in Section 2, we explain the proposed DRAPS framework. The
main design issues of DRAPS including the mechanisms for assurance and also
reconfiguration algorithm are presented in Section 3. In Section 4, we describe
the performance evaluation of the algorithm. Section 5 concludes the paper.

2 DRAPS Overview

DRAPS (Dynamic Reconfigurable Architecture for Protocol Stack) is an extendable middleware framework[1] that presents synchronous dynamic reconfiguration
for two communicating protocol stacks. Architectural components of DRAPS
are shown in Figure 1. The framework has been built out from a core framework and some plug-in components. Core framework is responsible to perform
synchronous dynamic reconfiguration and consist of three components, namely,
Reconfiguration Management and Control (RMC), Stack Factory (SF) and Execution Environment (EE). RMC is responsible for coordinating dynamic and
synchronous reconfigurations. SF is a component that is responsible to initialize protocols specifically when they are started from non-initial states. EE is a
component for installation and execution of the protocol components.

Plug-in components in DRAPS present extendability for the framework. They
perform supplementary tasks for the dynamic reconfiguration.

For synchronous and dynamic reconfiguration of two peer stacks in two systems, DRAPS frameworks in two systems cooperate. RMCs in both frameworks
implement a distributed algorithm for the reconfiguration. They send or receive
messages through the stacks to perform the reconfigurations.

3 DRAPS Design

In following subsections, we explain important design issues of DRAPS.

3.1 Protocol Component Model

We consider every protocol component as a processing unit that takes input
packets and produces output packets. The component has two interfaces; an

---

[1] The source code of the framework is available at
http://mehr.sharif.edu/~niamanesh/RG.htm

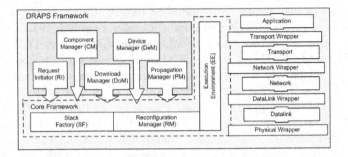

Fig. 1. Architecture of DRAPS including core components and some plug-ins

interface with the upper layer and an interface with the lower layer that are also buffers for the component to send or receive packets.

Protocol components in DRAPS should provide some functionalities to support dynamic reconfiguration. For this reason, DRAPS presents an implementation-level component model for reconfigurable protocols. Every protocol component should implement the `ReconfigurableComponent` interface. As shown in flowing `saveState()` and `restoreState()` methods are used for state transferring. Methods `start()` and `stop()` are used to start and stop execution of the component. Method `semiFreeze()` helps the component to start reporting its state to the framework. Method `setStateListener()` sets a listener to use it in semiFreeze stage for reporting the component state.

```
public interface ReconfigurableComponent {
    void saveState(String path);
    void restoreState(String path);
    void start();
    void stop();
    void semiFreeze();
    void setStateListener(StateListener listener);
}
```

3.2 Protocol Wrappers

A wrapper is a component that implements the interface of a service in component protocol. It is used to provide an indirect communication between two components in order to present a transparent run-time reconfiguration. Every reconfigurable component in DRAPS should have one wrapper that handles requests for the component delivering that service. For example, as depicted in Figure 2, TCP wrapper that implements TCP interface, manages application requests to the TCP component.

Several applications may request a reliable transport protocol. All these requests are managed by a wrapper using Java synchronized mechanism. The wrapper may be a general wrapper such as, Reliable Transport Wrapper (RTW) or a specific wrapper such as, UDP wrapper that provides services of UDP protocol. General wrapper presents a general interface to the upper layer to manage more than one protocol component.

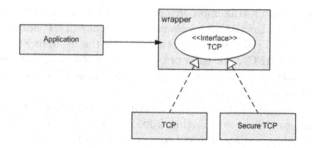

Fig. 2. TCP wrapper for TCP and Secure TCP components

3.3   DRAPS Plug-in Components

Five types of plug-in components exist in the framework to satisfy supplementary requirements for dynamic reconfigurable protocol stacks:

Request Initiator (RI). This type of component is responsible to detect the need for a reconfiguration.

Condition Checker (CC). In every reconfiguration to preserve required correctness properties and avoid inconsistencies some conditions should be checked before the reconfiguration process. A CC component checks situation and context to start the reconfiguration.

Component Provider (CP). Given the name or service name of a protocol, CP component can deliver the right component or components that match.

Installation Assistant (IA). An IA component is responsible for provisioning of the installation. It performs operations before and after the change.

Execution Assistant (EA). An EA component performs required operation before and after the re-execution of a component.

Plug-in components are options that can be added to DRAPS core framework. They are used by the RMC component to present reacher set of features.

3.4   Stack Factory

Stack Factory (SF) component provides all required knowledge for initializing the starting state (the non-initial state in which the component should be executed) in the new component; For this purpose, it has three responsibilities; first, it contains state mapping functions (MF) that each function is used for one reconfiguration and maps the states of the old component to some corresponding states in the new one. Second, SF should valuate the starting state in the new component to start the execution. Third, SF should prepare and initialize some parts of the state of the peer component as well. For example, SF may require to send the port number to the peer stack to establish a connection.

To model the state of a protocol we introduce protocol control block (PCB) that contains state information of a protocol component. This information is about the connection state, its associated local process, and other parameters about the connection's transmission properties that are stated in the protocol standard. Moreover, for the protocols in one category (TCP and its extensions) we define Basic PCB (BPCB) that is the PCB for the basic protocol specified in the standards and RFCs. For example, for TCP protocol and its extensions we consider TCP control block for the original TCP (RFC793) as the BPCB that contains the state of TCP connection.

To store the mapping functions, for each reconfiguration from one protocol to another one, for instance changing from protocol P_1 into P_2, SF has a table that maps the states[2] of P_1 protocol to a corresponding states of P_2. This table explains a mapping function between P_1 and P_2.

For transferring the state of the old component to the new one, we use BPCB as the temporary data structure to transfer the PBC of the old component to the PCB of new component. Three sources exist for filling the PCB entries; first, BPCB that is initialized based on the old PCB; second, user-defined handlers that should be provided through the reconfiguration adminstration; third, remote peer component that sends required parameters value to the component.

3.5   Reconfiguration Management and Control

The reconfiguration process is started upon receiving a reconfiguration command, which comprises of all necessary information to perform the reconfiguration. The information includes a map that describes the change, a state for the freezing and starting the reconfiguration, and some initialization parameters to valuate the starting state in the new component. The map for the reconfiguration includes set of reconfiguration operations for changing such as adding, or removing of components. It is provided by a reconfigurer. The state for the reconfiguration can be either provided by the reconfiguration administrator or can be determined by the framework.

Finding a Global Safe State. We define safe reconfiguration point (SRP) as a point of execution of a component in which the component is in the beginning or at the end of the processing input packet. In another words, the states just after writing a packet in the output buffer or before reading a packet from the input buffer are SRP. In these points, either no operation is started on the packet or all the operations are completed. In fact, we do not limit the buffers to be free in SRP. Developers of protocol components should determine and set some SRPs in the source code of reconfigurable components.

However, not every SRP in a component is safe state for the peer component either. A state in a component is safe for the peer component if it can satisfy the requirements of the current state of the peer after the reconfiguration. In other words, SRP state s in the currently running component is a global SRP if the mapped state $MF(s)$ (the starting state in the new component) has a compatible state in the new peer component in the peer stack.

---

[2] It is not necessary to define the mapping function for all states of the component. We consider only states that exist in the standard for the specification.

To freeze a component in a SRP point, we introduce "semiFreezing" mode for execution of a component. In this mode which should be implemented by protocol developers, the component reports its state in every pre-defined SRP point. For each reported state, we check whether $MF(s)$ has a compatible state in the new component. If so, the reported state together with its compatible state in the peer component is the global SRP for the reconfiguration. Two states from two components are called compatible if all inputs and outputs of the components on those states "match" with each other [6].

3.6   Reconfiguration of Communicating Peers

Now, we explain the proposed distributed algorithm for reconfiguration of communicating peer components. The algorithm uses 3 types of message (START, RECON and READY) for communication between two RMCs in two peer systems. Message START is the command for reconfiguration and consists of the elements stated in Subsection 3.5. Message RECON, is an announcement that the initiator stack sends to itself and the peer to indicate that the reconfiguration can be started. Message READY is a control message that each RMC sends to the peer after finishing the reconfiguration.

The algorithm is started upon receiving a reconfiguration command to a RMC. The RMC prepares a proper reconfiguration command and sends it to its peer and then starts installing the new component determined in the reconfiguration command. The peer stack upon receiving the command, starts this algorithm too. Each stack after sending START message to its peer and installing new component waits for a response message.

The initiator stack, upon receiving a START message, prepares a RECON message and sends it to own and its peer stack. Each stack upon receiving the RECON message, invokes semiFreeze() to enter semi-freeze mode and then freezes the execution by stop() and finally transfers the state using saveState(), and restoreState() methods. Afterwards each stack sends a READY message to its peer and finally waits for receiving a READY message from its peer. Both stacks upon receiving the READY message execute the new component by invoking start() method.

```
Algorithm 1 Synchronous Reconfiguration of Two Peers
               (Code of RMC Component)
//initializations: set active reconfiguration lists empty
//Peer_i as a initiator, Peer_j
  upon receive START = (m_i, s_i, delta_i, id) message
      If id is not in active reconfiguration list
(1)     s_j = find compatible state with s_i in the peer
(2)     m_j = find the corresponding change in the peer
(3)     delta_j = set of remote parameters initialization
        send START = (m_j, s_j, delta_j, id) to the peer
        put id in active reconfiguration list
        install new components
        wait for response message from the peer
      else
        Send RECON to yourself and the Peer_j
//Peer_i, Peer_j:
  upon receive RECON from the peer
        semi-Freeze the current component
```

```
(4)     find a global SRP
        freeze the current component
(5)     transfer the state
        send READY message to the peer
        wait for READY message from the peer
//Peer_i, Peer_j:
  upon receive READY message
        re-execute the new component
        remove id from active reconfiguration list
```

4   Implementation and Evaluation

We have implemented a prototype of DRAPS framework to demonstrate the feasibility of our approach as well as to test the basic functionalities of the architecture. The configuration of the experimental environment is a Celeron 1.5 GHz IBM personal computer with 256 MB memory and Linux (Debian 3.1 distribution) is the operating system. We have considered two peer stacks, $Stack_1$ and $Stack_2$, as two communicating stacks. Applications on the top each stack exchange data with each other. Both applications use a light version of TCP protocol for the transport layer. The IP layer is simulated using two Linux FIFOs, one for outgoing data and the other for incoming data.

For a file transfer, we measure its time in a normal transfer (as t_1) and in a situation that transfer layers (TCP) of both stacks during the file transfer are changing to a secure version (Secure TCP) (as t_2). Overall reconfiguration time (t_R), includes the time for installation (t_I), semi-freezing (t_S), freezing (t_F) and waiting time for receiving the response from the peer. Note that, only freeze time (t_F) is the time that the application is blocked.

Table 1 shows our 8 experiments with two different file sizes. Numbers in columns 2-5 are the times in milliseconds for each phase of reconfiguration. Overhead of the dynamic reconfiguration in DRAPS can be calculated by t_1/t_2 ratio, in which it is in average 5 percentage in our experiments.

For the experiments, we have set the input buffer of TCP component ("send buffer" parameter in TCP standard) to 180Kb; however, by restricting the TCP "send buffer" to become empty for starting a reconfiguration our experiments shows that the average amount of t_F is very low and less than 5 ms.

Table 1. The performance of synchronous reconfiguration of TCP with SecureTCP

FILE-SIZE	t_1	t_2	t_R	t_F	t_I
222K	2281	2320	372	99	32
222K	2175	2182	366	97	33
222K	2181	2305	376	103	31
222K	2198	2314	366	89	31
152K	1517	1655	306	47	129
152K	1514	1580	308	42	62
152K	1544	1581	302	40	71
152K	1509	1655	312	45	118

5 Conclusion

This paper proposed a framework for dynamic-reconfigurable protocol stack to overcome the limitation of current dynamic protocol stacks. DRAPS offers extendability in framework by means of plug-in components. Compared with other frameworks, DRAPS is based on the realistic requirements for reconfiguration of communicating protocol components; related frameworks have not considered peer components in a dynamic reconfiguration of a protocol component. Our experimental results on dynamic reconfigurations show that an acceptable transparency can be maintained using DRAPS.

References

1. Satyanarayanan, M.: Pervasive computing: Vision and challenges. In: IEEE PCM, pp. 10–17. IEEE Computer Society Press, Los Alamitos (2001)
2. Niamanesh, M., Dehkordi, F.H., Nobakht, N.F., Jalili, R.: On validity assurance of dynamic reconfiguration in component-based program. In: FSEN 2005. Proceedings of IPM International Workshop on Foundations of Software Engineering (Theory and Practice), vol. (7) (October 2005)
3. Stewart, R., Xie, Q., Morneault, K., Sharp, C., Schwarzbauer, H., Taylor, T., Rytina, I., Kalla, M., Zhang, L., Paxson, V.: Stream control transmission protocol. RFC 2960 (October 2000)
4. AN, L., Pung, H.K., Zhou, L.: Design and implementation of a dynamic protocol framework. Journal of Computer Communications (2005)
5. Lee, Y., Chang, R.: Developing dynamic-reconfigurable communication protocol stacks using java. Software Practice Experience 6(35), 601–620 (2005)
6. Niamanesh, M., Jalili, R.: Formalizing compatibility and substitutability in communication protocols using i/o-constraint automata. In: FSEN 2007. IPM International Workshop on Foundations of Software Engineering (Theory and Practice) (April 2007) (accepted)

Vulnerability Analysis in VGBPS Using Prolog

Mohammad Ebrahim Rafiei[1], Mohsen Taherian[1], Hamid Mousavi[1],
Ali Movaghar[2], and Rasool jalili[2]

[1] CE Department, Sharif University of Technology, Tehran, Iran
{rafiei,tahrian,h_mousavi}@ce.sharif.edu
[2] CE Department, Sharif University of Technology, Tehran, Iran
{movaghar,jalili}@sharif.edu

Abstract. Vulnerabilities are now part of all software systems. To handle vulnerabilities, many approaches have been proposed till now. Many of these approaches try to analyze vulnerabilities based on model checking techniques. However, the models used in these approaches handle authorized and unauthorized rules separately. This basically cause in weaker modeling abilities and consequently weaker vulnerability analysis. From authorized and unauthorized rules, we mean those emanated from access control model and those originated from vulnerabilities respectively. Currently, a new general graph-based protection system concentrating on vulnerabilities called VGBPS is proposed to overcome the mentioned problem. VGBPS combines vulnerabilities and their related rules in an access control system, in a way that no extra effort is needed to handle them. In contrast, vulnerability analysis in this model can be done by answering safety problem. Using this model, we propose a new approach for vulnerability analysis based on Prolog inference engine. In this approach, we show how to express modeling graph and rules set of a VGBPS model using Prolog facts and rules. Safety problem is also defined by Prolog rules. Finally, we use Prolog inference engine to answer safety problem which is the base of vulnerability analysis in VGBPS. We provide a case study to show how this approach can help us find possible exploits of a specific configuration in a system. Using Prolog, we can also find all possible scenarios of these exploits which can be used in many security analyses.

Keywords: Protection System, Safety Problem, Vulnerability Analysis, Prolog.

1 Introduction

Vulnerabilities are those software failures which may allow unauthorized access to attackers [1]. It is almost impossible to implement a software component without bugs or failures. Thus, some approaches are required to deal with specifying, designing, and implementing a computer system without vulnerabilities, discovering unknown vulnerabilities, and detecting possible exploits of them. This is usually referred to as *vulnerability analysis*. One of the usual ways to analyze vulnerabilities is to use model checking approaches. Generally in these approaches, an abstract model of the designated system will be constructed, and security constraints of the model will be specified formally. Using a model checker, it is examined whether the model meets its specified security conditions or not.

F. Arbab and M. Sirjani (Eds.): FSEN 2007, LNCS 4767, pp. 404–411, 2007.

Till now, various models have been proposed to deal with safety problem and vulnerability analysis in operating systems and computer networks. Some of these approaches employ logics such as Computational Tree Logic (CTL) or Linear Temporal Logic (LTL) to express their models and verify them. Gutteman *et al.* analyzed information flow in the access control system of SELinux using a tool called SLAT [2] and [3]. In their approach, the security policies of the access control are expressed by a formal language.

One of the first tools for modeling vulnerabilities and their interactions is COPs [4]. Later, many other works have been proposed to analyze vulnerabilities and to realize their effects using model checkers [5], [6], [7], and [8].

Centric problem in model checkers is the state explosion problem. To alleviate this problem, one can use a descriptive language to define his access control rules. He can then employ the inference engine of some tools such as Prolog and Clips to check his model. A good example of this approach is the one proposed in [9]. In this approach, vulnerabilities emanated from bad configuration of some commercial products such as Adobe and Multimedia in Windows are analyzed. Similarly, Ramakrishnan and Seker proposed a model based on Prolog and attempted to use a new model checking approach to identify vulnerabilities in a part of UNIX [8]. They claimed that using this approach, they can solve the state explosion problem partially.

The models used in these approaches are usually weak in modeling the interaction of different types of rules. In protection systems, two main types of rules should be considered; authorized and unauthorized rules. From the former, we mean those emanated from access control model. The latter one indicates those emanated from vulnerabilities. Previous models mostly deal with these two types of rules separately. This basically cause in weaker modeling abilities and consequently weaker vulnerability analysis. Currently, a new general graph-based protection system concentrating on vulnerabilities called VGBPS is proposed to overcome this problem [10]. VGBPS combines vulnerabilities and their related rules in an access control system in a way that no extra effort is required to handle them.

In this paper, introducing protection system VGBPS, we will propose a new approach to automatically answer the safety problem in VGBPS. In this approach, we express VGBPS models using Prolog language, and verify some specific security policies in it using Prolog inference engine. The main advantage of this approach is that we can automatically analyze vulnerabilities considering all possible interactions between authorized and unauthorized rules in the protection system containing them. Using Prolog inference engine can also alleviate the problem of state explosion [8]. Moreover, knowing that most of attack scenarios are containing a limited number of steps, we can reduce these states to a reasonable number. Another important feature of the approach is that we can find all possible scenarios of attacks. This kind of information is very important in vulnerability analyses. For example, with this information, we can find weak points of the system which are those parts participating in many scenarios of possible attack.

The paper is organized as follows; in section 2, we describe VGBPS in brief. We show how VGBPS can be expressed by Prolog rules and facts, and how we can define the safety problem in VGBPS using this language in section 3. Section 4 contains a case study of our approach. Finally, we conclude the paper in section 6.

2 VGBPS Protection System

In this part, we explain VGBPS protection system briefly. Formally, VGBPS is defined as a tuple (G, R), where G is the current modeling graph and R is the set of rules indicating how G can be changed. In this section, we discuss the modeling graph G, the rules set R, and the safety problem in VGBPS respectively.

Let V_{all} be all entities (vertices or nodes) in the system and E_{all} be all potential edges. G(V, E) is the modeling graph where $V \subseteq V_{all}$ and $E \subseteq E_{all}$. For the sake of simplicity, edges are defined as a triple (v, u, l) in G, where v and u are source and destination vertices (nodes) and l denotes the edge's associated label. The label set L consists of four sets L_{vul}, L_{attr}, L_{rgt}, and L_{rel}, to demonstrate vulnerabilities, attributes, access rights, and relations respectively.

Using this definition of edges, vulnerabilities, attributes, access rights, and relations can be dealt with similarly. To depict that a node v has *read* access over u, we can use the edge $(v, u, read)$. To demonstrate a vulnerability *vul* in node a, the loop edge (a, a, vul) can be used. To assign an attribute *attr* to the node a, the loop edge $(a, a, attr)$ may be employed. Having a relation *rel* between a and b, the edge (a, b, rel) can be used.

Edge pattern plays an important role in VGBPS rule definition. An *edge pattern* is a triple (a, b, t) where a and b belongs to the set of defined phrase called *PV* (Pattern Variables), and $t \in L$. Set of all possible edge patterns are referred as EP. The most important concern regarding edge patterns is to identify edges matching an edge pattern.

Definition 1. We say edge $e(v, u, l)$ *matches* edge pattern $ep(a, b, t)$; if and only if l and t be identical and if $a = b$ then $v = u$. In this case, we say a and b respectively match v and u or vice versa. Formally:

$$match: EP \times E_{all} \rightarrow \{true, false\}$$
$$match((a, b, t), (v, u, l)) = true \Leftrightarrow t = l \wedge (a = b \rightarrow v = u) \tag{1}$$

For example, the edge pattern $ep(a, b, r)$ matches all edges labeled r, or $ep(a, a, o)$ matches all loop edges labeled o. An edge pattern is not individually useful in rule definition; a set of edge patterns is required to be matched with a set of edges.

Definition 2. Suppose that EPS is a subset of EP, (that is EPS is a set of edge patterns). EPS matches with $E_m \subseteq E_{all}$, if and only if:

$$|E_m| = |EPS| \wedge$$
$$\forall ep \in EPS \,|\, (\exists e \in E_m \,|\, match(ep, e)) \wedge$$
$$\forall ep_1, ep_2 \in EPS, e_1, e_2 \in E_m \,|\, match(ep_1, e_1) \wedge match(ep_2, e_2) \rightarrow$$
$$((ep_1.a = ep_2.a \rightarrow e_1.a = e_2.a) \wedge \tag{2}$$
$$(ep_1.b = ep_2.b \rightarrow e_1.b = e_2.b) \wedge$$
$$(ep_1.a = ep_2.b \rightarrow e_1.a = e_2.b))$$

where $e.a$ and $e.b$ are the first and the second items of tuple e. We call E_m a setmatch of EPS. The definition implies that if any $a \in PV$ matched with a vertex v in one of the edge-match, it can not match with any other vertex.

Definition 3. Rule set R is the set of rules that each of them is a tuple (EP_e, EP_n, EP_a, EP_d) where EP_e, EP_n, EP_a, EP_d are all subsets of EP.

Informally, EP_e and EP_n are two sets of edge patterns indicating which edges should exist/not exist in order that the rule can be applied, and EP_a and EP_d respectively represent new edges which will be added to and the edges which will be removed from graph G after the rule application.

Although safety problem is not part of the model, we define it in this section. Before defining the safety problem we should first understand the concept of witness and also predicate can•share [11]. Having a protection system $PS(G_0, R)$, a *witness* is a sequence of rules, $r_1, r_2 \ldots r_n$ ($r_i \in R$, $1 \le i \le n$) which the first one is applicable to the current modeling graph G_0 and r_{i+1} is applicable to the resulted modeling graph after application of the first i rules in the sequence. That is $G_0 \mapsto_{r_1} G_1 \mapsto_{r_2} G_2 \ldots \mapsto_{r_n} G_n$.

Let l be a label ($l \in L$) and, v and u be two vertices in the protection system $PS(G, R)$. Predicate can•share(v, u, l) is true in PS if and only if there is a witness whose application to modeling graph G generates a new graph containing the edge (v, u, l). Having the protection system $PS(G, R)$ and a set of can•share predicate P, the *Safety Problem* is the problem of finding witness w whose application to graph G violates (makes true) at least one of the predicates included in P.

We can define other predicates for P set too. Another important predicate is can•revoke which can be define as follows; Let v and u be two vertices in the modeling graph G_0 of protection system $PS(G_0, R)$ and there is an edge between v and u labeled $r \in L$. Predicate can•revoke(v, u, r) is true in PS if and only if there is a witness whose application to G_0 generates a new graph containing no edge from v to u labeled r.

3 Expressing VGBPS Using Prolog

In this section, we show how a VGBPS protection system can be expressed using Prolog language. To this end, we divide the section into 3 parts; 1) expressing modeling graph G of VGBPS, 2) rules set R, and 3) safety problem in VGBPS.

3.1 Expressing Modeling Graph G

First of all, we should express basics of graphs which are vertices and edges using Prolog rules. To express vertex v and an edge from v to u labeled r, we use `ver-tex(v)` and `edge(v, u, r)` rules in Prolog respectively.

For simplicity, we define four primitives; `exists`, `not-exist`, `add`, and `de-lete`. Using `exists` and `not-exist`, we can check for the existence and absence of an edge respectively. To add a new edge and remove an exiting edge, `add` and `delete` predicates should be used respectively. The definitions of these rules are as follows.

```
exists(v, u, r) :- vertex(v), vertex(u), edge(v, u, r).
not-exist(V, U, R) :- \+ vertex(V).
not-exist(V, U, R) :- \+ vertex(U).
not-exist(V, U, R) :- \+ edge(V, U, R).
```

```
add(v, u, r) :- vertex(v), vertex(u),
   \+ edge(v, u, r), assert(edge(v, u, r)).
delete(v, u, r) :- vertex(v), vertex(u),
   edge(v, u, r),        retract(edge(v, u, r)).
```

3.2 Expressing Rules

Till now, we showed how to express the modeling graph of VGBPS. In this part, we show how to express a rule in VGBPS with Prolog rules. Suppose that $Rule1(EP_e, EP_n, EP_a, EP_d)$ is a rule in VGBPS where $EP_e=\{P_{e1}, P_{e2}, ...\}$, $EP_n=\{P_{n1}, P_{n2}, ...\}$, $EP_a=\{P_{a1}, P_{a2}, ...\}$, and $EP_d=\{P_{d1}, P_{d2}, ...\}$. We can express $Rule_1$, with following one in Prolog:

```
Rule₁ (Pₐ₁.A, Pₐ₁.B, Pₐ₁.r, ... ,
        P_d1.A, P_d1.B, P_d1.r, ...)
:-      exists(P_e1.A, P_e1.B, P_e1.r), ...,
        not-exist(P_n1.A, P_n1.B, P_n1.r), ...,
        add(Pₐ₁.A, Pₐ₁.B, Pₐ₁.r), ...,
        delete(P_d1.A, P_d1.B, P_d1.r), ... .
```

where P.A and P.B indicate the first and the second elements of pattern P, and P.r shows the related label of the pattern P. The only remaining thing is that for each rule we need another rule to remove its effects from the modeling graph:

```
rev-Rule₁ (Pₐ₁.A, Pₐ₁.B, Pₐ₁.r, ... ,
           P_d1.A, P_d1.B, P_d1.r, ...)
:-         delete(Pₐ₁.A, Pₐ₁.B, Pₐ₁.r),   ...,
           add(P_d1.A, P_d1.B, P_d1.r), ... .
```

3.3 Expressing the Safety Problem

As already mentioned, we usually define safety problem using can●share and\or can●revoke predicates. In other words, to answer safety problem, we should be able to answer these two predicates. Consider that PS is a VGBPS model with rule set R=$\{rule_1, rule_2, ...\}$. Thus, we can define can●share(v, u, r) predicate as follows.

```
can-share (V, U, r, depth) :- exists(V, U, r).
can-share (V, U, r, depth) :- depth = 0, !.
can-share (V, U, r, depth) :- rule₁(A, B, C, ...),
    can-share (V, U, r, depth-1) -> write('Rule₁');
    rev-rule₁(A, B, C, ...), fail.
can-share (V, U, r, depth) :- rule₂(A, B, C, ...),
    can-share (V, U, r, depth-1) -> write('Rule₂');
    rev-rule₂(A, B, C, ...), fail.
... .
```

In this definition, we used depth to limit the number of states in the model. Note that since the rules can both increase and decrease edges to and from the model, without definition of depth, the recursive rule can•share may never be ended. We used a simple mechanism to print the scenario of the exploits using `write` command. Finally, we remove effect of each rule before moving to next clause. Similarly, can•revoke(v, u, r) predicate can be also defined.

4 Case Study

In this part, we propose a simple case study. Modeling graph G in this protection system is depicted in Fig. 1. As you can see, there is a node m monitoring all other nodes in the system. Two nodes n_2 and n_3 have buffer overflow vulnerability. Other access rights are shown in the figure. The protection system contains following rules in its rule set R too:

$r_{TakeFromChild}$ ({(P, C, take), (P, C, parent), (C, O, R)}, $\varnothing$, {(P, O, R)}, $\varnothing$)

$r_{ManagedGrant}$ ({(B, A, grant), (B, O, own), (B, O, R)}, $\varnothing$, {(A, O, R)}, $\varnothing$)

$r_{UnmanagedGrant1}$ ({(B, O, own), (B, O, R)}, {(M, B, mntr)}, {(A, O, R)}, $\varnothing$)

$r_{UnmanagedGrant2}$ ({(B, A, grant), (B, O, R)}, {(M, B, mntr)}, {(A, O, R)}, $\varnothing$)

r_{bof} ({(A, App, execute), (App, App, bof)}, $\varnothing$, {(A, App, comp)}, $\varnothing$)

r_{WXComp} ({(A, App, write), (B, App, execute)}, $\varnothing$, {(A, B, comp)}, $\varnothing$)

$r_{TakeCompRight}$ ({(A, B, comp), (B, O, R)}, $\varnothing$, {(A, O, R)}, $\varnothing$)

Using the definition of rules, you can easily understand the meaning of each rule. For example, the first rule indicates that if there exist any 3 vertex P, C, and O and any right (label) R where P has *take* access over C, P is the parent of C, and C has access R over O then P can gain (*take*) access R over O. Informally, this rule shows how a node can take the access rights of another one. Comparing to Take-Grant Model (TG) [11], in this system, only can parents take the access rights of their children.

The system also has three kinds of grant rules. In managed grant (*ManagedGrant*), node B can grant its access rights over those nodes that B is their owner. Of course, B should have *grant* access to the node it wants to grant in this rule. We have also two types of unmanaged grants. In the first type (*UnmanagedGrant1*), Attacker A can gain access rights of a node B over those nodes which B owns if B is not being monitored.

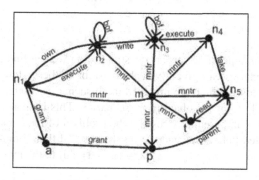

Fig. 1. Modeling graph for the case study

Similarly, in second type of unmanaged grant rules (*UnmanagedGrant2*), node *B* can grant its access rights to *A* if *B* is not being monitored and *B* has *grant* access over *A*. Another rule (*bof*) is considered to deal with access leakage because of buffer overflow vulnerability. Other vulnerability can be dealt with in a similar way too.

You should note that this is actually a very simple case. In more complex models, rules may have decreasing nature too. In that case, the safety problem will be a harder problem, usually a NP-Complete one. That is where our approach can be beneficial.

Using the approach introduced in previous section, we can define VGBPS rules in this case study using following Prolog rules. Because of the lack of space, we include only three of these rules here. Other rules can be defined similarly:

```
rule_take_from_child(P, C, O, R)  :-
    exists(P, C, take), exists(P, C, parent),
    exists(C, O, R), add(P, O, R).
rule_managed_grant(B, A, O, R):-
    exists(B, A, grant), exists(B, O, own),
    exists(B, O, R), add(A, O, R).
rule_unmanaged_grant(B, A, O, R)  :-
    exists(B, O, own), exists(B, O, R),
    not_exists(M, B, monitor), add(A, O, R).
```

Completing the translation of modeling graph and rules to Prolog language, we should specify the security policy too. For example in the proposed system, it is desired that node p be not able to gain read access over target node t (Fig. 1.). To check this out, we can use predicate can•share(p, t, read). This is equivalent to the rule can_share(p, t, read, d) in Prolog, where d is a reasonable depth. Using Prolog inference engine, it can be understood that this predicate is true. In other worlds, the security policy can be violated. The scenario of this attack is as follows:

```
rule_managed_grant       (n1, a, n2, execute)
rule_bof                 (a, n2)
rule_taking_comp_right   (a, n2, n3, write)
rule_w_xcomp             (a, n3, n4)
rule_taking_comp_right   (a, n4, n5, take)
rule_unmanaged_grant2    (a, p, n5, take)
rule_take_from_child     (P, n5, t, read)
```

This is not the only possible scenario. Using prolog we can find all other scenarios. The computed scenarios can give a valuable insight of the system. For example, we can find nodes or edges which are involved in all scenarios. In this case, edges (n_1, a, grant) and (n_2, n_2, bof) are involved in all scenarios. This basically shows that eliminating one of these can potentially resolve the problem of the leakage of *read* access on node t. We tested both cases and the results showed that eliminating one of them makes predicate can_share(p, t, read, d) fail in the model.

5   Conclusion and Future Works

Introducing the protection system VGBPS, we proposed a new approach to solve the safety problem in VGBPS automatically. In this approach, we use Prolog language to express both the model and the safety problem. After, we use Prolog inference engine to answer safety problem in VGBPS. We also provide a simple case study to show the approach in practice. We showed how we can resolve possible attacks in the system.

Knowing the possible scenario of an attack in a system gives a valuable insight of the system. In this paper, we showed how these scenarios can be found automatically, but a good future work is to use these peaces of information to analyze the status of a system from the security respects. As an example, one can give weight to edges resulting from different rules and find more probable scenarios of attack in a way.

References

1. Shahriari, H.R., Sadoddin, R., Jalili, R., Zakeri, R., Omidian, A.R.: Network vulnerability analysis through vulnerability Take-Grant model (VTG). In: 7th International Conference on Information and Communications Security (2005)
2. Guttman, J., Herzog, A., Ramsdell, J.: SLAT: Information flow in security enhanced Linux. Included in the SLAT distribution (2003)
3. Guttman, J., Herzog, A., Ramsdell, J., Skorupka, C.: Verifying Information Flow Goals in Security-Enhanced Linux. Journal of Computer Security 13, 115–134 (2005)
4. Farmer, D., Spafford, E.H.: The Cops Security Checker System. Technical Report CSDTR-993, Purdue University (1991)
5. Ramakrishnan, C.R., Sekar, R.: Model-Based Analysis of Configuration Vulnerabilities. Journal of Computer Security, 189–209 (2002)
6. Fithen, W.L., Hernan, S.V., O'Rourke, P.F., Shinberg, D.A.: Formal Modeling of Vulnerabilities. Bell Lab's Technical Journal, 173–186 (2004)
7. Ritchey, R.W., Ammann, P.: Using Model Checking to Analyze Network Vulnerabilities. In: 2000 IEEE Symposium on Security and Privacy, pp. 156–165. IEEE Computer Society Press, Los Alamitos (2000)
8. Ramakrishnan, C., Sekar, R.: Model-Based Vulnerability Analysis of Computer Systems. In: 2nd International Workshop on Verification, Model Checking and Abstract Interpretation (1998)
9. Govindavajhala, S., Appel, A.: Windows Access Control Demystified. Technical Report, Princeton University (2006)
10. Rafiei, M.E., Jalili, R., Mousavi, H.: Vulnerability Analysis through a General Graph-Based Protection System. International Journal of Computer Science and Network Security 6(12), 311–319 (2006)
11. Bishop, M.: Conspiracy and Information Flow in the Take-Grant Protection Model. Journal of Computer Security, 331–360 (1996)

An Alternative Algorithm for Constraint Automata Product

Bahman Pourvatan and Nima Rouhy

AmirKabir University of Technology, Tehran, Iran
pourvtan@ce.aut.ac.ir, ruhy@ce.aut.ac.ir

Abstract. Reo is a language for exogenous coordination of component connectors based on a calculus of channels. Constraint automata has been proposed as Reo formal semantics. The corresponding constraint automata of a Reo circuit is compositionally constructed by the product of all the constituent constraint automata. We introduce a simple alternative algorithm for computing product of two constraint automata in this paper. We also give a greedy algorithm for finding the order of selection of two constraint automata when we have to compute product of more than two constraint automata. The order of our algorithm is less than the other algorithms proposed earlier by a constant factor. We propose an algebraic representation for constraint automata which our product algorithm is based on. Input and output of the provided tool are consistent with the other tools supporting Reo join and constraint automata product.

Keywords: Reo, Constraint Automata, Constraint Automata Product.

1 Introduction

Components that work together need to be synchronized. Instead of endogenous component synchronization in which components should obey mutual exclusion rules themselves, Reo [1,2] uses exogenous component synchronization mechanism. It introduces an open-ended set of channels which data can move through. Channel-ends can be collocated in a node which has special rules for passing data through itself. Building automated tools to address such concerns as equivalence or containment of the behavior of two given connectors, and verification of the behavior of a connector requires an operational semantics model suitable for model checking. Constraint automata which are introduced in [3,4] give a solution to this problem. Using constraint automata that describe the input/output behavior at the ports of the components it is possible to check Reo models.

Working with constraint automata as a compositional semantics of Reo, we need to construct the product of constraint automata. Tools and the corresponding algorithms are introduced in [5] and [6]. In this paper our main concern is to introduce an algorithm for computing product of two constraint automata which is simpler to understand, easier to implement, and also faster than the algorithm in [6] by a constant factor. We use a dynamic programming algorithm

F. Arbab and M. Sirjani (Eds.): FSEN 2007, LNCS 4767, pp. 412–422, 2007.
© Springer-Verlag Berlin Heidelberg 2007

in the case that we have to compute product of more than two constraint automata which is based on better selection of constraint automata to be joined. We propose an algebraic representation for constraint automata which is the basis of our algorithm. This representation makes the intuition of the constraint automata product more clear. Basic algorithms in automata theory are considered in our work [7,8,9]. We also implement a tool to construct the product of two constraint automata. It gets the input in XML format and produces the result again in XML format, which makes it more portable to the other tools. Using this tool we compare our algorithm with the one in [6].

Plan of the paper. The rest of this paper is organized as follows. Section 2 and 3 is a brief overview of Reo and constraint automata, respectively. In Section 4 we show our algebraic representation for constraint automata. Then in Section 5 we explain our alternative algorithm for computing product of two constraint automata based on the algebraic representation introduced in Section 4. A small example is used to show the approach. We present our algorithm for better selection of constraint automata to be joined, in Section 6. In Section 7 we show a case study and explain our experimental results, comparing the running time of our algorithm with the one used in [6]. We conclude in Section 8, by pointing out our current and future work on building the product of two automata, and the methods for building larger and more complex constraint automata in a more structural way.

2   Reo: A Coordination Language

Reo is a model for building component connectors in a compositional manner [1,2]. It allows modeling the behavior of such connectors, formally reasoning about them, and once proven correct, automatically generating the so-called glue code from the specification. Each connector in Reo is, in turn, constructed compositionally out of simpler connectors, which are ultimately composed out of primitive channels.

A channel is a primitive communication medium with exactly two ends, each with its own unique identity. There are two types of channel ends: source end through which data enters and sink end through which data leaves a channel. A channel must support a certain set of primitive operations, such as I/O, on its ends; beyond that, Reo places no restriction on the behavior of a channel. This allows an open-ended set of different channel types to be used simultaneously together in Reo, each with its own policy for synchronization, buffering, ordering, computation, data retention/loss, etc.

Channels are connected to make a circuit. Connecting (or *joining*) channels is putting channel ends together in a *node*. So, a *node* is a set of channel ends. A node in Reo has certain semantics: for all the source channel ends on a node, a fork operation takes place which is copying the outgoing data to all the channel ends; for all the sink channel ends on a node, a merge operation takes place which is a nondeterministic choice between incoming data.

A component can write data items to a source node that it is connected to. The write operation succeeds only if all (source) channel ends coincident on the node accept the data item, in which case the data item is transparently written to every source end coincident on the node. A source node, thus, acts as a *replicator*. A component can obtain data items, by input operation, from a sink node that it is connected to. A take operation succeeds only if at least one of the (sink) channel ends coincident on the node offers a suitable data item; if more than one coincident channel end offers suitable data items, one is selected nondeterministically. A sink node, thus, acts as a nondeterministic *merger*. A mixed node nondeterministically selects and takes a suitable data item offered by one of its coincident sink channel ends and replicates it into all of its coincident source channel ends.

3   Constraint Automata: Compositional Semantics of Reo

Using constraint automata as an operational model for Reo connectors, the automata states stand for the possible configurations (e.g., the contents of the FIFO-channels of a Reo connector) while the automata-transitions represent the possible data flow and its effect on these configurations. The operational semantics for Reo presented in [2] can be reformulated in terms of constraint automata. Constraint automaton of a given Reo connector can be defined in a *compositional* way. For this, composition operators for constraint automata corresponding to the Reo connector primitives are presented.

The definition of constraint automata is as follows:

Definition 1. *[Constraint automata]* A constraint automaton (over the data domain *Data*) is a tuple $\mathcal{A} = (Q, \mathcal{N}ames, \longrightarrow, Q_0)$ where

- Q is a set of states,
- $\mathcal{N}ames$ is a finite set of names,
- $\longrightarrow$ is a subset of $Q \times 2^{\mathcal{N}ames} \times DC \times Q$, called the transition relation of $\mathcal{A}$, where DC is the set of data constraints,
- $Q_0 \subseteq Q$ is the set of initial states.

We write $q \xrightarrow{N,g} p$ instead of $(q, N, g, p) \in \longrightarrow$. We call N the name-set and g the guard of the transition. For every transition

$$q \xrightarrow{N,g} p$$

we require that (1) $N \neq \emptyset$ and (2) $g \in DC(N, Data)$. $\mathcal{A}$ is called finite iff Q, $\longrightarrow$ and the underlying data domain *Data* are finite.   □

3.1   Constraint Automata for the Basic Channels

Figure 1 shows the constraint automata for some of the standard basic channel types: synchronous channels with source a and sink b, synchronous drain with

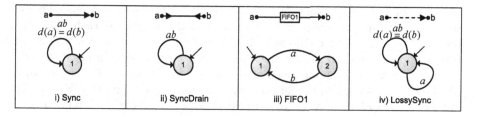

Fig. 1. Some primitive Reo's channels, and their constraint automata

sources a and b, FIFO1 channels with source a and sink b, lossy synchronous channels with source a and sink b. In all the cases the automata are deterministic. There are operators defined on constraint automata that capture the meaning of Reo join operator [4,3] which will be explained next.

3.2   Product of Two Constraint Automata

Definition 2. *[Product-automaton (join)]* The product-automaton of the two constraint automata $\mathcal{A}_1 = (Q_1, \mathcal{N}_1, \longrightarrow_1, Q_{0,1})$ and $\mathcal{A}_2 = (Q_2, \mathcal{N}_2, \longrightarrow_2, Q_{0,2})$, is:

$$A_1 \bowtie A_2 = (Q_1 \times Q_2, \mathcal{N}_1 \cup \mathcal{N}_2, \longrightarrow, Q_{0,1} \times Q_{0,2})$$

where $\longrightarrow$ is defined by the following rules:

$$\frac{q_1 \xrightarrow{N_1,g_1}_1 p_1, q_2 \xrightarrow{N_2,g_2}_2 p_2, N_1 \cap \mathcal{N}_2 = N_2 \cap \mathcal{N}_1}{\langle q_1, q_2 \rangle \xrightarrow{N_1 \cup N_2, g_1 \wedge g_2} \langle p_1, p_2 \rangle}$$

and

$$\frac{q_1 \xrightarrow{N,g}_1 p_1, N \cap \mathcal{N}_2 = \varnothing}{\langle q_1, q_2 \rangle \xrightarrow{N,g} \langle p_1, p_2 \rangle}$$

In the next section we will show our algebraic notation based on Definition 1 and in Section 5 the product algorithm based on Definition 2 is explained. It is shown that in our approach instead of computing two intersections of $N_1 \cap \mathcal{N}_2$ and $N_2 \cap \mathcal{N}_1$, we only need to compute one intersection at each step and hence reduce the order of the computation with a constant factor.

4   An Algebraic Representation for Constraint Automata

To have a simple product algorithm, we show a constraint automaton as the sum of transitions. Each transition is tagged by its name-set N and its guard g. The main difference is that in the name-set of each transition we also include the negation of absent names, $\mathcal{N} - N$. For that we introduce an expanded name set for a constraint automata which also includes the negation of each name. We show the set of negated names as $\overline{\mathcal{N}}$ and the expanded set is $\mathcal{N} \cup \overline{\mathcal{N}}$. For every transition we include all the names either in their positive form or negated form.

Our approach is that for each transition $\longrightarrow$ in $(Q, \mathcal{N}, \longrightarrow, Q_0)$ we expand its name-set N by adding negation of $\mathcal{N} - N$ to it. For example if $N = \{a, b\}$ and $\mathcal{N} = \{a, b, c\}$ then N is going to be $\{a, b, \overline{c}\}$. We show negation of i by $\overline{i}$ which means non-existence of i in that transition. In addition for each q in Q, we add a new transition from q to itself with a set of names consisting the negation of all names in $\mathcal{N}$. This denotes staying in the state while no action (name) is present.

Definition 3. *[Constraint automata algebraic representation]* We show a constraint automaton (over the data domain *Data*) $\mathcal{A} = (Q, \mathcal{N}, \longrightarrow, Q_0)$ as

$$\sum_{\substack{i=1 \\ p,q \in Q}}^{m} (N_i, g_i)_q^p, \quad Q_0$$

where

- each $(N_i, g_i)_q^p$ denotes a transition ($\longrightarrow$) of constraint automata from state p to state q with the name-set N_i and guard g_i, e.g., $p \xrightarrow{N_i, g_i} q$,
- $\mathcal{N}ames$ is a finite set of names,
- each N_i is a logical product of names a in $\mathcal{N}$ appearing as a or $\overline{a}$ for every $a \in \mathcal{N}$,
- g_i is the corresponding data constraint for the transition i,
- p, q denote states of the constraint automata,
- m is the number of transitions in $\mathcal{A}$,
- Q_0 denotes set of initial states.   □

Note: For the sake of simplicity, when convenient, we abstract from data constraints in our discussions. Data constraints are essential components of constraint automata, but in our approach we cope with them exactly like the other existing approaches (according to the two rules in Definition 2).

It is clear from the definition that there is a simple one-to-one mapping from a constraint automata and its algebraic representation. For mapping a constraint automata to its algebraic representation we have the sum of the name-sets of all the transitions, and for each name-sets (transition) we write source and destination states as a superscript and subscript, respectively. For example in Figure 2-i there are two transitions in constraint automata with ab and $\overline{ab}$, so its algebraic representation is $ab_1^1 + \overline{ab}_1^1$. We also denote the initial state by $\{1\}$.

For the opposite directed; constructing a constraint automata from its algebraic notation is clear. Figure 2 shows some of the primitive channels with their corresponding constraint automata and their algebraic representation.

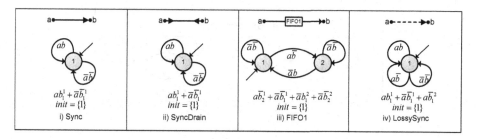

Fig. 2. Some primitive Reo channels, their constraint automata and algebraic representations

5 An Alternative Algorithm for Constraint Automata Production

Based on the Definition 3 and the mapping between constraint automata and its algebraic representation we have the following definition for finding the product of two constraint automata represented in the algebraic form.

Definition 4. *[Automaton-algebraic-product]* The product-automaton of the two constraint automata $\mathcal{A}_1 = (Q_1, \mathcal{N}_1, \longrightarrow_1, Q_{0,1})$ and $\mathcal{A}_2 = (Q_2, \mathcal{N}_2, \longrightarrow_2, Q_{0,2})$ is $\mathcal{A} = (Q, \mathcal{N}, \longrightarrow, Q_0)$ where

$$A_1 = \sum_{\substack{i=1 \\ p,q \in Q_1}}^{m_1} N_{1_i}{}^{p}_{q}, Q_{0,1} \quad , \quad A_2 = \sum_{\substack{i=1 \\ r,s \in Q_2}}^{m_2} N_{2_i}{}^{r}_{s}, Q_{0,2}$$

and

$$A = A_1 \bowtie A_2 = \sum_{\substack{i=1 \\ p,q \in Q_1}}^{m_1} N_{1_i}{}^{p}_{q} \times \sum_{\substack{i=1 \\ r,s \in Q_2}}^{m_2} N_{2_i}{}^{r}_{s}, Q_0 = \sum_{\substack{i=1 \\ t,u \in Q}}^{m_1 \times m_2} N_{i_u}{}^{t}, Q_0$$

where t and u are new combined source and destination states in result of logical product of two transitions with p and r as source and q and s as destination states. State $t \in Q$ is an initial state iff $p \in Q_{0,1}$ and $r \in Q_{0,2}$; and the new name set $\mathcal{N}$ is $\mathcal{N}_1 \cup \mathcal{N}_2$.

Logical product of two transitions (which are logical products themselves) produces a new transition according to the common rules, so we will have a new transition iff there is no name appears in both with different signs (e.g. x and $\bar{x}$). In a new transition with name set $\mathcal{N}$, the set of names appearing in the product is $\mathcal{N}_1 \cup \mathcal{N}_2$. All the names in $\mathcal{N}_1 \cup \mathcal{N}_2$ appear in all the transitions either in their positive or negative form. Data constraint of the new transition is the conjunction of data constraints of two corresponding transitions of A_1 and A_2 (not shown in the formulas).

Figure 3 gives an example for applying this algorithm on two FIFO1 channels connected to each other and making a FIFO2. Figures 3-*i* and *ii* show the

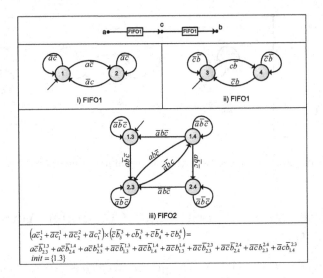

Fig. 3. Constraint automata for FIFO2 channels created by adding to FIFO1 channels to each others

constraint automata for FIFO1 channels, and *iii* shows the result. The algebraic representation is also included in the figure.

If we convert the algebraic representation of the result constraint automata to its corresponding diagram we will have a directed graph which can be unconnected. States that are not reachable from the initial states can be removed from the constraint automata. By using a simple graph traversal algorithm like DFS (Depth First Search) or BFS (Breadth First Search), it is possible to mark reachable states, and remove the other ones.

5.1   Pseudo Code of Our Algorithm

We use graph data structure to show each constraint automaton which enable us to produce reachable states without doing any extra computation (any graph traversal after constructing the constraint automata). Before explaining how this algorithm works, we explain the data structure containing a constraint automaton.

names	denotes	according to Definition 3
ca		the constraint automaton : $\mathcal{A}$
states		the set of states of constraint automaton : Q
init		the set of initial states of constraint automata : Q_0
names		the set of names in constraint automaton : $\mathcal{N}$
trans		the set of outgoing transitions for each state
dest		destination of each transition : q
fires		the set of names for ith transition : N_i

Now suppose we have two constraint automata ca_1 and ca_2, and want to compute their production. The following is the algorithm written as a pseudocode:

1. New constraint automata ca as the result
2. Add $ca_1.names$ and $ca_2.names$ to $ca.names$
3. New two empty sets set and tmp //set for current states and tmp for visited states
4. For all w in $(ca_1.init, ca_2.init)$ do
5.   add w to set and tmp
6. While set is not empty do
7.   Remove one pair of set as (s_1, s_2)
8.   New state s corresponding to (s_1, s_2)
9.   If s is not member of $ca.states$ Then
10.   Add s to $ca.states$
11.   If $s_1 \in ca_1.init$ and $s_2 \in ca_2.init$ Then
12.   Add s to $ca.init$
13.   For each transition t_1 in $s_1.trans$ and t_2 in $s_2.trans$ do
14.   New transition t
15. $t.fires = t_1.fires \times t_2.fires$ //according to Definition 4
16.   If $t.fires \neq \phi$ Then
17.   Add t to $s.trans$
18.   Set $t.dest$ to the state corresponding to $(t_1.dest, t_2.dest)$
19.   If pair of $(t_1.dest, t_2.dest)$ is not member of tmp Then
20.   Add $(t_1.dest, t_2.dest)$ to set and tmp
21.   End For
22. End While

5.2   The Order of the Algorithm

Using our algebraic representation, it is easy to compute the worst case running time of the algorithm. For computing product of constraint automata A_1 and A_2 which is defined in Definition 4 we need to compute product of each element N_{1_i} in A_1 with all N_{2_j} in A_2 where $i=1,m_1$, and $j=1,m_2$, and computing each product needs $|\mathcal{N}_1 \cup \mathcal{N}_2|$ operations. So the worst case running time of our algorithm is:

$$m_1 \times m_2 \times |\mathcal{N}_1 \cup \mathcal{N}_2|$$

Using graph notations for showing constraint automata improves running time of the algorithm in average case, and as mentioned earlier, because we only need to compute one product in each step and the algorithm used in [6] needs to compute two intersections, so, we expect that our algorithm be faster by at least a constant factor of two.

We have two constraint automata with n_1, n_2 for number of $names$; b_1, b_2 number of initial states; m_1, m_2 number of transitions; s_1, s_2 number of states; and $n_c = n_1 + n_2 - n$ where n is number of elements of $\mathcal{N}_1 \cup \mathcal{N}_2$ (n_c shows the number of common names of two constraint automata).

The probability in which product of two transition produced a new one is: 2^{-n_c}. And there are $\frac{m_1}{s_1}$ and $\frac{m_2}{s_2}$ transitions with the same state as their destination in each constraint automata. So the probability of producing a state is

$1 - (1 - 2^{-n_c})^{\frac{m_1 m_2}{s_1 s_2}}$. The upper bound for the average running time of algorithm is:

$$m_1 m_2 n \times \left[1 - \left(1 - 2^{-n_c}\right)^{\frac{m_1 m_2}{s_1 s_2}} \right]$$

6   Order of Selection of Two Constraint Automata

The result of product of more than two constraint automata does not depends on the order of selection of them, but the number of intermediate operations depends on the order of selection of two constraint automata.

The order of product of two constraint automata with m_1 and m_2 transitions respectively, is $m_1 \times m_2 \times |\mathcal{N}_1 \cup \mathcal{N}_2|$. Part $|\mathcal{N}_1 \cup \mathcal{N}_2|$ of this formula suggest to select those constraint automata which have more common names. We choose an order to decrease the number of $\mathcal{N}_1 \cup \mathcal{N}_2$ and increase the probability of ϕ in the product of two transitions. Dynamic programming is used in finding the two constraint automata with the largest set of common names.

7   Case Study and Experimental Results

In this section we show applying of the algorithm on a case study which computes the product of four constraint automata (Figure 4). In algebraic representation

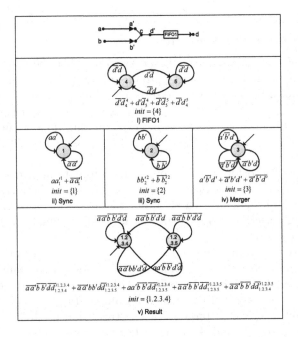

Fig. 4. Constraint automata for two Sync and one FIFO1 channel

of the result, a state named 1.2.3.4 shows that this state is made by joining states 1, 2, 3, and 4. In Figure 4-v you can see the states and transitions of the final constraint automata.

We implement a tool for constraint automata production based on the proposed representation and algorithm. We applied the tool on the same examples used in [6]. The result of this experiment confirms that our algorithm is two times faster than the one proposed in [6].

8   Conclusion and Future Work

In Reo, complex connectors are built out of simpler ones using join operator. Constraint automata is proposed as the compositional semantics of Reo. The composition operator in Reo, join, is captured by product of automata. In building the constraint automata of a connector we may reach to intermediate results with large number of transitions and states. So, we need efficient algorithms for generating automata product.

In this work, we proposed a simple and efficient algorithm for product. The algorithm is more efficient than the already proposed algorithms by a constant factor. We applied the algorithm on a set of examples and the experimental results clearly show the efficiency. We use an intuitive algebraic representation which simplifies the implementation. The representation can also help us when we are joining small automata by hand.

In our future work we will focus on the order of joining more than two constraint automata and how the structure of Reo circuits can be used to find a more efficient algorithm.

References

1. Arbab, F.: Abstract behavior types: A foundation model for components and their composition. In: de Boer, F.S., Bonsangue, M.M., Graf, S., de Roever, W.-P. (eds.) FMCO 2002. LNCS, vol. 2852, pp. 33–70. Springer, Heidelberg (2003)
2. Arbab, F.: Reo: A channel-based coordination model for component composition. Mathematical Structures in Computer Science 14, 329–366 (2004)
3. Arbab, F., Baier, C., Rutten, J.J., Sirjani, M.: Modeling component connectors in Reo by constraint automata (extended abstract). In: FOCLASA 2003. Proceedings of Second International Workshop on Foundations of Coordination Languages and Software Architectures. ENTCS, vol. 97, pp. 25–46. Elsevier, Amsterdam (2004)
4. Baier, C., Sirjani, M., Arbab, F., Rutten, J.J.: Modeling component connectors in reo by constraint automata. Science of Computer Programming 61, 75–113 (2006)
5. Mehta, N., Medvidovic, N., Sirjani, M., Arbab, F.: Modeling behavior in compositions of software architectural. In: ASE 2004, pp. 371–374 (2004)
6. Ghassemi, F., Tasharofi, S., Sirjani, M.: Automated mapping of reo circuits to constraint automata. In: FSEN 2005. Proceedings of the First International Conference on Fundamentals of Software Engineering. ENTCS, vol. 159, pp. 99–115. Elsevier, Amsterdam (2006)

7. Salomaa, A.: Computation and Automata. In: Encyclopedia of Mathematics and its Applications, Cambridge University Press, Cambridge (1985)
8. Hopcraft, J., Ulman, J.: Introduction to Automata Theory, Language and Computation. Addison-Wesley, Reading (1979)
9. Harison, M.: Introduction to Formal Language Theory. Addison-Wesley, Reading (1978)

A Review on Specifying Software Architectures Using Extended Automata-Based Models

Mehran Sharafi[1], Fereidoon Shams Aliee[2], and Ali Movaghar[3]

[1] Faculty of Engineering, Azad Islamic University- Najafabad branch,
PhD student, Tehran Science and Research branch, Iran
[2] Faculty of Computer Engineering, Shahid Beheshti University, Tehran, Iran
[3] Computer Engineering Department, Sharif University of Technology, Tehran 11365, Iran
Mehran_Sharafi@iaun.ac.ir, F_shams@sbu.ac.ir,
Movaghar@sharif.edu

Abstract. Applying an appropriate formal model to specify software architecture makes a reliable foundation to formally verify non-functional properties and therefore, leads to early detection of defects. In this paper we make a comparison between automata-based models and evaluate their abilities to model different aspects of components interaction in software architectures. We try to use Team automata as a middleware to formally specify well-known architectural descriptions in UML2.0. A Limitation of current automata models, so called "actions interleaving" is also discussed and some approaches to overcome this limitation described.

Keywords: Software architectures, Automata-based models, Components interaction.

1 Introduction

Software architecture has become one of the most active research areas in software engineering during recent years. Well designed software architecture may provide: better understanding of system structure, multiple levels of reuse, clear dimensions for system evolution, and ease for system management [1]. Additionally, a rigorous approach toward specifying the software architecture can be used to evaluate non-functional attributes of the software even before implementation and leads to early detection and correction of errors, thus to reduce overall development cost.

Formally specifying of software architecture makes it possible to use formal verification tools to support automatic verification of both functional and non-functional aspects which can be deduced from overall structure and the interactions between components. A key feature of these descriptions is the ability to specify the dynamics. Finite state machines (FSMs), Petri nets or labeled transition systems (LTSs) can be used to model the dynamics of software architectures, describing the set of all possible behaviors as a whole.

In this paper we make a comparison between automata-based models and their capabilities and drawbacks in specifying software architectures. The paper is organized as follows. In Section 2, three of extended automata models which are suitable for

F. Arbab and M. Sirjani (Eds.): FSEN 2007, LNCS 4767, pp. 423–431, 2007.

describing interactions in a component-based system are briefly introduced. These models are: I/O automata, Interface automata and Team automata. In Section 3, benefits and drawbacks of each model is considered and their abilities are compared based on a software architecture point of view, in this section an example of modeling components interaction by team automata also will be taken. We try to show how can create TA model of an architecture modeled by UML2.0 diagrams. In Section 4, a general limitation of all described models in the specification of architectural artifacts i.e. action interleaving is discussed and a solution to overcome this limitation is introduced. Conclusions and future work are discussed in Section 5.

2 Automata-Based Models for Specifying Software Architectures

Automata-based models have been widely used in the literature for the specification of behavioral properties of systems. Since software architecture refers to software components and interconnections between them (i.e. connectors), the behavioral aspects of components and interaction through connectors need to be effectively modeled for further evaluations. Therefore applying automata-based models in the field of software architecture has emerged [2],[3],[4],[5].

Despite the many abilities, some of the extended automata models have been less take in to consideration by software engineers. This is because of the models complexity and difficult use of them for practical purposes. However, specification and verification of various features of components interaction in software architectures needs more powerful formal models. In this section we briefly introduce three of those models that are used in the literature for purposes which are related to model cooperating components.

2.1 Input/Output Automata

I/O automata model was defined by Nancy A. Lynch and Mark R. Tuttle in [6] as a labeled transition system. I/O automata provide an appropriate model for discrete event systems consisting of concurrently operating components with different input, output and internal actions. I/O automata can be composed to form a higher-level I/O automaton and thus form a hierarchy of components of the system.

Definition 1. A (safe) I/O automaton is a tuple $A = (Q, \Sigma_{inp}, \Sigma_{out}, \Sigma_{int}, \delta, I)$, where:

- Q is a set of states.
- $\Sigma_{inp}, \Sigma_{out}, \Sigma_{int}$ are pair wise disjoint sets of input, output and internal actions, respectively. Let $\Sigma = \Sigma_{inp} \bigcup \Sigma_{out} \bigcup \Sigma_{int}$ be called a set of actions.
- $\delta \subseteq Q \times \Sigma \times Q$ is a set of labeled transitions such that for each a $a \in \Sigma_{inp}$ an $q \in Q$ there is a transition $(q, a, q') \in \delta$ (input enableness).
- $I \subseteq Q$ is a nonempty set of initial states.

2.2 Interface Automata

An interface automaton (IA) [7], introduced by de Alfaro and Henzinger, is an automata-based model suitable for specifying component-based systems. The two main characteristics of IA are that they assume a helpful environment and support top-down design. A helpful environment for an interface provides the inputs it needs and always accepts all its outputs. Therefore, interfaces are optimistic, and do not usually specify all possible behaviors of the systems. For example, they often do not include fault scenarios. Top-down design is based on a notion of refinement, which relates two instances of a model. A refinement of a model can be substituted for the original. This feature can be considered as a benefit of IA over the other models, and makes the modeling of hierarchical nature of the architectures easier.

The composition of two IAs consists of all possible interleaved transitions of the two IAs, except for those actions that are shared. Two IAs are composable if they do not take any of the same inputs, do not produce any of the same outputs and the hidden actions of the two components do not overlap. A hidden action is created through the composition of IA when an output action of one component is internally consumed by an input action of another component.

2.3 Team Automata

The Team automata model was first introduced in [8] by Clarence A. Ellis. This complex model is primary designed for modeling groupware systems with communicating teams but can be also used for modeling component-based systems. The main difference of Team automata, compared with previous models, is the freedom of choosing the transition set of the automaton obtained when composing a set of automata, and thus are not limited to one synchronization only. M.H. ter Beek et. al. in [9] have a detailed introduction of Team automata which we do not present in this paper because of the limitation of space.

Component automata are the basic building blocks of team automata. A component automaton is a labeled transition system. The labels represent the actions of the automaton. Three types of actions are distinguished. Component automata interact by synchronizing on common actions. Not all automata sharing an action have to participate in each synchronization on that action. This leads to the notion of a complete transition space, consisting of all possible combinations of identically labeled transitions.

Definition 2. Let $\Gamma \subseteq N$ be a finite set and let for each $i \in \Gamma$ and let S be a composable set of component automata. Then a *team automaton* over S is a transition system $T = \left(Q, \left(\Sigma_{inp}, \Sigma_{out}, \Sigma_{int} \right), \delta, I \right)$, with set of states $Q = \Pi_{i \in \Gamma} Q_i$ and set of initial states $I = \Pi_{i \in \Gamma} I_i$, actions $\Sigma = \bigcup_{i \in \Gamma} \Sigma_i$ specified by $\Sigma_{int} = \bigcup_{i \in \Gamma} \Sigma_{i,int}$, $\Sigma_{out} = \bigcup_{i \in \Gamma} \Sigma_{i,out}$, $\Sigma_{inp} = (\bigcup_{i \in \Gamma} \Sigma_{i,inp}) \setminus \Sigma_{out}$ and transitions $\delta \subseteq Q \times \Sigma \times Q$ such that $\delta \subseteq \Delta(S)$ and moreover $\delta_a = \Delta_a(S)$ for all $a \in \Sigma_{int}$. $\Delta_a(S)$ is the complete transition space of action a is S, and $\Delta(S) = \bigcup_{a \in \Sigma} \Delta_a(S)$.

3 Comparing Models, Based on Software Architecture View

In this section we compare abilities of automata-based models introduced in section 2, for the purpose of modeling software architectures. In this way their benefits and drawbacks regarding to different aspects of component interactions will be discussed.

I/O Automata. I/O automata are input enabled in all states; they can never block the input. Some limitations are to be mentioned regarding to this feature; For example suppose that a component A is ready to send output action a to a component B which is not ready to receive it (e.g. needs to finish some computation first), we are unable to directly model such situations with IOA.

Moreover, as it is defined in [6], a set of I/O automata is strongly compatible if the sets of output actions of component automata are pair wise disjoint and the set of internal actions of every component automaton is disjoint with the action sets of all other component automata. Therefore a set of automata where two or more automata have the same output action is not strongly compatible and cannot be composed according to the definition. Suppose that two components are using the same service of another component, this situation could be modeled without relabelling of the transitions.

Another drawback that could be mentioned about this model is that in the composition of strongly compatible I/O automata each input action a, for which an appropriate output action a exists, is removed to preserve the condition of disjoint input and output action sets. The input actions then cannot be used in a higher level of composition. It is a weakness for modeling hierarchical structure of components.

Interface Automata. Firstly, IA needs not to be input enabled and therefore it dos not have the limitation which mentioned about Input/Output Automata. Secondly, important benefit of IA over I/O Automata is the binary operator *composition* and the refinement *relation* that are introduced in the literature of IA. These approaches allow stepwise refinements of models into their more concrete equivalents. It is obvious that, the feature would be effective in architectural design of software systems.

IA has also the similar drawback of I/O Automata : each input (output) action after linking to an appropriate output (input) action becomes internal action and therefore is not allowable for other linking. Additionally in the literature of Interface automata the composition, is defined for only two IA, therefore it not be directly used for modeling interaction between more than two components, so in the literature of software architecture we can use it only to model client-server styles and it is difficult to generalized IA for example, for multicast/broadcast communications between components.

Moreover, because of the assumption of a helpful environment, neither component should have to wait to synchronize, i.e., if one component is ready to send an action, the other should be ready to receive the action immediately. A state of the product where one component would have to wait is considered an illegal state and is eliminated (with transitions leading to it) from the composed IA, hence this type of interaction would be difficult to model with IA.

Another shortcoming of this approach is the explicit indication of erroneous behavior (illegal states) that limits it to modeling solely the component-based systems with equivalent notion of what is and is not considered as an error (respecting one type of synchronization) [2].

Team Automata. One of the important and useful properties of TA compared with other models is that there is no unique Team automata composed over a set of component automata, but a whole range of Team Automata distinguishable only by their synchronizations can be composed over this set of component automata. This feature enables Team automata to be architecture and synchronization configurable, moreover, makes it possible to define a wide variety of protocols for the interaction between components of a system. TA in comparing with other models has more benefits (almost all of the benefits previously mentioned) and is flexible enough to be best fit for modeling different situations of components interaction.

For representing how TA can be used for modeling component interactions in software architecture, let us consider an example. In Figure 1, two components Merge and Sort are shown in UML2.0 notation [10]. Each of these components has its own *required* and *provided* interfaces and communicates through its ports. These components can be composed and create an aggregate component called MergAndSort which has new interfaces and ports. In UML2.0 one can define *protocol state machines* for specifying detailed behaviors of each port. Suppose that component Merge receives actions a and b through ports P1 and P2 respectively and sends an action c to the component Sort through port P3. Component Sort receives action c through its port, P4 and sends action d through port P5. Component Automata A1, A2 (equations 1 and 2) are models of components Merge and Sort from Figure 1, respectively:

$$A_1 = (\{m_0, m_1\}, \{a, b\}, \{c\}, \phi, \delta_1, \{m_0\}),\tag{1}$$

$where\, \delta_1 = \{(m_0, a, m_0), (m_0, b, m_0), (m_0, c, m_1)\}$

$$A_2 = (\{s_0, s_1\}, \{c\}, \{d\}, \phi, \delta_2, \{s_0\}),\tag{2}$$

$where\, \delta_2 = \{(s_0, c, s_1), (s_1, d, s_1)\}$

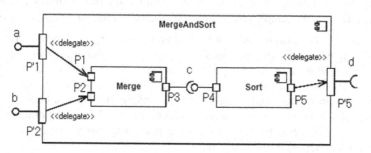

Fig. 1. Composition of components (UML2.0)

According to definition of TA we can define a set of Team Automata over component automata A1 and A2, differing by their transition relation. Each of those TAs could be used for modeling specific design of interaction between components. We choose TA showing in Figure 2. Note that the complete state space of Team automata in this case includes four states but because of ignoring some transitions, two of related states (which are not reachable) are also eliminaed.

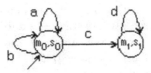

Fig. 2. TA for MergeAndSort component

Team automata of Figure 2. is the external behavioral model of composed component, MergeAndSort which could be in its turn a constituent component automata of a higher level Team automata. Another point in modeling software components by TA is that, whenever we model the *assembly* connectors between components [10], i.e. one component provides a services which is requested by another components (Like the connector that exists between tow components Merge and Sort in Figure 1.) one can consider that output action (request) is consumed by receiving component and it must not appear as output action of composed component. As we can see from definition 2, such actions consider as output actions of Team automata. However a useful operator introduced in the literature of Team automata i.e. *hide* operator has made the model more flexible and can solve previous problem. Let us define hide operator from [9]:

Definition 3. Let $T = \left(Q, \left(\Sigma_{inp}, \Sigma_{out}, \Sigma_{int}\right), \delta, I\right)$ be a TA and let $\tau \subseteq \Sigma_{ext}$. Then $hide_\tau(T) = \left(Q, \left(\Sigma_{inp} - \tau, \Sigma_{out} - \tau, \Sigma_{int} \cup \tau\right), \delta, I\right)$.

In $hide_\tau(T)$, the subset of τ of external actions of T have thus become unobservable for other TA by turning them in to internal actions. By this definition, action c of composed TA in our example could be turn to internal, using $hide_{\{c\}}(MergAndSort)$.

Hide operator can also be used for a more important purpose which is discussed as follow: Composition of automata hides every input action that is also an output action of some other automata in the composition, therefore the input action can not be used on a higher level of compositional hierarchy later on. Hence it may be necessary to internalized certain external actions of a TA before using this TA as a building block in order to prohibit the use of these actions on a higher level of the abstraction. In this way, hide operator could be used to make the needed actions unobservable for other TAs by turning them in to internal actions.

In addition to architectural aspects described and comparisons made over the models in this section, there is an important weakness that all of the introduced models are involved. This weakness is that all of actions execution in a system should be considered to be interleaved. This would be a limitation to model some software architecture artifacts. Interleaving and necessity of extending current models and ways to overcome this limitation will be discussed in next Section.

4   Interleaving and Necessity of Extending Current Models

In this section we describe a limitation which is common between all the mentioned models and many other formalisms, i.e. *Interleaving*. This limitation makes it difficult to model some important aspects of software architectures. Interleaving is a common choice to model the concurrent behavior between components and relies on a very basic assumption of "atomicity" of actions. Atomicity means that an action is indivisible in time. Interleaving means that at each point in time only one component takes a step. The result is all possible interleaving of the actions of the components. Many formalisms, both algebraic and non-algebraic, have adopted interleaving semantics. For example Lamport, L. in [11] indicates that messages exchanged among distributed components can always be totally ordered we can refer to [12], [13], [14],[15] as another examples.

However, interleaving is not always appropriate to characterize the behavior of software architectures accurately because it can be a limitation to model some software artifacts. Software artifacts which have multiple constituent elements but represent a single one, thus, we may wish to group multiple actions such that their behavior cannot be interleaved with the behavior of another component. If in the software architecture, we can realize a certain level of abstraction that all components can be modeled in, then interleaving allows us to model concurrency very nicely. Process algebras (CCS, CSP) all are based on a notion of concurrency, or the famous model checker SPIN is a pure asynchronous/interleaving formalism. But, if we cannot agree on a certain level of atomicity, then we face some limitations of applying common models [16].

In component-based systems, at its signature level, a method of a component can be characterized by the method's name and a set of parameters. Some formalism chooses to model methods by abstracting away their details using, for example, only its name, e.g., [7]. To model the details of the parameter communication, the arrival of the inputs should not be interleaved with the behavior of another component. Thus, we have difficulties to model the semantics of the concurrent behavior of component-based systems at this level of detail.

Speaking in terms of message passing, we may consider a message not merely a single indivisible item; rather it is a sequence of items that arrive as one complex action. One can say, why don't we interleave those small actions? The answer is that we don't want and we cannot, since it will change the semantics of the system which is being modeled. In Web services, for example, an XML message may consist of multiple parts, but those parts are not really independent messages. In fact, we receive either the whole message or none. By limiting interleaving we can try to capture these requirements .Of course, this result in more complexity, but that's a separate issue

All of the models mentioned in Section 2 of this paper, follow the principle of Interleaving and therefore have limitations for modeling of software architectures. S. Esmaeilsabzali et al. in [16] introduced an extended Interface Automata with complex actions. These actions extend interface automata with the ability to declare a sequence of transitions to be a complex action, which cannot be interleaved with transitions from another component in composition. This extension makes the model more powerful for modeling real interactions between software components.

5   Conclusion and Future Work

An appropriate formal model for specifying software architecture makes a reliable foundation to formally verify non-functional properties. In this paper, automata–based models suitable for modeling software architectures was compared and their robustness and weakness, regarding to different aspects of interactions between software components was described. The characteristics of the models described in this paper make their applicability for the full description of interactions in software architecture difficult. It is natural because studied models were often designed for a slightly different purpose. Among the compared models, Team automata has more abilities and less limitations because of its unique properties especially freedom of choosing the transition set what allows its configurability according to the architecture description.

Interleaving was also discussed and its limitation in modeling of real interactions was described. This limitation is common between other introduced models; so, extending Team Automata (as selected model) with complex action one can create a powerful formal model suitable for specifying architectures.

We are trying to develop a framework for transforming well-known architectural descriptions like UML2.0 diagrams to TA formal model and to exploit and evaluate non-functional properties such as security and performance at the architectural level of software design.

References

1. Shaw, M.: The coming-of-age of software architecture research. In: Proceedings of International Conference on Software Engineering, Toronto, pp. 656–664 (2001)
2. Brim, L., Cern, I., Varekov, P., Zimmerova, B.: Component Interaction Automata as a Verification Oriented Component-Based System Specification. In: SAVCBS. Workshop of Specification and Verification of Component-based Systems (2005)
3. Li, J., Horgan, J.R.: Applying formal description techniques to software architectural design. The journal of Computer Communications 23, 1169–1178 (2000)
4. ITU-T, Recommendation Z.100: specification and description language SDL, International Telecommunication Union, Geneva (1989)
5. Li, J.J., Micallef, J., Horgan, J.R.: Automatic simulation to predict software architecture reliability. In: ISSRE 1997. Proceedings of the IEEE Eigth International Symposium on Software Reliability Engineering, pp. 110–120. IEEE Computer Society Press, Los Alamitos (1997)
6. Lynch, N.A., Tuttle, M.R.: An introduction to input/output automata. CWI Quarterly 2(3), 219–246 (1989)
7. de Alfaro, L., Henzinger, T.: Interface Automata. In: Gruhn, V. (ed.) ESEC/FSE 2001. Proceedings of the Joint 8th European Software Engeneering Conference and 9th ACM SIGSOFT Symposium on the Foundation of Software Engeneering, September 10-14. Software Engineering Notes, vol. 26(5), pp. 109–120. ACM Press, New York (2001)
8. Ellis, C.: Team Automata for Groupware Systems. In: GROUP 1997. Proceedings of the International ACM SIGGROUP Conference on Supporting Group Work: The Integration Challenge, pp. 415–424. ACM Press, New York (1997)
9. Beek, M., Ellis, C., Kleijn, J., Rozenberg, G.: Synchronizations in Team Automata for Groupware Systems. Computer Supported Cooperative Work, The Journal of Collaborative Computing 12(1), 21–69 (2003)
10. Ivers, J., Clements, P., Garlan, D., Nord, R., Schmerl, B., Silva, O.: Documenting Component and Connector Views with UML 2.0. Technical report, CMU/SEI, TR-008 ESC-TR-2004-008 (2004)

11. Lamport, L.: Time, clocks, and the ordering of events in a distributed system. Communications of the ACM 21, 558–565 (1978)
12. Lynch, N.A., Tuttle, M.R.: Hierarchical correctness proofs for distributed algorithms. In: Proceedings of the 6th ACM Symposium on Principles of Distributed Computing, pp. 519–543. ACM Press, New York (1987)
13. Holzmann, G.J.: The model checker Spin. IEEE Trans. Soft. Eng. 23(5), 279–295 (1997)
14. Manna, Z., Pnueli, A.: The Temporal Logic of Reactive and Concurrent Systems: Specification. Springer, New York (1991)
15. Milner, R.: Communication and Concurrency. International Series in Computer Science. Prentice Hall. SU Fisher Research 511/24 (1989)
16. Esmaeilsabzali, S., Mavaddat, F., Day, N.A.: Interface Automata with Complex Actions. ENTCS, pp. 79–97. Elsevier, Amsterdam (2005)

ArchC#: A New Architecture Description Language for Distributed Systems

Saeed Parsa and Gholamreza Safi

Department of Computer Engineering,
Iran University of Science and Technology
Narmak, Tehran, Iran 16765-163
parsa@iust.ac.ir,
safireza@comp.iust.ac.ir

Abstract. In this paper a new architecture description language called ArchC#, is introduced. ArchC# is an extension of ArchJava for C#. It is mainly focused on describing architecture of distributed systems. ArchC# provides built-in constructs for describing distributed components and their interconnections. Specific features of distributed code such as remote asynchronous calls and activation of remote objects can be described in ArchC#. ArchC# unifies software architecture with an object-oriented implementation.

1 Introduction

ADLs describe the structure of software systems, enabling more effective design, program understanding and formal analysis. Despite, the growing application of distributed programming, there has not been many considerations for the development of architecture description languages (ADLs) covering specific architectural features of distributed code. There are a few ADLs for distributed systems. However, these ADLs are mostly domain-specific and focus on specific architectural issues [1, 2, 3, 4, 5, 6]. This article is aimed at the design and implementation of an ADL called ArchC# to describe the architecture of distributed programs code implemented in C#. Most of the existing ADLs decouple implementation from architecture, allowing inconsistencies, causing confusion, violating architectural properties and inhibiting software evolution. ArchC# embeds software architecture into source code and guarantees that there is no inconsistency between implemented code and the designed architecture.

ArchC# is an extension of ArchJava[1]. ArchC# models architectures using *components*, communicating through *connection ports* like ArchJava[1, 7]. Unlike ArchJava, it provides built-in constructs to define asynchronous calls within distributed environments. ArchJava does not include any built-in feature for defining asynchronous calls and the software designer has to define a subclass of its Connector class that supports asynchronous calls. Within a distributed environment remote objects are either server activated or client activated. This clarification of object types is not considered by current ADLs such as C2[8], ArchJava [1, 7, 9, 10], ComponetJ [2] and also ComponentC [11]. As described in Section 2, in ArchC# to enhance

F. Arbab and M. Sirjani (Eds.): FSEN 2007, LNCS 4767, pp. 432–439, 2007.

reusability of architectural components, certain component connection configurations such as address of the server or client, physical layer protocol, remote object type and object activation type, can be defined in a separate XML file.

In Section 3, a new scheme for code generation from an architecture description is presented. It is shown, in this Section that the resultant code may run faster than the code generated by ArchJava. The specific capabilities and features of ArchC# makes it possible to have an architectural plan of distributed systems and components that are strongly coupled with the implementation code. As described in Section 2, ArchC# makes it possible to model remote components, asynchronous method calls and many other things which are required to describe architecture of a distributed system. Section 4 presents a worked example to demonstrate the applicability of ArchC# in describing the architecture of a real software system.

2 ArchC# and Distributed Systems

ArchC# implements distributed systems using .Net Remoting [12]. We have enhanced some of the .Net Remoting capabilities. Although we use .Net Remoting in code generation phase of ArchC# compiler for distributed systems, it is possible to apply other technologies like Indigo[13] by making some changes to the compiler. The structures that will be introduced in the following sections are designed so that the change of technology makes no effect on the written code.

2.1 Remote Components in ArchC#

In ArchC# the keyword "remote component" is used to declare those components which may be accessed, remotely. Whenever, a class within a component is declared as a remote class, its instances can be created, remotely. ArchC#, facilitates the use of .Net Remoting, by automatically creating the required set of instructions to access and use it. To define a class as a remote class using .Net Remoting in C#, the class has to be defined as a subclass of MarshalbyRef class[12]. Therefore, since multiple inheritances are not allowed in C#, a remote class can not be a subclass. The difficulty is resolved in ArchC# compiler by applying the approach applied in Eiffel [14]. Eiffel makes use of interfaces to generate code for remote classes. Below, is the definition of a remote component in ArchC#.

```
public remote component class RemoteSellClient {
public port WantMainList { requires public DataSet
getMainList(); }... }
```

2.2 Defining Distributed Architectures in ArchC#

Within a distributed environment client and server ports facilitate communications between a program components. Each server port is defined as a class which can be accessed, remotely. Within a server port the communication protocols and the type of connections with the clients is also defined. Client ports define the address of the server port, the type of remote objects and also some information about the connection with the server. In ArchC# every component that has a server port can be used as a server. There can be more than one server ports defined in a component.

Both client/server and peer to peer architectures can be constructed by defining the interconnections between client and server ports. In Figure 1, the interconnection between a shopping center component and a main shop is shown. The ShoppingCenter component has one client port, MainList, which manages the connection to MainShopCenter for retrieving the items list. It has also one server port which provides information about sailed items for the clients.

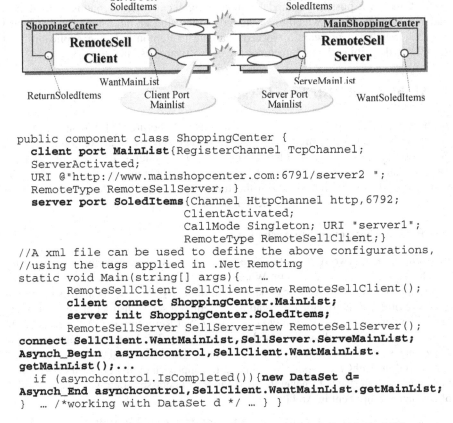

```
public component class ShoppingCenter {
    client port MainList{RegisterChannel TcpChannel;
    ServerActivated;
    URI @"http://www.mainshopcenter.com:6791/server2 ";
    RemoteType RemoteSellServer; }
    server port SoledItems{Channel HttpChannel http,6792;
                           ClientActivated;
                           CallMode Singleton; URI "server1";
                           RemoteType RemoteSellClient;}
    //A xml file can be used to define the above configurations,
    //using the tags applied in .Net Remoting
    static void Main(string[] args){  …
        RemoteSellClient SellClient=new RemoteSellClient();
        client connect ShoppingCenter.MainList;
        server init ShoppingCenter.SoledItems;
        RemoteSellServer SellServer=new RemoteSellServer();
    connect SellClient.WantMainList,SellServer.ServeMainList;
    Asynch_Begin  asynchcontrol,SellClient.WantMainList.
    getMainList();...
        if (asynchcontrol.IsCompleted()){new DataSet d=
    Asynch_End asynchcontrol,SellClient.WantMainList.getMainList;
    }  …  /*working with DataSet d */ …  } }
```

Fig. 1. The architecture of a distributed shopping system defined in ArchC#

As shown in Figure 1, a **server** keyword is inserted before the definition of the server port class. In a server port definition, the first element defines the channel type that the server may use. A server can define multiple channels. In the above server port definition, there is one channel called *http* which uses HTTP protocol to deliver messages between client and server. The HTTP channel uses port number 6792 to listen to client connections. After declaration of channels, ClientActivated primitive can be used to enable clients to activate remote objects. Applying this primitive, the client can mange the life time of the remote object on the server. If the remote object is to be activated by the server, then the next element to define is the connection type.

If the connection type is defined as Singleton, then the remote object will be created at the server side when the first request is received from one of the clients. The same remote object will be used for the next requests from other clients. Locking may be required for preventing deadlocks. On the other hand, if the connection type is defined as SingleCall then the server will not keep any history of the client and no client state will be persisted on the server side.

To define the name of a server port, the keyword URI followed by a string name is inserted in the server port, after the connection type definition. RemoteType keyword is used to define remote object types. The server port starts listening to the connection requests, after the following primitive is executed: server init {portname};

It is possible to use an xml file to define the configuration of server and client ports. The structure of this xml file is very similar to the one used by .Net Remoting for defining server and client configurations. A component may have more than one client port because of different remote objects that it needs. It is also possible that a component class has both client and server ports. As it is shown in Figure 1, the RegisterChannel keyword is used to define the channel type through which the client may connect to the server. The ServerActivated keyword enables the server to activate remote objects. Server activated objects are especially useful when the remote object acts like a service such that the state of the remote object is not required after the completion of the remote call. The server receives a request and replies the request and does not keep any information about the request and its response. To get a client port ready for remote access the primitive *"client connect"* can be used.

2.3 Asynchronous Remote Method Calls

In ArchC#, the Async_Begin keyword is inserted before any call statement which is supposed to be performed asynchrony. The keyword is followed by a state variable which is used by the clients to monitor the progress of the asynchronous call. The Asynch_End keyword highlights the position where the caller waits for the termination of the callee to receive the returned value from the called remote method. As an example, refer to Figure 1. Polyphonic C# [15] is an extension of C# which supports asynchronous method calls. However, Polyphonic C# does not provide any primitive for collecting the values returned or affected by asynchronous remote method calls.

3 ArchC# Implementation

The ArchC# compiler is implemented by applying a parser generator called Coco/R [16]. The compiler translates ArchC# files (.archc) into C# source code. Each component class is translated into a separate class in C#, leaving the fields and method bodies substantially unchanged. The component ports are translated into inner classes. Also, the ArchC# compiler automatically delegates the required and provided methods of each component port to the inner classes in the component. Delegate primitive in C# is similar to the function pointers in C++.

In ArchJava each connection is compiled into a "connection class" that implements all the interfaces of the connected ports. The connect expression returns a new connection object, passing the connected components to the connection object's constructor. The constructor assigns the connected components to the internal fields of the class component. Whenever a required method is invoked through the connection object, the object invokes the corresponding provided method on the targeted component [1]. In ArchC# in order to increase the speed of the connection between the components, the connection object is not created by the compiler. Instead the ArchC# compiler sets all the required delegates to point to the provided methods of the targeted component. ArchC# compiler also generate an XML file which includes information about component, ports, connections and other language structures in the ArchC# code. It also provides information about these architectural blocks. Using a XSLT document, some graphical plan about system architecture will be generated.

4 Online Shopping Systems Architecture

In this section an example of applying ArchC# to describe the architecture of a real distributed system is presented. In order to demonstrate the applicability of ArchC# , the architecture of a shopping center C# code described in ArchC# is presented. The code was reverse engineered and its class dependency graph and architecture was extracted. In Figure 2.a the overall architecture of the online shopping center is sketched. The architecture of each shopping center is also sketched in Figure 2.b by the developers. Many developers draw something on the paper and then start the implementation of the drawing. The implemented architecture may be quite different[17]. The overall architecture of the shopping center application software is shown in Figure 1.

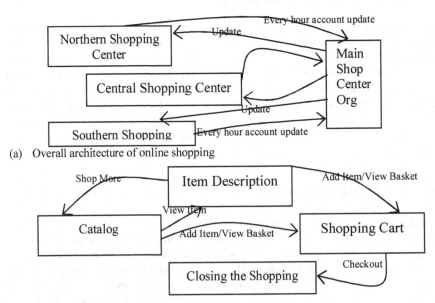

(a) Overall architecture of online shopping

(b) The architecture of an online shopping center

Fig. 2. The sketch of the architecture of an online shopping center drawn by developer

```
public component class MainShopCenter{client port ShopCenter{
… } server port MainShopCenterServerForOthherShopCenters{...}
public port ConnectToShopCenters{requires public DataSet
SelledItems(…); provides update(…){…} } …}
```

Fig. 3. ArchC# description of the architecture of the main shopping center

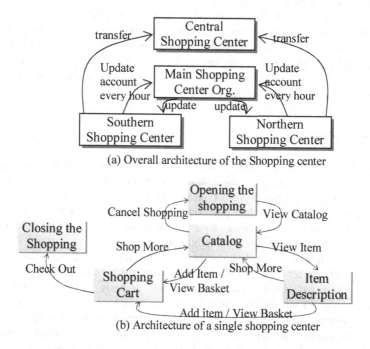

(a) Overall architecture of the Shopping center

(b) Architecture of a single shopping center

Fig. 4. Architecture of the shopping center system software

As shown in Figure 2.a the shopping center distributed software architecture consists of four components. These components interact with each other remotely. Every hour the information stored in the main center computer is directly updated by the shopping centers. Also, the information stored in any one of the shopping centers could be directly updated by the main center computer. The structure of the online shopping center software system made the reengineering process difficult. For instance it was not obvious where in the code and how a remote method call appears. A major difficulty has been to find and identify dependencies between different classes.

After examining the code we understood that a new component, called opening the shopping, could be augmented to the architecture of the shopping centers. We also set the relation between shopping centers and the main center to be server activated, because it is very similar to a web service and the server does not need to save the state. In the main office the type of connection was client activated. If there were so many differences between the sketched architecture which is drawn by the developers and the implemented code then it would take us longer to perform the reengineering process. This work took us fifty hours.

In Figure 1, an ArchC# description of the architecture of the application software for a distributed shopping center application software is given. The ArchC# description of the architecture of the main shopping center software is presented in Figure 3. The ShoppingCenter client port is used to connect to a shopping center remotely. In this code there is also a server port to serve connection requests from the shopping centers to the main center.

In Figure 4.a and 4.b the architecture of the shopping center program code considering the ArchC# description presented in Figure 3, is shown. This architecture model is more precise in compare with the one shown in Figure 2. Apparently, when adding ArchC# primitives to a program code, to describe the program architecture, the program code can be tracked easier and the architecture of the program code can be easily extracted from within the code.

5   Conclusions

There are certain features of distributed system architectures which acquire specific ADL primitives. As a part of distributed architecture plan, it may be required to clarify whether remote objects are server activated or client activated. When defining asynchronous calls, the very last position where the caller may proceed in parallel with the callee, should be defined as a part of the program architecture description. In order to enhance reusability of architectural components, certain component connection configurations such as address of the server or client, physical layer protocol, remote object type and object activation type, can be defined in a separate XML file. A software system source code should embody its architectural plan and the compiler should ensure that there are no violations of the planned architecture within the program code. ArchC# embeds architecture description within the source code and guarantees that there are no inconsistencies between the implemented code and the designed architecture. In ArchC#, a remote class may extend any other class. This is an enhancement made to .net remoting.

Acknowledgments. We would like to thank Jonathan Aldrich for his helpful comments.

References

1. Aldrich, J., Chambers, C., Notkin, D.: Architectural Reasoning in ArchJava. In: European Conference on Object Oriented Programming, Málaga, Spain (June 10-14, 2002)
2. Costa Seco, J., Caires, L.: A basic model of typed components. In: Proceedings of the European Conference on Object-Oriented Programming (2000)
3. Binns, P., Engelhart, M., Jackson, M., Vestal, S.: Domain-Specific Software Architectures for Guidance, Navigation, and Control, Int'l. J. Software Eng. and Knowledge Eng. 6(2) (1996)
4. Garlan, D., Monroe, R., Wile, D.: ACME: An Architecture Description Interchange Language. In: Proc. CASCON 1997 (November 1997)

5. Luckham, D.C., Kenney, J.J., Augustin, L.M., Vera, J., Bryan, D., Mann, W.: Specification and Analysis of System Architecture Using Rapide. IEEE Trans. Software Eng. 21(4), 336–355 (1995)
6. Medvidovic, N., Taylor, R.: A Classification and Comparison Framework for Software Architecture Description Languages. IEEE Trans. Software Engineering 26(1), 70–93 (2000)
7. Aldrich, J., Sazawal, V., Chambers, C., Notkin, D.: Language Support for Connector Abstractions. In: European Conference on Object Oriented Programming (2003)
8. Medvidovic, N., Oreizy, P., Robbins, J., Taylor, R.: Using Object-Oriented Typing to Support Architectural Design in the C2 Style. In: ACM SIGSOFT Fourth Symp., Foundations Software of Eng., pp. 24–32 (1996)
9. Aldrich, J.: Using Types to Enforce Architectural Structure. PHD thesis. Computer Science department, University of Washington (2003)
10. Zheng, K.: Lin Liao. ArchJava Evaluation Report. CSE503 Tool Evaluation Report 8/6/2002
11. Costa Seco, J.: Type safe composition in .NET. In: First Microsoft Research Summer Workshop, Cambridge (2002)
12. Rammer, I.: Advanced .Net Remoting. Apress (2002) ISBN: 1590590252
13. Chappell, D.: Introducing Indigo: An Early Look. Web services and other Distributed Technology Developer Center, Microsoft Developers Network (February 2005)
14. Simon, R., Stapf, E.: Full Eiffel on the .NET Framework, Interactive Software Engineering Santa Barbara, California (July 2002)
15. Benton, N., Cardelli, L., Fournet, C.: Modern Concurrency Abstractions for C#, Microsoft Research (July 2003)
16. Mössenböck, H., Kepler, J.: The Compiler Generator Coco/R, University Linz Institute of System Software (June 2005)
17. Hoffer, A., et al.: Modern Systems Analysis and Design, 3rd edn. Prentice-Hall, Englewood Cliffs (2002)

Relationships Meet Their Roles
in Object Oriented Programming

Matteo Baldoni[1], Guido Boella[1], and Leendert van der Torre[2]

[1] Dipartimento di Informatica - Università di Torino - Italy
baldoni@di.unito.it guido@di.unito.it
[2] Computer Science and Communications (CSC) - University of Luxembourg
leendert@vandertorre.com

Abstract. In this paper we study how roles can be added to patterns modelling relationships in Object Oriented programming. Relationships can be introduced in programming languages either by reducing them to attributes of the objects which participate in the relationship, or by modelling the relationship itself as a class whose instances have the participants of the relationships among their attributes. However, even if roles have been recognized as an essential component of relationships, also in modelling languages like UML, they have not been introduced in Object Oriented programming when it is necessary to model relationships. Introducing roles allows to add attributes and behaviors to the participants in the relationship, rather than to the relationship itself, and to distinguish the natural types of the participants in the relationships from the roles the participants acquire in the relationships. We show how the role model of the language powerJava can be used to endow the relationship as attribute pattern with roles.

1 Introduction

The need of introducing the notion of relationship as a first class citizen in Object Oriented (OO) programming, in the same way as this notion is used in OO modelling, has been argued by several authors, at least since Rumbaugh [1]. Rumbaugh [1] claims that relationships are complementary to, and as important as, objects themselves. For example, a student can be related to a university by an enrollment relationship, he can attend a course, and have a tutor. Thus, relationships should not only be present in modelling languages, like ER or UML, but they should also be available in programming languages, either as primitives, or, at least, represented by means of suitable patterns.

Two main alternatives have been proposed for modelling relationships by means of patterns, e.g., by Noble [2]:

- The relationship as attribute pattern: the relationship is modelled by means of an attribute of the objects which participate in the relationship. E.g., the Attend relationship between a Student and a Course can be modelled by means an attribute attended of the Student and of an attribute attendee of the Course.
- The relationship object pattern: the relationship is modelled as a third object linked to the participants Student and Course. A class Attend must be created and its instances related to each pair of objects in the relationship. This solution underlies programming languages introducing primitives for relationships, e.g., [3].

F. Arbab and M. Sirjani (Eds.): FSEN 2007, LNCS 4767, pp. 440–448, 2007.

```
class Student {                    class BasicCourse {
  String name;                       String code, title;
  int number;                        HashSet<Student> attendees;
  HashSet<BasicCourse> attends;      void enrol(Student s) {
                                       attendees.add(s);
}                                      s.attends.add(this); }}
```

Fig. 1. The relationship as attribute pattern

These two solutions have different pros and cons, as Noble [2] discusses. But they both fail to capture an important modelling and practical issue. If we consider the kind of examples used in the works about the modelling of relationships, we notice that relationships are also essentially associated with another concept: students are related to tutors or professors [3,4], courses are basic courses and advanced courses [4], customers buy from sellers [5], employees are employed by employers, underwriters interact with reinsurers [2], *etc.* From the ontological point of view these concepts are not natural kinds like person or organization: rather, they all are roles involved in a relationship [6].

Roles have different properties than natural kinds, and, thus, are difficult to model with classes: they are dynamically acquired, they depend on other entities - the relationship they belong to and their players - and they add properties and behaviors to the objects playing roles. Moreover, roles can be played by objects of different classes. In particular, when an object of some natural type plays a certain role in a relationship, it acquires new properties and behaviors. For example, a student in a course has a tutor, he can give the exam and get a mark for the exam, another property which exist only as far as he is a student of that course.

As Steimann [7] argues, there is an intrinsic role of roles as intermediaries between relationships and the objects that engage in them. Thus, in this paper, we focus on the following research question: How to introduce roles in relationships? And as subquestion: Which are the advantages given by roles in the relationship as attribute pattern?

In this paper as methodology we use our model of roles in OO programming languages which has been added to an extension of the Java programming language, called powerJava, described in [8,9].

The language powerJava introduces roles as a way to structure the interaction of objects (callee) with other objects calling their methods (caller). Roles express the possibilities of interaction offered by a callee to another one, i.e., the methods it can call. First, these possibilities change according to the class of the caller of the methods. Second, a role maintains the state of the interaction with a certain caller. As roles have a state and a behavior, they share some properties with classes. However, roles can be dynamically acquired and released by an object playing them. Moreover, they can be played by different types of classes. This is why roles in powerJava can be added to model relationships, where the behavior of an object changes when it enters a relationship until it subsequently abandons it.

In Section 2 we discuss how relationships are introduced in OO programming. In Section 3 we summarize our model of roles in powerJava and in Section 4 we use it to introduce roles in the relationship as attribute pattern.

2   Introducing Relations in OO

We will describe in this section the relationship as attribute pattern with reference to a university domain. Consider a student who can attend different kinds of courses: basic ones and advanced ones. The same course can be a basic one in the curriculum of a senior student and an advanced one for junior student. A student can give the exam of the basic course he is attending, and his mark is reported on a registry, and it is possible to send a message to the student of the course. Finally, a course is associated with a tutor if it is taken as a basic course; the tutor, which is not present in advanced courses, can be different for every student attending a given course.

The relationship as attribute pattern is described in Figure 1: the relationship between a student and a course he attends is modelled by means of an attribute `attends` of the instances of class `Student` which participate in the relationship. The type of the attribute is a set of `BasicCourses`. Symmetrically, the `Student` appears in the attribute `attendees` of the type set of `Students` in the class `BasicCourse`.

This solution, however, does not allow to add a state and behavior to the pairs of elements related by the relationship. For example, it is not possible to specify a different tutor for each `Student` of the `BasicCourse`.

This is possible in the alternative pattern, the relationship object, where the participants in the relationship are linked to an object representing a relationship instance. This alternative solution can be modelled in UML, which specifies information proper of an association via an association class, which can be endowed with properties and behaviors. An association class has exactly one instance for each set of objects linked through the association and a lifetime delimited by the existence of the association. If a link is dissolved, the association class instance is destroyed. Due to the association, certain information exists that is specific to the association.

But the relationship object solution shares with the relationship as attribute a limitation. We would like to model the scenario introducing natural types like `Person` rather than the `Student` class only. The reason for such modelling choice is that a `Person` is not always a `Student`, but only as long as he attends courses. Moreover, he can give exams or receive communications concerning the course, only if he is registered and, thus, related by the relationship with a `Course` which he follows as a `BasicCourse`. He has different marks in different exams, and even different students can have different tutors for the same course. Analogously a `Course` has a tutor only if it plays the role of `BasicCourse`. Note that `Person` instances can play also other roles while they are `Student`, like, e.g., employee.

Moreover, even if the relationship object pattern allows to add new properties and behaviors, it does not allow to satisfy completely the requirement that properties and behaviors are associated to the participants: this pattern does not distinguish which properties and behaviors belong to the `Student` and which ones to the `Course`. All properties and behaviors are associated to the instance of the class representing the relationship.

We leave modelling this pattern for future work, even if its realization in powerJava is straightforward.

```
class Printer {                    role User playedby UserReq
  private int printedTotal;          { void print();
                                       int getPrinted(); }
  definerole User {                interface UserReq
   private int printed;              { String getName();
   public void print(){ ...           String getLogin();}
    printed = printed + pages;      jack = new AuthPerson();
    printedTotal = printedTotal     laser1 = new Printer();
                  + printed;        laser1.new User(jack);
    Printer.print(that.getName());  ((laser1.User)jack).print();
}}}
```

Fig. 2. A role User inside a Printer

3 Roles in Powerjava

Baldoni *et al.* [8,9] introduce roles in powerJava, an extension of the object oriented programming language Java. Java is extended with:

1. A construct specifing the role with its name, the methods required to play the role, and the operations it offers to its players.
2. The implementation of a role, inside another object and according to its definition.
3. How an object can play a role and invoke the operations offered by the role.

Figure 2 shows the use of roles in powerJava by means of the example of a printer which can be accessed via roles, e.g. User. First of all, a role is specified as a sort of interface (role - right column) by indicating via an interface which classes can play the role (playedby) and which are the operations acquired by playing the role (e.g., print). Second (left column), a role is implemented inside an object as a sort of inner class which realizes the role specification (definerole). The inner class implements all the methods required by the role specification as it were an interface.

In the bottom part of the right column of Figure 2, the use of powerJava is depicted. First, the candidate player jack of the role is created. It implements the requirements of the roles (the class AuthPerson implements UserReq). Before the player can play the role, however, an instance of the object hosting the role must be created first (a Printer laser1). Once the Printer is created, the player jack can become a User too. Note that the User is created inside the Printer laser1 (laser1.new User(jack)) and that the player jack is an argument of the constructor of role User of type UserReq, which becomes the value of the special variable that, thus allowing to refer to the player from the role implementation.

The player jack to act as a User must be first classified as a User by means of a so-called *role casting* ((laser1.User) jack). Note that jack is not classified as a generic User but as a User of Printer laser1. Once jack is casted to its User role, it can exercise its powers, in this example, printing (print()). Such method is called a power since, in contrast with usual methods, it can access the state of

```
role Student playedby Person {int giveExam(String work);}
role BasicCourse playedby Course {void communicate(String text);}

class Person{
 String name;
 private Queue messages;
 private HashSet<BasicCourse> attended; //BasicCourse followed
 definerole BasicCourse {
  Person tutor;
  // the method communicate access the state of the outer class
  void communicate (String text) {Person.this.messages.add(text);}
  BasicCourse(Person t){
   tutor=t;
   Person.this.attended.add(this); }//add link
  }
}
class Course {
 String code;
 String title;
 private HashSet<Student> attendees; //students of the course
 private HashTable registry = new HashTable();
 private int evaluate(String x){...}
 definerole Student {
  int number;
  int mark;
  int giveExam(String work){ mark = Course.this.evaluate(work);
                 registry.set(that.name.hashCode(), mark); ... }
  Student (){ Course.this.attendees.add(this); }}}//add link
```

Fig. 3. Relationship-role as attribute pattern in powerJava

other objects: the role namespace shares the one of the object including the role (called institution). In the example, the method `print()` can access the private state of the `Printer` and invoke `Printer.print()` or modify `printedTotal`.

4   The Relationship-Role as Attribute Pattern

In this section we describe how a new pattern for modelling relationships with roles can be defined, in analogy with the relationship as attribute pattern. We will use the example of Section 2 to present it.

First of all, using powerJava we can distinguish natural types like `Person` and `Course` from the respective roles `Student` and `BasicCourse`. `Person` and `Course` become, respectively, `Student` and `BasicCourse` when they enter the relationship. Roles are represented in powerJava by instances dynamically associated with the players of the roles, which include the state and behaviors acquired by the

```
class University{
 public static void main (String[] args){
  Course c = new Course();
  Person p = new Person();
  Student s = c.new Student(p); //create role Student for p
  BasicCourse b = p.new BasicCourse(c,tutor);
  //p as a Student of Course c gives the exam by submitting work
  ((c.Student)p).giveExam(work);
  //a message  is sent to p since he attends c as a BasicCourse
  ((p.BasicCourse)c).communicate(text); }
```

Fig. 4. Using the relationship-role as attribute in powerJava

players of the roles in the relationship (see Figures 3 and 5 where the UML representation is illustrated[1]).

Second, in the relationship as attribute pattern, a relationship is reduced only to two symmetric attributes attended and attendees. In the new pattern, the relationship is modelled also by means of a pair of roles implemented in the two classes representing the natural types. Thus, the attribute attendees in Course of type Student in Course becomes Course.Student, and its values will be role instances which are played by instances of type Person. The role Student is associated with players of type Person in the role specification, which specifies that a Student can give an exam (giveExam). Analogously, the attribute attended of Person becomes of type Person.BasicCourse and its values are associated with players of type Course as in the role specification, which specifies that a Course can communicate with the attendee.

The role Student is implemented locally in the class Course by the class Course.Student, and, viceversa, the role BasicCourse is implemented locally in the class Person by the class Person.BasicCourse. Note that this is not contradictory, since roles describe the way an object offers interaction to another one: a Student represents what a Course offers a Person to interact with it, and, thus, the role is implemented inside the class Course. Moreover the methods associated with the role Student, i.e., giving exams, and implemented in Course.Student, modify the state of the class including the role (Course) or call its private methods, thus violating the standard encapsulation. Analogously, the communicate method of Person.BasicCourse, implementing the method signature specified in the role BasicCourse, modifies the state of the Person hosting the role by adding a message to the queue. These methods, in powerJava terminology, exploit the full potentiality that powers have of violating the standard encapsulation of objects.

To associate a Person and a Course in the relationship, the role instances must be created starting from the objects offering the role, e.g.: c.new Student(p) (see the main in Figure 4) where the player p is passed as a parameter.

When the player of a role must invoke a power it must be first role casted to the role. For example, to invoke the method giveExam of Student, the Person must

[1] The arrow starting from a crossed circle, in UML, represents the fact that the source class can be accessed by the arrow target class.

first become a `Student`. To do that, however, also the object offering the role must be specified, since the `Person` can play the role `Student` in different instances of `Course`; in this case the `Course` c: `((c.Student)p).giveExam(...)`.

The pattern has different pros and cons; the following list integrates Noble [2]'s discussions on them. Advantages of the Relationship-role as attribute pattern:

- It allows simple one-to-one relationships: it does not require a further class and its instance to represent the relationship between two objects.
- It allows to introduce a state and operations to the objects entering the relationship, which was not possible without roles in the relationship as attribute pattern.
- It allows the integration of the role and the element offering it by means of powers.
- It allows to show which roles can be offered by a class, and, thus, in which relationships they can participate, since they are all defined in the class.

Disadvantages of the Relationship-role as attribute pattern:

- It requires that the roles are already implemented offline inside the classes which participate in the relationship.
- It does not assure coherence of the pair of roles like student-course, buyer-seller, bidder-proponent, since they are defined separately in two different classes.
- The role cast to allow a player to invoke a power of its role requires to know the identity of the other participant in the relationship.
- It does not allow to distinguish which is the role played in the other object participating in the relationship (e.g., a `Student` in the `attendees` set of a `Course` can follow the `Course` as a `BasicCourse` or an `AdvancedCourse`).

In summary, we can define an informal program transformation, to add roles to the relationship as attribute pattern using powerJava:

1. Identify the natural types of the objects playing the roles (e.g., `Person` for `Student`, or `Person` and `Organization` for `Customer`).
2. Change the type of the classes which participate in the relationship from the name of the role to the name of the natural kinds playing the role (now there can be more than one class playing the role); e.g., the class `Student` becomes `Person`.
3. Add a role definition relating the role to the natural types which can play the role, or to an interface implemented by these natural types, and insert in the role specification the signature of the powers (e.g., `communicate`, `giveExam`).
4. Identify the two links to the participants in the relationships in the classes representing the participants (e.g., `attendees` of type `Student` in `Course`), now of natural types.
5. In the same class the link belongs to, add a role class implementing the role definition with the same name as the type of the link (e.g., `Student` in the `BasicCourse` class which is now called `Course`). Add to this role class the attributes and the implementation, according to the role specification, of the powers.
6. In the code which relates the two participant instances to the relationship, instead of adding the players to the links, first create two roles instances played by the

respective players (of natural types), and, second, add these instances to the links modelling the relationship in the class of the players, e.g., `Person` (this can be done in the role constructors).

7. When a method added by the relationship must be invoked, first, make a role cast from the object playing the role to the role it plays.

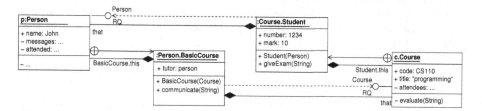

Fig. 5. The UML representation of the relationship-role as attribute pattern example

5   Conclusion

In this paper we discuss why roles need to be introduced when relationships are modelled in OO programs: it is possible to distinguish between the natural type of objects populating the program and the roles they play, and objects acquire new states and behaviors when they participate in a relationship. The state and behaviors which are dynamically acquired are modelled by roles.

Using the language powerJava, a role endowed version of Java, we show how to introduce roles in the the relationship as attribute pattern and we discuss the pros and cons of the pattern when roles are introduced. In particular, we show that the relationship as attribute pattern extended with roles enables to model the extension of behavior of the objects entering a relationship, without the introduction of a further class modelling the relationship. Future work is introducing roles in the relationship as object pattern and designing new patterns where both patterns can be considered at the same time.

References

1. Rumbaugh, J.: Relations as semantic constructs in an object-oriented language. In: Procs. of OOPSLA, pp. 466–481 (1987)
2. Noble, J.: Basic relationship patterns. In: Pattern Languages of Program Design 4, Addison-Wesley, Reading (2000)
3. Bierman, G., Wren, A.: First-class relationships in an object-oriented language. In: Black, A.P. (ed.) ECOOP 2005. LNCS, vol. 3586, pp. 262–286. Springer, Heidelberg (2005)
4. Albano, A., Bergamini, R., Ghelli, G., Orsini, R.: An object data model with roles. In: VLDB 1993. Procs. of Very Large DataBases, pp. 39–51 (1993)
5. Noble, J., Grundy, J.: Explicit relationships in object-oriented development. In: Beilner, H., Bause, F. (eds.) MMB 1995 and TOOLS 1995. LNCS, vol. 977, Springer, Heidelberg (1995)

6. Masolo, C., Vieu, L., Bottazzi, E., Catenacci, C., Ferrario, R., Gangemi, A., Guarino, N.: Social roles and their descriptions. In: KR 2004. Procs. of Conference on the Principles of Knowledge Representation and Reasoning, pp. 267–277. AAAI Press, Stanford (2004)
7. Steimann, F.: On the representation of roles in object-oriented and conceptual modelling. Data and Knowledge Engineering 35, 83–848 (2000)
8. Baldoni, M., Boella, G., van der Torre, L.: Interaction between Objects in powerJava. Journal of Object Technology 6, 7–12 (2007)
9. Baldoni, M., Boella, G., van der Torre, L.: Interaction among objects via roles: sessions and affordances in powerJava. In: PPPJ 2006. Procs. of Principles and Practice of Programming in Java, pp. 188–193. ACM, New York (2006)

Author Index

Lecture Notes in Computer Science

Sublibrary 2: Programming and Software Engineering

For information about Vols. 1–4143
please contact your bookseller or Springer

Vol. 4468: M.M. Bonsangue, E.B. Johnsen (Eds.), Formal Methods for Open Object-Based Distributed Systems. X, 317 pages. 2007.

Vol. 4467: A.L. Murphy, J. Vitek (Eds.), Coordination Models and Languages. X, 325 pages. 2007.

Vol. 4454: Y. Gurevich, B. Meyer (Eds.), Tests and Proofs. IX, 217 pages. 2007.

Vol. 4444: T. Reps, M. Sagiv, J. Bauer (Eds.), Program Analysis and Compilation, Theory and Practice. X, 361 pages. 2007.

Vol. 4440: B. Liblit, Cooperative Bug Isolation. XV, 101 pages. 2007.

Vol. 4408: R. Choren, A. Garcia, H. Giese, H.-f. Leung, C. Lucena, A. Romanovsky (Eds.), Software Engineering for Multi-Agent Systems V. XII, 233 pages. 2007.

Vol. 4406: W. De Meuter (Ed.), Advances in Smalltalk. VII, 157 pages. 2007.

Vol. 4405: L. Padgham, F. Zambonelli (Eds.), Agent-Oriented Software Engineering VII. XII, 225 pages. 2007.

Vol. 4401: N. Guelfi, D. Buchs (Eds.), Rapid Integration of Software Engineering Techniques. IX, 177 pages. 2007.

Vol. 4385: K. Coninx, K. Luyten, K.A. Schneider (Eds.), Task Models and Diagrams for Users Interface Design. XI, 355 pages. 2007.

Vol. 4383: E. Bin, A. Ziv, S. Ur (Eds.), Hardware and Software, Verification and Testing. XII, 235 pages. 2007.

Vol. 4379: M. Südholt, C. Consel (Eds.), Object-Oriented Technology. VIII, 157 pages. 2007.

Vol. 4364: T. Kühne (Ed.), Models in Software Engineering. XI, 332 pages. 2007.

Vol. 4355: J. Julliand, O. Kouchnarenko (Eds.), B 2007: Formal Specification and Development in B. XIII, 293 pages. 2006.

Vol. 4354: M. Hanus (Ed.), Practical Aspects of Declarative Languages. X, 335 pages. 2006.

Vol. 4350: M. Clavel, F. Durán, S. Eker, P. Lincoln, N. Martí-Oliet, J. Meseguer, C. Talcott, All About Maude - A High-Performance Logical Framework. XXII, 797 pages. 2007.

Vol. 4348: S. Tucker Taft, R.A. Duff, R.L. Brukardt, E. Plödereder, P. Leroy, Ada 2005 Reference Manual. XXII, 765 pages. 2006.

Vol. 4346: L. Brim, B. Haverkort, M. Leucker, J. van de Pol (Eds.), Formal Methods: Applications and Technology. X, 363 pages. 2006.

Vol. 4344: V. Gruhn, F. Oquendo (Eds.), Software Architecture. X, 245 pages. 2006.

Vol. 4340: R. Prodan, T. Fahringer, Grid Computing. XXIII, 317 pages. 2007.

Vol. 4336: V.R. Basili, D. Rombach, K. Schneider, B. Kitchenham, D. Pfahl, R.W. Selby (Eds.), Empirical Software Engineering Issues. XVII, 193 pages. 2007.

Vol. 4326: S. Göbel, R. Malkewitz, I. Iurgel (Eds.), Technologies for Interactive Digital Storytelling and Entertainment. X, 384 pages. 2006.

Vol. 4323: G. Doherty, A. Blandford (Eds.), Interactive Systems. XI, 269 pages. 2007.

Vol. 4322: F. Kordon, J. Sztipanovits (Eds.), Reliable Systems on Unreliable Networked Platforms. XIV, 317 pages. 2007.

Vol. 4309: P. Inverardi, M. Jazayeri (Eds.), Software Engineering Education in the Modern Age. VIII, 207 pages. 2006.

Vol. 4294: A. Dan, W. Lamersdorf (Eds.), Service-Oriented Computing – ICSOC 2006. XIX, 653 pages. 2006.

Vol. 4290: M. van Steen, M. Henning (Eds.), Middleware 2006. XIII, 425 pages. 2006.

Vol. 4279: N. Kobayashi (Ed.), Programming Languages and Systems. XI, 423 pages. 2006.

Vol. 4262: K. Havelund, M. Núñez, G. Roşu, B. Wolff (Eds.), Formal Approaches to Software Testing and Runtime Verification. VIII, 255 pages. 2006.

Vol. 4260: Z. Liu, J. He (Eds.), Formal Methods and Software Engineering. XII, 778 pages. 2006.

Vol. 4257: I. Richardson, P. Runeson, R. Messnarz (Eds.), Software Process Improvement. XI, 219 pages. 2006.

Vol. 4242: A. Rashid, M. Aksit (Eds.), Transactions on Aspect-Oriented Software Development II. IX, 289 pages. 2006.

Vol. 4229: E. Najm, J.-F. Pradat-Peyre, V.V. Donzeau-Gouge (Eds.), Formal Techniques for Networked and Distributed Systems - FORTE 2006. X, 486 pages. 2006.

Vol. 4227: W. Nejdl, K. Tochtermann (Eds.), Innovative Approaches for Learning and Knowledge Sharing. XVII, 721 pages. 2006.

Vol. 4218: S. Graf, W. Zhang (Eds.), Automated Technology for Verification and Analysis. XIV, 540 pages. 2006.

Vol. 4214: C. Hofmeister, I. Crnković, R. Reussner (Eds.), Quality of Software Architectures. X, 215 pages. 2006.

Vol. 4204: F. Benhamou (Ed.), Principles and Practice of Constraint Programming - CP 2006. XVIII, 774 pages. 2006.

Vol. 4199: O. Nierstrasz, J. Whittle, D. Harel, G. Reggio (Eds.), Model Driven Engineering Languages and Systems. XVI, 798 pages. 2006.

Vol. 4192: B. Mohr, J.L. Träff, J. Worringen, J.J. Dongarra (Eds.), Recent Advances in Parallel Virtual Machine and Message Passing Interface. XVI, 414 pages. 2006.

Vol. 4184: M. Bravetti, M. Núñez, G. Zavattaro (Eds.), Web Services and Formal Methods. X, 289 pages. 2006.

Vol. 4166: J. Górski (Ed.), Computer Safety, Reliability, and Security. XIV, 440 pages. 2006.

Vol. 4158: L.T. Yang, H. Jin, J. Ma, T. Ungerer (Eds.), Autonomic and Trusted Computing. XIV, 613 pages. 2006.

Vol. 4157: M. Butler, C.B. Jones, A. Romanovsky, E. Troubitsyna (Eds.), Rigorous Development of Complex Fault-Tolerant Systems. X, 403 pages. 2006.